REMEMBERING THEIR SACRIFICE IN THE GREAT WAR

ARDS

Compiled by Barry Niblock

Published 2011 by
Barry Niblock
www.barryniblock.co.uk

First Edition
First Impression

Designed by April Sky Design, Newtownards
Tel: 028 9182 7195
Web: www.aprilsky.co.uk

Printed by W&G Baird Ltd, Antrim

ISBN 978-0-9570627-1-9

Dedication and Thanks

This Book of Honour is dedicated to the memory of all those people from the Ards area who died on active service or from causes attributable to service during the Great War. Some of them died in the most appallingly awful circumstances.

The Rev Geoffrey Studdert Kennedy MC from Ireland was a Church of England priest who became a Chaplain to the Forces during the Great War. He was better known as Woodbine Willie – the nickname given to him by the troops because of his practice of distributing New Testaments and cigarettes to men who were going into battle. In poetry, sermons and books he struggled to articulate a relevant pastoral response to the horrendous suffering he encountered and he said:

> 'The brutality of war is literally unutterable.
> There are no words foul and filthy enough to describe it.'

Today it behoves us all to remember the sacrifice of those who died.

> 'Greater love hath no man than this,
> that a man lay down his life for his friends'
> St. John 15:13

This book could not have been written without help from a great many people and a list of acknowledgements is included towards the back of the book. Here, at the outset, I want to put on record my particular thanks to the following:

Ards Borough Council for financial support; **Austen Lennon** of Austen Lennon Web Design www.AustenLennon.co.uk for developing and maintaining my website; **Lester Morrow** for so generously sharing his encyclopaedic military knowledge and expertise; **Derek Smyth** for his unfailing encouragement, constructive suggestions and guided battlefield tour; **Doreen Walker** of the North of Ireland Family History Society www.nifhs.org for her time-consuming and painstaking work in researching family information; **Wesley Johnston** of April Sky Design www.aprilsky.co.uk for his customer-care and attention to detail; **my wife Anne** for her patience, help with research and proof-reading and support in so many other ways throughout the project.

For our grand-children Ella, Sophie, Jason and Brugh

May they and children everywhere be able to live in peace

Author's Preface – A Tribute

Lists of names on War Memorials are a poignant reminder of lives lost during the Great War but on their own the lists do not convey the human tragedy behind each death. This Book of Honour seeks to establish the context of the deaths and in so doing to pay tribute to all those people with Ards connections who died.

There has been extensive publicity during the information-collecting stage of this project and exhaustive efforts have been made to ensure that the list of names is as complete as possible. That said, it is accepted that some names may yet be missing. If that is the case and, where evidence is provided to support their inclusion, such names will be included in any future edition of the book. New names, together with additional information collected about people already listed in this book, will be added to the *War Dead of North Down and Ards* website which may be found at www.barryniblock.co.uk This website is interactive and readers are invited to use it to provide new information.

Every death in war is a tragic loss of life. It will be noticed that there is more information in this book about some people than about others. That is simply a reflection of the data available at the time of writing and the objective is to increase the amount of information in those cases where there is currently very little written. That said, space constraints in this book dictate that not everything known about some of those who died has been included. In such cases additional information may be included on the website and it is hoped that the details published there, and in this book, will provide a useful starting point for family historians and others wishing to pursue additional research.

In this book we remember the sacrifice of those who died and the impact on generations of their families left behind – grandparents; parents, uncles and aunts; brothers, sisters and cousins, spouses and children. It is beyond the scope of this book to pay tribute to all of the other Ards heroes who fought and survived the Great War. Some information about them may be added to the *War Dead of North Down and Ards* website on an ongoing basis.

A Book of Honour which pays tribute to those people from the North Down area who died on active service or from causes attributable to service in the Great War has also been written. It is entitled:

Remembering Their Sacrifice in the Great War – North Down

BARRY NIBLOCK

Contents

Introduction

Geographical Area

The geographical area covered by this Book of Honour is the Ards Borough Council area as it exists in 2011. A separate Book of Honour covering the present North Down Borough Council area is being published at the same time. Many of those who enlisted for service in the Great War gave their townland as their primary address. The townland is one of the most ancient land divisions in the country and now it is the smallest recognised unit in rural areas.

Some recruits from places like Ballygrainey, Ballysallagh, Conlig, Cottown and Craigantlet affiliated their townland with Newtownards whilst others from those places affiliated their townland with either Bangor or Donaghadee. In service records the spelling of townland names varies tremendously and local spelling sometimes differs from the official form. Generally in this Book of Honour the spelling used is that found in the Topographical Index. A new recruit's pronunciation of a place-name, together with a recruiting sergeant's interpretation of what he said, has led to some alternative spellings in service records. For example, *Killinchy* has been found written as both *Kilychi* and *Clinchy*, *Portaferry* has been found written as *Partargary* while *Kircubbin* has been found written as *Carcubin*.

Another outcome of townland names being associated with different towns is that some names of people who died on active service have been included on the War Memorials in more than one town or village. For example, Rifleman **James Brown** is listed on the War Memorials in both Newtownards and Bangor while Lance Corporal **William Drennan** is listed on the War Memorials in both Donaghadee and Groomsport.

There is another reason why some names are included on more than one War Memorial. Very simply, families didn't stay permanently in one place. Some families moved relatively short distances within an area, others moved further afield. As was the case throughout Ireland at that time, more children were growing up in Ards than could expect to gain a livelihood in that area.

Before the Great War a significant number of Ardsmen moved to Great Britain whilst others emigrated to Australia, Canada, New Zealand, South

Africa, the United States of America and elsewhere. Many young men growing up in large families with low incomes went to work on farms in Scotland.

Several instances have also been found where names are commemorated on more than one church War Memorial, for example, **David Gamble** who served with the Royal Irish Fusiliers (Regimental Service Number 2/8290) is commemorated in Conlig Presbyterian Church and in Greenwell Street Presbyterian Church Newtownards. Young men moving in search of work or moving after they got married were two amongst many reasons.

Service Numbers

Prior to 1920 each Regiment issued its own service numbers so the same number could be issued to other soldiers serving in different Regiments. When a serviceman was transferred he was given a new service number by his new Regiment.

Criteria for Inclusion

Criteria for including names in this Book of Honour have been set so that they are as inclusive as possible. Anyone who lost their life and had a demonstrable association with the Ards area has been included:

- Individuals who were born in the area – including those who subsequently moved out of the area

- Individuals who were born elsewhere but came to reside in the area

- Individuals who married into local families

- Individuals who had strong family connections with the area

There are cases where it is some other member of the deceased's family who had the clearest demonstrable association with the Ards area. There were times when the *Newtownards Chronicle* reported the deaths on active service of individuals whose parents, grandparents or other family members had stronger local connections than the individual did himself. Under the headline 'Kircubbin Officer Dies of Wounds in Germany' the *Newtownards Chronicle* reported that Second Lieutenant **Frederick Echlin** Royal Fusiliers and Royal Flying Corps had died of wounds in Germany on 26 September 1916. He was a son of the late Captain Frederick Echlin, Royal Navy of Echlinville, Kircubbin and grandson of the late Rev JR Echlin JP of Ardquin, Portaferry.

In some cases a casualty's only confirmed Ards connection is that he enlisted in the area, for example, **Alexander Beattie** who lived in Bessbrook, enlisted in Newtownards, served with the Royal Irish Fusiliers (19763) and died on 9 July 1916.

Sources of Information

In compiling the material for this Book of Honour a wide range of information sources has been tapped. Within the Ards Borough Council area names have been collected from Cenotaphs, Royal British Legion and Church Memorial Plaques, together with the Memorial Plaques in Loyal Orange Halls, Masonic Halls, Public Buildings, Schools, Sports Clubs, and Workplaces. The editions of the *Newtownards Chronicle* and *County Down Spectator* published during and after the war years have been very informative.

Information has been collected from a range of websites and databases including the Commonwealth War Graves Commission Debt of Honour, Soldiers Died in the Great War 1914 – 1919, de Ruvigny's Roll of Honour 1914 – 1918, the Presbyterian Church in Ireland Roll of Honour 1914 – 1919, the Grand Lodge of Free and Accepted Masons of Ireland Roll of Honour Great War 1914 – 1919, Ireland's Memorial Records World War One 1914 – 1918 and World War One Irish Soldiers – Their Final Testament. Information has been obtained from Church Records, the 1901 Census (taken on 31 March 1901), the 1911 Census (taken on 2 April 1911), Regimental Museums, the National Archives in Britain and Military Archives in Australia, Canada, New Zealand, South Africa and the United States of America.

War diaries and attestation papers have been very useful and it is interesting to note in passing what doctors looked for when they examined volunteers for fitness to serve. For example, in Australia the examining doctor signed a pro-forma confirming that the volunteer did not present any of the following conditions: scrofula, phthisis, syphilis, impaired constitution, defective intelligence, defects of vision, voice or hearing, hernia, haemorrhoids, varicose veins, marked varicocele with unusually pendant testicle, inveterate cutaneous disease, chronic ulcers, traces of corporal punishment, evidence of having been marked with the letters D (Deserter) or BC (Bad Character), contracted or deformed chest or any abnormal curvature of the spine.

A series of public appeals for information has generated a good response. That said, and as has already been stated, it is not possible to say beyond all doubt that the list of names included in this Book of Honour has no omissions. Furthermore, to date it has not been possible to find definitive information about some of the people whose names are listed on War

Memorials in the Ards Borough Council area. This book contains a lengthy list of acknowledgments and amongst them are many experts who have given advice on the interpretation of data. In cases where it has not been possible to corroborate information they have helped me to draw conclusions. That said, any errors in the book are mine and mine alone.

I decided that, unless there was a compelling reason to do so, any information obtained concerning illegitimacy, deaths by suicide and deductions from pay because of misdemeanours or because of illnesses caused by sexually transmitted diseases would not be included in this Book of Honour. None of those shot for desertion or disobedience during the Great War came from the Ards area.

Erection of First World War Memorial Plaques in the Ards Area

In some instances a considerable amount of time elapsed after the cessation of hostilities before First World War Memorials were erected in towns and villages in the Ards area. Some families died out and in other cases surviving family members moved away and this provides a partial explanation as to why the names of some Ardsmen who died have not been listed. Given the inclusivity of the criteria set for the inclusion of names in this Book of Honour it is *not* being suggested that all of the additional names recorded in this book should be added to local War Memorials. However, a precedent has already been set with the addition of some names since the original memorials were unveiled, for example **James Gregory** on Newtownards and District War Memorial, and so the additional names in this book ought at least to be *considered* for addition – against a set of predetermined criteria.

Greyabbey and District War Memorial

On Saturday afternoon **2 April 1921** a War Memorial Stone for the men from Greyabbey and District who fell in the Great War was dedicated by the Church of Ireland Lord Bishop of Down and Connor. The stone was constructed by Messrs Purdy and Millard of Belfast in Peterhead granite and was placed in the outer wall of Greyabbey Parish Church of Ireland (St Saviour). This tablet was the gift of Major-General WE Montgomery DL. The Rector of the Church was the Rev Canon WLT Whatham who had been the Rector

in Newtownards during the war years and who had been a key figure in compiling lists of names of the men from Newtownards who served in the Great War.

Ballywalter and District War Memorial

Ballywalter and District War Memorial by PC Bantham of London takes the form of a Rifleman cast in bronze standing atop a Mourne granite pedestal and it was unveiled on Wednesday **25 October 1922** by Lady Dunleath of Ballywalter Park.

Comber and District War Memorial

Comber and District War Memorial sculpted by LS Merrifield takes the form of a bronze infantryman on a granite pedestal. It was unveiled by Mrs Lawrence Arthur Hind (nee Andrews) and dedicated on Saturday **14 April 1923**. Her husband **Lawrence Arthur Hind** was killed in action on 1 July 1916.

Donaghadee and District War Memorial

Donaghadee and District War Memorial takes the form of a Connemara marble obelisk and it was unveiled on Thursday **1 July 1926** by the Marchioness of Londonderry.

Newtownards and District War Memorial

Newtownards and District War Memorial takes the form of a Mourne granite obelisk constructed by Messrs Purdy and Millard of Belfast. It was unveiled by the Marquis of Londonderry KG and dedicated on Saturday **26 May 1934**.

In January 1919 a committee of officers from the 4th Battalion Royal Irish Rifles (Royal North Downs) was formed to promote a War Memorial in Newtownards. The committee entered discussions with the Urban Council and there followed a series of public meetings. Public views were also collected through the letters column of the *Newtownards Chronicle* and there were many suggestions as to what form the memorial should take. These included a Public Park named Falhero Park, a terrace of houses for servicemen widows and children (Falhero Terrace), Public Baths and a Monument. Suggestions for the location of a monument included the Bowling Green, Movilla Cemetery and Conway Square.

Time passed and decisions kept being postponed. The question of how to raise a sufficient sum of money kept being asked and there was increasing public frustration with the delay. More public meetings were held in 1923 and in March 1924 ex-soldiers from Newtownards built a snow memorial in the Bowling Green. A concert was organised in 1925 to augment funds and that year a temporary cenotaph was erected in Conway Square for the Battle of the Somme commemoration.

For several years the Newtownards Branch of the Royal British Legion had a temporary memorial in the grounds of their headquarters on Victoria Avenue. In 1933 some decisions were taken regarding a permanent structure. It was decided to erect a permanent War Memorial in the Bowling Green but first to build a temporary structure to gauge what the permanent memorial would look like. Discussions continued as to the dimensions of the permanent memorial and what direction it should face and at the same time Mr RP Dorrian of 15 East Street had responsibility for compiling the list of names to be inscribed. In the 23 and 30 September 1933 editions of the *Newtownards Chronicle* two lists of names were published 'with the object of ensuring that all the names of men from Newtownards and District who were killed in the Great War or who died as the result of wounds received or disease contracted in the campaign are included'. Relatives were requested to report any omissions or mistakes.

The timing of this process explains in part why some of the servicemen who are commemorated on Newtownards and District War Memorial died after the official ending of the Great War (31 August 1921) and, as a consequence of that, their names are not included in the Commonwealth War Graves Commission (CWGC) Debt of Honour.

Conflicting Information

During the course of the research for this Book of Honour several instances of conflicting information have been found and these need to be pointed up. Service details in newspaper reports were not always in accord with the details contained in military records. In such cases military records have been given precedence. The same is true in cases where service details provided by family members are at variance.

In some cases variations have been found between the spelling of surnames in the CWGC Debt of Honour, in 1901 Census returns, in 1911 Census returns, in newspaper reports, in attestation papers and in church records. Examples include Bailie, Baillie, Bailey; Cairnduff and Carnduff; Majury and McJury; Mawhinney and McWhinney; McVey, McVeagh and McVeigh; Smith and Smyth. Reasons for these variations include literacy issues and miscommunication due to misheard pronunciation.

Variations have been found in the recorded ages of individuals and in some cases this is probably accidental. Families with many children, numeracy issues and simple memory lapses are three of the reasons which account for at least some of the variations between 1901 and 1911 Census returns. In other cases there may have been a deliberate attempt to mislead – a very young recruit adding years to his age to exaggerate maturity and an older recruit subtracting years to exaggerate physical fitness. Where they are available, baptismal records have been taken to be the most reliable indicator of age at death.

'Soldiers Died in the Great War 1914 – 1919' provides information about where casualties were born, where they lived and where they enlisted. In cases where this information conflicts with information from other sources the difference has been pointed up in the text.

The 'Presbyterian Church in Ireland Roll of Honour 1914 – 1919' contains over 24,000 names and was produced by the Presbyterian Historical Society from returns made by Presbyterian Congregations in Ireland. It is a valuable resource even though in its own words it is 'far from complete' and 'probably 2,000 names are wanting'. Variations have been found for some congregations between the names listed in the Roll of Honour and the names listed on the Church War Memorial.

Cases have also been highlighted where people listed on church and other Rolls of Honour as having 'served and survived' actually died – together with those instances where people listed as 'died on active service' actually survived.

Population Statistics

In each of the war years a new edition of the *Newtownards and County Down Illustrated Almanac and Directory* was published by the *Newtownards Chronicle* newspaper. Amongst other information this Almanac incorporated data taken from the 1911 Census and so provided some interesting insights to the Ards and North Down areas. The overall population of County Down in 1911 was stated to be 191,719 and individual figures were provided for some of the main population centres:

Place	Population	Males	Females
Ballygowan	209	102	107
Ballyhalbert	421	170	251
Ballywalter	575	258	317
Bangor	7776	3207	4569
Carrowdore	310	141	169
Comber	2589	1190	1399
Conlig	239	111	128
Crawfordsburn	89	42	47
Donaghadee	2213	945	1268
Dundonald	114	52	62
Grey Abbey	572	278	294
Groomsport	239	111	128
Holywood	4035	1806	2229
Killinchy	173	79	94
Kircubbin	591	253	338
Millisle	258	105	153
Newtownards	9587	4409	5178
Portaferry	1518	674	844
Totals	31508	13933	17575

It will be noted that, without exception, in every population centre throughout the Ards and North Down areas, females outnumbered males in 1911. This disparity in numbers between the sexes was further exacerbated when more than 800 men with Ards connections lost their lives in the Great War. No female casualties were identified during this study.

Local Industry and Trade at the Beginning of the Great War

In the Almanacs the chief source of industry in **Ballygowan** was stated to be square set making at the different blue stone quarries in the neighbourhood. In Ballygowan and elsewhere women did exquisite hand embroidery. **Ballywalter** was a flourishing seaport with many of the vessels owned by local merchants. **Comber** was noted for its superior whiskey making and extensive flax spinning. **Donaghadee** was a market and seaport town where many families came to spend the summer months. **Greyabbey** was another popular place for Belfast folk to visit. **Kircubbin** was a small seaport used for the importation of coal and the export of grain and potatoes. **Newtownards** was an important commercial and market town. It was the second largest town in County Down, only Newry with a population of 11,963 being larger. **Portaferry** was a thriving seaport and market town with a considerable trade in coal, timber, corn, potatoes and agricultural produce. A herring fishery operated from June to September and there was a flax scutching mill in the nearby townland of Ballyherley. Throughout the whole of the Ards area agriculture was an important source of employment.

Employment

In addition to the data describing family relationships, the 1901 and 1911 Census returns have provided an interesting insight into the types of work providing the *main* source of income for Ards casualties and their families prior to the Great War. The following analysis is based on available data for more than 70% of the casualties:

Agriculture and Horticulture   27%
This includes farmers, agricultural labourers, farm servants and gardeners.

General Labouring   22%
This includes labouring in distilleries, quarries, on the roads and in factories.

Professional and other services   13%
This includes bankers, ministers of religion, clerks, doctors, engineers, gas workers, insurance agents, policemen, postal workers, railway employees, solicitors, teachers and telegraphers.

Textile Industry   12%
This includes flax scutchers, mill workers and weavers.

Trades   9%
This includes blacksmiths, carpenters, mechanics, painters, plasterers, saddlers, shoemakers, umbrella-makers and watchmakers.

Armed Forces   8%
This includes those who served in the Army and Royal Navy before the Great War.

Retail   5%
This includes butchers, chemists, drapers, grocers, hardware merchants and publicans.

Maritime Work   4%
This includes fishermen, coastguards, lightship-men and merchant mariners.

Family Size

From information provided by family members, together with information extracted from 1901 and 1911 Census returns, it has been possible to compile indicative data about family size for approximately two-thirds of the casualties with Ards connections. For Ards servicemen who died in the Great War, their parents had *at least* the following numbers of children:

Number of Children	% of Families
1 or 2	4
3 or 4	16
5 or 6	25
7 or 8	23
9 or 10	19
11 or 12	8
13 or 14	4
15	1

Approximately 48% of the families had five to eight children with seven being the overall average number of children per family.

Community Spirit

There was always great pride in any community or street where there were many members of a family on active service. It was reported proudly in the *Newtownards Chronicle* that one Newtownards lady had six brothers and four nephews in the army. There were many instances of fathers and sons serving in the Great War and in some cases both died, for example, **James and Archie Campbell**. In this Ards Book of Honour five sets of three brothers and 45 sets of two brothers who died are commemorated. Having demonstrable connections with both areas, the three **Angus brothers – James, John Blair and Robert** – are commemorated in this Ards Book of Honour and also in the North Down Book of Honour.

Soldiers serving in far-flung parts of Europe sometimes got unexpected reminders of home. Hay made in Ireland was transported to the front to feed the horses and mules and on one occasion a ration-cart driver from Newtownards opened a new bundle of hay on the Western Front only to find a label that indicated the hay had been produced on a farm near Newtownards by a farmer whom he knew.

A Spirit of Patriotism

Patriotism shown by local people was extolled and this included the Ardsmen who emigrated before the outbreak of war. The case of Robert George who had lived in Balfour Street, Newtownards before emigrating to the United States of America was cited. He was working as a plasterer in the city of Mobile, Alabama when 'he responded to the call of the Empire by travelling 1400 miles to Toronto in Canada to enlist'. At that point in time the USA had not entered hostilities.

The Comforts Committees

People at home worked hard to collect items for inclusion in parcels sent out to the Ardsmen on active service and most local communities established Comforts Committees. The Newtownards Comforts Committee appealed for gifts of jerseys, mufflers, mittens, socks and money to buy soap, candles, towels and razors 'for their boys'. Each local Committee provided a central collection point, organised fundraising events and kept records of all the men to whom parcels were sent.

It was customary for the recipients of parcels to write letters of acknowledgement and these were published regularly in the *Newtownards Chronicle*. Sometimes via the letters column men at the front asked for specific items, including musical instruments such as mouth organs and melodeons. In September 1915 it was reported that 'a group of Newtownards boys at the front asked the girls of Castle Gardens Spinning Mill to raise money and send out a melodeon'. The girls raised enough money to send out 'the best melodeon on the market' and along with it they sent 'cigarettes and safety matches'. In their published letter of thanks the Newtownards boys begged readers at home not to throw away their old *Chronicles* but instead to send them out for the boys at the front to read.

Some lads from Newtownards who were serving with the Royal Irish Fusiliers in Gallipoli asked the Comforts Committee for 'a few smokes and some hard tobacco'. They said that they could not smoke the local cigarettes because 'they were very bad.'

Delays in News Reaching Home

Sometimes news about a death on active service reached the bereaved family very quickly while on other occasions a considerable period of time might elapse. When a family was informed that a relative was missing in action the following explanation was included:

"The term 'Missing' does not necessarily mean that the soldier is killed or wounded. He may be an unwounded prisoner or temporarily separated from his Regiment. Any further information received will be at once sent on to you."

There was always the risk that the Authorities might get it wrong and cause unnecessary distress if someone who was missing in action was reported killed in action too soon and subsequently turned up alive. Under the heading 'A Grim Error' the *Newtownards Chronicle* reported a case in May 1915 where a mother was informed that her son had died, only to be told some time later that he was still alive. In another case a Portaferry rifleman who came home on sick-leave after being wounded had the experience of reading an official communication to his mother announcing his death.

Due to cases such as these there were times when news of a death reached a bereaved family unofficially in a letter written by a surviving comrade before the family heard the news officially. Sometimes a full year or more elapsed between a 'missing in action' report and the dreaded 'killed in action' official intimation.

The *Newtownards Chronicle* was read avidly by soldiers at the front and by those who were recuperating in military hospitals. Very often when a soldier was posted as missing in action and no more letters from him were received, the family at home requested information from readers of the paper – both those serving at the front and those recuperating in military hospitals.

The Aftermath of War

Many Ardsmen who were on active service in the Great War and survived the experience came home suffering from serious physical and/or mental infirmities. For many of the survivors, gas poisoning, lost limbs, the effects of malaria and other tropical diseases, shell shock, blindness, deafness and nightmarish memories made working impossible and severely curtailed their quality of life after the cessation of hostilities. These men were living memorials to the sacrifice made by those who died. Some survivors died prematurely from causes attributable to service and other survivors spent the remainder of their lives in institutions then called 'lunatic asylums'.

Any disability impacted on employability after the war and there was a human dimension to every injury. Private Samuel McTear lost a hand in the fighting at Ypres on 6 January 1915 and this only a very short time after receiving the news that his wife had given birth to twins. Other soldiers lost fingers and toes because of frostbite. Life was hard, physically and financially, for such men when they came home from war and cases were reported in the *Newtownards Chronicle* of ex-servicemen sent to jail after being found guilty of begging on the streets.

Life in the Trenches

Entrenchments ran through towns, villages, farms and fields. Trench types varied depending on their geographical location. In the Somme area the ground was chalky and easier to dig so the trenches were deeper with reinforced walls. In the Ypres area where the water table was high the trenches were shallower. Trenches zigzagged following the contours of the land.

Life in the trenches was never easy but during the winter months conditions could be appalling. A report written in November 1914 referred to the conditions as being 'wretched beyond description.' This was after four days of incessant rain that turned to snow. Instead of standing knee-deep in liquid mud, men were standing knee-deep in freezing slush. Lice-infested clothes that remained perpetually wet; incessant deafening noise; the appalling stench of rotting horse and human flesh and plagues of rats stealing food and crawling over soldiers as they tried to rest were all part of the daily routine. Primitive latrines were situated in close proximity to the trenches.

In the face of such terrible hardship and adversity there were occasional flashes of humour in the letters written by soldiers serving at the front. When Lance Corporal Samuel Wright of the 2nd Battalion Royal Irish Rifles wrote to his wife Lizzie who lived at 2 Robert Street (Front Shuttlefield), Newtownards he told her about having been wounded in the leg. To that piece of information he added laconically, 'And I have lost my set of good teeth.'

Causes of Death

The causes of death for Ardsmen on active service were many and varied. For some, death from a gunshot, an explosion or a bayonet thrust could be instantaneous. Others died slowly and painfully from wounds sustained. Loss of blood and infections took their toll. One of the ways that the Girl Guides in Newtownards did their bit for the war effort was by collecting Sphagnum moss which they sent to the Sphagnum Moss Depot in Belfast. Because of its antiseptic and absorptive qualities Sphagnum moss was used for wound cleansing and as a wound dressing during the First World War.

Death by drowning, death as a result of the privations suffered in prisoner of war camps, death by suicide, death from disease and death caused by accidents on land, at sea and in the air all happened to Ardsmen.

'Why me?' might be thought by the dying while others might ask, 'Why not me?' when a tragedy occurred. Engineer John Savage of Barr Hall, Portaferry who was aboard the SS *Minneapolis* when she was torpedoed on 23 March 1916 had two lucky escapes. Having survived the explosion he was getting away in one of the lifeboats when another lifeboat fell on top of his boat killing five men who were sitting alongside him.

The Commonwealth War Graves Commission (CWGC)

The Commission was founded by Sir Fabian Ware and it was officially established by Royal Charter in 1917 as the Imperial War Graves Commission with its headquarters at 82 Baker Street in London. It became the Commonwealth War Graves Commission in 1960 and for simplicity that is the name used throughout this book. In its Debt of Honour the Commission commemorates those who died in service or from causes attributable to service during the designated war years – from 4 August 1914 to 31 August 1921. Some interim dates are significant and provide an explanation as to why War Memorials differ in the time period they cite for the duration of the Great War – some memorials commemorate deaths between 1914 and 1918, others between 1914 and 1919 and others between 1914 and 1921.

Germany signed an **Armistice** with the Allies and the guns fell silent on the Western Front at 11.00 am on **11 November 1918**. The **Termination of the Present War (Definition) Act** received Royal Assent on **21 November 1918**. This Act provided for an Order in Council to be made specifying the date upon which the war would officially end. The **Treaty of Versailles** was signed on **28 June 1919** by the Allied Powers and Germany and this treaty brought to an end the state of war that existed between those countries. Finally, on 10 August 1921 the Order was made specifying that **the Great War would officially end on 31 August 1921**.

When the Commonwealth War Graves Commission was making preparations for the erection of a CWGC headstone Major General Fabian Ware wrote to the next-of-kin informing them about the proposed wording for the service inscription and seeking confirmation that it was accurate. Families were given the opportunity to add a short personal inscription on the headstone at their own expense. This was limited to 66 letters (including the spaces between words) at a cost of 3½d (1½p) per letter – equivalent to around £1 per letter today.

Most of the Ardsmen commemorated in this Book of Honour died within the designated war years. Also included in the book are those men who died after 31 August 1921 and whose names were inscribed on War Memorials in the Ards area. The author has taken the view that it would be inappropriate to exclude anyone from this Book of Honour whose name has already been listed on a War Memorial in the area. One such casualty whose name is listed on Newtownards and District War Memorial is **Robert McKimm** who died on 22 November 1922.

In addition to members of the British forces who died, the CWGC Debt of Honour commemorates service personnel from Australia, Canada, India, New Zealand and South Africa who died. Those countries have their own War Memorials and Rolls of Honour and it is beyond the scope of this book to describe them all in detail. By way of example, South African forces fought in German South-West Africa, in German East Africa and in Europe on the Western Front where their heaviest losses were sustained in the summer of 1916 during the Battle of Delville Wood. The South African National Memorial was unveiled there on 10 October 1926 and it bears no names.

The American Battle Monuments Commission (ABMC)

In the United States of America the American Battle Monuments Commission (ABMC) was established by Congress in 1923 to commemorate the service, achievements and sacrifice of US armed forces during the Great War. After the USA entered the war on 6 April 1917 some Ardsmen served in the US Army and three of them lost their lives – **James Reid** and **Niven Boyd Stewart** from Carrowdore and **Robert John Ireland** from Comber.

Deaths in the Local Military Hospital

Not everyone on active service who died in the Ards area was a local person. The first soldier from the Newtownards Camp to die in the local Military Hospital was Private William James Bacon of the 12th Battalion Royal Irish Rifles. The deceased, who died of pneumonia on Saturday 7 February 1915, was a native of Portrush and he left behind a wife and family. Full military honours were conferred as his coffin was carried by relays of his comrades along the Belfast Road in Newtownards to meet the motor hearse that conveyed his remains to Portrush for burial. Private Bacon is commemorated on page 16 of *Portrush Heroes* compiled and edited by Robert Thompson.

Military Weddings in Newtownards

A happier result of the presence of a Military Camp in Newtownards was the number of military weddings that took place in the town during the war years. On one occasion, in January 1916, when the wedding of a Highland Light Infantryman and a Newtownards girl had to be postponed for a day an old Yorkshire saying was recalled:

'A wedding postponed means a monarch dethroned'

To this old saying was added the quip:

'And may the words prove true of the Emperor of the Huns'

Battalions Stationed in Newtownards

At different times different Battalions were stationed in Newtownards. In January 1916 the 10th Battalion of the Royal Irish Fusiliers arrived from Lurgan and they marched through the town. They were headed by a brass band led by the two Regimental mascots – a brindled Great Dane and a Goat. Afterwards it was reported somewhat anthropomorphically that the animals had both 'comported themselves with dignity.'

HMS *Bayano*

Not everyone who is buried in a Commonwealth War Grave in the Ards area was a local person. Seven men from HMS *Bayano* whose bodies were washed ashore along the coastline of the Ards Peninsula are buried in graveyards located within the Ards area.

HMS *Bayano* was a merchant ship that was commissioned by the Admiralty as an Armed Merchant Cruiser in 1914 and she served with 10th Cruiser Squadron. HMS *Bayano* sank off Carswell Point, Stranraer around 4.45 am on Thursday 11 March 1915 after being hit by a torpedo fired from the German submarine U-27. It was pitch dark at the time and many of the crew were asleep.

Out of a crew of around 220 only about 10% were saved. Survivors clung to wreckage in the water for more than four hours before being picked up. HMS *Bayano* disappeared within about three minutes of being torpedoed and the majority of those who perished were sucked into the vortex created by the rapidly sinking ship.

An unidentified 'Royal Marine of the Great War' from HMS *Bayano* is buried in the North-East part of Ballyhalbert (St Andrew) Church of Ireland Churchyard at Ballyeasborough. Also buried in that Churchyard is **Edgar J Spracklin** (1113X) who was a Leading Seaman in the Newfoundland Royal Naval Reserve. Aged 36 and married with children his body was found on the shore at Portavogie.

Frederick William Chater (Tyneside Z/501), a British Able Seaman in the Royal Naval Volunteer Reserve, is buried near the middle of the South-East boundary of Whitechurch Graveyard, Ballywalter. His widow's name was Sarah and he was 30 years of age when he died.

In Ballyphilip Church of Ireland Churchyard, Portaferry there are the graves of two unidentified sailors from HMS *Bayano*. Their headstones affirm that they are '*Known Unto God*'. Also buried in that Churchyard is **AG Bain** (PO/7542), a Private in the Royal Marine Light Infantry. He is buried in Grave 197 and he was identified by means of a letter in his pocket. The fourth casualty from HMS *Bayano* who is buried there is **WA Wellstead** (179706), a British Able Seaman in the Royal Navy. He had his name on his belt and he is buried in Grave 198.

Ireland at the Outbreak of War

When the Great War commenced in August 1914 around 30,000 Irishmen from all four of its Provinces (Ulster, Munster, Leinster and Connaught) were in the regular forces and a similar number of Reservists were called up. Not all were serving in 'Irish' units. At that time there were seventeen units in the British Army that could be classified as 'Irish'; an eighteenth, the Tyneside Irish, was raised in November 1914:

- Eight infantry units based in Ireland – the Royal Irish Regiment, the Royal Inniskilling Fusiliers, the Royal Irish Rifles, the Royal Irish Fusiliers, the Connaught Rangers, the Leinster Regiment, the Royal Munster Fusiliers and the Royal Dublin Fusiliers

- Three infantry units based in Great Britain – the Liverpool Irish, the London Irish Rifles and the Tyneside Irish

- The Irish Guards in the Brigade of Guards

- Two cavalry units based in Ireland – the North Irish Horse and the South Irish Horse

- Four cavalry units based in Great Britain – the 4th Royal Irish Dragoon Guards, the 5th Royal Irish Lancers, the 6th (Inniskilling) Dragoons and the 8th (King's Royal Irish) Hussars.

In addition to those who were serving in the Army, many Irishmen were serving or Reservists in the Royal Navy and many others were seamen who manned the Mercantile Marine. Following the outbreak of the Great War, Lord Kitchener was appointed British Secretary of State for War and he set about recruiting a 'New Army'. Ardsmen volunteered for many different reasons including a sense of patriotic duty, outrage at the invasion of Belgium, escape from poverty, seeking adventure and peer pressure. During the Great War approximately 150,000 Irishmen from the four Provinces enlisted making a total contribution of more than 210,000. More than one New Army was raised.

The 10th, 16th and 36th Divisions

New recruits were placed in new infantry battalions, artillery batteries, cavalry squadrons and companies of the Royal Engineers, Army Service Corps and Royal Army Medical Corps. These units made up a number of new divisions which formed the basis of the New Armies that were successfully raised by Kitchener. Two of the new divisions, the 10th and the 16th were known as 'Irish' Divisions and one, the 36th, was known as the 'Ulster' Division.

The term 'Division' and some other military terms are defined in the 'Abbreviations and Glossary of Terms' section in this book.

The 10th (Irish) Division was formed in Ireland in August 1914 as part of the First New Army and it comprised three Infantry Brigades, the 29th, 30th and 31st. Training took place at the Curragh, Newbridge and Kildare and in May 1915 the Division moved to Basingstoke in England. The 10th was the first Irish Division to take part in the war and saw active service in Gallipoli, the Balkans and Palestine. On 6/7 August 1915 the Division landed at Suvla Bay and ANZAC Cove, Gallipoli and made attacks at Chocolate Hill, Sari Bair and Hill 60. Under the intense heat of the summer sun and tortured by insects, some of those who lost their lives at Gallipoli died of thirst, sunstroke and dysentery. On 25 September 1915 the Division withdrew from Gallipoli and moved via Mudros to Salonika where they fought until August 1917. In the freezing cold of the Balkan Mountains some soldiers died after their uniforms froze to their bodies. Other soldiers died from malaria contracted in the mosquito-ridden swamps of the Struma Valley. On 18 August 1917 the 10th Division moved from Salonika to Egypt and fought in the Palestine campaign against the Turks. They left Palestine between April and June 1918 and were sent to France

The 16th (Irish) Division was raised in Ireland in September 1914 as part of the Second New Army formed by Lord Kitchener and it comprised three Infantry Brigades, the 47th, 48th and 49th. Training took place at Fermoy and Buttevant and in September 1915 the Division moved to Aldershot in England. The Division went to the Western Front in December 1915 and remained there until June 1918. On 27 April 1916 at Hulluch they endured the horrors of gas warfare and there were reports of corpses grotesquely twisted into all kinds of tragic attitudes, 'some holding hands like children in the dark'. Survivors of the attack were plagued by hordes of half-poisoned rats. Other notable engagements included Guillemont and Ginchy in 1916, Messines and Langemarck in 1917 and St Quentin and Rosieres in 1918.

The 36th (Ulster) Division was raised in the province of Ulster in September

1914 and it comprised three Infantry Brigades, the 107th, 108th and 109th, each comprising four Battalions. Thirteen of the battalions in the Ulster Division were comprised of men, the majority of whom were members of the Ulster Volunteer Force (UVF). The UVF was formally established in January 1913 to resist the introduction of Home Rule in Ireland. Organised along British Army lines the UVF was a trained and practised force and Sir Edward Carson negotiated with the British Government for UVF members to be kept as a single unit. Training took place in Ulster and in July 1915 the Division moved to Seaford on the coast of Sussex. The Division went to the Western Front in October 1915 and it remained there throughout the war. The 36th (Ulster) Division suffered dreadful casualties during the Battle of the Somme, most notably on the first day. The 13th Battalion Royal Irish Rifles was formed in County Down and in November 1917 the 11th Battalion (formed in County Antrim) and the 13th Battalion were amalgamated. They were disbanded in February 1918 with many of the troops going to the 22nd Entrenching Battalion.

The Easter Rising

The Home Rule debate in Ireland continued after the outbreak of the Great War with Nationalists in favour and Unionists against. The Ulster Volunteer Force had been formed to resist Home Rule while the Irish Volunteers formed in late 1913 were resolved to fight for it. On 18 September 1914 the Third Home Rule Bill was placed on the Statute Book but it was suspended for a year or until after the end of the war. That led to a split in the Irish Volunteers. One group calling itself the National Volunteers followed John Redmond, the leader of the Irish Parliamentary Party, and they went on to join the British Army. The other group which retained the title Irish Volunteers did not support the war effort and they advocated armed rebellion, leading to the Easter Rising in 1916.

On Easter Monday 24 April 1916 a force of some 1000 Irish Republicans occupied a number of strategic buildings in Dublin and proclaimed an Irish Republic. At that time there were about 400 British soldiers based in Dublin and reinforcements were brought in quickly. There was a week of intense fighting before the Republicans surrendered on 30 April 1916. More than 100 military personnel and 300 civilians died during the Easter Rising, or afterwards from their wounds. Rifleman **Alexander McClelland** died on 27 April 1916 and Rifleman **James McCullough** died on 2 May 1916.

Conscription

In January 1916 the British Government introduced the Military Service

Act which provided for conscription. Ireland was exempt from this Act and conscription in Ireland was never implemented. Every Irishman who enlisted, except for those living in Great Britain, was a Volunteer.

Theatres of War

The Great War was fought on land, at sea and in the air. Many of the Ardsmen on active service fought along the Western Front in France and Flanders while others fought in the other theatres of war across the globe. These included the Eastern Front, Africa, the Middle and Far-East, India, the Balkans, Greece and Turkey. More than 80% of the Ards casualties died as a result of fighting on the Western Front.

The Chaplaincy Service

During the Great War the spiritual needs of service personnel were catered for by clergy of all denominations who volunteered to serve as Military Chaplains. Their pastoral duties included looking after the wounded and rendering medical assistance at Casualty Clearing Stations. Some local clergymen served in other capacities during the Great War. John Blacker Aickin Hughes who was Vicar of Holy Trinity Church in Ballywalter from 1910 until his death on 16 February 1921 served from 1914 to Easter 1919 as Captain, RASC, 36th (Ulster) Division. He died aged 52 from causes not attributable to war service and he is commemorated on a personalised memorial plaque in Ballywalter Parish Church of Ireland and on the family grave headstone in Whitechurch Cemetery Ballywalter.

The Influenza Pandemic

Following the end of the Great War an influenza pandemic spread through Europe killing more people than were killed in the war. Some Ardsmen who had survived the exigencies of war fell victim to this pandemic.

Ards Fatalities on Active Service

Service	Fatalities	%
Army	773	93.0
Royal Navy	27	3.3
Mercantile Marine	11	1.3
Air Force	5	0.6
Not Known	15	1.8
Total	831	100

In addition to those who served with British forces, some Ardsmen served with Commonwealth and American forces:

Country	Number	%
Australia	12	1.4
Canada	49	5.9
India	1	0.1
New Zealand	9	1.1
South Africa	6	0.7
United Kingdom	732	88.1
USA	3	0.4
Not Known	19	2.3
Total	831	100

Men from Ards served in many Units of the British Army including:

Argyll and Sutherland Highlanders, Black Watch (Royal Highlanders), Border Regiment, Cameron Highlanders, Cameronians (Scottish Rifles), Cheshire Regiment, Connaught Rangers, Durham Light Infantry, Essex Regiment, Gordon Highlanders, Grenadier Guards, Hampshire Regiment, Highland Light Infantry, Irish Guards, King's (Liverpool Regiment), King's Own (Royal Lancaster Regiment), King's Own Scottish Borderers, King's Royal Rifle Corps, Labour Corps, Lancashire Fusiliers, Leicestershire Regiment, Lincolnshire Regiment, London Regiment, Loyal North Lancashire Regiment, Machine Gun Corps, Manchester Regiment, Middlesex Regiment, North Staffordshire Regiment, Northumberland Fusiliers, Princess Victoria's (Royal Irish Fusiliers), Queen's Own Hussars, Rifle Brigade (Prince Consort's Own), Royal Army Medical Corps, Royal Army Service Corps, Royal Army Veterinary Corps, Royal Dublin Fusiliers, Royal Engineers, Royal Field Artillery, Royal Fusiliers (City of London Regiment), Royal Garrison Artillery, Royal Inniskilling Fusiliers, Royal Irish Regiment, Royal Irish Rifles, Royal Munster Fusiliers, Royal Regiment of Artillery (Royal Horse and Royal Field Artillery), Royal Scots, Royal Scots Fusiliers, Royal Sussex Regiment, Royal Welsh Fusiliers, Scots Guards, Seaforth Highlanders, Sherwood Foresters (Notts & Derby Regiment), South Staffordshire Regiment, South Wales Borderers, Tank Corps and Welsh Regiment.

More than 50% of the Ards casualties served with the Royal Irish Rifles.

From time to time Army personnel were transferred from one Regiment or Battalion to another and it is beyond the scope of this book to chronicle every move. Where transfers are not chronicled it will *normally* be the Regiment/Battalion in which a casualty was serving when he died that is given.

Age Profile

Inconsistencies between the ages of casualties taken from different sources have already been pointed up and for a number of Ards casualties reliable information about age at death has not been found to date. Using the best available data the age profile for 667 of the Ards casualties is as follows:

Age Range	Number	Percentage
17 to 20	143	21.4
21 to 25	191	28.6
26 to 30	153	22.8
31 to 35	78	11.7
36 to 40	57	8.6
41 to 45	21	3.2
46 to 50	11	1.7
51 to 55	8	1.2
56 to 61	5	0.8

Half of the Ards servicemen who died were aged 25 or under.

Fatalities by Month/Year

To date it has not been possible to pinpoint the date of death for 72 of the men with Ards connections who are commemorated in this book. The following analysis relates to the remaining 759.

Month	1914	1915	1916	1917	1918	1919	1920	1921	After 1921
Jan		4	3	4	2	3	2	0	
Feb		0	7	7	4	5	0	0	
Mar		8	5	10	28	1	3	0	
Apr		9	12	20	19	0	0	2	
May		26	12	13	5	0	0	3	
June		3	13	13	6	1	0	2	
July		5	164	12	10	1	0	1	
Aug	2	13	13	52	12	1	2	0	
Sept	4	11	25	8	11	0	1	0	
Oct	11	4	13	12	20	0	2	0	
Nov	8	9	9	14	11	1	1	0	
Dec	5	5	6	11	1	1	0	0	
Total	**30**	**97**	**282**	**176**	**129**	**14**	**11**	**8**	**12**

The two months in which the greatest number of fatalities occurred were July 1916, with many men dying during the Battle of the Somme, and August 1917, with many men dying at Langemarck during the Third Battle of Ypres.

The first Ardsmen to die in the Great War were Privates **Samuel Ritchie** and **William Warnock** who served with the 2nd Battalion Royal Inniskilling Fusiliers and they were killed in action on Wednesday 26 August 1914.

Medals

Two types of medal were awarded – those awarded for gallantry and those awarded for service:

Gallantry Medals

Two of the men with Ards connections who died on active service were awarded the **Victoria Cross (VC)**. This was the highest military decoration for gallantry and was awarded for most conspicuous bravery, a daring or pre-eminent act of valour, self-sacrifice or extreme devotion to duty in the presence of the enemy. The VC could be awarded posthumously and all ranks were eligible.

Second Lieutenant **Edmund De Wind**
Lieutenant **William David Kenny**

Four of the men with Ards connections who died on active service were awarded the **Distinguished Service Order (DSO)**. This was the second highest military decoration for gallantry, typically awarded to commissioned officers ranked Major (or its equivalent) or higher. A gold bar was added to the ribbon for each subsequent award to the holder.

Captain **George James Bruce**
Major **Meyrick Myles Magrath**
Lieutenant Colonel **Francis Savage Nesbitt Savage-Armstrong**
Major **William Maxwell Shaw**

Five of the men with Ards connections who died on active service were awarded the **Military Cross (MC)**. This was the third highest military decoration for gallantry in the field, typically awarded to commissioned officers ranked Captain or below. Warrant Officers were also eligible for this award. Silver bars were awarded for further acts of gallantry. The award was instituted in 1914.

Captain **George James Bruce (and Bar)**
Lieutenant **Henry McDonnell Anderson**
Lieutenant **Robert Davison**
Lieutenant Colonel **Lawrence Arthur Hind**
Captain **Elliott Johnston**

Three of the men with Ards connections who died on active service were awarded the **Distinguished Conduct Medal (DCM)**. Equivalent to the DSO for commissioned officers, this medal was instituted to recognise gallantry within 'other ranks' and silver laurelled bars were awarded for further acts of gallantry. Sergeant James Armstrong Kelly held the award for gallant conduct in the South African War.

Second Lieutenant **Hugh Charles Allen**
Corporal **Gerald Marcus Huston**
Captain **Walter Percy O'Lone**

Nine of the men with Ards connections who died on active service were reported to have been awarded the **Military Medal (MM)**. In two cases evidence to substantiate these reports has not been found to date. Instigated in March 1916 for 'other ranks', the MM was equivalent to the MC awarded to commissioned officers. Silver laurelled bars were awarded for subsequent acts of bravery and devotion under fire. On the back it bore the words 'For Bravery in the Field'.

Sergeant **Alexander Colville**
Rifleman **Joseph Crooks (unsubstantiated to date)**
Lance Corporal **James Gregory**
Rifleman **Thomas James Harrison**
Corporal **Lowry Jordan**
Private **John Maidens**
Private **David H McMillan (unsubstantiated to date)**
Corporal **William John Peake**
Rifleman **Henry Quigley (and Bar)**

Eleven of the men with Ards connections who died on active service were **Mentioned in Despatches (MID)**. This happened when a senior officer mentioned a subordinate officer or soldier who performed some noteworthy action. The recipient was entitled to wear an emblem of bronze oak leaves on the ribbon of the Allied Victory Medal. MID could be awarded posthumously.

Private **Jonathan Ardill**
Captain **George James Bruce (x3)**
Company Sergeant **Major David Ferris**
Lieutenant Colonel **Lawrence Arthur Hind (x2)**
Lieutenant **John Joseph Leo Morgan**
Captain **Robert James O'Lone**
Captain **Walter Percy O'Lone**
Captain **Hamilton Orr (×2)**
Captain **Mervyn Stronge Richardson**
Lieutenant Colonel **Francis Savage Nesbitt Savage-Armstrong (x2)**
Major **William Maxwell Shaw**

One of the men with Ards connections who died on active service received an award under the Most Excellent Order of the British Empire. Such awards were for outstanding services of a non-combatant nature. There are five classes of award and **Captain John McMath** became an **Officer of the Order of the British Empire (OBE)**.

At least four of the men with Ards connections who died on active service held the **Long Service and Good Conduct Medal (LS&GC)**:

Colour Sergeant John Isaac Cutler
Sergeant William John Doherty
Company Sergeant Major David Ferris
Lieutenant Samuel Valentine Morgan

Service Medals

Generally, the service medals awarded to Ards servicemen who lost their lives in the Great War were either 'trios', 'pairs' or 'singles'.

The **1914 Star** was awarded to those who served in France or Belgium between 5 August 1914 and midnight on 22/23 November 1914. Those who were under fire were awarded a bar to this star; those who were not under fire received the star without a bar. The star bore the inscription '5th AUG – 22nd NOV 1914'. The **1914 – 1915 Star** (5th August 1914 – 31st December 1915) was awarded to all who served in any theatre of war against the Central Powers between 5 August 1914 and 31 December 1915 – except those who were eligible for the 1914 Star (these two stars were never issued together). It bore the inscription '1914 – 15'.

The **British War Medal** was awarded to personnel who rendered service during the First World War and there were circumstances when this medal could be awarded on its own. The **Mercantile Marine War Medal** (along with the British War Medal) was issued to members of the Mercantile Marine who served one or more voyages through a danger zone.

The **Allied Victory Medal 1914 – 18** was awarded to all those who received the 1914 or 1914 – 15 Star and also to those who served in a theatre of war up to 11 November 1918. It was also awarded to some personnel who served after 11 November 1918 in Russia or in mine-clearance operations in the North Sea. The design on the Allied Victory Medal varied depending on the country of issue and three men with Ards connections who died on active service were entitled to the medal issued by the United States of America (pictured opposite) – **Private Robert John Ireland**, **Private James Reid** and **Corporal Niven Boyd Stewart**.

The trio (Star, British War and Allied Victory Medals) became known as Pip, Squeak and Wilfred after characters in a Daily Mail cartoon of the period. Pairs were generally awarded to servicemen who served after 1915 and comprised the British War Medal and the Allied Victory Medal, popularly known as the 'Mutt and Jeff' pair.

A great many Ardsmen qualified for the **Silver War Badge** which was awarded to service personnel who were honourably discharged due to wounds or illness (either caused by service or not discovered at enlistment). The badge bore the words 'For King and Empire – Services Rendered'. The badge had to be applied for by the eligible person and one of its purposes was to discourage women from presenting a white feather (a symbol of cowardice) to men who looked like they were capable of enlisting when in fact they had been honourably discharged because of wounds or illness.

In October 1916 the British Government decided that some form of recognition should be given to the next-of-kin of those who had fallen. A committee was formed and in August 1917 it was announced that the memorial should take the form of a bronze plaque accompanied by a memorial scroll. A public competition was instigated to find a suitable design and the winner was Carter Preston of the Sandon Studios Society in Liverpool. Entitled 'Pyramus', the

bronze plaque measured 120mm in diameter. The memorial plaque and memorial scroll were posted to the next-of-kin accompanied by a letter from King George V. This plaque became known as the 'Death Plaque', 'Death Penny' or 'Dead Man's Penny'.

Names in Chronological Order

In this Section the names of men with Ards connections are presented chronologically in the context of the Great War.

The Outbreak of the Great War

The historical background to the Great War is complex but it is generally agreed that the assassination of Archduke Franz Ferdinand, heir to the Austro-Hungarian throne, along with his wife Duchess Sophie of Hohenberg, was one of the defining moments. Prior to these murders committed by Gavrilo Princep on 28 June 1914 in Sarajevo there had been a long succession of territorial disputes and conflicts in Europe and, as a consequence, several treaties and alliances were established. It is beyond the scope of this Book of Honour to describe all of these European conflicts and alliances in detail. The main reason for including reference to *some* of them is to provide a context for the deaths of Ards servicemen during the Great War.

After the Franco-Prussian War of 1870/71 France lost the provinces of Alsace and Lorraine to the newly formed German Reich as the then German Chancellor Otto von Bismarck set about creating a unified German Empire in Europe. After Bismarck left office in 1890 Kaiser Wilhelm II set about establishing Germany as a colonial power in Africa and the Pacific. Germany began a massive shipbuilding programme to produce a naval fleet that would rival in size the British fleet. Britain responded by increasing her own naval strength. In 1902 Britain agreed a military alliance with Japan and on 8 April 1904 Britain and France reached an understanding known as the 'Entente Cordiale'. Each acknowledged the other's interests in Africa, Asia and the Pacific and in 1907 Russia (then suffering difficulties arising from the 1905 revolution) joined Britain and France to form the 'Triple Entente'. In the Great War these three countries comprised the **Allied Powers**. Germany and Austria-Hungary were allied by treaty and these countries, joined by Turkey and Bulgaria, comprised the **Central Powers** during the Great War.

There was ongoing conflict in and around the Balkan Peninsula. In 1912 Turkey lost Libya, Rhodes and the Dodecanese Islands to Italy. In 1913 Turkey was at war with Greece, Serbia, Bulgaria and Montenegro, losing Crete and other European territories. In 1913 Bulgaria lost territory back to Turkey and tensions in the Balkans remained high. After the murder of Archduke Franz Ferdinand, Austria-Hungary issued an ultimatum to Serbia and, not being satisfied with the response, declared war with Serbia on 28 July

1914. Austria-Hungary bombarded Belgrade the following day. Russia was allied by treaty to Serbia and mobilised its army in her defence. Germany was allied by treaty to Austria-Hungary and declared war with Russia on 1 August 1914; Austria-Hungary declared war with Russia on 6 August 1914. Germany declared war with France on 3 August 1914 and invaded neutral Belgium that day with a view to reaching Paris by the shortest possible route. The initial plan was to swing west of the city, sever any help from Britain via the channel ports and then attack the bulk of the French forces massed on the German Border. Instead, under Commander von Kluck, the German forces swerved east of Paris leaving themselves vulnerable to attack by the French forces surging eastwards out of the city – the Miracle of the Marne. France declared war with Austria-Hungary on 12 August 1914.

Allied by treaty to France and obligated by treaty to defend neutral Belgium, Britain declared war with Germany on 4 August 1914. Britain's colonies and dominions abroad – Australia, Canada, India, New Zealand and the Union of South Africa – provided immediate assistance. The United States of America declared a policy of neutrality which remained in force until 6 April 1917 when the USA entered the war, partly in response to Germany's policy of unrestricted submarine warfare and partly in response to the Zimmermann Telegram to Mexico. This note urged Mexico to wage war against the United States and was intercepted by the British. Japan honoured a military agreement with Britain and declared war with Germany on 23 August 1914. Two days later Austria-Hungary responded by declaring war with Japan. Italy, although allied to both Germany and Austria-Hungary, declared a policy of neutrality in 1914 and then in 1915 Italy sided with the Allied Powers against the Central Powers.

That the Great War was truly a world war can be seen from the following list of declarations of war and it should be noted that these do not include instances where countries simply severed relations with other countries.

Country Declaring War	With	Date
Austria-Hungary	Serbia	28 July 1914
Germany	Russia	1 August 1914
Germany	France	3 August 1914
Germany	Belgium	4 August 1914
United Kingdom	Germany	4 August 1914
Liberia	Germany	4 August 1914
Montenegro	Austria-Hungary	5 August 1914
Austria-Hungary	Russia	6 August 1914

Country Declaring War	With	Date
Serbia	Germany	6 August 1914
Montenegro	Germany	8 August 1914
France	Austria-Hungary	12 August 1914
United Kingdom	Austria-Hungary	12 August 1914
Japan	Germany	23 August 1914
Japan	Austria-Hungary	25 August 1914
Austria-Hungary	Belgium	28 August 1914
Serbia	Turkey	2 November 1914
Russia	Turkey	2 November 1914
United Kingdom	Turkey	5 November 1914
France	Turkey	5 November 1914
Italy	Austria-Hungary	23 May 1915
San Marino	Austria-Hungary	3 June 1915
Italy	Turkey	21 August 1915
Italy	Germany	28 August 1915
Bulgaria	Serbia	14 October 1915
United Kingdom	Bulgaria	15 October 1915
Montenegro	Bulgaria	15 October 1915
France	Bulgaria	16 October 1915
Russia	Bulgaria	19 October 1915
Italy	Bulgaria	19 October 1915
Germany	Portugal	9 March 1916
Austria-Hungary	Portugal	15 March 1916
Romania	Austria-Hungary	27 August 1916
Turkey	Romania	30 August 1916
Bulgaria	Romania	1 September 1916
United States of America	Germany	6 April 1917
Cuba	Germany	7 April 1917
Panama	Germany	7 April 1917
Greece	Austria-Hungary	27 June 1917
Greece	Bulgaria	27 June 1917
Greece	Germany	27 June 1917
Greece	Turkey	27 June 1917
Siam	Austria-Hungary	22 July 1917
Siam	Germany	22 July 1917
China	Germany	14 August 1917

Country Declaring War	With	Date
China	Austria-Hungary	14 August 1917
Brazil	Germany	26 October 1917
United States of America	Austria-Hungary	7 December 1917
Panama	Austria-Hungary	10 December 1917
Guatemala	Germany	23 April 1918
Nicaragua	Austria-Hungary	8 May 1918
Nicaragua	Germany	8 May 1918
Costa Rica	Germany	23 May 1918
Haiti	Germany	12 July 1918
Honduras	Germany	19 July 1918

The Great War was fought across many fronts and servicemen with Ards connections were involved in most of them:

African Wars

Germany had two colonies in West Africa – Togoland (surrendered in August 1914) and German Cameroon (surrendered in 1916).

German and Portuguese forces clashed along the border between German South-West Africa and Portuguese Angola; German South-West Africa fell to South African forces in May 1915.

General Paul Emil von Lettow-Vorbeck commanded the German forces in German East Africa and he evaded British and South African forces for four years. He surrendered on 23 November 1918 and returned to Berlin a hero.

Balkan Front – Macedonian Front – Salonika Front

The Austro-Hungarian bombardment of Belgrade began on 29 July 1914 and many battles were fought in Serbia. Belgrade was taken in December 1914 and soon thereafter it was re-taken by the Serbians. The Balkan region was significant too in the wider context of the Great War. Turkey's supply route from Germany ran through then neutral Romania and in October 1915 Bulgaria joined the Central Powers with the aspiration of taking Macedonia. Greece mobilised in response to the Bulgarian threat to Serbia and requested Allied assistance. In October 1915 a combined French/British force landed at Salonika (today called Thessalonika). The expedition arrived too late to prevent the fall of Serbia and in a change of position Greece declared neutrality. Serbia and Montenegro were occupied by the Central Powers. The Allied forces in Salonika took up a defensive stance against possible attack and they suffered heavy casualties from malaria and other illnesses. This was an unpopular place to serve. The front stretched from the Albanian Adriatic coast to the Struma River (a river rising in the mountains of Bulgaria and flowing through Greece to the Aegean Sea). Greece entered the war on the Allied side in June 1917 and the great Allied offensive in September 1918 resulted in the capitulation of Bulgaria on 30 September and the liberation of Serbia.

Eastern Front (Russia)

This theatre of war extended from the Baltic Sea in the west to Minsk in the east and from St Petersburg in the north to the Black Sea in the south. In 1914 Russia invaded East Prussia and suffered defeat at the Battle of Tannenberg. At the same time Russia successfully invaded Galicia only to be driven back in 1915 when the Central Powers transferred more troops to the area. There were significant Russian advances in 1916 and then in 1917, because of the financial strain of the war effort, the Russian economy almost collapsed. The Russian Revolution is a collective term for a series of revolutions in Russia in 1917 which led to the abdication of the Tsar and the formation of the Soviet Union. The Tsar abdicated and was replaced by a provisional government in March 1917 (Gregorian calendar; February in the older Julian calendar which was in use in Russia at the time) and under Alexander Kerensky the new Government remained committed to pursuing the war. In July 1918 the Tsar and his family were murdered. In October (Julian) the provisional government was overthrown by the Communist Bolsheviks under Vladimir Lenin. He declared that there should be peace with any necessary reparations or annexations. The Germans continued to advance into Russia and Lenin ordered Trotsky to conclude a peace agreement with whatever concessions were necessary. In March 1918 the Treaty of Brest-Litovsk was signed. The Eastern Front ceased to be a war zone in the Great War and this enabled the Germans to transfer forces and mount the 'Michael' offensive on the Western Front. However, there continued to be civil unrest in Russia and the Russian Civil War lasted from 1917 to 1921 (with skirmishes continuing until 1923) between Bolshevik and anti-Bolshevik protagonists. Allied forces remained in the region during this time.

Far East

Engagements in the Far East included bombardment of the German colony of Tsingtao in China (today called Qingdao) by Japanese and British forces and the Battle of Bita Paka in German New Guinea.

Gallipoli Front (Dardanelles)

Turkey entered the Great War on the side of the Central Powers at the end of October 1914 and closed the Dardanelles, a stretch of water between the Mediterranean and the Sea of Marmara that had considerable strategic significance. The main engagements in this theatre of war are outlined later in this section.

Italian Front

This front opened in May 1915 when Italy entered the war on the Allied side after the Treaty of London promised substantial annexations of Austro-Hungarian territory. There were two main objectives – to hold the Trentino Salient which butted into Italy and to attack the Isonzo Salient which jutted into Austria. Italy suffered huge losses in 1917 and both Britain and France sent reinforcements. In October/November 1918 British, French and Italian forces defeated the Austro-Hungarian armies with the Battle of Vittorio Veneto being decisive.

Middle East – Mesopotamian Front (present-day Iraq)

Britain invaded Mesopotamia and Basra fell on 23 November 1914. Accompanied by reinforcements from India, British forces advanced towards Baghdad in May 1915. Kut-el-Amara was taken in September 1915 but the further push towards Baghdad was halted and Allied forces retreated to Kut. After a lengthy siege British forces surrendered Kut on 29 April 1916. Engagements continued at Baku and the Mosul oilfields and in February 1917 Kut was retaken by the British forces followed by Baghdad the following month.

Middle East – Palestine Front (including Gaza and Jerusalem)

Britain had possession of the Suez Canal and successfully repelled a Turkish attack in February 1915. Britain pushed defences into the Sinai Peninsula and repelled a further Turkish attack in August 1916. Arab guerrillas caused ongoing problems for the Turks. British forces advanced towards Gaza and Beersheba; Jerusalem fell on 8 December 1917. In September 1918 the Turks were defeated at the Battle of Megiddo and in October 1918 Damascus and Beirut were taken by the Allied forces.

War at Sea

German maritime colonies in the Pacific fell quickly at the start of the Great War and Admiral Maximilian von Spee sailed towards South America with the intention of returning to Germany via the Atlantic. German ships attacked British ships and the Battle of Coronel was fought on 1 November 1914 off the coast of Chile. In February 1915 Germany initiated a submarine campaign against all merchant shipping in all waters around the British Isles. Following the sinking of the SS *Lusitania* on 7 May 1915 off the south coast of Ireland with the loss of 1198 lives (128 of them American) there were strong protests from the USA and on 1 September 1915 Germany suspended unrestricted submarine warfare.

In February/March 1915 Allied ships were involved in the Dardanelles campaign and in 1916 Germany resumed unrestricted submarine attacks in February, suspending them again in May. There were hit-and-run raids by the German Navy at Lowestoft and Yarmouth in April 1916 and on 31 May 1916 the Battle of Jutland began. This battle was inconclusive with both sides claiming victory. More British ships and men were lost in this battle but the German fleet returned to port and German naval resources thereafter were concentrated on the U-boat campaign. Germany resumed unrestricted submarine warfare in February 1917 and this tactic was countered by the Allied convoy system. The USA entered the Great War on the side of the Allies on 6 April 1917.

After the Armistice was signed on 11 November 1918 the German High Seas Fleet was interned at the Royal Navy Base, Scapa Flow while negotiations continued as to the fate of the ships. There was a skeleton crew of German sailors aboard each ship and to prevent the ships being used by the Allied Powers the German commander Admiral Ludwig von Reuter decided to scuttle the fleet. This he did on 21 June 1919 and more than fifty vessels sank.

War in the Air

The Royal Flying Corps (RFC) was created in May 1912 from the Air Battalion Royal Engineers which had been formed as a kite-balloon unit. Naval aviators formed part of the Corps until July 1914 when the Royal Naval Air Service (RNAS) was formed and then, at the outbreak of war, all available RFC machines were sent to France. The RFC and RNAS were merged on 1 April 1918 to form the Royal Air Force (RAF).

Western Front (France and Flanders)

During the Great War most of the deaths of servicemen with Ards connections occurred in France and Flanders and the main engagements in this theatre of war are outlined later in this section. Some men were killed in action while others died later of wounds or illness – either on the battlefield or in a designated centre somewhere along the treatment chain between the battlefield and home.

Treatment Chain for Wounded Soldiers

Front-line units were able to provide only the most basic first aid in the Regimental Aid Posts (RAPs) located near the front line. A wounded man might walk in on foot or be stretchered there. Facilities were limited and casualties were moved on to the Advanced Dressing Stations (ADSs) that comprised the Field Ambulance (FA). Here wounds were dressed and some emergency operations carried out. At times wounded men had to lie in the open on stretchers for a considerable length of time before being moved on down the line to a Casualty Clearing Station (CCS). These were better-equipped medical facilities that kept wounded soldiers who were unfit for further travel; treated and returned to the front line those who had less serious wounds and evacuated all the rest. In some cases groups of clearing stations were given nicknames by the troops, for example, in the locality of Poperinge, West-Vlaanderen in Belgium: Mendinghem (mending them), Dozinghem (dosing them) and Bandaghem (bandaging them).

The CCS comprised tents or huts and was usually located beside a railway line. More serious operations such as limb amputations were carried out there. Casualties moved from the CCS either to a Base Hospital (BH) or directly to a port of embarkation to Britain. Given the very serious nature of many of the wounds it was inevitable that some casualties died and beside each CCS there was a large military cemetery. This is how Mendinghem, Dozinghem and Bandaghem Military Cemeteries got their names (these three cemeteries together contain more than 6300 Commonwealth burials for the Great War). Base Hospitals were located at Boulogne, Le Havre, Rouen, Le Touquet and Etaples and casualties whose wounds did not prevent them from travelling would often be moved back to a hospital in the United Kingdom for treatment.

Hospitals in the UK included existing Military Hospitals, Territorial Force General Hospitals and the War Hospitals. Pre-war asylums and other buildings (Red Cross, St John's Ambulance, auxiliary and private hospitals) were converted for military use. Large numbers of public and private buildings (often large houses) were turned over for use as small hospitals, most of which operated as annexes to nearby larger hospitals. Some hospitals became specialist units – mental hospitals, units for limbless men, neurological units, orthopaedic units, cardiac units, typhoid units and venereal disease units.

Convalescent hospitals for recovering service personnel were under military control and there were several in Ireland. These included the Belfast War Hospital (formerly the Belfast District Lunatic Asylum); the Ulster Volunteer Force Hospital in Belfast; Holywood Military Convalescent Hospital; the

Duke of Connaught's Auxiliary Hospital (formerly located in Princess Patricia Hospital in Bray); the Richmond War Hospital (formerly the Richmond District Asylum in Dublin); the King George V Hospital in Dublin; Portobello Military Hospital in Dublin and the Irish Counties War Hospital at Glasnevin in Dublin.

Battles

It is beyond the scope of this Book of Honour to provide a detailed account of all the battles fought during the Great War. *Some* of the major engagements of the Great War are listed below in chronological order showing the month when they took place or, in the case of longer engagements, when they began. Sources vary as to the precise date on which some of the engagements commenced and ended and in this Book of Honour the dates given should be regarded as indicative rather than definitive. Some of the battles were components of other battles.

Engagement	Theatre of War	Date Started
1914		
Austrian Bombardment of Belgrade	Balkan Front	29 July 1914
Battle of Liege	Western Front	05 August 1914
Konigin Luise (1st German loss)	War at Sea	05 August 1914
HMS *Amphion* (1st British loss)	War at Sea	06 August 1914
Battle of Mulhouse	Western Front	07 August 1914
Russian Invasion of East Prussia	Eastern Front	07 August 1914
Battle of Haelen	Western Front	12 August 1914
Battle of Lorraine	Western Front	14 August 1914
German Capture of Liege	Western Front	16 August 1914
Battle of Stalluponen	Eastern Front	17 August 1914
Russian Invasion of Galacia	Eastern Front	18 August 1914
Battle of Gumbinnen	Eastern Front	20 August 1914
German Capture of Brussels	Western Front	20 August 1914
Battle of the Ardennes	Western Front	21 August 1914
Battle of Charleroi	Western Front	21 August 1914
Battle of the Sambre	Western Front	22 August 1914
Battle of Mons	Western Front	23 August 1914
Capture of Namur	Western Front	23 August 1914
Destruction of Louvain	Western Front	25 August 1914

Engagement	Theatre of War	Date Started
Battle of Le Cateau	Western Front	26 August 1914
Battle of Tannenberg	Eastern Front	26 August 1914
German Surrender of Togoland	African Wars	26 August 1914
German Capture of Lille	Western Front	27 August 1914
Battle of Heligoland Bight	War at Sea	28 August 1914
Battle of Guise	Western Front	29 August 1914
Siege of Tsingtao	Far East	02 September 1914
First Battle of the Marne	Western Front	06 September 1914
First Battle of Masurian Lakes	Eastern Front	09 September 1914
Battle of Bita Paka	Far East	11 September 1914
First Battle of the Aisne	Western Front	12 September 1914
Loss of *Aboukir, Cressy & Hogue*	War at Sea	22 September 1914
First Battle of Albert	Western Front	25 September 1914
Battle of Sandfontein	African Wars	26 September 1914
Siege of Antwerp	Western Front	01 October 1914
First Battle of Arras	Western Front	01 October 1914
Battle of La Bassee	Western Front	10 October 1914
Battle of Messines	Western Front	12 October 1914
Battle of Warsaw	Eastern Front	15 October 1914
Battle of Armentieres	Western Front	16 October 1914
Battle of the Yser	Western Front	18 October 1914
First Battle of Ypres	Western Front	19 October 1914
Battle of Langemarck	Western Front	21 October 1914
Battle of Gheluvelt	Western Front	29 October 1914
Battle of Coronel	War at Sea	01 November 1914
Battle of Tanga	African Wars	03 November 1914
British Capture of Basra	Mesopotamia	23 November 1914
Battle of Qurna	Mesopotamia	03 December 1914
Battle of the Falkland Islands	War at Sea	08 December 1914
Battle of Givenchy	Western Front	18 December 1914
First Battle of Champagne	Western Front	20 December 1914

1915

Battle of Dogger Bank	War at Sea	24 January 1915
Battle of Bolimov	Eastern Front	31 January 1915
Turkish Attack on the Suez Canal	Palestine Front	03 February 1915

Engagement	Theatre of War	Date Started
Second Battle of Masurian Lakes	Eastern Front	07 February 1915
Allied Bombardment of Dardanelles	Gallipoli Front	19 February 1915
Battle of Neuve-Chapelle	Western Front	10 March 1915
Battle of St Eloi	Western Front	14 March 1915
Battle of Shaiba	Mesopotamia	11 April 1915
Second Battle of Ypres	Western Front	22 April 1915
Battle of St Julien	Western Front	24 April 1915
Landings at Helles/Anzac Cove	Gallipoli Front	25 April 1915
First Battle of Krithia	Gallipoli Front	28 April 1915
Second Battle of Krithia	Gallipoli Front	06 May 1915
Battle of Aubers	Western Front	09 May 1915
Capture of Windhoek	African Wars	12 May 1915
Battle of Festubert	Western Front	15 May 1915
Turkish attack at Anzac Cove	Gallipoli Front	19 May 1915
Battle of Bellewaarde	Western Front	24 May 1915
Allied Capture of Amara	Mesopotamia	31 May 1915
Third Battle of Krithia	Gallipoli Front	04 June 1915
First Battle of the Isonzo	Italian Front	23 June 1915
Battle of Nasiriyeh	Mesopotamia	27 June 1915
Battle of Gully Ravine	Gallipoli Front	28 June 1915
German Surrender of SW Africa	African Wars	09 July 1915
Allied Attack on Achi Baba	Gallipoli Front	12 July 1915
Second Battle of the Isonzo	Italian Front	18 July 1915
Landings at Suvla Bay	Gallipoli Front	06 August 1915
Battle of Lone Pine	Gallipoli Front	06 August 1915
Battle of Sari Bair	Gallipoli Front	06 August 1915
Battle of the Nek	Gallipoli Front	06 August 1915
Battle of Kirich Tepe	Gallipoli Front	15 August 1915
Battle of Hill 60	Gallipoli Front	21 August 1915
Battle of Scimitar Hill	Gallipoli Front	21 August 1915
Battle of Loos	Western Front	25 September 1915
British Capture of Kut-al-Amara	Mesopotamia	28 September 1915
Battle of Es Sinn	Mesopotamia	28 September 1915
Austro-German Invasion of Serbia	Balkan Front	06 October 1915
Third Battle of the Isonzo	Italian Front	18 October 1915

Engagement	Theatre of War	Date Started
Fourth Battle of the Isonzo	Italian Front	10 November 1915
Battle of Ctesiphon	Mesopotamia	22 November 1915
Turkish Siege of Kut-al-Amara	Mesopotamia	07 December 1915
Evacuation of Suvla & Anzac	Gallipoli Front	19 December 1915

1916

Battle of Sheikh Sa'ad	Mesopotamia	06 January 1916
Evacuation of Helles	Gallipoli Front	08 January 1916
Battle of the Wadi	Mesopotamia	13 January 1916
Battle of Hanna	Mesopotamia	21 January 1916
German Surrender, Cameroon	African Wars	18 February 1916
Battle of Verdun	Western Front	21 February 1916
Battle of Dujaila	Mesopotamia	08 March 1916
Fifth Battle of the Isonzo	Italian Front	09 March 1916
Battle of Lake Naroch	Eastern Front	18 March 1916
First Battle of Kut	Mesopotamia	05 April 1916
Battle of Hulluch	Western Front	27 April 1916
British Surrender of Kut	Mesopotamia	29 April 1916
Battle of Asiago	Italian Front	15 May 1916
Battle of Jutland	War at Sea	31 May 1916
Battle of Lutsk	Eastern Front	04 June 1916
Capture of Mecca, Arab Revolt	Palestine Front	10 June 1916
Battle of the Somme	Western Front	01 July 1916
Battle of Albert	Western Front	01 July 1916
Battle of Bazentin Ridge	Western Front	14 July 1916
Battle of Delville Wood	Western Front	15 July 1916
Battle of Pozieres Ridge	Western Front	23 July 1916
Battle of Romani	Palestine Front	03 August 1916
Sixth Battle of the Isonzo	Italian Front	06 August 1916
Battle of Gorizia	Italian Front	06 August 1916
Battle of Guillemont	Western Front	03 September 1916
Battle of Ginchy	Western Front	09 September 1916
Seventh Battle of the Isonzo	Italian Front	14 September 1916
Battle of Flers-Courcelette	Western Front	15 September 1916
Battle of Le Transloy	Western Front	01 October 1916
Eighth Battle of the Isonzo	Italian Front	10 October 1916

Engagement	Theatre of War	Date Started
Battle of the Ancre	Western Front	13 October 1916
Ninth Battle of the Isonzo	Italian Front	01 November 1916
Austro-German Capture of Bucharest	Eastern Front	06 December 1916
Second Battle of Kut	Mesopotamia	13 December 1916

1917

Engagement	Theatre of War	Date Started
Battle of Khadairi Bend	Mesopotamia	09 January 1917
Battle of Nahr-al-Kalek	Mesopotamia	26 February 1917
British Capture of Baghdad	Mesopotamia	11 March 1917
British Seizure of Fallujah	Mesopotamia	19 March 1917
First Battle of Gaza	Palestine Front	26 March 1917
Battle of Vimy Ridge	Western Front	09 April 1917
Battle of Shiala	Mesopotamia	11 April 1917
Second Battle of the Aisne	Western Front	16 April 1917
Second Battle of Gaza	Palestine Front	17 April 1917
Battle of Istabulat	Mesopotamia	21 April 1917
Battle of the Boot	Mesopotamia	30 April 1917
Tenth Battle of the Isonzo	Italian Front	12 May 1917
Battle of Otranto Straits	War at Sea	14 May 1917
Battle of Messines	Western Front	07 June 1917
Third Battle of Ypres	Western Front	31 July 1917
Battle of Langemarck	Western Front	16 August 1917
Eleventh Battle of the Isonzo	Italian Front	19 August 1917
Battle of Polygon Wood	Western Front	26 September 1917
Battle of Ramadi	Mesopotamia	28 September 1917
Battle of Poelcapelle	Western Front	09 October 1917
Battle of Passchendaele	Western Front	12 October 1917
Twelfth Battle of the Isonzo	Italian Front	24 October 1917
Battle of Caporetto	Italian Front	24 October 1917
Third Battle of Gaza	Palestine Front	31 October 1917
Battle of Beersheba	Palestine Front	31 October 1917
British Capture of Tikrit	Mesopotamia	05 November 1917
Battle of Mughar Ridge	Palestine Front	13 November 1917
Battle of Cambrai	Western Front	20 November 1917
British Capture of Jerusalem	Palestine Front	08 December 1917

Engagement	Theatre of War	Date Started
1918		
German 'Michael' Offensive	Western Front	21 March 1918
Battle of St Quentin	Western Front	21 March 1918
Battle of Bapaume	Western Front	24 March 1918
Battle of Arras	Western Front	28 March 1918
Battle of the Lys	Western Front	02 April 1918
Battle of Hazebrouck	Western Front	12 April 1918
Battle of Bailleul	Western Front	13 April 1918
Battle of Kemmel	Western Front	17 April 1918
Battle of Bethune	Western Front	18 April 1918
Allied Raid on Zeebrugge	War at Sea	23 April 1918
Third Battle of the Aisne	Western Front	27 May 1918
Battle of Cantigny	Western Front	28 May 1918
Battle of Chateau-Thierry	Western Front	03 June 1918
Battle of Belleau Wood	Western Front	06 June 1918
Battle of Piave River	Italian Front	15 June 1918
Battle of Le Hamel	Western Front	04 July 1918
Second Battle of the Marne	Western Front	15 July 1918
Allied Hundred Days Offensive	Western Front	08 August 1918
Battle of Amiens	Western Front	08 August 1918
Battle of St Mihiel	Western Front	12 September 1918
Battle of Havrincourt	Western Front	12 September 1918
Battle of Epehy	Western Front	18 September 1918
Battle of Courtrai	Western Front	14 October 1918
Battle of Vittorio Veneto	Italian Front	23 October 1918
Battle of Sharqat	Mesopotamia	29 October 1918
Battle of the Sambre	Western Front	04 November 1918
Armistice	Western Front	11 November 1918
German Surrender in East Africa	African Wars	25 November 1918

Ards Casualties in Chronological Order

At the beginning of the Great War the German strategy was to contain Russia on the Eastern Front and to make a lightning strike on France through Belgium. On 9 August 1914 the British Expeditionary Force (BEF) landed in

France and on 23 August the BEF met the full force of the advancing German army at the Battle of Mons. The BEF was forced to retreat southwards and it was during the retreat from Mons that the first two Ardsmen died on the Western Front:

| 26 August 1914 | Private **Samuel Ritchie** | Newtownards |
| 26 August 1914 | Private **William Warnock** | Newtownards |

The German advance was halted in early September 1914 by a counterattack on the River Marne – the Miracle of the Marne. The Germans established positions along the River Aisne and the Battle of the Aisne was fought between 14 and 28 September 1914. Three more Ardsmen died on the Western Front during September 1914 together with one Royal Navy man who was serving with the Coastguard at Tara War Signal Station, Portaferry:

1 September 1914	Private **John Arthur Bell**	Comber
20 September 1914	Leading Boatman **John Hogan**	Portaferry
22 September 1914	Private **Andrew Russell**	Newtownards
27 September 1914	Bandsman **George Coulter Gunning**	Ballywalter

One of the German objectives was to seize the Channel ports. The Allies were equally determined to prevent this and so began the 'race to the sea' during which each army tried to out-flank the other. It was at this point in the war that trench warfare began and eventually the Western Front became a continuous trench system extending for more than 400 miles from the Belgian channel town of Nieuport to the Swiss border. Dugouts, fire steps, lookout posts, listening posts, machine gun positions and mortar pits were constructed. In No Man's Land between the trenches, coils of barbed wire were spread out with machine guns sighted on gaps in the wire to funnel the enemy into the 'killing zones'. Men died attacking the enemy, holding the line against enemy attack and undertaking raids and reconnaissance patrols at night.

During the Great War, men with Ards connections also served in the Royal Navy and in the Mercantile Marine. At the beginning of the Great War many Royal Navy ships were moored at Scapa Flow in Scotland and from there they sought to control the North Sea and blockade German ports. There was also a Royal Navy destroyer flotilla deployed in the English Channel. Merchant ships, singly and in convoys, transported vital supplies throughout the war. Two of the greatest threats to Royal and Merchant Navy vessels came from German mines and submarines. Able Seaman **Robert Algie** who was serving aboard HMS *Hawke* when that ship was torpedoed in the North Sea was the first Ards seaman to be killed in action during the Great War.

Memorials each with an identical design were erected after the war at three manning ports in Great Britain – Chatham, Plymouth and Portsmouth – to commemorate those members of the Royal Navy who have no known grave. The Tower Hill Memorial in London commemorates those members of the Merchant Navy and Fishing Fleets who have no known grave.

During October and November 1914 there was intense fighting along the Western Front during a series of battles at places like La Bassee, Armentieres, Yser, Langemarck, Passchendaele, Broodseinde, Gheluvelt and Nonne Boshen. The Germans captured Messines Ridge and the First Battle of Ypres ended on 22 November.

During the period from October to December 1914 twenty-two Ardsmen died on the Western Front and two died in the war at sea:

15 October 1914	Able Seaman **Robert Algie**	Newtownards
23 October 1914	Lance Corporal **James Stevenson Poag**	Donaghadee
26 October 1914	Sergeant **Richard Henry Martin**	Newtownards
26 October 1914	Lance Corporal **Thomas Gray Mellefont**	Millisle
26 October 1914	Rifleman **William John Pritchard**	Ballywalter
26 October 1914	2nd Lieutenant **Donald SS Smurthwaite**	Portaferry
27 October 1914	Rifleman **William Hurley**	Newtownards
27 October 1914	Lance Corporal **Hector Claude Marsh**	Newtownards
28 October 1914	Private **James Best**	Newtownards
28 October 1914	Private **Thomas Russell**	Newtownards
30 October 1914	Private **William Tompsett**	Comber
1 November 1914	Able Seaman **Samuel Johnston**	Donaghadee
1 November 1914	Captain **The Hon Andrew Mulholland**	Ballywalter
6 November 1914	Private **John Lynch**	Comber
9 November 1914	Rifleman **John Irvine**	Newtownards
15 November 1914	Private **James McBlain**	Newtownards
15 November 1914	Rifleman **Hamilton Orr (James Street)**	Newtownards
16 November 1914	Lance Corporal **Robert Stannage**	Newtownards
23 November 1914	Lance Corporal **Thomas Harris**	Newtownards
6 December 1914	Captain **Bertram Allgood**	Newtownards
14 December 1914	Rifleman **William Robert Bell**	Newtownards
18 December 1914	Rifleman **John Foster**	Newtownards
18 December 1914	Rifleman **William John Majury**	Newtownards
30 December 1914	Rifleman **George Smyth**	Newtownards

On Christmas Day 1914 an unofficial truce was declared by soldiers along the Western Front. South of Ypres at Ploegsteert Wood a game of football was played between the Seaforth Highlanders and the German Royal Saxon Regiment. So far as is known none of the players was from the Ards area.

At the beginning of 1915 Germany decided to hold the Western Front and to concentrate resources in the East. Four soldiers with Ards connections died on the Western Front during January 1915:

1 January 1915	**Sapper Nathaniel Ferguson**	Comber
17 January 1915	**Rifleman William Vance**	Newtownards
25 January 1915	**Private John McBride**	Kircubbin
30 January 1915	**Rifleman James Mackenzie Irwin**	Newtownards

Turkey entered the Great War on the side of the Central Powers at the end of October 1914 and closed the Dardanelles. By closing the Dardanelles to Allied shipping, supply lines to Russia were severed and both Russia and Britain declared war on Turkey. Britain annexed Cyprus and invaded Mesopotamia. During February and March 1915 there was a series of British and French naval actions aimed at destroying the Turkish fortifications guarding the Dardanelles but these operations were not successful.

On 2/3 February 1915 Turkey launched an offensive on the Suez Canal which at that time was under British control. This attack was repelled but the threat of further attacks occupied resources that were needed in the Dardanelles. The first major British offensive of 1915 on the Western Front was at Neuve-Chapelle from 10 to 13 March and after that at St Eloi. Four soldiers with Ards connections died on the Western Front during March 1915 and seven of the men who died aboard HMS *Bayano* (three of whom were unidentified) were buried in the Ards Peninsula that month:

10 March 1915	**Rifleman James Carnduff**	Newtownards
11 March 1915	**Private A G Bain**	Portaferry
11 March 1915	**Able Seaman Frederick William Chater**	Ballywalter
11 March 1915	**Rifleman Alexander Gibson**	Newtownards
11 March 1915	**Bugler William John McWhinney**	Newtownards
11 March 1915	**Leading Seaman Edgar J Spracklin**	Ballyhalbert
11 March 1915	**Able Seaman W A Wellstead**	Portaferry
12 March 1915	**Rifleman James Fisher**	Newtownards

After the naval operations aimed at opening the Dardanelles failed, a decision was taken to send in ground troops and the Allies landed on the Gallipoli peninsula on 25 April 1915. The British forces landed at Cape Helles on the southern tip of the peninsula while the Anzacs (the Australians and the New Zealanders) landed 15 miles further north at what became known as Anzac Cove. There were heavy casualties during the landings and during the weeks that followed. In many cases bodies were never recovered. There were also many deaths caused by disease. For the next eight months the Royal Navy supported the ground troops and then provided the means for the eventual evacuation of troops off the Peninsula.

On 22 April 1915 the Germans launched a major attack on the Western Front at Ypres. This Second Battle of Ypres lasted until 25 May and there was heavy fighting at places including Gravenstafel, St Julien, Frezenberg, Bellewaarde, Aubers and Festubert. It was during the Battle of St Julien that the Germans used poison gas for the first time on the Western Front. Gases caused a range of injuries depending on the type of gas used – some victims died quickly, others more slowly as their lungs collapsed and filled with liquid. Blindness, skin lesions and respiratory problems beset those who survived. When a soldier died, enemy numbers were reduced by one; when a soldier was wounded, additional army resources were tied up caring for that soldier. As well as men, many thousands of horses died from the effects of gas poisoning. For some soldiers who died months or even years later, their deaths could be attributed to the effects of gas poisoning during the Great War.

The year 1915 saw the opening of another front as a result of Italy entering the war on the side of the Allies. During the period April to June 1915 another 39 men with Ards connections died in the various theatres of war, including those who died of wounds in dressing stations, casualty clearing stations, base hospitals and war hospitals in Britain, Malta and elsewhere:

2 April 1915	Private William Robinson	Donaghadee
4 April 1915	Driver Samuel Walker	Newtownards
18 April 1915	Rifleman William James McCluskey	Portaferry
22 April 1915	Private Thomas Alexander Keith	Donaghadee
25 April 1915	Private Alexander Martin	Donaghadee
25 April 1915	2nd Lieutenant John Stanley Williamson	Donaghadee
25 April/3 May 1915	Private Robert Douglas Niblock	Comber
29 April 1915	Private Thomas Best	Newtownards
29 April 1915	Private Robert Matear	Donaghadee
29 April 1915	Farrier Sergeant Robert McDonald	Newtownards
30 April 1915	Private Robert Coulter	Donaghadee
1/23 May 1915	Private James Beck	Newtownards

5 May 1915	Rifleman **Francis Orr**	Carrowdore
9 May 1915	Private **Albert Edward Gregory**	Donaghadee
9 May 1915	Lance Corporal **William Charles Gregory**	Donaghadee
9 May 1915	Sergeant **William Hanna**	Ballyhalbert
9 May 1915	Lance Corporal **Robert Johnston (Snr)**	Newtownards
9 May 1915	Rifleman **Robert Johnston (Jnr)**	Newtownards
9 May 1915	Rifleman **Edward Kelly**	Newtownards
9 May 1915	Corporal **Daniel Matier**	Newtownards
9 May 1915	Corporal **John Hill McKibbin**	Newtownards
9 May 1915	Corporal **John Patrick Quinn**	Newtownards
13 May 1915	Stoker 1st Class **William Ernest Beringer**	Portaferry
13 May 1915	Boy 1st Class **Alfred Henry Victor Gadd**	Newtownards
13 May 1915	Stoker 1st Class **Hector Hiles**	Comber
16 May 1915	Private **William Francis**	Newtownards
16 May 1915	Lieutenant **John Joseph L Morgan MID**	Newtownards
17 May 1915	Private **Hugh McTear**	Newtownards
17 May 1915	Private **Hugh Orr**	Carrowdore
17 May 1915	Private **Robert Stewart**	Donaghadee
18 May 1915	Private **Patrick Daly**	Newtownards
19 May 1915	Lance Sergeant **Robert Bell Harrison**	Newtownards
22 May 1915	Private **William Morris**	Newtownards
22 May 1915	Private **Samuel James Reid**	Newtownards
24 May 1915	Lance Corporal **Robert McKee**	Newtownards
29 May 1915	Lance Corporal **Sidney Lane**	Newtownards
15 June 1915	Private **John Hanna**	Newtownards
16 June 1915	Rifleman **James Heron**	Newtownards
16 June 1915	Private **Daniel Maclean Keith**	Newtownards

Sometimes soldiers who were killed in action died instantly whilst others suffered a painful, lingering death. Some soldiers died from wounds sustained in action a few hours, or several days, previously. In an effort to minimise the anguish suffered by bereaved families, the reports by officers of deaths in action usually intimated that death was instantaneous or else that pain and suffering were minimal. This was a period of time when British forces suffered from a shortage of ammunition on the Western Front.

In August 1915 there was another British landing on the Gallipoli Peninsula at Suvla Bay and, when further British and Anzac offensives at Suvla, Lone Pine and Kirich Tepe failed to make progress, a decision was taken to evacuate the peninsula. Suvla and Anzac were evacuated on 19/20 December 1915 and Helles was evacuated on 8/9 January 1916.

During September and October 1915 the Battles of Champagne and Loos were fought on the Western Front and in December 1915 Sir Douglas Haig replaced Sir John French as British Commander-in-Chief.

Fighting on the Balkan Front in the Great War had begun on 29 July 1914 with the Austro-Hungarian bombardment of Belgrade and this theatre of war assumed additional strategic importance in 1915. Both the Allied and Central powers sought Bulgarian support and, after the Allied reverses at the Dardanelles, Bulgaria sided with the Central Powers with the objective of securing Macedonia. Greece mobilised in response to the Bulgarian threat to Serbia and requested Allied assistance. An expeditionary force landed at Salonika on 9 October but then Greece declared neutrality and the Allied forces were unable to proactively help the Serbs. Serbia and Montenegro were occupied by the Central Powers.

During the period July to December 1915 forty-seven men with Ards connections died in the various theatres of war including Salonika:

12 July 1915	Private Andrew Kerr	Newtownards
12 July 1915	Private Francis Smythe	Comber
13 July 1915	Private William Maddock	Newtownards
19 July 1915	Rifleman James Burns	Newtownards
29 July 1915	Rifleman George Jamison	Newtownards
2 August 1915	2nd Lieutenant Mark William McDonald	Portaferry
3 August 1915	Lance Corporal James Holland	Greyabbey
9 August 1915	Private Patrick Hamill	Newtownards
9 August 1915	Private William Henry Thompson	Newtownards
11 August 1915	Rifleman John Crossen	Ballygowan
11 August 1915	Lance Corporal William Moore	Newtownards
11 August 1915	Rifleman Neil McLean Mulholland	Ballywalter
15 August 1915	Private Hamilton McWhinney	Newtownards
21 August 1915	Private Robert Marshall	Newtownards
21 August 1915	Corporal Daniel Rea	Newtownards
25 August 1915	Rifleman Charles Thompson	Newtownards
27 August 1915	Greaser James Jamison	Millisle
28 August 1915	Rifleman Thomas Dines	Newtownards
1 September 1915	Captain Herbert Vesey Scott	Portaferry

3 September 1915	**2nd Lieutenant Irvine Johnston Smyth**	Newtownards
8 September 1915	**Lance Corporal Richard C Chasty**	Portaferry
10 September 1915	**Private Ellis Oliver**	Comber
20 September 1915	**Captain John William Field**	Newtownards
25 September 1915	**Private William Blair**	Ballywalter
25 September 1915	**Captain Walter Percy O'Lone DCM MID**	Newtownards
25 September 1915	**Sergeant Albert Edward Young**	Comber
27 September 1915	**Private James Bell**	Greyabbey
27 September 1915	**Private William Roseman**	Newtownards
30 September 1915	**Private Patrick Docherty**	Kircubbin
1 October 1915	**Rifleman James Brown**	Newtownards
18 October 1915	**Rifleman Thomas Davidson**	Donaghadee
20 October 1915	**Regimental Sgt Major Charles J Cherry**	Newtownards
27 October 1915	**Driver Hugh Andrew McKee**	Millisle
1 November 1915	**Chief Gunner John David Sumner**	Portaferry
5 November 1915	**Sapper Arthur McKeown**	Newtownards
8 November 1915	**Sergeant James Armstrong Kelly DCM**	Newtownards
10 November 1915	**Private Robert John Lightbody**	Newtownards
11 November 1915	**Captain Robert James O'Lone MID**	Newtownards
19 November 1915	**Lance Corporal Valentine Cairnduff**	Newtownards
21 November 1915	**Private James Carser**	Newtownards
27 November 1915	**Rifleman Joseph Porter**	Newtownards
28 November 1915	**Lance Sergeant James Mullan**	Newtownards
7 December 1915	**Corporal Gerald Marcus Huston DCM**	Killinchy
10 December 1915	**Lance Corporal James Cardy**	Newtownards
11 December 1915	**Company Sgt Major Francis McMath**	Donaghadee
16 December 1915	**Rifleman William Boyd**	Newtownards
24 December 1915	**Sergeant George Hamilton**	Newtownards

The first soldier from Ards to die on the Western Front in 1916 was killed on 6 January when he was working as a stretcher bearer. Between 21 February and 18 December 1916 a series of German offensives comprised the Battle of Verdun and between 2 and 13 June the Battle of Mount Sorrell was fought.

In all theatres of war fifty-three men with Ards connections died during the first six months of 1916, including those who died in Dublin during the suppression of the Easter Rising:

6 January 1916	Rifleman **Andrew McDonald**	Newtownards
12 January 1916	Chief Stoker **William John Reains**	Donaghadee
23 January 1916	Rifleman **Thomas McTaggart**	Newtownards
7 February 1916	Rifleman **James Calvert**	Killinchy
7 February 1916	Rifleman **David McConnell**	Newtownards
7 February 1916	Rifleman (Bandsman) **Charles Newell**	Newtownards
7 February 1916	Rifleman **John P K Tate**	Newtownards
14 February 1916	Rifleman **Hugh Shanks**	Newtownards
22 February 1916	2nd Lieutenant **Rowan Shaw**	Kircubbin
27 February 1916	CQMS **David John Stratton**	Newtownards
13 March 1916	Rifleman **Frederick H Trousdale**	Comber
19 March 1916	Lieutenant **George B Keeling**	Millisle
19 March 1916	Captain **Mervyn Stronge Richardson MID**	Newtownards
22 March 1916	Company Sergeant Major **Martin Brown**	Newtownards
27 March 1916	Lance Corporal **Samuel Orr**	Portaferry
4 April 1916	Rifleman **Joseph Oswald**	Donaghadee
9 April 1916	2nd Lieutenant **George Knox**	Newtownards
11 April 1916	Rifleman **Patrick Mullen**	Newtownards
12 April 1916	Private **James Downes**	Newtownards
25 April 1916	Private **Edward McMullan**	Portaferry
25 April 1916	Private **Thomas Patton**	Newtownards
26 April 1916	Private **Joseph Craig**	Greyabbey
27 April 1916	Rifleman **William Cardy**	Newtownards
27 April 1916	Private **James Healy**	Comber
27 April 1916	Rifleman **Alexander McClelland**	Kircubbin
28 April 1916	Rifleman **James Glover Mackey**	Newtownards
29 April 1916	Private **Patrick Gilmore**	Newtownards
2 May 1916	Driver **George Casey**	Comber
2 May 1916	Rifleman **James McCullough**	Donaghadee
6 May 1916	Rifleman **John Henry McBratney**	Comber
8 May 1916	Private **James J Corrigan**	Portaferry
10 May 1916	Rifleman **Charles Francis Hill**	Ballygowan
17 May 1916	Rifleman **Charles Pollock**	Donaghadee
18 May 1916	Private **William Boal alias McHugh**	Newtownards
19 May 1916	Rifleman **William Smyth (Greenwell St)**	Newtownards
27 May 1916	Rifleman **David Scott**	Newtownards
28 May 1916	Private **Robert Lennon**	Newtownards

30 May 1916	Rifleman **William John Thompson**	Comber
31 May 1916	Stoker First Class **David Magee**	Ballyhalbert
31 May 1916	Stoker First Class **John Moreland**	Ballyhalbert
5 June 1916	Surgeon **Hugh Francis McNally**	Portaferry
8 June 1916	Corporal **John Norish Chasty**	Portaferry
10 June 1916	Private **John Price**	Comber
11 June 1916	Rifleman **William Tanner**	Donaghadee
13 June 1916	**Robert McConnell**	Donaghadee
16 June 1916	Rifleman **Joseph McDowell**	Newtownards
17 June 1916	Rifleman **Alexander Dodds**	Portaferry
23 June 1916	Lance Corporal **Robert John McDowell**	Ballygowan
25 June 1916	Rifleman **William Semple**	Donaghadee
26 June 1916	Lance Sergeant **William John Brown**	Comber
27 June 1916	Lance Corporal **John McCracken**	Newtownards
29 June 1916	Rifleman **James Morrison**	Comber
30 June 1916	Private **Robert Watson McMillan**	Newtownards

Saturday 1 July 1916 is described by some commentators as 'the bloodiest day in the history of the British Army'. British forces attacked in waves towards the German wire, much of which was undamaged despite a huge preparatory bombardment. The first day of the Battle of the Somme was indeed a bloody day for Ards when at least 129 soldiers and one airman with Ards connections died in the carnage. Many of them served with the 13th Battalion Royal Irish Rifles in 108th Brigade of the 36th (Ulster) Division and from Thiepval Wood they attacked German positions to the south of the River Ancre between the river and the heavily fortified Schwaben Redoubt.

1 July 1916	Private **Edward Adair**	Newtownards
1 July 1916	Rifleman **Robert Hugh Allen**	Newtownards
1 July 1916	Rifleman **William Anderson**	Newtownards
1 July 1916	Rifleman **William Angus**	Donaghadee
1 July 1916	Rifleman **John Blair Angus**	Donaghadee
1 July 1916	Rifleman **James Auld**	Comber
1 July 1916	Lance Corporal **James Bailie**	Portaferry
1 July 1916	Lance Corporal **Thomas John Ballance**	Kircubbin
1 July 1916	Rifleman **William Bell**	Kircubbin
1 July 1916	Private **James Bennett**	Ballygowan
1 July 1916	Corporal **Edward Bennett**	Newtownards
1 July 1916	Sergeant **Alfred Blythe**	Newtownards

1 July 1916	Rifleman Alexander Boland	Newtownards
1 July 1916	Private Richard Boucher	Newtownards
1 July 1916	Lance Corporal George Taylor Boyd	Comber
1 July 1916	Sergeant Henry Burgess	Comber
1 July 1916	Rifleman George Burns	Newtownards
1 July 1916	Sapper Robert James Burrows	Ballygowan
1 July 1916	Rifleman William James Calvert	Killinchy
1 July 1916	Lance Corporal Alexander Campbell	Donaghadee
1 July 1916	Rifleman Archibald Thomas Campbell	Newtownards
1 July 1916	Rifleman Alexander Carlisle	Newtownards
1 July 1916	Rifleman Samuel Carnduff	Newtownards
1 July 1916	Rifleman John Cathcart	Comber
1 July 1916	Rifleman Edward Corry	Ballywalter
1 July 1916	Private William John Dalzell	Newtownards
1 July 1916	Rifleman Andrew John Dempster	Comber
1 July 1916	Rifleman Robert Dempster	Comber
1 July 1916	Sergeant Samuel DeVoy	Newtownards
1 July 1916	Corporal James Neil Doggart	Newtownards
1 July 1916	Rifleman Thomas Maddock Doggart	Newtownards
1 July 1916	Rifleman James Donaldson	Comber
1 July 1916	Rifleman John Donaldson	Comber
1 July 1916	Rifleman Samuel Donaldson	Comber
1 July 1916	Private John Dornan	Newtownards
1 July 1916	Lance Corporal James Dorrian	Newtownards
1 July 1916	Rifleman John Dorrian	Newtownards
1 July 1916	Lance Corporal William Drennan	Donaghadee
1 July 1916	Rifleman John Dynes	Killinchy
1 July 1916	Rifleman James Fisher	Comber
1 July 1916	Rifleman John Ralston Fitzsimmons	Kircubbin
1 July 1916	Sergeant Henry Foster	Newtownards
1 July 1916	Rifleman William John Fowles	Newtownards
1 July 1916	Rifleman Thomas Gilliland	Newtownards
1 July 1916	Lance Corporal Walter Gunning	Ballywalter
1 July 1916	Rifleman John Irvine Hamilton	Donaghadee
1 July 1916	Rifleman Thomas James Harrison MM	Newtownards
1 July 1916	Lt Col Lawrence Arthur Hind MC MID	Comber
1 July 1916	Private Andrew Johnston	Newtownards

1 July 1916	Rifleman James Stevenson Johnston	Comber
1 July 1916	Private William Johnston	Newtownards
1 July 1916	Captain Elliott Johnston MC	Newtownards
1 July 1916	Rifleman Samuel Wallace Jordan	Ballygowan
1 July 1916	Rifleman William George Kelly	Newtownards
1 July 1916	Lance Corporal David Lamont	Newtownards
1 July 1916	Rifleman Samuel Hugh Ledgerwood	Newtownards
1 July 1916	Rifleman Robert Lowry	Newtownards
1 July 1916	Rifleman John Magill	Comber
1 July 1916	Lance Corporal George Mahaffy	Newtownards
1 July 1916	Rifleman Andrew Marshall	Newtownards
1 July 1916	Rifleman John Martin	Newtownards
1 July 1916	Rifleman John Magilton McAvoy	Newtownards
1 July 1916	Lance Corporal James McCann	Donaghadee
1 July 1916	Rifleman Robert McCartney	Newtownards
1 July 1916	Rifleman David McConnell	Donaghadee
1 July 1916	Lance Corporal William James McCoy	Newtownards
1 July 1916	Rifleman Daniel McCutcheon	Donaghadee
1 July 1916	Rifleman John McCutcheon	Comber
1 July 1916	Rifleman James McGimpsey	Newtownards
1 July 1916	Rifleman John McIlveen	Comber
1 July 1916	Rifleman Robert McKibbin	Donaghadee
1 July 1916	Lance Corporal James McNeilly	Newtownards
1 July 1916	Rifleman William McQuiston	Newtownards
1 July 1916	Private William John Melville	Donaghadee
1 July 1916	Private Joseph Miller	Comber
1 July 1916	Rifleman John Mills	Ballygowan
1 July 1916	Rifleman James Morrow	Carrowdore
1 July 1916	Private Walter Mulholland	Newtownards
1 July 1916	Rifleman Alexander Mullan	Comber
1 July 1916	Rifleman David Swan Mullan	Newtownards
1 July 1916	Rifleman (Bandsman) Thomas Newell	Newtownards
1 July 1916	Private Thomas Norris	Newtownards
1 July 1916	Corporal John O'Neill	Newtownards
1 July 1916	Rifleman John O'Neill	Ballywalter
1 July 1916	Rifleman Robert James Orr	Comber
1 July 1916	Rifleman David Bell Patterson	Newtownards

1 July 1916	Lance Corporal **James Patterson**	Comber
1 July 1916	Rifleman **Robert Patterson**	Comber
1 July 1916	Corporal **William James Patterson**	Newtownards
1 July 1916	Rifleman **William Patton**	Donaghadee
1 July 1916	Lieutenant **John Luddington Peacock**	Newtownards
1 July 1916	Corporal **William John Peake MM**	Ballywalter
1 July 1916	Rifleman **William Haire Poole**	Newtownards
1 July 1916	Rifleman **James Porter**	Newtownards
1 July 1916	Rifleman **David Rainey**	Ballygowan
1 July 1916	Rifleman **Robert Regan**	Ballywalter
1 July 1916	Rifleman **Alexander Robinson**	Newtownards
1 July 1916	Rifleman **Samuel Robinson**	Donaghadee
1 July 1916	Rifleman **John Russell (Frederick St)**	Newtownards
1 July 1916	Rifleman **Alexander Russell**	Newtownards
1 July 1916	Rifleman **William Semple**	Donaghadee
1 July 1916	Rifleman **David Shanks**	Carrowdore
1 July 1916	Rifleman **John Shannon**	Newtownards
1 July 1916	Lance Corporal **William Simpson**	Newtownards
1 July 1916	Rifleman **John Sinclair**	Kircubbin
1 July 1916	Rifleman **George Sloan**	Comber
1 July 1916	Rifleman **William Sloan**	Newtownards
1 July 1916	Rifleman **David John Smyth**	Comber
1 July 1916	Rifleman **David Smyth**	Comber
1 July 1916	Rifleman **William John S Snodden**	Killinchy
1 July 1916	Lance Corporal **John Milliken Spence**	Comber
1 July 1916	Private **Robert Stewart**	Donaghadee
1 July 1916	Rifleman **Robert Stewart**	Donaghadee
1 July 1916	Rifleman **Samuel Strain**	Donaghadee
1 July 1916	Sergeant **James Tate**	Killinchy
1 July 1916	Company Sgt Major **William Taylor**	Portaferry
1 July 1916	Rifleman **William Robert Taylor**	Donaghadee
1 July 1916	Rifleman **James Thompson**	Kircubbin
1 July 1916	Private **William James Thompson**	Newtownards
1 July 1916	Rifleman **Charles Thompson**	Donaghadee
1 July 1916	Lance Corporal **David John Thompson**	Newtownards
1 July 1916	Corporal **William John Thompson**	Newtownards
1 July 1916	Lance Corporal **Henry Edward Victor**	Donaghadee

1 July 1916	Private **John Walker**	Comber
1 July 1916	Rifleman **James Walsh**	Comber
1 July 1916	Captain (Pilot) **Gilbert Watson Webb**	Newtownards
1 July 1916	Rifleman **John Weir**	Newtownards
1 July 1916	Rifleman **William Wilson**	Killinchy
1 July 1916	2nd Lieutenant **Matthew John Wright**	Newtownards
1 July 1916	Rifleman **James Young**	Newtownards

Despite the heavy losses sustained on the first day Sir Douglas Haig decided to press on with the attack and the Battle of the Somme continued until 18 November 1916. There were major battles at many places including High Wood, Delville Wood, Pozieres, Guillemont, Ginchy and the Ancre. Armoured vehicles were used for the first time on 15 September 1916 at Flers-Courcelette and on 27 September the village of Thiepval was taken.

In the days and weeks that followed the opening day of the Battle of the Somme soldiers with Ards connections continued to die on the Western Front and in other theatres of war. In all, 100 Ardsmen are recorded as having died between 2 July 1916 and the end of the year. In the heat of battle the 8th Battalion Royal Irish Rifles did not make a casualty return on 1 July 1916 and many military historians agree that those 8th Battalion casualties listed on the 2 July return were actually killed in action on 1 July.

2 July 1916	Rifleman **James Bowman**	Newtownards
2 July 1916	Rifleman **David Cromie**	Killinchy
2 July 1916	Rifleman **Robert Finlay**	Newtownards
2 July 1916	Rifleman **Samuel Kennedy**	Newtownards
2 July 1916	Rifleman **Robert McClements**	Killinchy
2 July 1916	Rifleman **John McCulloch**	Comber
2 July 1916	Rifleman **James McIlwrath alias Harris**	Comber
2 July 1916	Rifleman **Samuel McMillan**	Newtownards
2 July 1916	Rifleman **Samuel Miskelly**	Newtownards
2 July 1916	Rifleman **Alexander Palmer**	Newtownards
2 July 1916	Rifleman **Thomas Quinn**	Newtownards
2 July 1916	Rifleman **William Ravey**	Greyabbey
2 July 1916	Private **Robert Thompson**	Killinchy
3 July 1916	Rifleman **Samuel Heslip Gordon**	Newtownards
4 July 1916	Rifleman **James Robinson**	Donaghadee
7 July 1916	Rifleman **Robert Henderson**	Newtownards
7 July 1916	Corporal **Bryan McCloone**	Portaferry

7 July 1916	Lance Cpl Robert James McGreechan	Newtownards
8 July 1916	Rifleman David John Gamble	Comber
8 July 1916	Rifleman James Croskery Stevenson	Newtownards
9 July 1916	Lance Corporal Robert Angus	Donaghadee
9 July 1916	Private Alexander Beattie	Newtownards
9 July 1916	Rifleman Joseph Miskimmin	Donaghadee
11 July 1916	Captain Henry Cooke Lowry	Greyabbey
12 July 1916	Rifleman Edward Ferguson McAvoy	Newtownards
12 July 1916	Sergeant Thomas Millar	Ballygowan
14 July 1916	Private Redmond Joseph Diver	Newtownards
15 July 1916	Private Richard Rae	Newtownards
18 July 1916	Private George Laidlaw	Ballyhalbert
18 July 1916	Private John Smyth	Portaferry
20 July 1916	Private Mason Simonton	Comber
21 July 1916	Private James Aloysius Kinlay	Portaferry
30 July 1916	Private Joseph M Scarr	Newtownards
31 July 1916	Rifleman Andrew Orr	Ballywalter
9 August 1916	Trooper Herbert Alexander Bell	Newtownards
9 August 1916	Corporal John Clark	Donaghadee
9 August 1916	Rifleman James Smyth	Newtownards
16 August 1916	Private David Greer Cooke	Newtownards
19 August 1916	Stoker First Class Robert Ennis	Ballyhalbert
19 August 1916	Rifleman William John Smyth (Mill St)	Newtownards
20 August 1916	Lance Corporal Henry J Parfitt	Newtownards
23 August 1916	Rifleman Robert Stratton	Newtownards
24 August 1916	Lance Corporal Andrew Clarke	Comber
25 August 1916	Private David Gamble	Newtownards
26 August 1916	Private John Maidens MM	Newtownards
29 August 1916	Lance Corporal William McDowell	Newtownards
30 August 1916	Rifleman Alexander Dines	Newtownards
1 September 1916	Rifleman Robert Douglas	Ballygowan
1 September 1916	Rifleman David Pyper	Ballyhalbert
3 September 1916	Private William O'Neill	Newtownards
3 September 1916	Private James Runaghan	Newtownards
3 September 1916	Private David Smyth	Portaferry
6 September 1916	Private John Joseph McMullan	Portaferry
9 September 1916	Private Thomas Guiney	Portaferry

9 September 1916	Rifleman James Hughes	Comber
9 September 1916	Lance Corporal Robert Russell Irvine	Newtownards
9 September 1916	Private Hugh McGreevy	Killinchy
9 September 1916	2nd Lieutenant John Ross Moore	Newtownards
9 September 1916	Private Joseph Murphy	Newtownards
11 September 1916	Private James Angus	Donaghadee
15 September 1916	Private Beresford Addy	Ballyhalbert
15 September 1916	Lt Col Charles William R Duncombe	Greyabbey
15 September 1916	Sergeant Andrew Heron	Newtownards
15 September 1916	Private James McGaffin	Donaghadee
15 September 1916	Private Robert Sloane McGaffin	Donaghadee
15 September 1916	Private John Stewart	Carrowdore
16 September 1916	Private Collins Alexander Cooke	Newtownards
16 September 1916	Private Samuel Grant	Ballygowan
16 September 1916	Rifleman David John Keilty	Newtownards
17 September 1916	Gunner William Dickson	Comber
21 September 1916	Private James Edgar Drake	Comber
27 September 1916	Lt Frederick St John Ford North Echlin	Kircubbin
8 October 1916	Lieutenant Robert Davison MC	Newtownards
10 October 1916	Private James Gorman	Newtownards
11 October 1916	Private Francis Haire	Newtownards
12 October 1916	Colour Sgt John Isaac Cutler LS&GC	Newtownards
12 October 1916	Private James McKimm	Newtownards
17 October 1916	Lance Corporal Robert Fitzsimons	Killinchy
20 October 1916	Horseman Hugh Muckle	Donaghadee
22 October 1916	Rifleman Hugh McClure	Newtownards
22 October 1916	Private Hugh Mullan	Newtownards
23 October 1916	Rifleman Robert Buckley	Newtownards
24 October 1916	Rifleman Charles Gorman	Newtownards
25 October 1916	Private Hugh Moore	Newtownards
26 October 1916	Rifleman John Waring	Donaghadee
4 November 1916	Captain Archibald H Hamilton	Killinchy
13 November 1916	Corporal Francis Geddis	Comber
13 November 1916	Lance Cpl Herbert Henry MacMahon	Newtownards
13 November 1916	Private William Wadham Robinson	Newtownards
13 November 1916	Sergeant Patrick P Spain	Newtownards
14 November 1916	Lance Corporal John Adair	Ballywalter

14 November 1916	Private **Ernest Ludgate Hill**	Greyabbey
19 November 1916	Private **David McKittrick**	Newtownards
27 November 1916	Lieutenant **William Hamilton Mitchell**	Comber
10 December 1916	Rifleman **Thomas McBride Patton**	Donaghadee
14 December 1916	Private **John Donnan**	Kircubbin
16 December 1916	Private **David Taylor**	Newtownards
19 December 1916	Private **James Gray**	Donaghadee
26 December 1916	Rifleman **Robert Carpenter**	Ballywalter
31 December 1916	Rifleman **John Harvey**	Newtownards

The first Ardsman to die in 1917 was Rifleman **John Ledgerwood**. He had been severely wounded on 11 December 1916 and he died after having one of his legs amputated. From February to April 1917 the Germans fell back in stages to the heavily fortified Hindenburg Line. As they retreated they laid booby traps and destroyed bridges, buildings and communications. On 6 April 1917 the United States of America declared war with Germany and in June the first US troops began to arrive in France. During April and May the Battle of Arras was fought. From the beginning of January 1917, up to and including 6 June, 56 men with Ards connections died in all theatres of war, including the war in Africa.

6 January 1917	Rifleman **John Ledgerwood**	Newtownards
10 January 1917	Private **William Martin**	Newtownards
28 January 1917	Petty Officer **John Joseph Sheals**	Portaferry
30 January 1917	Seaman **John McClement**	Kircubbin
6 February 1917	Lance Corporal **William Edwin Logan**	Comber
6 February 1917	Private **Thomas Reilly**	Donaghadee
9 February 1917	Private **Andrew McCutcheon Mayne**	Newtownards
14 February 1917	Lance Corporal **Robert H Marshall**	Comber
14 February 1917	Rifleman **William McKittrick**	Newtownards
15 February 1917	Rifleman **Robert Robinson**	Donaghadee
16 February 1917	Rifleman **Thomas Strickland**	Comber
1 March 1917	Corporal **William Menown**	Portaferry
2 March 1917	Private **John Kinnaird**	Newtownards
4 March 1917	Private **Hugh McConnell**	Newtownards
5 March 1917	Private **William McLaughlin**	Newtownards
7 March 1917	Rifleman **George Hamilton**	Donaghadee
8 March 1917	Private **Joseph Murray**	Newtownards

17 March 1917	Private **Hugh Charles H McLean**	Newtownards
22 March 1917	Rifleman **William Beers**	Comber
24 March 1917	Rifleman **Thomas Blackadder**	Newtownards
24 March 1917	Rifleman **William Gunning**	Newtownards
5 April 1917	Rifleman **Thomas Martin Horner**	Killinchy
9 April 1917	Private **Frederick G Beringer**	Portaferry
9 April 1917	Private **Henry Douglas Ritchie**	Comber
9 April 1917	Lt **Basil Llewellyn Boyd Thomas**	Ballywalter
10 April 1917	Private **William Montgomery**	Newtownards
11 April 1917	Private **Andrew Lyttle**	Killinchy
11 April 1917	Private **William Savage Montgomery**	Killinchy
11 April 1917	Private **Alexander White**	Newtownards
14 April 1917	Private **John Joseph Delaney**	Portaferry
14 April 1917	Private **James Arthur Drennan**	Donaghadee
14 April 1917	Sergeant **James McKee**	Millisle
16 April 1917	Private **George Fisher**	Portaferry
17 April 1917	Carpenter **Robert Hughes**	Portavogie
18 April 1917	Major **John Campbell Galway**	Comber
23 April 1917	Gunner **James Campbell**	Newtownards
23 April 1917	2nd Lieutenant **Hugh Charles Allen DCM**	Newtownards
23 April 1917	Private **James McGimpsey**	Greyabbey
23 April 1917	Lt Col **F Savage-Armstrong DSO MID**	Cloughey
25 April 1917	Private **James Paton**	Newtownards
28 April 1917	Sergeant **John Quinn**	Comber
3 May 1917	Private **William Donnan**	Kircubbin
7 May 1917	Private **John Boyd**	Newtownards
8 May 1917	Private **John McMillan**	Newtownards
10 May 1917	Corporal **Edward Atkin**	Cloughey
10 May 1917	Lance Corporal **Thomas S Swanger**	Newtownards
17 May 1917	Rifleman **Robert John Corry**	Newtownards
18 May 1917	Private **James Martin**	Newtownards
24 May 1917	Lance Sergeant **James Clegg**	Newtownards
27 May 1917	Driver **Hugh Crouch Houston**	Newtownards
29 May 1917	Lance Corporal **Samuel John Gregg**	Newtownards
29 May 1917	Sapper **Joseph Hare**	Comber
29 May 1917	Major **William Maxwell Shaw DSO MID**	Kircubbin
29 May 1917	Rifleman **John Swindle**	Comber

5 June 1917	**Corporal William Francis Cumming**	Greyabbey
5 June 1917	**Private Thomas Donnan**	Cloughey

On 7 June 1917 the Battle of Messines began on the Western Front when British forces detonated 19 huge mines in tunnels they had excavated under the German trenches and advanced under a creeping barrage to capture Messines Ridge. The explosions which killed more than 10,000 Germans were heard in London. Men from the 16th (Irish) and 36th (Ulster) Divisions fought side by side. It was in this battle that Major Willie Redmond of the 16th (Irish) Division, an Irish Nationalist MP and a brother of Joseph Redmond, was fatally wounded. He was brought in by stretcher bearers from the 36th (Ulster) Division and, amongst many other people, Sir Edward Carson paid tribute to his memory.

Preceded by a heavy preliminary bombardment which began on 18 July 1917 the Third Battle of Ypres was launched by the Allied forces on 31 July 1917 (the First and Second Battles of Ypres were launched by the Germans in 1914 and 1915). The Third Battle continued until the fall of Passchendaele village on 6 November 1917 with battles at many places including Langemarck, Polygon Wood, Poelcapelle and Hill 60. Weather conditions were atrocious with soldiers advancing through a muddy quagmire. Many who died or fell wounded were swallowed up by the mud. In all, 95 men with Ards connections died on the Western Front and in other theatres of war between 7 June and the end of October 1917.

7 June 1917	**Rifleman Robert James Dempster**	Comber
7 June 1917	**Rifleman Frederick McKee**	Newtownards
7 June 1917	**Corporal William Barry Ritchie Millar**	Ballygowan
7 June 1917	**Corporal Robert Boyd Rainey**	Newtownards
7 June 1917	**Rifleman Hugh Tate**	Donaghadee
8 June 1917	**Sergeant George Brankin**	Newtownards
12 June 1917	**Gunner Thomas Simpson alias Harvey**	Comber
17 June 1917	**Private Alexander McClean**	Donaghadee
18 June 1917	**Rifleman Alexander Doggart**	Newtownards
22 June 1917	**Driver Alexander Gibson**	Newtownards
26 June 1917	**Rifleman William Regan**	Newtownards
1 July 1917	**Gunner Hugh Stevenson**	Newtownards
7 July 1917	**Private Roland Hugh Mason**	Portaferry
7 July 1917	**Corporal Francis McAlpine**	Newtownards
9 July 1917	**Stoker First Class Hugh Fisher**	Portaferry

14 July 1917	**Rifleman John Campbell**	Newtownards
17 July 1917	**Rifleman James McCullough**	Donaghadee
20 July 1917	**Second Mate Thomas Lewis Nicholas**	Ballywalter
25 July 1917	**Rifleman Samuel Gibson**	Ballygowan
27 July 1917	**Private James McGilton Brett**	Newtownards
31 July 1917	**Private Catherwood Moore**	Donaghadee
31 July 1917	**Corporal John Russell**	Newtownards
31 July 1917	**Captain Alfred Squire Taylor**	Comber
1 August 1917	**Lance Corporal James Irvine**	Newtownards
2 August 1917	**Rifleman John Kennedy**	Newtownards
3 August 1917	**Rifleman Thomas Corry**	Newtownards
3 August 1917	**Rifleman Robert McGimpsey**	Millisle
4 August 1917	**Rifleman David Cromie**	Ballywalter
6 August 1917	**Rifleman William James Gibson**	Newtownards
6 August 1917	**Rifleman James McClelland**	Newtownards
6 August 1917	**Rifleman John Smyth**	Comber
7 August 1917	**Rifleman James Jones**	Newtownards
8 August 1917	**Rifleman George Edgar Edmonds**	Ballywalter
8 August 1917	**Rifleman Alexander Pagan**	Newtownards
8 August 1917	**Rifleman Reuben Peake**	Ballywalter
9 August 1917	**Company Sgt Major James Campbell**	Newtownards
10 August 1917	**Lieutenant S Valentine Morgan LS&GC**	Newtownards
11 August 1917	**Rifleman John McPhillips**	Newtownards
12 August 1917	**Rifleman Hans Hamilton**	Donaghadee
12 August 1917	**Rifleman Joseph McConnell**	Donaghadee
13 August 1917	**Lance Corporal Andrew Donaldson**	Portaferry
13 August 1917	**Rifleman Alexander McIlwrath**	Comber
13 August 1917	**Second Lieutenant Thomas McRoberts**	Comber
15 August 1917	**Private John McDonnell**	Kircubbin
15 August 1917	**Rifleman James Stewart**	Kircubbin
16 August 1917	**Rifleman James Campbell**	Donaghadee
16 August 1917	**Lance Corporal Thomas Coey**	Comber
16 August 1917	**Rifleman William Coleman**	Comber
16 August 1917	**Lance Corporal William John Cromie**	Killinchy
16 August 1917	**Private Hugh Dalzell**	Newtownards
16 August 1917	**Sergeant William John Doherty LS&GC**	Newtownards
16 August 1917	**Rifleman John Fullerton**	Newtownards

16 August 1917	Rifleman **Alexander Hamill**	Newtownards
16 August 1917	Lance Corporal **John A Hare**	Comber
16 August 1917	Private **Vincent Hendley**	Newtownards
16 August 1917	Rifleman **Thomas Johnston**	Ballywalter
16 August 1917	Private **William James Johnston**	Kircubbin
16 August 1917	Rifleman **Hugh Kelly**	Comber
16 August 1917	Rifleman **John Kennedy**	Newtownards
16 August 1917	Second Lieutenant **Joseph Laverty**	Newtownards
16 August 1917	Rifleman **William McBride**	Newtownards
16 August 1917	2nd Lieutenant **James Wilson McBurney**	Comber
16 August 1917	Rifleman **Duncan McLean**	Newtownards
16 August 1917	Company Sgt Major **W Harold Medland**	Newtownards
16 August 1917	2nd Lieutenant **William Moore**	Newtownards
16 August 1917	Private **George Morrow**	Newtownards
16 August 1917	Rifleman **Samuel Murray**	Newtownards
16 August 1917	Sergeant **James Proctor**	Comber
16 August 1917	Lance Corporal **Thomas Stevenson**	Newtownards
16 August 1917	Corporal **John Thompson**	Donaghadee
16 August 1917	Rifleman **James Vance**	Newtownards
16 August 1917	Rifleman **James Wright**	Newtownards
17 August 1917	Rifleman **William Thomas Miller**	Newtownards
18 August 1917	Company Sgt Major **Robert H Wallace**	Newtownards
19 August 1917	Private **George Stevenson**	Newtownards
5 September 1917	Gunner **Alexander McDonnell**	Portaferry
5 September 1917	Sapper **Robert Morrison**	Newtownards
14 September 1917	Private **Hugh Samuel Bailie**	Ballyhalbert
18 September 1917	Private **James McCutcheon**	Newtownards
20 September 1917	Sergeant **Robert Thompson**	Ballywalter
21 September 1917	Lieutenant **William Angus Browne**	Kircubbin
22 September 1917	Private **Adam Donaldson**	Newtownards
22 September 1917	Private **David Harvey**	Newtownards
3 October 1917	Corporal **Hamilton Moore**	Newtownards
4 October 1917	Private **Hugh John M Dorrian**	Portaferry
10 October 1917	Private **Thomas Emerson**	Portaferry
11 October 1917	Private **Hamilton Bennett**	Newtownards
11 October 1917	Private **Samuel Gilmour**	Newtownards
19 October 1917	2nd Lieutenant **James Campbell Watters**	Newtownards

26 October 1917	Sergeant John Gracie	Newtownards
26 October 1917	Captain John Sibbald Simms	Newtownards
27 October 1917	Acting Bombardier George E Mulholland	Newtownards
29 October 1917	Rifleman Thomas James Fisher	Comber
29 October 1917	Private Robert Saunders	Donaghadee
31 October 1917	Lance Corporal Samuel Horace Nelson	Newtownards

On 5 November 1917 the Supreme War Council was established and this comprised the Prime Ministers of Britain, France and Italy, together with the President of the USA. On 20 November 1917 British forces on the Western Front attacked at Cambrai, using tanks to good effect. In all, 25 men with Ards connections died during November and December 1917 on the Western Front and in the other theatres of war.

1 November 1917	Private Samuel McKee	Comber
16 November 1917	Able Seaman James Skilling	Donaghadee
18 November 1917	Rifleman James Lundy	Ballygowan
22 November 1917	Rifleman John Allen	Comber
22 November 1917	Private James Fitzsimmons	Portaferry
22 November 1917	Lieutenant Alexander McKee	Newtownards
22 November 1917	Rifleman Albert Edward Nelson	Comber
22 November 1917	Rifleman John Orr	Ballywalter
22 November 1917	Lance Corporal Gilbert (Bertie) Paden	Newtownards
23 November 1917	Rifleman David McMaster	Kircubbin
23 November 1917	Lance Corporal James Gordon Whyte	Ballywalter
24 November 1917	Rifleman William George Clifford	Comber
25 November 1917	Sergeant Samuel George Miskimmin	Killinchy
30 November 1917	Gunner James Francis Simpson	Carrowdore
1 December 1917	Private William James Donnan	Portaferry
1 December 1917	Company Sgt Major Hugh McCallum	Greyabbey
8 December 1917	Rifleman Robert John Black	Comber
8 December 1917	Corporal Henry Earney	Comber
8 December 1917	Rifleman Robert James Semple	Donaghadee
15 December 1917	Petty Officer Stoker John Croskery	Portaferry
17 December 1917	Corporal Leonard Edward J Parker	Newtownards
21 December 1917	Pte DH McMillan (MM not substantiated)	Newtownards
23 December 1917	Private John Hall	Newtownards
30 December 1917	Rifleman Charles McKeown	Newtownards
31 December 1917	Able Seaman Samuel Crooks	Newtownards

The first Ardsman to die in 1918 was Company Sergeant Major **David Smyth** from Newtownards and he died of disease on 16 January in what is now Tanzania. During the spring and summer of 1918 the Germans initiated a series of offensives on the Western Front in which they suffered defeat; on 21 March 1918 the 'Michael' offensive began (St Michael being the patron saint of Germany) and the series of battles that followed comprised the Second Battle of the Somme. Amongst other places there were battles at St Quentin, Bapaume, Arras and Ancre. During the Lys offensive in April there were battles at Lys, Estaires, Messines, Hazebrouck, Bailleul and Kemmel. Battles also took place along the Western Front at Villers-Brettoneux, Aisne, Lassigny, Marne, Amiens, Albert, Bapaume, St Mihiel, Arras, Le Cateau, Champagne, Ypres, Courtrai and the Sambre. By July the Germans were on the defensive and the Allied forces pursued a relentless advance against all sections of the German line.

On 7 November 1918 a German delegation sought peace, the Kaiser abdicated and an armistice was signed in a railway carriage at Compiegne. It came into effect at 1100 hours on 11 November 1918. That day Private **James McCully** from Newtownards died and at the same time, in Pasewalk Hospital near Stettin in Pomerania, a young German Corporal was undergoing treatment for the effects of mustard gas poisoning. His name was Adolf Hitler.

In all the theatres of war, 120 men with Ards connections died during 1918, up to and including the date of the armistice.

16 January 1918	**Company Sergeant Major David Smyth**	Newtownards
20 January 1918	**Fireman William Oliver**	Newtownards
14 February 1918	**Private James Henry Rilley**	Newtownards
17 February 1918	**Private James O'Neill Dorrian**	Ballywalter
19 February 1918	**Lance Corporal Joseph Croan**	Newtownards
28 February 1918	**Rifleman Samuel Hugh Regan**	Ballywalter
8 March 1918	**Rifleman Robert McConnell**	Donaghadee
21 March 1918	**Rifleman Alexander Courtney**	Comber
21 March 1918	**2nd Lieutenant Edmund De Wind VC**	Comber
21 March 1918	**Corporal Thomas McCann**	Newtownards
21 March 1918	**Rifleman Samuel Montgomery**	Comber
21 March 1918	**Private Robert Robson**	Newtownards
21 March 1918	**Rifleman Alexander Skillen**	Comber
23 March 1918	**Rifleman Edward Mooney**	Newtownards
23 March 1918	**Lance Corporal Henry Quigley MM**	Killinchy

24 March 1918	Private William Thomas McBride	Newtownards
24 March 1918	Rifleman Hugh McGinn	Newtownards
24 March 1918	Rifleman Robert McVea	Portavogie
24 March 1918	Rifleman Andrew McWilliams	Donaghadee
24 March 1918	Rifleman David Robinson	Newtownards
26 March 1918	Rifleman Robert Carnduff	Newtownards
26 March 1918	Coy Sgt Maj David Ferris LS&GC MID	Newtownards
27 March 1918	Rifleman George Chambers	Newtownards
28 March 1918	Rifleman James Armour	Greyabbey
28 March 1918	Lance Corporal Thomas Griffin	Donaghadee
28 March 1918	Rifleman David John McDonnell	Portaferry
29 March 1918	Corporal James Charles Burrows	Millisle
29 March 1918	Rifleman William Hewitt McIlveen	Comber
29 March 1918	Rifleman James Patton	Comber
29 March 1918	Lance Corporal Francis M Ritchie	Killinchy
29 March 1918	Rifleman John Meharry Sheppard	Newtownards
30 March 1918	Master Robert Murphy	Ballywalter
31 March 1918	Rifleman Robert James Pyper	Ballyhalbert
6 April 1918	Private Henry Young	Ballygowan
9 April 1918	Private Alexander McDowell	Newtownards
10 April 1918	Lance Corporal James Gregory MM	Newtownards
10 April 1918	Private George Turner McAlpine	Newtownards
11 April 1918	Rifleman William Fryers	Newtownards
12 April 1918	Private Bernard Kerr	Portaferry
12 April 1918	Rifleman John McCartan	Newtownards
13 April 1918	Private James Campbell McGimpsey	Newtownards
15 April 1918	Rifleman Robert McKay	Greyabbey
15 April 1918	Lance Corporal Henry Alan Murray	Newtownards
15 April 1918	Lance Corporal James Henry Quail	Newtownards
16 April 1918	Jnr 2nd Engineer Officer Alfred J Rice	Newtownards
18 April 1918	Private Dupree William McWha	Carrowdore
19 April 1918	Rifleman George Birney	Greyabbey
23 April 1918	Private Maxwell Aiken	Donaghadee
24 April 1918	Private George Young	Ballygowan
27 April 1918	Corporal James Munn Dugan	Comber
27 April 1918	Private Hugh McCullough	Newtownards
29 April 1918	Lance Corporal John McKee	Newtownards

Date	Name	Place
1 May 1918	Gunner Henry Shaw	Newtownards
6 May 1918	First Mate Michael Collins	Portaferry
26 May 1918	Private Samuel Gourley	Newtownards
27 May 1918	Private Patrick Moore alias McConnell	Newtownards
30 May 1918	Lt Henry McDonnell Anderson MC	Portaferry
1 June 1918	Rifleman Robert Allen	Comber
9 June 1918	Lance Corporal Frederick McCann	Newtownards
10 June 1918	Rifleman Thomas Calderwood	Newtownards
13 June 1918	Lance Corporal William John Branch	Ballywalter
27 June 1918	Rifleman Robert Hamilton	Donaghadee
28 June 1918	Rifleman Robert Orr	Newtownards
1 July 1918	Rifleman Arthur Rickwood Broderick	Newtownards
3 July 1918	Rifleman John Dickson	Newtownards
4 July 1918	Private William Woods	Kircubbin
16 July 1918	Rifleman Thomas Edward Ingram	Comber
16 July 1918	Captain John (Jack) McMath OBE	Portaferry
18 July 1918	2nd Corporal Dennis de Courcey Shaw	Kircubbin
20 July 1918	Private Thomas Devlin	Newtownards
20 July 1918	Gunner Daniel McNeice	Donaghadee
22 July 1918	Corporal Lowry Jordan MM	Ballygowan
24 July 1918	Driver Samuel Forbes Patton	Newtownards
2 August 1918	Major Meyrick Myles Magrath DSO	Ballywalter
8 August 1918	Private Robert Marshall	Comber
11 August 1918	Private Alexander Boyle	Ballywalter
12 August 1918	Private John Pollock	Newtownards
18 August 1918	Rifleman Thomas McMullan	Killinchy
23 August 1918	Private Jonathan Ardill MID	Newtownards
25 August 1918	Rifleman James Morrison McCready	Donaghadee
27 August 1918	Private Arthur Todd	Newtownards
27 August 1918	Private Charles Tomelty	Portaferry
28 August 1918	Private James Hamilton	Greyabbey
28 August 1918	Private John Bassett Shanks	Portaferry
29 August 1918	George Todd	Newtownards
2 September 1918	Rifleman Albert Hawthorne	Newtownards
2 September 1918	Rifleman William Smyth (Regent St)	Newtownards
6 September 1918	Rifleman Robert Heaney	Newtownards
6 September 1918	Rifleman James McCandless	Newtownards

19 September 1918	Lieutenant **Samuel McKee Geddis**	Comber
19 September 1918	Private **Andrew Lowry**	Killinchy
21 September 1918	Sergeant **Alexander Colville MM**	Carrowdore
24 September 1918	Captain **John Singleton Henry Robinson**	Newtownards
27 September 1918	Private **Robert Hewitt**	Killinchy
27 September 1918	Private **William Stratton**	Kircubbin
29 September 1918	Private **Samuel Logan**	Newtownards
1 October 1918	Private **Thomas Bailie**	Donaghadee
1 October 1918	Private **William Cooper**	Newtownards
1 October 1918	Rifleman **Robert Regan**	Greyabbey
2 October 1918	Captain **George J Bruce DSO MC MID**	Comber
2 October 1918	Private **William Holland Kennedy Ellison**	Comber
2 October 1918	Lance Corporal **Hugh Kerr**	Newtownards
3 October 1918	Private **Patrick McGreevy**	Killinchy
4 October 1918	Rifleman **David Coey**	Comber
4 October 1918	Rifleman **Alfred Johnston**	Newtownards
5 October 1918	Sergeant **Samuel Taylor**	Donaghadee
11 October 1918	Private **Robert John Ireland**	Comber
13 October 1918	Lance Corporal **Samuel Esler Fenton**	Newtownards
14 October 1918	Rifleman **Frederick Parkes**	Newtownards
15 October 1918	Private **Robert Whiteside**	Newtownards
20 October 1918	Private **James Gabbey**	Comber
20 October 1918	Sapper **James Hutton**	Newtownards
20 October 1918	Sergeant **Samuel Scott**	Newtownards
22 October 1918	Rifleman **William John Dorman**	Ballyhalbert
22 October 1918	Rifleman **Thompson Mathers**	Newtownards
31 October 1918	Rifleman **James Montgomery**	Newtownards
4 November 1918	Private **Charles Hugh Parke Wilson**	Portaferry
8 November 1918	Private **Charles William Henry Hall**	Donaghadee
10 November 1918	Corporal **Niven Boyd Stewart**	Carrowdore
11 November 1918	Private **James McCully**	Newtownards

After the armistice was signed in Compiegne, men with Ards connections continued to die from causes attributable to service (wounds and disease) and by being killed in action in other areas of conflict and theatres of war. Between 12 November 1918 and 31 August 1921 when the Great War officially ended, 41 men with Ards connections died.

12 November 1918	Lieutenant Francis Cinnamond	Newtownards
12 November 1918	Rifleman Robert Harvey	Newtownards
19 November 1918	Private Samuel Blakely Dunn Donnan	Carrowdore
19 November 1918	Driver Hugh McGreeghan	Comber
24 November 1918	Lieutenant Samuel Gatensby	Donaghadee
27 November 1918	Captain Cyril Gerrard Haselden	Comber
29 November 1918	Rifleman John McChesney	Newtownards
7 December 1918	Private James Pollock	Donaghadee
13 January 1919	Private Archibald Nisbet	Newtownards
19 January 1919	Private James Finlay	Comber
25 January 1919	Private Robert McDermott	Carrowdore
9 February 1919	Rifleman Alexander Glover	Comber
11 February 1919	Private DJ Dempster	Comber
17 February 1919	Rifleman James Parkhill	Newtownards
22 February 1919	Lance Corporal William James Quail	Comber
25 February 1919	Private Albert Connolly	Ballygowan
7 March 1919	Private James Reid	Carrowdore
26 June 1919	Private Michael McMillan	Newtownards
2 July 1919	Engineer Lieutenant Edward McBurney	Comber
20 August 1919	Lance Corporal William James Caughey	Newtownards
26 November 1919	Rifleman Thomas Dowdell	Newtownards
16 December 1919	Rifleman Hamilton McKibben	Newtownards
2 January 1920	Lieutenant William David Kenny VC	Donaghadee
7 January 1920	Rifleman Frederick (Frew) Shaw	Killinchy
14 March 1920	Rifleman Samuel Robinson	Newtownards
19 March 1920	Joseph Burns	Newtownards
28 March 1920	Rifleman Robert Kane	Newtownards
15 August 1920	Rifleman James Graham	Newtownards
20 August 1920	Rifleman John Thompson	Newtownards
29 September 1920	Private John Brennan Waugh	Newtownards
26 October 1920	Rifleman Wm John Jamison (Armour)	Newtownards
31 October 1920	Captain David Mitchell	Comber
9 November 1920	Rifleman Thomas Millar	Newtownards
6 April 1921	Driver Robert Davidson Robinson	Killinchy
8 April 1921	Captain Hamilton Orr (North St) MID	Newtownards
6 May 1921	Private Hugh Graham Ritchie	Ballyhalbert
9 May 1921	John Russell	Newtownards

27 May 1921	**David Bennett**	Newtownards
7 June 1921	**Rifleman John Milligan**	Kircubbin
13 June 1921	**Rifleman James Kerr**	Ballywalter
21 July 1921	**Rifleman Thomas Glendinning**	Newtownards

At least 12 people listed on Newtownards and District War Memorial died after 31 August 1921:

12 July 1922	**William John Cairns**	Newtownards
22 November 1922	**Rifleman Robert McKimm**	Newtownards
23 June 1923	**Petty Officer Hugh Ferguson**	Newtownards
21 January 1924	**Petty Officer Joseph McClure**	Newtownards
17 September 1924	**Company QMS David Condon**	Newtownards
31 August 1926	**Private Archibald Cairns**	Newtownards
10 November 1927	**William Bell**	Newtownards
7 August 1928	**James Adair**	Newtownards
15 October 1928	**James Algie**	Newtownards
11 April 1929	**John McCready**	Newtownards
10 November 1929	**Henry Stratton**	Newtownards
4 May 1932	**Joseph Crooks MM (not substantiated)**	Newtownards

At the time of writing it has not been possible to confirm the date of death for 71 men with Ards connections who are listed on War Memorials in the Ards area. The author hopes that publication of this Book of Honour will stimulate readers who have further information to provide it via the interactive website **www.barryniblock.co.uk** with a view to having the information added (once validated) to that website and then included in any future edition of this book.

Rifleman William J Allen	Newtownards and District War Memorial
Rifleman William Auld	Newtownards and District War Memorial
Rifleman David Bell	Newtownards and District War Memorial
QMS Andrew Boyd	Newtownards (Served with Canadians)
Private Samuel Boyd	Newtownards and District War Memorial
Rifleman James Brankin	Newtownards and District War Memorial
Rifleman Hugh Brown	Newtownards and District War Memorial
Pte A Edward Campbell	Comber and District War Memorial
Sergeant Henry Campbell	Newtownards and District War Memorial
John Campbell	Killinchy Parish Church of Ireland
RSM Patrick Campbell	Newtownards and District War Memorial
Rifleman William Campbell	Newtownards and District War Memorial

Sergeant George Carson	Newtownards and District War Memorial
Rifleman James Casey	Comber and District War Memorial
James Clarke	Ballygowan Presbyterian Church
Private William Clarke	Newtownards and District War Memorial
Thomas Clegg	Donaghadee and District War Memorial
Robert Close	Kircubbin Parish Church of Ireland
Sergeant Hugh Crowe	Newtownards and District War Memorial
Robert Dempster	Comber (Ireland's Memorial Records)
Rifleman Thomas Dorrian	Newtownards and District War Memorial
Private Alfred Fenton	Newtownards and District War Memorial
Rifleman Samuel Gilmore	Newtownards and District War Memorial
Rifleman Thomas Girvin	Newtownards and District War Memorial
A Gracey	*Newtownards Chronicle* Roll of Sacrifice
Sapper Thomas Griffiths	Newtownards and District War Memorial
Samuel Hamilton	Carrowdore Parish Church of Ireland
Stephen Johnson	Killinchy Parish Church of Ireland
Rifleman Robert Kemp	Newtownards and District War Memorial
Corporal Hugh Lawson	Newtownards and District War Memorial
Corporal George Ledlie	Ballyeasborough Parish Church of Ireland
James Majury	Donaghadee and District War Memorial
Rifleman George Mallon	Newtownards and District War Memorial
Rifleman James McClure	Newtownards and District War Memorial
Rifleman John McCullough	Shore St Presbyterian Church Donaghadee
Gunner John McDonagh	Newtownards and District War Memorial
James W McDowell	Ballygowan Presbyterian Church
Rifleman John T McDowell	Ballywalter and District War Memorial
Private Thomas McGimpsey	Newtownards and District War Memorial
Gunner Samuel McKendry	Newtownards and District War Memorial
Private John McKenna	Newtownards and District War Memorial
Rifleman David McKimm	Newtownards and District War Memorial
Private George McKnight	Newtownards and District War Memorial
Rifleman Patrick McMullan	Newtownards and District War Memorial
Rifleman William McMullan	Newtownards and District War Memorial
Private Andrew McTaggart	Newtownards and District War Memorial
Sergeant James Monks	Newtownards and District War Memorial
Private Walter Morrison	Newtownards and District War Memorial
Rifleman James Neill	Newtownards and District War Memorial

Private **Robert Palmer**	Newtownards and District War Memorial
Sergeant **Charles Pegg**	Newtownards and District War Memorial
Rifleman **Robert James Poole**	Newtownards and District War Memorial
Private **Charles Quigley**	Newtownards and District War Memorial
W Regan	Newtownards Parish Church of Ireland
William Rice	Cloughey Presbyterian Church Records
Rifleman **Robert Russell**	Newtownards and District War Memorial
T Scott	*Newtownards Chronicle* Roll of Sacrifice
Robert Stannage	Newtownards Parish Church of Ireland
Rifleman **James Stewart**	Newtownards and District War Memorial
Robert D Stewart	Donaghadee and District War Memorial
Rifleman **William R Strain**	Newtownards and District War Memorial
Rifleman **David Stratton**	Newtownards and District War Memorial
Rifleman **George Stratton**	Newtownards and District War Memorial
Rifleman **Henry Stratton**	Newtownards and District War Memorial
John Thompson	Killinchy Parish Church of Ireland
Rifleman **William Vance (East St)**	Newtownards and District War Memorial
Captain **GAC Ward CBE**	Ballywalter and District War Memorial
Adam White	Kircubbin Parish Church of Ireland
Private **James Wilson**	Newtownards and District War Memorial
T Woodside	*Newtownards Chronicle* Roll of Sacrifice
Rifleman **Charles Young**	Newtownards and District War Memorial

Names in Alphabetical Order

In this Section the names of men with Ards connections are presented alphabetically by surname.

For names marked with an asterisk (*) some additional information may be found in the Section beginning on Page 767.

Adair, Edward
Private
No. 27059, 10th Battalion, Royal Inniskilling Fusiliers
Killed in action on Saturday 1 July 1916 (aged 20)
Thiepval Memorial, France (Pier and Face 4 D and 5 B)

Edward Adair was born on 30 July 1895 in Newtownards and he was the youngest son of Robert and Maggie Adair (nee Mullen) who lived at 12 Robert Street. Before that the Adair family lived in the townland of Ballyharry. Robert and Maggie Adair were married on 11 November 1890 in Ballyblack Presbyterian Church and they had at least five children all of whom were baptised in First Newtownards Presbyterian Church – Kathleen, James, Edward, Alice and Ann Jane Bleakley. Both Edward Adair and his father worked as agricultural labourers.

A

Edward Adair enlisted in November 1914, he joined the 10th Battalion Royal Inniskilling Fusiliers and he went to France in October 1915. He served with 109th Brigade in the 36th (Ulster) Division. On 1 July 1916 Edward was posted as missing in action and one year later it was officially confirmed that he had been killed in action on that date or since.

> **FOR KING AND COUNTRY.**
> ADAIR—Missing since 1st July, 1916, now reported killed on or since that date, Private Edward Adair, 10th Royal Inniskilling Fusiliers, youngest and beloved son of Robert and Maggie Adair. Deeply regretted by his sorrowing Father, Mother, Sisters, Brother, and Brother-in-Law (both the latter on active service).
> 12 Robert St., Newtownards.

Edward's elder brother James served as a Gunner in the Royal Field Artillery and he also had a brother-in-law on active service. The Adair family placed a 'For King and Country' notice in the 21 July 1917 edition of the *Newtownards Chronicle*. Private Edward Adair is commemorated on Newtownards and District War Memorial and in First Newtownards Presbyterian Church.

Adair, James *

The name James Adair is listed on Newtownards and District War Memorial and in the booklet produced for the Unveiling and Dedication Ceremony held on Saturday 26 May 1934 he is described as a Gunner in the Royal Garrison Artillery. Desk searches and public appeals to date have yielded no further information.

Adair, John
Lance Corporal
No. 17/765, 10th Battalion, Royal Irish Rifles
Died of wounds on Tuesday 14 November 1916 (aged 30)
St. Quentin Cabaret Military Cemetery, Belgium (Grave I.C. 35)

John Adair was born on 7 June 1886 in Ballywalter and he was the eldest son of George and Anna Adair. George Adair worked as a fisherman and he and Anna had at least seven children – Elizabeth (died 21 January 1881 aged 4), Campbell (died 11 March 1881 aged 2), George, Lilian (Lily), John, Samuel (died 25 March 1900 aged 9) and Ellen. The children were baptised in Ballywalter Parish Church of Ireland and their father George died on 19 December 1906 aged 53. Their mother Anna died on 16 January 1931.

John Adair enlisted in Belfast, he served with the 10th Battalion Royal Irish Rifles in 107th Brigade of the 36th (Ulster) Division and he died of wounds on 14 November 1916. Lance Corporal John Adair is commemorated on Ballywalter and District War Memorial; in Ballywalter Church of Ireland (Holy Trinity) and on the family grave headstone in Whitechurch Cemetery. This headstone bears the verse:

'Call him not dead who fell at duty's feet
And passes through light where earth and heaven meet
For radiant rest'

Addy, Beresford
Private
No. 71566, 27th Battalion, Canadian Infantry (Manitoba Regiment)
Killed in action on Friday 15 September 1916 (aged 23)
Vimy Memorial, France

Beresford Addy was born on 6 August 1893 in Pettigo, Co Fermanagh and he was the youngest son of William and Sarah Jane Addy. The Rev William Addy was a Methodist Clergyman and he and Sarah Jane had at least ten children including Lilian, Beresford, Kathleen, Wilhelmina Gladys, Victoria and Georgina Violet. The Rev William Addy ministered in a number of Methodist churches including Glastry and he died on 20 December 1923.

A

Beresford Addy attended Methodist College Belfast and before moving to Canada he worked as an apprentice to the pharmaceutical chemist in Connor's of Hill Street, Newry. Beresford was the youngest of three Addy brothers who served with the Canadian Forces. He enlisted in Winnipeg, Manitoba on 28 October 1914 and he cited his father as his next-of-kin. It was noted in his attestation papers that he was 5 feet 8½ inches tall.

Private Beresford Addy died on 15 September 1916 at Flers-Courcelette and at the time of his death one of his sisters was a teacher in Dungannon Royal School. He is commemorated on the Memorial Plaque in Methodist College Belfast.

Aiken, Maxwell
Private
No. 30133, 11th (Lonsdale) Battalion, Border Regiment
Died of disease on Tuesday 23 April 1918 (aged 21)
St. Sever Cemetery Extension, France (Grave P. IX. B. 1A)

Maxwell Aiken was born on 29 March 1897 in Donaghadee and he was a son of Henry and Agnes Aiken who lived at 8 Railway Street. Henry Aiken was a gas works manager and he and Agnes had at least seven children –

 Henry, Madeline, Thomas McMinn, Maxwell, Jane, Desmond and Kennedy. Maxwell Aicken was baptised in Donaghadee Parish Church of Ireland. Sometime after April 1911 the Aiken family moved to 5 Skiddaw Street, Silloth, Cumberland.

Maxwell Aiken enlisted in Carlisle and joined the 3rd Line Battalion of the Territorial Force of the 5th Battalion of the Border Regiment. In late 1916 he was transferred to the 11th Battalion and went to France.

Maxwell is reported as 'died' and Tony Goddard, the Assistant Curator in Cumbria's Military Museum, has concluded that this probably means he died of disease. Although Rouen was behind the lines it was frequently bombed by the enemy. There were several base hospitals there and St Sever was the cemetery used by these hospitals when necessary.

The war diary for the period indicates that the 11th Battalion of the Border Regiment was relieved from the front line by the 1st Dorsets in February 1918. The men were bathed, deloused and issued with straw, palliasses and an extra blanket. They had musketry, bombing and Lewis Gun training and they played a football match against the 10th Argyll and Sutherland Highlanders. They lost by one goal.

The 11th Battalion of the Border Regiment went back into the front line from 3 to 21 March 1918 and during that period suffered some casualties, as they did during the German 'Michael' offensive. The alternating pattern of front line service and recuperation continued through April and it was on 23 April 1918 that Private Maxwell Aiken died. He is commemorated on Donaghadee and District War Memorial and in Donaghadee Parish Church of Ireland.

Algie Brothers, Robert and James

The Algie family came originally from Scotland with a company that was setting up a linen print-works in Newtownards. Robert and James Algie were sons of John and Mary Algie (nee Connor) who were married on 15 April 1870 in Albert Street Presbyterian Church Belfast. They lived in James Street, Newtownards. John Algie worked as a print cutter and he and Mary had at least six children including James, Lizzie, Polly, Nellie, Robert and John C. John Algie Senior died on 20 July 1917. Robert Algie was the first of the two brothers to die:

Algie, Robert

Able Seaman
No. SS/40, (RFR/CH/B/5311) HMS *Hawke*, Royal Navy
Killed in action on Thursday 15 October 1914 (aged 28)
Chatham Naval Memorial, Kent (Panel 1)

Before the war Robert Algie was a Reservist in the Royal Navy and he had been at home for about five years when he was called up. He was employed as a mechanic in the hem-stitching factory belonging to Messrs Freeland & Ferguson and he and his wife Mary Jane (nee Russell) lived at 124 Greenwell Street, Newtownards. They were married on 6 December 1911 in Ballygrainey Presbyterian Church and they had two children. Robert was born on 24 September 1912 and Madge (Maggie) was born on 23 July 1914. Both children were baptised in Greenwell Street Presbyterian Church Newtownards.

Robert Algie served aboard HMS *Hawke*, a Cruiser which was torpedoed by the German submarine U-9 in the northern waters of the North Sea on the afternoon of 15 October 1914. The ship sank in a few minutes with the loss of her captain and some 530 officers and men. Only around 65 officers and men were saved.

On Monday 19 October 1914 Mary Jane Algie received a telegram from the Admiralty informing her that her husband was not amongst those who had been saved. This news was made all the more painful because the previous Saturday she had received three letters from her husband each stating that he was well. She was left a widow with two small children, one of them a babe in arms.

On 31 October 1914 Robert's widow placed a 'For King and Country' notice in the *Newtownards Chronicle*, as did his father and his sisters. Every year thereafter Mary Jane placed an 'In Memoriam' notice in the *Newtownards Chronicle* on behalf of herself and her two children. Other relatives did the same from time to time and these included Robert's uncle John Russell, his sister and brother-in-law Polly and Hugh Dunlop and his sister Nellie Algie.

Able Seaman Robert Algie is commemorated on Newtownards and District War Memorial and in the PCI Roll of Honour for Greenwell Street Presbyterian Church Newtownards.

A

Algie, James *
Battery Sergeant Major
Royal Field Artillery
Died in 1923 of disease contracted in service (aged 51)

James Algie and Elizabeth Adair were married on 27 January 1903 in Second Newtownards Presbyterian Church and they had two sons – John and Joseph Norman. After Elizabeth died James Algie married Mary Finlay on 27 March 1909 in Newington Presbyterian Church Belfast and they had four children – James, Samuel, William and Nellie. In civilian life James Algie worked as a print cutter.

During the Great War James Algie served with the Royal Field Artillery in India. There he contracted malaria and was invalided home. He was discharged from the army on medical grounds and it is recorded in the family archives that he died in 1923. Battery Sergeant Major James Algie is commemorated on Newtownards and District War Memorial.

A

Allen, Hugh Charles
Distinguished Conduct Medal
Second Lieutenant
1st/7th (Fife) Battalion (Territorial), Black Watch (Royal Highlanders)
Killed in action on Monday 23 April 1917 (aged 27)
Brown's Copse Cemetery, France (Grave II. B. 28)

Hugh Charles Allen was the youngest son of Hugh Wallace Allen and Charlotte Allen (nee Camlin) who were married on 23 July 1878 in Kirkinriola Parish Church of Ireland Ballymena. When Hugh Wallace Allen was the Principal of Ekenhead National School in Belfast the Allen family lived at Glencot, Glenburn Park, Belfast and after Hugh retired they lived at 'Ulsterville' in Newtownards.

Hugh Charles Allen worked as a commercial traveller for Messrs Black & Company of Glasgow. In April 1913 he enlisted in the Black Watch Territorials and he was called up in 1914. That year he was awarded the title of 'Best Shot' in his

Battalion. On 2 May 1915 he went to France with his Battalion and while serving in the ranks he was wounded five times.

Newtownards Resident's Son Killed.

Second-Lieutenant Hugh Charles Allen, Black Watch, killed in action on 23rd April, was the youngest son of Mr. Hugh W. Allen, retired principal of Ekenhead N.S., Belfast, and late of Glencot, Glenburn Park, Belfast, and now of Ulsterville, Newtownards. Deceased, who was a Belfast man, enlisted in the Territorials in 1913, was called up on mobilisation in 1914, and was five times wounded serving in the ranks. Holding the rank of sergeant, he was awarded the D.C.M. last winter for leading his platoon with great courage and initiative, and, although wounded, continuing to do so until the capture of the enemy front line was effected. Deceased was promoted to a commission in February, 1917, and transferred to another battalion of the Black Watch. In civil life he was a commercial traveller for Messrs. Black & Co., Glasgow.

In January 1917 when he held the rank of Sergeant (1381) Hugh Charles Allen was awarded the Distinguished Conduct Medal for conspicuous gallantry in action. 'He led his platoon with great courage and initiative and, although wounded, continued to do so until the capture of the enemy front line was affected'. Sergeant Allen was commissioned in February 1917 and he transferred to another Battalion of the Black Watch. Second Lieutenant Hugh Charles Allen was killed in action on 23 April 1917. He had made his will and his property and effects were received by his father. He is commemorated on Newtownards and District War Memorial and in the Belfast Book of Honour (Page 8).

A

Allen, John
Rifleman
No. 17142, 'B' Company, 13th & 12th Battalions, Royal Irish Rifles
Killed in action on Thursday 22 November 1917 (aged 22)
Bailleul Road East Cemetery, France (Grave II. J. 11)

John Allen was a son of Henry and Rebecca Allen (nee Ferguson) who lived at 4 High Street, Comber. They were married on 13 January 1888 in Dundonald Presbyterian Church. Henry Allen worked as a garden labourer and he and Rebecca had at least ten children including James, Agnes Jane, William, John, Rebecca, Hugh, Isabella, Mary and Henrietta.

Prior to enlisting in Comber John Allen worked as a farm labourer. He served with the 13th Battalion Royal Irish Rifles in 108th Brigade of the 36th (Ulster) Division and he was wounded on 1 July 1916 at the Battle of the Somme. During his recuperation he was posted to the 18th Battalion and when he was fit again for service he was posted to the 12th Battalion Royal Irish Rifles. On 24 August 1917 he made his will at Clandeboye.

Rifleman John Allen was killed in action on 22 November 1917 and his property and effects were received by his sister Agnes Jane Allen. He is commemorated on Comber and District War Memorial and in Second Comber Presbyterian Church.

Allen, Robert
Rifleman
No. 17135, 'B' Company, 13th Battalion, Royal Irish Rifles
Died of wounds on Saturday 1 June 1918 (aged 24)
Vevey (St. Martin's) Cemetery, Switzerland (Grave 65)

Robert Allen was born in Belfast, he enlisted in Comber and he served with the 13th Battalion Royal Irish Rifles in 108th Brigade of the 36th (Ulster) Division. He was wounded in action and taken prisoner, probably during the German 'Michael' offensive that began on 21 March 1918. Deemed to be unfit for further active service, he was being repatriated through Switzerland when he died of his wounds.

Allen, Robert Hugh (Robert)
Rifleman
No. 17143, 'B' Company, 13th Battalion, Royal Irish Rifles
Killed in action on Saturday 1 July 1916 (aged 20)
Thiepval Memorial, France (Pier and Face 15 A and 15 B)

A

Robert Allen was born on 28 May 1896 in Newtownards and he was the eldest son of James and Mary Ann Allen (nee McChesney) who lived at 28 John Street Lane. They were married on 22 December 1893 in Ballygilbert Presbyterian Church. James Allen worked as a general labourer and he and Mary Ann had at least seven children – Esther (Essie), Robert Hugh, James, Lizzie McChesney, David (died), Samuel and David. The children were baptised in Greenwell Street Presbyterian Church Newtownards.

Robert Allen enlisted in Newtownards after the outbreak of the Great War. He joined the 13th Battalion Royal Irish Rifles (1st County Down Volunteers) and he went to France in October 1915. He served with 108th Brigade in the 36th (Ulster) Division. First reported as missing in action on 1 July 1916 it wasn't until July 1917 that Robert's father heard officially that Robert was 'regarded as having been killed on that date or since'.

Deeply regretted by his father, mother, sisters and brothers, the family placed a 'For King and Country' notice in the *Newtownards Chronicle* on 7 July 1917. Reflecting the anguish they endured during the year that Robert was missing in action it contained the following verse:

> *'Weary and long have we waited*
> *For his coming, but all in vain,*
> *Asking ourselves this hopeless question,*
> *Will he ever return again?'*

Rifleman Robert Allen was killed in action and he is commemorated on Newtownards and District War Memorial; in the PCI Roll of Honour for Greenwell Street Presbyterian Church Newtownards and in the Belfast Book of Honour (Page 9).

Allen, William J

The name William J Allen is listed on Newtownards and District War Memorial and in the booklet produced for the Unveiling and Dedication Ceremony held on Saturday 26 May 1934 he is described as a Rifleman in the Royal Irish Rifles. A discharged soldier from Newtownards named William Allen who died of consumption on 28 March 1921 was buried in Section 3 of Movilla Old Cemetery. Desk searches and public appeals to date have yielded no further information.

Allgood, Bertram
Captain
1st Battalion, Royal Irish Rifles
Killed in action on Sunday 6 December 1914 (aged 40)
Estaires Communal Cemetery and Extension, France (Grave I. B. 2)

Bertram Allgood was born on 11 February 1874 and he was the second son of Major-General George Allgood CB (died 1907) and Elizabeth Allgood (died 1874). Major-General George Allgood served in the Indian Army and became Chief Constable of Northumberland. Bertram was educated at Eton and became a career soldier serving in both India and Ireland. On 19 December 1911 he was appointed Adjutant of the 4th Battalion Royal Irish Rifles in Newtownards and in April 1913 he and Isa Cochrane Bayley were married in London. In February 1914 Bertram Allgood retired from the Army and joined the Reserve of Officers.

In August 1914 he was called up for service and in the same month his daughter was born. He went to the front on 7 November 1914 with the 1st Battalion Royal Irish Rifles and a month later Captain Bertram Allgood was shot through the heart by a sniper while he was taking his men into the

A

trenches. The death of Captain Bertram Allgood ex-Adjutant 4th Battalion Royal Irish Rifles was reported in the *Newtownards Chronicle*:

> Captain B. Allgood, ex-adjutant, 4th R. I. Rifles, Newtownards, killed in action in France.

Anderson, Henry McDonnell (Harry)
Military Cross
Lieutenant
'D' Company, 5th Battalion, Northumberland Fusiliers attached 63rd Battalion, Machine Gun Corps
Killed in action on Thursday 30 May 1918 (aged 25)
Bagneux British Cemetery, France (Grave III. A. 9)

Henry McDonnell Anderson was born on 6 June 1892 in Portaferry and he was a son of John and Mary (Minnie) Anderson (nee Begley) who were married on 14 July 1885 in Townsend Presbyterian Church Belfast. John Anderson worked as a hardware merchant and he and Mary had at least six children. They were all baptised in Portaferry Presbyterian Church – Mary, Sarah Gladys, George Rollo Begley, Henry McDonnell, William and John Thompson. Prior to the outbreak of the Great War Henry worked as an apprentice municipal clerk.

Lieutenant Henry McDonnell Anderson served with the Northumberland Fusiliers and when he was killed in action on 30 May 1918 during the German 'Michael' offensive his parents were living at 32 Dargle Road, Drumcondra, Dublin. Lieutenant Anderson's name is not commemorated on the Anderson family grave in Ballymanish Cemetery Portaferry. For a time Henry McDonnell Anderson lived in Fitzwilliam Street, Belfast and he is commemorated in Elmwood Presbyterian Church Belfast (now Elmwood Hall, Queen's University) and in the Belfast Book of Honour (Page 11).

Anderson, William
Rifleman
No. 8563, 'A' Company, 1st Battalion, Royal Irish Rifles
Killed in action on Saturday 1 July 1916 (aged 26)
Thiepval Memorial, France (Pier and Face 15 A and 15 B)
William Anderson was born on 24 March 1890 in Newtownards and he was a son of Thomas and Agnes Anderson (nee McKnight) who lived in the

townland of Ballywatticock. They were married on 18 August 1882 in First Newtownards Presbyterian Church. Thomas and William Anderson both worked as agricultural labourers. Thomas and Agnes Anderson had at least eight children all of whom were baptised in First Newtownards Presbyterian Church – Ellen, Jane, David, John, William, Samuel, Henry Crawford Orr and Agnes. Thomas Anderson died on 13 April 1932.

William Anderson enlisted in Belfast and he served with the 1st Battalion Royal Irish Rifles. He was killed in action near Ovillers on the first day of the Battle of the Somme and he is commemorated on Newtownards and District War Memorial and in First Newtownards Presbyterian Church.

Angus Brothers: James, John Blair and Robert

James, John Blair and Robert Angus were sons of Alexander and Mary Angus (nee Murphy) who lived in the townland of Cottown, Donaghadee with Alexander's parents Robert and Ellen Angus. Their father and grandfather both worked as agricultural labourers. Alexander and Mary were married on 26 February 1885 in Shore Street Presbyterian Church Donaghadee and they had at least nine children – James, Agnes, Rose, Robert, John Blair, Ellen, Emily, Janie and Sarah Ann. The children were baptised in Shore Street Presbyterian Church Donaghadee. Alexander and his family moved from Cottown, Donaghadee to 20 Albert Street, Bangor after the outbreak of the Great War.

Robert Angus was the second of the three Angus brothers to be killed in action although his was the first of the three deaths to be confirmed. James Angus was the third of the three Angus brothers to be killed in action although his was the second of the three deaths to be confirmed. Blair Angus was the first of the three Angus brothers to be killed in action although his was the last of the three deaths to be confirmed:

Angus, Robert
Lance Corporal
No. 20885, 2nd Battalion, Royal Scots Fusiliers
Killed in action on Sunday 9 July 1916 (aged 22)
Thiepval Memorial, France (Pier and Face 3 C)

Robert Angus was born on 6 September 1893 and he was the second son of Alexander and Mary Angus. Like his father and grandfather Robert worked as an agricultural labourer. Robert moved to Scotland, he enlisted in Irvine, Ayrshire and he served with the 2nd Battalion Royal Scots Fusiliers.

Lance Corporal Robert Angus was killed in action on 9 July 1916 during the Battle of the Somme and his parents placed a notice in the *County Down Spectator*. It contained the verse:

> *'It was hard to lose you, Robert dear,*
> *But God, Who knoweth best,*
> *Held wide His loving arms and said,*
> *"Come unto Me and rest".'*

Angus, James
Private
No. 75229, 29th Battalion, Canadian Infantry (British Columbia Regiment)
Killed in action on Monday 11 September 1916 (aged 29)
Vimy Memorial, France

A

James Angus was born on 16 July 1887 and he was the eldest son of Alexander and Mary Angus. He moved to Canada and he enlisted in Vancouver on 9 November 1914. He cited his mother Mary as his next-of-kin and it was noted in his attestation papers that he was 5 feet 6 inches tall. He served with the British Columbia Regiment of the Canadian Infantry and he was killed in action on 11 September 1916.

Angus, John Blair (Blair)
Rifleman
No. 17155, 'A' Company, 13th Battalion, Royal Irish Rifles
Killed in action on Saturday 1 July 1916 (aged 19)
Thiepval Memorial, France (Pier and Face 15 A and 15 B)

John Blair Angus was born on 10 July 1896 and he was the youngest son of Alexander and Mary Angus. He enlisted in Bangor and he served with the 13th Battalion Royal Irish Rifles in 108th Brigade of the 36th (Ulster) Division. His prowess as a rat catcher led to his appointment as Assistant Rat-Killer in his Platoon.

Rifleman Blair Angus was posted as missing in action after the first day of the Battle of the Somme and in

June 1917 it was officially confirmed that he had been killed in action on 1 July 1916. By then his family knew that Robert and James were dead and his parents placed a notice in the County Down Spectator. It contained the verse:

'God is good, He will give us grace
To bear our heavy cross,
He is the only one who knows
How bitter is our loss.'

The three brothers died within a three-month period and their mother Mary died on 26 March 1920.

Lance Corporal Robert Angus, Private James Angus and Rifleman Blair Angus are all commemorated on Donaghadee and District War Memorial; on Bangor and District War Memorial; on the RBL Bangor Branch Memorial Plaque; in the RBL Album in North Down Museum (Pages 9 & 10); in Shore Street Presbyterian Church Donaghadee and in Trinity Presbyterian Church Bangor. They are also commemorated on the family grave headstone in Bangor New Cemetery.

A

Angus, William
Rifleman
No. 16172, 'A' Company, 13th Battalion, Royal Irish Rifles
Killed in action on Saturday 1 July 1916 (aged 18)
A.I.F. Burial Ground, France (Grave X. A. 4)

William Angus was born on 20 February 1898 in Donaghadee and he was a son of James and Sarah Angus (nee Haisley) who lived in Warren Road. They were married on 24 January 1889 in Greenwell Street Presbyterian Church Newtownards. James Angus worked as a carpenter and he and Sarah had at least twelve children – Mary Caroline, Margaret, John Haisley, Richard, Francis, William (died in infancy), William, James, Lorimer, George Albert, Sarah and Harold (died in infancy). All twelve children were baptised in Shore Street Presbyterian Church Donaghadee. William's mother Sarah died on 28 February 1910 aged 44 and she was buried in Donaghadee Parish Church Graveyard alongside her two infant sons.

William Angus enlisted in Donaghadee, he served with the 13th Battalion Royal Irish Rifles in 108th Brigade of the 36th (Ulster) Division and he was killed in action on the first day of the Battle of the Somme. Rifleman William Angus is commemorated on Donaghadee and District War Memorial and in Shore Street Presbyterian Church Donaghadee. He is also commemorated on the family grave headstone in Donaghadee Parish Church Graveyard. CWGC records show that William Angus was 22 when he was killed; church baptismal records show that he was 18 so it is likely that he overstated his age when he enlisted. William's father James died on 26 November 1916 aged 54 and he was buried alongside his wife and two infant sons.

Ardill, Jonathan (John)
Mentioned in Despatches
Private
No. 25007, 7th (South Irish Horse) Battalion, Royal Irish Regiment
Died in a Prisoner of War Camp on Friday 23 August 1918 (aged 25)
Roisel Communal Cemetery Extension, France (Grave Sp. Mem. 3)

A

Jonathan Ardill was born in Aghancon, King's County and he was the second son of John and Alice Ardill (nee Lawder). John Ardill Senior worked as a land-steward and he and Alice had four children – Thomas, Jonathan, George and Albert. The Ardill family moved from Aghancon to Ballysallagh, Newtownards.

John Ardill enlisted in Coolderry, Queen's County and he served with the Royal Irish Regiment. He was taken prisoner and died in a prisoner of war camp on 23 August 1918. His CWGC headstone bears the inscription:

'Their glory shall not be blotted out'

Armour, James
Rifleman
No. 1036, 'B' Company, 13th Battalion, then 11th/13th Battalion, Royal Irish Rifles, then 22nd Entrenching Battalion
Killed in action on Thursday 28 March 1918 (aged 24)
Pozieres Memorial, France (Panel 74 to 76)

James Armour was born on 22 October 1893 in Newtownards and he was a son of Robert and Mary Jane Armour (nee McLoughlin) who lived in the townland of Ballybryan, Greyabbey. They were married on 20 January 1882 in Newtownards Parish Church of Ireland. Robert Armour worked as a flax scutcher and he and Mary Jane had at least six children – George, William, Isabella, Alexander, James and Margaret. Robert Armour drowned in Strangford Lough.

James Armour enlisted in Belfast and he served with the 13th Battalion Royal Irish Rifles in 108th Brigade of the 36th (Ulster) Division. In November 1917 the 11th and 13th Battalions were amalgamated and when they were disbanded in February 1918 James was transferred to the 22nd Entrenching Battalion. He was killed in action on 28 March 1918 during the German 'Michael' offensive. Rifleman James Armour had made a will and his property and effects were received by his widow Margaret Armour (nee Robinson) who lived in Greyabbey (they were married in Ballyfrenis Presbyterian Church Carrowdore and they had one son named James Robert who was born on 12 May 1915). After the war Margaret Armour and Samuel McCready were married on 11 February 1920 in Newtownards Registry Office.

Rifleman James Armour is commemorated on Greyabbey and District War Memorial located on the outside wall of Greyabbey Parish Church of Ireland (St Saviour).

Armour, William John (see Jamison, William John)
William John Armour is commemorated on Newtownards and District War Memorial as Jamison, William John.

Atkin, Edward
Corporal
No. 233149, Inland Water Transport, Royal Engineers
Died on Thursday 10 May 1917
Cloughey Presbyterian Church Graveyard, Co. Down
(Grave 182 at North end)

Corporal Edward Atkin served with Inland Water Transport, Royal Engineers and he died on 10 May 1917. His grave in Cloughey Presbyterian Church Graveyard has a CWGC headstone. Desk searches and public appeals to date have yielded no further information.

Auld, James
Rifleman
No. 17162, 'A' Company, 13th Battalion, Royal Irish Rifles
Killed in action on Saturday 1 July 1916 (aged 23)
Thiepval Memorial, France (Pier and Face 15 A and 15 B)

A

James Auld was born in Comber and he was the youngest son of Andrew and Susanna Auld (nee Mason) who lived in the townland of Ballykeel and later Cherryvalley, Comber. They were married on 15 July 1874 in Tullynakill Parish Church of Ireland. Andrew Auld worked as an agricultural labourer and he and Susanna had at least seven children including Margaret, Francis, Jane, James and Mary. Susanna Auld died in 1898 aged 41.

James Auld worked as a farm servant for John and Eleanor Boyd in the townland of Ballyalton and he and Margaret Moore were married on 2 October 1914 in Dundonald Presbyterian Church. James Auld enlisted in Holywood and he joined the 13th Battalion Royal Irish Rifles. He went to France in October 1915 and he served in 108th Brigade of the 36th (Ulster) Division. Two of his brothers were also on active service.

Rifleman James Auld was killed in action on the first day of the Battle of the

Somme. His widow was living in the townland of Craigogantlet (commonly Craigantlet) and James is commemorated on Comber and District War Memorial; in First Comber Presbyterian Church; in Dundonald Presbyterian Church; on Holywood and District War Memorial and in Ballykeel Defenders LOL No. 417.

Auld, William *

The name William Auld is listed on Newtownards and District War Memorial and in the booklet produced for the Unveiling and Dedication Ceremony held on Saturday 26 May 1934 he is described as a Rifleman in the Royal Irish Rifles.

DEATHS.

AULD—April 15th, 1924, at his residence, 74 Mill Street, Newtownards, William Auld. His remains were interred in the family burying-ground, Movilla, on Thursday, 17th inst. Deeply regretted by his sorrowing Wife and Family.

The death of a William Auld on 15 April 1924 was reported in the *Newtownards Chronicle*. In the 1911 census a William Auld aged 34 lived in Mill Street, Newtownards with his wife Sarah and daughter Margaret.

Desk searches and public appeals to date have not confirmed a connection between these data and the soldier commemorated on Newtownards and District War Memorial.

A
B

Bailie, Hugh Samuel (Hugh)
Private
No. 40631, 2nd Battalion, Royal Scots Fusiliers
Killed in action on Friday 14 September 1917 (aged 20)
Derry House Cemetery No. 2, Belgium (Grave II. E. 3)

Hugh Samuel Bailie was born on 22 March 1897 in Portavogie, he was a son of Agnes Bailie and he was baptised in Glastry Presbyterian Church. In the *Newtownards Chronicle* it was reported that it was his sister Eliza Jane Bailie who received official notification of his death. In the 1911 census Eliza Jane is recorded as Hugh's aunt and she had at least two brothers and one sister – Robert, James and Sarah.

Private Hugh Bailie served in the Royal Scots Fusiliers and he was the servant of Second Lieutenant Nisbet. It was Second Lieutenant Nisbet who wrote to Eliza Jane to convey his sympathy. He told her that Hugh had been faithful in all his duties. Second Lieutenant Nisbet also assured her that Hugh's death had been instantaneous and painless when he was killed by an exploding shell.

Eliza Jane Bailie placed an 'Our Heroes – In Memoriam' notice in the 14 September 1918 edition of the *Newtownards Chronicle*. 'In loving memory of my dear brother' and it contained the following verse:

'Boy of the smiling eyes, I'll not forget,
Though you will not return, Life's not done yet;
In my heart you live, never to die:
Courage to give me as years slip by.
Boy of the smiling eyes, it sometimes seems,
That you have never gone – just into dreams.
Strange but you often seem here at my side,
Toddling, a baby still, my joy and pride.
I think upon your smile, dream of your face,
Remember your merry heart, your boyish grace;
So for your sake I smile, boy – boy so dear,
That makes it seem to me still you are near.'

Private Hugh Bailie is commemorated in Glastry Presbyterian Church.

B

Bailie, James
Lance Corporal
No. 18867, 'A' Company, 13th Battalion, Royal Irish Rifles
Killed in action on Saturday 1 July 1916 (aged 22)
Thiepval Memorial, France (Pier and Face 15 A and 15 B)

James Bailie was born in Portaferry and he was a son of John and Jane Bailie (nee Smith) who lived in the townland of Priest Town. They were married on 30 August 1876 in Ardquin Parish Church of Ireland Portaferry. John Bailie was a farmer and he and Jane had at least five children – Lois and Nellie (both died in infancy), Jeannie, Bessie and James. John Bailie died on 1 October 1930 and Jane died on 23 July 1935.

James Bailie enlisted in Ballywalter and he joined the 13th Battalion Royal Irish Rifles. He went to France in October 1915, he served with 108th Brigade in the 36th (Ulster) Division and he was killed in action on the first day of the Battle of the Somme. Lance Corporal James Bailie is commemorated in Portaferry Presbyterian Church and on the family grave headstone in Ballymanish Graveyard Portaferry.

Bailie, Thomas
Private
No. 3033371, 4th Battalion, Canadian Infantry (Central Ontario Regiment)
Killed in action on Tuesday 1 October 1918 (aged 41)
Sancourt British Cemetery, France (Grave I. D. 32)

Thomas Bailie was born on 19 April 1877 (at attestation he declared his date of birth to be 28 March 1878) and he was a son of William and Catherine Bailie (nee Kimm) who lived in Donaghadee. They were married on 15 August 1872 in Newtownards Parish Church of Ireland and they had at least three children – Thomas, Hugh and Ellen. The children were baptised in Donaghadee Parish Church of Ireland.

Thomas Bailie and Agnes Bennett were married on 28 September 1896 in Ballycopeland Presbyterian Church, they lived at 9 Hunter's Lane, Donaghadee and they had at least six children – Elizabeth, Agnes Bennett, Catherine, Samuel, Almira and Henrietta. The children were baptised in Donaghadee Parish Church of Ireland. Thomas Bailie worked as a general labourer and Agnes worked as an embroiderer.

Thomas Bailie moved to the USA and he was living in Sioux City, Iowa when he made the journey to enlist in Toronto on 21 January 1918. In his attestation papers he cited his wife Agnes, who was still living at 9 Hunter's Lane in Donaghadee, as his next of kin. He stated that he was a farmer and it was noted that Thomas Bailie was 5 feet 6½ inches tall.

B

FOR KING AND COUNTRY.

BAILIE—Killed in action on 1st October, 1918, Private Thomas Bailie (3033371), Canadian Infantry, the dearly-loved husband of Agnes Bailie.

God is good, He'll give me grace
     To bear my heavy cross ;
He is the Only One Who knows
     How bitter is my loss.
We mourn the absent voice and face,
     That made home doubly dear,
But memory fills the vacant place,
     And keeps him ever near.

Deeply regretted by his sorrowing Wife and Family.
                    AGNES BAILIE.
9 Hunter's Lane,
     Donaghadee.

BAILIE—Killed in action on 1st October, 1918, Private Thomas Bailie (3033371), Canadian Infantry.

We have lost the dearest father,
     And we mourn his absence sore ;
His loving form and kindly smile
     We'll see on earth no more.
And with the morn, those
     Angel faces smile
Which we have loved
     Long since, and lost awhile.

Sadly missed by his sorrowing Daughter and Son-in-law.
     ANNIE and JOSEPH M'CHESNEY
          (The latter on Active Service).
25 Bow Street,
     Donaghadee.

After Private Thomas Bailie was killed in action on 1 October 1918 Agnes placed a 'For King and Country' notice in the *Newtownards Chronicle* and it contained the verse:

'God is good, He'll give me grace
To bear my heavy cross;
He is the Only One Who knows
How bitter is my loss.
We mourn the absent voice and face,
That made home doubly dear,
But memory fills the vacant place,
And keeps him ever near'

At the time of Thomas Bailie's death his son-in-law Joseph McChesney was also on active service. Private Thomas Bailie is commemorated on Donaghadee and District War Memorial and in Donaghadee Parish Church of Ireland. On his CWGC headstone his age is inscribed as 42.

Bain, AG
Private
No. PO/7542, (RMR/PO/1024), Royal Marine Light Infantry, HMS *Bayano*
Died on Thursday 11 March 1915
Ballyphilip Church of Ireland Churchyard, Portaferry (Grave 197)

Seven crew members from HMS *Bayano* are buried in graveyards on the Ards Peninsula.

Spracklin, Edgar J and **one unidentified Royal Marine** are buried in Ballyhalbert Church of Ireland (St Andrew) Graveyard Ballyeasborough.

Chater, Frederick William is buried in Whitechurch Graveyard Ballywalter.

B

Bain, AG; **Wellstead, WA** and **two unidentified sailors** are buried in Ballyphilip Church of Ireland Churchyard Portaferry.

Ballance, Thomas John (Thomas)
Lance Corporal
No. 18870, 'D' Company, 13th Battalion, Royal Irish Rifles
Killed in action on Saturday 1 July 1916 (aged 20)
Thiepval Memorial, France (Pier and Face 15 A and 15 B)

Thomas John Ballance was born in Kilkeel and he was a son of William and Susanna Ballance who lived at 13 Stanley Terrace, Harbour Road. William Ballance worked as a fisherman and he and Susanna had at least six children including George, Thomas John, William Henry, Leticia Jane and Margaret.

Thomas Ballance worked as an agricultural labourer and in 'Soldiers Died in the Great War 1914 – 1919' it is recorded that he lived in Kircubbin. Desk searches and public appeals to date have not found evidence to corroborate this. Thomas enlisted in Newry and he joined the 13th Battalion Royal Irish Rifles. He went to France in October 1915 and he served with 108th Brigade in the 36th (Ulster) Division. Lance Corporal Thomas John Ballance was killed in action on the first day of the Battle of the Somme.

Beattie, Alexander
Private
No. 19763, 9th Battalion, Princess Victoria's (Royal Irish Fusiliers)
Died of wounds on Sunday 9 July 1916
Doullens Communal Cemetery Extension No. 1, France (Grave IV. D. 7)

Alexander Beattie lived in Bessbrook and he serves as an example of a soldier who enlisted in Newtownards. He served with the 9th Battalion Royal Irish Fusiliers in 108th Brigade of the 36th (Ulster) Division and he died of wounds on 9 July 1916. Alexander's brother James enlisted in Belfast, served with the 13th Battalion Royal Irish Rifles (16222) in 108th Brigade of the 36th (Ulster) Division and was killed in action on the first day of the Battle of the Somme. Private Alexander Beattie is commemorated in Bessbrook Presbyterian Church as is Private James (Jimmy) Brown (18560) who also enlisted in Newtownards. Jimmy served with the 9th Battalion Royal Irish Fusiliers in 108th Brigade of the 36th (Ulster) Division and he too was killed in action on the first day of the Battle of the Somme.

Beck, James Davidson (James)
Private

B

No. 8/328, Otago Regiment, NZEF
Killed in action between Saturday 1 May and Sunday 23 May 1915 (aged 24)
Lone Pine Memorial, Gallipoli, Turkey (Panel 75)

James Beck was born on 16 May 1891 and he was a son of James and Mary Anne Beck (nee Kelly) who lived in the townland of Ballyblack, Newtownards. They were married on 1 October 1886 in Greenwell Street Presbyterian Church Newtownards. James Beck Senior worked as an agricultural labourer and he and Mary Anne had at least nine children – Thomas, William Kelly, James Davidson, Sarah, David, Margaret, Anne Mary, John and Elizabeth. They were all baptised in Greenwell Street Presbyterian Church.

James Davidson Beck moved to New Zealand and when he enlisted he served with the Otago Regiment of the New Zealand Expeditionary Force. In June 1915 he was posted as missing in action at Gallipoli and his family appealed for information about him.

In May 1916 it was officially confirmed that Private James Beck had been killed in action between 1 and 23 May 1915. His family placed 'Our Heroes – In Memoriam' notices in the *Newtownards Chronicle* in 1916 and 1917

OUR HEROES—IN MEMORIAM.

BECK—In fond and loving memory of our dear son (8,328), Private Jas. Beck, Otago Infantry, N.Z., missing after action at Gallipoli, Turkey, since 1st May, 1915, now believed killed in action.

It is well we can't draw the curtain,
  Or our hearts would sink with doubt,
But just as our strength can bear it
  Our portion He meteth out.
Inserted by his loving Father, Mother, Sisters and Brothers.
  Ballyblack.

and one of them contained the verse:

'It is well we can't draw the curtain,
Or our hearts would sink with doubt,
But just as our strength can bear it
Our portion He meteth out.'

Private James Beck is commemorated on Newtownards and District War Memorial and in the PCI Roll of Honour for Greenwell Street Presbyterian Church Newtownards. James's father died on 4 April 1929 and he is buried in Movilla Old Cemetery (Grave 4. 167).

Beers, William
Rifleman
No. 18/624, 11th Battalion, Royal Irish Rifles attached 108th Trench Mortar Battery, 36th (Ulster) Division
Killed in action on Thursday 22 March 1917 (aged 28)
Kemmel Chateau Military Cemetery, Belgium (Grave M. 84)

B

William Beers was born on 14 March 1889 in Comber and he was the eldest son of Robert and Margaret Beers (nee Smiley) who lived in Railway View, Belfast Road. They were married on 28 January 1886 in Killinchy Presbyterian Church. Robert Beers worked as a car driver and Margaret died in the late 1800s. Robert Beers had four children – Minnie, William, Robert and Eliza. William was baptised in First Comber Presbyterian Church.

Prior to the Great War William Beers worked as a van driver and he was a member of the Ulster Volunteer Force. He enlisted in Newtownards, he served with the 11th Battalion Royal Irish Rifles attached to 108th Trench Mortar Battery in the 36th (Ulster) Division and he was killed in action on 22 March 1917.

After William's death an officer wrote a letter of sympathy to his father. In it the officer wrote, 'Your son was on sentry duty at the time of his death, which was caused by shrapnel, and was instantaneous. I have always found him a keen and willing soldier. He always displayed marked coolness under the most trying circumstances and will be greatly missed by all in the battery.' Rifleman William Beers is commemorated on Comber and District War Memorial and in First Comber Presbyterian Church.

Bell, David

The name David Bell is listed on Newtownards and District War Memorial and in the booklet produced for the Unveiling and Dedication Ceremony held on Saturday 26 May 1934 he is described as a Rifleman in the Royal Irish Rifles.

In the PCI Roll of Honour for Greenwell Street Presbyterian Church Newtownards Private David Bell 13th Battalion Royal Irish Rifles who lived at 22 Wallace's Street No. 1 is commemorated. In the 1901 census a David Bell aged 18 who worked as a labourer was living with his mother Mary Smylie at 6 Wallace's or Brown's Lane, Newtownards.

Desk searches and public appeals to date have yielded no further information and no evidence has been found as yet in service records to confirm that a David Bell from Newtownards and District served in the 13th Battalion Royal Irish Rifles.

Bell, Herbert Alexander (Bertie)
Trooper
No. 932, 10th Australian Light Horse Regiment, AIF
Killed in action on Wednesday 9 August 1916 (aged 22)
Kantara War Memorial Cemetery, Egypt (Grave B. 75)

B

Herbert Alexander Bell was a son of John Turtle Bell and Emma Jane Bell. John Bell worked as a cashier in the Newtownards branch of the Ulster Bank and he married Emma Jane Patton from the townland of Ballywatticock on 18 August 1892 in First Holywood Presbyterian Church. John resigned from the bank and became a merchant in Moira, Co Down before moving to Western Australia. The Bell family lived at 2 Oswald Street, Victoria Park and later in Keane Street, Peppermint Grove, Cottesloe, Western Australia.

Prior to the outbreak of the Great War Bertie Bell worked as a warehouseman. He enlisted in Perth on 11 January 1915 and it was noted in his attestation papers that he had a small scar on his forehead and that he was 5 feet 6½ inches tall. In July 1915 he arrived in Gallipoli and in September he was admitted to hospital with influenza. He arrived in Alexandria on Christmas Day.

In 1916 Trooper Bertie Bell went to Egypt and on 22 August 1916 he was killed in action during the Hassanein engagement in the Suez Canal Zone. Shortly before he was killed he came upon a wounded comrade. He told his comrade to lie still and said that he would come back and bring him in. Trooper Bell was buried on the battlefield and a Chaplain, the Rev Collick, was in attendance. The position of his grave was carefully recorded and later his body was exhumed and re-interred in Kantara War Memorial Cemetery.

Trooper Bertie Bell's personal effects were posted to his father and they amounted to one scarf, one military book, one dictionary, a piece of stone, buttons, badges, numerals, a piece of shell, ammunition pouch, letters, photos, post cards, newspaper cuttings, testament, plume, notebook and one field service pocket book. Trooper Bertie Bell is commemorated on Newtownards and District War Memorial.

Bell, James
Private
No. 9885, 2nd Battalion, Argyll & Sutherland Highlanders
Killed in action on Monday 27 September 1915 (aged 26)
Cambrin Churchyard Extension, France (Grave C. 5)

B

James Bell was born on 7 January 1889 and he was the second son of Hugh and Ellen Bell (nee Stewart) who lived in Greyabbey. They were married on 29 April 1872 in Newtownards Parish Church of Ireland. Hugh Bell worked as a carpenter and he and Ellen had at least seven children – Robert, James, Anna Matilda (died 1911), Mary Eleanor, Margaret Elizabeth, Harriett and Agnes. Ellen Bell died on 18 March 1896 and Hugh Bell died on 10 June 1905. Both are buried in Greyabbey Old Graveyard. On 25 September 1905 James enlisted at Kirkintilloch, Dumbarton. He served with the Argyll and Sutherland Highlanders (Princess Louise's) and he was stationed in South Africa for three years.

Private James Bell landed in France with the first British Expeditionary Force on 9 August 1914. From then until his death on 27 September 1915 James was continuously at the front with the exception of a one-week furlough in August 1915 which he spent in Greyabbey. When he was at home it was noted how haggard he looked and this was attributed to the length of time he had spent in the trenches.

James's brother Robert Bell lived in Church Street, Greyabbey. His four sisters – Mary Eleanor Bryce, Margaret Elizabeth Filson, Agnes Adair and Harriett Reid – also lived in Greyabbey and in September 1916 they placed an 'Our Heroes – In Memoriam' notice in the *Newtownards Chronicle*.

It contained the following verse:

'Duty called him, he was there,
To do his bit and take his share;
His heart was good, his spirit brave,
His resting-place a soldier's grave.'

Private James Bell is commemorated on Greyabbey and District War Memorial located on the outside wall of Greyabbey Parish Church of Ireland (St Saviour) and also on the family grave headstone in Greyabbey Old Graveyard.

Bell, John Arthur
Private
No. 3568, 1st Battalion, Irish Guards
Killed in action on Tuesday 1 September 1914 (aged 23)
La Ferte-Sous-Jouarre Memorial, France

John Arthur Bell was born in County Antrim and he was a son of John Arthur Bell. He enlisted in Antrim before the outbreak of the Great War, he served with the Irish Guards and he went to France on 13 August 1914. He was killed in action on 1 September 1914 and at the time of his death his father was living at 'Gwenville', Comber. Private John Arthur Bell is commemorated in Comber Parish Church of Ireland (St Mary).

B

Bell, William
Rifleman
No. 18876, 'B' Company, 13th Battalion, Royal Irish Rifles
Killed in action in France on Saturday 1 July 1916 (aged 22)
Thiepval Memorial, France (Pier and Face 15 A and 15 B)

William Bell was born in Kircubbin and he was a son of Mrs Agnes Reid who lived in Blackhall Street. He enlisted in Ballywalter and joined the 13th Battalion Royal Irish Rifles. He went to France on 6 October 1915 and he served with 108th Brigade in the 36th (Ulster) Division. Rifleman William Bell was killed in action on the first day of the Battle of the Somme and he is commemorated in Kircubbin Parish Church of Ireland (Holy Trinity).

Bell, William *
The name William Bell is listed on Newtownards and District War Memorial and in the booklet produced for the Unveiling and Dedication Ceremony held on Saturday 26 May 1934 he is described as a Rifleman in the Royal

Irish Rifles. Desk searches and public appeals to date have not confirmed conclusively whether or not this William Bell is the same William Bell (18876) who is commemorated in Kircubbin Parish Church of Ireland (Holy Trinity).

Bell, William Robert (Cully)
Rifleman
No. 12487, 1st Battalion, Royal Irish Rifles
Killed in action on Monday 14 December 1914 (aged 40)
Le Touret Memorial, France (Panel 42 and 43)

William Robert Bell was born in Newtownards. He joined the ranks of the Royal Inniskilling Fusiliers on 5 November 1892 and served abroad for eight years. He was invalided home and discharged from the army on 22 December 1901. His army record was unblemished, he was a first-class marksman and he had earned the Indian Frontier medal with two clasps in 1895. He was known to his friends as Cully Bell and when he came home he lived at 9 Little Francis Street, Newtownards with his grandmother Mrs Martha O'Brien. Cully Bell was a member of Loyal Orange Lodge No. 1948 in Newtownards.

B

In September 1914 he re-enlisted in Newtownards and joined the 3rd Battalion Royal Irish Rifles. In October 1914 he was drafted to the 1st Battalion and went to Winchester Camp in England. From there he went to the front in November 1914 and he was killed in action on 14 December 1914. At that time, because of persistent rain, the soldiers in some parts of the trenches were up to their thighs in mud and frostbite was a problem. Cully Bell was killed by a German sniper.

OUR HEROES—IN MEMORIAM.
BELL—In memory of Rfm. Wm. Robert Bell, 1st Batt. R. I. Rifles, who was killed in action in France on 14th Dec., 1914.
One long and dreary year has passed Since this great sorrow fell ;
The shock that we received that day We still remember well.

Although we're in a far off land, And your grave we cannot see, As long as life and memory lasts We shall remember thee.
Inserted by his Brother and Sister-in-Law.
JAMES AND MARY ANN BELL.
25 Queen St., Newtownards.

Rifleman Cully Bell made a will and his property and effects were received by his brother James Bell who lived at 25 Queen Street, Newtownards. In December 1915 James Bell and his wife Mary Ann placed an 'Our Heroes – In Memoriam' notice in the *Newtownards Chronicle*. It contained the verse:

'One long and dreary year has passed
Since this great sorrow fell;
The shock that we received that day
We still remember well.

Although we're in a far off land
And your grave we cannot see,
As long as life and memory lasts
We shall remember thee.'

Rifleman William Robert Bell is commemorated on Newtownards and District War Memorial (in the booklet produced for the Unveiling and Dedication Ceremony held on Saturday 26 May 1934 he is described as a Private in the Royal Irish Regiment) and also in Newtownards Parish Church of Ireland (St Mark).

Bennett Brothers: Edward and Hamilton

Edward and Hamilton Bennett were sons of John and Annabella Bennett (nee Boland) who were married on 12 October 1891 in Greenwell Street Presbyterian Church. John and Annabella had at least five children – James, John, Hamilton, Edward and Isabella. The Bennett family lived in Downpatrick before they moved to Frederick Street, Newtownards. Annabella Bennett was widowed around 1900 and she lived at 11 Pound Street, Newtownards. Edward was the first of the two brothers to die:

B

Bennett, Edward
Corporal
No. 18/578, 'B' Company, 13th Battalion, Royal Irish Rifles
Killed in action on Saturday 1 July 1916 (aged 18)
Thiepval Memorial, France (Pier and Face 15 A and 15 B)

> **FOR KING AND COUNTRY.**
> BENNETT—Killed in action, 1st July, 1916, Corpl. Edward Bennett, 13th Battalion R.I. Rifles, youngest son of Annabella Bennett, Pound Street, Newtownards.
> Sadly missed by his loving Mother, Sister, and Brothers (two of the latter on active service.)

Edward Bennett was Annabella Bennett's youngest son and she was around 50 years of age when Edward died. In October 1915 Edward Bennett enlisted at Clandeboye and he joined the 18th Battalion Royal Irish Rifles. He was drafted to the 1st County Down Volunteers and he went to France in 1916. He served with 108th Brigade in the 36th (Ulster) Division and he was posted as missing in action after the first day of the Battle of the Somme. Just over a year later it was officially confirmed that he had been killed in action on that date or since.

When Corporal Edward Bennett died two of his brothers were also on active service. John Bennett was serving in Egypt and Hamilton Bennett was serving with the Machine Gun Corps. Some three months after it was confirmed that Corporal Edward Bennett had been killed Private Hamilton Bennett was also killed in action.

Bennett, Hamilton
Private
No. 32413, Royal Scots Fusiliers transferred to (104993) 213th Company, Machine Gun Corps (Infantry)
Killed in action on Thursday 11 October 1917 (aged 21)
Strand Military Cemetery, Belgium (Grave IX. P. 2)

Hamilton Bennett was Annabella Bennett's third son and he enlisted in Stevenston, Ayr. He joined the Royal Scots Fusiliers (32413) and was subsequently transferred to the Machine Gun Corps. Major Ruard commanded the section and it was he who wrote to Hamilton's mother to express his condolences and to tell her that Private Hamilton Bennett had been killed at 3.00 am on 11 October 1917 whilst on sentry duty. Hamilton Bennett was engaged to be married and Major Ruard asked for his condolences to be conveyed to Hamilton's fiancée.

Corporal William Campbell also wrote a letter of sympathy to Hamilton's mother. He told her that Hamilton had been killed by an exploding shell and that his death had been instantaneous. His comrades buried him close to the gun position where he fell and they placed a cross to mark the spot.

Private Hamilton Bennett had made a will and his property and effects were received by his mother. She placed a 'For King and Country' notice in the *Newtownards Chronicle* and it contained the verse:

> **FOR KING AND COUNTRY.**
> BENNETT—Killed in action on 11th October, 1917, Private Hamilton Bennett, Machine Gun Section, third son of Mrs. Bennett, 11 Pound Street, Newtownards.
> But we hope to meet in heaven above,
>   On that eternal shore,
> We hope to meet him in that land—
>   The land for rich and poor—
> Where peace shall reign eternally,
>   And wars shall be no more.
> Inserted by his sorrowing Mother, Sister, Isabella, and Brothers, James and John (the latter serving in Egypt).

'But we hope to meet in heaven above,
On that eternal shore,
We hope to meet him in that land –

B

The land for rich and poor –
Where peace shall reign eternally,
And wars shall be no more.'

Both Corporal Edward Bennett and Private Hamilton Bennett are commemorated on Newtownards and District War Memorial and in the PCI Roll of Honour for Greenwell Street Presbyterian Church Newtownards.

Bennett, David *

On 28 May 1921 a retired soldier named David Bennett who had died of cardiac failure was buried in Movilla New Cemetery (Grave 2. 25). Desk searches and public appeals to date have yielded no further information.

Bennett, James
Private
No. 18099, 11th Battalion, Royal Inniskilling Fusiliers
Killed in action on Saturday 1 July 1916
Connaught Cemetery, France (Grave I. A. 20)

In 'Soldiers Died in the Great War 1914 – 1919' it is recorded that James Bennett was born in Ballygowan and he enlisted in Belfast. He served with the 11th Battalion Royal Inniskilling Fusiliers and he was killed in action with 109th Brigade in the 36th (Ulster) Division on the first day of the Battle of the Somme. Private James Bennett's wife Lizzie lived in Capital Street, Belfast and he is commemorated in the Belfast Book of Honour (Page 37).

Beringer Brothers: Frederick G and William Ernest
Frederick and William Beringer were sons of Frederick and Elizabeth Beringer (nee James) who lived in High Street, Portaferry. They were married on 13 September 1882 in Ballyphilip Parish Church of Ireland Portaferry. Frederick Beringer Senior worked as a watchmaker and jeweller and he and Elizabeth had at least seven children – Frederick, John, William, Richard, Helena, Thomas and Elizabeth. William was the first of the two brothers to die:

Beringer, William Ernest (Willie)
Stoker First Class
No. 309949, HMS *Goliath*, Royal Navy
Killed in action on Thursday 13 May 1915 (aged 28)
Chatham Naval Memorial, Kent, England (Panel 11)

William Ernest Beringer was born on 2 November 1886 and he was the third son of Frederick and Elizabeth Beringer. He worked as a servant before he

B

joined the Royal Navy on 25 April 1906 and he signed on for 12 years. Willie Beringer was killed at around 1.00 am on 13 May 1915 when HMS *Goliath* was torpedoed by a Turkish destroyer while she was anchored in Morto Bay off Cape Helles. There was a massive explosion and of the 750 men on board 570 were lost as the ship sank.

Stoker First Class Willie Beringer was one of three men with Ards connections who were killed aboard HMS *Goliath*. The others lost that night were Boy First Class **Alfred Henry Victor Gadd** and Stoker First Class **Hector Hiles**.

Stoker First Class Willie Beringer is commemorated in Ballyphilip Parish Church of Ireland Portaferry (surname spelt Berringer). Willie's older brother Fred served with the Canadian Infantry and he was killed in action less than two years later. Their brother John served in the Mercantile Marine and he survived the war.

B

Beringer, Frederick G (Fred)
Private
No. 144208, 87th Battalion, Canadian Infantry (Quebec Regiment)
Killed in action on Monday 9 April 1917 (aged 33)
Cabaret-Rouge British Cemetery, France (Grave VIII. E. 12)

> **Portaferry-Canadian Missing.**
> Mr. F. Berringer, jeweller, High Street, Portaferry, has been notified that his son, Fred, of the Canadians, is posted as missing since 9th April. In business in the Dominion for about five years, he joined the Canadian forces at the outbreak of war, and has been in the firing line for about twelve months. Another son, William, in the Navy, was lost at the Dardanelles.

Frederick G Beringer was born on 19 July 1883 and he was the eldest son of Frederick and Elizabeth Beringer. After leaving school Fred worked with his father as a watchmaker and clock repairer. Fred moved to Canada around 1911 where he worked as a farmer before he enlisted in Ottawa, Ontario on 4 August 1915. It was noted in his attestation papers that he was 5 feet 4¼ inches tall.

Private Fred Beringer was killed in action on 9 April 1917 and he is commemorated in Ballyphilip Parish Church of Ireland Portaferry (surname spelt Berringer).

Best Brothers: James and Thomas
James and Thomas Best were born in Newtownards and they were sons of John and Agnes Best (nee Gaw). John Best was a soldier and he and Agnes

were married on 8 June 1878 in Newtownards Parish Church of Ireland. They had at least five children – James, Lizzie, Samuel, Martha and Thomas. The Best family lived in George's Street and Greenwell Street, Newtownards before moving to Scotland where they lived at 62 Rumford Street, Glasgow. James was the first of the two brothers to die in the Great War:

Best, James
Private
No. 6530, 2nd Battalion, Scots Guards
Killed in action on Wednesday 28 October 1914 (aged 29)
Ypres (Menin Gate) Memorial, Belgium (Panel 11)

James Best was born on 21 May 1885 and he enlisted on 24 May 1906 in Glasgow. He and his wife Elizabeth were married on 31 December 1913 in Rutherglen and they lived at 77 Greenhill Road, Rutherglen, Glasgow.

Private James Best served with the Scots Guards and he was killed in action on 28 October 1914. He is commemorated on Newtownards and District War Memorial and in Newtownards Parish Church of Ireland (St Mark).

B

Best, Thomas
Private
No. 8879, 2nd Battalion, Scots Guards
Killed in action on Thursday 29 April 1915 (aged 20)
Aubers Ridge British Cemetery, France (Grave V. B. 13)

Thomas Best was born on 25 January 1895 and he was educated at Bridgeton, Glasgow. He enlisted on 23 February 1914 in Glasgow and he served with the Scots Guards.

Private Thomas Best was killed in action on 29 April 1915 (recorded as 1918 in the CWGC Debt of Honour) and he is commemorated on Newtownards and District War Memorial and in Newtownards Parish Church of Ireland (St Mark).

OUR HEROES—IN MEMORIAM.
BEST—In loving memory of Private Thomas Best (No. 8,879), 2nd Batt. Scot's Guards, killed in action in France on 29th April, 1915.
Deeply regretted by his loving Friends,
M. A. GREGORY and L. M'NEILLY,
94 Greenwell Street, Newtownards.

In the 29 April 1916 edition of the *Newtownards Chronicle* his friends MA Gregory and L McNeilly placed an 'Our Heroes – In Memoriam' notice.

Birney, George

Rifleman
No. 18877, 'A' Company, 13th & 12th Battalions, Royal Irish Rifles
Killed in action on Friday 19 April 1918 (aged 30)
Tyne Cot Memorial, Belgium (Panel 138 to 140 & 162 to 162A & 163A)

George Birney was born in Arva, Co Cavan and he was a son of William and Ann Birney. William Birney worked as a general labourer and he and Ann had at least seven children – William, James, George, Henry, Thomas, Annie and Josephine.

For a time George Birney lived in Armagh and he enlisted in Ballywalter. Private George Birney served with the 13th Battalion Royal Irish Rifles in 108th Brigade of the 36th (Ulster) Division and in November 1917 the 11th and 13th Battalions were amalgamated. When they were disbanded in February 1918 he was transferred to the 12th Battalion. He was killed in action on 19 April 1918 (16 April 1918 in some records) and he is commemorated on Greyabbey and District War Memorial located on the outside wall of Greyabbey Parish Church of Ireland (St Saviour) and also on a headstone in Greyabbey Old Graveyard.

Black, Robert John

Rifleman
No. 18879, 'B' Company, 13th Battalion, Royal Irish Rifles
Killed in action on Saturday 8 December 1917 (aged 20)
Thiepval Memorial, France (Pier and Face 15 A and 15 B)

Robert John Black was born in the townland of Ballyscullion, Co Londonderry and he was a son of Robert and Mary Black (nee Wherry). They were married on 8 October 1895 in First Comber Presbyterian Church. Robert John worked as a machine boy and he lived with his widowed grandmother Jane S Wherry in Brownlow Street, Comber. He enlisted in Belfast, he served with the 13th Battalion Royal Irish Rifles in 108th Brigade of the 36th (Ulster) Division and he was killed in action on 8 December 1917. His mother Mary lived in 'Laurencetown House', Laurencetown, Co Down. Rifleman Robert John Black is commemorated on Comber and District War Memorial and in First Comber Presbyterian Church.

B

Blackadder, Thomas
Rifleman
No. 17/709, 9th Battalion, Royal Irish Rifles
Killed in action on Saturday 24 March 1917 (aged 32)
Pond Farm Cemetery, Belgium (Grave L. 13)

Thomas Blackadder was born in 1885 in Newtownards and he was the eldest son of Annie Blackadder. Annie Blackadder was widowed in the late 1800s and she worked as a yarn reeler in a mill. She had three children – Thomas, Jane and John.

Prior to the outbreak of the Great War both Thomas and John worked as brush makers and after Thomas enlisted in Belfast he served with the 9th Battalion Royal Irish Rifles in 107th Brigade of the 36th (Ulster) Division. When Rifleman Thomas Blackadder was killed in action on 24 March 1917 his mother was living at 34 Tobergill Street, Belfast and before that the family lived in Urney Street, Belfast. He is commemorated in the Belfast Book of Honour (Page 43).

Blair, William
Private
No. 18115, 12th Battalion, Highland Light Infantry
Killed in action on Saturday 25 September 1915
Loos Memorial, France (Panel 108 to 112)

In 'Soldiers Died in the Great War 1914 – 1919' it is recorded that William Blair was born in Ballywalter and he enlisted in Clydebank. He served with the Highland Light Infantry and he was killed in action on 25 September 1915.

Blythe, Alfred
Sergeant
No. 16197, 'B' Company, 13th Battalion, Royal Irish Rifles
Killed in action on Saturday 1 July 1916 (aged 29)
Thiepval Memorial, France (Pier and Face 15 A and 15 B)

Alfred Blythe was born in Newtownards and he was a son of Robert and Agnes Blythe (nee Jackson) who were married on 5 September 1874 in Newtownards Parish Church of Ireland. Alfred and his widowed mother lived at 22 Thomas Street, Newtownards and after that in West Street. Prior to the outbreak of the Great War Alfred Blythe worked as a labourer. He enlisted in Belfast, he served with the 13th Battalion Royal Irish Rifles in 108th

B

Brigade of the 36th (Ulster) Division and he was posted as missing in action after the first day of the Battle of the Somme.

Is He a Newtownards Volunteer?

In "Thompson's Weekly News," published in Glasgow, there appears in last Saturday's issue a photograph which has given rise to much local speculation as to who is the original. The suggestion is that it may be Sergeant A. Blythe, 1st County Down Volunteers, of West Street, Newtownards, who it is said to represent very strongly in the features. Sergeant Blythe was in the push at 1st July, 1916, and has not been heard of since. The wording underneath the photograph published is :—" This soldier is a prisoner in Gefangenlager, Scheidmuill, Posen. He has lost his memory and his name; regiment, &c., are not known. Who is he?" We understand local inquiries are being made for the purpose of elucidating the identity of the soldier.

As in every case where a soldier was posted as missing in action family and friends at home retained the hope that Alfred had not been killed. This hope received a boost in July 1917 when a photograph of a soldier who was being held prisoner in Gefangenlager, Scheidmuill, Posen was published in the Glasgow newspaper *Thompson's Weekly News*. It was reported that this prisoner had lost his memory and he couldn't remember his name or his regiment. When people in Newtownards looked at the photograph they saw a very strong resemblance to Sergeant Blythe and enquiries were made. However, hopes were dashed when it was officially confirmed that Sergeant Blythe had been killed in action at the Battle of the Somme and he is commemorated on Newtownards and District War Memorial.

Boal, William (served as McHugh, William)
Private
No. 3356, 1st Battalion, Scots Guards
Died in a Prisoner of War camp on Thursday 18 May 1916 (aged 38)
Niederzwehren Cemetery, Germany (Grave IX. F. 8)

William Boal and Mary Jane Hanna were married on 12 November 1902 in Greenwell Street Presbyterian Church Newtownards. By then William's father John who had been a career soldier was dead. William and Mary Jane Boal had at least five children – William, Mary, James, Ernest and John. Three of them were baptised in Greenwell Street Presbyterian Church.

The 4 March 1916 edition of the *Newtownards Chronicle* carried an article under the headline 'Crown Princess of Sweden and a Newtownards Scots Guardsman'. Her Royal Highness The Crown Princess of Sweden was the daughter of Prince Arthur, Duke of Connaught, third son of Queen Victoria and in the article it was reported that Private William Boal whose wife and children lived at 11 Balfour Street and who had 17 years service in the Scots Guards had been taken prisoner and was being held in Gottingen Prisoner of War Camp. The report carried a quotation from a letter received by Mrs Boal:

'The Crown Princess of Sweden wishes to let you know that she sends your husband, Private William Boal, Scots Guards, frequent parcels to Gottingen, which he seems most grateful for. He asked the Crown Princess to let you know this and that he is well'.

On 15 July 1916 the *Newtownards Chronicle* published a letter from Private Vester Viney (7958) of the 1st Wiltshire Regiment to Mary Jane Boal in which he informed her that her husband William Boal (3356) Scots Guards had died from heart failure.

DIED A PRISONER OF WAR.

Guardsman W. M'Hugh (No. 3,356), of the Scots Guards, who was previously reported as missing, is now reported died as prisoner of war.

In the 2 September 1916 edition of the *Newtownards Chronicle* it was reported that Guardsman W McHugh (3356) Scots Guards who was previously reported as missing was now reported died as a prisoner of war.

Guardsman William Boal who enlisted in Hamilton Lanark and served as William McHugh is commemorated on Newtownards and District War Memorial and in the PCI Roll of Honour for Greenwell Street Presbyterian Church Newtownards. He is buried in Niederzwehren Cemetery, as is Private Vester Viney who died on 13 November 1918.

B

Boland, Alexander
Rifleman
No. 14098, 10th Battalion, Royal Irish Rifles
Killed in action on Saturday 1 July 1916 (aged 21)
Thiepval Memorial, France (Pier and Face 15 A and 15 B)

Alexander Boland was born in Newtownards on 10 January 1895 and he was a son of Charles and Martha Boland (nee Kirkpatrick) who lived at 28 James Street. They were married on 19 October 1891 in First Newtownards Presbyterian Church. Charles Boland worked as a grocer and Martha worked as a dressmaker before the family moved to Belfast. Charles and Martha had at least eleven children including Maggie, Alexander, Robert Charles, Arthur, Annie, Elizabeth, David John, Catherine and Albert. Alexander was baptised in First Newtownards Presbyterian Church.

Prior to the outbreak of the Great War Alexander Boland worked as a printer and after he enlisted in Belfast he served with the 10th Battalion Royal Irish Rifles in 107th Brigade of the 36th (Ulster) Division. He was killed in action on the first day of the Battle of the Somme and at that time the Boland family was living at 21 Gosford Street, Belfast. Rifleman Alexander Boland is commemorated in the Belfast Book of Honour (Page 48) and in the PCI Roll of Honour for Crescent Presbyterian Church Belfast.

Boucher, Richard
Private
No. 23663, 1st Battalion, Royal Inniskilling Fusiliers
Killed in action on Saturday 1 July 1916 (aged 23)
Thiepval Memorial, France (Pier and Face 4 D and 5 B)

Richard Boucher was born in Newtownards and he was the youngest son of William and Elizabeth (Eliza) Boucher (nee Neill) who lived at 7 Canal Row. They were married on 20 April 1889 in Regent Street Methodist Church Newtownards. William Boucher worked as a labourer on the railway and he and Eliza had at least nine children – Elizabeth, Robert, Richard, Isabella, Sarah, Jane, Agnes, James and Miriam.

Prior to the outbreak of the Great War Richard Boucher worked as a machine printer and after enlisting in Newtownards he served with the 1st Battalion Royal Inniskilling Fusiliers. He went to Gallipoli on 17 October 1915 and he served there with 87th Brigade of the 29th Division before going to France.

FOR KING AND COUNTRY.
BOUCHER—Killed in action, 1st July, 1916 (23663) Private Richard Boucher, 1st Inniskilling Fusiliers, youngest and dearly-beloved son of William and Eliza Boucher.
Although we're in a far-off land,
    And your grave we cannot see;
As long as life and memory lasts,
    We shall remember thee.
Inserted by his Father, Mother, Brothers
        and Sisters.
7 Canal Row,
    Newtownards.

Private Richard Boucher was killed in action on the first day of the Battle of the Somme and in January 1917 his father, mother, brothers and sisters placed a 'For King and Country' notice in the *Newtownards Chronicle*. It contained the verse:

'Although we're in a far-off land,
And your grave we cannot see;
As long as life and memory lasts,
We shall remember thee.'

Private Richard Boucher is commemorated on Newtownards and District War Memorial and in Regent Street Methodist Church Newtownards.

Bowman, James
Rifleman
No. 12601, 8th Battalion, Royal Irish Rifles
Killed in action on Sunday 2 July 1916 (aged 21)
Thiepval Memorial, France (Pier and Face 15 A and 15 B)

James Bowman was born in Newtownards and he was a son of John and Margaret (Maggie) Bowman (nee McKibbin). They were married on 25 January 1893 in First Newtownards Presbyterian Church. John Bowman worked as a house painter and he and Maggie had at least ten children including James, George, John, Mary, Edward, Elizabeth, William, Margaret and Robert.

Prior to the outbreak of the Great War James Bowman worked as an apprentice house painter. When James enlisted he joined the East Belfast Volunteers and he served as a Rifleman and Signaller with the 8th Battalion Royal Irish Rifles in 107th Brigade of the 36th (Ulster) Division. In the CWGC Debt of Honour it is recorded that he died on 2 July 1916. In the heat of battle the 8th Battalion Royal Irish Rifles did not make a casualty return on 1 July 1916 and many military historians agree that those 8th Battalion casualties listed on the 2 July return were killed in action on 1 July.

B

FOR KING AND COUNTRY.

BOWMAN—Killed in action 2nd July, 1916, Signaller James Bowman, Royal Irish Rifles (East Belfast Volunteers), beloved son of John and the late Maggie Bowman, Sandown Road, Ballyhackamore, and nephew of E. and M. M'Kibben, 20 North Street, Newtownards.

At that time his widowed father lived at 30 Sandown Road, Ballyhackamore, Belfast and his uncle and aunt E and M McKibben lived at 20 North Street, Newtownards. Collectively they placed a 'For King and Country' notice in the *Newtownards Chronicle*. Rifleman James Bowman is commemorated in the Belfast Book of Honour (Page 51).

Boyd, Andrew
Quartermaster Sergeant

A further proof of the care taken by the Canadian military authorities of the soldiers in their jurisdiction has been shown in Newtownards this week by the long and interesting letter sent to Mrs. Boyd, of Church Street, by Mr. E. C. Lemieux, of the Department of Militia and Defence, in which he conveys sympathy with her on the death of her son, Quartermaster-Sergeant Andrew Boyd. The deceased soldier had excellent military service abroad, having served during the South African war, for which he received the Queen's Medal. He had also been granted the Long Service and Good Conduct Medal. Sergeant Boyd died in hospital in Ottawa, and was accorded the honour of a military funeral.

In the 13 May 1916 edition of the *Newtownards Chronicle* it was reported that Mrs Boyd of Church Street, Newtownards had received a letter from the Canadian military authorities. Mr EC Lemieux of the Department of Militia and Defence conveyed his sympathy on the death of her son. Quartermaster Sergeant Andrew Boyd had served during the South African

War for which he received the Queen's Medal. He had also been awarded the Long Service and Good Conduct Medal. He died in Ottawa and was accorded the honour of a military funeral. Desk searches and public appeals to date have not confirmed whether this soldier served in the Great War or not.

Boyd, George Taylor (George)
Lance Corporal
No. 17293, 'B' Company, 13th Battalion, Royal Irish Rifles
Killed in action on Saturday 1 July 1916 (aged 21)
Thiepval Memorial, France (Pier and Face 15 A and 15 B)

George Taylor Boyd was born in Scotland and he was a son of Hugh and Marion Boyd who lived in High Street, Comber after they came to Ireland from Scotland in the 1890s. Hugh Boyd worked as a butcher and he and Marion had at least three children including George and Grace.

Prior to the outbreak of the Great War George Boyd worked as a labourer in a spinning mill. He enlisted in Comber and he served with the 13th Battalion Royal Irish Rifles in 108th Brigade of the 36th (Ulster) Division. Lance Corporal George Boyd was killed in action on the first day of the Battle of the Somme and there is a story in the family archives that George's death was witnessed at very close quarters by local man Girvan Strange when George's body fell on top of him. Lance Corporal George Boyd is commemorated on Comber and District War Memorial and in First Comber Presbyterian Church.

Boyd, John
Private
No. 790538, 47th Battalion, Canadian Infantry (Western Ontario Regiment)
Killed in action on Monday 7 May 1917 (aged 35)
Vimy Memorial, France

> **NEWTOWNARDS MEN MAKE THE SUPREME SACRIFICE.**
>
> Mr. Wm. Boyd, 61 Church Street, Newtownards, received word on the 2nd inst. that his brother, Private John Boyd, according to latest information, was reported killed in action on 3/7th May, 1917. Private Boyd enlisted in the 47th Canadian Batt. in February, 1916, and pro-

John Boyd was born on 22 October 1881 in Baltinglass, Co Wicklow. When he was killed on 7 May 1917 his brother William was living at 61 Church Street, Newtownards. His death was reported in the *Newtownards Chronicle* along with the death of Private **James Martin** under the headline 'Newtownards Men Make the Supreme Sacrifice'.

John Boyd enlisted in New Westminster British Columbia on 5 February 1916. Prior to that he had been working as a labourer in Canada and he and his wife Sarah lived at 330 Strand Avenue, New Westminster. It was noted in his attestation papers that John Boyd was 5 feet 11 inches tall and that he had a scar on the calf of his left leg. Private John Boyd went to the front on 27 November 1916 and he was killed in action on 7 May 1917.

Boyd, Samuel

The name Samuel Boyd is listed on Newtownards and District War Memorial and in the booklet produced for the Unveiling and Dedication Ceremony held on Saturday 26 May 1934 he is described as a Private in the Colonials. Private Samuel Boyd is also commemorated in Newtownards Parish Church of Ireland (St Mark). Desk searches and public appeals to date have yielded no further information.

Boyd, William
Rifleman
No. 7025, 1st Battalion, Royal Irish Rifles
Died in hospital on Thursday 16 December 1915 (aged 29)
Ste. Marie Cemetery, France (Div. 19. N. 2)

B

William Boyd was born in the townland of Ballymacarrett in Belfast and he was a son of Mary Jane Boyd who worked as a handkerchief stitcher when William's father died. Mary Jane Boyd had at least five children – Annie, Agnes, John, William and Thomasina. They all lived in Balfour Street, Newtownards with Agnes Rooney, Mary Jane's widowed mother. William Boyd worked as a labourer and he and Elizabeth Weir were married on 5 July 1909 in Newtownards Registry Office. They lived in George's Street with Elizabeth's father Thomas Weir. William Boyd enlisted in Holywood and at that time his mother was living at 1 Talbot Street, Newtownards.

William Boyd joined the Royal North Downs and he went to the front in April 1915. He served with 25th Brigade in the 8th Division, he lost his hearing in the trenches and he underwent an operation in No. 2 General Hospital at Le Havre. He died at 4.30 am on 16 December 1915 after having been unconscious for many hours.

William had made a will and when he died his property and effects were received by his wife who was living at 81 William Street, Newtownards with their young son. At the time Rifleman William Boyd's brother John was serving with the Royal Inniskilling Fusiliers.

A year after William's death his widow and little son placed an 'Our Heroes – In Memoriam' notice in the *Newtownards Chronicle*. There was another one from his mother, grandmother, sisters and brother John. The notice placed by his widow contained the verse:

'Oh, call it not death, it is life begun,
The battle's fought, the victory won;
The ransomed soul has reached the shore
Where he will weep, and suffer, and sin no more.
God knows the way, He holds the key,
He Guides us with unerring hand;
And soon with tearless eyes we'll see,
Yes there, up there, we'll understand.'

Rifleman William Boyd is commemorated on Newtownards and District War Memorial; in Newtownards Parish Church of Ireland (St Mark); in the PCI Roll of Honour for Greenwell Street Presbyterian Church Newtownards and in the Belfast Book of Honour (Page 54).

B

Boyle, Alexander (Alex)
Private
No. 6769, 20th Battalion, Australian Infantry, AIF
Killed in action on Sunday 11 August 1918 (aged 29)
Villers-Bretonneux Military Cemetery, France (Grave X. F. 6)

Alexander Boyle was born on 26 August 1888 and he was the third son of Robert and Agnes Jane Boyle (nee Hamilton) who lived in the townland of Kilbright, Carrowdore. They were married on 6 August 1884 in Raffrey Presbyterian Church. Robert Boyle was a farmer and he and Agnes Jane had at least five children – William, James, Alexander, Mary Agnes and Joseph. They were baptised in Ballywalter Presbyterian Church. Alexander Boyle's mother Agnes Jane died on 18 January 1916 aged 62. His father Robert died on 7 May 1940 aged 93.

Alex Boyle worked as an electrical engineer before he moved to Australia around 1909. There he worked as a telephone mechanic before he enlisted in Sydney, New South Wales on 5 April 1917. In his attestation papers it was noted that Alex Boyle was 5 feet 11 inches tall and the Medical Officer pronounced him fit to serve.

Private Boyle was posted to England to complete his training and from there he was granted leave to visit his family at home. He went to France on 30 April 1918 and he was killed in action four months later on 11 August 1918.

Alex Boyle was unmarried and when he made his will on 13 June 1917 he bequeathed all of his property and effects to his father. These items were duly itemised and forwarded to Robert Boyle in a sealed parcel – two metal mirrors, one photometer in a purse, one notebook, two wallets, one tobacco pouch, two discs, one metal ring, one silver wrist watch and strap, photographs, letters, cards, one cloth badge and odd papers.

When Private Alex Boyle was killed he was buried in Lamotte-en-Santerre Communal Cemetery Extension, 4¾ miles south east of Corbie. The Rev RG Crawford officiated. Later his body was exhumed and reinterred in Villers-Bretonneux Military Cemetery. Private Alex Boyle is commemorated on Ballywalter and District War Memorial; on the family grave headstone in Whitechurch Cemetery and in Ballywalter Presbyterian Church.

Branch, William John
Lance Corporal

No. 28663, 11th Battalion, Essex Regiment
Died of wounds on Thursday 13 June 1918 (aged 19)
Longuenesse (St. Omer) Souvenir Cemetery, France (Grave V. B. 62)

B

William John Branch was born on 15 May 1899 in Ballywalter and he was a son of William and Hannah Miriam Branch (nee Hart) who were married in the first quarter of 1892 in Epping, Essex. William Branch worked as a coastguard and he and Hannah had at least five children – William Gordon (died aged 3 months and buried in Whitechurch Cemetery Ballywalter), William John, Albert Edward, Ivy and Bernard. William John Branch was baptised in Ballywalter Parish Church of Ireland.

William John Branch enlisted in Colchester and he served with the 11th Battalion Essex Regiment. When he died his parents were living at 7 Florence Cottages, Brightlingsea, Essex.

Brankin, George
Sergeant

No. 16204, 14th Battalion, Royal Irish Rifles
Died of wounds on 8 June 1917 (aged 30)
Hazebrouck Communal Cemetery, France (Grave I. F. 11)

George Brankin was born on 3 March 1887 in Newtownards and he was a son of James and Agnes Brankin (nee Savage) who were married on 24 June 1871 in Newtownards Parish Church of Ireland. His parents were in the drapery business and they had at least five children – John, Elizabeth Jane, George, Agnes Anna and Jessie. Prior to the outbreak of the Great War George Brankin was employed in the Davidson & Company Sirocco Works Belfast and at that time he and his wife Mary lived in Seventh Street, Belfast. At the outbreak of war George enlisted in Belfast, he went to France in October 1915 and he was wounded during the Battle of the Somme.

After a period of convalescence George served at Ballykinler Camp before being posted back to the Western Front some five weeks before he died. He served with the 14th Battalion Royal Irish Rifles in 109th Brigade of the 36th (Ulster) Division and he died of wounds sustained during the Battle of Messines. At the time of his death his mother was living at 20 William Street, Newtownards and his wife and four surviving children were living at 59 Frederick Street, Newtownards. They placed a joint 'For King and Country' notice in the Newtownards Chronicle and it contained the verse:

'God is good, He will give me grace
To bear my heavy cross;
He is the only one who knows
How bitter is my loss.
Dearest children, I have left you
To the care of God above;
Do not let my absence grieve you.
For my sake each other love.'

In subsequent years family members placed 'Our Heroes – In Memoriam' notices in the Chronicle, including one from Annie and George Weber – his sister and brother-in-law who lived in Vancouver, Canada. George Weber was also on active service. Sergeant George Brankin is commemorated on Newtownards and District War Memorial; in Newtownards Parish Church of Ireland (St Mark); on the Davidson & Co Memorial (now in the Somme Heritage Centre, 233 Bangor Road, Newtownards) and in the Belfast Book of Honour (Page 60).

Brankin, James

The name James Brankin is listed on Newtownards and District War Memorial and in the booklet produced for the Unveiling and Dedication Ceremony held on Saturday 26 May 1934 he is described as a Rifleman in the Royal Irish Rifles. He is also commemorated in Newtownards Parish Church of Ireland (St Mark). Church records show that James Brankin born on 27 July 1893 was a son of William James and Eliza Jane Brankin who lived in John Street. Desk searches and public appeals to date have yielded no further information.

Brett, James McGilton (James)
Private
No. 2135 Highland Light Infantry, transferred to (91125), 13th Battalion, Machine Gun Corps
Died of wounds on Friday 27 July 1917 (aged 18)
Maroeuil British Cemetery, France (Grace IV. E. 15)

James McGilton Brett was born on 15 December 1898 in Newtownards and he was the youngest son of Robert and Anna Maria Brett (nee McGilton) who lived in Greenwell Street. They were married on 21 January 1882 in Newtownards Parish Church of Ireland and they had at least six children – Robert John, Edward, Mary Anne, Margaret, Richard and James McGilton. James enlisted in Glasgow and at that time he was living at Maryhill, Glasgow. When he died of wounds on 27 July 1917 he was serving with the Machine Gun Corps and before that he served with the Highland Light Infantry (2135).

B

FOR KING AND COUNTRY.

BRETT—Killed in action on 27th July, 1917, Private Jas. Brett, Machine-Gun Corps, youngest son of the late Anna and Robert Brett, Greenwell Street, Newtownards, aged eighteen years.

Inserted by his sorrowing Sisters and Brothers.

Private James Brett made a will and his property and effects were received by his sister who lived at 96 Vernon Street, Maryhill, Glasgow; both of his parents were dead. His sisters and brothers placed a 'For King and Country' notice in the *Newtownards Chronicle* and he is commemorated on Newtownards and District War Memorial.

Broderick, Arthur Rickwood (Arthur)
Rifleman
No. 44742, 3rd Battalion, Royal Irish Rifles
Died of pneumonia on Monday 1 July 1918 (aged 28)
Fulham Palace Road Cemetery, London (Grave 8B. D. 40)

Arthur Rickwood Broderick was born in Fulham and at the time of his death his wife Laura Jane was living at 33 Adela Avenue, West Barnes Lane, New Malden, Surrey. For some time Rifleman Arthur Broderick was a patient in the Military Hospital Newtownards and while he was there he became well-known in Newtownards and District as the leading organiser of a series of military concerts in the Guild Hall. When he was discharged from hospital he was sent to Belfast to await orders about rejoining his unit. He fell victim to the 'flu epidemic and was admitted to the Military Hospital in Victoria Barracks Belfast where he developed double-pneumonia and died on 1 July 1918.

FOR KING AND COUNTRY.

BRODERICK—On July 1st, 1918, at the Military Hospital, Victoria Barracks, Belfast (of pneumonia), Rifleman Arthur R. Broderick, Royal Irish Rifles (late Newtownards Military Hospital). Inserted by Matron, Staff, and Patients. Military Hospital, Newtownards.

The Matron, staff and patients of the Military Hospital Newtownards placed a 'For King and Country' notice in the *Newtownards Chronicle* and an article in that newspaper reported on the 'sincere regret that would be felt in Newtownards on account of his death'.

Brown, Hugh

The name Hugh Brown is listed on Newtownards and District War Memorial and in the booklet produced for the Unveiling and Dedication Ceremony held on Saturday 26 May 1934 he is described as a Rifleman in the Royal Irish Rifles. Hugh Brown who served with the Coldstream Guards (1512) during the South African War enlisted in Newtownards on 17 September 1914 and he joined 'B' Company of the 13th Battalion Royal Irish Rifles (17325). He was Church of Ireland and he declared his age to be 38 years 6 months. Prior to enlisting he worked as a bricklayer and he was a member of 'A' Company in the Newtownards branch of the Ulster Volunteer Force. Hugh and his wife Mary Brown had at least five children including Madge and John and they lived at 72 Movilla Street, Newtownards. Before that the Brown family lived in William Street and also at 37 Greenwell Street.

In November 1917 the 11th and 13th Battalions of the Royal Irish Rifles were amalgamated and after they were disbanded in February 1918 Hugh Brown was transferred to the 12th Battalion. Desk searches and public appeals to date have not confirmed a connection between these service data and the soldier who is commemorated on Newtownards and District War Memorial.

Brown, James
Rifleman
No. 6389, 2nd Battalion, Royal Irish Rifles
Died of wounds on Friday 1 October 1915 (aged 26)
Le Touquet-Paris Plage Communal Cemetery, France (Grave II. A. 30)

James Brown was born in Newtownards on 25 April 1889 and he was baptised in First Newtownards Presbyterian Church. He was a son of William and Jane (Jennie) Brown (nee Robinson) who were married on 2 June 1876 in Ballyfrenis Free Church of Scotland. William Brown worked as a farm labourer and he and Jennie had at least three children – William, Samuel and James. The Brown family lived at 1 Price's Lane, Newtownards before moving to 68 Abbey Street, Bangor. James Brown was a Reservist who was recalled at the outbreak of the Great War. Before that he worked in Morrow's posting establishment in Bangor.

James Brown served with the 2nd Battalion Royal Irish Rifles and he was wounded in action on 25 September 1915. Both of his legs were badly injured, the right leg so seriously that it had to be amputated. Rifleman James Brown died in Hooge Hospital on 1 October 1916 and in his will he had bequeathed all of his property and effects to his widowed mother. He is commemorated on Newtownards and District War Memorial; on Bangor and District War Memorial; in Strean Presbyterian Church Newtownards; on the RBL Bangor Branch Memorial Plaque and in the RBL Album in North Down Museum (Page 64).

B

Brown, Martin
Company Sergeant Major
No. 1149, 'B' Company, 17th Battalion, Royal Irish Rifles
Died on Wednesday 22 March 1916 (aged 52)
Blaris Old Burial Ground, Co. Down (Grave 194A)

A son of Mr W and Mrs S Brown of Lisburn, Company Sergeant Major Martin Brown died suddenly at the Victoria Barracks Belfast on Wednesday 22 March 1916. He was a career soldier with 22 years of service in the Royal Irish Rifles and had served for a number of years in India. Subsequent to that he had served as a Sergeant on the Permanent Staff of the Royal North Downs at Newtownards. While he lived in Newtownards Martin Brown was a member of both the Orange and Masonic Orders.

In 1905, after he left the Army, Martin Brown was appointed caretaker with the Central Presbyterian Association and he held that position until the outbreak of the Great War. He re-enlisted, joined the 8th Battalion Royal Irish Rifles (East Belfast Volunteers) and then transferred to the Reserve Battalion in January 1915. When Company Sergeant Major Martin Brown died his wife was living at 94 Marlborough Park, Belfast. They had six children, the eldest of whom was serving as a Lance Corporal with the Royal Irish Rifles at Ballykinlar. Company Sergeant Major Martin Brown is commemorated in Fountainville Presbyterian Church Belfast and in the Belfast Book of Honour (Page 67).

Brown, William John
Lance Sergeant
No. 17314, 'B' Company, 13th Battalion, Royal Irish Rifles
Killed in action on Monday 26 June 1916 (aged 20)
Authuile Military Cemetery, France (Grave G. 8)

William John Brown was born in Comber and he was the fourth son of Robert and Margaret Jane Brown (nee McIlveen) who lived in 'Millview Cottage'. They were married on 23 December 1887 in Second Comber Presbyterian Church. Robert Brown worked as a labourer and he and Jane had at least eight children – Joseph, Robert, David, William John, Hugh, Jane, James and Samuel.

> **Comber Volunteer Killed.**
> Lance-Sergeant W. '. Brown, Royal Irish Rifles (1st Co. Down Regiment), killed on 27t hult., was the 4th son of Mr. Robert Brown, Millview, Comber. He had served in the Ulster Division since its formation, and had two brothers at the front.

Prior to the outbreak of the Great War William John Brown worked in a factory. He enlisted in Comber, he joined the 13th Battalion Royal Irish Rifles and he served in 108th Brigade of the 36th (Ulster) Division. Lance Sergeant Brown was killed in action on 26 June 1916 and at that time two of his brothers were serving at the front. He is commemorated on Comber and District War Memorial and in Second Comber Presbyterian Church.

Browne, William Angus
Lieutenant
8th Battalion Royal Inniskilling Fusiliers attached 53rd Squadron, Royal Flying Corps
Killed in action on Friday 21 September 1917 (aged 24)
Pont-du-Hem Military Cemetery, France (Grave IV. G. 25)

William Angus Browne was born on 2 April 1893 and he was the younger son of William and Ellen Johnstone Browne (nee Davidson) of 'Tubber-na-carrig', Kircubbin. They were married on 24 April 1876 in Inishargie Parish Church Balligan and they had at least six children all of whom were baptised in Kircubbin Parish Church of Ireland – John Boyd, Harriet Selena Hatton, Helen Lyle, Lucy Caroline, Sara Miriam and William Angus. William Angus Browne's father died on 17 June 1907, his mother died on 15 January 1909 and both are buried in Kircubbin Parish Church graveyard.

William Angus Browne was commissioned on 9 October 1915. He served with the 8th Battalion Royal Inniskilling Fusiliers and was attached to the 53rd Squadron of the Royal Flying Corps.

FOR KING AND COUNTRY.

BROWNE—Previously reported missing 21st September, 1917, now reported killed on that date, William Angus Browne, Lieutenant Royal Inniskilling Fusiliers (attached Royal Flying Corps), younger son of the late Wm. Browne, Tubber-na-carrig, Kircubbin. 113 Agincourt Av., Belfast.

Lieutenant Browne was initially posted as missing in action on 21 September 1917 and then in February 1918 it was officially confirmed that he had been killed in action. The 'For King and Country' notice in the *Newtownards Chronicle* was submitted by his sister Miss Lucy Browne who lived at 113 Agincourt Avenue, Belfast and it was she who received the medal pair to which he was entitled.

Lieutenant Browne is commemorated in Kircubbin Parish Church of Ireland (Holy Trinity) and on the family grave headstone in the adjoining graveyard. He is also commemorated on the QUB War Memorial and in the QUB Book of Remembrance (Page 11).

Bruce, George James
Distinguished Service Order
Military Cross and Bar
Mentioned in Despatches (3 times)
Captain
'B' Company, 13th Battalion Royal Irish Rifles
Brigade Major
109th Infantry Brigade, 36th (Ulster) Division
Killed in action on Wednesday 2 October 1918 (aged 37)
Dadizeele New British Cemetery, Belgium (Grave III. E. 14)

George James Bruce was a son of Samuel and Julia Bruce of Norton Hall, Campden, Gloucestershire. He was born in County Cork and on 25 September 1907 he married Hilda Blakiston-Houston, a daughter of John Blakiston-Houston JP DL. They were married in Knockbreda Parish Church of Ireland. George and Hilda Bruce had four children including Michael

Robert and Mary Annie and for a time the Bruce family lived in the townland of Multyhogy, Pottinger, Belfast.

George James Bruce started as 'B' Company Commander in the 13th Battalion Royal Irish Rifles and later as a Staff Officer he was attached to the 16th (Irish) Division. During the Battle of Langemarck in August 1917 he was awarded a 16th (Irish) Division Gallantry Certificate. He returned to 109th Brigade of the 36th (Ulster) Division and on 2 October 1918 Captain George James Bruce was killed in action. Afterwards his widow Hilda moved to Corriewood, Castlewellan, Co Down and she died on 4 November 1935. Captain Bruce is commemorated on Comber and District War Memorial; in Comber Parish Church of Ireland (St Mary); on the North of Ireland [Rugby] Football Club Memorial Plaque and in Comber Masonic Lodge No. 46. He is also commemorated along with Second Lieutenant Edmund De Wind VC and Second Lieutenant Thomas McRoberts on the Banner of Comber Ulster Defenders LOL No. 100.

B

Buckley, Robert
Rifleman
No. 18/848, 11th Battalion, Royal Irish Rifles
Died of wounds on Monday 23 October 1916 (aged 25)
City of London Cemetery & Crematorium, Essex (Screen Wall. 235. 34A)

Robert Buckley was born on 14 September 1891 in Dundonald and he was a son of Samuel and Maria Buckley (nee Milligan). They were married on 22 February 1889 in Gilnahirk Presbyterian Church. Robert was baptised in Dundonald Parish Church of Ireland (St Elizabeth). After his father died Robert and his brother Samuel and their widowed mother lived in Mill Street, Comber.

> **FOR KING AND COUNTRY.**
> BUCKLEY—Died at Mile End Military Hospital, London, on 22nd October, 1916, from wounds received in action. Rifleman Robert Buckley, Royal Irish Rifles, beloved husband of Ellen Jane Buckley.
> A loving husband, true and kind,
>   Missed by those he left behind;
> Forget him? No, I never will,
>   As time rolls on I love him still.
> He gave his life for his country.
> What more could he do?
>   Inserted by his loving Wife,
>   ELLEN JANE BUCKLEY.
> 43 East Street,
>   Newtownards.

Robert Buckley and his wife Ellen Jane lived at 43 East Street, Newtownards and he enlisted in Newtownards. He made his will on 6 March 1916 and when he died his property and effects were received by his widow. Robert died at Mile End Military Hospital in London as a result of wounds received in action. Ellen Jane placed a 'For King and Country' notice in the 11 November 1916 edition of the *Newtownards Chronicle* and it contained the verse:

'A loving husband, true and kind,
Missed by those he left behind;
Forget him? No, I never will,
As time rolls on I love him still.
He gave his life for his country,
What more could he do?'

Five weeks after Rifleman Robert Buckley's death another tragedy befell his family. On Thursday 30 November 1916 his three year old son, also called Robert, fell into a pot of boiling water and died two days later. At the time of the accident Ellen Jane Buckley was washing clothes. She took the pot of boiling water off the fire and placed it on the floor beside the fireplace. There was a lid on the pot. Her son Robert was in the kitchen with her and when she turned round to put coal on the fire the child fell backwards onto the lid of the pot which gave way and he fell into the boiling water. Ellen Jane stripped off his clothes and called for a neighbour. Dr Jamison was sent for and he dressed the scalds before an ambulance arrived to take the child to the Infirmary. There the child was examined by Dr Warnock, Medical Officer of the Workhouse, who found scalding on the child's lower abdomen, between his legs and hips, on the upper part of his thighs and on the lower part of his back. Robert seemed to be holding his own during Thursday and Friday but he died of shock in the early hours of Saturday morning. There was a verdict of accidental death.

B

Rifleman Robert Buckley is commemorated on Newtownards and District War Memorial and in Newtownards Parish Church of Ireland (St Mark).

Burgess, Henry (Harry)
Sergeant
No. 17341, 'B' Company, 13th Battalion, Royal Irish Rifles
Killed in action on Saturday 1 July 1916 (aged 29)
Thiepval Memorial, France (Pier and Face 15 A and 15 B)

Henry Burgess was born in Comber and he was the third son of Samuel and Sarah Jane Burgess (nee Maxwell) who lived at 17 Brownlow Street. They were married on 15 July 1881 in Granshaw Presbyterian Church. Samuel Burgess worked as a farm labourer and he and Sarah Jane had nine children – Mary Jane, Samuel, James, Henry, Alexander, Clara, Robert, Sarah and Agnes Eva.

Prior to the outbreak of the Great War Harry Burgess worked as a farm labourer. He enlisted in Comber and served with the 13th Battalion Royal Irish Rifles in 108th Brigade of the 36th (Ulster) Division. Sergeant Harry Burgess was killed in action on the first day of the Battle of the Somme and he is commemorated on Comber and District War Memorial and in Comber Non-Subscribing Presbyterian Church.

Burns, George
Rifleman
No. 18/551, 'D' Company, 13th Battalion, Royal Irish Rifles
Killed in action on Saturday 1 July 1916 (aged 20)
Thiepval Memorial, France (Pier and Face 15 A and 15 B)

George Burns was born in Newtownards and he was the eldest son of Robert John and Elizabeth Burns (nee Morrison) of Conlig. They were married on 30 April 1892 in Greenwell Street Presbyterian Church Newtownards and they had at least three children - Lillie, George and Allan. Robert Burns worked as an agricultural labourer and George worked as an apprentice bricklayer.

George Burns enlisted at Clandeboye, he joined the 13th Battalion Royal Irish Rifles and he served with 108th Brigade in the 36th (Ulster) Division. He was killed in action on the first day of the Battle of the Somme and like so many others his body was not recovered. Rifleman George Burns is commemorated on Bangor and District War Memorial; on the RBL Bangor Branch Memorial Plaque; in the RBL Album in North Down Museum (Page 30) and in Conlig Presbyterian Church.

Burns, James
Rifleman
No. 9287, Depot, Royal Irish Rifles
Died of wounds on Monday 19 July 1915 (aged 23)
Bangor Old Abbey Churchyard, Co. Down (South-West part)

James Burns was a son of Joseph and Georgina Burns (nee Patterson) of Conlig who were married on 26 September 1884 in St Anne's Church of

Ireland Belfast. Joseph Burns was a sailor and he and Georgina had at least eight children – Josephina, Lizzie, Catherine, James, John, William Theodore, Ruth and Joseph. Joseph Burns remarried in 1903 and his second wife's name was Annie.

Rifleman James Burns died of wounds at home in Conlig on 19 July 1915 and he is commemorated on Bangor and District War Memorial; on the RBL Bangor Branch Memorial Plaque; in the RBL Album in North Down Museum (Page 31) and in the PCI Roll of Honour for Conlig Presbyterian Church.

Burns, Joseph *
Private
No. 4606, 2nd Battalion, Royal Inniskilling Fusiliers
Died as a result of gas poisoning

Joseph Burns served with the 2nd Battalion Royal Inniskilling Fusiliers and he went to France on 28 December 1914. He was discharged from the Army on 16 June 1916 and a family member has said that this was for medical reasons resulting from gas poisoning. His Silver War Badge is recorded on List B/393 Royal Inniskilling Fusiliers. Private Joseph Burns is commemorated on Newtownards and District War Memorial.

B

Burrows, James Charles
Corporal
No. 14547, Royal Scots Fusiliers, transferred to (40235), 13th Battalion, Royal Irish Rifles and (412316) Labour Corps
Died of wounds on Friday 29 March 1918 (aged 27)
Abbeville Communal Cemetery Extension, France (Grave II. A. 30)

James Charles Burrows was born on 1 August 1890 in Carrowdore and he was a son of William Robert Burrows and Maggie Burrows (nee Ritchie) who lived in the townland of Ballyfrenis. They were married on 7 May 1886 in Ballycopeland Presbyterian Church. William Robert Burrows worked as a farm labourer and he and Maggie had at least six children – William John, David, Mary Eliza, Margaret Jane, James Charles and Robert. James Charles Burrows was baptised in Carrowdore Presbyterian Church.

 In September 1914 James Charles Burrows enlisted at Lochans near Stranraer in Scotland. He joined the Royal Scots Fusiliers (14547) and went to Bristol for training. In August 1915 he went to France and in November 1915 he was severely wounded. In 1916 he returned to France and was transferred to the 13th Battalion Royal Irish Rifles, then to the 894th Garrison Area Employment Company of the Labour Corps (412316).

Corporal Burrows was acting as a stretcher bearer in the 45th Casualty Clearing Station when it was bombed and he was seriously wounded. He was taken to the 3rd General Australian Hospital at Abbeville where he died of his wounds on 29 March 1918. He was buried the following day with full military honours. At the time of James Burrow's death his brother Robert was on active service in the Royal Navy.

After James Burrows died two 'For King and Country' notices were placed in the *Newtownards Chronicle*. One was placed by his father-in-law and mother-in-law James and Eliza Ann Robson along with his three children John, William and Jeannie. The other was placed by his mother, brothers and sisters and it contained the verse:

'Sleep on, dear son, sleep and take thy rest,
Lay down thy head upon the Saviour's breast;
We love thee well, but Jesus loves thee best:
Good night! Good night! Good night!
Calm is thy slumber as an infant's sleep,
But thou shalt wake no more to toil and weep;
Thine is a perfect rest, secure and deep:
Good night! Good night! Good night!

Corporal James Charles Burrows is commemorated on Donaghadee and District War Memorial and in Carrowdore Presbyterian Church.

Burrows, Robert James
Sapper
No. 57416, 150th Field Company, Royal Engineers, 36th (Ulster) Division
Killed in action on Saturday 1 July 1916 (aged 32)
Thiepval Memorial, France (Pier and Face 8 A and 8 D)

Robert James Burrows was born on 13 August 1883 in the townland of Drumreagh, Ballygowan and he was a son of William and Martha Burrows (nee Burgess). They were married on 24 June 1881 in Spa Presbyterian Church

and they had at least four children – Robert James, Alexander, Rebecca Mills and Elizabeth.

Robert James Burrows enlisted in Belfast, he served with the 150th Field Company Royal Engineers in the 36th (Ulster) Division and he was killed in action on the first day of the Battle of the Somme. Sapper Robert James Burrows is commemorated in Ballygowan Presbyterian Church; in Megain Memorial Presbyterian Church Belfast and in the Belfast Book of Honour (Page 76).

Cairnduff, Valentine (Val)
Lance Corporal
No. 4596, 2nd Battalion, Royal Inniskilling Fusiliers
Killed in action on Friday 19 November 1915 (aged 20)
Suzanne Communal Cemetery Extension, France (Grave B. 10)

Valentine Cairnduff was born in 1895 in Newtownards. He was a son of Jane Cairnduff who worked as a spinner and they lived in John Street Lane with Jane's parents James and Emily. James worked as a horse dealer and he and Emily had at least eleven children including Jane, Lizzie, Sarah, Eleanor, Robert, Bella, Malcolm and William James. There is some variation in the spelling of the family surname. In census records it is spelt Carnduff. On Newtownards and District War Memorial, on the Church War Memorial, in Newspaper notices and in the CWGC Debt of Honour it is spelt Cairnduff.

C

Prior to the outbreak of the Great War Valentine Cairnduff worked as a shoemaker and on 5 December 1914 he married Marion McNurney in First Londonderry Presbyterian Church. He made a will and after he died his property and effects were received by his widow who lived at 27 Elmwood Terrace, Londonderry. Sergeant J Snodden wrote to Lance Corporal Valentine Cairnduff's mother to express his sympathy and he told her that Valentine had died on the night of 19 November 'without suffering of any kind'. Lance Corporal H McClurg also wrote to her and he enclosed a blood-stained photo of Valentine's wife Marion – 'enriched by the blood shed by her husband for his God and country'. The photograph was printed on a postcard and on the back of it Valentine had written his last and subsequently bloodstained message of love.

After Valentine Cairnduff died his mother Jane was living at 13 Pound Street, Newtownards. She placed a 'Killed in Action' notice in the *Newtownards Chronicle* and it contained the verse:

'No loved one stood around him
To hear his last farewell;
No parting kisses could he give
To those he loved so well.'

Lance Corporal Valentine Cairnduff is commemorated on Newtownards and District War Memorial and in Newtownards Parish Church of Ireland (St Mark).

Cairns, Archibald (Archie)
Private
No. 7565, 3rd Battalion, Royal Inniskilling Fusiliers
Died of blood poisoning on Tuesday 31 August 1926 (aged 40)
Newtownards (Movilla) Cemetery, Co. Down (Grave 13. 145)

C

Archibald Cairns was born in 1886 in Newtownards and he was a son of John and Annie Cairns who lived at 9 Ford Street. John Cairns worked as a linen weaver and he and Annie had at least nine children including Ellen Jane, Annie, Samuel, Archibald and David. Archibald worked as a Nursery Hand in Newtownards and later in the nursery of Messrs W & T Samson in Kilmarnock. An Army Reservist, Archie was called up at the commencement of the Great War and he went to France on 4 September 1914 with the 2nd Battalion Royal Inniskilling Fusiliers.

In the 23 January 1915 edition of the *Newtownards Chronicle* there was a report under the headline 'Newtownards Soldier in English Hospital'. The report stated that Private A Cairns (7565) 3rd Battalion Royal Inniskilling Fusiliers whose wife lived at 43 James Street, Newtownards had been wounded in the head and left unattended in the trenches during the fighting at Ypres in October 1914 because initially he was presumed to be dead.

While Archie was in a convalescent hospital in England (it had been the home of 'Mr Tillingworth brother of late Chief Liberal Whip') at Wydale, Bromley in Yorkshire he wrote a letter to Mr RK Sillars, foreman of the Greenhouse Department in Samson's Nursery, and outlined some of his experiences. He said that while he was in the trenches at Ypres he was struck on the head and he lay all night wounded and unable to help himself. His comrades thought that he was dead and he lost a lot of blood. In the morning when he was found to be still alive he was picked up and taken to hospital in Boulogne where he underwent an operation. From there he was transferred to England to convalesce and his head wound was kept open by the doctors in charge in order to extract a piece of broken bone. As a result of his injuries Archie Cairns was no longer fit for war service and he was discharged from the Army in 1915.

 He returned to Newtownards and in the 1920s Archie worked as weigh-master at the Urban Council weigh-bridge. He and his wife and eight children lived in William Street. Archie Cairns died of blood poisoning on 31 August 1926 and he was buried in grave 13.145 in Movilla New Cemetery. The name Cairns is inscribed on the grave-surround but there is no headstone.

Cairns, William John *
The name William John Cairns is listed on Newtownards and District War Memorial and in the booklet produced for the Unveiling and Dedication Ceremony held on Saturday 26 May 1934 he is described as a Rifleman in the Royal Irish Rifles. Desk searches and public appeals to date have yielded no further information.

C

Calderwood, Thomas (Tom)
Rifleman
**No. 17392, 'B' Company, 13th Battalion, Royal Irish Rifles
Died on Monday 10 June 1918 (aged 26)
Cologne Southern Cemetery, Germany (Grave XVII. B. 32)**

 Tom Calderwood was born on 9 December 1891 in the townland of Ballyblack and he was the youngest son of Robert and Margaret (Maggie) Calderwood (nee McCallion) who were married in 1883. Robert Calderwood worked as a general labourer and he and Maggie had at least seven children – Robert Geddis, Eleanor (died young), Jane (died 24 May 1909 aged 25), William Charles McCallion, Thomas, Susanna Ewart and Mary Morgan. The older children including Thomas were baptised in Greenwell Street Presbyterian Church Newtownards and the younger ones in Ballyblack Presbyterian Church. The Calderwood family lived at 157 Greenwell Street and at 5 Brownlow Place, John Street, Newtownards. Robert died on 27 February 1921 aged 67 and Margaret died on 25 October 1941 aged 81.

Tom Calderwood enlisted in Newtownards and he joined the 1st County Down Volunteers shortly after the outbreak of war. He proceeded to the front in October 1915 and served with 108th Brigade in the 36th (Ulster) Division. He was reported missing in action after the advance at the Somme on 1 July 1916 and then it was officially confirmed that he had been captured by the Germans. He was held prisoner for almost two years and he died in a German prisoner of war camp on 10 June 1918. His parents, brothers and sisters placed a 'For King and Country' notice in the *Newtownards Chronicle* with a request for the American papers to carry it. It contained the verse:

> *'His weary hours and days of pain,*
> *His troubled nights are passed;*
> *His ever-patient, worn-out frame*
> *Has found sweet rest at last'*

News of Tom's death reached his mother in a letter dated 15 June 1918 from the British Help Committee, Prisoners of War, Rennbahn Camp near Munster in Westphalia Germany. The letter stated that despite every attention in the Camp Hospital Tom had succumbed to a lung infection on the evening of 10 June. Tom was interred on 15 June in the Allied Prisoners of War Cemetery near Munster City and the grave number was 933. The letter continued, 'There was a beautiful floral offertory and we are sending you the ribbons from it and a photograph of the cemetery. If you want it you can ask for a photograph of the individual grave.'

The letter informed Mrs Calderwood that, 'In accordance with regulations the effects of the deceased (excepting small mementoes which will be sent to you after the war) have been disposed of and the sum realised, 343 marks 60 pfennigs, will be remitted to you by the authorities'.

Rifleman T Bennett of the 8th City of London Rifles who was a prisoner in the same camp also wrote to Tom's mother, 'Your son's death took place at 7.00 pm on Monday. I had the pleasure of knowing Tom for two years and Rifleman Quigley of the 2nd Battalion Royal Irish Rifles and I used to visit him in hospital. Tom never appeared to suffer and always had a smile on his face whenever we entered his room. The English medical corporal in whose charge Tom was placed assured me that Tom's end was peaceful'.

At the close of the morning service in Ballyblack Presbyterian Church on Sunday 21 July 1918 the congregation conveyed a resolution of sympathy to Robert and Maggie Calderwood on the death of their son. Tom's name had been among the first to be entered on the Roll of Honour in Ballyblack Church.

A week after Tom's death the Rev R Graham received a postcard from Tom that he had written shortly before he died. In it Tom thanked the members of Ballyblack Church for the last parcel that they had sent to him.

Rifleman Thomas Calderwood is commemorated on Newtownards and District War Memorial; in Ballyblack Presbyterian Church; in the PCI Roll of Honour for Greenwell Street Presbyterian Church Newtownards and on the family grave headstone in Ballyblack Presbyterian Church graveyard. The inscription on his CWGC headstone is:

'Still loved and remembered at home'

Calvert, James
Rifleman
No. 17394, 'B' Company, 13th Battalion, Royal Irish Rifles
Killed in action on Monday 7 February 1916 (aged 19)
Mesnil Ridge Cemetery, France (Grave G. 5)

James Calvert was born in the townland of Ballymacreelly, Killinchy and he was a son of James and Sarah Calvert (nee Morrison) who lived in the townland of Ballybredagh, Killinchy. They were married on 26 November 1892 in Raffrey Presbyterian Church. James Calvert Senior worked as an agricultural labourer and he and Sarah had at least nine children including Robert, Lizzie, James, William, David John, Sarah, Hans and Annie May. Prior to the outbreak of the Great War James worked for Joseph Gilmore of Toye and also for Mr J Prentice of 'Beechbank', Killinchy. He was a member of the Killinchy Ulster Volunteer Force and he enlisted in September 1914 in Downpatrick.

Rifleman James Calvert was one of four Ardsmen who were killed in action together on 7 February 1916. They were all members of the 13th (Service) Battalion of the Royal Irish Rifles (1st Co Down Volunteers) serving with 108th Brigade in the 36th (Ulster) Division. The others were Rifleman **David McConnell** of 22 Wallace's Street No. 2, Newtownards, Bandsman **Charlie Newell** of South Street, Newtownards and Rifleman **Jack Tate** of Frances Street and North Street, Newtownards.

The officer in charge of the platoon was Lieutenant **Elliott Johnston** who was a son of Samuel Johnston JP Glen Printing and Finishing Works in Newtownards. Elliott described the circumstances of their deaths. During a heavy bombardment a shell from the German lines exploded in the midst of a party of men killing three and wounding three. James Calvert, David McConnell and Charlie Newell were killed outright and Jack Tate died later from his injuries. The three men who died immediately were laid to rest together and the burial service was conducted by one of the brigade chaplains, the Rev Charles Campbell Manning, Rector of Comber. On that occasion Lieutenant Johnston escaped injury but he was killed in action five months later on the first day of the Battle of the Somme.

The letter from Lieutenant Johnston to Sarah Calvert was delivered to her on the same day as the last letter James had written to her. In his letter James told her that he was in good form and looking forward to being home soon on leave. Sarah Calvert was a widow when James was killed and the family lived in the townland of Tullycore, Killinchy. Sarah placed a 'For King and Country' notice in the *Newtownards Chronicle* and it contained the line:

'He now seeth greater things.'

James Calvert had been training to become a Signaller and when he died his brother William was with 18th Battalion Royal Irish Rifles at Clandeboye. Rifleman James Calvert is commemorated on Killyleagh War Memorial; in Killinchy Presbyterian Church and also in Killinchy Parish Church of Ireland.

Calvert, William James
Rifleman
No. 17395, 'C' Company, 13th Battalion, Royal Irish Rifles
Killed in action on Saturday 1 July 1916
Thiepval Memorial, France (Pier and Face 15 A and 15 B)

William James Calvert was born in the townland of Ballygoskin and he enlisted in Downpatrick. He served with the 13th Battalion Royal Irish Rifles in 108th Brigade of the 36th (Ulster) Division and he was killed in action on the first day of the Battle of the Somme. Rifleman William James Calvert is commemorated in Killinchy Parish Church of Ireland and in the PCI Roll of Honour for First Killyleagh Presbyterian Church.

Campbell, A Edward
Under the headline 'Comber Fusilier Killed' there was a report in the 20 October 1917 edition of the *Newtownards Chronicle*:

'Mrs A Campbell, 28 Railway Street, Comber is in receipt of news that her son Private AE Campbell Royal Fusiliers has been killed in action. Deceased enlisted since the outbreak of hostilities prior to which he was employed at the spinning mills of Messrs John Andrews & Company Ltd Comber'.

In 1901 Edward Campbell was living in Belmont Road Belfast and he was a son of Archibald and Ellen Campbell (nee Hewitt). They were married on 1 February 1896 in Comber Parish Church of Ireland. Archibald Campbell came from Scotland and he worked as a gardener. He and Ellen (who came from County Cavan) had at least three children – Annie, Edward and Frank. By 1911 Ellen was widowed and the family moved to Railway Street, Comber. Ellen worked as a charwoman and Edward aged 12 worked as a mill boy.

Private A Edward Campbell was killed in action in 1917 and he is commemorated on Comber and District War Memorial (as Edward Campbell); on the Andrews Mill Memorial Plaque (as A Edward Campbell) and as Edward Campbell on the Memorial Plaque in Comber Parish Church of Ireland (St Mary).

Campbell, Alexander
Lance Corporal
No. 16321, 'A' Company, 13th Battalion, Royal Irish Rifles
Killed in action on Saturday 1 July 1916 (aged 24)
Suzanne Military Cemetery No. 3, France (Grave II. D. 12)

C

Alexander Campbell was born on 18 February 1892 in Donaghadee and he was the youngest son of David and Sarah Jane Campbell (nee Smyth) who lived in Railway Street. They were married on 30 December 1886 in First Holywood Presbyterian Church. David Campbell worked as a railway ganger and he and Sarah Jane had at least three sons and one daughter – William, Hugh, Alexander and Mary. Alexander was baptised in Shore Street Presbyterian Church Donaghadee. Alexander's mother died in the 1890s and after leaving school Alexander worked as a general labourer. Both William and Hugh Campbell were railway workers.

Alexander Campbell enlisted in Donaghadee and he served with the 13th Battalion Royal Irish Rifles in 108th Brigade of the 36th (Ulster) Division. He was killed in action on the first day of the Battle of the Somme and he is commemorated on Donaghadee and District War Memorial and in Shore Street Presbyterian Church Donaghadee.

Campbell Family: Archibald Thomas and James
Archibald Thomas Campbell was James Campbell's son.

James Campbell was born in Newtownards and he was the eldest son of

Thomas and Margaret Campbell (nee Foster) who lived in Greenwell Street. They were married on 12 October 1866 in Ballycopeland Presbyterian Church. Thomas Campbell worked as a carpenter and he and Margaret had at least six children including James, Mary Sophia and Margaret.

James Campbell also worked as a carpenter and he and Jeanie Irwin were married on 9 August 1895 in Donaghadee Methodist Church. They had one son called Archibald Thomas and he was very young when his mother Jeanie died. During the Great War Archie died before his father James:

Campbell, Archibald Thomas (Archie)
Rifleman
No. 17404, 'B' Company, 13th Battalion, Royal Irish Rifles
Killed in action on Saturday 1 July 1916 (aged 19)
Thiepval Memorial, France (Pier and Face 15 A and 15 B)

Archibald Thomas Campbell was born on 22 June 1897 in the townland of Ballymacarrett, Belfast and he was baptised in Mountpottinger Methodist Church. After his mother died Archie and his father lived at 37 Court Street, Newtownards and then Archie went to live with his grandmother Eliza Irwin and his great-aunt Sarah Bell at 84 Little Frances Street, Newtownards.

Prior to the outbreak of the Great War Archie worked as an apprentice painter with Robert Thompson of High Street in Newtownards. In September 1914 he enlisted in Newtownards and joined the 1st County Downs. When he was in camp at Clandeboye he won several athletic events and he went to France in October 1915 where he served in 108th Brigade of the 36th (Ulster) Division.

Archie Campbell belonged to the fourth generation of soldiers in his family. His father Private James Campbell served with the Royal Garrison Artillery and he died of wounds in Egypt on 23 April 1917. His great grandfather William Fearney was a Crimean War veteran who had served with the Royal Horse Artillery and who was buried with military honours in Movilla Cemetery Newtownards. His maternal grandfather Thomas Irwin had also been a soldier.

It was Sarah Bell who received official news from the Army Council in July 1917 that her great-nephew, who had been reported as missing in action on the first day of the Battle of the Somme, had been killed in action 'on that day or since'.

Several of Archie's relations placed 'Our Heroes – In Memoriam' notices in the *Newtownards Chronicle* when his death was officially confirmed. These included his great-aunt Sarah Bell; his aunt and uncle Mary Sophia and John Askin of Greyabbey; his grandmother and aunt Margaret and Maggie Campbell of 3 Greenwell Street, Newtownards. The last of these contained the verse:

> *'Just as manhood days were dawning*
> *On the lad we loved so well,*
> *He was taken from amongst us,*
> *To his heavenly home to dwell,*
> *Taken away in his early youth,*
> *Taken from those he loved,*
> *From serving his King on earth below,*
> *To serve his great King above'*

Rifleman Archie Campbell is commemorated on Newtownards and District War Memorial; on the Memorial Plaque in Regent Street Methodist Church Newtownards and in the Belfast Book of Honour (Page 84).

Campbell, James
Gunner
No. 6649, 91st Heavy Battery, Royal Garrison Artillery
Died of wounds on Monday 23 April 1917 (aged 51)
Cairo War Memorial Cemetery, Egypt (Grave F. 217)

James Campbell enlisted in Newtownards and he served as a Gunner with the Royal Garrison Artillery. He made his will on 15 November 1916 and when he died his property and effects were received by his sister Maggie Campbell who lived at 3 Greenwell Street, Newtownards.

It was reported in the *Newtownards Chronicle* that first intimation of Gunner Campbell's death reached Newtownards in a letter to the Rev Jones Whitla dated 23 April 1917. The letter was written by the Rev Munro from the Wesleyan Church Rooms in Sharia Manakh, Cairo immediately after he conducted Gunner Campbell's funeral. In his letter the Rev Munro explained that James Campbell had been admitted to hospital on Friday 20 April 1917 and that he had passed away at 6.00 am on 23 April. He had been shot through the left temple and he had only very occasional and brief moments of consciousness thereafter. During one such moment James Campbell told the Rev Munro that he was married, he was from Newtownards and he was a Presbyterian. In his letter the Rev Munro asked the Rev Whitla to try to locate James Campbell's family and pass on the news of his death.

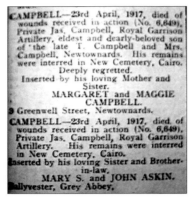

CAMPBELL—23rd April, 1917, died of wounds received in action (No. 6,649). Private Jas. Campbell, Royal Garrison Artillery, eldest and dearly-beloved son of 'the late T. Campbell and Mrs. Campbell, Newtownards. His remains were interred in New Cemetery, Cairo. Deeply regretted. Inserted by his loving Mother and Sister.
MARGARET and MAGGIE CAMPBELL.
9 Greenwell Street, Newtownards.

CAMPBELL—23rd April, 1917, died of wounds received in action (No. 6,649). Private Jas. Campbell, Royal Garrison Artillery. His remains were interred in New Cemetery, Cairo.
Inserted by his loving Sister and Brother-in-law.
MARY S. and JOHN ASKIN.
Ballyvester, Grey Abbey.

When James Campbell died on 23 April 1917 his widowed mother Margaret was in her 70s. She and James's sister Maggie lived in Greenwell Street, Newtownards and they placed a 'For King and Country' notice in the *Newtownards Chronicle*. So too did his sister and brother-in-law Mary Sophia and John Askin of Ballyvester, Greyabbey.

James Campbell's son Archie was killed in action on 1 July 1916 but James did not know that his son was dead. Initially Archie was reported as missing in action and it wasn't until July 1917, three months after James died, that Archie's death was officially confirmed. Gunner James Campbell is commemorated on Newtownards and District War Memorial.

Campbell, Henry

The name Henry Campbell is listed on Newtownards and District War Memorial and in the booklet produced for the Unveiling and Dedication Ceremony held on Saturday 26 May 1934 he is described as a Sergeant in the Royal Garrison Artillery. Desk searches and public appeals to date have yielded no further information.

Campbell, James
Rifleman
No. 105, 'A' Company, 13th Battalion, Royal Irish Rifles
Killed in action on Thursday 16 August 1917
Tyne Cot Memorial, Belgium (Panel 138 to 140 & 162 to 162A & 163A)

James Campbell was born in Donaghadee and he enlisted in Belfast. He served with the 13th Battalion Royal Irish Rifles in 108th Brigade of the 36th (Ulster) Division and he was killed in action on 16 August 1917 at Langemarck during the Third Battle of Ypres.

Initially Rifleman James Campbell was posted as missing in action and when his wife Maggie was officially informed in April 1918 that James had been killed in action she and their children were living at 16 West Street, Newtownards.

Maggie Campbell placed a 'For King and Country' notice in the *Newtownards Chronicle* and it contained the verse:

'The news was sad, the blow was hard,
God's will it must be done;
With a manly heart he did his part,
My dear beloved James.
He fell at his post, like a soldier brave,
He answered his Master's call;
He sleeps far away in a hero's grave,
For his country's cause he did fall.
In the pride of life death claimed him,
In the pride of his manhood days;
None knew him but to love him,
None mentioned his name but with praise.'

Rifleman James Campbell is commemorated on Donaghadee and District War Memorial and in Donaghadee Parish Church of Ireland.

Campbell, James
Company Sergeant Major
No. 4842, 7th Battalion, Royal Irish Rifles
Killed in action on Thursday 9 August 1917
Ypres (Menin Gate) Memorial, Belgium (Panel 40)

C

Two Popular "North Down" W.O.'s Killed.

With deep regret we record the deaths of two warrant officers who were for a long time past on the permanent staff of the Royal North Down Rifles, Newtownards. They are C.-S.-M. James Campbell, formerly of Ann Street, Newtownards, and C.-S.-M. Robert H. Wallace, formerly of John Street, Newtownards.

James Campbell lived in Ann Street Newtownards and he joined the Royal Irish Rifles in 1896. He served in India and Africa after which he was posted to the permanent staff of the Royal North Down Rifles in Newtownards. He and Margaret Reid were married on 21 May 1915 in Newtownards Parish Church of Ireland and Margaret lived in James Street, Newtownards with her sister Mrs Sharkey whose husband was also on the permanent staff of the Royal North Down Rifles. Shortly after James Campbell was transferred to Carrickfergus Margaret moved there and she lived at 3 Victoria Street. Company Sergeant Major James Campbell was killed in action on 9 August 1917 during the Third Battle of Ypres.

Campbell, John
Rifleman
No. 6712, 14th Battalion, Royal Irish Rifles
Died of wounds on Saturday 14 July 1917 (aged 28)
Belfast (Dundonald) Cemetery, Co. Down (Grave E5. 843)

Newtownards Rifleman Dies in Dublin Hospital.

The funeral took place on Tuesday with military honours from the Gt. Northern Railway Terminus, Belfast, to Dundonald Cemetery of Rifleman John Campbell, Royal Irish Rifles. Deceased, who passed away at Richmond Hospital, Dublin, leaves a widow and little son, who live at 33½ William Street, Newtownards.

John Campbell lived in Newtownards, he enlisted in Belfast and he served with the 14th Battalion Royal Irish Rifles in 109th Brigade of the 36th (Ulster) Division.

Rifleman John Campbell was wounded in action and he died of his wounds at Richmond Hospital in Dublin on 14 July 1917. The funeral cortege travelled from the Great Northern Railway Terminus in Belfast to Dundonald Cemetery on Tuesday 17 July and Rifleman John Campbell was buried with military honours.

John Campbell had made his will on 31 March 1916 and his property and effects were received by his widow Norah Lillan Campbell. She lived with their young son at 33½ William Street, Newtownards. Rifleman John Campbell is commemorated on Newtownards and District War Memorial.

Campbell, John

The name John Campbell is commemorated in Killinchy Parish Church of Ireland where it is recorded that he served with the Cameronians. Desk searches and public appeals to date have yielded no further information.

Campbell, Patrick

The name Patrick Campbell is listed on Newtownards and District War Memorial and in the booklet produced for the Unveiling and Dedication Ceremony held on Saturday 26 May 1934 he is described as a Regimental Sergeant Major in the Royal Irish Rifles.

In August 1917 it was reported in the *Newtownards Chronicle* that Company Sergeant Major P Campbell Royal North Down Rifles of Ann Street, Newtownards had been killed in action. His name is not recorded in the CWGC Debt of Honour. Desk searches and public appeals to date have yielded no further information.

Campbell, William

The name William Campbell is listed on Newtownards and District War Memorial and in the booklet produced for the Unveiling and Dedication Ceremony held on Saturday 26 May 1934 he is described as a Rifleman in the Royal Irish Rifles. Desk searches and public appeals to date have yielded no further information.

Cardy Brothers: James and William

James and William Cardy were born in Newtownards and they were sons of William and Jane Cardy (nee Turbit) who were married on 16 March 1875 in Newtownards Parish Church of Ireland and who lived at 115 Mark Street. William Cardy Senior worked as a linen weaver and he and Jane had at least ten children including Jane, Mary, William, Alexander, James, Elizabeth, Sarah and John. James was the first of the two brothers to die in the Great War:

Cardy, James (Jim)
Lance Corporal
No. 4/7078, 6th Battalion, Royal Irish Rifles
Died of wounds on Friday 10 December 1915 (aged 29)
Doiran Military Cemetery, Greece (Grave III. E. 11)

Prior to the outbreak of the Great War James Cardy worked as a tenter in the Ards Weaving Company Newtownards. He and Isabella McCamley were married on 30 May 1913 in First Bangor Presbyterian Church and they had two children – Evelyn and James. James Cardy enlisted in Newtownards, he joined the 4th Battalion Royal Irish Rifles and in August 1915 he went to Gallipoli with the 6th Battalion Royal Irish Rifles in 29th Brigade of the 10th (Irish) Division.

C

Lance Corporal James Cardy served in the Machine Gun Section of the Battalion and he went from Gallipoli to Salonika in October 1915. In late November and early December 1915 the 6th Rifles were holding a line on Kosturino Ridge near Lake Dorian. Conditions were dreadful; in the bitter cold uniforms froze solid and some soldiers died of hypothermia. Jim Cardy was wounded and he died of wounds on 10 December 1915.

At the time of his death Lance Corporal James Cardy had three brothers, two brothers-in-law and two nephews on active service. Four months later, on 27 April 1916, James Cardy's brother William was killed in action.

James Cardy's widow Bella and their two young children, the younger of whom was only seven months old, lived at 10 Thomas Street, Newtownards. Bella placed a 'Killed in Action' notice in the *Newtownards Chronicle* and on his headstone are the words:

'We do not know, we cannot tell, what pain he had to bear
Peace perfect peace'

Cardy, William
Rifleman
No. 6751, 2nd Battalion, Royal Irish Rifles
Killed in action on Thursday 27 April 1916 (aged 30)
Ecoivres Military Cemetery, France (Grave I. G. 14)

William Cardy was born on 25 July 1885 in Mark Street, Newtownards. Prior to the outbreak of the Great War he worked as a block printer and on 29 December 1906 he and Lydia Adeline Edmunds were married in First Donaghadee Presbyterian Church. He and Lydia had at least five children including William John and Lydia Adeline. William Cardy enlisted in Newtownards and he served with the 4th Battalion and then the 2nd Battalion Royal Irish Rifles. In the winter of 1914/15 he suffered frostbite when he was in the trenches and he was invalided home for a period.

William made a will on 24 November 1915 and after he died his property and effects were received by his widow Lydia who lived at 107 Mark Street, Newtownards. Four of their children were still alive. Rifleman William Cardy died on 27 April 1916 when he was killed by shell-fire, some four months after his brother James had died of wounds. William's brother Alexander (Sandy) was with him when he died.

C

FOR KING AND COUNTRY.
CARDY—Killed in action in France, on 27th April, 1916, Rifleman Wm. Cardy, of the Royal Irish Rifles, beloved husband of Lydia Cardy, 107 Mark Street, second son of William and Jane Cardy, 115 Mark Street, Newtownards.
Inserted by his sorrowing Father, Mother, Sisters and Brothers, Wife and Family.

William had been a member of LOL No. 1055 and after his death the secretary wrote to Lydia on behalf of members to express their sympathy. William's wife, parents, brothers and sisters placed a 'For King and Country' notice in the *Newtownards Chronicle*.

In April 1917 Lydia placed an 'Our Heroes – In Memoriam' notice in the *Newtownards Chronicle* and it contained the verse:

'I little thought when he left home
That he would ne'er return;
That he so soon in death would sleep,
And leave me here to mourn,
But now, alas! with sorrowing heart,
Through life's dark veil I tread;
The dearest one to me on earth
Lies numbered with the dead.'

Lance Corporal James Cardy and Rifleman William Cardy are both commemorated on Newtownards and District War Memorial and in

Newtownards Parish Church of Ireland (St Mark). Jim Cardy is named on the Roll of Honour in Regent Street Methodist Church Newtownards as having served. Sandy Cardy died on Remembrance Sunday 1935 aged 47.

Carlisle, Alexander
Rifleman
No. 294, 'A' Company, 9th Battalion, Royal Irish Rifles
Killed in action on Saturday 1 July 1916 (aged 28)
Thiepval Memorial, France (Pier and Face 15 A and 15 B)

Alexander Carlisle was born in Newtownards and he was the eldest son of Alexander and Ellen Carlisle (nee Gamble) of Arthur Street, Conlig. They were married on 6 May 1881 in Ballysillan Presbyterian Church Belfast. Alexander Carlisle Senior worked as a general labourer and he and Ellen had at least seven children including Martha, Alexander, Mary, James and Helen.

Like his father, Alexander Carlisle Junior worked as a general labourer before the outbreak of the Great War. He was an Orangeman and in 1908 the two Lambeg drums in his Lodge were placed in his charge. In Lodge records it is noted that on 12 July that year the Orangemen marched from Conlig to Greyabbey and back again.

Alexander Carlisle enlisted in Newtownards and he served with the 9th Battalion Royal Irish Rifles in 107th Brigade of the 36th (Ulster) Division. He was killed in action on the first day of the Battle of the Somme and he is commemorated on Bangor and District War Memorial; in the RBL Album in North Down Museum (Page 33) and on the Memorial Plaques in the RBL Bangor Branch, Conlig Presbyterian Church and Conlig Orange Hall.

Carnduff, James (Tibs)
Rifleman
No. 9294, 1st Battalion, Royal Irish Rifles
Killed in action on Wednesday 10 March 1915
Le Touret Memorial, France (Panel 42 and 43)

James Carnduff was born in Newtownards and he enlisted in Newtownards. Prior to the outbreak of the Great War he had been a member of the North Downs and when war broke out he rejoined the colours. He went to France on 6 November 1914 and on successive days in March 1915 two men from

Newtownards were killed in action at Neuve Chapelle where the Allied objective was to take Aubers Ridge – Riflemen James Carnduff on 10 March and Rifleman **Alexander Gibson** on 11 March. First news of their deaths reached Newtownards in a letter written by Rifleman John Weir (7496) to his uncle James Weir of Mill Street, Newtownards.

James Carnduff left a wife and six children the eldest of whom was 15 years old. Before the war the Carnduffs lived in George's Street and when James enlisted his wife and family moved to Mill Street to live with the children's grandmother. Later they lived at 34 Greenwell Street.

OUR HEROES—IN MEMORIAM.

CARNDUFF—In loving memory of my dear son, Rifleman James Carnduff (No. 9,924), 2nd R. I. Rifles, killed at the battle of Neuve Chapelle, on 10th March, 1915.

Far, far away thy grave to see,
But not too far to think of thee.
No morning dawns, no light returns,
But what, dear son, I think of thee.
We cannot, Lord, Thy purpose see,
But all is well that's done by Thee.

Deeply regretted by his loving Mother, Brothers and Sisters, also Wife and Family.
27 Frederick Street,
Newtownards.

C

In March 1916 James Carnduff's mother, brothers, sisters, wife and family placed an 'Our Heroes – In Memoriam' notice in the *Newtownards Chronicle* and it contained the verse:

'Far, far away thy grave to see,
But not too far to think of thee,
No morning dawns, no light returns,
But what, dear son, I think of thee.
We cannot, Lord, Thy purpose see,
But all is well that's done by Thee.'

Rifleman James Carnduff is commemorated on Newtownards and District War Memorial and in Newtownards Parish Church of Ireland (St Mark) where his surname is spelt Cairnduff.

Carnduff, Robert
Rifleman
No. 17388, 13th & 12th Battalions, Royal Irish Rifles
Killed in action on Tuesday 26 March 1918 (aged 26)
Pozieres Memorial, France (Panel 74 to 76)

Robert Carnduff was born in Newtownards and he was a son of Samuel and Ann Jane Carnduff who lived in Mill Street (20 Greenhill Terrace in the CWGC Debt of Honour). Samuel Carnduff worked as a general labourer and he and Ann Jane had at least five children – Lizzie, Samuel, Febby, James and Robert.

Robert Carnduff enlisted in Newtownards and he served with the 13th Battalion Royal Irish Rifles in 108th Brigade of the 36th (Ulster) Division.

He was wounded during the Battle of Langemarck in August 1917, he was transferred to the 12th Battalion and he was killed in action on 26 March 1918 during the German 'Michael' offensive. At the time of Robert's death his wife Sarah was living at 39 Robert Street, Newtownards. Later she moved to High Street, Portaferry.

In some military records Robert's surname is spelt Cairnduff. Rifleman Robert Carnduff is commemorated on Newtownards and District War Memorial and in Second Newtownards Presbyterian Church.

Carnduff, Samuel
Rifleman
No. 17416, 'B' Company, 13th Battalion, Royal Irish Rifles
Killed in action on Saturday 1 July 1916
Cerisy-Gailly Military Cemetery, France (Grave III. C. 9)

Samuel Carnduff was born in Newtownards and he enlisted in Newtownards. He served with the 13th Battalion Royal Irish Rifles in 108th Brigade of the 36th (Ulster) Division and he was killed in action on the first day of the Battle of the Somme. Rifleman Samuel Carnduff is commemorated on Newtownards and District War Memorial and in Newtownards Parish Church of Ireland (St Mark) where his surname is spelt Cairnduff.

C

Carpenter, Robert
Rifleman
No. 18/766, 11th Battalion, Royal Irish Rifles
Died of wounds on Tuesday 26 December 1916 (aged 26)
Bailleul Communal Cemetery Extension (Nord), France (Grave III. A. 152)

Robert Carpenter was born in Ballywalter on 8 July 1890 and he was the fourth child and the third son of Edward and Alice Carpenter (nee Bell). They were married on 7 January 1884 in Newtownards Parish Church of Ireland. Edward Carpenter worked as an agricultural labourer and he and Alice had five other children – Mary Eliza, John, Jane, Thomas and Edward. They were baptised in Ballywalter Parish Church of Ireland.

Robert Carpenter also worked as an agricultural labourer and he was a member of the Ulster Volunteer Force. He enlisted on 9 November 1915 in Newtownards and he served with the 11th Battalion Royal Irish Rifles in 108th Brigade of the 36th (Ulster) Division. He and Jane Keenan were married on 20 April 1910 in St Anne's Church of Ireland Belfast and they had six children – Hugh, Thomas John, Edward, Alice and Bella (twins) and Jane. They were all baptised in Ballywalter Parish Church of Ireland.

Rifleman Robert Carpenter was wounded in action on 18 December 1917 and he died eight days later. He had made a will and his widow received his property and effects. Jane Carpenter placed a 'For King and Country' notice in the *Newtownards Chronicle* on 20 January 1917. Rifleman Robert Carpenter is commemorated on Ballywalter and District War Memorial and in Ballywalter Parish Church of Ireland (Holy Trinity). His brother Edward also served and he survived the Great War.

Carser, James (Jim)
Private
No. 3351, 6th City of Glasgow Battalion, Highland Light Infantry
Died of wounds on Sunday 21 November 1915 (aged 24)
Lancashire Landing Cemetery, Gallipoli, Turkey (Grave H. 38)

James Carser was born on 1 November 1890 and he was the third son of David and Sarah Jane Carser (nee McDonald) who lived in the townland of Ballycullen, Newtownards and later at 33 Balfour Street, Newtownards. They were married on 29 July 1881 in Trinity Presbyterian Church Bangor. David Carser worked as an agricultural labourer and he and Sarah Jane had at least nine children including Isabella, William Henry, John Andrew, James, Robert Hugh, David and Samuel. James was baptised in First Newtownards Presbyterian Church.

James Carser worked as an agricultural labourer and on 11 April 1911 he and Margaret Anne Miskelly were married in First Newtownards Presbyterian Church and that is where their children David and Robert were baptised. In May 1915 James enlisted in Glasgow and he served with the Highland Light Infantry in Gallipoli. During November 1915 there was heavy rain and sleet and the temperature fell. Men wore all the clothes they had and with little to shelter under, together with the cloying mud underfoot, conditions were very uncomfortable.

Private Jim Carser died at No. 17 Stationary Hospital on 21 November 1915 from wounds sustained in action at Gallipoli and at that time his wife was living with her parents at 32 Little Frances Street, Newtownards. Annie Carser and Jim's parents placed separate 'For King and Country' notices in the *Newtownards Chronicle* and Annie's contained the verse:

> *'If love and care could death prevent,*
> *Thy days would not so soon have been spent.*
> *Some day, some time my eyes shall see*
> *Thy face I loved so well;*
> *Some day my hand shall clasp in thine,*
> *And ne'er bid farewell'.*

Private Jim Carser is commemorated on Newtownards and District War Memorial and in First Newtownards Presbyterian Church.

Carson, George *

The name George Carson is listed on Newtownards and District War Memorial and in the booklet produced for the Unveiling and Dedication Ceremony held on Saturday 26 May 1934 he is described as a Sergeant in the Royal Irish Rifles. Desk searches and public appeals to date have yielded no further information.

Casey, George
Driver
No. T4/092961, 251st Company, Army Service Corps
Died of wounds on Tuesday 2 May 1916 (aged 22)
Beauval Communal Cemetery, France (Grave E. 13)

George Casey was born on 23 March 1894 in Ballygowan and he was a son of William and Margaret Casey (nee Swindle) who later lived in the townland of Ballyrickard, Comber. William Casey worked as an agricultural labourer and he and Margaret had at least eleven children including John, William, Annie, Lizzie, George, Thomas, Jane and Maria. George was baptised in Ballygowan Presbyterian Church.

George Casey worked as a farm servant for Robert Bell in the townland of Cattogs, Comber, he enlisted in Belfast and he served with the Army

C

Service Corps. He died of wounds on 2 May 1916 and he is commemorated on Comber and District War Memorial and in First Comber Presbyterian Church.

Casey, James

The name Rifleman James Casey is listed on Comber and District War Memorial and he is listed as James Cassey in the PCI Roll of Honour for First Comber Presbyterian Church. Desk searches and public appeals to date have yielded no further information.

Cathcart, John
Rifleman
No. 19429, 'B' Company, 13th Battalion, Royal Irish Rifles
Killed in action on Saturday 1 July 1916
Thiepval Memorial, France (Pier and Face 15 A and 15 B)

John Cathcart was born in Portaferry, he lived in Comber and he enlisted in Belfast. He served with the 13th Battalion Royal Irish Rifles in 108th Brigade of the 36th (Ulster) Division and he was killed in action on the first day of the Battle of the Somme. Rifleman John Cathcart is commemorated on Comber and District War Memorial.

Caughey, William James (William) *
Lance Corporal
No. 12048, 'A' Company, 2nd Battalion, Royal Scots Fusiliers
Died of consumption on Wednesday 20 August 1919 (aged 33)
Newtownards (Movilla) Cemetery, Co. Down (Grave 11. 132)

William James Caughey was born on 17 March 1886 in Newtownards (aged 32 in CWGC Debt of Honour) and he was a son of John and Martha Caughey (nee Wilson). They were married on 24 June 1884 in Killinchy Non-Subscribing Presbyterian Church.

William Caughey worked as a labourer and he moved to Scotland where he lived in Shore Road, Stevenston, Ayrshire. He and Annie Bowman McClinton were married on 31 December 1906 in Greenwell Street Presbyterian Church Newtownards and they lived in Scotland, then in Church Street, Newtownards and later at 38 Frederick Street, Newtownards. They had at least three children – George

C

Alexander McClinton Caughey born in 1907 in Scotland, Martha Wilson Galway Caughey born in 1914 and James Galway Caughey born in 1917. All three children were baptised in Greenwell Street Presbyterian Church.

William Caughey enlisted in Ayr on 26 August 1914 and he served with the 6th Battalion Royal Scots Fusiliers before being transferred to the 2nd Battalion and going to France on 2 November 1914. He was seriously wounded on 22 December 1914 and transported to England for hospital treatment. There was serious damage to his lower bowel and he had to have a colostomy. In May 1915 he was discharged from the Army on medical grounds and granted a small pension. Regularly thereafter he was required to appear before a medical board for an assessment of his physical condition and to confirm his eligibility to continue to receive his army pension.

William Caughey died of consumption on 20 August 1919 and he is buried in Movilla Cemetery. His widow Annie paid for the following inscription on his CWGC headstone:

'My beloved is mine
And I am his'

C

Lance Corporal William Caughey is commemorated on Newtownards and District War Memorial. In the PCI Roll of Honour for Greenwell Street Presbyterian Church Newtownards he is recorded as having served and survived.

Chambers, George
Rifleman
No. 18/1674, 2nd Battalion, Royal Irish Rifles
Died of wounds on Wednesday 27 March 1918 (aged 19)
Grand-Seraucourt British Cemetery, France (Cugny German Cem. Mem. 30)

George Chambers was born in 1899 in the townland of Ballyalton, Newtownards and he was the fourth son of John Martin Chambers and Mary Chambers (nee Whitla). They were married on 15 December 1884 in St Anne's Church of Ireland Belfast. John Martin Chambers worked as a farmer and he and Mary had fourteen children including James, John, Annie, Lizzie, Henry, Margaret, George, Edith, Edward, Hugh and William Thomas.

In February 1917 George Chambers enlisted at Clandeboye and he joined the 18th Battalion Royal Irish Rifles. He left for France on 12 March 1918 to join the 2nd Battalion and fifteen days later he died in a German Field Hospital at Cugny. He had been severely wounded in the head during the German 'Michael' offensive.

FOR KING AND COUNTRY.

CHAMBERS—March 27th, 1918, at a German Field Hospital, Rifleman George Chambers, fourth and dearly-loved son of the late John Martin Chambers, Ballyalton, Comber, and of Mary Chambers, 17 Mill Street, Newtownards.
Deeply regretted by his sorrowing Mother, Brothers, and Sisters.

George's father died in the early 1900s and at the time of George's death his mother was living at 17 Mill Street, Newtownards. She placed a 'For King and Country' notice in the *Newtownards Chronicle*. Rifleman George Chambers is commemorated on Newtownards and District War Memorial and in the PCI Roll of Honour for both Greenwell Street and Regent Street Presbyterian Churches Newtownards.

Chasty Brothers: John and Richard

John and Richard Chasty were sons of James and Clara Lucretia Chasty. James Chasty was born in Devon and he worked as a Chief Boatswain in the Coastguard. He served a total of 38 years from 1876 to 1914 in the Royal Navy. James Chasty and Clara Lucretia How were married in 1881 in Stoke Damerel, Devon. Clara was born in Newfoundland and she and James had at least five children – Ellen, William, Richard, John and Alice. The Chasty family moved from Portaferry in County Down to Moville in County Donegal and then to Bray in County Wicklow. Richard was the first of the two brothers to die on active service in the Great War:

Chasty, Richard Christopher (Richard)
Lance Corporal
No. 9834, 1st Battalion, Royal Inniskilling Fusiliers
Died of wounds on Wednesday 8 September 1915 (aged 22)
Netley Military Cemetery, Hampshire, England (Grave C. E. 1721)

Richard Christopher Chasty was born on 24 August 1893 in Portaferry and he was educated in Strangford Co Down, Moville Co Donegal and Belmullet Co Mayo. Richard Chasty enlisted in Dublin in 1909 and he served with the 1st Battalion Royal Inniskilling Fusiliers in 87th Brigade of the 29th Division. He went to Gallipoli in April 1915 and on 22 May he was wounded in action. He died of wounds in Netley Hospital on 8 September 1915.

Chasty, John Norish (John)
Corporal
No. 12207, 1st Battalion, Royal Inniskilling Fusiliers
Died of wounds on Thursday 8 June 1916 (aged 21)
Louvencourt Military Cemetery, France (Plot 1. Row C. Grave 45)

John Norish Chasty was born on 26 October 1894 in Portaferry and when the Chasty family lived in Bray John worked as a boot boy in a hotel at 2 Cloonada Terrace.

John Chasty enlisted on 1 September 1914 and he joined the 5th (Service) Battalion Royal Inniskilling Fusiliers. In April 1915 he went to Basingstoke and on 14 July he left Devonport with his Battalion to join the Mediterranean Expeditionary Force as part of 31st Brigade in the 10th (Irish) Division. He was promoted to the rank of Corporal in September 1915 and he was injured during the evacuation of Gallipoli. After spending some time in hospital in Liverpool he joined the 3rd (Reserve) Battalion of his Regiment on 27 February 1916. He was transferred to the 1st Battalion and he went to France on 23 March 1916. His Battalion had been holding the line for 10 days when he was wounded on 7 June. It was a serious abdominal wound caused by a shell fragment and he was taken to a dressing station and then to a field ambulance at Louvencourt where he died the following day.

C

Chater, Frederick William
Able Seaman
No. Tyneside Z/501, HMS _Bayano_, Royal Naval Volunteer Reserve
Killed in action on Thursday 11 March 1915 (aged 30)
Whitechurch Graveyard, Ballywalter, Co. Down (Middle of South-East boundary)

Frederick William Chater was the husband of Sarah Dixon (formerly Chater) of 114 Chester Road Sunderland.

Seven crew members from HMS _Bayano_ are buried in graveyards on the Ards Peninsula.

Spracklin, Edgar J and **one unidentified Royal Marine** are buried in Ballyhalbert Church of Ireland (St Andrew) Graveyard Ballyeasborough.

Chater, Frederick William is buried in Whitechurch Graveyard Ballywalter.

Bain, AG; Wellstead, WA and **two unidentified sailors** are buried in Ballyphilip Church of Ireland Churchyard Portaferry.

Cherry, Charles James
Regimental Sergeant Major
No. 5881, 1st Battalion, Manchester Regiment
Died on Wednesday 20 October 1915
Madras 1914-1918 War Memorial, Chennai, India (Face 21)

Charles James Cherry was born in Newtownards and he was the youngest son of Sergeant Robert Cherry who for many years was on the Permanent Staff of the Royal North Downs at Newtownards.

Local Soldier's Death in India.—The death is reported from Bangalore of Sergeant-Major Charles J. Cherry, Bangalore Rifles. Deceased was the youngest son of the late Sergt. Robert Cherry, who was on the Permanent Staff of the Royal North Downs, at Newtownards, for many years prior to his death.

Charles James Cherry enlisted in Belfast and he served in India with the 1st Battalion Manchester Regiment. It was in India that Sergeant Major Charles James Cherry died on 20 October 1915. His death was reported in the 20 November 1915 edition of the *Newtownards Chronicle* under the headline 'Local Soldier's Death in India'.

Cinnamond, Francis (Frank)
Lieutenant
2nd Battalion, Royal Inniskilling Fusiliers
Died on Tuesday 12 November 1918 (aged 25)
Poznan Old Garrison Cemetery, Poland (Grave II. B. 5)

Francis Cinnamond was a son of Robert and Martha Cinnamond who lived at 7 Church Street, Cavan. Robert Cinnamond was a merchant in Cavan and prior to the outbreak of the Great War Frank Cinnamond worked as assistant accountant in the Newtownards branch of the Ulster Bank.

Lieutenant Frank Cinnamond served with the Royal Inniskilling Fusiliers and after he was taken prisoner in April 1918 he was held in House I, Room 77, Officer Prisoner of War Camp Grandenz. It was there that he died on 12 November 1918 although a month elapsed before his father received official confirmation that Frank had died.

Lieutenant Frank Cinnamond's death was reported in the 14 December 1918 edition of the *Newtownards Chronicle* under the headline 'Former Newtownards Banker Reported Dead'. Only a few days earlier, on 3 December, the Manager of the Ulster Bank in Newtownards had received a postcard from

Ards Officer's Fate.—Confirmation has now been received of the death in Germany of Second-Lieutenant Frank Cinnamond, Royal Inniskilling Fusiliers, who, before the war, was assistant accountant in the Ulster Bank, Newtownards. Deceased was a son of Mr. Robert Cinnamond, Main Street, Cavan. He joined the R. Rifles as a cadet over two years ago, and had been at the front a year in April last, when he was reported missing, and subsequently a prisoner.

Frank Cinnamond. The postcard was dated 22 October and in it Frank expressed kind regards to all the staff. He wrote, 'We all hope to see the homeland again soon'. Lieutenant Frank Cinnamond is commemorated on the Ulster Bank War Memorial Plaque and in the Royal Bank of Scotland Group Book of Remembrance (Page 34).

Clark, John
Corporal
No. 18524, 1st Battalion, Royal Inniskilling Fusiliers
Died of wounds on Wednesday 9 August 1916
Lijssenthoek Military Cemetery, Belgium (Grave VIII. D. 4)

In 'Soldiers Died in the Great War 1914 – 1919' it is recorded that John Clark was born in Cromer, Norfolk, he lived in Donaghadee and he enlisted in Newtownards. Corporal John Clark served with the 1st Battalion Royal Inniskilling Fusiliers in 87th Brigade of the 29th Division and he died of wounds on 9 August 1916 during the Battle of the Somme.

Clarke, Andrew
Lance Corporal
No. 6647, 1st Battalion, Royal Irish Rifles
Killed in action on Thursday 24 August 1916 (aged 20)
Vermelles British Cemetery, France (Grave III. O. 6)

In 'Soldiers Died in the Great War 1914 – 1919' it is recorded that Andrew Clarke was born in Comber, he lived in Dublin and he enlisted in Belfast.

In the 1901 census Andrew Clarke aged five who was a son of Robert James and Lizzie Clarke lived at 10 The Square, Comber. Robert James Clarke and Elizabeth Horner were married on 21 November 1894 in Comber Parish Church of Ireland. Robert James Clarke worked as a labourer and he and Lizzie had at least seven children including Robert John, Lizzie, Andrew, Susanna, Mary Jane, James and William. In 1911 the Clarke family was living at 6 Castle Street, Comber.

Desk searches and public appeals to date have not confirmed a connection between these 1901 census data and the soldier who died on 24 August 1916. He was killed in a bomb explosion whilst holding the line against a German attack. Andrew Clarke's wife Mrs S Clarke lived at 34 Chamberlain Street in

C

Belfast and Lance Corporal Andrew Clarke is commemorated in the Belfast Book of Honour (Page 101).

Clarke, James

The name James Clarke is listed on the Memorial Plaque in Ballygowan Presbyterian Church and in the PCI Roll of Honour he is described as a Private in the 19th Battalion Royal Irish Rifles. Possibly his number is 19/494. Desk searches and public appeals to date have yielded no further information.

Clarke, William

The name William Clarke is listed on Newtownards and District War Memorial and in the booklet produced for the Unveiling and Dedication Ceremony held on Saturday 26 May 1934 he is described as a Private in the Highland Light Infantry. In the records for Movilla Cemetery Newtownards it is noted that William Clarke from Newtownards, an army pensioner, died on 17 March 1921 (Grave 7.137). Desk searches and public appeals to date have not confirmed a connection between the Movilla burial record and the soldier commemorated on Newtownards and District War Memorial.

C

Clegg, James (Jim)
Lance Sergeant
No. 242618, 1st/6th Battalion, North Staffordshire Regiment
Killed in action on Thursday 24 May 1917 (aged 27)
Arras Memorial, France (Bay 7 and 8)

James Clegg was the eldest son of James and Margaret Clegg (nee Matchett) who lived in the townland of Federnagh, Poyntzpass, Co Armagh. They were married on 25 May 1887 in Crewmore Presbyterian Church. James Clegg Senior worked as a labourer and he and Margaret had at least five children including James, Samuel, Joseph and Mary Elizabeth.

FOR KING AND COUNTRY.

CLEGG—Killed in action on the 25th May, 1917, Sergeant James Clegg, North Staffordshire Regiment, eldest son of James and Margaret Clegg, Federnaugh, Poyntzpass, Co. Armagh.

Somewhere abroad our brother fell,
Beneath the roar of shot and shell;
When days are dark, and friends are few,
Dear Jim, it's then we'll long for you.

Deeply regretted by his loving Brother and Sister.
W. J. and M. CLEGG.
Greenwell Street, Newtownards.

Jim Clegg Junior worked as a gamekeeper and he enlisted in Longton, Staffordshire. He served with the Prince of Wales's (North Staffordshire Regiment) and he was killed in action on 24 May 1917.

After Jim died his brother and sister who lived in Greenwell Street, Newtownards placed a 'For King and Country' notice in the *Newtownards Chronicle*. It contained the verse:

'Somewhere abroad our brother fell,
Beneath the roar of shot and shell;
When days are dark, and friends are few,
Dear Jim, it's then we'll long for you.'

Lance Sergeant Jim Clegg is commemorated on Newtownards and District War Memorial.

Clegg, Thomas

The name T Clegg is listed on Donaghadee and District War Memorial and on the Memorial Plaque in Donaghadee Methodist Church the name Thomas Clegg Mercantile Marine is listed. Desk searches and public appeals to date have yielded no further information.

Clifford, William George (William)
Rifleman
No. 18912, 'C' Company, 13th Battalion, Royal Irish Rifles
No. 19/239, 10th Battalion, Royal Irish Rifles
Killed in action on Saturday 24 November 1917 (aged 21)
Cambrai Memorial, France (Panel 10)

William George Clifford was born in the townland of Moneyreagh and he was a son of William and Sarah Anne (Annie) Clifford (nee Duncan). They were married on 18 January 1892 in St Anne's Church of Ireland Belfast. William Clifford Senior worked as a labourer and he and Annie had at least seven children including John, William George, Mary Agnes, James and Rachel Ann.

William Clifford Junior worked as a labourer before he enlisted in Belfast on 24 September 1914. He joined the 13th Battalion Royal Irish Rifles (18912) and was discharged on 17 June 1915 at Clandeboye Camp as being physically unfit because of defective vision.

He re-enlisted in November 1915 in Belfast and served with the 10th Battalion Royal Irish Rifles in 107th Brigade of the 36th (Ulster) Division. He was killed in action on 24 November 1917 and at the time of his death his parents were living at 7 Wayland Street, Castlereagh Road, Belfast. Rifleman William Clifford is commemorated in the Belfast Book of Honour (Page 106).

Close, Robert

The name Robert Close is listed on the Memorial Plaque in Kircubbin Parish Church of Ireland (Holy Trinity). Information from one source suggests that Robert was born on 26 December 1891 or 1892 and that he was a son of James and Elizabeth Close who had at least two other children – Maggie born in 1885 and Agnes born in 1899. These three children were baptised in Kircubbin Parish Church of Ireland. Desk searches and public appeals to date have yielded no further information.

Coey Brothers: David and Thomas

David and Thomas Coey were born in Comber and they were sons of David and Elizabeth Coey (nee Miller) who lived in Mill Street. They were married on 28 October 1892 in Dundonald Presbyterian Church. David Coey Senior worked as a labourer and he and Elizabeth had at least six children including Thomas, Elizabeth, David, Archibald and James. Thomas was the first of the two brothers to die on active service during the Great War:

Coey, Thomas
Lance Corporal
No. 17459, 'B' Company, 13th Battalion, Royal Irish Rifles
Killed in action on Thursday 16 August 1917 (aged 21)
Harlebeke New British Cemetery, Belgium (Grave XII. A. 4)

Thomas Coey was the eldest son, he enlisted in Comber, he served with the 13th Battalion Royal Irish Rifles in 108th Brigade of the 36th (Ulster) Division and he was killed in action on 16 August 1917 at the Battle of Langemarck.

Coey, David
Rifleman
No. 10327, 1st Battalion, Royal Irish Rifles
Killed in action on Friday 4 October 1918 (aged 19)
Dadizeele New British Cemetery, Belgium (Grave IV. D. 7)

David Coey enlisted in Belfast, he served with the 1st Battalion Royal Irish Rifles and he was killed in action on 4 October 1918 during the Allied offensive against all sections of the German line.

Both Rifleman David Coey and Lance Corporal Thomas Coey are commemorated on Comber and District War Memorial and in Second Comber Presbyterian Church.

C

Coleman, William
Rifleman
No. 17462, 'B' Company, 13th Battalion, Royal Irish Rifles
Killed in action on Thursday 16 August 1917 (aged 26)
Tyne Cot Cemetery, Belgium (Grave V. H. 14)

William Coleman was born around 1891 and he was educated in a boarding school in Ballygowan. Prior to the outbreak of the Great War he worked as a farm servant for Joseph Berkeley in the townland of Ballyloughan, Comber.

William Coleman enlisted in Comber, he served with the 13th Battalion Royal Irish Rifles in 108th Brigade of the 36th (Ulster) Division and he was killed in action on 16 August 1917 during the Battle of Langemarck. Rifleman William Coleman is commemorated on Comber and District War Memorial and in Second Comber Presbyterian Church.

Collins, Michael
First Mate
SS *Eveleen* (Belfast), Mercantile Marine
Presumed drowned on Monday 6 May 1918 (aged 61)
Tower Hill Memorial, London, England

C

Michael Collins was born in the townland of Ballymarter, Quintin, Portaferry and he was a son of Owen and Eliza Collins. Owen Collins worked as an agricultural labourer and he was in his 90s when he died. Michael Collins was baptised on 9 November 1856 in Portaferry Roman Catholic Church (St Patrick's Ballyphilip) and he had at least two sisters – Margaret and Elizabeth.

Michael Collins worked as a seaman and he and his wife Jane (nee McGann) lived at 61 Corporation Street Belfast. Michael and Jane Collins had at least fifteen children including Lizzie, Mary, Kate, Michael, John, Jane and Robert.

Michael Collins served aboard the SS *Eveleen* which sailed from Ayr on 6 May 1918 bound for Belfast. SS *Eveleen* was a cargo steamer built in 1891 by Workman, Clark & Co Ltd Belfast and may have been torpedoed by a German U-boat. There were no survivors when the ship sank and First Mate Michael Collins is commemorated in the Belfast Book of Honour (Page 112).

Colville, Alexander
Military Medal
Sergeant
No. 240686, 1st/5th Battalion, Royal Scots Fusiliers
Died of wounds on Saturday 21 September 1918 (aged 23)
Sunken Road Cemetery, France (Grave II. D. 24)

Alexander Colville was born on 18 June 1895 and his mother's name was Margaret. He was baptised in Carrowdore Parish Church of Ireland and he lived with his grandparents James and Mary Colville (nee Gillan) in the townland of Ballyhaskin, Carrowdore. Then in his 70s James Colville was an  army pensioner who had served in the Royal Artillery. Alexander Colville was a nephew of Francis and Bessie Colville of Ballyhaskin, Carrowdore. Mary Colville died in 1904 and James died in 1911.

Before the Great War Alexander Colville worked as an agricultural labourer and he moved to Scotland. He enlisted in Dalmellington, Ayrshire, he served with the Royal Scots Fusiliers and he was awarded the Military Medal for gallantry. Sergeant Alexander Colville died of wounds on 21 September 1918 and he is commemorated in Carrowdore Parish Church of Ireland (Christ Church).

Condon, David
C
Company Quartermaster Sergeant
No. 19033, Royal Dublin Fusiliers, transferred to (336041), Labour Corps
Died on Wednesday 17 September 1924
Killysuggan Graveyard, Newtownards, Co Down

The name David Condon is listed on Newtownards and District War Memorial and in the booklet produced for the Unveiling and Dedication Ceremony held on Saturday 26 May 1934 he is described as a Company Sergeant Major in the Labour Corps.

Military records show that David Condon served as a Company Quartermaster Sergeant (19033) with the Royal Dublin Fusiliers and he went to France on 19 December 1915. Subsequently he transferred to the Labour Corps (336041) and he was discharged from the army on 18 December 1918.

David Condon and Isabella Riordan were married on 1 October 1918 in Donaghadee Roman Catholic Church. David Condon was described as a widower, a son of Thomas Condon (Royal Irish Constabulary), a Quartermaster in the Labour Corps and his address was given as Camp, Newtownards. Isabella was described as a widow, a daughter of Hugh McAlea (Publican) and her address was given as 42 Ann Street, Newtownards.

David Condon died on 17 September 1924 at 59 North Street, Newtownards and his wife Isabella placed a death notice in the *Newtownards Chronicle*.

CONDON—September 17, 1924, at 59, North Street, Newtownards, David Condon.—R.I.P. The remains of my beloved husband were interred in Killysuggan on Friday, 19th inst.
ISABELLA CONDON.

David is commemorated on Newtownards and District War Memorial and on the family grave headstone in Killysuggan Graveyard where the inscription reads 'died 1922'.

Connolly, Albert
Private
No. M2/117563, Mechanical Transport, Army Service Corps attached 110th Field Ambulance, Royal Army Medical Corps
Died of pneumonia on Tuesday 25 February 1919 (aged 22)
Tourcoing (Pont-Neuville) Communal Cemetery, France (Grave M. 2)

Albert Connolly was born on 21 September 1896 and he was the youngest son of James John and Mary Elizabeth Connolly (nee Wallace) who lived in the townland of Ravara, Ballygowan. They were married on 1 June 1882 in Holywood Presbyterian Church. James Connolly worked as a farmer and he and Mary had ten children including James G, William John, Mary Jane, Hugh Henry, Ruth, Euphemia, Albert and Madge Isabella. Albert's father died when Albert was a young child. Albert was educated at Ballycloughan, Saintfield and prior to the Great War he worked as a mechanical engineer

C

Death of Ballygowan Soldier.
Driver Albert Connolly, M.T., A.S.C., died of pneumonia at No. 10 Casualty Clearing Station, France, on February 25. Driver Connolly, who had four years' service, was the youngest son of Mrs. Connolly, Ravara, Ballygowan, who has also another son serving with the Australian Forces.

He enlisted on 26 May 1915, he joined the Army Service Corps and he went to France in October 1915. Private Albert Connolly was attached to the 110th Field Ambulance as a Despatch Rider and he died of pneumonia at No. 10 Clearing Station in France on 25 February 1919. One of his brothers served with the Australian Forces.

Cooke Brothers: Collins Alexander and David Greer
Collins and David Cooke were sons of Robert and Mary Ann Cooke who lived at 11 Court Street, Newtownards. Robert Cooke was a Sergeant in the Royal Irish Constabulary and for many years he was stationed in Newtownards. Robert and Mary Ann Cooke had at least twelve children including William R, Frances, Collins Alexander, David Greer, Sarah, John Orme, Margaret, Mary Kathleen and Madeline. David was the first of the two Cooke brothers to die on active service in the Great War:

Cooke, David Greer (David)
Private
No. 159661, 2nd Battalion, Canadian Mounted Rifles
Killed in action on Wednesday 16 August 1916 (aged 28)
Railway Dugouts Burial Ground, Belgium (Grave VI. K. 18)

David Greer Cooke was born in County Down on 28 December 1887 less than a year after his brother Collins Alexander. Around 1904 David Cooke moved to America where he worked as a machinist before the outbreak of the Great War. He took out his naturalisation papers and became an American citizen. David was unmarried when he enlisted in Toronto on 7 January 1916 and in his attestation papers it was noted that he was 5 feet 7 inches tall.

David Cooke joined the Canadian Mounted Rifles and in May 1916 he sailed to England. His brother Collins was in England at the same time and the brothers asked for home leave to visit their parents in Newtownards. David hadn't seen them for seven years. The urgent need for more soldiers to fight at the front meant that their request was denied and they were compelled to sail for France without visiting their parents.

When Private David Cooke completed his first period of trench warfare and was back in rest camp he wrote a letter to his brother William who lived at 321 Wister Street, Germantown, Philadelphia. David was dead by the time the letter was delivered. On the first day of his second period of duty in the trenches David was struck down by a shell and killed. Collins Cooke saw his brother fall and he was a member of the burial party. One month later Collins Cooke was also killed in action.

FOR KING AND COUNTRY.
COOKE—Killed in action, on August 16, 1916, Lance-Corporal David Greer Cooke (159,661), 4th Canadian Mounted Rifles, third and dearly-beloved son of Robert Cooke, Ex-Sergeant R.I.C., 11, Court Street, Newtownards.
Deeply regretted.

When Private David Greer Cooke died his father placed a 'For King and Country' notice in the *Newtownards Chronicle*. So too did Lord Londonderry's Own CLB Flute Band in Newtownards of which David had been a member. David's brother William wrote a letter of tribute to Messrs Henry Brothers *Newtownards Chronicle*. The letter stated that David had been a member of the Masonic Fraternity and also the Stonemen's Fellowship in America. The founder of this Order, the Rev HC Stone paid glowing tribute to David Cooke in a speech delivered in the Grand Opera House of Philadelphia to an audience in excess of 5000 people.

Cooke, Collins Alexander (Collins)
Private
No. 158053, 4th Battalion, Canadian Mounted Rifles
Killed in action on Saturday 16 September 1916 (aged 29)
Serre Road Cemetery No. 1, France (Grave IX. A. 19)

Collins Alexander Cooke was born in County Tyrone on 22 January 1887 and he was the second son. He was a keen sportsman and an active member of both the Ards Lacrosse Hockey Team and the Ards Football Club. Collins was one of at least four Cooke brothers who moved to the United States of America, the others being William, David and John. For a time Collins and David Cooke lived with their aunt Miss Sarah J Greer at 5629 Stokes Street in Germantown, Philadelphia in Pennsylvania.

C

Collins Cooke was unmarried and before the outbreak of the Great War he worked as a supervisor in a jute mill. He travelled to Canada on Labour Day 1915 and he enlisted in Toronto on 9 September 1915. In his attestation papers it was noted that he was 5 feet 7¼ inches tall and he had a birth mark at the end of his spine. He joined the 4th Battalion Canadian Mounted Rifles – the same Battalion that his brother John had joined earlier that year.

For several months after his enlistment Collins Cooke travelled throughout Canada with a recruitment officer giving exhibition drills. Since boyhood each of the Cooke brothers had been trained by their father in the use of firearms. Collins Cooke died on 16 September 1916 just one month after his brother David was killed in action.

> **OUR HEROES—IN MEMORIAM.**
> COOKE—In proud and loving memory of my dear sons, Lance-Corporal David Greer Cooke, C.M.R., killed in action 16th August, 1916, and Private Collins Alexander Cooke, C.M.R., killed in action 16th September, 1916.
> "They loved honour and duty more than they feared death."
> ROBT. COOKE, Ex-Sergt R.I.C.

When Private Collins Alexander Cooke died his father placed a 'For King and Country' notice in the *Newtownards Chronicle*. So too did Lord Londonderry's Own CLB Flute Band Newtownards of which he had been a member.

In August 1917 Robert Cooke placed an 'Our Heroes – In Memoriam' notice in the *Newtownards Chronicle* in proud and loving memory of his two sons David and Collins Cooke. It contained the tribute:

'They loved honour and duty more than they feared death.'

Both Private David Cooke and Private Collins Cooke are commemorated on Newtownards and District War Memorial and in Newtownards Parish Church of Ireland (St Mark).

Cooper, William
Private
No. 16031, 9th Battalion, Border Regiment
Died of pneumonia on Tuesday 1 October 1918 (aged 26)
Mikra British Cemetery, Greece (Grave 464)

William Cooper was born in Newtownards and before the Great War he worked as a labourer. He was 22 years of age when he enlisted at Shiney Row, Sunderland on 6 September 1914. In his attestation papers it was noted that he was 5 feet 6 inches tall, he weighed 133 lbs and he had a sallow complexion, blue eyes and brown hair. His mother's name was Polly Stewart but William didn't know her address. He didn't know where his father lived and he didn't know anything about his grandparents. He didn't know if he had any brothers or sisters and he declared that he had no wife or children of his own. He stated that he was a nephew by marriage of Thomas Pearson. Thomas and his wife Alice lived at 3 Bell Street, Old Penshaw, Co Durham and when William Cooper made his will he left everything to his uncle Thomas Pearson.

Private William Cooper was on active service in France from 7 September 1915 and subsequently he was posted to Salonika. Military records show that in late September 1918 William was suffering from vomiting, a sore throat and a cough. With his previous history of malaria he was admitted to hospital at the end of the month. His heart action was weak and he died on 1 October 1918. The cause of death was influenza and pneumonia.

Corrigan, James J
Private
No. 23910, 8th Battalion, Royal Inniskilling Fusiliers
Died of wounds on Monday 8 May 1916 (aged 20)
Kilclief Roman Catholic Churchyard, Co. Down (South-west of Church)

James J Corrigan was a son of Thomas and Annie Corrigan (nee Curran) who lived in Castle Street, Strangford. They were married on 31 January

1882 in Killough Roman Catholic Church. Thomas Corrigan worked as a farm servant and he and Annie had at least eleven children including Jennie, William, James J, Nora, Kathleen, Alice, Annie and Mary. Prior to the outbreak of the Great War James Corrigan worked as a farm servant.

James Corrigan enlisted in Downpatrick and he joined the 8th Battalion Royal Inniskilling Fusiliers. He went to France in February 1916 with the 49th Brigade of the 16th (Irish) Division and he was wounded in action. He was taken to the hospital for war casualties at Gosforth in Newcastle-upon-Tyne and he died on 8 May 1916. Private James Corrigan had made a will and his property and effects were received by his mother Annie who was living in Cottage 662 in the townland of Tullyboard, Portaferry. His sisters Nora and Annie also lived in Portaferry.

Corry Brothers: Robert John and Thomas
Robert John and Thomas Corry were sons of David and Maggie Corry (nee Irvine) who lived at 46 East Street, Newtownards. They were married on 14 October 1893 in Regent Street Methodist Church Newtownards. David Corry worked as a linen weaver and he and Maggie had at least eight children, including Robert John, Mary, Thomas, Henry, William Morris, David and James. Robert John was the first of the two brothers to die in the Great War:

C

Corry, Robert John
Rifleman
No. 9877, 2nd Battalion and Depot, Royal Irish Rifles
Died of consumption on Thursday 17 May 1917 (aged 23)
Newtownards (Movilla) Cemetery, Co. Down (Grave 11. 43)

Robert John Corry worked for John Gowdy (a local grocer) as a carter and van driver before he joined the 4th Battalion Royal Irish Rifles. After nine months he was transferred to the 2nd Battalion on 11 January 1912. He served in the British Expeditionary Force with 'D' Company from 15 August 1914 and on 18 September 1914 he sustained a gunshot wound to his right arm. He suffered a compound fracture of the humerus which left him 'permanently unfit for war service' and he was discharged from the army on 22 July 1915. Some time later Robert John Corry re-enlisted and joined the 5th Battalion Royal Irish Rifles. It was reported that 'his spirit was willing' but he was discharged again owing to the state of his health.

Robert John Corry and Elizabeth Graham were married on 13 October 1915 in Newtownards Parish Church of Ireland and they had two children both of whom died in infancy. Rifleman Robert John Corry died on 17 May 1917 at

CORRY—In fond and loving memory of Private Robert John Corry, 2nd Royal Irish Rifles, eldest and dearly-loved son of David and Maggie Corry, who passed away on 17th May, 1917, and was interred in Movilla Cemetery.

Dear is the spot where our loved one is laid.

Sweet is the memory that never shall fade ;

Fond is the hope that again we shall meet,

All kneeling together at Jesus' feet.

Those that think of you to-night

Are those that loved you best.

Ever remembered by his sorrowing Father, Mother, Sister and Brothers. 46 East Street, Newtownards.

12 Windmill Row, Newtownards and the following Saturday he was buried with military honours in Movilla Cemetery. The band of the 10th Royal Irish Fusiliers played the music and there was a firing party from the 20th Royal Irish Rifles. The Rev WLT Whatham conducted the service and three volleys were fired over the open grave. Buglers sounded *The Last Post*.

Elizabeth Corry lived at 3 Mary Street, Newtownards and she placed 'Our Heroes – In Memoriam' notices in the *Newtownards Chronicle*. One contained the verse:

> *'I have lost my soul's companion,*
> *A life linked with my own,*
> *One in hope, in love, in feeling,*
> *Death divided – now alone;*
> *At the river's crystal brink*
> *Christ shall join each broken link.'*

C

Robert John's father, mother, sister and brothers also placed 'Our Heroes – in Memoriam' notices. Less than three months later Robert John's brother Thomas was killed in action.

Corry, Thomas
Rifleman
No. 4/7253, 8th Battalion, Royal Irish Rifles
Killed in action on Friday 3 August 1917 (aged 21)
Ypres (Menin Gate) Memorial, Belgium (Panel 40)

Prior to the outbreak of the Great War Thomas Corry worked in a factory. In August 1914 he enlisted in Newtownards and he served with the 8th Battalion Royal Irish Rifles in 107th Brigade of the 36th (Ulster) Division. He went to the front on 5 July 1915 and was wounded in September that year. In July 1916 he returned to the front and was wounded in October 1916. In July 1917 he went to the front for the third time and less than a month later he was killed in action while his Battalion was holding the line.

Lieutenant Kennedy, the officer who commanded Thomas Corry's company, wrote to Thomas's mother to express his sympathy and in his letter he outlined the circumstances of Thomas's death. Thomas was on his way up to the trenches at night when an enemy shell landed in the middle of his platoon. Lieutenant Kennedy gave an assurance that Rifleman Thomas Corry's death had been instantaneous.

Thomas Corry had made his will on 3 July 1917 and his property and effects were received by his mother. His father, mother, sister and brothers placed a 'For King and Country' notice in the *Newtownards Chronicle*, as did his sister-in-law, aunt, grandmother and cousin Minnie. At the time of his death his brother Henry was being held as a Prisoner of War in Germany.

Both Rifleman Robert John Corry and Rifleman Thomas Corry are commemorated on Newtownards and District War Memorial and in Newtownards Parish Church of Ireland (St Mark).

Corry, Edward
Rifleman
No. 18892, 'B' Company, 13th Battalion, Royal Irish Rifles
Killed in action on Saturday 1 July 1916 (aged 31)
Thiepval Memorial, France (Pier and Face 15 A and 15 B)

C

Edward Corry was born on 1 February 1885 in Ballywalter and he was a son of Robert and Ellen Corry. He was baptised in Ballywalter Parish Church of Ireland. Robert Corry worked as a farm labourer and he and Ellen had at least five children including Edith, Minnie, Edward and Willie. Ellen Corry died on 20 July 1916 less than three weeks after Edward was killed in action.

Prior to the outbreak of the Great War Edward Corry worked as a stone mason and he and Ellie Adair were married on 10 March 1911 in Ballywalter Parish Church of Ireland. They had four children, Robert who was born in 1911, Edward who was born in 1912 and who died aged three months, John who was born in 1913 and Edna who was born on 5 February 1916. Edna was less than four months old when her father died. Their mother Ellie Corry died on 9 February 1933 aged 43.

Edward Corry enlisted in Ballywalter and he served with the 13th Battalion Royal Irish Rifles in 108th Brigade of the 36th (Ulster) Division. Rifleman Edward Corry was killed in action on the first day of the Battle of the Somme and he is commemorated on Ballywalter and District War Memorial; in

Ballywalter Parish Church of Ireland (Holy Trinity) and on the family grave headstone in Whitechurch Cemetery Ballywalter.

Coulter, Robert
Private
No. 10051, 1st Battalion, Royal Dublin Fusiliers
Killed in action on Friday 30 April 1915 (aged 29)
V Beach Cemetery, Gallipoli, Turkey (Special Memorial A. 28)

Robert Coulter was born on 2 July 1886 in Donaghadee and he was a son of John and Margaret Coulter (nee Agnew). They were married on 16 February 1882 in Donaghadee Parish Church of Ireland. For many years John Coulter was the manager of the local Gas Works and he and Margaret had at least six children – Sarah, John, Robert, Thomas, James and Ellen Annabella. They were baptised in Donaghadee Methodist Church. Robert Coulter's father died on 2 October 1898, his mother died on 11 October 1904, his sister Ellen Annabella died on 17 July 1910 and his sister Sarah died on 27 April 1911.

C

> **Gave His Life for His Country.**—The sad intelligence reached Donaghadee during the week that Rifleman Coulter had been killed in action, somewhere in France, and the news was received with general regret, as the young man was widely known and esteemed. Deceased was on the regular army, 1st Batt. Royal Irish Rifles, and had spent years in India, and he was home on a few days' leave prior to leaving for the front, where, as stated, he has laid down his life in the service of his King and country. He was a son of the late Mr. John Coulter, who for years was manager of the Gas Works. The greatest sympathy has been extended to the relatives in their bereavement.

In May 1915 it was reported in the *Newtownards Chronicle* that, prior to the outbreak of the Great War, Robert Coulter had served in India with the 1st Battalion Royal Irish Rifles. It was in the ranks of the Royal Dublin Fusiliers that Private Robert Coulter died on 30 April 1915 when he was on active service at Gallipoli and he is commemorated on Donaghadee and District War Memorial and in Donaghadee Methodist Church. He is also commemorated on the family grave headstone in Donaghadee Parish Church Graveyard where his date of death is inscribed as 11 May 1915.

Courtney, Alexander
Rifleman
No. 9167, 1st Battalion, Royal Irish Rifles
Killed in action on Thursday 21 March 1918
Pozieres Memorial, France (Panel 74 to 76)

In 'Soldiers Died in the Great War 1914 – 1919' it is recorded that Alexander Courtney was born in Comber and that he enlisted in Belfast. He served with the 1st Battalion Royal Irish Rifles and he was killed in action on 21 March

1918 at the beginning of the German 'Michael' offensive. Alexander Courtney was a son of Mrs Mary Courtney who lived at 54 Donegall Road, Belfast and Rifleman Alexander Courtney is commemorated in the Belfast Book of Honour (Page 122).

Craig, Joseph
Private
No. 81186, 2nd Battalion, Canadian Infantry (Eastern Ontario Regiment)
Killed in action on Wednesday 26 April 1916 (aged 24)
Woods Cemetery, Belgium (Grave II. E. 5)

Joseph Craig was born on 6 September 1891 and he was the eldest son of Robert and Margaret Craig (nee Mason) who were married on 11 November 1890 in Ballymacarrett Parish Church of Ireland. For many years Royal Irish Constabulary Sergeant Robert Craig was stationed in Greyabbey and he and Margaret had at least six children – Joseph, Mary Ann, Margaret, Robert Francis, Albert Ernest and James Alexander.

Joseph Craig left Greyabbey in October 1912 and went to Toronto where he remained until March 1913. From Toronto he went to Saskatchewan to take up a Government appointment as a school teacher. On 16 December 1914 he enlisted in Winnipeg and in his attestation papers it was noted that he was 5 feet 8½ inches tall. After a period of training he was posted to the Western Front in May 1915.

With the exception of a one-week furlough in February 1916 which he spent in Greyabbey, Private Joseph Craig served at the Western Front continuously until he met his death in a front trench. He was killed when an enemy mine exploded. During the morning of the day Joseph died he wrote a letter to his parents. He had returned at 4.00 am from a bombing expedition in a German trench and in the letter he told his parents that he had just heard the cuckoo for the first time that year. At foot of this letter Joseph's Sergeant added a note stating that Joseph had been killed in action that very day.

In an article in the *Newtownards Chronicle* Private Joseph Craig was described as a devoted son and brother and an 'extremely fine specimen of youthful manhood – mentally, morally and physically'. He is commemorated on Greyabbey and District War Memorial located on the outside wall of Greyabbey Parish Church of Ireland (St Saviour).

Croan, Joseph
Lance Corporal
No. 241192, 1st/5th Battalion, Seaforth Highlanders
Died of wounds on Tuesday 19 February 1918 (aged 20)
Grevillers British Cemetery, France (Grave X. E. 15)

Joseph Croan was the eldest son of William and Elizabeth Croan (nee Tibbs) who lived at 34 Mark Street, Newtownards. They were married on 29 December 1896 in Donaghadee Roman Catholic Church. Joseph's grandmother and aunt lived at 125 Mark Street, Newtownards. William Croan worked as a labourer and he and Elizabeth had at least five children including Joseph, Madge, Elizabeth and May.

Joseph Croan enlisted in Belfast and he served with the Seaforth Highlanders. In September 1916 he was wounded and had treatment for shell shock. He was wounded in action again on 18 February 1918 and admitted to a Casualty Clearing Station. The following day he died in Grevillers Hospital near Bapaume. Matron TM Rice wrote to Joseph's mother and assured her that Joseph had slept peacefully away without any pain. The Chaplain, Rev WP Young, described how Joseph had been hit by a 'chance shell' while he was in charge of a working party. His arm had been very badly smashed. A few days before going back into the trenches Lance Corporal Croan had distinguished himself by achieving second place in the Brigade Cross-Country Race. He is commemorated on Newtownards and District War Memorial.

Cromie, David
Rifleman
No. 16359, 'B' Company, 13th Battalion, Royal Irish Rifles
Died of wounds on Saturday 4 August 1917 (aged 24)
Mendinghem Military Cemetery, Belgium (Grave IV. A. 3)

David Cromie was born on 31 March 1893 in Ballywalter and he was a son of David and Ann Jane (Annie) Cromie (nee Harkness). They were married in 1892 in Ballywalter Presbyterian Church. David Cromie Senior worked as an agricultural labourer and he and Annie (who worked as an embroiderer) had at least four children – David, Thomas, Robert James and Albert. David was baptised in Ballywalter Presbyterian Church.

David Cromie Junior worked as agricultural labourer for Lord Dunleath in

Ballywalter Park and on 14 November 1916 he and Annie Reid were married in Ballywalter Parish Church of Ireland.

In September 1914 David Cromie enlisted in Belfast and he joined the 13th Battalion Royal Irish Rifles. He was sent to Clandeboye Camp for training and he went to the front in September 1915 with 108th Brigade of the 36th (Ulster) Division. On 26 May 1916 Rifleman Cromie was wounded in the left leg when he was struck by fragments of a shell while he was in his billet. He was transferred to hospital in Bristol for treatment. At that time two of Robert's brothers were also on active service – Thomas with the 13th Royal Irish Rifles (16315) and Robert James with the Cyclist Corps. David Cromie returned to the front and he was mortally wounded by shellfire on 4 August 1917 during the Third Battle of Ypres. He died in a Casualty Clearing Station.

After she received the official news that David had died of wounds his wife Annie placed a 'For King and Country' notice in the *Newtownards Chronicle* and it contained the verse:

C

> 'Somewhere in France my husband fell,
> Amidst the roar of shot and shell;
> When days are dark, and friends are few,
> Oh David, how I long for you.
> I prayed that God would keep you,
> And shield you in the fray;
> But, alas, my hopes were blighted
> When the sad news came that day.
> As dawn crept o'er the trenches
> He fell 'midst shot and shell;
> My only grief, I was not there
> To bid him a last farewell.
> He fought his battle, for his country he fell,
> Defending his home he was struck by a shell.'

Rifleman David Cromie is commemorated on Ballywalter and District War Memorial and in Ballywalter Presbyterian Church.

Cromie, David
Rifleman
No. 17/989, 8th Battalion, Royal Irish Rifles
Killed in action on Sunday 2 July 1916 (aged 31)
Thiepval Memorial, France (Pier and Face 15 A and 15 B)

David Cromie was born on 16 April 1885 in Killinchy and he was a son of David and Jane Cromie (nee Geddis) who lived in the townland of Ballyminstra. They were married on 18 September 1874 in First Killyleagh Presbyterian Church. David Cromie Senior worked as a scutcher in a flax mill and he and Jane had at least four children – William, Alexander, Margaret Lowry Coulter and David. David Cromie was baptised in Killinchy Presbyterian Church and he was just 20 months old when his mother died on 8 December 1886 at the age of 30. His brother William died on 22 March 1906 aged 30 years.

Prior to the outbreak of the Great War David Cromie worked as a general labourer and he and Margaret Houston were married on 19 October 1907 in Willowfield Parish Church of Ireland. They lived at 35 Rathmore Street, Belfast. He enlisted and served with the 8th Battalion Royal Irish Rifles in 107th Brigade of the 36th (Ulster) Division. In the CWGC Debt of Honour it is recorded that Rifleman David Cromie died on 2 July 1916. In the heat of battle the 8th Battalion Royal Irish Rifles did not make a casualty return on 1 July 1916 and many military historians agree that those 8th Battalion casualties listed on the 2 July return were killed in action on 1 July.

Rifleman David Cromie is commemorated in Killinchy Presbyterian Church and in the Belfast Book of Honour (Page 130). He is also commemorated on the family grave headstone in Killinchy Presbyterian Church Graveyard where his date of death is inscribed as 1 July 1916 and his age as 32.

Cromie, William John (William)
Lance Corporal
No. 17506, 'C' Company, 13th Battalion, Royal Irish Rifles
Killed in action on Thursday 16 August 1917 (aged 20)
New Irish Farm Cemetery, Belgium (Grave XVIII. B. 9)

William John Cromie was a son of Robert and Sarah Cromie who lived in the townland of Ballybunden, Killinchy. Robert Cromie worked as a farm labourer and he and Sarah had at least eleven children including Maggie, Hugh, Usilla, Robert, William John, Nathaniel, Alexander and Grace. William Cromie's father died and, prior to enlisting, William worked on his mother's farm at Killinchy. His brother Robert was also on active service.

Lance Corporal William Cromie was killed in action on 16 August 1917 during the Third Battle of Ypres and after he died 'his loving friends Eva Thompson and Private D Hanna (on active service)' placed a 'For King and Country' notice in the 1 September 1917 edition of the *Newtownards Chronicle*. It contained the verse:

'For a noble cause his life he gave,
And fell at his post like a soldier brave.'

Lance Corporal William Cromie is commemorated in Killinchy Parish Church of Ireland.

Crooks, Joseph *

The name Joseph Crooks MM is listed on Newtownards and District War Memorial and in the booklet produced for the Unveiling and Dedication Ceremony held on Saturday 26 May 1934 he is described as a Rifleman in the Royal Irish Rifles who was awarded the Military Medal. Desk searches and public appeals to date have yielded no further information.

Crooks, Samuel
Able Seaman
No. 224561, HMS *Thunderer*, Royal Navy
Died on Monday 31 December 1917 (aged 32)
Ford Park Cemetery (formerly Plymouth Old Cemetery)
(Pennycomequick), Devon, England (Grave General K. 26. 36)

Samuel Crooks was a son of Andrew and Jane Crooks (nee Arnold) who lived at 69 Balfour Street Newtownards. They were married on 10 July 1883 in First Newtownards Presbyterian Church. Andrew Crooks worked as a wool and cotton weaver and he and Jane had at least seven children including Samuel, Jane, Alice and Ellen.

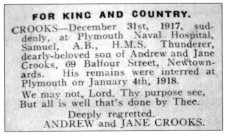

FOR KING AND COUNTRY.
CROOKS—December 31st, 1917, suddenly, at Plymouth Naval Hospital, Samuel, A.B., H.M.S. Thunderer, dearly-beloved son of Andrew and Jane Crooks, 69 Balfour Street, Newtownards. His remains were interred at Plymouth on January 4th, 1918.
We may not, Lord, Thy purpose see, But all is well that's done by Thee.
Deeply regretted.
ANDREW and JANE CROOKS.

Able Seaman Samuel Crooks served aboard the battleship HMS *Thunderer*. He died suddenly in Plymouth Naval Hospital on 31 December 1917 and he was buried on 4 January 1918. After Samuel died his parents placed a 'For King and Country' notice in the *Newtownards Chronicle* and it contained the verse:

C

'We may not, Lord, Thy purpose see,
But all is well that's done by Thee.'

Able Seaman Samuel Crooks is commemorated on Newtownards and District War Memorial and in Second Presbyterian Church Newtownards.

Croskery, John
Petty Officer Stoker
No. K/10685, HMS *Arbutus*, Royal Navy
Killed in action on Saturday 15 December 1917 (aged 25)
Portsmouth Naval Memorial, Hampshire, England (Panel 26)

John Croskery was a son of William and Elizabeth Croskery (nee Beattie) who lived in Church Street Portaferry. They were married on 27 May 1883 in Portaferry Roman Catholic Church. William Croskery worked as a general labourer and he and Elizabeth had at least nine children – James, William, Thomas, Ellen Jane, John, Hugh, Sarah (Sally), Elizabeth and Joseph. All of the children were baptised in Portaferry Roman Catholic Church, John on 30 October 1892.

C

John Croskery joined the Royal Navy and he served aboard HMS *Arbutus*. Built in 1917 this special service vessel was torpedoed by German submarine UB-65 during very rough weather on 15 December 1917 in St George's Channel and nine men, including the Captain, perished. It was reported that if the weather not been so bad the ship might have been saved.

Crossen, John
Rifleman
No. 11113, 6th Battalion, Royal Irish Rifles
Killed in action on Wednesday 11 August 1915
Helles Memorial, Gallipoli, Turkey (Panel 177 and 178)

In 'Soldiers Died in the Great War 1914 – 1919' it is recorded that John Crossen was born in Ballygowan and he enlisted in Belfast. He served with the 6th Battalion Royal Irish Rifles in 29th Brigade of the 10th (Irish) Division in Gallipoli and it was reported that they were plagued by flies and a shortage of water. Rifleman John Crossen was killed in action on 11 August 1915 in the advance on Chunuk Bair during the Battle of Sari Bair.

Crowe, Hugh
The name Hugh Crowe is listed on Newtownards and District War Memorial and in the booklet produced for the Unveiling and Dedication Ceremony

held on Saturday 26 May 1934 he is described as a Sergeant in the Royal Irish Rifles. Desk searches and public appeals to date have yielded no further information.

Cumming, William Francis (William)
Corporal
No. 40964, 1st Battalion, Royal Scots Fusiliers (formerly Ayrshire Yeomanry)
Killed in action on Tuesday 5 June 1917 (aged 28)
Arras Memorial, France (Bay 5)

William Francis Cumming was born on 12 July 1888 and he was the only child of John and Isabella Cumming (nee McMaster) who lived in Greyabbey. They were married on 14 October 1887 in Innishargie Church of Ireland Balligan. John Cumming worked as a wool weaver and his wife Isabella died on 18 December 1893 when William was 5 years old.

During his teenage years William Cumming moved to Scotland and prior to the outbreak of the Great War he worked there as a gardener. William won several prizes and medals for his essays on horticultural subjects.

William Cumming joined the Ayrshire Yeomanry in September 1915 and he was promoted to the rank of Sergeant some ten months later. He qualified First Class as a machine gunner and also First Class in musketry. After that he was appointed as instructor at the Ayrshire Yeomanry School of Musketry.

On learning that his Regiment was not going to France he secured a transfer to the Royal Scots Fusiliers in December 1915 and immediately thereafter he volunteered for active service. In April 1917 Corporal Cumming was wounded by a shell at Arras and he had only rejoined his Regiment for a short time when he was killed in action on 5 June 1917.

Newspaper reports after his death paid tribute to William Cumming's 'bright and cheery disposition, his Christian principles and his intellectual qualities'. Corporal William Cumming is commemorated on Greyabbey and District War Memorial located on the outside wall of Greyabbey Parish Church of Ireland (St Saviour).

Cutler, John Isaac (Jack)
Long Service and Good Conduct Medal
Colour Sergeant
No. G/1228, 2nd (Garrison) Battalion, Royal Irish Fusiliers
Died of heart disease on Thursday 12 October 1916 (aged 53)
Salonika (Lembet Road) Military Cemetery, Greece (Grave 576)

Colour Sergeant John Isaac (Jack) Cutler was born in 1863 in London and he spent some time in St Mary Orphanage and Certified Poor Low School, North Hyde, Houndslow, West Heston. He served for more than 28 years in the Army of which 26 were spent in the Royal Irish Rifles. Details of his army career were published in the 28 October 1916 edition of the *Newtownards Chronicle*. He served in many parts of the world and held the Long Service and Good Conduct Medal. The latter part of his service was on the permanent staff of the 4th Battalion Royal Irish Rifles (Royal North Downs) at Newtownards.

C
D

When Jack Cutler left the army he was employed by the Comber Distilleries Company Ltd. He was a member of the Ulster Star Masonic Lodge No. 133 in Comber and he was an instructor for the Ballygowan and Comber companies of the Ulster Volunteer Force. Later he held a similar position with the Ballynafeigh and Newtownbreda Battalions.

After the outbreak of the Great War Jack Cutler rejoined the Royal Irish Rifles. He was 51 years of age and initially he was stationed at the Depot in Victoria Barracks Belfast. Subsequently he transferred to a Garrison Battalion of the Royal Irish Fusiliers and left for Egypt in August 1916. He had only been there for about two months when he died at Alexandria.

Jack Cutler's widow Kathleen and their four children including Mabel, John Isaac and Margaret lived at 61 Belvoir Street Belfast. Colour Sergeant Jack Cutler is commemorated in the Belfast Book of Honour (Page 140).

Daly, Patrick
Private
No. 1301, 1st Battalion, Irish Guards
Killed in action on Tuesday 18 May 1915 (aged 33)
Le Touret Memorial, France (Panel 4)

Patrick Daly was born in Aughlisnafin, between Clough and Castlewellan, in County Down and he was a son of Daniel and Jessie Daly. Daniel Daly

NEWTOWNARDS IRISH GUARDSMAN KILLED IN ACTION.

SON OF EX-SERGT. DALY, R.I.C.

We much regret to announce that Private Patrick Daly, of Newtownards, of the 1st Battalion of the Irish Guards, has been killed in action. The official news reached his father, Mr. D. Daly, Ann Street (ex-sergeant R.I.C.), on Wednesday, stating that his son Patrick had met his death in action on 18tth May. We sincerely sympathise with Mr. Da and his family in the bereavement which has befallen them.

was a Sergeant in the Royal Irish Constabulary and when he was stationed in Newtownards the Daly family lived in Ann Street.

Daniel and Jessie Daly had at least eight children – Patrick, Lizzie, Mary, William, Daniel, Jessie, Norah and Amelda. Patrick Daly enlisted in Belfast and he served with the Irish Guards. He was killed in action on 18 May 1915 and he is commemorated on Newtownards and District War Memorial.

Dalzell, Hugh
Private
No. 24114, 9th Battalion, Princess Victoria's (Royal Irish Fusiliers)
Killed in action on Thursday 16 August 1917 (aged 20)
Tyne Cot Memorial, Belgium (Panel 140 to 141)

D

Hugh Dalzell was born on 15 April 1897 in Newtownards and he was a son of Hugh and Selina Dalzell (nee Gordon) who were married on 17 December 1884 in Newtownards Parish Church of Ireland. They had at least six children – James Gordon, Agnes Jane, John, Martha, William Gordon and Hugh, all of whom were baptised in Newtownards Parish Church of Ireland. Hugh Dalzell served with the 9th Battalion Royal Irish Fusiliers in 108th Brigade of the 36th (Ulster) Division and when he was killed in action on 16 August 1917 during the Third Battle of Ypres his parents were living at 76 Paris Street, Belfast. Private Hugh Dalzell is commemorated in the Belfast Book of Honour (Page 142).

Dalzell, William John
Private
No. 26091, 9th Battalion, Royal Inniskilling Fusiliers
Killed in action on Saturday 1 July 1916
Thiepval Memorial, France (Pier and Face 4 D and 5 B)

William John Dalzell was born in Newtownards and he and Lavinia Cowan were married on 11 May 1915 in Regent Street Methodist Church Newtownards.

William John Dalzell enlisted in Newtownards and he served with the 9th Battalion Royal Inniskilling Fusiliers in 109th Brigade of the 36th (Ulster)

Division. He was posted as missing in action after the first day of the Battle of the Somme and in May 1917 it was officially confirmed that he had been killed in action on that date.

Private William John Dalzell's wife Lavinia lived at 3 Movilla Street, Newtownards and she placed a 'For King and Country' notice in the *Newtownards Chronicle*. It contained the verse:

'For King and country well he stood,
Unknown to coward's fears;
With a manly heart he did his part
With the Inniskilling Fusiliers.
He sleeps beside his comrades
In a hallowed grave unknown;
But his name is written with letters of gold
On the hearts he left at home.'

D

Private William John Dalzell is commemorated on Newtownards and District War Memorial and in Newtownards Parish Church of Ireland (St Mark).

Davidson, Thomas
Rifleman
Royal Irish Rifles
Died on Monday 18 October 1915 (aged 30)
Donaghadee Parish Church of Ireland Graveyard

Thomas Davidson was born on 9 October 1885 in Donaghadee and he was a son of John and Jane Davidson who lived at 19 Back Street, then 3 Meetinghouse Street and then 8 Saltwork Street. John Davidson worked as a seaman and then as a fish dealer and he and Jane had at least eleven children including John (died young), Thomas, David, Ellen (died 22 February 1912), Agnes (died 4 September 1922 aged 25), John, Adelaide, Martha and Matilda (died 23 July 1922 aged 16). Thomas was baptised in Donaghadee Methodist Church.

Prior to the outbreak of the Great War Thomas Davidson worked as a tramway conductor in Belfast and he and Agnes Rubina Martin were married on 29 April 1908 in St Mark's Parish Church of Ireland Dundela. They lived in Ribble Street, Belfast and they had a number of children including Ellen.

Thomas Davidson enlisted and served with the Royal Irish Rifles. Due to ill health he was discharged from the army and he died on 18 October 1915 after a prolonged illness. His brothers David and John were also on active service. John served with the Royal Engineers and David served with the Canadian Infantry. While David's regiment was undergoing training in England David was granted a short period of home leave. He arrived home in Donaghadee on the day that Thomas died. Later David was very severely wounded.

It was reported in the *Newtownards Chronicle* that Thomas Davidson had left 'a widow and several young children'. His funeral took place on 20 October 1915 and it was conducted by the Rev MHG Willis MA, Rector of Donaghadee Parish Church.

Thomas's surname is spelt Davidson in newspaper reports, in his own 1911 census return and on the family grave headstone. In the 1901 and 1911 census returns for John, Jane and their children the surname is spelt Davison.

Rifleman Thomas Davidson is commemorated on Donaghadee and District War Memorial and on the family grave headstone in Donaghadee Parish Church of Ireland.

D

Davison, Robert
Military Cross
Lieutenant, 12th (Service) Battalion, King's (Liverpool Regiment)
Died of wounds on Sunday 8 October 1916 (aged 20)
Grove Town Cemetery, France (Grave I. O. 4)

Robert Davison was the only son of Dr John Robert Davison and Lizzie Davison (nee Dickson) of 'Romanov', Ormeau Road, Belfast and he was educated at Coleraine Academical Institution. At the outbreak of The Great War he joined the Young Citizen Volunteer Battalion of the Ulster Division and within a week he received a commission in the King's Liverpool Regiment.

Newtownards Family Bereaved.
Official intimation was received on Tuesday that Lieutenant Robert Davison, the King's Liverpool Regiment, was killed in action on the 8th inst. He was

On 8 October 1916 Lieutenant Robert Davison died of wounds sustained at Gueudecourt during the Battle of the Somme. His death was reported in the *Newtownards Chronicle* under the headline 'Newtownards Family Bereaved'. His mother Lizzie Davison was the eldest daughter of George Dickson JP, Royal Nurseries, Newtownards.

Robert Davison was awarded the Military Cross for conspicuous gallantry during operations. 'He showed great determination when consolidating the position of his company close to the enemy under heavy machine-gun and shell fire. He displayed great coolness and set a fine example'.

Robert Davison is commemorated in Cooke Centenary Presbyterian Church Belfast; on the North of Ireland [Rugby] Football Club Memorial Plaque; on the QUB War Memorial; in the QUB Book of Remembrance (Page 17) and in the Belfast Book of Honour (Page 146).

De Wind, Edmund
Victoria Cross
Private
No. 79152, 31st Battalion, Canadian Expeditionary Force
Second Lieutenant
15th Battalion, Royal Irish Rifles
Killed in action on Thursday 21 March 1918 (aged 34)
Pozieres Memorial, France (Panel 74 to 76)

D

Edmund De Wind was born on 11 December 1883 and he was the youngest son of Arthur Hughes De Wind (who was born in Malacca, Bengal, India) and Margaret Jane De Wind (nee Stone). They were married on 12 April 1863 in Comber Parish Church of Ireland. The De Wind family lived in Castle Street, Comber and then in 'Kinvara', Killinchy Road, Comber. Arthur De Wind worked as Chief Engineer on the Belfast & County Down Railway and he and Margaret Jane had at least nine children including Catherine Anne, Edith Caroline, Louise, Alice Maud, Florence, Norman and Edmund. After attending Campbell College Edmund worked as a bank official in the Cavan branch of the Bank of Ireland before he moved to Canada. There he worked for the Canadian Bank of Commerce. On 16 November 1914 he enlisted in Edmonton and joined the 31st Battalion of the Canadian Expeditionary Force (he had six months previous service in the Queen's Own, Toronto). On 29 May 1915 he embarked for England aboard the SS *Northland* and he went to France on 19 September 1915 with the Machine Gun Section of the 31st Battalion. On 20 March 1917 he transferred to Cadet School with a view to obtaining a commission and on 25 September 1917 he was discharged to a commission with the 15th Battalion Royal Irish Rifles. Edmund's father had died some seven months earlier on 22 February 1917. His mother died on 8 April 1922.

Second Lieutenant Edmund De Wind was killed in action on 21 March 1918 at Grugies, St Quentin and he was awarded the Victoria Cross. Details were published in the *London Gazette* dated 13 May 1919: 'For most conspicuous bravery and self-sacrifice on 21 March 1918, at the Race Course Redoubt, near Grugies. For seven hours he held this most important post, and though twice wounded and practically single-handed, he maintained his position until another section could be got to his help. On two occasions, with two NCOs only, he got out on top under heavy machine gun and rifle fire, and cleared the enemy out of the trench, killing many. He continued to repel attack after attack until he was mortally wounded and collapsed. His valour, self-sacrifice and example were of the highest order.' On 28 June 1919 Margaret Jane De Wind received her son's Victoria Cross from King George V at Buckingham Palace and when she returned to Comber the town was decorated with flags in honour of the occasion.

After the Great War a large German gun was presented to the town and placed in The Square as a memorial to him. This gun was removed to provide scrap metal during the Second World War. The metal plates bearing the inscription are preserved in the porch of the Parish Church. He is commemorated on Comber and District War Memorial; in Comber Parish Church of Ireland (St Mary); on Campbell College War Memorial and on a Marble Plaque in the grounds of the Ulster Tower near Thiepval. A column at the West Front of St Anne's Cathedral Belfast is dedicated to him and he is named with Captain **George James Bruce** and Second Lieutenant **Thomas McRoberts** on the Banner of LOL No. 100 (Comber Ulster Defenders). Mount de Wind in Jasper National Park, Alberta in Canada is named after him.

Delaney, John Joseph (John)
Private
No. 21940, 1st Battalion, Princess Victoria's (Royal Irish Fusiliers)
Died of wounds on Saturday 14 April 1917 (aged 20)
Aubigny Communal Cemetery Extension, France (Grave II. E. 19)

John Joseph Delaney was born in Ballywalter, the eldest son of William and Theresa Delaney (nee Mason) who lived at Quintin, Portaferry. They were married on 4 October 1893 in Bryansford Roman Catholic Church. William Delaney worked as a light keeper on a lightship and he and Theresa had at least six children – Sarah Ann, John Joseph, Margaret, Mary, William and Kathleen.

Portaferry Fusilier Dies of Wounds.
Private J. Delaney (No. 21,940), Royal Irish Fusiliers, is reported to have died of wounds.

John Delaney lived in Portaferry, he enlisted in Newtownards and he served with the 1st Battalion Royal Irish

Fusiliers in 10th Brigade of the 4th Division. Private John Delaney died of wounds on 14 April 1917.

Dempster, Andrew John (Andrew)
Rifleman
No. 17568, 'C' Company, 13th Battalion, Royal Irish Rifles
Killed in action on Saturday 1 July 1916 (aged 24)
Suzanne Military Cemetery No. 3, France (Grave II. D. 11)

Andrew John Dempster was born on 12 August 1891 and he was a son of Hugh and Elizabeth Dempster (nee Lappin) who lived in the townland of Moneyreagh. They were married on 4 August 1879 in Second Comber Presbyterian Church. Hugh Dempster was a farmer and he and Elizabeth had at least eight children – James, Agnes, Lizzie, Jane, William, Andrew John, Hugh and Samuel. They were all baptised in Granshaw Presbyterian Church. His eldest brother James lived at 95 Thorndyke Street, Belfast.

Pte. Andrew Dempster, County Down Volunteers, killed in action in France July 1. Deceased was a son of Mr. Hugh Dempster, Moneyrea, Comber, and brother of Mr. James Dempster, 95 Thorndyke Street, Belfast.

Andrew Dempster enlisted in Belfast and he served with the 13th Battalion Royal Irish Rifles in 108th Brigade of the 36th (Ulster) Division. He went to France on 6 October 1915. Rifleman Andrew John Dempster was killed in action on the first day of the Battle of the Somme and he is commemorated on Comber and District War Memorial; in the PCI Roll of Honour for Granshaw Presbyterian Church and on the family grave headstone in Moneyreagh Non-Subscribing Presbyterian Church Graveyard.

Dempster, DJ
Private
No. 30861, Royal Air Force
Died on Tuesday 11 February 1919
Comber New Cemetery, Co. Down (Grave 5. 305)

Private DJ Dempster served in the Royal Air Force, he died on 11 February 1919 and he is buried in Comber New Cemetery. In some records his number is 308611. Desk searches and public appeals to date have yielded no further information.

Dempster, Robert
Rifleman
No. 16412, 14th Battalion, Royal Irish Rifles
Killed in action on Saturday 1 July 1916 (aged 35)
Thiepval Memorial, France (Pier and Face 15 A and 15 B)

Robert Dempster was born in 1881 in the townland of Moneyreagh and he enlisted in Belfast. He served with the 14th Battalion Royal Irish Rifles in 109th Brigade of the 36th (Ulster) Division and he was killed in action on the first day of the Battle of the Somme.

Prior to the outbreak of the Great War Robert Dempster worked as a lamplighter in Belfast and on 30 April 1900 he and Mary Bell were married in St Stephen's Parish Church of Ireland Millfield, Belfast. Robert and Mary Dempster had at least five children – William, Robert, Hugh, Edward and Samuel.

When Rifleman Robert Dempster died on 1 July 1916 his wife and children were living at 22 Dover Street, Belfast and he is commemorated in the Belfast Book of Honour (Page 149).

D

Dempster, Robert
Rifleman
No. 16433, 'B' Company, 13th Battalion, Royal Irish Rifles

In 'Soldiers Died in the Great War 1914 – 1919' it is recorded that Rifleman Robert Dempster (16433) served with the 13th Battalion Royal Irish Rifles and that he was killed in action in France on Thursday 21 March 1918. It is also recorded there that he was born in Comber, he lived in Comber and he enlisted in Belfast.

Military records show that Rifleman Robert Dempster (16433) enlisted on 21 September 1914 aged 23 years 2 months and that he cited as his next-of-kin his widowed mother Elizabeth who was living at 32 High Street, Comber. He was posted to the 13th Battalion Royal Irish Rifles and he was wounded in the foot on 10 May 1916. He was posted to Depot, then to the 20th Battalion, then back to the 13th Battalion. At the end of March 1918 Rifleman Robert Dempster (16433) sustained a gunshot wound to his hand and had to have a finger amputated. He was posted to Depot and on 22 November 1918 he was discharged from the army as being no longer physically fit for war service. He qualified for an army pension.

Dempster, Robert James
Rifleman
No. 910, 8th Battalion, Royal Irish Rifles
Killed in action on Thursday 7 June 1917 (aged 28)
Ypres (Menin Gate) Memorial, Belgium (Panel 40)

Robert James Dempster was the eldest son of James and Isabella Dempster (nee Patterson) who lived in the townland of Carnasure, Comber. They were married on 28 February 1888 in Comber Non-Subscribing Presbyterian Church. James Dempster worked as an agricultural labourer and he and Isabella had seven children including Robert James, Emily, Isabella, William Stewart and Alexander.

Comber Rifleman Killed.

Rifleman Robert J. Dempster, Royal Irish Rifles, killed in action on 7th inst., was the eldest son of Mr. Jas. Dempster, Carnesure, Comber.

Robert James Dempster enlisted at Clandeboye and on 10 October 1916 he made his will at Clandeboye Camp. He was killed in action on 7 June 1917, the first day of the Battle of Messines, and after he died his property and effects were sent to his father. Rifleman Robert James Dempster is commemorated on Comber and District War Memorial and in Comber Non-Subscribing Presbyterian Church.

Devlin, Thomas
Private
No. 28515, Royal Inniskilling Fusiliers, transferred to (18538), 2nd Battalion, Royal Irish Regiment
Killed in action on Saturday 20 July 1918
Hawthorn Ridge Cemetery No.1, France (Grave B. 59)

In 'Soldiers Died in the Great War 1914 – 1919' it is recorded that Thomas Devlin was born in 'St Malachy's', Antrim, he lived in Newtownards and he enlisted in Hamilton, Lanarkshire. It is also recorded that he served with the Royal Inniskilling Fusiliers (28515) before being transferred to the Royal Irish Regiment.

Private Thomas Devlin was killed in action on 20 July 1918 and at the time of his death one of his brothers was living at 14 Hardcastle Street, Belfast. Private Thomas Devlin is commemorated in the Belfast Book of Honour (Page 150).

D

DeVoy, Samuel (Sammy)
Sergeant
No. 17563, 'B' Company, 13th Battalion, Royal Irish Rifles
Killed in action on Saturday 1 July 1916 (aged 29)
Thiepval Memorial, France (Pier and Face 15 A and 15 B)

Samuel DeVoy was a son of John and Eleanor Maria DeVoy (nee McCracken) who lived in South Street, Newtownards. They were married on 28 June 1882 in First Newtownards Presbyterian Church. John DeVoy worked as a saddler and he and Maria had at least six children – James, Mary, Samuel, Agnes Jane, John Forbes and Eleanor Maria. Three of the children were baptised in Strean Presbyterian Church Newtownards.

Prior to the outbreak of the Great War Samuel DeVoy worked as a draper's assistant. He enlisted in 1914 and served with the 13th Battalion Royal Irish Rifles in 108th Brigade of the 36th (Ulster) Division. Sergeant Samuel DeVoy was killed in action on the first day of the Battle of the Somme and his widowed mother placed a 'For King and Country' notice in the *Newtownards Chronicle*. So too did his chum George Whalley who lived in Court Square, Newtownards.

D

Sergeant Samuel DeVoy is commemorated on Newtownards and District War Memorial and in the PCI Roll of Honour for Strean Presbyterian Church Newtownards.

Dickson, John
Rifleman
No. 18/1697, 12th Battalion, Royal Irish Rifles
Died in a Prisoner of War Camp on Wednesday 3 July 1918 (aged 40)
Hautmont Communal Cemetery, France (Grave V. B. 4)

John Dickson was born around 1878 and he was a son of William and Charlotte Dickson (nee Quinn). They were married on 2 November 1877 in Ballygowan Presbyterian Church and they lived at 9 Mill Street, Newtownards. Charlotte was widowed sometime before 1901 and she had eleven children including Annie, William, John, Grace, James Campbell, and Mary Eleanor. The two youngest children were baptised in First Newtownards Presbyterian Church. Charlotte Dickson worked as a 'sewer and embroiderer' and John worked as a labourer in a bleach works when he lived in Newtownards.

189

John Dickson and Caroline (Carrie or Kerry) Taylor were married in 1914 in Newtownards Reformed Presbyterian Church and their daughter Grace was born on 14 February 1915. She was baptised in First Newtownards Presbyterian Church. John Dickson enlisted in February 1915 and he trained at Clandeboye with the 18th Battalion Royal Irish Rifles. He was posted to the 12th Battalion and he went to France on 4 October 1915 in 108th Brigade of the 36th (Ulster) Division. He was taken prisoner by the Germans and held at Lager Hautmont where he died of heart failure on 3 July 1918.

It was not until January 1919 that John's mother heard what had happened to him. On 31 December 1918 Charlotte Dickson wrote to the Enquiry Department for Wounded, Missing and Prisoners of War. This Department was part of the British Red Cross Society at 51 Dawson Street, Dublin. She received a reply dated 4 January 1919 from Edmund Troughton, Honorary Secretary of the Department and in it she read the dreaded news that her son was dead, 'We deeply regret to inform you that the Central Prisoners of War Committee state that your son died at Lager Hautmont on 3 July last from heart trouble. They are surprised to learn that the War Office had not informed his next-of-kin. Should we get further particulars we have noted your name to receive them at once'.

At the time of John's death his wife Carrie was living at The Butts, Kilwinning in Scotland. Charlotte Dickson placed a 'For King and Country' notice in the 18 January 1919 edition of the *Newtownards Chronicle* on behalf of John's wife and family, his mother, his sisters and his brothers. Rifleman John Dickson is commemorated on Newtownards and District War Memorial.

Dickson, William
Gunner
No. 86122, 5th Brigade, Canadian Field Artillery
Killed in action on Sunday 17 September 1916 (aged 44)
Pozieres British Cemetery, France (Grave II. F. 35)

William Dickson was born on 18 July 1872 and he was a son of James and Mary Dickson (nee Shields). They were married on 5 May 1866 in First Comber Presbyterian Church and they lived in the townland of Ballymagaughey, later in the townland of Ballywilliam, Comber. James Dickson worked as a farm servant and he and Mary had at least four children including William, John and Sarah. William moved to Canada where he worked as a shoemaker.

He enlisted on 8 December 1914 in Winnipeg where he and his wife Annie were living at 619 Alverstone Street. In his attestation papers it was noted that he was 5 feet 7½ inches tall and that he had served for 19 years in the Royal Garrison Artillery. When Gunner William Dickson was killed in action on 17 September 1916 his wife was living at 549 Simcoe Street, Winnipeg in Manitoba.

Dines Brothers: Alexander and Thomas

In some records the family surname is spelt Dynes.

Alexander and Thomas Dines were sons of William and Ellen Dines (nee Kennedy) who lived at 19 Irish Street, Killyleagh. They were married on 3 February 1886 in Newtownards Registry Office. William Dines worked as a general labourer and he and Ellen had at least ten children including Mary Alice, Martha, Hugh, George, Alexander, Thomas, William and Nellie. The Dines family moved from Killyleagh to 16 Ann Street, Newtownards and subsequently to Brownlow Street, Comber. Thomas was the first of the two brothers to die on active service in the Great War:

Dines, Thomas
Rifleman
No. 10418, 2nd Battalion, Royal Irish Rifles
Killed in action on Saturday 28 August 1915 (aged 18)
Ypres (Menin Gate) Memorial, Belgium (Panel 40)

D

Thomas Dines was born in Killyleagh, he enlisted in Newtownards and he served with the Royal Irish Rifles. He made a will and after he was killed in action at Hooge his property and effects were received by his mother. At the time of his death his brothers Alexander and George were also on active service. George was wounded in the leg at Mons and subsequently went to Victoria Barracks in Belfast. One year after Thomas Dines died, almost to the day, Alexander Dines was killed in action.

Dines, Alexander (Alex) *
Rifleman
No. 6741, 1st Battalion, Royal Irish Rifles attached 25th Light Trench Mortar Battery
Killed in action on Wednesday 30 August 1916 (aged 23)
Vermelles British Cemetery, France (Grave VI. E. 5)

COMBER.

Mrs. Ellen Dines, Brownlow Street, Comber, has received intimation that her son, Private Alexander Dines, Royal Irish Rifles (attached Trench Mortar Battery), has been killed in action. Another son, Private Thomas Dines, R.I.R., was killed at Hooge on the 28th May, 1915, and a third son, Private Geo. Dines, was wounded in the leg at Mons, and is now in the Victoria Barracks, Belfast. A photo found in the pocket of Alexander was sent to Mrs. Dines by his captain on 3rd inst., also a letter intimating his death.

Alexander Dines was born in Killyleagh, he enlisted in Ballykinlar and he served with the Royal Irish Rifles. On the day that he was killed in action Rifleman Alex Dines made a will and after he died his property and effects were received by his mother. An officer wrote to Alex's mother and said, 'Your son was killed instantaneously. My only words of comfort to you can be that he died fighting, a noble and brave soldier. His death means a great loss to me, as during the time he was with me he was one of my most reliable men. Apart from his fighting qualities and wonderful bravery, his cheerful disposition helped the other men to face many a black hour. I can only tell you that you are the mother of one of the nation's heroes'.

Riflemen Alex and Thomas Dines are commemorated on Newtownards and District War Memorial; on Killyleagh War Memorial (as Dynes) and in the PCI Roll of Honour for First Killyleagh Presbyterian Church (as Dynes). Rifleman Alex Dines is also commemorated on Comber and District War Memorial.

Diver, Redmond Joseph (served as Wheeler, Albert)
Private
No. 2748, 1st Battalion, Black Watch (Royal Highlanders)
Killed in action on Friday 14 July 1916 (aged 19)
Thiepval Memorial, France (Panel Pier and Face 10 A)

Redmond Joseph Diver was a son of James and Margaret Diver who came from Letterkenny in County Donegal. James Diver was a Constable in the Royal Irish Constabulary and it was while he was stationed in Newtownards that Redmond Joseph Diver was born. James and Margaret Diver had at least five children – Mary Alice, Bridgetta T, Redmond Joseph, Charles and John Coyle. The Diver family lived in John Street Newtownards.

PORTAFERRY.

Private A. Wheeler (No. 2,748), Black Watch, killed.

Redmond Joseph Diver served with the 1st Battalion Black Watch using the alias Albert Wheeler and he was killed in action on 14 July 1916 during the Battle of the Somme.

Docherty, Patrick
Private
No. 16702, 2nd Battalion, Royal Scots Fusiliers
Killed in action on Thursday 30 September 1915
Loos Memorial, France (Panel 46 to 49)

In 'Soldiers Died in the Great War 1914 – 1919' it is recorded that Patrick Docherty was born in Kircubbin (spelt Carcubin; spelt Kircubbin in 'Ireland's Memorial Records'), he lived in Ardrossan, Ayrshire and he enlisted in Ayr. He served with the Royal Scots Fusiliers and he was killed in action on 30 September 1915 during the Battle of Loos. Prior to the outbreak of the Great War he had worked as a seaman. Private Patrick Docherty is commemorated on Ardrossan War Memorial

Dodds, Alexander
Rifleman
No. 16438, 'C' Company, 10th Battalion, Royal Irish Rifles
Killed in action on Saturday 17 June 1916 (aged 30)
Hamel Military Cemetery, France (Grave I. B. 20)

D

Alexander Dodds was born on 23 July 1885 in Portaferry and he was a son of William and Elizabeth Dodds (nee Vance) who lived in the townland of Derry, Portaferry. They were married on 3 November 1875 in Portaferry Presbyterian Church. William and Elizabeth Dodds had at least six children – William, Samuel, John, Sarah, Alexander and Lizzie. Alexander was baptised in Portaferry Presbyterian Church and his father died when he was a small child.

Prior to the outbreak of the Great War Alexander Dodds worked in Belfast. He enlisted in Belfast and served with the 10th Battalion Royal Irish Rifles in 107th Brigade of the 36th (Ulster) Division. Alexander's mother died after his Battalion went to France. Rifleman Alexander Dodds died on 17 June 1916 when he was killed by shell fire in a front line trench. He had made a will and his property and effects were received by his sister Lizzie. His headstone bears the inscription:

'O death where is thy sting
O grave where is thy victory'

Rifleman Alexander Dodds is commemorated in Portaferry Presbyterian Church.

Doggart Brothers: Alexander, James and Thomas

Alexander, James and Thomas Doggart were sons of Hugh and Agnes Doggart (nee McCullough) who lived at 46 East Street, Newtownards. They were married on 23 March 1882 in Newtownards Parish Church of Ireland. Hugh Doggart worked as a painter and decorator and he and Agnes had at least eight children – Hugh, James Neil, Thomas M, Adam, Jemima, William, Mary Jane McCullough and Alexander. They were baptised in Newtownards Parish Church of Ireland. After Agnes died Hugh Doggart Senior married Eleanor (Ellen) Jane McChesney on 25 April 1908 in Newtownards Parish Church of Ireland.

All six of Hugh Doggart's sons were on active service during the Great War and three of them – James, Thomas and Alexander – were killed in action.

Bugler Adam Doggart served with the Royal Irish Rifles and was invalided out of service because of injuries; after that he worked as a motorman on Belfast City Tramways.

Rifleman Alexander Doggart served with the Royal Irish Rifles and he was killed in action on 18 June 1917.

D

Seaman-Gunner Hugh Doggart served on a Minesweeper.

Corporal James Neil Doggart served with the Royal Inniskilling Fusiliers and was killed in action on 1 July 1916.

Rifleman Thomas Maddock Doggart served with the 13th Battalion Royal Irish Rifles and was killed in action on 1 July 1916.

Private William Doggart served with the Royal Scots Fusiliers.

James and Thomas died on the same day, Alexander less than a year later:

Doggart, James Neil (James)
Corporal
No. 8496, 1st Battalion, Royal Inniskilling Fusiliers
Killed in action on Saturday 1 July 1916 (aged 30)
Thiepval Memorial, France (Pier and Face 4 D and 5 B)

James Neil Doggart was born in 1886 and he was the second son of Hugh and Agnes Doggart. According to newspaper reports James Doggart joined the Connaught Rangers around 1909 and was subsequently transferred to the Royal Inniskilling Fusiliers. After the outbreak of the Great War he was recalled from India and on 17 March 1915 he went to the Dardanelles where he was wounded on 14 May 1915. He recovered from his wounds and, like his brother Thomas, Corporal James Doggart was killed in action on the first day of the Battle of the Somme.

Doggart, Thomas Maddock (Thomas)
Rifleman
No. 16418, 'B' Company, 13th Battalion, Royal Irish Rifles
Killed in action on Saturday 1 July 1916 (aged 28)
Thiepval Memorial, France (Pier and Face 15 A and 15 B)

Thomas Maddock Doggart was born on 2 December 1887 and he was the third son of Hugh and Agnes Doggart. Thomas worked as a shipyard labourer and he and his wife Agnes (nee Patterson) lived at 6 Oakdale Street, Belfast. They were married on 10 July 1909 in St Clement's Parish Church of Ireland Belfast. Shortly after the outbreak of the Great War Thomas Doggart enlisted in Belfast and he joined the 1st County Down Volunteers. He served with 108th Brigade of the 36th (Ulster) Division and he was killed in action on the first day of the Battle of the Somme. Initially posted as missing in action it was not until July 1917 that he was officially reported as having been killed on 1 July 1916.

At the time Rifleman Thomas Maddock's death was reported his wife and their three young children (Elizabeth was the eldest) were living at 20 James Street, Newtownards. Agnes placed a 'For King and Country' notice in the *Newtownards Chronicle* and it contained the verse:

> *'Father, in Thy gracious keeping,*
> *Leave we now our loved one sleeping.'*

Doggart, Alexander
Rifleman
No. 18/389, 2nd Battalion, Royal Irish Rifles
Killed in action on Monday 18 June 1917 (aged 18)
Ypres (Menin Gate) Memorial, Belgium (Panel 40)

Alexander Doggart was born on 14 August 1898 and he was the sixth son of Hugh and Agnes Doggart. Prior to the outbreak of the Great War he worked at the Glen Printing and Finishing Works. Alexander enlisted in July 1915 in Newtownards and he trained with the 18th Battalion Royal Irish Rifles at Clandeboye. He was posted to the 2nd Battalion Royal Irish Rifles and he was killed in action on 18 June 1917 in the front line west of Warneton. Rifleman

D

Alexander Doggart had made his will on 12 December 1916 and when he died his property and effects were received by his brother Adam Doggart who lived at 2 Matlock Street, Belfast.

Rifleman Alexander Doggart, Rifleman Thomas Doggart and Corporal James Doggart are commemorated on Newtownards and District War Memorial and on the Memorial Plaque in Newtownards Parish Church of Ireland (St Mark). Rifleman Alexander Doggart is also commemorated in the Belfast Book of Honour (Page 156).

Doherty, William John (William)
Long Service and Good Conduct Medal
Sergeant
No. 4476, 1st Battalion, Royal Irish Rifles
Died on Thursday 16 August 1917 (aged 40)
Tyne Cot Memorial, Belgium (Panel 138 to 140 & 162 to 162A & 163A)

William John Doherty was born in Belfast and he was a career soldier. He was a Bugler in the Royal Irish Rifles and he served in India and in the South African Campaign. He was awarded the Long Service and Good Conduct Medal.

William Doherty and Sarah Carnduff were married on 8 December 1903 in Newtownards Parish Church of Ireland, they lived at 52 James Street, Newtownards and they had at least five children – Robert James (born 1905), Sarah Elizabeth (born 1906), Agnes Jane (born 1908, Eleanor and William John (twins born 1910).

Sergeant William Doherty died on 16 August 1917 during the Third Battle of Ypres and at the time of his death his family lived at Tullywest, Saintfield. He is commemorated on Newtownards and District War Memorial and in the Belfast Book of Honour (Page 157).

Donaldson, Adam (Addie)
Private
No. 85849, 228th Company, Machine Gun Corps (Infantry)
Killed in action on Saturday 22 September 1917 (aged 22)
Tyne Cot Memorial, Belgium (Panel 154 to 159 and 163A)

Adam Donaldson was the youngest son of William Henry and Mary Jane Donaldson (nee Allen) who lived in the townland of Whitespots, Newtownards. They were married on 9 February 1869 in Regent Street

Presbyterian Church Newtownards. William Donaldson was a farmer and he and Mary Jane had at least thirteen children – Elizabeth (died in infancy), George, Joseph, William Henry, Mary Jane, James, Hugh, John, Samuel, Maggie, Thomas, Adam and Lizzie. Nine of the children were baptised in Greenwell Street Presbyterian Church Newtownards.

Adam Donaldson worked as a tenter in the Glen Print Works before he went to the United States of America for a short time. After he came back from America Adam went to Scotland and it was there, in Rutherglen, Lanarkshire, that he enlisted in December 1916.

Private Addie Donaldson had been at the Western Front for around three months when he was killed in action on 22 September 1917.

DONALDSON—In loving memory of Private Addie Donaldson, M.G.C., killed in action September 22nd, 1917, youngest son of William Donaldson. Deeply regretted by his Father, Sisters, and Brothers (two of the latter on active service and one prisoner of war).
25 Victoria Avenue, Newtownards.

Lieutenant EC Thorburn of the Machine Gun Corps wrote to Addie's father to express his sympathy and in the letter he described the circumstances of Addie's death. Lieutenant Thorburn said that a shell had burst in Addie's dugout killing him instantly. The Lieutenant paid tribute to Private Addie Donaldson by saying that he was indifferent to danger; he was always merry and joking and the evening before he died he distinguished himself by carrying up ammunition to his gun through a heavy German barrage.

When Addie was killed his mother was already dead and his father was living at 25 Victoria Avenue, Newtownards with Addie's married sister Mrs Joseph Robinson. Three of Addie's brothers were on active service:

Private William Donaldson MT Army Service Corps; Rifleman John Donaldson Royal Irish Rifles and Rifleman Thomas Donaldson who had been gassed on the first day of the Battle of the Somme and was being held as a Prisoner of War.

Private Addie Donaldson is commemorated on Newtownards and District War Memorial and in the PCI Roll of Honour for Greenwell Street Presbyterian Church Newtownards.

Donaldson, Andrew (Andy)
Lance Corporal
No. 18937, 'A' Company, 13th Battalion, Royal Irish Rifles
Killed in action on Monday 13 August 1917 (aged 43)
New Irish Farm Cemetery, Belgium (Grave XIX. C. 12)

Andrew Donaldson was born on 3 July 1874 in Portaferry and he was a son of Samuel and Ellen Jane Donaldson (nee Davison). They were married on 12 January 1872 in Portaferry Presbyterian Church and they had at least two children – Samuel and Andrew. Both were baptised in Portaferry Presbyterian Church. Andrew's father died sometime before 1901.

Andrew Donaldson and Ruth Ellen Johnston were married on 12 December 1905 in Ballyphilip Parish Church of Ireland Portaferry and they had at least eight children including Annie Elizabeth, Andrew, David and Ruth. Both generations of the Donaldson family lived in the townland of Thomastown, Portaferry.

> **Died for His Country.**—Mrs. Donaldson, Thomastown, Portaferry, has just been informed that her husband, Andrew Donaldson, was killed in action in France on the 16th August. Much sympathy is felt for the widow and eight surviving children of the deceased soldier. Andy Donaldson was one of the brave Ulster Volunteers who enlisted in the Ulster Rifles at the outbreak of hostilities.

Andy Donaldson enlisted in Ballywalter, he served with the 13th Battalion Royal Irish Rifles in 108th Brigade of the 36th (Ulster) Division and he was killed on 13 August 1917 while the Battalion was holding the line prior to the Battle of Langemarck. Lance Corporal Donaldson was wounded whilst in the line and he walked to a dressing station for treatment. He was killed there when the dressing station was hit by a shell and he is commemorated in Portaferry Presbyterian Church and in Ballyphilip Parish Church of Ireland Portaferry.

On the day he was wounded Andy was accompanied to the dressing station by Rifleman William McMullan from Portaferry who also served with 'A' Company 13th Battalion Royal Irish Rifles (19117). Rifleman McMullan left the dressing station and returned to the line just before the shell hit. He was wounded in action on 16 August 1917 at the Battle of Langemarck and he was discharged from the Army on 31 January 1919. He died in 1957.

Donaldson Brothers: James, John and Samuel

James, John and Samuel Donaldson were sons of John and Mary Donaldson (nee Potts) who lived in the townland of Ballyloughan, Comber and formerly in Ballyalton, Newtownards. They were married on 18 August 1894 in Ballygowan Presbyterian Church. John Donaldson Senior worked as an agricultural labourer and he and Mary had at least nine children – William, Jane, Eliza, Mary Eleanor, John, James, Samuel, Elizabeth and Robert Hugh. Seven of the children, including John, James and Samuel were baptised in First Newtownards Presbyterian Church. John was born on 9 May 1890, James was born on 15 September 1892 and Samuel was born on 17 July 1894.

Prior to the outbreak of the Great War John and James worked in the shipyard at Queen's Island Belfast and Samuel worked in Andrew's Mill in Comber. They were members of the Ulster Volunteer Force and the three brothers enlisted together in Comber where they were allocated consecutive battalion numbers. They served in 'B' Company 13th Battalion Royal Irish Rifles (1st County Down Volunteers) in 108th Brigade of the 36th (Ulster) Division and the three brothers fought and died side by side on the first day of the Battle of the Somme.

Donaldson, James
Rifleman
No. 18960, 'B' Company, 13th Battalion, Royal Irish Rifles
Killed in action on Saturday 1 July 1916 (aged 23)
Thiepval Memorial, France (Pier and Face 15 A and 15 B)

Donaldson, John
Rifleman
No. 18958, 'B' Company, 13th Battalion, Royal Irish Rifles
Killed in action on Saturday 1 July 1916 (aged 26)
Thiepval Memorial, France (Pier and Face 15 A and 15 B)

D

Donaldson, Samuel
Rifleman
No. 18959, 'B' Company, 13th Battalion, Royal Irish Rifles
Killed in action on Saturday 1 July 1916 (aged 21)
Thiepval Memorial, France (Pier and Face 15 A and 15 B)

John Donaldson   James Donaldson   Samuel Donaldson

Initially there was uncertainty about the fate of the three brothers and they were posted as missing in action. There were rumours that James was being held as a prisoner of war and in the 15 July 1916 edition of the *Newtownards Chronicle* there was a report that John and Samuel had been killed. At home the Donaldson family feared the worst and this accentuated a decline in the health of their 60 year old father. John Donaldson Senior died on Sunday 1 October 1916.

In August 1917 the widowed Mary Donaldson was officially informed that her three sons, Riflemen James, John and Samuel Donaldson, had all been killed in action on 1 July 1916. On 25 August 1917 Mary Donaldson and her remaining sons and daughters placed a 'For King and Country' notice in the *Newtownards Chronicle* and it contained the verse:

D

> DONALDSON—Reported missing since July 1st, 1916, now officially reported killed on that date, Riflemen John, James, and Samuel Donaldson, 13th Battalion Royal Irish Rifles (1st Co. Down Volunteers), beloved sons of the late John Donaldson.
> Sometimes we often sit and think
> Of our loved ones far away,
> Who left their home at duty's call,
> And fell in the battle's fray.
> They were true Britons every inch,
> Unknown to coward's fears;
> "Somewhere in France" they did their part
> With the Ulster Volunteers.
> We do not grudge their sacrifice,
> For this we know full well,
> They helped to keep the flag unstained,
> And like true soldiers fell.
> Inserted by their loving Mother, Sisters, and Brothers.
> MARY DONALDSON.
> Ballyloughan, Comber.

'Sometimes we often sit and think
Of our loved ones far away,
Who left their home at duty's call,
And fell in the battle's fray.

They were true Britons every inch,
Unknown to coward's fears;
'Somewhere in France' they did their part
With the Ulster Volunteers.

We do not grudge their sacrifice,
For this we know full well,
They helped to keep the flag unstained,
And like true soldiers fell.'

Riflemen James, John and Samuel Donaldson are commemorated on Comber and District War Memorial and in Second Comber Presbyterian Church. Samuel Donaldson is also commemorated on the Andrew's Mill Memorial Plaque.

Donnan, John
Private
No. 22817, 7th/8th Battalion, Princess Victoria's (Royal Irish Fusiliers)
Died on Thursday 14 December 1916 (aged 28)
St. Pol Communal Cemetery Extension, France (Grave C. 15)

John Donnan was born in the townland of Ballyfrench, Ballyhalbert and he was a son of Hugh Donnan who later moved to the townland of Kirkistown, Kircubbin. John Donnan enlisted in Belfast and he served with the 7th Battalion Royal Irish Fusiliers in 49th Brigade of the 16th (Irish) Division. The 7th and 8th Battalions were amalgamated on 15 October 1916 and Private John Donnan died on 14 December 1916.

Donnan, Samuel Blakely Dunn (Samuel)
Private
No. 27299, 11th Battalion, Royal Inniskilling Fusiliers
Died on Tuesday 19 November 1918 (aged 22)
Berlin South-Western Cemetery, Germany (Grave X. C. 5)

In the CWGC Debt of Honour the surname is spelt Donnon.

Samuel Blakely Dunn Donnan was born on 9 February 1896 in Millisle and he was a son of Robert and Elizabeth Donnan (nee Robinson) who lived in the townland of Ballyrolly, Carrowdore. They were married on 2 November 1894 in Carrowdore Parish Church of Ireland. Robert Donnan worked as an agricultural labourer and he and Elizabeth had two children – Samuel and William John. Samuel was baptised in Carrowdore Parish Church of Ireland. Elizabeth Donnan died in the early 1900s and prior to the outbreak of the Great War Samuel worked as an errand boy. He enlisted in Donaghadee and served with the 11th Battalion Royal Inniskilling Fusiliers in 109th Brigade of the 36th (Ulster) Division. Private Samuel Blakely Dunn Donnan died on 19 November 1918 and he is commemorated on Donaghadee and District War Memorial and in Carrowdore Parish Church of Ireland (Christ Church).

D

Donnan, Thomas
Private
No. 14080, Canterbury Regiment, NZEF
Killed in action on Tuesday 5 June 1917 (aged 24)
Strand Military Cemetery, Belgium (Grave V. A. 16)

Thomas Donnan was born on 16 August 1892 and he was a son of James and Elizabeth Donnan (nee Agar) who lived in the townland of Ardkeen Kircubbin. They were married on 6 February 1884 in Cloughey Presbyterian Church. James Donnan was a sailor and he and Elizabeth had at least eight children including Maggie (6 October 1884), David (6 November 1886), Agnes (19 November 1888), James (27 February 1890; served in the Great War and was discharged on medical grounds), Thomas (16 August 1892), William (16 may 1894), Alexander (12 July 1897; lost at sea on 18 December 1919) and Samuel (5 January 1901). These children were all baptised in Cloughey Presbyterian Church. James Donnan Senior died on 18 July 1926 and Elizabeth died on 12 May 1946.

Thomas Donnan worked as an agricultural labourer before and after he moved to New Zealand. He enlisted in Ashburton, Canterbury in the South Island and in his attestation papers he cited his mother Elizabeth as his next-of-kin. He sailed from Wellington to Devonport before going to the Western Front where he served with the Canterbury Regiment of the New Zealand Expeditionary Force.

Private Thomas Donnan was killed in action on 5 June 1917 and he is commemorated in the PCI Roll of Honour for Cloughey Presbyterian Church. He is also commemorated on the Ashburton War Memorial in New Zealand and on the family grave headstone in Cloughey Presbyterian Church Graveyard where the date of death and his age are inscribed as 7 June 1917 and 27.

Donnan, William (Willie)
Private
No. 911995, 46th Battalion, Canadian Infantry (Saskatchewan Regiment)
Killed in action on Thursday 3 May 1917 (aged 44)
Villers Station Cemetery, France (Grave V. G. 9)

William Donnan was born on 28 July 1872 and he was the only son of Robert and Margaret Donnan (nee Boyd) who lived in the townland of Ballycran, Kircubbin. They were married on 28 December 1869 in Innishargie Church of Ireland Balligan. Robert Donnan JP was a farmer and he and Margaret had five children – Mary Elizabeth, William, Margaret Robina, Jane Boyd and Anna Helena. The four girls were baptised in Kircubbin Presbyterian Church. William's mother Margaret died on 18 June 1891 and his father Robert died on 7 January 1920.

Kircubbin-Canadian Killed.

The death of Private Wm. Donnan, of the Canadian Infantry, who was killed in action on 3rd inst., has been reported. Mr. Donnan was a brilliant student, and had a distinguished career. He emigrated to America some years ago, and took up teaching as a profession. He has now made the supreme sacrifice, and the sympathy of the whole community of the Ards will go out to his much respected mother and father, Mr. Robert Donnan, J.P., Kircubbin, and other members of his family. The following letter has been received by Mr. Donnan from the chaplain of the battalion:—" Dear Mr. Donnan,—Just a hurried note to extend to you my warm sympathy in the heroic death of your son, Private W. Donnan, No. 911,995, of the 46th Canadian Infantry Battalion. He was instantly killed while at his post of duty on May 3rd, 1917, and was buried by me to-day in the Villiers-au-Bois Military Cemetery. His grave will be marked by a neat wooden cross suitably inscribed. He did his duty nobly, and you have every reason to feel proud of your gallant boy, who was a worthy son of the Empire.—Yours very sincerely, Chas. B. Cumming, Chaplain."

William Donnan moved to Canada where he worked as a teacher before he enlisted on 20 May 1916 in Nanairns, British Columbia. In his attestation papers it was noted that he was unmarried, he was 5 feet 9 inches tall and he had a large brown mole on the back of his neck.

Private Willie Donnan died on 3 May 1917 when 'he was killed instantly while at his post of duty'. These were the words used by Rev Charles B Cumming, the Chaplain who buried him and who then wrote to William's parents to express his sympathy.

Private William Donnan is commemorated in Kircubbin Presbyterian Church and on the family grave headstone in the adjoining graveyard.

Donnan, William James (William)
Private
No. 23726, 5th Royal Irish Lancers, transferred to (G/61958), 23rd Battalion, Royal Fusiliers (City of London Regiment)
Killed in action on Saturday 1 December 1917 (aged 19)
Cambrai Memorial, France (Panel 3 and 4)

William James Donnan was born in Portaferry and he was a son of Hugh and Jane Donnan (nee Chermside) who lived in the townland of Kearney, Quintin, Portaferry. They were married on 16 August 1895 in Ballyphilip Parish Church of Ireland Portaferry. Hugh Donnan was a seaman (during the Great War he served in the RNVR) and he and Jane had at least two children – William James and Sarah Elizabeth.

William Donnan enlisted in Dublin and he served with the 5th Royal Irish Lancers (23726) before being transferred to the 23rd Battalion Royal Fusiliers (City of London Regiment). Private William Donnan was killed in action on 1 December 1917 and he is commemorated in Ballyphilip Parish Church of Ireland Portaferry (St James).

D

Dorman, William John
Rifleman
No. 240, 16th Battalion, Royal Irish Rifles, transferred to (593769) 459th Company, Labour Corps
Died on Tuesday 22 October 1918 (aged 32)
Stirling (Mar Place) Cemetery, Scotland (Grave YZ. 13)

In 'Soldiers Died in the Great War 1914 – 1919' and in 'Ireland's Memorial Records 1914 – 1918' it is recorded that William John Dorman was born in the townland of Ballyeasborough, Ballyhalbert. He was a son of Carlisle and Alice Dorman (nee Mateer) who were married on 7 October 1885 in Lisburn Registry Office. Carlisle Dorman worked as a farmer and the Dorman family lived at Carnbane, Maze. Carlisle and Alice had five children – William John, Emily Jane, Caroline, Howard and David James. Alice Dorman died in the early 1900s.

Rifleman William John Dorman enlisted in Lurgan and he served with the 16th Battalion Royal Irish Rifles in the 36th (Ulster) Division before being transferred to the 459th Company Labour Corps. He died on 22 October 1918 and he is commemorated in 'Lisburn's Dead 1914 – 1919' (Friends School Lisburn WW1 Research Project).

Dornan, John
Private
No. 12779, 2nd Battalion, Royal Inniskilling Fusiliers
Killed in action on Saturday 1 July 1916 (aged 29)
Thiepval Memorial, France (Pier and Face 4 D and 5 B)

John Dornan was born in Newtownards and he was a son of William and Mary Ann Dornan (nee McNally). They were married on 27 March 1883 in Newtownards Parish Church of Ireland and they had at least four children – Maggie, Eliza, John and Thomas. William Dornan died in the late 1800s and the Dornan family moved to 19 Roseberry Street, Connswater in Belfast.

Prior to the outbreak of the Great War John Dornan worked as a carpenter. When he enlisted he served with the 2nd Battalion Royal Inniskilling Fusiliers, by then in 96th Brigade of the 32nd Division and he was killed in action on the first day of the Battle of the Somme. Private John Dornan is commemorated in the Belfast Book of Honour (Page 162).

Dorrian, Hugh John M *
Private
No. 29513, 1st Battalion, Royal Dublin Fusiliers
Killed in action on Thursday 4 October 1917 (aged 20)
Cement House Cemetery, Belgium (Grave XIV. C. 12)

Hugh John M Dorrian was born in Portaferry and he was a son of John and Eliza Jane Dorrian (nee Maguire) who lived in Knocknagow. They were married on 20 October 1887 in Portaferry Roman Catholic Church. John Dorrian worked as a farm labourer and he and Eliza Jane had at least eight children including William, Daniel, Mary, Thomas, Hugh John, James and Francis. Hugh John M Dorrian enlisted and served with the 1st Battalion Royal Dublin Fusiliers and he was killed in action on 4 October 1917.

Dorrian, James
Lance Corporal
No. 16420, 'B' Company, 13th Battalion, Royal Irish Rifles
Killed in action on Saturday 1 July 1916 (aged 32)
Thiepval Memorial, France (Pier and Face 15 A and 15 B)

James Dorrian was the eldest son of William John and Ellen Dorrian (nee Crawford) who lived at 4 Talbot Street, Newtownards. They were married on 5 March 1881 in Newtownards Parish Church of Ireland. William John Dorrian worked as a quarryman and he and Ellen had thirteen children

D

including Sarah Elizabeth, James, William John, Jane, Robert, Susanna, Charles Thomas and Mary Ellen. James Dorrian and Jane Oliver were married on 15 April 1905 in Newtownards Registry Office and they had six children – Catherine Oliver born in 1906, William John born in 1908, James born in 1909, Robert Joseph born in 1911 and twins Harry and Charles born in 1912. They were baptised in Newtownards Parish Church of Ireland.

James Dorrian worked as a general labourer and at the outbreak of hostilities he enlisted in Belfast. He served with the 13th Battalion Royal Irish Rifles in 108th Brigade of the 36th (Ulster) Division and he was killed in action on the first day of the Battle of the Somme. At that time he had two brothers on active service.

Initially James Dorrian was reported as missing in action and in June 1917 it was officially confirmed that he had been killed on 1 July 1916. His family placed a 'For King and Country' notice in the *Newtownards Chronicle* and it contained the verse:

D

'Dear son, it makes our hearts sore
To think in this life we shall meet you no more;
It was thy sad fate to be killed by the Huns
'Midst the splinter of shells and the roar of the guns.
Dear son of my bosom, you sleep 'mong the brave,
Where no tears of a mother can drop on thy grave;
In the red fields of France you are laid far away,
Still our tribute of love to thy memory we pay.
Although we regret that so early in life
It was thy misfortune to fall in the strife,
Yet it may give thy friends consolation to know
That you died in the field with your face to the foe.
But as long as we are allowed to remain here behind,
Dear son, we will always bear thee in mind;
The bugles may sound, and the cannons may roar,
But you will be found in the conflict no more.'

Lance Corporal James Dorrian is commemorated on Newtownards and District War Memorial and in Newtownards Parish Church of Ireland (St Mark).

Three Newtownards families related by marriage suffered bereavement during the first two weeks of the Battle of the Somme when four men who are commemorated in this book died:

- **James Dorrian** (16420)

- His sister Susanna's husband **Robert McCartney** (13/343)

- His sister Jane's husband **Edward McAvoy** (18125)

- Edward's brother **John McAvoy** (18183)

Three women living at 4 Talbot Street were widowed.

Dorrian, James O'Neill (Jim)
Private
No. 291603, 44th Battalion, Canadian Infantry (New Brunswick Regiment)
Killed in action on Sunday 17 February 1918 (aged 29)
Sucrerie Cemetery, France (Grave II. D. 4)

D

James Dorrian was born on 30 January 1889 and he was a son of William and Lizzie Dorrian (nee O'Neill) who lived in Main Street Ballywalter. They were married on 11 May 1880 in Newtownards Parish Church of Ireland. William Dorrian worked as an agricultural labourer and he and Lizzie had at least eleven children – Mary Anne, George (born in 1884 and died in 1905 aged 20), Agnes McCance, James O'Neill, Minnie, John, William, Lizzie, Samuel (died in June 1918 aged 17), Essie and George (born in 1905). All of the children were baptised in Ballywalter Presbyterian Church.

Jim Dorrian moved to Canada where he worked as a teamster. He and his wife and two children lived in Suite 12, Wallar Block, Norwood, Winnipeg in Manitoba. Jim enlisted in Winnipeg on 8 February 1916 and in his attestation papers it was noted that he was 5 feet 6¾ inches tall. He declared his date of birth to be 19 January 1892.

Jim's brother John also enlisted in Winnipeg and he too joined the 44th Battalion (291602). John lived with Jim and his family and he also worked as a teamster prior to the outbreak of the Great War. John saw continuous service on the Western Front and was awarded the Military Medal for bravery in the field and devotion to duty.

Private Jim Dorrian fought on the Western Front and in April 1916 he was wounded in the chest. He was transported to hospital in England where he remained until September 1916. He returned to the front and he was killed in action on 17 February 1918. In February 1919 Jim's father, mother, sisters and brothers placed an 'Our Heroes – In Memoriam' notice in the *Newtownards Chronicle* and it contained the verse:

'Taken away in his early youth,
Taken from those he loved;
From serving his King on earth below
To serve his great King above'

Private Jim Dorrian is commemorated on Ballywalter and District War Memorial; on the family grave headstone in Whitechurch Cemetery Ballywalter (where the date of death is inscribed as 1 July 1916) and in Ballywalter Presbyterian Church.

Dorrian, John
Rifleman
No. 17582, 'B' Company, 13th Battalion, Royal Irish Rifles
Killed in action on Saturday 1 July 1916 (aged 18)
Thiepval Memorial, France (Pier and Face 15 A and 15 B)

John Dorrian was born in Newtownards and there is evidence from one source that he was a son of Samuel George and Sarah Dorrian (nee McCully) who lived in Greenwell Street. They were married on 23 February 1884 in Newtownards Registry Office. Samuel George Dorrian worked as a general labourer and he and Sarah had at least five children including George, Robert, James and John.

Prior to the outbreak of the Great War John Dorrian worked as a factory clerk and he enlisted in Newtownards. He served with the 13th Battalion Royal Irish Rifles in 108th Brigade of the 36th (Ulster) Division and he was killed in action on the first day of the Battle of the Somme. Rifleman John Dorrian is commemorated on Newtownards and District War Memorial.

Dorrian, Thomas
The name Thomas Dorrian is listed on Newtownards and District War Memorial and in the booklet produced for the Unveiling and Dedication Ceremony held on Saturday 26 May 1934 he is described as a Rifleman in the Royal Irish Rifles. Thomas Dorrian (3/17583) enlisted on 17 September 1914 and he went to France on 16 April 1915. Being unfit for further active service as a result of being wounded in action he was discharged from the army on 3 December 1915. Desk searches and public appeals to date have yielded no further information.

Douglas, Robert
Rifleman
No. 18/767, 11th Battalion, Royal Irish Rifles
Killed in action on Friday 1 September 1916 (aged 20)
Ration Farm (La Plus Douve) Annexe, Belgium (Grave II. C. 27)

Robert Douglas was born in Kilmood (Kilwood in census) and he was a son of John Kerr Douglas and Agnes Douglas (nee Carse). They were married on 29 September 1893 in First Comber Presbyterian Church and they had at least five children – Robert, Susan Carse, David Carse, William and Hugh Brown. Four of the children were baptised in Ballygowan Presbyterian Church.

Robert Douglas lived in Belfast and he enlisted in Newtownards. He served with the 11th Battalion Royal Irish Rifles in 108th Brigade of the 36th (Ulster) Division and he was killed in action on 1 September 1916. At that time his parents were living at 13 Eversleigh Street, Belfast. Rifleman Robert Douglas is commemorated in Ballygowan Presbyterian Church and in the Belfast Book of Honour (Page 164).

D

Dowdell, Thomas (Tommy)
Rifleman
No. 9595, 3rd Battalion, Royal Irish Rifles
Died on Wednesday 26 November 1919 (aged 23)

The name Thomas Dowdall is listed on Newtownards and District War Memorial. In all of the Army papers where his signature appears he spelt his surname Dowdell.

Thomas Dowdell was born in Magherafelt on 13 November 1896 and he was the son of Andrew and Mary Dowdell (nee Henry), both of whom worked as servants. They were married on 11 December 1890 in Magherafelt Roman Catholic Church. Andrew Dowdell went to Glasgow to work as a sanitary labourer and when he died there on 28 October 1898 Tommy Dowdell and his widowed mother lived with her parents, Hugh and Mary Henry. Hugh Henry worked as a shoemaker. The Henry family moved to Belfast and then for a time Tommy and his widowed mother lived at Ardkeen in County Down. In 1911 Mary Dowdell married local man John Drysdale.

Tommy Dowdell worked as a labourer and when he enlisted on 15 August 1916 at Bridge End in Belfast he was living at 63 Louisa Street, Belfast. It was noted in his attestation papers that he was 5 feet 4½ inches tall and weighed

104 lbs. He was assigned to the 3rd (Reserve) Battalion Royal Irish Rifles.

On 24 October 1916 Thomas Dowdell was admitted to Ward 6 of the Military Hospital in Belfast with a gun shot wound to the head. He was described as being dangerously ill and the Medical Officer was of the opinion that his injury would, in all probability, 'interfere with his future efficiency as a soldier'. It was stated that a bullet had entered his head, just to the right of the bridge of his nose, penetrated the skull and probably lodged in his brain.

On 25 October 1916 a Court of Enquiry was set up to investigate the circumstances in which the injury occurred. It happened during a session of musketry training at Victoria Barracks in Belfast and several witnesses gave evidence. The soldiers were engaged in snap shooting practice after having come in from range practice where live ammunition was being used. Tommy had been taking his turn to hold the target for his comrades to aim at and everyone should have been using dummy rounds. Somehow there was a ball cartridge among the dummy rounds and Tommy Dowdell was shot in the head.

By 15 November 1916 his condition had improved sufficiently for Tommy to be pronounced 'out of danger'. The Court of Enquiry was reconvened and Tommy himself was called to give evidence. He stated that he and Rifleman James Smyth, the soldier who had fired the ball cartridge, were on good terms. He said that he had no reason to think that the shot had been fired intentionally and he was satisfied that what had happened was an accident.

On 16 December 1916 Tommy Dowdell was transferred to Mountstewart Hospital near Greyabbey to recuperate and on 15 January 1917 the Court of Enquiry delivered its Opinion that 'the occurrence was a pure accident' and that 'neither 9595 Rifleman Thomas Dowdell nor 9514 Rifleman James Smyth was to blame in the matter'.

Tommy Dowdell returned to service and he was posted to France on 1 September 1917. He was wounded in the arm in December that year and he was transported to Eastleigh Hospital in England. On 22 December 1917 he was transferred to the Irish Counties War Hospital at Glasnevin in Dublin and on 22 January 1918 he was sent home on furlough for five weeks.

After being at home for about two weeks he developed paralysis and needed ongoing medical attention thereafter. Tommy's mother stated later that she had reported his state of health to Victoria Barracks in April 1918 and that she had handed in a Medical Certificate to an Official there. No trace of this certificate was found amongst Tommy Dowdell's service papers.

D

On 25 February 1918, at the end of his five-week furlough, when Tommy Dowdell did not report to the Officer Commanding he was declared by the Army to be a Deserter. It is unclear from his records what steps were taken to find him. Tommy Dowdell died on 26 November 1919 'from epileptic convulsions and syncope following a gun shot wound in the head'. At the time of his death his address was stated to be 31 Springmount Street, Belfast. Even after his death letters kept arriving, advising him to report to the nearest Military Barracks. Afterwards the Army apologised for this as his mother continued her efforts to have Tommy's name cleared. Finally, on 31 May 1922, the Army Council confirmed in writing that Thomas Dowdell was 'no longer to be regarded by the Army as a Deserter'.

D

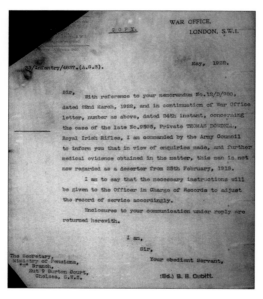

Thomas Dowdell's name had been cleared but his details were never recorded on the CWGC Debt of Honour. As a result of correspondence during 2010 the Ministry of Defence has approved his commemoration but, for a CWGC headstone to be erected, his grave needs to be located. Enquiries to date have drawn a blank at the following burial grounds: Belfast City Cemeteries; Milltown Cemetery Belfast; Killysuggan Graveyard Newtownards; Movilla Cemetery Newtownards and Mount St Joseph's Graveyard Ballycranbeg.

Downes, James
Private
No. 436344, 4th Battalion, Canadian Infantry (Central Ontario Regiment)
Died of wounds on Wednesday 12 April 1916 (aged 31)
Lijssenthoek Military Cemetery, Belgium (Grave VI. B. 6A)

James Downes was born on 14 August 1884 and he was a son of Andrew and Anne Downes (nee Beers) who lived in the townland of Milecross Newtownards. They were married on 2 November 1881 in Newtownards Parish Church of Ireland. Andrew worked as a surface-man on the roads and he had at least six children. There is some variation in the spelling of the family surname. It is spelt Downs on the Memorial Plaque in Newtownards Parish Church of

Ireland (St Mark) and that is the form that Andrew used when he signed his name on form A for the 1911 census. It is spelt Downes on Newtownards and District War Memorial and that is the form that James used when he signed his name on the attestation papers.

James Downes moved to Canada where he worked as a labourer. He was unmarried when he enlisted on 11 January 1915 in Edmonton and he cited his father as his next-of-kin. It was noted in his attestation papers that he was 5 feet 7½ inches tall.

Private James Downes went with the Central Ontario Regiment of the Canadian Infantry to France in September 1915 and he died of wounds on 12 April 1916. The Rev AB Brooker, Military Chaplain, wrote a letter from No. 10 Casualty Clearing Station to James Downes's parents expressing his sympathy and outlining the circumstances of James's death:

James died around 7.30 am on 12 April 1916 having been brought in about three hours earlier with serious wounds to his head and chest. He was unconscious when he was brought in and despite every effort being made to save him he died without regaining consciousness and without being able to leave a message.

D

FOR KING AND COUNTRY.

DOWNES—Died in hospital in France, on 12th April, 1916, as the result of wounds, Private James Downes, of the Canadian Expeditionary Force, eldest son of Andrew and Mrs. Downes, Milecross, Newtownards. His remains were interred in the Military Cemetery on the Poperinghe-Boeschepe Road, France.

The family placed a 'For King and Country' notice in the *Newtownards Chronicle* and Private James Downes is commemorated on Newtownards and District War Memorial and as James Downs in Newtownards Parish Church of Ireland (St Mark).

Drake, James Edgar (Edgar)
Private
No. 151617, 43rd Battalion, Canadian Infantry (Manitoba Regiment)
Killed in action on Thursday 21 September 1916 (aged 23)
Courcelette British Cemetery, France (Grave VIII. B. 9)

James Edgar Drake was born on 2 May 1893 and he was a son of Samuel B and Sarah Drake (nee Paisley) who lived in Mill Street, Comber. They were married on 13 October 1887 in First Bangor Presbyterian Church. Samuel Drake worked as a draper and he and Sarah had five children including Thomas J, James Edgar, Robert and Samuel D. James Edgar Drake also worked as a draper before he moved to Canada around 1912. He was a member of the North Down Hockey Club.

Private E. Drake.—Rev. Thos. M'Connell, B.A., made touching reference in Second Comber Presbyterian Church on Sunday last to the death in action of Private Edgar Drake, of the Canadian Force. Deceased, whose father is an elder in the congregation, before going out to Canada some four years ago, was actively attached to the congregation. He had served his apprenticeship to a business in Belfast. In sporting circles he was very popular, and was a valued member of the North Down Hockey Club. He, like many other Ulster lads, joined the forces on the outbreak of war, and now he has made the supreme sacrifice.

James Edgar Drake enlisted in Brandon Manitoba on 21 September 1915 and it was noted in his attestation papers that he was 5 feet 8½ inches tall. Exactly one year later Private Drake was killed in action on 21 September 1916. Private James Edgar Drake is commemorated on Comber and District War Memorial and in Second Comber Presbyterian Church.

His father Samuel died on 27 January 1923.

Drennan, James Arthur
Private
No. 22820, 1st Battalion, Princess Victoria's (Royal Irish Fusiliers)
Died of wounds on Saturday 14 April 1917 (aged 18)
Etaples Military Cemetery, France (Grave XXII. H. 22)

D

James Arthur Drennan was born on 20 March 1899 and he was a son of John and Annie Maria Drennan (nee McKeag) who lived at 2 Victoria Terrace, William Street, Donaghadee. They were married on 19 September 1890 in Ballyblack Presbyterian Church.

John Drennan worked as a labourer and Annie Maria worked as a seamstress. They had at least eleven children – David John, Hugh, Georgina Dunbar Buller, James Arthur, Maggie Eleanor, Annie Catherine, Frederick Ernest, Thomas White, Georgina, Albert and Jane McCauley. The Drennan family moved to Woburn Road, Millisle and it was in Millisle Presbyterian Church that the children were baptised.

James Arthur Drennan enlisted in Belfast and he served with the 1st Battalion Royal Irish Fusiliers. He was wounded in action and he died of his wounds on 14 April 1917. Private James Arthur Drennan is commemorated on Donaghadee and District War Memorial and in Millisle Presbyterian Church.

Drennan, William
Lance Corporal
No. 17591, 11th Battalion, Royal Irish Rifles
Killed in action on Saturday 1 July 1916
Thiepval Memorial, France (Pier and Face 15 A and 15 B)

William Drennan was born in Downpatrick, he lived in Donaghadee and he enlisted in Bangor. He served with the 11th Battalion Royal Irish Rifles in 108th Brigade of the 36th (Ulster) Division and he was killed in action on the first day of the Battle of the Somme. Lance Corporal William Drennan is commemorated on Groomsport and District War Memorial; on Donaghadee and District War Memorial and on the Memorial Plaques in Groomsport Parish Church of Ireland and Donaghadee Parish Church of Ireland.

Dugan, James Munn
Corporal
No. 14500, 10th Battalion Royal Irish Rifles, transferred to 21st Entrenching Battalion
Died of wounds on Saturday 27 April 1918 (aged 28)
Brandhoek New Military Cemetery No. 3, Belgium (Grave I. O. 30)

James Munn Dugan was born in Comber and he worked as a clerk before the outbreak of the Great War. He and Jemima Watson Nelson were married on 2 November 1910 in Mountpottinger Presbyterian Church and they lived in High Street, Comber.

D

James enlisted in Belfast and he served with the 10th Battalion Royal Irish Rifles in 107th Brigade of the 36th (Ulster Division) before being transferred to the 21st Entrenching Battalion in February 1918. Corporal James Munn Dugan died of wounds on 27 April 1918 and he is commemorated on Comber and District War Memorial and in Comber Non-Subscribing Presbyterian Church.

Duncombe, Charles William Reginald
Lieutenant Colonel
Yorkshire Hussars Yeomanry commanding 21st Battalion King's Royal Rifle Corps
Killed in action on Friday 15 September 1916 (aged 37)
A.I.F. Burial Ground, France (Grave III. L. 29)

The reason for including Lieutenant Colonel Charles William Reginald Duncombe in this book is because there is an interesting connection with Mountstewart, Greyabbey. In the 30 September 1916 edition of the *Newtownards Chronicle* the death on active service of Lieutenant Colonel the Earl of Feversham was reported. Charles William Reginald Duncombe, 2nd

Dowager Lady Londonderry's Nephew Killed.

Lieutenant-Colonel the Earl of Feversham, King's Royal Rifle Corps, killed in action on the 15th September, whilst leading his battalion, was a nephew of the Dowager Marchioness of Londonderry. His Lordship, who was better known as Viscount Helmsley, M.P., succeeded to the earldom on the death of his grandfather in January, 1915, and was a frequent visitor at Mountstewart.

Earl of Feversham was a nephew of the Dowager Marchioness of Londonderry and he was also known as Viscount Helmsley. It was reported that he was a frequent visitor to Mountstewart and was very well known in the area.

Dynes, John
Rifleman
No. 1112, 9th Battalion, Royal Irish Rifles
Killed in action on Saturday 1 July 1916 (aged 48)
Thiepval Memorial, France (Pier and Face 15 A and 15 B)

John Dynes was born in Killinchy and on 31 January 1898 he and Elizabeth (Lizzie) Stuart were married in Killinchy Presbyterian Church. For a time they lived in Killyleagh and they had at least two children – George and John. The Dynes family moved from Killyleagh to Belfast where they lived at 30 Ardgowan Street.

John Dynes enlisted in Belfast, he served with the 9th Battalion Royal Irish Rifles in 107th Brigade of the 36th (Ulster) Division and he was killed in action on the first day of the Battle of the Somme. At the time of John's death Lizzie and their two sons were living at 8 Lecale Street, Donegall Road, Belfast. John Dynes Junior worked as a brakeman on the railway and he died on 11 January 1919. Lizzie Dynes died on 2 June 1919 and George Dynes died on 8 March 1941. Rifleman John Dynes is commemorated in Broadway Presbyterian Church Belfast and in the Belfast Book of Honour (Page 173).

Earney, Henry (Harry)
Corporal
No. 25882, 7th/8th Battalion, Royal Inniskilling Fusiliers
Died of wounds on Saturday 8 December 1917 (aged 20)
Villers-Faucon Communal Cemetery Extension, France (Grave I. C. 10)

Henry Earney was born on 7 June 1897 in Rademon, Crossgar and he was the third son of Walter James and Rose Earney (nee Rogers). Walter Earney worked as a gamekeeper and both he and his wife were born in England. They were married in 1894 in Alderbury, Wiltshire and they had at least seven children including Harry, Fred, Edith, Walter and Ellen.

Prior to the Great War Harry Earney worked as a gardener and he was a member of the South Down Battalion of the Ulster Volunteer Force. In the UVF Harry was awarded a medal for being the best shot. He enlisted on 26 August 1915 in Belfast and he went to France on 17 February 1916.

Corporal Harry Earney served with the Royal Inniskilling Fusiliers and on 8 December 1917 he died of wounds sustained the previous day. After he died his Commanding Officer wrote a letter to Harry's mother. The CO said that Harry was one of the youngest in his company when they arrived at the front and he paid tribute to Harry's 'splendid work in the sniping section'. At the time of Harry's death his parents were living in the townland of Carnasure, Comber. Corporal Harry Earney is commemorated on Comber and District War Memorial and in Comber Parish Church of Ireland (St Mary).

Echlin, Frederick St John Ford North (Frederick)
Lieutenant
70th Squadron, Royal Flying Corps and Royal Fusiliers
Died of wounds on Wednesday 27 September 1916 (aged 27)
Achiet-Le-Grand Communal Cemetery Extension, France (Grave IV. H. 7)

> **Kircubbin Officer Dies of Wounds in Germany.**
>
> Sec.-Lieut. F. St. J. F. N. Echlin, Royal Fusiliers and Royal Flying Corps, whose death was unofficially announced last October, is now officially reported to have died of wounds in German hands on 26th September, 1916. He was a son of the late Captain Frederick Echlin, R.N., of Echlinville, Kircubbin, and grandson of the late Rev. J. R. Echlin, J.P., of Ardquin.

Under the headline 'Kircubbin Officer Dies of Wounds in Germany' the death of Lieutenant Frederick St John Ford North Echlin was reported in the 10 March 1917 edition of the *Newtownards Chronicle*. He was the only son of the late Captain Frederick Echlin (died 1906) Royal Navy from the townland of Echlinville, Rubane, Kircubbin and he was a grandson of the late Rev J R Echlin JP of Ardquin, Portaferry. He could trace his lineage back to the Right Rev Henry Echlin Bishop of Down and Connor in the 17th Century. Lieutenant Echlin was the husband of Dorothy Blanche Echlin (nee Dobree) of 'The Anchorage', Doyle Road, Guernsey in the Channel Islands. They were married for only a short time before Frederick died; they had one child.

Prior to the outbreak of the Great War Frederick Echlin had been working in the Federated Malay States. He volunteered for service and was commissioned on 6 March 1915 to the 5th Battalion Royal Fusiliers. He joined

the Royal Flying Corps on probation on 27 October 1915 and he obtained his pilot's certificate. He died of wounds in German hands on 27 September 1916. Another descendant of the Right Rev Henry Echlin, Private Richard Brabazon More Echlin (4431) 1st Battalion Irish Guards, was killed in action on 1 November 1914 and he is commemorated on the Ypres (Menin Gate) Memorial.

Edmonds, George Edgar
Rifleman
No. 10707, 7th Battalion, Royal Irish Rifles
Killed in action on Wednesday 8 August 1917 (aged 24)
Tyne Cot Cemetery, Belgium (Grave LIV. D. 2)

George Edgar Edmonds was born on 16 May 1893 in Ballywalter and he was a son of William and Kate Edmonds. William Edmonds worked as the Mate on a Light Ship and he and Kate had at least five children – Edith, Catherine, William, Edwin Edward (baptised in Ballywalter Parish Church of Ireland) and George Edgar (baptised in Kircubbin Parish Church of Ireland).

George Edgar Edmonds enlisted in Belfast and he served with the 7th Battalion Royal Irish Rifles in 48th Brigade of the 16th (Irish) Division. He was killed in action on 8 August 1917 when his Battalion was holding the line ahead of the Third Battle of Ypres. At the time of his death his father was living at 214 Roden Street, Belfast and Rifleman George Edgar Edmonds is commemorated in the Belfast Book of Honour (Page 175).

Ellison, William Holland Kennedy (William)
Private
No. 49736, 9th Battalion, Princess Victoria's (Royal Irish Fusiliers)
Killed in action on Wednesday 2 October 1918 (aged 19)
Tyne Cot Memorial, Belgium (Panel 140 to 141)

William Holland Kennedy Ellison was born in Comber and he was a son of John and Agnes Ellison who lived at 59 Mill Street. John Ellison worked as an agricultural labourer and he and Agnes had at least two children – John and William. Later the Ellison family moved to Lisburn Street,

Ballynahinch. William Ellison served with the 9th Battalion Royal Irish Fusiliers in 108th Brigade of the 36th (Ulster) Division and he was killed in action on 2 October 1918 during the Allied offensive against all sections of the German line.

Emerson, Thomas
Private
No. 11473, 1st Battalion, Irish Guards
Killed in action on Wednesday 10 October 1917
Tyne Cot Memorial, Belgium (Panel 10 to 11)

Thomas Emerson was born in the townland of Ballyphilip, Portaferry and he enlisted in Belfast. He served with the 1st Battalion Irish Guards and he was killed in action on 10 October 1917.

Ennis, Robert (Bob)
Stoker First Class
No. K/16955, HMS *Nottingham*, Royal Navy
Killed in action on Saturday 19 August 1916 (aged 23)
Plymouth Naval Memorial, Devon, England (Panel 15)

E
F

Robert Ennis was a son of David and Mary Ennis (nee McCann) who lived at Butterlump, Ballyhalbert. They were married on 19 April 1898 in Newtownards Registry Office. David Ennis worked as an engine driver and he and Mary had at least two other children – Adam born in 1899 and David George born in 1914. Both were baptised in Glastry Presbyterian Church. Prior to the outbreak of the Great War Robert Ennis worked as a farm servant.

Stoker First Class Robert Ennis served aboard the light cruiser HMS *Nottingham*. Launched in 1913 this ship was involved in the Battles of Heligoland Bight, Dogger Bank and Jutland. On 19 August 1916 she was engaged in a sweep of the North Sea in thick mist to the south-east of the Firth of Forth. At 6.00 am she was hit by two torpedoes fired by U-Boat U-52 and then by a third some thirty minutes later. At 7.10 am HMS *Nottingham* sank and among those crewmembers that died was Stoker First Class Robert Ennis. He is commemorated in Glastry Presbyterian Church and on the family grave headstone in Kircubbin Presbyterian Church Graveyard.

Fenton, Alfred *
The name Alfred Fenton is listed on Newtownards and District War Memorial and in the booklet produced for the Unveiling and Dedication

Ceremony held on Saturday 26 May 1934 he is described as a Private in the Royal Army Medical Corps. Leonard Alfred Fenton was born in Loughborough, he enlisted on 12 September 1914, he served with the 67th Field Ambulance Royal Army Medical Corps (33237) and he was discharged from the army on 5 May 1919. Desk searches and public appeals to date have not confirmed a connection between these service data and the soldier who is commemorated on Newtownards and District War Memorial.

Fenton, Samuel Esler (Samuel)
Lance Corporal
No. 17628, then 22473, 12th Battalion, Royal Irish Rifles
Died of wounds on Sunday 13 October 1918 (aged 24)
Dadizeele Communal Cemetery, Belgium (Grave II. 1)

Samuel Esler Fenton was the second son of James and Elizabeth Fenton (nee Adair) who lived at Mount Pleasant, Whitehouse, Co Antrim. They were married on 31 May 1889 in Ballynure Presbyterian Church. James Fenton worked as a linen finisher in a bleach works and he and Elizabeth had at least twelve children including Robert James, Samuel Esler, Margaret, Isabella, Charles, Albert Edward and Elizabeth.

Prior to the outbreak of the Great War Samuel worked as a railway porter and in 1914 he enlisted in Mossley. He served with the 12th Battalion Royal Irish Rifles and he went to France with 108th Brigade of the 36th (Ulster) Division on 6 October 1915. After being wounded he was invalided home and stationed at Clandeboye. It was reported in the *Newtownards Chronicle* that he had a 'magnificent baritone voice' and whilst stationed at Clandeboye he sang in the choir of St Mark's Parish Church of Ireland Newtownards.

He was engaged to be married to a girl from Newtownards and arrangements were being made for their wedding to take place in September 1918. However Lance Corporal Samuel Fenton was not granted leave to get married and he was posted back to the front. He died in a casualty clearing station on 13 October 1918 as a result of wounds sustained during the Allied offensive against all sections of the German line.

Ferguson, Hugh
Petty Officer
Royal Navy
Died on Saturday 23 June 1923
Bangor New Cemetery, Newtownards Road, Bangor, Co. Down (Grave 4. R)

F

FERGUSON—June 23, 1923, at the U.V.F. Hospital, Belfast, Hugh Ferguson, dearly-beloved husband of Mary Ferguson, and third son of the late Hugh Ferguson, 10, South Street, Newtownards. His remains were removed from his late residence, 32, Springfield Road, Bangor, for interment in Bangor New Cemetery on Monday, the 25th inst.

Inserted by his sorrowing Wife and Family.

Hugh Ferguson was the third son of Hugh Ferguson who lived at 10 South Street, Newtownards and during the Great War he served in the Royal Navy. Hugh Junior and his wife Mary lived at 32 Springfield Road, Bangor and they had at least two children – Edward (died 12 October 1988) and Mary (died 29 September 2005). His widow Mary died on 9 January 1959.

Petty Officer Hugh Ferguson died on 23 June 1923 in the UVF Hospital in Belfast and he is commemorated on Newtownards and District War Memorial.

Ferguson, Nathaniel
Sapper
No. 30118, Postal Section, Corps of Royal Engineers
Died of blood poisoning on Friday 1 January 1915 (aged 36)
Ste. Marie Cemetery, France (Div. 14. I. 2)

F

Nathaniel Ferguson was born in Comber and he was a son of John and Jane Ferguson (nee Ferguson). They were married on 28 November 1876 in Comber Non-Subscribing Presbyterian Church. Prior to the outbreak of the Great War Nathaniel Ferguson worked as a sorting clerk and telegrapher. He and his wife Elizabeth (Lillie) McCaw Ferguson lived in Belmont Church Road, Belfast and they had at least one child whose name was Marion.

Nathaniel Ferguson enlisted in London, he served in the Postal Section of the Corps of Royal Engineers and he died of blood poisoning on 1 January 1915. At the time of his death his wife and family were living in Kilrea, Co Londonderry. Sapper Nathaniel Ferguson is commemorated on Comber and District War Memorial and in Comber Non-Subscribing Presbyterian Church.

Ferris, David
Long Service and Good Conduct Medal
Mentioned in Despatches
Company Sergeant Major
No. 4849, 'G' Company, 2nd Battalion, Royal Irish Rifles
Died of wounds on Tuesday 26 March 1918 (aged 39)
Thiepval Memorial, France (Pier and Face 15 A and 15 B)

In the CWGC Debt of Honour his date of death is recorded as 20 March 1918.

David Ferris was a career soldier. He was a son of William Ferris who worked as a labourer and he was born in the townland of Glasker, Banbridge, Co Down. David Ferris and Elizabeth Emily Crawford were married on 21 November 1911 in Helen's Bay Presbyterian Church and they lived at 86 Church Street, Newtownards. On 10 March 1910 David Ferris was presented with a gold watch on the occasion of his leaving the 2nd Battalion Royal Irish Rifles to take up duty on the Permanent Staff of the Royal North Downs (4th Battalion Royal Irish Rifles).

David was an all-round sportsman and had acknowledged soccer skills. He was on the Royal Irish Rifles team that won the All-Army Challenge Football cup and for that he received a gold medal and a silver cup. He won at least fourteen other medals on the soccer field. When he was posted to Newtownards David Ferris readily gave his services to Ards Football Club.

In 1914 he was awarded the Long Service and Good Conduct Medal and on 9 January 1915 he was promoted to the rank of Company Sergeant Major. It was reported in the press that he was offered a commission at a later stage but he declined saying that he 'preferred to stay in the ranks with his comrades'. On 26 January 1916 Company Sergeant Major David Ferris was posted back to his old Battalion – the 2nd Royal Irish Rifles. He went to the front and fought through several battles. He was granted two weeks home leave in February 1918 and less than a month later he died of wounds sustained in action.

FOR KING AND COUNTRY.

FERRIS—March 26th, 1918, in a field hospital, at Flavy le Martel, from wounds received in action, Company Sergeant-Major David Ferris, 2nd Batt. Royal Irish Rifles (late of the Permanent Staff, 4th Royal Irish Rifles), beloved husband of Elizabeth Ferris, 86 Church Street, Newtownards.

Elizabeth Ferris first heard unofficially that David had been mortally wounded but she retained some hope that he was still alive. This hope was eventually dashed some ten months later when she received official confirmation that he had died just five days after the start of the German 'Michael' offensive which began on 21 March 1918. In a letter dated 28 January 1919 from the Infantry Record Office in Dublin the circumstances of his death were described. His captain was killed, and in an attempt to stem the onrush of the Germans when they broke through the line at St Quentin, David Ferris led an attack on a nest of enemy machine guns. He received such serious injuries from shell and machine gun fire that both of his legs were shattered.

He and his comrades were taken prisoners of war and they carried him on an improvised stretcher to a German field hospital at Flavy-le-Martel where he died some six hours later without regaining consciousness. Company Sergeant Major David Ferris is commemorated on Newtownards and District War Memorial and in the PCI Roll of Honour for Regent Street Presbyterian Church Newtownards. Elizabeth Emily Ferris died on 24 June 1939 and she, her husband David, Colour Sergeant H Crawford and Sergeant William McVeigh are all commemorated on a headstone in Movilla New Cemetery, Newtownards.

F

Field, John William (Dick)
Captain
1st Battalion, Royal Irish Rifles
Died of wounds on Monday 20 September 1915 (aged 40)
Cabaret-Rouge British Cemetery, France (Grave XXI. C. 6)

John William Field was born in 1875 in County Cavan, he enlisted on 13 June 1892 in Wexford and he joined the 5th Battalion Royal Irish Rifles. He served in the South African War and on 10 December 1903 he and Elizabeth Henry were married in Christchurch Parish Church of Ireland Belfast. On 13 June 1904 he re-enlisted and re-joined the 5th Battalion. He received promotions and prior to the outbreak of the Great War he served with the 4th Battalion Royal Irish Rifles (Royal North Downs). During that time he and his family lived in Newtownards and before that they lived in Downpatrick.

It was reported in the *Newtownards Chronicle* that John William Field had over twenty years of army service and he could have remained in Newtownards during the Great War. Instead he volunteered to serve at the front and he went to France on 1 May 1915. He was promoted to the rank of Captain on 5 July 1915. It was also reported that his wife Elizabeth became seriously ill and he was granted leave to come home to Holywood where she was living at 6 Marine Parade (she had also lived at 52 Carlisle Street, Belfast). They had at least five children including Robert Hugh, Isabella Sarah and Elizabeth Rae.

Captain Field returned to the front and he was killed on 20 September 1915 during a night reconnaissance when he was shot in the head and chest. He is commemorated on Newtownards and District War Memorial and in Newtownards Parish Church of Ireland (St Mark).

Finlay, James (Jimmy)
Private
No. 3189, 2nd Battalion, Royal Inniskilling Fusiliers
Sergeant
No. 17617, 'B' Company, 13th Battalion, Royal Irish Rifles
Died on Sunday 19 January 1919 (aged 51)
Comber New Cemetery, Co. Down (Grave 5. 74)

F

James Finlay was born in Comber and he was a son of Frank and Catherine Finlay (nee Dickson). They were married on 6 August 1859 in Newtownards Registry Office. James served for more than 16 years with the 2nd Battalion Royal Inniskilling Fusiliers and he saw active service in many parts of the world including India and South Africa. In civilian life he worked as a flax dresser and also as an engine driver.

James Finlay and his wife Lizzie had one surviving son named Frank. Lizzie Finlay had two daughters – Jane and Lizzie – from a previous marriage. They all lived at 4 High Street, Comber and later at 4 Braeside, Comber.

Prior to the outbreak of the Great War Jimmy Finlay was an instructor for the Comber Companies of the Ulster Volunteer Force and after the war began he joined the 13th Battalion Royal Irish Rifles and served in 108th Battalion of the 36th (Ulster) Division.

Sergeant Finlay died on 19 January 1919 of an illness contracted during service and the effects of a shell explosion. He was buried with military honours in Comber New Cemetery on 21 January 1919. There was a firing party in attendance and buglers sounded *The Last Post*. James Finlay is commemorated in First Comber Presbyterian Church.

Finlay, Robert
Rifleman
No. 3528, 8th Battalion, Royal Irish Rifles
Killed in action on Sunday 2 July 1916
Thiepval Memorial, France (Pier and Face 15 A and 15 B)

In 'Soldiers Died in the Great War 1914 – 1919' it is recorded that Robert Finlay was born in Newtownards and he enlisted in Belfast. He served with the 8th Battalion Royal Irish Rifles in 107th Brigade of the 36th (Ulster) Division and in the CWGC Debt of Honour it is recorded that Rifleman Robert Finlay died on 2 July 1916. In the heat of battle the 8th Battalion Royal Irish Rifles did not make a casualty return on 1 July 1916 and many military historians agree that those 8th Battalion casualties listed on the 2 July return were killed in action on 1 July.

F

Fisher Brothers: George and Hugh *
George and Hugh Fisher were sons of George and Jane Fisher (nee McGrattan), who were married on 15 October 1887 in a Belfast Roman Catholic Church and they had at least three children – Hugh, George and Mary. After George Fisher Senior died Jane Fisher married John Berry on 1 May 1900 in Portaferry Roman Catholic Church. They lived in the townland of Keentagh, Quintin, Portaferry and they had at least five children – Sarah Jane, Jennie, John, Dominic and Isabel. George was the first of the two brothers to die in the Great War:

Fisher, George
Private
No. 724696, 38th Battalion, Canadian Infantry (Eastern Ontario Regiment)
Died of wounds on Monday 16 April 1917 (aged 28)
Belfast (Dundonald) Cemetery, Co. Down (Grave F5. 501)

George Fisher was born on 10 August 1888. He moved from Portaferry to Belfast where he worked as a labourer and he and Elizabeth Fisher were married on 19 August 1912 in St Anne's Church of Ireland Belfast. They lived at 67 Lord Street, Belfast. George Fisher moved to Canada and on 7 December 1915 he enlisted in Lindsay, Ontario. In his attestation papers it was noted that he was 5 feet 8 inches tall and that he had previous military experience. Private George Fisher was wounded in action at Vimy Ridge and he died in hospital in Farnham on 16 April 1917. He was buried on 21 April 1917 in Dundonald Cemetery.

Fisher, Hugh
Stoker First Class
No. K/33119, HMS *Vanguard*, Royal Navy
Killed in action on Monday 9 July 1917 (aged 26)
Chatham Naval Memorial, Kent, England (Panel 23)

By the age of eleven Hugh Fisher was working as a farm servant in the townland of Ballyfounder, Quintin, Portaferry. Prior to the outbreak of the Great War both Hugh Fisher and his step-father John Berry worked as agricultural labourers. Hugh Fisher joined the Royal Navy and he served aboard HMS *Vanguard*. This battleship was involved throughout the Battle of Jutland and did not suffer any damage or casualties. Just before midnight on Monday 9 July 1917 at Scapa Flow there was a massive explosion on board. The reason for the explosion has never been proved but most experts agree that the likely cause was cordite in one of the magazines overheating to a dangerous level because of a fire in an adjacent compartment. The ship sank almost immediately with the loss of more than 840 lives. There were only two survivors and afterwards there were gruesome reports about a nearby trawler being splattered with blood and pieces of human flesh.

Fisher, James (Jim)
Rifleman
No. 7191, 1st Battalion, Royal Irish Rifles
Killed in action on Friday 12 March 1915 (aged 24)
Le Touret Memorial, France (Panel 42 and 43)

James Fisher was born in Newtownards around 1891 and he was a son of William and Margaret Fisher. William Fisher worked as a hand loom weaver and he and Margaret had at least thirteen children including Mary, William and James. They lived at 15 East Street, Newtownards and prior to the outbreak of the Great War Jim worked as a tenter.

Jim Fisher and Margaret Davis were married on 28 November 1911 in Regent Street Methodist Church Newtownards. They lived in Court Street, Newtownards and they had at least one child. Jim enlisted in Newtownards on 24 August 1914 and he joined the Royal North Downs. He went to France on 26 December 1915 and he was attached to 'D' Company of the 1st Battalion Royal Irish Rifles.

In early April 1915 unofficial news reached Newtownards that Rifleman James Fisher of the 4th Battalion of the Royal Irish Rifles attached to the 1st Battalion had died of wounds. The first intimation came in a letter from Jim's comrade Hugh McConnell, also from Newtownards. Jim Fisher had been a regular letter writer and, significantly, his letters stopped coming. His family feared that Jim had died during the Battle of Neuve Chapelle which commenced on 10 March 1915 with the objective of recapturing the town and also the overlooking Aubers Ridge. In another letter home Hugh McConnell described the charge to the German trenches as 'terrible' and he imparted the news that Jim had been shot in the stomach. 'Very few live after getting injured there', Hugh had added.

During April and May 1915 Jim's wife and the Rev WLT Whatham both tried without success to get definitive information from the War Office as to Jim's whereabouts. Then, in a letter to Jim's mother, Rifleman T Stitt (another of Jim's comrades) informed her that when Jim was wounded he had been too close to the German lines for the stretcher bearers to get to him under the sustained enemy fire and Jim had died on the battlefield.

In late May 1915 Rifleman James Fisher was reported as wounded and missing in action and it was not until March 1916 that it was officially confirmed he had been killed in action on 12 March 1915 during an attack on the enemy trenches. That day more than 50 men of the 1st Battalion Royal Irish Rifles died. Rifleman James Fisher is commemorated on Newtownards and District War Memorial and on the Memorial Plaques in both Newtownards Parish Church of Ireland (St Mark) and Regent Street Methodist Church Newtownards.

Fisher, James
Rifleman
No. 810, 11th Battalion, Royal Irish Rifles
Killed in action on Saturday 1 July 1916 (aged 35)
Thiepval Memorial, France (Pier and Face 15 A and 15 B)

James Fisher was a son of Moore and Elizabeth (Lizzie) Fisher (nee McCullough) who lived in the townland of Ballymalady, Moneyreagh. They were married on 4 October 1883 in Moneyreagh Non-Subscribing Presbyterian Church. Moore Fisher was a farmer and he and Lizzie had at least three children – James, Maggie and John. Prior to the outbreak of the Great War James Fisher worked as a shop assistant. He and Elizabeth (Lizzie) Jane McCalmont were married on 26 October 1906 in Moneyreagh Non-Subscribing Presbyterian

Church and they had at least two children – James and Mary Anne.

James Fisher enlisted in Belfast and he served with the 11th Battalion Royal Irish Rifles in 108th Brigade of the 36th (Ulster) Division. He was killed in action on the first day of the Battle of the Somme and he is commemorated on Comber and District War Memorial.

Fisher, Thomas James
Rifleman
No. 17637, 'B' Company, 13th Battalion, Royal Irish Rifles
Died on Monday 29 October 1917 (aged 20)
Comber New Cemetery, Co. Down (Grave 8. 203)

Thomas James Fisher was born on 12 July 1897 and he was a son of Robert James and Isabella Fisher (nee Ferguson) who lived in High Street, Comber. They were married on 13 May 1893 in Ballygowan Presbyterian Church. Isabella died when Thomas James was a child and the Head of the House in 1911 was his maternal grandfather James Ferguson. Both his father and grandfather worked as farm labourers. The other members of the household in which Thomas James Fisher grew up were two unmarried aunts Jane and Mary Ferguson, his brother George and his sisters Ellen Jane, Sarah and Rebecca.

Thomas James Fisher enlisted in Comber and he served with the 13th Battalion Royal Irish Rifles in 108th Brigade of the 36th (Ulster) Division. He died at home on 29 October 1917 and he is commemorated on Comber and District War Memorial and in First Comber Presbyterian Church.

Fitzsimmons, James *
Private
No. 4153, Royal Irish Regiment, transferred to (21942), 7th/8th Battalion, Princess Victoria's (Royal Irish Fusiliers)
Died of wounds on Thursday 22 November 1917 (aged 42)
Bucquoy Road Cemetery, France (Grave II. E. 12)

In some records the surname is spelt Fitzsimons.

James Fitzsimmons was born in the townland of Ballyphilip, Portaferry and he was a son of George and Mary Fitzsimmons (nee Tomilty). They were

THE SUPREME SACRIFICE.

Portaferry Fusilier's Death.

It is officially announced that Private J. Fitzsimmons (No. 21,942), R. Irish Fusiliers, has died of wounds received in action.

married on 3 November 1866 in Portaferry Roman Catholic Church. James Fitzsimmons and Catherine McIlvenny were married on 22 March 1916 in a Belfast Roman Catholic Church and they lived in Knocknagow, Portaferry. James enlisted in Newtownards.

When Private James Fitzsimmons died of wounds on 22 November 1917 he was serving with the 7th/8th Battalion Royal Irish Fusiliers and before that he served with the Royal Irish Regiment (4153).

Fitzsimmons, John Ralston (Ralston)
Rifleman
No. 2368, 'A' Company, 13th Battalion, Royal Irish Rifles
Killed in action on Saturday 1 July 1916 (aged 19)
Thiepval Memorial, France (Pier and Face 15 A and 15 B)

F

John Ralston Fitzsimmons was born on 22 December 1896 and he was a son of Nicholas and Mary Jane Fitzsimmons (nee Sinclair) who lived in Main Street, Kircubbin. They were married on 2 March 1888 in Glastry Presbyterian Church. Nicholas Fitzsimmons worked as a grocer and he and Mary Jane had at least twelve children – Jane, Robert, Jennie, John Ralston, James, Florence, Mary, Eva, Stella, Thomas, Ellen Chambers and Clair. The children were baptised in Kircubbin Presbyterian Church.

Prior to the outbreak of the Great War John Ralston Fitzsimmons worked as a tailor's apprentice. He enlisted in Belfast and he served with the 13th Battalion Royal Irish Rifles in 108th Brigade of the 36th (Ulster) Division. He went to France on 6 October 1915 and he was killed in action on the first day of the Battle of the Somme. Rifleman John Ralston Fitzsimmons is commemorated in Kircubbin Presbyterian Church and on the family grave headstone (as Fitzsimmins) in the adjoining graveyard. His mother died on 9 October 1919 and his father died on 18 March 1947.

Fitzsimons, Robert
Lance Corporal
No. 6581, 2nd Battalion, Royal Irish Rifles
Killed in action on Tuesday 17 October 1916 (aged 40)
Thiepval Memorial, France (Pier and Face 15 A and 15 B)

Robert Fitzsimons was a son of Henry and Rosanna Fitzsimons (nee McFerran) who lived in Tower Street, Pottinger, Belfast. They were married on 7 October 1863 in York Street Presbyterian Church Belfast. Henry Fitzsimons worked as a carpenter and he and Rosanna had at least eleven children including Robert, Henry, Agnes and Rosanna.

Robert Fitzsimons and his wife Harriette had at least one child – Henry Seymour Fitzsimons – and they lived in the townland of Ballymorran, Killinchy along with Harriette's father Robert Morrison and Harriette's daughter Alice Montgomery.

> **KILLINCHY.**
> Lance-Corporal R. Fitzsimmons, (No. 6,581), R.I. Rifles, killed.

Lance Corporal Robert Fitzsimons served with the 2nd Battalion Royal Irish Rifles and he died on 17 October 1916. He is commemorated in Killinchy Parish Church of Ireland and in the Belfast Book of Honour (Page 194).

Foster Brothers: Henry and John

> **A Patriotic Newtownards Family.**
>
> **THE FOSTERS.**
>
> The record of the Foster family, Newtownards, in this war will, we think, be hard to beat. Mrs. Sarah Jane Foster, 76 James Street, Newtownards, has, or rather had, four sons, 5 grandsons, and 4 sons-in-law serving King and country, and she is certainly to be congratulated on the patriotism of her family. The following particulars will, no doubt, be read with interest, indicating, as they do, that some of the brave soldiers mentioned have already made the supreme sacrifice:—
>
> **Her Sons.**
>
> Sergeant H. Foster, 9th Royal Irish Rifles. Missing since 1st July, 1916.
> Rifleman John Foster, 1st Royal Irish Rifles. Missing since Mons, 1914.
> Rifleman Alex. Foster, Royal Irish Rifles. Wounded in July, 1916.
> Rifleman Thos. Foster, 17th Royal Irish Rifles. Now serving at Holywood.
>
> **Her Grandsons.**
>
> Rifleman John Foster (No. 6,234), 1st County Down Volunteers. Serving with the B.E.F., France.
> Rifleman Alex. Foster (No. 17,652), 1st County Down Volunteers. Serving with his battalion in France.
> Rifleman Harry Foster, 2nd Royal Irish Rifles. Wounded and discharged 1916.
> Private William Foster, Royal Irish Fusiliers. Serving in Salonica.
> Rifleman Jas. Logan, Royal Irish Rifles. Serving in France.
>
> **Her Sons-in-law.**
>
> Private Thos. Johnston, Royal Irish Fusiliers. Serving in France.
> Lance-Corporal John M'Neill, 9th Irish Fusiliers, now in 10th. Wounded.
> Rifleman Charles Reid, 1st Royal Irish Rifles. Killed 1st July, 1916.
> Rifleman Joseph Reid, Royal Irish Rifles. With B.E.F., France.

Henry and John Foster were sons of George and Sarah Jane Foster (nee Hainey) who were married on 21 January 1856 in Newtownards Parish Church of Ireland. Sarah Jane was widowed sometime before 1901 and she worked as a seamstress. She lived in North Street with her son Isaac and he worked as an umbrella maker. Sarah Jane had at least nine children including John, Alexander, Henry (Harry), Thomas, Isaac, Lena and Nellie.

In April 1917 an article published in the *Newtownards Chronicle* under the heading 'A Patriotic Newtownards Family' reported that Sarah Jane Foster had four sons, five grand-sons and four sons-in-law on active service.

Her sons on active service were named as John, Alexander, Thomas and Harry and two of them (John and Harry) were killed in action. Her sons-in-law on active service were named as Thomas Johnston, John McNeill, Charles Reid (served with the

1st Battalion Royal Irish Rifles and was killed in action on 1 July 1916) and Joseph Reid. Sarah Jane Foster's grand-sons who served in the Great War were named as John, Alex, Harry and William Foster and James Logan.

John Foster was the first of Sarah Jane's two sons to die on active service in the Great War:

Foster, John
Rifleman
No. 5623, 2nd Battalion, Royal Irish Rifles
Killed in action on Friday 18 December 1914 (aged 56)
Ypres (Menin Gate) Memorial, Belgium (Panel 40)

John Foster was born in 1858 in Newtownards and he and his wife Rose Ann lived in Whiteabbey, Co Antrim. John Foster worked as a labourer and he and Rose Ann had at least seven children including Mary, Henry, Annie, Sarah Jane, John and Alexander.

Rifleman John Foster was killed in action on 18 December 1914 during exchanges at the end of a spell of four days in the trenches and at that time his family was living at 35 Tyne Street, Belfast.

Foster, Henry (Harry)
Sergeant
No. 12770, 9th Battalion, Royal Irish Rifles
Killed in action on Saturday 1 July 1916 (aged 45)
Thiepval Memorial, France (Pier and Face 15 A and 15 B)

Harry Foster was born in 1871 in Newtownards and he and his wife Annie lived at 128 Canmore Street, Belfast. Harry Foster was a linen worker and he and Annie had at least two children, Harry and Alexander, both of whom were on active service.

Sergeant Harry Foster served with the 9th Battalion Royal Irish Rifles in 107th Brigade of the 36th (Ulster) Division and he was killed in action on 1 July 1916.

Both Henry and John Foster are commemorated in the Belfast Book of Honour (Pages 198 and 199).

Fowles, William John
Rifleman
No. 18/110, 'D' Company, 13th Battalion, Royal Irish Rifles
Killed in action on Saturday 1 July 1916 (aged 21)
Thiepval Memorial, France (Pier and Face 15 A and 15 B)

OUR ROLL OF HONOUR.

THE SUPREME SACRIFICE.

On Friday, 10th inst. Mrs. Elizabeth Fowles, 78 East Street, Newtownards, received official intimation that her eldest son, Rifleman Wm. John Fowles, who was reported missing in "the great push" of 1st July, 1916, may now be regarded as having been killed on that date. Rifleman Fowles, who has so gallantly given his all for King and country, was only 22 years of age. He enlisted on the County Down Volunteers (13th Royal Irish Rifles) in May, 1915, and with the Ulster Division proceeded to France in October of that year.

William John Fowles was born on 2 January 1895 in Newtownards and he lived at 78 East Street with his grandmother Ann Jane Fowles, his mother Lizzie Fowles and his brother Robert. He was baptised in Greenwell Street Presbyterian Church. Prior to the outbreak of the Great War William John Fowles was a mill worker. He enlisted in May 1915 and he served with the 13th Battalion Royal Irish Rifles in 108th Brigade of the 36th (Ulster) Division. He went to France on 5 October 1915.

After the first day of the Battle of the Somme Rifleman William John Fowles was posted as missing in action and more than a year later, in August 1917, it was officially confirmed that he had been killed on 1 July 1916. His grandmother, mother and brother placed an 'Our Heroes – In Memoriam' notice in the *Newtownards Chronicle*. It contained the verse:

'Dear son, it makes our hearts sore
To think in this life we shall meet you no more;
It was thy sad fate to be killed by the Huns,
Midst the splinter of shells and the roar of the guns.
Dear son of my bosom, you sleep 'mong the brave,
Where no tears of a mother can drop on thy grave;
In the red fields of France you are laid far away,
Still our tribute of love to thy memory we pay.
Although we regret that so early in life
It was thy misfortune to fall in the strife,
Yet it may give thy friends consolation to know
That you died in the field with your face to the foe.
But as long as we are allowed to remain here behind,
Dear son, we will always bear thee in mind;
The bugles may sound and the cannons may roar,
But you will be found in the conflict no more.'

Rifleman William John Fowles is commemorated on Newtownards and

F

District War Memorial and in Newtownards Parish Church of Ireland (St Mark).

Francis, William
Private
No. 7706, 2nd Battalion, Royal Inniskilling Fusiliers
Died of wounds on Sunday 16 May 1915 (aged 44)
Le Touret Memorial, France (Panel 16 and 17)

There is evidence that William Francis was born on 5 February 1871 in Newtownards and he was a son of Elisha and Elisa Francis (nee Simpson). They were married on 22 August 1866 in Newtownards Registry Office and they lived in Mark Street. Elisha Francis worked as a hand loom weaver and he and Elisa had at least four children – Elisha, William, Sarah and John.

William Francis and Agnes Boyd were married on 24 December 1907 in First Newtownards Presbyterian Church. They lived in James Street, Newtownards and they had at least two children – Mary Jane and William. They lived with Agnes's widowed grandmother Agnes Roney, her widowed aunt Mary Jane Boyd and her cousins Annie, John and Thomasina Boyd.

Prior to the outbreak of the Great War William Francis worked as a machine printer. He served with the 2nd Battalion Royal Inniskilling Fusiliers in 5th Brigade of the 2nd Division and he died of wounds on 16 May 1915.

Fryers, William
Rifleman
No. 14/7567, 2nd Battalion, Royal Irish Rifles
Died of wounds on 11 April 1918 (aged 33)
Haringhe (Bandaghem) Military Cemetery, Belgium (Grave II. B. 3)

Born in Shankill and a native of Belfast, William Fryers was a son of Agnes and the late Robert Fryers. William was a professional soldier and he and Lizzie Anderson were married on 30 August 1904 in Ballyblack Presbyterian Church. They lived at 36 Upper Movilla Street, Newtownards and later at 27 Queen Street, Newtownards. William and Lizzie had at least five children all of whom were baptised in Greenwell Street Presbyterian Church – William (1906), Lizzie (1908), Minnie (1910), Robert Greer (1911) and John Herbert McMillan (1914).

Prior to the outbreak of the Great War William Fryers was in civil employment and following his previous army experience he re-enlisted in

Newtownards in April 1915. He joined the Royal North Downs and went to France in January 1917.

After William Fryers died the Chaplain, Rev William H Leathem, wrote to William's wife Lizzie and described the circumstances of his death. Rifleman Fryers was brought in to No. 36 Casualty Clearing Station in the early morning of 11 April 1918. He was suffering from a gunshot wound to the head. He was unconscious and unable to convey any message and he died at 8.30 am.

Lizzie placed a 'For King and Country' notice in the 27 April 1918 edition of the *Newtownards Chronicle* and it contained the verse:

> 'Short was my race, long is my rest,
> God took me when He thought best;
> My time had come, I in a moment fell,
> And had not time to say farewell.
> Death to me short warning gave,
> But quickly took me to the grave;
> My weeping wife I left behind,
> I had not time to speak my mind.'

F

Rifleman William Fryers is commemorated on Newtownards and District War Memorial; in the PCI Roll of Honour for Greenwell Street Presbyterian Church Newtownards (as Fryars) and in the Belfast Book of Honour (Page 203).

Fullerton, John
Rifleman
No. 1011, 14th Battalion, Royal Irish Rifles
Killed in action on 16 August 1917 (aged 34)
Tyne Cot Memorial, Belgium (Panel 138 to 140 & 162 to 162A & 163A)

John Fullerton was born on 9 February 1883 in Kircubbin and he was a son of Thomas and Mary Fullerton (nee Cooper) who lived at 26 Court Street, Newtownards. They were married on 24 December 1880 in Ballywalter Presbyterian Church. Thomas Fullerton worked as a boot-maker and later as a carter. He and Mary had at least seven children – William, John, Robert, Maggie, Jane, Thomas and Joseph McMaster. William, John and Robert were baptised in Kircubbin Presbyterian Church and the others were baptised in Glastry Presbyterian Church. Prior to the outbreak of the Great War John Fullerton worked as a bricklayer's labourer.

John Fullerton enlisted in Newtownards and he served with the 14th Battalion Royal Irish Rifles in 109th Brigade of the 36th (Ulster) Division. In August

Missing, Now Reported Killed.

In the official casualty list published this week appears the name of Rifleman J Fullerton (No. 1,011), R.I. Rifles, of Newtownards, who, previously reported missing, is now reported killed.

1917 he was posted as missing in action during the Third Battle of Ypres and in December 1917 it was officially confirmed that he had been killed in action. Rifleman John Fullerton is commemorated on Newtownards and District War Memorial and in the PCI Roll of Honour for Greenwell Street Presbyterian Church Newtownards.

Gabbey, James
Private
No. 27524, 9th Battalion, Royal Inniskilling Fusiliers
Killed in action on Sunday 20 October 1918 (aged 27)
Harlebeke New British Cemetery, Belgium (Grave VIII. D. 4)

James Gabbey was the younger son of James Gabbey and the late Sarah Jane Gabbey (nee English). They were married on 16 December 1887 in Dundonald Presbyterian Church. James Gabbey Junior was born in Shankill during the time that his parents were living in Belfast. Both of his parents were born in Comber and in the 1890s they returned to Comber where they lived at 27 Railway Street. James Gabbey Senior had problems with his eyes and he worked as a gardener and a labourer. James and Sarah Gabbey had at least five children – John, James and Mary born in Belfast and then Lizzie and Sarah Jane born in Comber. Prior to the outbreak of the Great War James Gabbey Junior was unemployed and he enlisted in Newtownards.

G

Private James Gabbey was wounded in action in July 1917 but he recovered sufficiently to return to the front. He served with the 9th Battalion Royal Inniskilling Fusiliers in 109th Brigade of the 36th (Ulster) Division and he was killed in action on 20 October 1918. He is commemorated on Comber and District War Memorial; in Second Comber Presbyterian Church and in the Belfast Book of Honour (Page 205).

Gadd, Alfred Henry Victor (Victor)
Boy First Class
No. J/27246, HMS *Goliath*, Royal Navy
Killed in action on Thursday 13 May 1915 (aged 17)
Chatham Naval Memorial, Kent, England (Panel 10)

Alfred Henry Victor Gadd was the only son of Alfred Henry Gadd and Kathleen (Katie) Gadd (nee Cleland) who lived at 29 Queen's Avenue, Winchmore Hill, London. They were married on 9 July 1891 in St Andrew, Holborn (Church of England) in Middlesex. Victor's maternal grandparents, Thomas Cleland who was a woollen draper from Killyleagh and Marianne Brown, were married on 11 December 1861 in Regent Street Presbyterian Church, Newtownards. Victor Gadd's death was widely reported in the *Newtownards Chronicle* because he could trace his Newtownards connections back through three generations – his mother; his grandmother Mrs William Yeates and his great-grandfather John Brown who had been a leading merchant in the town.

Victor Gadd was just 17 years 11 months old when he was killed in action aboard HMS *Goliath*. HMS *Goliath* was torpedoed by a Turkish destroyer in the Dardanelles during the early hours of 13 May 1915 and of the 750 men on board 570 were lost. Boy First Class Alfred Henry Victor Gadd was one of three men with Ards connections who were killed in action aboard HMS *Goliath*. The others lost that night were Stoker First Class **Willie Beringer** and Stoker First Class **Hector Hiles**.

On 8 May 1915, only five days before he died, Victor Gadd wrote a cheery letter home to his parents. On 22 May 1915, some nine days after the sinking of HMS *Goliath*, Victor's parents received official notification from the Admiralty about his death. In May 1917 Boy First Class Victor Gadd's parents placed an 'Our Heroes – In Memoriam' notice in the *Newtownards Chronicle* and it contained the verse:

'In a foreign sea he sleeps today,
A mother's pride and joy;
He did his part with manly heart,
A brave, a noble boy'

G

Galway, John Campbell (John)
Major
'C' Company, 2nd Battalion, Canadian Pioneers
Killed in action on Wednesday 18 April 1917 (aged 40)
Ecoivres Military Cemetery, France (Grave VI. F. 10)

Comber Officer Killed.

Major John Campbell Galway, Canadian Pioneer Battalion, attached Canadian Engineers, killed in action on 18th April, was the only son of the late Mr. Thomas Galway, who was supervisor in the Inland Revenue at Comber twenty years ago. This officer, who belonged to the Western Ontario Regiment, obtained his lieutenancy on 6th December, 1915, was promoted to the rank of captain on 20th July, 1916, and was appointed major whilst commanding a company on 20th December, 1916.

John Campbell Galway was born on 18 June 1876 in South Molton, Devon. He was the only son of Thomas and Elizabeth Galway and when the family lived in Comber Thomas Galway was working as a supervisor in the Inland Revenue.

John Campbell Galway moved to Canada where he worked as a civil engineer. He and his wife Anna M Galway lived at 46 Leonard Avenue, Ottawa. He enlisted in Quebec, obtained his Lieutenancy on 6 December 1915, was promoted to the rank of Captain on 20 July 1916 and was appointed Major whilst commanding a company on 20 December 1916.

Major John Campbell Galway was killed in action on 18 April 1917 when he was hit by a high explosive shell whilst returning from Battalion HQ to 'C' Company along the road between Mont-St Eloi and Neuville-St Vaast.

At the time of his death his wife Anna was living at 'The Manse', Hulton Avenue, West Hartlepool in England. He is commemorated on the QUB War Memorial and in the QUB Book of Remembrance (Page 22).

Gamble, David
Private
No. 2/8290, 1st Battalion, Princess Victoria's (Royal Irish Fusiliers)
Died in a Prisoner of War Camp on Friday 25 August 1916 (aged 32)
Cologne Southern Cemetery, Germany (Grave VIII. E. 20)

David Gamble was born in Conlig and he was a son of Hugh and Mary Ann Gamble. Hugh Gamble worked as a general labourer and he and Mary Ann had three children – David, James and Hugh. Both parents, Hugh and Mary Ann, are buried in Bangor New Cemetery.

Prior to the outbreak of the Great War David Gamble worked as a general labourer and on 1 January 1909 he and Jane Dempster were married in Newtownards Registry Office. They had at least three children and they were

baptised in Greenwell Street Presbyterian Church Newtownards – James (born on 2 September 1910), Hugh (born on 4 December 1912) and William John (born on 1 July 1914). The Gamble family lived at 91 East Street, Newtownards along with David's stepdaughter Georgina and his stepson David.

David Gamble enlisted in Belfast and he served with the 1st Battalion Royal Irish Fusiliers. He was taken prisoner and died in a German Prisoner of War Camp on 25 August 1916. At the time of his death David's wife and family were living in the townland of Ballycullen, Newtownards.

Private David Gamble is commemorated on Bangor and District War Memorial and on Newtownards and District War Memorial; in the RBL Album in North Down Museum (Page 40) and on the Memorial Plaques in RBL Bangor Branch, Conlig Orange Hall and Conlig Presbyterian Church. He is also commemorated in the PCI Roll of Honour for Greenwell Street Presbyterian Church Newtownards.

G

Gamble, David John (David)
Rifleman
No. 18/115, 12th Battalion, Royal Irish Rifles
Died on Saturday 8 July 1916 (aged 17)
Caudry Old Communal Cemetery, France (Grave B. 4)

David John Gamble was the second son of Robert and Sarah Gamble (nee Mullan) who lived at 4 Brownlow Street, Comber. They were married on 17 September 1892 in Dundonald Presbyterian Church. Robert Gamble worked as a blacksmith and he and Sarah had at least six children including James, Jane, Frances, David John, Hugh and Samuel (all baptised in First Comber Presbyterian Church).

David John Gamble served with the 12th Battalion Royal Irish Rifles in 108th Brigade of the 36th (Ulster) Division and he was posted as missing in action after the first day of the Battle of the Somme. In December 1916 it was reported that he had been wounded during the advance and that he had been taken prisoner.

In May 1917 it was officially confirmed that Rifleman David John Gamble had died of his wounds while being held prisoner by the Germans. He was 17

COUNTY DOWN AND THE WAR.

Comber Rifleman Dies a Prisoner.

The death is reported while a prisoner in Germany of Rifleman J. Gamble, Royal Irish Rifles. Deceased, who was wounded during the advance on the Somme on July 1, 1916, was a son of Mr. Robert Gamble, 4 Brownlow Street, Comber.

years of age when he died and he is commemorated on Comber and District War Memorial and in First Comber Presbyterian Church.

Gatensby, Samuel
Lieutenant
15th Battalion, Royal Irish Rifles
Died of pneumonia on Sunday 24 November 1918 (aged 33)
Belfast City Cemetery (Grave Screen Wall. H3. 55)

Samuel Gatensby was born in Belfast and he was a son of Thomas and Mary Gatensby (nee Campbell). They were married on 15 April 1876 in Eglinton Street Presbyterian Church Belfast. Thomas Gatensby worked as a tenter and he and Mary had at least seven children including Annie, Minnie, Samuel and Elizabeth. Samuel was a young boy when his father died and the family moved to Donaghadee where they lived in Princess Gardens.

G

Prior to the outbreak of the Great War, Samuel Gatensby worked as a Sheriff's Clerk in Belfast. He enlisted in the Cyclist Company of the 36th (Ulster) Division and when he obtained a commission he was posted to the 15th Battalion Royal Irish Rifles in March 1917 as a Second Lieutenant. A few weeks later he went to the front with 107th Brigade of the 36th (Ulster) Division and twice he was wounded in action.

Donaghadee Officer's Death.

The death took place on Sunday, at his residence, Millisle Road, Donaghadee, of Lieut. Samuel Gatensby, 15th Batt. Royal Irish Rifles, who succumbed to pneumonia. Deceased was a son of Mr. Samuel Gatensby, Donaghadee, and was on the Belfast City Hall staff before joining the Army Cyclists Corps (Ulster Division) in 1914. He was afterwards promoted to a commission in the infantry, and served in France with the North Belfast Regiment, being twice wounded.

Lieutenant Samuel Gatensby suffered from gas poisoning and he died of pneumonia at his home in Donaghadee on 24 November 1918 three days after his mother Mary died of influenza. He is commemorated on Donaghadee and District War Memorial; in Donaghadee Methodist Church; on Belfast Corporation War Memorial Plaque in Belfast City Hall and in the Belfast Book of Honour (Page 210) where it is recorded that he was awarded the Military Cross (this award is not listed on his Medal Index Card).

Geddis, Francis (Frank)
Corporal
No. 10940, 8th Battalion, King's Own (Royal Lancaster Regiment)
Killed in action on Monday 13 November 1916 (aged 24)
Thiepval Memorial, France (Pier and Face 5 D and 12 B)

 Francis Geddis was born in Comber and he was the eldest son of Samuel and Catherine Geddis (nee Finlay). They were married on 22 April 1887 in Gilnahirk Presbyterian Church. Samuel Geddis worked as an insurance agent and he and Catherine had at least two children – Francis and Lizzie. When Catherine died Samuel, Francis and Lizzie lived with Samuel's father (also called Samuel Geddis) who worked as a night watchman and lived in High Street Comber.

Frank Geddis worked as a shipyard labourer and he lived with his uncle William James McKibbin in High Street, Comber. He enlisted in Belfast and in some records his surname is spelt 'Geddes'. He served with the 8th Battalion King's Own (Royal Lancaster Regiment) and he was killed in action on 13 November 1916. At the time of Frank's death his wife was living at 17 Brownlow Street, Comber and his sister Lizzie Loughran lived in High Street, Comber.

Frank Geddis suffered multiple wounds during the fighting at Ypres on 2 May 1915 and he was transferred to Leckhampton Court Hospital in England for treatment. He recovered sufficiently to be posted back to the front. After Frank was killed on 13 November 1916 his Commanding Officer wrote to Frank's widow to express his condolences. In the letter he commented that, had Frank survived, he would have been promoted to the rank of Sergeant.

In another letter the Church of England Chaplain explained how Frank had died. He was badly wounded at the German wire and he took cover in a shell hole. It was in the shell hole that Frank died and it was impossible to bring his body in. Corporal Frank Geddis is commemorated on Comber and District War Memorial and in First Comber Presbyterian Church.

Geddis, Samuel McKee (Sam)
Lieutenant
1st Battalion, Leicestershire Regiment
Died on Thursday 19 September 1918 (aged 25)
Trefcon British Cemetery, France (Grave C. 59)

Samuel McKee Geddis was the younger son of Andrew and Mary Jane (Minnie) Geddis (nee McKee) who lived in the townland of Tullynakill, Killinchy. They were married on 23 November 1883 in Downpatrick Registry Office. After Andrew died Minnie Geddis who was then in her forties ran the family farm. Samuel had an older brother called Andrew and an older sister called Winifred.

Before he enlisted Samuel worked as a Solicitor's Clerk with the firm of Messrs Moorhead & Wood in Rosemary Street, Belfast. Widely known amongst the members of the legal profession, he was also well-known as a member of the North Down Cricket and Hockey Clubs. In July 1915 Samuel Geddis obtained his commission through the Officers' Training Corps at Queen's University Belfast and he was gazetted to the Leicestershire Regiment. In November 1915 he went to France where he saw considerable service during which he was wounded twice and gassed once. Lieutenant Sam McKee Geddis died on 19 September 1918 and he is commemorated on Comber and District War Memorial; in both Second Comber Presbyterian Church and Killinchy Presbyterian Church; on the QUB War Memorial and in the QUB Book of Remembrance (Page 23).

G

Sam Geddis was engaged to be married to Jeannie McBurney of Comber and after Sam died Jeannie never married. Two of Jeannie's brothers **Jim and Teddy McBurney** also died.

Gibson, Alexander
Driver
No. 57742, 121st Field Company, Royal Engineers, 36th (Ulster) Division
Died of wounds on Friday 22 June 1917 (aged 25)
Boulogne Eastern Cemetery, France (Grave IV. A. 12)

In 'Soldiers Died in the Great War 1914 – 1919' it is recorded that Alexander Gibson was born in Newtownards and he enlisted in Belfast. He served as a Driver with the 121st Field Company Royal Engineers in the 36th (Ulster) Division and on 22 June 1917 he died of wounds sustained during the Battle of Messines. At the time of Alexander's death his wife was living at 16 Baywood Street, Belfast. Driver Alexander Gibson is commemorated in the Belfast Book of Honour (Page 212).

Gibson, Alexander
Rifleman
No. 7079, 1st Battalion, Royal Irish Rifles
Killed in action on Tuesday 11 March 1915 (aged 19)
Le Touret Memorial, France (Panel 42 and 43)

Alexander Gibson was born on 24 June 1895 and he was a son of William John and Margaret Gibson (nee Weir) who lived at 32 Movilla Street Newtownards. They were married on 17 July 1876 in Greenwell Street Presbyterian Church. William John Gibson worked as a horse dealer and he and Margaret had at least nine children – Mary, William John, Hugh, James, Margaret, David, James, Marquis and Alexander. Alexander was baptised in Fourth Newtownards Presbyterian Church.

TWO NEWTOWNARDS SOLDIERS KILLED IN ACTION.

FELL AT NEUVE CHAPELLE.

The casualties amongst the rank and file of our troops at the battle of Neuve Chapelle, which resulted in a glorious victory for the British Army, include quite a number of soldiers of the 1st Battalion Royal Irish Rifles, to which drafts of the Royal North Downs (4th R.I. Rifles) were attached. We hear that a number of Newtownards men are included in those who gallantly fought and fell in the defence of their King and country. Official news has not yet reached the relatives, but the following letter, written by Rifleman John Weir, of Newtownards, to his uncle, Mr. James Weir, of Mill Street, indicates that at least two brave Newtownards youths have fallen in action. The letter, which is undated, was received here on Tuesday morning, and runs as follows:—

"B" Company,
1st Batt. R.I. Rifles,
No. 4 Unit British Expeditionary Force.

Dear Uncle,—Just a line to let you know I am well, hoping this will find you all at home in the same state of good health. I suppose you have heard of the great British victory (Neuve Chapelle). Well, this will let you know I am safe yet, but poor "Tibs" Carnduff and Wm. John Gibson's son are killed. I haven't time to write any more, and will close.—From your affectionate nephew,
JOHN WEIR, No. 7496.

Alexander Gibson enlisted in Newtownards and he joined the North Downs. On successive days in March 1915 Rifleman **James Carnduff** and Rifleman Alexander Gibson from Newtownards were killed in action during the Allied attack at Neuve Chapelle which had as its objective to take Aubers Ridge. Neuve Chapelle had been the scene of heavy fighting the previous autumn and on 11 March 1915 the horrors of war were compounded during the intense bombardment when bodies buried in October 1914 were blown from their graves and scattered among the March 1915 casualties.

News of the deaths of Riflemen Carnduff and Gibson first reached Newtownards in a letter written by Rifleman John Weir (7496) to his uncle James Weir of Mill Street Newtownards. Rifleman Alexander Gibson is commemorated on Newtownards and District War Memorial and in the PCI Roll of Honour for Greenwell Street Presbyterian Church Newtownards.

Gibson, Samuel
Rifleman
No. 14/6881, No. 1 Company, 16th Battalion, Royal Irish Rifles
Killed in action on Wednesday 25 July 1917 (aged 25)
Dickebusch New Military Cemetery Extension, Belgium (Grave I. B. 9)

Samuel Gibson was born on 15 March 1892 in Ballygowan and he was the youngest son of Joseph and Agnes Gibson (nee Skillen). They were married on 5 January 1872 in Ballygowan Presbyterian Church. Joseph Gibson worked as the postmaster and when he died on 2 February 1908 Agnes continued as postmistress. Joseph and Agnes had seven children all of whom were baptised in Ballygowan Presbyterian Church – William Joseph Scott, Margaret, Jane, Robert, Agnes, John and Samuel.

FOR KING AND COUNTRY.
GIBSON—25th July, 1917, killed in action, Samuel, youngest and dearly-beloved son of Agnes and the late Joseph Gibson, The Post Office, Ballygowan.

Samuel Gibson enlisted in Belfast where he joined the 14th Battalion Royal Irish Rifles and later he was transferred to the 16th Battalion. He went to France on 5 October 1915 and served in 109th Brigade of the 36th (Ulster) Division. He was killed in action on 25 July 1917 and his mother placed a 'For King and Country' notice in the *Newtownards Chronicle*. Rifleman Samuel Gibson is commemorated in Ballygowan Presbyterian Church.

G

Gibson, William James
Rifleman
No. 17702, 'B' Company, 13th Battalion, Royal Irish Rifles
Killed in action on Monday 6 August 1917 (aged 25)
Potijze Chateau Grounds Cemetery, Belgium (Grave II. E. 23)

William James Gibson was born in 1892 in Newtownards and he was the youngest son of Samuel James and Margaret Gibson (nee Cameron). They were married on 6 October 1888 in Ballyblack Presbyterian Church. Samuel James Gibson worked as a carter and he and Margaret had at least five children – Annabella, Samuel, William James, Susan and Margaret. Samuel James Gibson was widowed in the late 1890s and he lived at 166 Greenwell Street, Newtownards.

William James Gibson enlisted in Newtownards, he served with the 13th Battalion Royal Irish Rifles (1st County Down Volunteers) in 108th Brigade of the 36th (Ulster) Division and he was killed in action on 6 August 1917 while holding the line at the beginning of the Third Battle of Ypres.

After Rifleman William James Gibson died his platoon officer Second-Lieutenant RW Craig wrote to Samuel Gibson to express sympathy and to assure him that his son's death had been instantaneous. On behalf of the whole family Samuel Gibson placed a 'For King and Country' notice in the *Newtownards Chronicle* and it contained the verse:

'A light is from our household gone,
The voice we loved now stilled;
A place is vacant in our home
Which never will be filled'
'Gone, but not forgotten'

William James Gibson's older brother Samuel was also on active service.

Rifleman William James Gibson is commemorated on Newtownards and District War Memorial and in the PCI Roll of Honour for Greenwell Street Presbyterian Church Newtownards.

G

Gilliland, Thomas
Rifleman
No. 18/171, 'A' Company, 13th Battalion, Royal Irish Rifles
Killed in action on Saturday 1 July 1916 (aged 19)
Thiepval Memorial, France (Pier and Face 15 A and 15 B)

Thomas Gilliland was just a baby when his father William died. His widowed mother Eliza Gilliland (nee McKee) worked as a seamstress and the family lived at 18 Wallace's Street No. 2, Newtownards. William and Eliza had at least seven children – Margaret Jane, John, Isabella, William, David, Hannah McMorran and Thomas. All but Thomas were baptised in Greenwell Street Presbyterian Church Newtownards.

PRISONER OF WAR.
Mrs. Gilliland, 18,· Wallace Street, No. 2, has been officially informed that her son, Rifleman T. Gilliland (N. 171), reported missing and wounded in our last issue, is now a prisoner of war at Dulmann Camp, Germany.

Thomas Gilliland enlisted in June 1915 in Belfast and he trained with the 18th Battalion Royal Irish Rifles before going to the front with the 13th Battalion in 108th Brigade of the 36th (Ulster) Division. He was killed in action on the first day of the Battle of the Somme. Initially it was reported that he was missing and wounded, then it was reported that he was a prisoner of war and finally it was confirmed that he had been killed.

Rifleman Thomas Gilliland is commemorated on Newtownards and District War Memorial and in the PCI Roll of Honour for Regent Street Presbyterian Church Newtownards.

Gilmore, Patrick
Private
No. 18805, 8th Battalion, Royal Dublin Fusiliers
Killed in action on Saturday 29 April 1916 (aged 31)
Loos Memorial, France (Panel 127 to 129)

Patrick Gilmore was born in Newtownards and he was a son of Michael and Susan Gilmore (nee McCormick) who lived at 26 Ann Street. They were married on 22 April 1882 in Newtownards Roman Catholic Church. Michael Gilmore worked as a gas fitter in Newtownards Gasworks and he and Susan had four children – Maggie, Patrick, John and James.

Prior to the outbreak of the Great War Patrick Gilmore worked as a linen lapper. He spent eleven years with the Ards Weaving Company and five years with the Bedford Street Weaving Company in Belfast. Whilst in Newtownards he was a member of the local swimming club.

G

Patrick Gilmore enlisted in Belfast and he served with the 8th Battalion Royal Dublin Fusiliers in 48th Brigade of the 16th (Irish) Division. He was killed in action on 29 April 1916 and at the time of his death his wife and family were living at 18 Belmont Avenue, Belfast. Private Patrick Gilmore is commemorated on Newtownards and District War Memorial.

Gilmour, Samuel
Private
No. 10405, 1st Battalion, Royal Irish Rifles transferred to (421490)
194th Company, Labour Corps
Killed in action on Thursday 11 October 1917 (aged 20)
Tyne Cot Memorial, Belgium (Panel 160 and 162A and 163A)

Samuel Gilmour was born in Edinburgh and he lived with his foster parents James and Mary Kerr at 27 George's Street, Newtownards. James Kerr worked as a general labourer and he and Mary had no children of their own. Samuel Gilmour also worked as a labourer.

Some four months before the outbreak of the Great War Samuel Gilmour

went to Belfast where he joined the 1st Battalion Royal Irish Rifles (10405) and he went to France on 19 January 1915. On 5 March 1917 Rifleman Samuel Gilmour suffered severe shrapnel wounds in both legs in action at Bouchavesnes and it was feared that his left leg would have to be amputated. However, after several months of nursing care in Netley Hospital and subsequently in the Mater and Victoria Barracks Hospitals in Belfast, his leg was saved but he was too severely incapacitated to resume service with the Royal Irish Rifles.

Samuel Gilmour joined the Labour Corps in September 1917 and he was immediately posted to the front. Less than a month later, Private Samuel Gilmour was killed in action. His foster mother and his two sisters, Annie Dodds and Agnes Gilmour, placed a 'For King and Country' notice in the *Newtownards Chronicle*. Private Samuel Gilmour is commemorated on Newtownards and District War Memorial and in the PCI Roll of Honour for Greenwell Street Presbyterian Church Newtownards.

G   In some newspaper reports the surname of Samuel Gilmour Labour Corps (421490) formerly Royal Irish Rifles (10405) is spelt Gilmore.

The names Samuel Gilmour and Samuel Gilmore are both listed on Newtownards and District War Memorial and in the booklet produced for the Unveiling and Dedication Ceremony held on Saturday 26 May 1934 Samuel Gilmour is described as a Private in the Labour Corps and Samuel Gilmore is described as a Rifleman in the Royal Irish Rifles. Desk searches and public appeals to date have not conclusively confirmed whether these two names on Newtownards and District War Memorial relate to the same person or to two different people.

Girvin, Thomas

The name Thomas Girvin is listed on Newtownards and District War Memorial and in the booklet produced for the Unveiling and Dedication Ceremony held on Saturday 26 May 1934 he is listed as Thomas Girvan and described as a Rifleman in the Royal Irish Rifles.

Thomas Girvin who enlisted on 29 September 1914 in Belfast stated that:

He was 34½ years old (he was in fact 37½ years old having been born on 3 March 1877), he was born in Newtownards, he was a Presbyterian, he was single and he was a labourer. He cited as his next-of-kin his mother Jane who lived at 7 Queen Street Newtownards. Thomas Girvin joined the 8th

Battalion Royal Irish Rifles (8/19518) but it transpired that he was wanted by the civil authorities. He was arrested and served one month in prison from 12 October 1914 until 11 November 1914. On release from prison he absented himself and he was apprehended again by the police 'for a misdemeanour'. He served a further term of imprisonment from 18 December 1914 until 17 February 1915. Thomas Girvin absented himself again and with no information available as to his whereabouts he was declared to be a deserter.

In September 1920 the military authorities wrote to Jane Girvin asking her for information about her son. The letter was returned marked 'deceased' and the military authorities referred the matter to the police in Belfast for investigation. The police provided the following information 'based on their enquiries': Thomas Girvin was dead; after deserting from the Royal Irish Rifles he had gone to Scotland, joined the Royal Scots Fusiliers in 1915 and he had drowned when the troopship taking him to the Dardanelles was torpedoed.

Then the military authorities asked the RIC in Belfast to determine Thomas's regimental number in the Royal Scots Fusiliers. The police in Belfast referred the case to RIC in Newtownards and officers there interviewed Thomas's father Henry Girvin. Henry Girvin made a statement saying that he believed his son to be dead. He told police that when Thomas went to Scotland he stayed with his aunt Eliza Burns at 6 John Street Lane off Main Street, Glasgow and that he joined the Scottish Rifles under the alias Thomas Coulter. Henry Girvin told police that some time previously he had received a letter from Eliza Burns informing him that Thomas had drowned when the troopship taking him to the Dardanelles was torpedoed. Eliza had said that she was told this by a comrade of Thomas's who had survived the torpedo attack. Henry told police that he had no papers relating to Thomas's enlistment in Scotland but he referred them to Patrick Burns – a son of the late Eliza Burns and Thomas's full cousin.

Military authorities wrote to Patrick Burns at 60 Franklin Street Bridgeton Glasgow and he furnished a copy of Thomas Girvin's birth certificate but could provide no documents relating to Thomas's service. Patrick Burns stated that Thomas had been serving as a fireman aboard the ship that was torpedoed and when Thomas signed up he had arranged for Eliza Burns to receive half of his pay on a regular basis.

Desk searches and public appeals to date have not confirmed that the Thomas Girvin described above is the Thomas Girvin who is listed on Newtownards and District War Memorial. No information has been found to confirm the death on active service of a Thomas Girvin or a Thomas Coulter who served in the Royal Scots Fusiliers, the Scottish Rifles (also known as the Cameronians), the Royal Navy or the Mercantile Marine.

Glendinning, Thomas
Rifleman
No. 10944, 'D' Company, 3rd Battalion, Royal Irish Rifles
Died on Thursday 21 July 1921 (aged 22)
Killysuggan Graveyard, Newtownards, Co. Down (Grave 1. 2. 23)

Thomas Glendinning was a son of John and Agnes Glendinning of Union Lane and before that Church Street, Newtownards. John Glendinning worked as a general labourer and he and Agnes had at least seven children – Rose Ann, Thomas, Margaret, Elizabeth, Agnes Mary, Eleanor and John.

Thomas Glendinning served as a Rifleman with the 3rd Battalion Royal Irish Rifles and he died on 21 July 1921. He is commemorated on Newtownards and District War Memorial and his headstone in Killysuggan Graveyard bears the inscription:

'On his soul sweet Jesus have mercy'

Glover, Alexander
Rifleman
No. 16/695, 16th Battalion, Royal Irish Rifles, transferred to (513447), 889th Area Employment Company, Labour Corps
Died of pneumonia on Sunday 9 February 1919 (aged 24)
Comber New Cemetery, Co. Down (Grave 5. 80)

Alexander Glover was a son of Alexander and Agnes Glover (nee Mullan) who lived in Castle Street, Comber. They were married on 22 November 1889 in Dundonald Presbyterian Church. Alexander Glover Senior worked as a car driver and he and Agnes had at least eleven children including Ruth, Alexander, Lizzie, John, Colville, Robert, George, Sarah and Fred.

Alexander Glover Junior worked as an oiler before he enlisted. He joined the 16th Battalion

Royal Irish Rifles and he went to France on 2 October 1915 with the 36th (Ulster) Division. He was wounded on 4 July 1916 and required surgery to his hand. He rejoined his battalion in August and the following year, after three periods of illness, he was transferred to the Labour Corps. He survived the war but died of pneumonia at home on 9 February 1919 and he is commemorated on Comber and District War Memorial and in First Comber Presbyterian Church.

Gordon, Samuel Heslip (Samuel)
Rifleman
No. 17733, 'B' Company, 13th Battalion, Royal Irish Rifles
Died of wounds on Monday 3 July 1916 (aged 28)
Puchevillers British Cemetery, France (Grave I. A. 26)

Samuel Heslip Gordon was born in the townland of Whitespots, Newtownards. By the age of thirteen he was working as a farm servant and he lived with his grandparents David and Sarah Dempster (nee McCreedy). They were married on 13 January 1863 in Newtownards Registry Office. After David Dempster died the family moved to 44 John Street, Newtownards. Samuel lived with his grandmother Sarah, his mother Elizabeth, his brother William and his sister Sarah. Prior to the outbreak of the Great War Samuel Gordon was a member of 'B' Company in the Newtownards contingent of the Ulster Volunteer Force and when he enlisted he served with the 13th Battalion Royal Irish Rifles in 108th Brigade of the 36th (Ulster) Division.

Newtownards Casualties.
DIED OF WOUNDS.
Rifleman S. H. Gordon (No. 17,733) is reported as having succumbed to wounds received in action. He enlisted on the 13th Royal Irish Rifles on the outbreak of the war, and had been with the Ulster Division throughout. He resided at John Street, and was a member of the local U.V.F. contingent.

On 3 July 1916 Rifleman Samuel Gordon died of wounds sustained on the first day of the Battle of the Somme and he is commemorated on Newtownards and District War Memorial and in Second Newtownards Presbyterian Church. In the CWGC Debt of Honour his initials are recorded as SM.

Gorman Brothers: Charles and James
Charles and James Gorman were born in Newtownards and they were

sons of Charles and Ann Gorman (nee Fairley) who were married on 26 September 1867 in Newtownards Registry Office. The Gorman family lived at 11 Windmill Row Newtownards and three brothers were on active service in the Great War. David served with the 3rd Battalion Royal Irish Rifles and survived. James was killed two weeks before his brother Charles was killed:

Gorman, James
Private
No. 911, 8th Battalion, Cameronians (Scottish Rifles)
Killed in action on Tuesday 10 October 1916 (aged 37)
Jerusalem Memorial, Israel (Panel 25)

In 'Soldiers Died in the Great War 1914 – 1919' it is recorded that James Gorman was born in Newtownards. He was born on 31 March 1879 and he was baptised in Greenwell Street Presbyterian Church. He enlisted in Glasgow, he served with the 8th Battalion Cameronians (Scottish Rifles) and he was killed in action on 10 October 1916.

Gorman, Charles
Rifleman
No. 7439, 1st Battalion, Royal Irish Rifles
Killed in action on Tuesday 24 October 1916 (aged 28)
Thiepval Memorial, France (Pier and Face 15 A and 15 B)

G

By the age of thirteen Charles Gorman was working as a news boy. He lived for a time in Glasgow, he enlisted in Belfast and he went to France with the 2nd Battalion Royal Irish Rifles on 27 August 1914. On 5 October 1914 he was admitted to No. 1 General Hospital in Boulogne with rheumatic fever and he was brought to England by hospital ship on 15 December 1914. When he returned to France he served with the 1st Battalion Royal Irish Rifles and he was killed in action between Gueudecourt and Le Transloy on 24 October 1916.

Rifleman Charles Gorman is commemorated on Newtownards and District War Memorial and both he and Private James Gorman are commemorated in the PCI Roll of Honour for Greenwell Street Presbyterian Church Newtownards.

Gourley, Samuel
Private
No. 6214, 25th Battalion, Australian Infantry, AIF
Died of pneumonia on Sunday 26 May 1918 (aged 26)
Vignacourt British Cemetery, France (Grave III. A. 11)

Samuel Gourley was a son of John and Agnes Gourley (nee Young) who lived in the townland of Ballyskeagh, Newtownards. They were married on 2 April 1869 in Castlereagh Presbyterian Church. John Gourley worked as an agricultural labourer and he and Agnes had at least six children including William, Robert, John, Elizabeth, Samuel and Hugh.

Like his father, Samuel Gourley worked as an agricultural labourer and he served for three months in the Ulster Volunteer Force before he moved to Australia. There he worked as a labourer before he enlisted in Brisbane, Queensland on 2 March 1916. In his attestation papers it is noted that he was 5 feet 9 inches tall and that he required dental treatment.

Private Samuel Gourley was hospitalised at Lytton Camp in Australia from 24 May until 25 October 1916. He boarded ship in Brisbane on 27 October and he reached Plymouth on 9 January 1917. He was in Bulford Hospital from 16 January until 12 March 1917 and he went to France on 24 April 1917. Private Samuel Gourley made his will on 7 June 1917 and his legatee was his brother Robert who lived in Cedar Street, Dunellan Estate, South Brisbane.

G

Private Samuel Gourley died of pneumonia in the 61ˢᵗ Casualty Clearing Station on 26 May 1918 and an inventory of his effects was made: one disc, one razor strop, one safety razor in case, one purse, one note case, one metal cigarette case, one pipe, one badge, one wallet, one tobacco pouch, one note book, letters and photos. At the time of Samuel's death his parents were living at 48 Vicarage Street, Belfast and he is commemorated in the Belfast Book of Honour (Page 224). He is also commemorated in the PCI Roll of Honour for Dundonald Presbyterian Church.

Gracey, A

The name A Gracey is listed along with that of John Gracey in the Roll of Sacrifice published in the 6 January 1917 edition of the *Newtownards Chronicle*. Desk searches and public appeals to date have yielded no further information.

Gracie, John (Johnnie)
Sergeant
No. 6573, 1st Battalion, Royal Irish Rifles
Killed in action on 26 October 1916 (aged 35)
Lonsdale Cemetery, France (Grave II. D. 20)

There is some variation in the spelling of John's surname: Gracey on Newtownards and District War Memorial and in some newspaper reports; Gracie in the CWGC Debt of Honour and in some other newspaper reports.

NEWTOWNARDS.
Killed.

Official word has been received that Sergeant John Gracey (No. 6,573), Royal North Downs, attached to the 1st Batt. R.I. Rifles, was killed in action on 26th October. He was a son of John Gracey, late of Greenwell Street, Newtownards, and was thirty-five years of age. Before he enlisted he was a collier in Scotland, and went to the front on December 26, 1914. He leaves behind a wife and five children, who reside in Glasgow. His brother, Andrew Gracey, resides at 81 Movilla Street, Newtownards.

John Gracie was a son of John Gracie who lived in Greenwell Street, Newtownards. Before he enlisted John Gracie Junior worked as a collier in Scotland and when he died on 26 October 1916 it was reported in the *Newtownards Chronicle* that he left a widow and five children living in Glasgow. He first went to the front on 26 December 1914.

Each year after Sergeant John Gracie died and close to the anniversary of his death various family members placed 'Our Heroes – In Memoriam' notices in the *Newtownards Chronicle*. These included his brother Andrew and his brother Joseph and sister-in-law Rachel who lived in Movilla Street, Newtownards. So too did his mother and his sisters Mary McNeilly and Maggie Davidson who lived in Mill Street, Bridgeton, Glasgow. One of the notices placed by his mother contained the verse:

'Often in the night time, when I hear the autumn breeze,
I think upon the bairn that played around my knees;
My bonnie brown-eyed laddie, who fought against the foe,
And died in France so gallantly, where now he lieth low;
But soon will come the happy time, when Jesus will unite,
And I shall see for evermore the boy who died for right.
Where no tears of a mother can drop on your grave;
In the red fields of France you are laid far away,
Still our tribute of love to your memory we pay.
Mourn not for me, my life is past,
You all loved me to the last;
Then haste to Christ, make no delay,

For no one knows their dying day.
Like ivy on the withered oak,
When all things else decay,
Your memory is as dear today
As at the hour you passed away.
We oft-times think of days gone by,
A shadow o'er our life is cast,
A dear one gone for ever.'

OUR HEROES—IN MEMORIAM.

GRACIE.—In loving remembrance of my dearly, beloved father, Sergeant John Gracie, who was killed in action between Oct. 23rd and 26th, 1916; also my dear mother, Mary Gracie, who died December 5th, 1909.

My grief the world can never know,
The thoughts of sadness that are mine;
As with the years I older grow
My heart for them will ever pine.

Sadly mourned by their loving Daughter,
23 Mill Street, MOLLIE.
Bridgeton,
Glasgow.

In 1919 his daughter Mollie placed an 'Our Heroes – In Memoriam' notice in the *Newtownards Chronicle* which also commemorated her mother who died on 5 December 1909. Sergeant John Gracie is commemorated on Newtownards and District War Memorial (as John Gracey).

Graham, James *

G

Rifleman
No. 12/6517, 12th Battalion, Royal Irish Rifles, transferred to (231684), 311th Home Service Works Company, Labour Corps
Died of inflammation on Sunday, 15 August 1920 (aged 52)
Newtownards (Movilla) Cemetery, Co. Down (Grave 3. 30)

James Graham and Elizabeth (Lizzie) Montgomery were married on 26 January 1890 in First Newtownards Presbyterian Church and they lived at 33 Balfour Place, Mark Street, Newtownards. They had at least six children including James, John Milliken, Mary Ann and Margaret. Four of their children died in infancy.

James Graham worked as a plasterer and he served with the 12th Battalion Royal Irish Rifles in 108th Brigade of the 36th (Ulster) Division before being transferred to the Labour Corps. He survived the war but died of inflammation on 15 August 1920 and he was buried the following day.

Grant, Samuel

Private
No. 424841, 29th Battalion, Canadian Infantry (British Columbia Regiment)
Died on Saturday 16 September 1916 (aged 34)
St. Sever Cemetery, France (Grave B. 19. 14)

Samuel Grant was born on 4 June 1882 and he was a son of Samuel and Jane Grant who lived in the townland of Ballyknockan, Ballygowan. Samuel Grant Senior worked as a corn miller and he and Jane had nine children – Samuel, Thomas, Robert, James, Lizzie, John, Annie, Mary and Jane. (John Grant served with the Royal Dublin Fusiliers and he was seriously wounded at Gallipoli in 1915. He was disabled for the rest of his life.)

Samuel Grant Junior worked as an assistant miller before he moved to Canada where he was employed as a railway foreman. He enlisted on 17 May 1915 at Portage la Prairie, Manitoba and in his attestation papers it was noted that he was 5 feet 6 inches tall. He declared his date of birth to be 4 June 1884. Private Samuel Grant died on 16 September 1916 and he is commemorated in Ballygowan Presbyterian Church and on the family grave headstone in Moneyreagh Non-Subscribing Presbyterian Church Graveyard. Samuel's mother Jane died on 12 March 1921 and his father Samuel died on 22 April 1929.

G

Gray, James
Guardsman
No. 14840, 2nd Battalion, Scots Guards
Killed in action on Tuesday 19 December 1916
A.I.F. Burial Ground, France (V. C. 30)

In 'Soldiers Died in the Great War 1914 – 1919' it is recorded that James Gray was born in Sorn, Ayrshire and in the CWGC Debt of Honour it is recorded that he was a son of William Gray who lived in the townland of Ballyvester, Donaghadee. James enlisted in Kilmarnock and he served with the 2nd Battalion Scots Guards. Guardsman James Gray was killed in action on 19 December 1916.

Gregg, Samuel John (Samuel)
Lance Corporal
No. 18/446, 10th Battalion, Royal Irish Rifles
Died of wounds on 29 May 1917 (aged 41)
Bailleul Communal Cemetery Extension (Nord), France (Grave III. B. 189)

Samuel John Gregg was born in Lurgan and he was a son of Allen and Rebecca Gregg who came to live in Newtownards. Prior to the outbreak of the Great War Samuel Gregg worked as a tailor. He and Margaret McFerran were married on 25 December 1895 in St Matthew's Church of Ireland Belfast. They had two sons, Alexander and William, and the Gregg family lived at 17 East Street, Newtownards. Samuel's son Alexander worked as a hairdresser.

Samuel Gregg served with the 10th Battalion Royal Irish Rifles in 107th Brigade of the 36th (Ulster) Division and he died of wounds on 29 May 1917. Alexander was 21 years old and William was nine years old when their father died. Lance Corporal Samuel Gregg is commemorated on Newtownards and District War Memorial and in Newtownards Parish Church of Ireland (St Mark).

G

Gregory Brothers: Albert Edward and William Charles

Albert Edward and William Charles Gregory were sons of William Charles and Esther Gregory (nee Robinson) who were married on 17 September 1890 in Toronto, Canada. William Charles and Esther Gregory had at least five children – Albert Edward, Ann Elizabeth and William Charles who were born in Donaghadee and baptised in Donaghadee Parish Church and then, after the Gregory family moved to England – Henry Ernest and Esther who were born and baptised in Kent. Albert Edward and William Charles served in the same regiment and both were killed in action on the same day:

Gregory, Albert Edward
Private
No. 9300, 2nd Battalion, Lincolnshire Regiment
Killed in action on Sunday 9 May 1915 (aged 21)
Ploegsteert Memorial, Belgium (Panel 3)

Albert Edward Gregory was born on 22 February 1894 in Donaghadee, he enlisted in London and he served with the 2nd Battalion Lincolnshire Regiment.

Gregory, William Charles
Lance Corporal
No. 8929, 2nd Battalion, Lincolnshire Regiment
Killed in action on Sunday 9 May 1915 (aged 23)
Ploegsteert Memorial, Belgium (Panel 3)

William Charles Gregory was born on 30 October 1892 in Donaghadee, he enlisted in London and he served with the 2nd Battalion Lincolnshire Regiment.

Private Albert Edward Gregory and Lance Corporal William Charles Gregory were both killed in action on 9 May 1915, the opening day of the Battle of Aubers Ridge. At the time of their deaths their parents were living in Bell Lane, Fenstanton, St Ives in Huntingdonshire

Gregory, James
Military Medal
Lance Corporal
No. 10991, 'C' Squadron, 4th (Queen's Own) Hussars
Died of wounds on Wednesday 10 April 1918 (aged 21)
St. Sever Cemetery Extension, France (Grave P. IX. J. 7B)

G

James Gregory was born on 1 February 1897 in George's Street, Newtownards and he was a son of Ellen Jane Gregory (nee Ferguson formerly McDowell and formerly Cairns). Around 1904 Ellen Jane married James Hutton and he, Ellen Jane and her two sons James and Hugh Gregory lived at 56 Chadolly Street, Belfast. James Hutton worked as a bricklayer and James Gregory worked as a message boy.

James Gregory enlisted in Belfast, he served with the Queen's Own Hussars and he was awarded the Military Medal. Lance Corporal James Gregory died of wounds in a military hospital on 10 April 1918 and he is commemorated on Newtownards and District War Memorial. His name, which was added later, is listed after those who died in the Second World War. James Gregory is also commemorated in the Belfast Book of Honour (Page 237). At the time of his death his mother was living at 11 Pound Street Newtownards.

During the Great War Lance Corporal James Gregory's brother Hugh served with the Royal Irish Fusiliers; he survived the war and died in 1961.

James Hutton (James Gregory's stepfather) served with the 150th Field Company Royal Engineers (64457) and he died on 2 October 1918, less than six months after James Gregory died. James Hutton was born in Belfast and he is commemorated in the Belfast Book of Honour (Page 237).

Griffin, Thomas
Lance Corporal
No. 57969, 36th (Ulster) Division Signalling Company, Royal Engineers
Killed in action on Thursday 28 March 1918
Pozieres Memorial, France (Panel 10 to 13)

Thomas Griffin was a son of the late Thomas Griffin and Mrs Hall of Dunmurry, Belfast. Thomas Jnr. and his wife lived at 16 Marguerette Terrace, Donaghadee. When Thomas was killed in action his wife was serving with the Women's Auxiliary Army Corps (WAAC). Following the heavy losses on the Western Front in 1916 there was concern about the reduced number of fighting soldiers in the British Army. It was concluded that too many men were doing so-called 'soft jobs' and it was decided to use women to replace men doing certain administrative jobs in Britain and France. These men could then be sent to fight at the front. In January 1917 the Government announced the establishment of the WAAC, a new voluntary service, and the plan was for these women to serve as clerks, telephonists, waitresses, cooks, and instructors in the use of gas masks.

Lance Corporal Thomas Griffin was killed in action on 28 March 1918 during the German 'Michael Offensive' and he is commemorated on Donaghadee and District War Memorial.

Griffiths, Thomas
The name Thomas Griffiths is listed on Newtownards and District War Memorial and in the booklet produced for the Unveiling and Dedication Ceremony held on Saturday 26 May 1934 he is described as a Sapper in the Royal Engineers. Desk searches and public appeals to date have yielded no further information.

G

Guiney, Thomas
Private
No. 2768, 'B' Company, 6th Battalion, Royal Irish Regiment
Killed in action on Saturday 9 September 1916 (aged 28)
Delville Wood Cemetery, France (Grave XXIII. G. 4)

Thomas Guiney was born in the townland of Ballyphilip, Portaferry and he was a son of Thomas and Eliza Jane Guiney. Eliza Jane Guiney worked as a seamstress and she and Thomas had four children – Elizabeth (died 10 February 1914), Mary Catherine, Thomas and Annie. Eliza Jane died on 2 August 1922.

Thomas Guiney Junior lived in Portaferry and he worked as a labourer. He was a member of the Irish National Volunteers before he enlisted in Newtownards. Private Thomas Guiney served with the 6th Battalion Royal Irish Regiment in 47th Brigade of the 16th (Irish) Division and he was killed in action on 9 September 1916 at Ginchy. He is commemorated on the family grave headstone in Ballyphilip Roman Catholic Graveyard Portaferry.

Newtownards Casualties.
Killed.
Private T. Guiney (No. 2,768), Royal Irish Regiment, is officially reported killed.

G

2768 PRIVATE
T. GUINEY
ROYAL IRISH REGIMENT
9TH SEPTEMBER 1916 AGE 28

Gunning, George Coulter
Rifleman
No. 6897, 2nd Battalion, Royal Irish Rifles
Died of wounds on Sunday 27 September 1914 (aged 28)
Terlincthun British Cemetery, France (X. A. B. 12)

KILLED IN ACTION.
GUNNING—Sept. 27th, 1914, died of wounds, at the Base Hospital, Angers, France, George Coulter Gunning, 2nd Batt. Royal Irish Rifles.
Deeply regretted by his sorrowing Wife,
ELIZABETH GUNNING.
Springvale, Ballywalter.

George Coulter Gunning was born in Newtownards and he and Elizabeth Brian were married on 17 January 1913 in Ballywalter Parish Church of Ireland. He was already on active service before the outbreak of the Great

War and he was posted to France where he died of wounds and tetanus at the Base Hospital in Angers on 27 September 1914. Five weeks later, on 1 November 1914, his daughter Georgina Elizabeth was born and she was baptised in Ballywalter Parish Church of Ireland.

George Coulter Gunning was a Bandsman and when he died his widow Elizabeth was living in the townland of Springvale, Ballywalter. He is commemorated on Ballywalter and District War Memorial and in Ballywalter Parish Church of Ireland (Holy Trinity).

Gunning, Walter
Lance Corporal
No. 18990, 'B' Company, 13th Battalion, Royal Irish Rifles
Killed in action on Saturday 1 July 1916 (aged 33)
Thiepval Memorial, France (Pier and Face 15 A and 15 B)

Walter Gunning was born on 21 December 1882 in Ballywalter and he was a son of Hugh and Mary Ann Gunning (nee Bowden). They were married on 13 March 1860 in Greyabbey Presbyterian Church. Hugh Gunning worked as a bootmaker and he and Mary Ann had fourteen children including Eliza Jane, William, Arthur (died aged 5 months), John, Annie, Robert, Charlotte Louisa, Walter, Angus (died aged 11 years) and Hugh Herbert (died aged 13 years). Walter Gunning was baptised in Ballywalter Presbyterian Church.

G

Walter Gunning and Mary Selina Sloan were married on 25 September 1908 in First Donaghadee Presbyterian Church. They lived in Ballywalter where Walter worked as a grocer and their son William, who was born on 1 September 1912, was baptised in Ballywalter Presbyterian Church. Walter's mother died on 14 March 1913 aged 71.

Walter Gunning enlisted in Ballywalter, he served with the 13th Battalion Royal Irish Rifles in 108th Brigade of the 36th (Ulster) Division and he was killed in action on the first day of the Battle of the Somme. Lance Corporal Walter Gunning is commemorated on Ballywalter and District War Memorial; in Ballywalter Presbyterian Church and in Ballywalter Masonic Lodge No. 386. He is also commemorated on the family grave headstone in Whitechurch Cemetery Ballywalter. His father died on 19 February 1920.

Gunning, William
Rifleman
No. 1462, 'B' Company, 13th Battalion, Royal Irish Rifles
Died of wounds on Saturday 24 March 1917 (aged 23)
Bailleul Communal Cemetery Extension (Nord), France (III. B. 24)

 William Gunning was born on 27 May 1893 in Newtownards and he was a son of David and Martha Gunning (nee Gray) who lived in Greenwell Street. They were married on 4 June 1877 in Newtownards Registry Office. David Gunning worked as a shoemaker and he and Martha had thirteen children including Charlotte, Charles, Thomas, David, William, Samuel, Martha and Sarah.

William Gunning and Sarah Jane Robinson were married on 28 June 1913 in Newtownards Parish Church of Ireland and they lived at 77 Movilla Street, Newtownards. Their daughter Sarah Ann Robinson Gunning was born in 1915. Shortly after the outbreak of war William enlisted in Belfast and he joined the 1st County Downs. He served with the 13th Battalion Royal Irish Rifles in 108th Brigade of the 36th (Ulster) Division and in January 1917 he was home from the front on ten days leave. On 26 March 1917 Sarah Jane was informed that her husband had been seriously wounded and the following day she received a telegram from the War Office informing her that he had died at 2nd Casualty Clearing Station in France at 2.00 am on 24 March.

Rifleman William Gunning's widow received letters of sympathy from his comrades and also from the Rev JR Beresford assuring her that William had passed away peacefully and that he had been buried with Church of England rites. She also received a letter of sympathy from Lieutenant **Max H Browne** who was killed in an accidental explosion a little over a year later on 21 June 1918. (Lieutenant Browne is commemorated on the War Memorial Plaque in Bangor Grammar School and in the Book of Honour *Remembering Their Sacrifice in the Great War – North Down*.)

Sarah Jane Gunning placed a 'For King and Country' notice in the 7 April 1917 edition of the *Newtownards Chronicle* and it contained the verse:

> *'Sleep on, dear husband, in a far-off land,*
> *In a grave I will never see;*
> *But as long as life and memory last*
> *I will remember thee'*

Rifleman William Gunning is commemorated on Newtownards and District War Memorial and in Newtownards Parish Church of Ireland (St Mark).

Haire, Francis (Frank)
Private
No. 622913, 1st Canadian Mounted Rifles Battalion, CEF
Killed in action on Wednesday 11 October 1916 (aged 23)
Vimy Memorial, France

Francis Haire was born on 22 June 1893 in Belfast and subsequently some members of the Haire family lived in Newtownards. Frank Haire moved to Canada where he worked as a mechanic before he enlisted on 16 September 1915 at Camp Hughes, Winnipeg. In his attestation papers it was noted that he was 5 feet 5 inches tall and he cited his brother James as his next-of-kin.

> **Killed.**
> Pte. Frank Haire, Canadian Mounted Rifles, was killed in action on the 11th ... He was a cousin of Mrs. Campbell, 33½, William Street, Newtownards.

Private Frank Haire served with the 1st Canadian Mounted Rifle Battalion and he was killed in action on 11 October 1916. His name is included in a Roll of Honour published on 4 November 1916 in the *Newtownards Chronicle*.

Hall, Charles William Henry (Charles)
Private
No. 8180, 2nd Battalion, North Staffordshire Regiment
Died on Friday 8 November 1918 (aged 29)
Nowshera Military Cemetery, India (Grave L. 27)
Delhi Memorial (India Gate), India (Face 23)

Charles William Henry Hall was born on 30 October 1889 in Donaghadee and he was a son of Charles and Louisa Hall. He was baptised in Donaghadee Parish Church of Ireland. Charles Hall served as a Drummer with the 2nd Battalion North Staffordshire Regiment and he died in India on 8 November 1918.

Hall, John
Private
No. 11300, 9th Battalion, Royal Inniskilling Fusiliers
Died of wounds on Sunday 23 December 1917 (aged 39)
Abbeville Communal Cemetery Extension, France (Grave III. G. 1)

> **COUNTY DOWN AND THE WAR.**
> **Newtownards-Inniskillinger Succumbs.**
> Private J. Hall (No. 11,300), R. Inniskilling Fusiliers, is officially reported to have died of wounds.

The death of Private John Hall was reported in the 2 February 1918 edition of the *Newtownards Chronicle* under the headline 'Newtownards-

H

Inniskillinger Succumbs'. Records show that John Hall was born in Newtownstewart, Co Tyrone and that he enlisted in Omagh. He served with the 9th Battalion Royal Inniskilling Fusiliers in 109th Brigade of the 36th (Ulster) Division and he died of wounds on 23 December 1917.

Hamill, Alexander
Rifleman
No. 17/322, 'A' Company, 13th Battalion, Royal Irish Rifles
Killed in action on Thursday 16 August 1917
Thiepval Memorial, France (Pier and Face 15 A and 15 B)

Alexander Hamill was born in Newtownards and he enlisted in Belfast. He served with the 13th Battalion Royal Irish Rifles in 108th Brigade of the 36th (Ulster) Division and he was killed in action on 16 August 1917 during the Battle of Langemarck.

Hamill, Patrick
Private
No. 13073, 6th Battalion, Princess Victoria's (Royal Irish Fusiliers)
Killed in action on Monday 9 August 1915
Helles Memorial, Gallipoli, Turkey (Panel 178 to 180)

Patrick Hamill was born in Newtownards and he served in the South African War. After the outbreak of the Great War he rejoined the colours in Belfast and served with the 6th Battalion Royal Irish Fusiliers in 31st Brigade of the 10th (Irish) Division. Private Patrick Hamill was killed in action at Gallipoli on 9 August 1915. His home address was 24 Alton Street, Belfast and he is commemorated in the Belfast Book of Honour (Page 244) where his rank is given as Lance Sergeant.

Hamilton, Archibald H (Archie)
Captain
13th Battalion, Royal Irish Rifles
Died on Saturday 4 November 1916 (aged 39)
Belfast City Cemetery (Grave C. 617)

Archibald H Hamilton was born in England and he was a son of Robert Hamilton who lived in London. He was a grandson of Robert Sinclair who was described in newspaper reports as a 'well-known engineer'. Archibald was educated at Shrewsbury School and he moved to Belfast where he worked

as a naval architect, serving his apprenticeship with Harland & Wolff. Later he became the director of a foundry and engineering company and he and his wife Gertrude lived in the townland of Carrigullian, Killinchy. Archie did much to promote yachting in Strangford Lough.

Archie Hamilton was a prominent member of the Ulster Volunteer Force and at the outbreak of war he received a commission in the 13th Battalion Royal Irish Rifles in 108th Brigade of the 36th (Ulster) Division. He was promoted to the rank of Captain in January 1915 before he had to be invalided home because of illness. He never recovered and he died on 4 November 1916. Military honours were accorded for his funeral to Belfast City Cemetery.

Captain Archie Hamilton is commemorated in Killinchy Parish Church of Ireland; in the Belfast Book of Honour (Page 244) and in Belfast Masonic Lodge No. 154.

Hamilton Brothers: George, Hans and Robert

George, Hans and Robert Hamilton were born in Donaghadee and they were sons of Robert and Margaret (Maggie) Hamilton (nee Maxwell) who lived in the townland of Hogstown and later at 30 Moat Street, Donaghadee. They were married on 7 April 1890 in Donaghadee Parish Church of Ireland. Robert Hamilton worked as a general labourer and he and Maggie had at least eight children – Eliza Jane, George, Hans, Robert, James, Maggie, Mary and Ernest. Hans and Robert were baptised in Donaghadee Parish Church of Ireland. George was the first of the three brothers to die, then Hans and then Robert:

Hamilton, George
Rifleman
No. 18/1088, 'A' Company, 12th Battalion, Royal Irish Rifles
Killed in action on Wednesday 7 March 1917 (aged 26)
St. Quentin Cabaret Military Cemetery, Belgium (Grave II. B. 8)

George Hamilton was the eldest son of Robert and Maggie Hamilton and at the time of the 1911 census he was aged 20. He worked as a general labourer before enlisting on 22 November 1915 in Donaghadee and serving with the 12th Battalion Royal Irish Rifles in 108th Brigade of the 36th (Ulster) Division. Rifleman George Hamilton was killed in action on 7 March 1917.

Hamilton, Hans
Rifleman
No. 18/998, 12th Battalion, Royal Irish Rifles
Killed in action on Sunday 12 August 1917 (aged 24)
Ypres (Menin Gate) Memorial, Belgium (Panel 40)

Hans Hamilton was born on 9 April 1893 and he was the second son of Robert and Maggie Hamilton. He worked as a general labourer before enlisting on 16 November 1915 in Belfast and serving with the 12th Battalion Royal Irish Rifles in 108th Brigade of the 36th (Ulster) Division. Rifleman Hans Hamilton was killed in action on 12 August 1917 during the Third Battle of Ypres.

Hamilton, Robert
Rifleman
No. 18/932, 12th Battalion, Royal Irish Rifles
Killed in action on Thursday 27 June 1918 (aged 22)
Premont British Cemetery, France (Grave IV. A. 26)

Robert Hamilton was born on 13 January 1896 and he was the third son of Robert and Maggie Hamilton. He worked as a general labourer before enlisting on 15 November 1915 in Belfast and serving with the 12th Battalion Royal Irish Rifles in 108th Brigade of the 36th (Ulster) Division. Rifleman Robert Hamilton was killed in action on 27 June 1918 during the German offensive that began in March.

Rifleman George Hamilton, Rifleman Hans Hamilton and Rifleman Robert Hamilton are all commemorated on Donaghadee and District War Memorial and in Donaghadee Parish Church of Ireland.

Hamilton, George
Sergeant
No. 330 Royal Irish Rifles, transferred to (398), 1st Garrison Battalion, Princess Victoria's (Royal Irish Fusiliers)
Died on Friday 24 December 1915
Grangegorman Military Cemetery, Co. Dublin (Grave CE. 607)

George Hamilton was born in Newtownards and he enlisted in Holywood. He served with the Royal Irish Rifles (330) before being transferred to the 1st Garrison Battalion Princess Victoria's (Royal Irish Fusiliers). Sergeant George Hamilton died in Wellington Barracks Dublin on 24 December 1915.

H

Hamilton, James
Private
No. 249365, 58th Battalion, Canadian Infantry (Central Ontario Regiment)
Killed in action on Wednesday 28 August 1918 (aged 23)
Vis-en-Artois British Cemetery, France (Grave X. A. 9)

James Hamilton was born on 15 July 1895 and he was the fourth son of Samuel and Margaret Hamilton (nee Kelly) of 'Mountstewart Lodge', Newtownards. They were married on 6 June 1884 in First Newtownards Presbyterian Church. Samuel Hamilton worked as a gardener's labourer and he and Margaret had at least eight children – John, Mary Ann, Samuel, William, Isabella, James, Margaret and Agnes Anna. Isabella died on 1 May 1892 aged 6 months and William died on 28 April 1903 aged 13 years. James Hamilton's mother Margaret died on 2 January 1913 and his father Samuel died on 22 February 1914.

James Hamilton worked as an office apprentice before he moved to Canada and there he worked as a policeman. James lived at 32 Brunswick Avenue, Toronto and he enlisted on 12 April 1916. It was noted in his attestation papers that he was 5 feet 11¼ inches tall and that he had scars on his forehead and on his right thumb. Vis-en-Artois is a village on the road between Arras and Cambrai and it was taken by the Canadian Corps on 27 August 1918. Private James Hamilton was killed in action there on 28 August 1918.

The Hamilton family burying ground is in Greyabbey Old Graveyard and in addition to the family members who are buried there James Hamilton is also remembered – *'Gone but not forgotten'*. He is commemorated on the Greyabbey and District War Memorial located on the outside wall of Greyabbey Parish Church of Ireland (St Saviour) and in the PCI Roll of Honour for Trinity Presbyterian Church Greyabbey.

Hamilton, John Irvine (John)
Rifleman
No. 14827, 9th Battalion, Royal Irish Rifles
Killed in action on Saturday 1 July 1916 (aged 21)
Thiepval Memorial, France (Pier and Face 15 A and 15 B)

John Irvine Hamilton was born on 14 April 1895 in Donaghadee and he was

H

a son of William and Lizzie Hamilton (nee Irvine) who lived at 9 Bow Street. They were married on 23 March 1892 in Greenwell Street Presbyterian Church Newtownards. William Hamilton worked as a bread server and he and Lizzie had at least seven children – Meta, John, Ernest, Ellen, Alexander, James and Agnes Irvine. Some of the children (including John) were baptised in Ballygrainey Presbyterian Church and others were baptised in Shore Street Presbyterian Church Donaghadee.

John Hamilton enlisted in Belfast, he served with the 9th Battalion Royal Irish Rifles in 107th Brigade of the 36th (Ulster) Division and he was killed in action on the first day of the Battle of the Somme.

Hamilton, Samuel

The name Samuel Hamilton, Canadian Expeditionary Force, is listed on the Memorial Plaque in Carrowdore Parish Church of Ireland (Christ Church) as one of those men from the Parish who gave their lives.

H

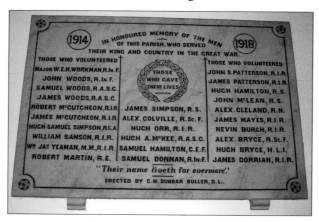

Only one Canadian casualty named Samuel Hamilton (788615) is listed in the CWGC Debt of Honour and on the Canadian Virtual War Memorial for the Great War. He was born in Glasgow. In the registers for Carrowdore Parish Church of Ireland there are two baptismal records for children named Samuel Hamilton:

- Samuel Hamilton born on 4 April 1881: his parents were Samuel and Ann Hamilton and they lived in the townland of Ballyblack; Samuel Hamilton and Ann Dickson were married on 28 May 1879 in Newtownards Parish Church of Ireland.

- Samuel Hamilton born on 22 November 1882: his parents were Hugh and Rose Anna Hamilton and they lived in the townland of Ballywhisken;

Hugh Hamilton and Rose Anna Orr were married on 7 June 1871 in Newtownards Registry Office.

The Canadian Expeditionary Force (CEF) database held by Library and Archives Canada lists twelve soldiers named Samuel Hamilton who served in the Great War. One of the attestation records correlates very well with the first of the two baptismal records in Carrowdore Parish Church of Ireland:

Samuel Hamilton (127313) who enlisted on 13 January 1915 at Galt, Ontario was born in the townland of Ballyblack, his father's name was Samuel and his declared date of birth was 5 April 1881. On the Coates family grave in Carrowdore Graveyard there is an inscription by 'James Hamilton in memory of his brother Samuel Hamilton who died at Galt, Ontario, Canada, 28th October 1918 aged 38 years'. Desk searches and public appeals to date have not confirmed a link between these data and the soldier who is commemorated on the Memorial Plaque in Carrowdore Parish Church of Ireland (Christ Church).

Hanna, John
Private

H

No. 10792, 1st Battalion, Royal Dublin Fusiliers
Killed in action on Tuesday 15 June 1915
Twelve Tree Copse Cemetery, Gallipoli, Turkey (Grave XI. E. 14)

John Hanna was born in Newtownards and he was a son of widowed Mary Hanna who lived with her daughters Sara and Maggie at 25 Front Shuttlefield (Robert Street), Newtownards. John enlisted in Newtownards and he served with the 1st Battalion Royal Dublin Fusiliers. He was killed in action at Gallipoli on 15 June 1915 and when he died a cheery letter that he had written to his mother was found in one of his pockets. This letter, in which he requested cigarettes, was sent on to her by Sergeant Kelly who informed her that John had been killed in action. At the same time she received official notification of his death.

OUR HEROES—IN MEMORIAM.

HANNA—In loving memory of Private John Hanna, 1st Royal Dublin Fusiliers, who was killed in action at Gallipoli, on 15th June, 1915.

"Greater love hath no man than this, that a man lay down his life for his friends."

Inserted by his sorrowing Mother and Sister.

25 Robert Street, Newtownards.

In June 1916 Private John Hanna's mother and sister placed an 'Our Heroes – In Memoriam' notice in the *Newtownards Chronicle* and it contained the text:

'Greater love hath no man than this, that a man lay down his life for his friends'

Private John Hanna is commemorated on Newtownards and District War Memorial and in the PCI Roll of Honour for Greenwell Street Presbyterian Church Newtownards.

Hanna, William
Sergeant
No. 8540, 1st Battalion, Royal Irish Rifles
Killed in action on Sunday 9 May 1915 (aged 32)
Ploegsteert Memorial, Belgium (Panel 9)

William Hanna was born in Cloughey and he and his mother Margaret lived in the townland of Ballyeasborough. Margaret Hanna worked as a seamstress and William worked as a farm servant before he joined the Army. William Hanna and Margaret Smyth were married on 3 August 1909 in Glastry Presbyterian Church and they lived in Shore Street Portaferry. Their son Francis Kitchener Hanna was born on 13 October 1914 and he was baptised three days later in Portaferry Presbyterian Church.

William Hanna served with the 1st Battalion Royal Irish Rifles and at one point he was hospitalised for eight weeks after being wounded in action in France. He returned to the Western Front and he was killed in action at Rouge Bancs on 9 May 1915. Sergeant William Hanna is commemorated in Glastry Presbyterian Church and in the PCI Roll of Honour for Portaferry Presbyterian Church.

Hare, John A
Lance Corporal
No. 17832, 'B' Company, 13th Battalion, Royal Irish Rifles
Killed in action on Thursday 16 August 1917 (aged 20)
Tyne Cot Memorial, Belgium (Panel 138 to 140 & 162 to 162A & 163A)

John Hare was born in Ballygowan and he was a son of James and Margaret Anna (Maggie) Hare (nee Snodden) who lived in Killinchy Street Comber. They were married on 10 July 1895 in Second Comber Presbyterian Church. James Hare worked as a labourer and he and Maggie had at least three children – Aggie, John and James.

John Hare enlisted in Comber and he served with the 13th Battalion Royal Irish Rifles in 108th Brigade of the 36th (Ulster) Division. He was killed in action at Langemarck during the Third Battle of Ypres.

266

Lance Corporal John Hare is commemorated on Comber and District War Memorial as John A Hare; on the Memorial Plaque in Second Comber Presbyterian Church as John Haire and in the PCI Roll of Honour for Second Comber Presbyterian Church as James Hare.

Hare, Joseph
Sapper
No. 64344, 150th Field Company, Royal Engineers, 36th (Ulster) Division
Died on Tuesday 29 May 1917
Bailleul Communal Cemetery Extension (Nord), France (Grave III. B. 182)

In 'Soldiers Died in the Great War 1914 – 1919' it is recorded that Joseph Hare was born in Comber and he enlisted in Belfast. He served with 150th Field Company Royal Engineers in the 36th (Ulster) Division and he died on 29 May 1917 during preparations for the Battle of Messines.

H

Harris, James (served as McIlwrath, James)
Rifleman
No. 13153, 8th Battalion, Royal Irish Rifles
Killed in action on Sunday 2 July 1916 (aged 21)
Thiepval Memorial, France (Pier and Face 15 A and 15 B)

James Harris who served as James McIlwrath was born in 1895 in Comber and he was a son of Robert and Susanna Harris (nee McIlwrath) who were married on 30 March 1891 in St Anne's Church of Ireland Belfast. Robert Harris worked as a general labourer and he and Susanna had at least two children – William and James. After their mother Susanna died William and James lived in Belfast with their maternal grandmother Jane McIlwrath and both worked as general labourers. Their father Robert Harris and Margaret Jane McClure were married on 10 September 1900 in Comber Parish Church of Ireland, they had at least five children including Christina and Lizzie. They lived in Bridge Street and later Railway Street, Comber.

James McIlwrath enlisted in Belfast and he served with the 8th Battalion

Royal Irish Rifles in 107th Brigade of the 36th (Ulster) Division. In the CWGC Debt of Honour it is recorded that Rifleman James McIlwrath died on the second day of the Battle of the Somme. In the heat of battle the 8th Battalion Royal Irish Rifles did not make a casualty return on 1 July 1916 and many military historians agree that those 8th Battalion casualties listed on the 2 July return were killed in action on 1 July. Rifleman James Harris alias McIlwrath is commemorated on Comber and District War Memorial and in Comber Parish Church of Ireland (St Mary).

Harris, Thomas
Lance Corporal
No. 9590, 'B' Company, 1st Battalion, Connaught Rangers
Killed in action on Monday 23 November 1914 (aged 26)
Le Touret Memorial, France (Panel 43)

H

Thomas Harris was born on 21 December 1887 in Newtownards and he was the fourth son of Thomas and Ellen Harris (nee Welsh) who lived at 142 Mill Street. They were married on 12 July 1879 in First Newtownards Presbyterian Church. Thomas Harris Senior worked as a general labourer and he and Ellen had seven children including Henry, James, Agnes, Thomas, Andrew and Edward.

Thomas Harris enlisted in Dundalk and he served with the 1st Battalion Connaught Rangers. Lance Corporal Thomas Harris was killed in action at Festubert in France on 23 November 1914 and he is commemorated on Newtownards and District War Memorial and in First Newtownards Presbyterian Church.

A year after his death his family placed an 'In Memoriam' notice in the *Newtownards Chronicle* and it contained the verse:

'No loved one stood around him
To hear his last farewell;
No parting kisses could he give
To those he loved so well.
We mourn the loss of our dear son,
So good, so kind, so brave;
Died on the battlefield of France,
Now lies in a hero's grave.'

Harrison, Robert Bell (Robert)
Lance Sergeant
No. 2249, 1st Battalion, Irish Guards
Died of wounds on Wednesday 19 May 1915 (aged 30)
Bethune Town Cemetery, France (Grave III. D. 87)

Robert Harrison was born on 29 September 1884 in Newtownards and he was a son of Robert and Margaret Ann (Maggie) Harrison (nee Black). They were married on 6 December 1877 in Newtownards Parish Church of Ireland. Robert Harrison Senior worked as a general labourer and he and Maggie had at least seven children – James, Robert, Isabella Jane, Annie, John, David and Mabel. All four brothers were on active service during the Great War.

Robert Harrison Junior worked as a plasterer and he enlisted in Newtownards. He served with the 1st Battalion Irish Guards and he died of wounds on 19 May 1915. Lance Sergeant Robert Harrison is commemorated on Newtownards and District War Memorial.

H

Harrison, Thomas James (Thomas)
Military Medal
Rifleman
No. 17838, 'B' Company, 13th Battalion, Royal Irish Rifles
Killed in action on Saturday 1 July 1916 (aged 27)
Thiepval Memorial, France (Pier and Face 15 A and 15 B)

Thomas James Harrison was the youngest son of Samuel and Grace Harrison (nee Armour) who lived at the Masonic Hall, Regent Street, Newtownards. They were married on 23 September 1869 in First Newtownards Presbyterian Church. Sam Harrison worked as a foreman for Newtownards Urban Council and he and Grace had at least ten children including Samuel, William John, Joseph Bradshaw, Thomas James, Elizabeth and Grace.

Immediately prior to the outbreak of the Great War Thomas Harrison worked in the Urban Council Gas Works. Before that he had worked in William Gill's quarries. Thomas Harrison was a member of the Ulster Volunteer Force and a member of Mill Street Heroes Loyal Orange Lodge No. 1908.

He enlisted shortly after war commenced and after completing his training he proceeded to France in October 1915 with the 13th Battalion Royal Irish Rifles in 108th Brigade of the 36th (Ulster) Division. In May 1916 Rifleman Thomas Harrrison was the first County Down Volunteer to be awarded a Military Medal for 'bravery in the field in carrying wounded comrades to safety'. At that time two of his brothers were also serving with the Royal Irish Rifles, William John in the 13th Battalion and Samuel in the 18th Battalion. Two of Thomas Harrison's nephews, James and Samuel Gordon, were also serving in the Army.

Rifleman Thomas Harrison did not live long enough to receive his Military Medal in person. After the first day of the Battle of the Somme he was posted as missing in action and a year later he was officially reported as having been killed in action.

On Friday 3 August 1917 Sam and Grace Harrison received the Military Medal on their son's behalf. Just over a month later, on 16 September 1917, Sam Harrison died at the age of 73 years. He carried out his duties with the Urban Council up until a few days before his death. Rifleman Thomas Harrison is commemorated on Newtownards and District War Memorial.

H

Harvey Brothers: David, John and Robert

David, John and Robert Harvey were born in Newtownards and they were sons of William and Mary Harvey (nee Service) who were married on 8 May 1866 in Newtownards Parish Church of Ireland. They lived at 9 Upper Movilla Street. William Harvey worked as a wool weaver and he and Mary had thirteen children including Robert, William, John, Edward, Susanna, George, Hugh, Margaret, David and Mary. John was the first of the three brothers to die, then David and then Robert:

Harvey, John (Jock)
Rifleman
No. 17790, 'B' Company, 13th Battalion, Royal Irish Rifles
Died of consumption on Sunday 31 December 1916 (aged 36)
Newtownards (Movilla) Cemetery, Co. Down (Grave 1. 279)

John Harvey worked as a house painter and decorator before the outbreak of the Great War and he and Martha McManus were married on 11 May 1906 in Second Newtownards Presbyterian Church. They lived at 77 Mark Street Newtownards and they had at least four children – David, William, John and Mary Eleanor. Aged 34, John Harvey enlisted on 17 September 1914 in Belfast and he joined the 13th Battalion Royal Irish Rifles. After training at

Clandeboye he went to England where he became ill and was hospitalised. He recovered and was posted to the 18th Battalion. He went to France on 22 November 1915 where he served with the 12th Battalion and again he became seriously ill. Suffering from pulmonary tuberculosis Jock Harvey was hospitalised in England and later in Forster Green Hospital Belfast. On 14 May 1916 he was discharged from the army because he was no longer fit for active service.

Ex-Rifleman John Harvey died of consumption on 31 December 1916 and on 2 January 1917 he was accorded a full military funeral. The coffin was wrapped in the Union Jack and the band of the 10th Royal Irish Fusiliers under Drum Major F May played funeral marches on the way to Movilla Cemetery. The services in the house and at the graveside were conducted by the Rev JAF Young of Second Newtownards Presbyterian Church. When the funeral cortege was passing along the Donaghadee Road a cow broke through the crowd, knocked several mourners to the ground and then galloped ahead of the procession. No-one was seriously injured.

Rifleman John Harvey is commemorated on Newtownards and District War Memorial and in Second Newtownards Presbyterian Church.

H

Harvey, David
Private
No. 241092, 1st/5th Battalion, Seaforth Highlanders (Ross-shire Buffs, the Duke of Albany's)
Killed in action on Saturday 22 September 1917 (aged 25)
Cement House Cemetery, Belgium (Grave XI. D. 22)

> HARVEY—In loving memory of David Harvey, 1/5th Seaforth Highlanders, youngest son of William and Mary Harvey, No. 9 Upper Movilla Street, Newtownards, killed in action in France on 22nd September, 1917.

Like his brother Jock, David Harvey worked as a house painter and decorator before the outbreak of the Great War. He enlisted in Belfast, he served with the Seaforth Highlanders (Ross-shire Buffs, the Duke of Albany's) and he was killed in action on 22 September 1917.

He is commemorated on Newtownards and District War Memorial and in the PCI Roll of Honour for Greenwell Street Presbyterian Church Newtownards.

Harvey, Robert
Rifleman
No. 18/976, 18th Battalion, Royal Irish Rifles, transferred to (275368)
Labour Corps
Died of influenza on Tuesday 12 November 1918 (aged 48)
Newtownards (Movilla) Cemetery, Co. Down (Grave 12. 89)

Robert Harvey worked as a wool weaver before the outbreak of the Great War and he and Mary Jane Boyce were married on 24 December 1903 in Greenwell Street Presbyterian Church Newtownards. They lived in Upper Movilla Street, Newtownards and they had at least five children two of whom died in infancy. The others were Thomas Boyce, Mary (Maria) and Jessie and they were baptised in Greenwell Street Presbyterian Church.

Robert Harvey served with the 18th Battalion Royal Irish Rifles before being transferred to the Labour Corps (275368). Robert Harvey was discharged from the army and he died of influenza on 12 November 1918. His daughter Maria died of pneumonia and she was buried in the same grave at the same time as her father.

Harvey, Thomas (see Simpson, Thomas)
Thomas Simpson from Comber served as Thomas Harvey.

Haselden, Cyril Gerrard
Captain
Royal Engineers attached Australian Corps HQ
Died on Wednesday 27 November 1918 (aged 40)
Maubeuge (Sous-le-Bois) Cemetery, France (Grave DD. 7)

The reason for including Captain Cyril Gerrard Haselden in this book is simply because there is an interesting connection with the Andrews family of Comber. His widow married James Andrews, the brother-in-law of Lieutenant Colonel **Lawrence Arthur Hind** who is commemorated on Comber and District War Memorial.

Cyril Gerrard Haselden was a son of Thomas and Emma Haselden of Bolton Lancashire, he served with the Royal Engineers and he died on 27 November

MARRIAGE.

ANDREWS—HASELDEN—May 17th, 1922, at Spettisbury Church, near Blandford, Dorset, by the Rev. Arthur Field, M.A., James Andrews, Lord Justice of Appeal for Northern Ireland, third son of the late Right Honourable Thomas Andrews, D.L., and Mrs. Andrews, Ardara, Comber, to Jane Lawson Haselden, widow of Captain Cyril Herard Haselden R.E., of Spettisbury, and daughter of the late Joseph Ormrod and Mrs. Ormrod, of Bolton, and Lytham, Lancashire.

1918. On 17 May 1922 his widow Jane Lawson Haselden (nee Ormrod) and James Andrews who was Lord Justice of Appeal in Northern Ireland were married in Spetisbury Church, Blandford, Dorset. James and Jane Andrews lived at 'Eusemere', Comber.

Hawthorne, Albert
Rifleman
No. 2534, 12th Battalion, Royal Irish Rifles
Killed in action on Monday 2 September 1918 (aged 24)
Messines Ridge British Cemetery, Belgium (Grave I. C. 41)

Albert Hawthorne was born in the townland of Magheragall, Lisburn and he was a son of William and Eliza Ann Hawthorne (nee Dixon). They were married on 10 October 1869 in Magheragall Parish Church of Ireland. William Hawthorne worked as a corn miller and he and Eliza Ann had at least twelve children. Albert Hawthorne worked as a farm labourer before he enlisted in Lisburn. He served with the 12th Battalion Royal Irish Rifles in 108th Brigade of the 36th (Ulster) Division and he was killed in action on 2 September 1918 during the Allied offensive against all sections of the German line.

H

Newtownards Losses.—News has been received by Mr. T. Johnston, 18 Church Street, Newtownards, that his son, Sapper R. Johnston, Royal Engineers, who had been admitted to hospital in Boulogne suffering from severe gas poisoning, is now in hospital in England. Mrs. Alice Robinson, 3 Castle Place, Newtownards, has been officialy notified that her son, Rifleman David Robinson, who was reported missing since 24th March, 1918, is now regarded as having been killed on that date. It is officially intimated that Rifleman Albert Hawthorne has been killed in action. He is a brother of Mr. Samuel Hawthorne, 135 Mill Street, Newtownards, and was a son of the late Mr. Wm. Hawthorne, Magheragall, Lisburn.

Albert Hawthorne's brother Samuel lived at 135 Mill Street, Newtownards and he also worked as a corn miller. Their father died before Albert was killed in action and it was Samuel who was informed of Albert's death. This was reported in the *Newtownards Chronicle* under the headline 'Newtownards Losses'. Rifleman Albert Hawthorne is commemorated in Lisburn's Dead 1914 – 1919 (Friends' School Lisburn WW1 Research Project).

Healy, James
Private
No. 5154, 2nd Battalion, Royal Munster Fusiliers
Killed in action on Thursday 27 April 1916
Bully-Grenay Communal Cemetery, French Extension, France (Grave A. 81)

In some records and newspaper reports the surname is spelt Healey.

James Healy was born in Killyleagh and his sister Mrs Annabel McBratney lived at 28 Brownlow Street, Comber. Private Healy enlisted in Downpatrick and in 'Soldiers Died in the Great War 1914 – 1919' it is recorded that he served with the Royal Inniskilling Fusiliers (16984) before being transferred to the 2nd Battalion Royal Munster Fusiliers. He was killed in action on 27 April 1916 and just nine days later his nephew **John Henry McBratney** was also killed in action.

H

Heaney, Robert
Rifleman
No. 20/330, Royal Irish Rifles transferred to London Regiment (London Irish Rifles)
Killed in action on Friday 6 September 1918 (aged 18)
Peronne Communal Cemetery Extension, France (Grave V. H. 1)

There is some variation between CWGC Debt of Honour records and 'Soldiers Died in the Great War 1914 – 1919' records concerning Robert Heaney's service details. According to 'Soldiers Died' Robert Heaney enlisted in Londonderry and he served with the Royal Inniskilling Fusiliers (29464) before being posted to the 1st/18th London Regiment (London Irish Rifles).

Robert Heaney was born in 1900 in Drumachose, Limavady, Co Londonderry and he was a son of Matilda Heaney who worked as a linen weaver. They lived with Matilda's parents Joseph and Margaret Ann Heaney (nee Anderson) in Isle of Man Street, Limavady. Joseph and Margaret Ann were married on 1 August 1876 in Drumachose Parish Church of Ireland. Robert's grandfather Joseph Heaney worked as a hairdresser and he and Margaret had six children. Matilda Heaney, Robert's mother, married Peter Rogers on 1 June 1905 in Drumachose Parish Church of Ireland and they had at least four children including Thomas and William.

Newtownards Rifleman Killed in Action.

Mrs. Martha Heaney, 77 Mark Street, Newtownards, has received official intimation from the War Office that her husband (No. 330) Rifleman Robert Heaney, Royal Irish Rifles (London Regiment), was killed in action in France on 6th September, 1918. He was previously wounded in the arm.

Robert Heaney and Martha Crawford were married on 18 March 1918 in Newtownards Parish Church of Ireland and they lived at 77 Mark Street, Newtownards. Wounded in the arm on a previous occasion Rifleman Robert Heaney was killed in action on 6 September 1918, less than six months after he was married. Robert's widow subsequently remarried and as Martha Rush she lived at 7 Stanley Cottages, Elm Road, Hook in Surrey.

Rifleman Robert Heaney is commemorated on Newtownards and District War Memorial and in Newtownards Parish Church of Ireland (St Mark) and he provides an example of a soldier who probably enlisted when he was underage. In the CWGC Debt of Honour his age is recorded as 21. In the 1901 census his age is recorded as 8 months and so he was 18 years old when he died.

Henderson, Robert
Rifleman
No. 2587, 2nd Battalion, Royal Irish Rifles
Killed in action in France on Friday 7 July 1916 (aged 34)
Thiepval Memorial, France (Pier and Face 15 A and 15 B)

H

Robert Henderson was born in Newtownards and he was a son of James and Ann Henderson (nee McCormick) who lived in Mill Street. They were married on 20 May 1871 in Fourth Newtownards Presbyterian Church. James Henderson worked as a general labourer and he and Ann had at least eight children including John, Robert, Henry and Samuel.

Robert Henderson worked as general labourer and he married Prudence Clarke on 13 July 1903 in Greenwell Street Presbyterian Church Newtownards. Robert and Prudence had two children – Sarah born on 20 September 1904 and James born on 3 December 1905. Both were baptised in Greenwell Street Presbyterian Church. After his wife died Robert lived with his parents in Mill Street and the two children lived in Queen Street with Sarah Clarke their maternal grandmother.

KILLED.

Rifleman Robert Henderson, 2nd Batt. Royal Irish Rifles, is officially reported to have been killed in action on 7th July. He joined the regular army about 18 months ago, and his mother-in-law, Mrs. Clarke, resides in Queen Street.

Robert Henderson enlisted in Newtownards and he served with the 2nd Battalion Royal Irish Rifles. He was killed in action on 7 July 1916 during the Battle of the Somme while the

Battalion was holding a section of the front line captured from the enemy. Rifleman Robert Henderson is commemorated on Newtownards and District War Memorial and in Newtownards Parish Church of Ireland (St Mark).

Hendley, Vincent
Private
No. 20813, 7th/8th Battalion, Princess Victoria's (Royal Irish Fusiliers)
Killed in action on Thursday 16 August 1917 (aged 20)
Tyne Cot Memorial, Belgium (Panel 140 to 141)

Vincent Hendley was born in Newtownards and he was a son of James and Margaret Hendley who moved to Belfast where they lived first in Rosapenna Street and later in Rosevale Street. Originally from County Cork, James Hendley worked as an insurance agent after he retired from the army. He and Margaret had at least eleven children including Edward, James, Cyril, Violet, Lewis, Vincent, Winifred, Mary and John.

Vincent Hendley enlisted in Belfast and when he died he was serving with the 7th/8th Battalion Royal Irish Fusiliers in 49th Brigade of the 16th (Irish) Division (the 7th and 8th Battalions were amalgamated in October 1916). He was killed in action on 16 August 1917 at Langemarck during the Third Battle of Ypres and at the time of his death his parents were living in Glenaan, Cushendall, Co Antrim.

Heron, Andrew
Sergeant
No. 4/7271, 4th Battalion, Royal Irish Rifles
Died of Bright's disease on Friday 15 September 1916 (aged 48)
Newtownards (Movilla) Cemetery, Co. Down (Grave 9. 111)

Andrew Heron enlisted on 20 November 1885 and he served with the Liverpool Regiment before being transferred in April 1889 to the 1st Battalion Royal Irish Rifles. Andrew went to the Army Reserve in 1892 and he rejoined the Royal Irish Rifles in 1900. He fought in the South African War and was awarded the Queen's South Africa Medal with two clasps and the King's South Africa Medal with one clasp. His service record was 'exemplary'. Andrew was discharged from the Army in 1902 and he worked as a publican and spirit merchant.

Andrew Heron and Elizabeth Ritchie were married on 16 March 1910 in First Donaghadee Presbyterian Church and they lived at 40 Frances Street, Newtownards. They had at least four children including David, Andrew, Archibald and Elizabeth.

Prior to the outbreak of the Great War Andrew Heron had around 17 years of service in the army. On 16 September 1914 he re-enlisted in Holywood and he served with the 4th Battalion Royal Irish Rifles at home until he was discharged on 31 December 1915 as being no longer physically fit for war service. He was suffering from valvular disease of the heart (VDH). He was ill for some months before he died of Bright's disease (kidney disease) on 15 September 1916.

> **THANKS.**
>
> Mrs. HERON and FAMILY desire to express their gratitude to the Officers Commanding 10th Royal Irish Fusiliers and 20th Royal Irish Rifles for the excellent military arrangements for the funeral of her late husband; also the many friends who sent floral tributes, including the Sergeants of the 4th Royal Irish Rifles (Royal North Downs). They hope this notice will be accepted as an acknowledgment of their sincere appreciation.
> 40, Frances Street,
> Newtownards.

Andrew Heron's funeral was accorded military honours and the brass band of the 10th Royal Irish Fusiliers under Bandmaster F May preceded the funeral cortege. His coffin was covered with the Union Jack and the mourners included representatives from the Masonic and Orange Orders. A firing party furnished by the 20th Battalion Royal Irish Rifles fired the customary three volleys over his open grave.

Amongst the mourners were Andrew's brothers James, John, David and Alex. Sergeant Andrew Heron is commemorated on Newtownards and District War Memorial; in Newtownards Parish Church of Ireland (St Mark) and in Newtownards Masonic Lodge No. 198.

Heron, James
Rifleman
No. 7153, 2nd Battalion, Royal Irish Rifles
Killed in action on Wednesday 16 June 1915 (aged 26)
Ypres (Menin Gate) Memorial, Belgium (Panel 40)

James Heron was born in Newtownards and he was a son of William John and Mary Heron who lived at 24 West Street. William John Heron worked as a carter and he and Mary had at least four children – Willie, Nellie, Thomas and James.

James Heron enlisted in Newtownards and he served

with the 2nd Battalion Royal Irish Rifles. Rifleman James Heron was killed in action on 16 June 1915 during an attack on Bellewaarde Spur and he is commemorated on Newtownards and District War Memorial.

Hewitt, Robert
Private
No. 235130, 44th Battalion, Canadian Infantry (New Brunswick Regiment)
Killed in action on Friday 27 September 1918 (aged 29)
Vimy Memorial, France

Robert Hewitt was born on 14 July 1889 and when he moved to Canada he worked as a teamster. He enlisted on 29 May 1916 in Winnipeg, Manitoba and in his attestation papers it was noted that he was 5 feet 9 inches tall and he cited his mother Florence Hewitt as his next-of-kin.

Private Robert Hewitt served with the 44th Battalion Canadian Infantry (New Brunswick Regiment) and he was killed in action on 27 September 1918 during the Allied offensive against all sections of the German line. He is commemorated in the PCI Roll of Honour for Killinchy Presbyterian Church.

H

Hiles, Hector
Stoker First Class
No. SS/109881, HMS *Goliath*, Royal Navy
Killed in action on Thursday 13 May 1915 (aged 35)
Chatham Naval Memorial, Kent, England (Panel 11)

Hector Hiles was a son of Thomas Hamilton Hiles and Anna Maria Hiles (nee Carson) who lived in Mill Street, Comber. They were married on 28 January 1865 in Newtownards Registry Office. Thomas Hiles worked in the Comber Spinning Company for over fifty years and he and Maria had at least four children – Ellen, Agnes, Thomas George and Hector. Maria Hiles died in the early 1900s.

Before he joined the Royal Navy Hector Hiles worked as a railway engine cleaner. He and Cassandra Catherine Crossen were married on 28 September 1907 in Dundela Presbyterian Church and they lived at 48 Derwent Street, Newtownards Road, Belfast. Stoker First Class Hector Hiles was killed in action when HMS *Goliath* was torpedoed by a Turkish destroyer in the

Dardanelles during the early hours of 13 May 1915. Of the 750 men on board 570 were lost.

Hector Hiles was known to be a fine swimmer and initial reports suggested that he might be amongst those who had been saved. Hopes were dashed when it was officially confirmed that he had died. Stoker First Class Hector Hiles was one of three men with Ards connections who were killed aboard HMS *Goliath*. The others lost that night were Boy First Class **Alfred Henry Victor Gadd** and Stoker First Class **Willie Beringer**.

Stoker First Class Hector Hiles is commemorated on Comber and District War Memorial; on the Memorial Plaque in Comber Parish Church of Ireland (St Mary); in the PCI Roll of Honour for Megain Memorial Presbyterian Church Belfast and in the Belfast Book of Honour (Page 268).

Hill, Charles Francis (Charles)
Rifleman
No. 17876, 'C' Company, 13th Battalion, Royal Irish Rifles
Killed in action on Wednesday 10 May 1916 (aged 18)
Authuile Military Cemetery, France (Grave A. 12)

H

Charles Francis Hill was born in Saintfield and he was a son of Charles Hill and a stepson of Catherine Hill who lived in the townland of Ravara, Ballygowan. Like his father, Charles Francis Hill worked as a farm labourer and his older brother John worked as a general dealer. John Hill planned to enlist but was unable to do so after he lost an arm in a threshing machine accident.

Charles Francis Hill enlisted in Comber, he trained at Clandeboye and he served with the 13th Battalion Royal Irish Rifles in 108th Brigade of the 36th (Ulster) Division. He was killed by shellfire during the night of 10/11 May 1916 and he is commemorated in Ballygowan Presbyterian Church.

Hill, Ernest Ludgate (Ernest)
Private
No. 5048, 26th Battalion, Australian Infantry, AIF
Killed in action on Tuesday 14 November 1916 (aged 18)
Villers-Bretonneux Memorial, France

Ernest Ludgate Hill was born in the first quarter of 1898 and he was the second son of Marshall and Sarah Louisa Hill (nee Ludgate) both of whom worked as National School Teachers in Greyabbey. They were married on 24 December 1894 in Greyabbey Parish Church of Ireland. Marshall and Sarah Hill had at least seven children – Arthur, Ernest, Edgar, Thomas Jeffrey, Evelyn Mary, Vera Kathleen and Doris Ellinor Louisa. Doris was born in 1915, the year before Ernest died. All except Ernest were baptised in Greyabbey Parish Church of Ireland.

Ernest Hill moved to New South Wales in Australia where he worked on a sheep station. He enlisted on 2 February 1916 at Lismore and it was recorded in his attestation papers that he was 21 years 1 month old, he was 5 feet 9⅞ inches tall and he weighed 147 lbs. Ernest Ludgate Hill had exaggerated his age; he was 18 years old when he enlisted.

After initial training he proceeded with his unit to England and he was granted a short period of home leave. He arrived in Belfast late one night, walked to Greyabbey and had to be back on board ship early the following day. That was the last time that his family saw him. Private Hill was sent to France and he went to the front on 3 October 1916. On 18 November 1916 he was posted as missing in action and it was noted on his service record that he was being held as a prisoner of war at Limburg. Later this note was amended when it was confirmed that he had been killed in action on 14 November 1916.

Some time later his family received a few of Ernest's personal effects from a German soldier who forwarded them after Ernest died. The German soldier whose forename was Ernst had come upon Ernest's body on the battlefield and had recovered the items from the pockets of Ernest's uniform. Private Ernest Ludgate Hill is commemorated on Greyabbey and District War Memorial located on the outside wall of Greyabbey Parish Church of Ireland (St Saviour) and on family grave headstones in both Bangor New Cemetery and Greyabbey Old Graveyard.

Hind, Lawrence Arthur (Lawrie)
Military Cross
Mentioned in Despatches (twice)
Lieutenant Colonel
1st/7th Battalion, Sherwood Foresters, (Nottinghamshire and Derbyshire Regiment)
Killed in action on Saturday 1 July 1916 (aged 38)
Thiepval Memorial, France (Pier and Face 10 C 10 D and 11 A)

Lawrence Arthur Hind was the third son of Jesse and Eliza Hind and he was born on 18 October 1877 in Edwalton, Nottingham. Jesse and Eliza Hind had at least five children – Oliver Watts, Harold, Lawrence Arthur, Ethel and Edith. A solicitor by profession (he obtained his law degree at Trinity Hall Cambridge where he was also middleweight boxing champion) Lawrie Hind worked in the family law firm of Messrs Wells & Hind before he joined the Army. He was appointed Lieutenant in the Robin Hood Rifles on 16 February 1901, promoted to the rank of Captain on 4 February 1903 and in 1914 he was appointed Captain in the 7th (Robin Hood) Battalion of the Sherwood Foresters. Promoted to the rank of Major in 1915 he obtained a field commission and became temporary Lieutenant Colonel on 25 July 1915. His Trench Diary for this period has been preserved.

H

Lawrie Hind and Eliza Montgomery (Nina) Andrews were married in the Unitarian Church Comber on Thursday 26 April 1906 at 1.30 pm. Nina Andrews was a daughter of the Right Honourable Thomas Andrews DL of 'Ardara', Comber. Thomas and Eliza Andrews (nee Pirrie and sister of Lord Pirrie, principal owner of Harland & Wolff) had at least five children – John Miller (who became Prime Minister of Northern Ireland), Thomas (who became Managing Director of Harland & Wolff and Head Designer of RMS *Titanic* and who died when the ship sank on 14 April 1912), Eliza Montgomery (Nina), James (who became Lord Justice of Appeal for Northern Ireland) and William.

There were more than 300 guests at Lawrie and Nina's wedding and the reception was held in the grounds of 'Ardara' in a large marquee with a polished wooden floor. The menu included Soup, Mayonnaise of Salmon, Prawns in Aspic, Chicken Patties, Game Pie, Bechamel Chicken, Roast Lamb, Spring Chicken, Pressed Beef, Limerick Ham, Ox Tongue and Lobster Salad followed by Trifle, Pineapple Cream, Pistachio Cream, Fruit Jellies,

Meringues and Ices. Lawrie and Nina Hind went to live in Ruddington and they had three daughters – Eileen, Edith and Doreen.

Lieutenant Colonel Hind was wounded in the head at Zouave Wood, Hooge on 31 July 1915. He recovered and it was on Saturday 1 July 1916 at the Battle of the Somme that he was killed in action. He was killed at Gommecourt when he was shot in the head by a German sniper.

The 7th Battalion War Diary covering 1 July 1916 indicates that the Battalion was in trenches and that they were ordered to attack enemy trenches in five waves commencing at 7.30 am. It was during this action that Major (Temporary Lieutenant Colonel) Hind was reported 'missing believed killed'. Afterwards the Hind family sought clarification as to the circumstances of his death and they received the following details:

'Major Hind was in command and was making a charge. Private Tomlinson was detailed to attend upon his Major and he did so. During the charge the Battalion was pretty severely punished but all went well with Major Hind until he and Tomlinson were within fifty yards of the German trenches when they were held up owing to the wire entanglements not having been completely swept away by the Artillery fire. Major Hind and Tomlinson lay down flat side by side. In a few minutes the Major raised himself on his hands and knees to look for a place in the entanglements where he could get through and when he was in that position he was shot through the forehead and immediately dropped. Tomlinson lay still and spoke to him and touched him but he was satisfied that death was instantaneous.' Private Tomlinson was injured but he escaped after nightfall.

Lieutenant Colonel Hind is commemorated on the War Memorials in Edwalton Parish Church of England where he grew up; Ruddington where he lived after he and Nina were married; Uppingham Public School and Trinity Hall Cambridge where he was educated; Comber where his wife's family lived and Comber Unitarian Church where he was married.

Lieutenant Colonel Hind's widow unveiled the Memorial Tablet in Comber Non-Subscribing Presbyterian Church on Sunday 23 April 1922 and she also unveiled the Comber and District War Memorial on 14 April 1923.

Hogan, John
Leading Boatman
No. 194182 (Dev), Tara War Signal Station, Royal Navy
Died of illness on Sunday 20 September 1914 (aged 35)
Portaferry Roman Catholic Churchyard (Near South Boundary)

John Hogan was a son of John and Ellen Hogan and he and his wife Catherine (nee O'Connell) lived at Derry Cottages, Portaferry. John Hogan worked as a seaman before he joined the Royal Navy and he and Catherine had at least three children – William (1906), Mary Ellen (1913) and Kathleen who was born after her father died. She was baptised on 9 January 1915.

Leading Boatman John Hogan was stationed at Tara War Signal Station, Portaferry where he monitored shipping and he died of illness on 20 September 1914. He was buried in Portaferry Roman Catholic Churchyard and he is commemorated there on the family grave headstone.

Holland, James
Lance Corporal
No. A/189, 8th Battalion, King's Royal Rifle Corps
Killed in action on Tuesday 3 August 1915 (aged 20)
Ypres (Menin Gate) Memorial, Belgium (Panel 51 and 53)

James Holland was born in Greyabbey and he was the second son of William and Lizzie Holland (nee Regan). They were married on 25 July 1886 in St Mary's Star of the Sea Roman Catholic Church at Nunsquarter, Kircubbin. William Holland worked as a silk weaver and he and Lizzie had at least four children including Eliza Anne and James. His mother Lizzie died while James was a young child and later he moved to Llanelli in Wales where he was employed in the tinplate works.

H

James enlisted in Llanelli and he served with the 8th Battalion King's Royal Rifle Corps. Lance Corporal James Holland was wounded by shellfire and after a period in hospital he returned to the firing line in July 1915. Two weeks later, on 3 August 1915, he was killed in action and it was reported at the time that his death was instantaneous. In August 1916 his father, brother and sisters placed an 'Our Heroes – In Memoriam' notice in the *Newtownards Chronicle* and it contained the verse:

'His warfare o'er, his battle fought;
His victory won, though dearly bought;
He fought so well, he was so brave,
His soul at rest in a soldier's grave'

Lance Corporal James Holland is commemorated on Greyabbey and District War Memorial located on the outside wall of Greyabbey Parish Church of

Ireland (St Saviour) and on the family grave headstone in Greyabbey Old Graveyard.

Horner, Thomas Martin (Tom)
Rifleman
No. 18/1073, 8th Battalion, Royal Irish Rifles
Killed in action on Thursday 5 April 1917 (aged 19)
Pond Farm Cemetery, Belgium (Grave M. 15)

There is substantial evidence to support the conclusion that Thomas Martin Horner had a connection with 'Killinchy Woods Crossgar' rather than with 'Killinchy'. In both 'Ireland's Memorial Records 1914 – 1918' and 'Soldiers Died in the Great War 1914 – 1919' Tom's surname is spelt Homer and he is listed as having been born in Killinchy. In the CWGC Debt of Honour Tom's surname is spelt Horner and he is described as the son of Elizabeth Homer of Killinchy Woods Crossgar. In newspaper reports Tom is described as the eldest son of Thomas Horner and the address given is Killinchy Woods, Crossgar.

H

> **Killinchy Woods Rifleman Killed.**
> Mr. Thos. Horner, Killinchy Woods, Crossgar, has received intimation that his eldest son, Rifleman Thos. Martin Horner, Royal Irish Rifles, was killed in action on 8th April.

Thomas Martin Horner was the eldest son of Thomas and Elizabeth Horner who lived in the townland of Barnamaghery, Derryboye. Thomas Horner Senior worked as an agricultural labourer and he and Lizzie had at least six children – Tom, John, Robert, Maggie, David and Agnes.

Tom Horner enlisted at Clandeboye and he served with the 8th Battalion Royal Irish Rifles in 107th Brigade of the 36th (Ulster) Division. Rifleman Tom Horner was killed in action on 5 April 1917 and at the time of his death his parents were living in Killinchy Woods Crossgar.

Houston, Hugh Crouch (Hugh)
Driver
No. L/306, 'C' Battery, 64th Brigade, Royal Field Artillery
Died of wounds on Sunday 27 May 1917 (aged 21)
Brandhoek Military Cemetery, Belgium (Grave I. A. 14)

Hugh Crouch Houston was born in 1896 in Newtownards and he was a son of David and Annie Williamson Houston (nee Crouch). They were married on 19 February 1890 in Carrickfergus Parish Church of Ireland (St Nicholas) and they lived in William Street, Newtownards. David Houston worked as a printer and he and Annie had at least nine children – David, Alexander,

Hugh, Frederick, Henrietta, William, Queenie, Bertie and Bobbie. The Houston family moved from Newtownards to Lancashire where they lived at 10 King Street, Church near Accrington. Hugh Houston enlisted in Accrington and he served with the Royal Field Artillery. Driver Hugh Houston died of wounds on 27 May 1917 and at the time of his death his parents were living at 32 York Street, Church near Accrington in Lancashire.

Hughes, James
Rifleman
No. 5932, 7th Battalion, Royal Irish Rifles
Killed in action on Saturday 9 September 1916
Thiepval Memorial, France (Pier and Face 15 A and 15 B)

James Hughes was born in Comber, he lived at 52 Douglas Street, Belfast and he enlisted in Belfast. He served with the 7th Battalion Royal Irish Rifles in 48th Brigade of the 16th (Irish) Division and he was killed in action on 9 September 1916 at Ginchy. Lance Corporal **Robert Irvine** was killed in the same action. Rifleman James Hughes is commemorated in the PCI Roll of Honour for McQuiston Memorial Presbyterian Church Belfast and in the Belfast Book of Honour (Page 278).

H

Hughes, Robert
Carpenter
SS *Donegal* (Belfast), Mercantile Marine
Killed in action on Tuesday 17 April 1917 (aged 40)
Tower Hill Memorial, London

Robert Hughes was born on 9 February 1877 in Portavogie and he was a son of James and Catherine Hughes (nee McClements). They were married on 14 January 1865 in Glastry Presbyterian Church. James and Catherine Hughes had at least ten children – John McLiment, William, Mary Jane, Margaret (died in infancy), Alice Gowan, Margaret, James, Robert, Lizzie and Hugh. Robert's father James Hughes died sometime before 1911.

Robert Hughes worked as a ship's carpenter and he and Nellie Emma Fleming were married on 1 August 1904 in St Augustine's Parish Church of Ireland in Londonderry. They lived in Ballyhalbert before moving to Portavogie. Robert and Nellie Hughes had at least seven children three of whom died in infancy. The others were Hester, Lizzie, Walter and Robert.

Robert Hughes was killed in action when the SS *Donegal* was torpedoed without warning by a German submarine on 17 April 1917. The attack happened 19 miles south of the Dean Light Vessel in the English Channel and as a result SS *Donegal* sank.

SS *Donegal* was launched in 1904 and was originally used as a passenger steamship. She was requisitioned by the Admiralty and converted for use as a hospital ship. SS *Donegal* was used to ferry wounded soldiers back to England from France and in the attack on 17 April 1917 eleven crew members died as did 29 of the wounded soldiers who were aboard.

> **Portavogie Carpenter on Roll of Honour.**
> The Board of Trade has issued a list of officers and seamen in British merchant and sailing vessels whose deaths have been reported as caused by enemy action. The list contains the name of Robert Hughes, carpenter, Portavogie (17th April, 1917).

Robert Hughes's body wasn't found and initially he was posted as missing in action. His widow applied to the courts to presume her husband's death and in October 1917 the case was heard in Dublin. An affidavit was read in which a seaman by the name of Mullan stated that he had seen Robert Hughes lying dead on the deck. The application was granted. In August 1918 the Board of Trade issued a list of merchant seamen whose deaths were caused by enemy action. This list contained the name of Robert Hughes.

H

Hurley, William
Rifleman
No. 5138, 2nd Battalion, Royal Irish Rifles
Killed in action on Tuesday 27 October 1914 (aged 28)
Le Touret Memorial, France (Panel 42 and 43)

William Hurley was born in Athy, Co Kildare and he was a son of John and Mary Hurley. John Hurley worked as a general labourer and he and Mary had at least twelve children including William, Matthew, Christopher, Kate, Martin, Michael, James and Anne. William Hurley was a married man and he was a member of the band of the Royal North Downs when the Hurley family lived in Newtownards.

After the intense fighting on 27 October 1914 at Neuve Chapelle Rifleman William Hurley was reported as missing in action and over the next 18 months his wife sought information through the pages of the *Newtownards Chronicle* and in other ways as to what had happened to him. At that stage she and their four children were living at 8 Maralin Street, Belfast. Later it was officially confirmed that Rifleman William Hurley had been killed in action and he is commemorated on Newtownards and District War Memorial and in the Belfast Book of Honour (Page 283).

Huston, Gerald Marcus (Gerald)
Distinguished Conduct Medal
Corporal
No. 28763, 7th Signal Company, Royal Engineers
Died on Tuesday 7 December 1915 (aged 19)
Beauval Communal Cemetery, France (Grave C. 31)

Gerald Marcus Huston was born in Shankill, Belfast and he was a son of Mr WW and Mrs EV Huston of 'Ashville', Killinchy in County Down. He enlisted in Belfast, he served with the 7th Signal Company Royal Engineers and he was awarded the Distinguished Conduct Medal. Corporal Gerald Marcus Huston died on 7 December 1915 and he is commemorated in the Belfast Book of Honour (Page 284).

Hutton, James
Sapper
No. 64457, 150th Field Company, Royal Engineers, 36th (Ulster) Division
Died on Sunday 20 October 1918 (aged 40)
Harlebeke New British Cemetery, Belgium (Grave VII. A. 16)

H
I

James Hutton was born in the townland of Ballymacarrett, Belfast and James, his wife Ellen Jane and his stepsons James and Hugh Gregory lived at 56 Chadolly Street, Belfast. Later the Hutton family lived at 1 Pound Street, Newtownards.

James Hutton enlisted in Belfast and he served with 150th Field Company Royal Engineers in the 36th (Ulster) Division. Sapper James Hutton died on 20 October 1918 during the Allied offensive against all sections of the German line and he is commemorated in the Belfast Book of Honour (Page 285). His stepson **James Gregory** died of wounds on 10 April 1918.

Ingram, Thomas Edward (Thomas)
Rifleman
No. 45212, 1st Battalion, 3rd New Zealand Rifle Brigade, NZEF
Killed in action on Tuesday 16 July 1918
Hebuterne Military Cemetery, France (Grave I. L. 8)

Thomas Ingram was the younger son of Thomas and Sarah Ingram (nee Cairns) who lived in Ballyloughan House, Comber. They were married on 5 June 1878 in Strean Presbyterian Church Newtownards. After the Ingram family moved to New Zealand two of Thomas Ingram Junior's aunts – Jane and Agnes Ingram – continued to live in Ballyloughan House. Thomas Ingram's uncle, the Rev Thomas Cairns, was at one time Moderator of the Presbyterian Church of Australia.

Prior to the outbreak of the Great War Thomas Ingram worked in New Zealand as a farmer. He joined the New Zealand Expeditionary Force and on 26 April 1917 he sailed aboard a troopship from Wellington to Plymouth. Before he went to France he visited friends and family members in Comber. These included his aunt Miss Ingram of Ballyloughan House. Rifleman Thomas Ingram was killed in action on 16 July 1918 and at that time his widowed mother was living at 112 Humber Street, Oamaru, South Island, New Zealand.

Ireland, Robert John
Private, US Army
325th Infantry Regiment, 82nd Division American Expeditionary Force
Died of wounds on Friday 11 October 1918
Meuse-Argonne American Cemetery, France (Plot D Row 20 Grave 21)

Robert John Ireland moved from Comber to New York and it was there that he joined the US Army. He served with the 325th Infantry Regiment in 82nd Division American Expeditionary Force and he died of wounds on 11 October 1918 during the Allied offensive against all sections of the German line. Private Robert John Ireland is commemorated on Comber and District War Memorial and in Second Comber Presbyterian Church.

Irvine family: James, John and Robert
James and John Irvine were brothers and Robert Irvine was their nephew (he was a son of their brother Samuel).

James and John Irvine were born in Newtownards and they were sons of

Samuel and Margaret Irvine who lived in Dobbin's Row and then Upper Movilla Street. Samuel and Margaret Irvine had at least six children – Samuel, Robert, James, William, John and Margaret.

John was the first of the three family members to die on active service in the Great War, then Robert and then James:

Irvine, John
Rifleman
No. 7587, 2nd Battalion, Royal Irish Rifles
Died of wounds on Monday 9 November 1914 (aged 29)
Poperinghe Old Military Cemetery, Belgium (Grave I. M. 55)

John Irvine was a Reservist who had previously served with the 1st Battalion Royal Irish Rifles in India. He was called up to the 2nd Battalion and he went to the front at the outbreak of hostilities. He died in Poperinghe Hospital on 9 November 1914 as a result of wounds received in action on 3 November 1914. Ironically, Rifleman John Irvine had sent a postcard dated 3 November 1914 to his brother Samuel intimating that he was well. Samuel Irvine lived at 152 Leopold Street, Belfast.

Around the time of John Irvine's death, news came through that his brother Rifleman James Irvine had been wounded in action. After John died his mother Margaret placed a 'Killed in Action' notice in the *Newtownards Chronicle* and it contained the verse:

'Though my heart may break with sorrow,
By the grief so hard to bear,
I shall meet him some bright morning
In our Father's mansion fair'

Rifleman John Irvine is commemorated on Newtownards and District War Memorial and in the Belfast Book of Honour (Page 288).

Irvine, Robert Russell (Robert)
Lance Corporal
No. 5952, 7th Battalion, Royal Irish Rifles
Killed in action on Saturday 9 September 1916 (aged 18)
Thiepval Memorial, France (Pier and Face 15 A and 15 B)

Robert Irvine was born on 14 June 1898 in Newtownards and he was a son of Samuel and Jemima Irvine (nee McGraw) who lived in Greenwell Street before they moved to 152 Leopold Street, Belfast. They were married on 18 May 1896 in Greenwell Street Presbyterian Church Newtownards. Samuel Irvine worked in a mill as a carding master and he and Jemima had at least four children – John, Robert Russell, Samuel and Hugh. These children were all baptised in Greenwell Street Presbyterian Church Newtownards.

Robert Irvine enlisted in Belfast, he served with the 7th Battalion Royal Irish Rifles in 48th Brigade of the 16th (Irish) Division and he was killed in action on 9 September 1916 at Ginchy. Rifleman **James Hughes** was killed in the same action.

Lance Corporal Robert Irvine is commemorated in the PCI Roll of Honour for Crumlin Road Presbyterian Church Belfast and in the Belfast Book of Honour (Page 288).

Irvine, James
Lance Corporal
No. 18392, 7th/8th Battalion, King's Own Scottish Borderers
Killed in action on Wednesday 1 August 1917 (aged 40)
Ypres (Menin Gate) Memorial, Belgium (Panel 22)

James Irvine and Margaret Milligan were married on 7 August 1901 in St Anne's Church of Ireland Belfast and prior to the outbreak of the Great War they lived in Victoria Avenue, Newtownards. They had at least five children – Grace, Robert, James, Agnes and Frederick Harold. James Irvine worked as a linen weaver and he was a member of the Newtownards Miniature Rifle Club where he won many prizes for rifle shooting. A letter to a friend back home was published in the 4 December 1915 edition of the *Newtownards Chronicle* and in it he described the part of the trenches where he was stationed as 'a very bad spot'. It was the place where he had previously sustained head injuries but he said 'they were not bad enough for me to be sent home'. He went on, 'But I got my own back, as I got shelter and I just thought I was on the 'Rec' shooting for the 'Bell' medal. And I have not forgotten what I learnt in the Newtownards Miniature Rifle Club. The enemy were thick and I helped to thin them out a bit'.

When Lance Corporal James Irvine was killed in action his Platoon Officer, Second Lieutenant EMS Houston wrote to James's widow to express his sympathy. He told her that her husband had been hit by a sniper's bullet during the afternoon of 1 August 1917 and that his death had been instantaneous.

At the time of James's death his wife and family were living at 191 Leopold Street in Belfast.

Lance Corporal James Irvine is commemorated on Newtownards and District War Memorial; in Newtownards Masonic Lodge No. 198 and in the Belfast Book of Honour (Page 288).

Irwin, James Mackenzie (James)
Rifleman
No. 6446, 2nd Battalion, Royal Irish Rifles
Died of wounds on Sunday 31 January 1915 (aged 19)
Kemmel Chateau Military Cemetery, Belgium (Grave B. 35)

James Mackenzie Irwin was born in Dublin and he was a son of James M Irwin. When James Mackenzie Irwin lived in Newtownards he boarded with Nathaniel and Sarah Ledgerwood at 73 Greenwell Street. He enlisted in Newtownards, he joined the Royal North Downs and on 3 December 1914 he went to the front with the 2nd Battalion Royal Irish Rifles in 7th Brigade of the 3rd Division. Rifleman James Irwin died of wounds received in the action at Kemmel and his death was reported in the 6 March 1915 edition of the *Newtownards Chronicle* under the headline 'Another Newtownards Man Meets a Soldier's Fate'. In the previous week's edition of the newspaper there was a death notice inserted by 'his companions N Ledgerwood and J Francis'.

Rifleman James Irwin's sister Mrs White received a letter dated 8 February 1915 from Lieutenant JR Tuckett. In the letter he informed her that her brother, who had been his orderly, had asked him to write to her and tell her what had happened. Lt Tuckett wrote, 'I was walking up to the trenches with him and my servant at 10.00 pm on 20 January when he was hit by a stray bullet, there being hundreds about that night, about 1000 yards behind the firing line. The bullet passed through from the left side and out the right side just below the ribs. We bound him up and carried him to the nearest farm and sent for the nearest stretcher party. He was quite conscious when he left soon after 11.00 pm'. Lt Tuckett went on to describe how brave and uncomplaining James Irwin had been and he told her that James had died of his wounds on 31 January 1915.

Rifleman James Irwin is commemorated on Newtownards and District War Memorial and in Newtownards Parish Church of Ireland (St Mark).

Jamison, George
Rifleman
No. 10409, 1st Battalion, Royal Irish Rifles
Killed in action on Thursday 29 July 1915 (aged 20)
Y Farm Military Cemetery, France (Grave K. 35)

George Jamison was born in Carrowdore and he was a son of James and Sarah Jamison who lived at 159 Greenwell Street, Newtownards. James Jamison worked as a general labourer and he and Sarah had at least nine children including Thomas, David, George, Jennie and John.

George Jamison worked as an apprentice weaver before the outbreak of the Great War. He enlisted in Belfast and he served with the 1st Battalion Royal Irish Rifles. Rifleman George Jamison was killed in action on 29 July 1915 while his Battalion was holding the line and the Rev MWT Cowan, Church of England Chaplain 95th Infantry Brigade conducted his funeral that same day. From 20th Field Ambulance in 8th Division of the British Expeditionary Force the Rev Cowan wrote a letter of sympathy to George Jamison's mother the following day.

J

In an article in the *Newtownards Chronicle* the Rev WLT Whatham, Church of Ireland Rector in Newtownards described Rifleman George Jamison as 'the soldier who died with a smile on his face'. This description was based on a comment made in a letter of sympathy to his parents written by Lance Corporal D Wilkinson (6888). He wrote, 'We all miss him badly here, he was such a real good fellow, always in the best of spirits. I might tell you that he died with a smile. He and I were just after passing a joke. He was showing me the rose and handkerchief you had sent him, then he sat down to write a letter. I don't think he got it finished. He got up again to have a shot at them, as he said, when he was hit. He got it right through the head. He did not suffer any pain for he was laughing when he was hit, and that is how he fell – smiling'.

KILLED IN ACTION.

JAMISON—July 29, 1915 (killed in action) in France, 10409, Rifleman George Jamison, 1st Batt. Royal Irish Rifles.

We in suffering : they in crime,
Wait the just reward of time,
Wait the vengeance that is due.
Not in vain a heart shall break,
Not a tear for Freedom's sake
Fall unheeded ; God is true.

Inserted by his sorrowing father and mother, sister (Jennie) and brother (John).
159 Greenwell Street,
Newtownards.

His family placed a 'Killed in Action' notice in the 7 August 1915 edition of the *Newtownards Chronicle* and it included the verse:

'We in suffering, they in crime
Wait the just reward of time,
Wait the vengeance that is due.
Not in vain a heart shall break,
Not a tear for Freedom's sake
Fall unheeded; God is true'

Rifleman George Jamison is commemorated on Newtownards and District War Memorial and in Newtownards Parish Church of Ireland (St Mark).

Jamison, James
Greaser
R.M.S. *Redbreast*, Mercantile Marine Reserve
Died of dysentery on Friday 27 August 1915 (aged 60)
Plymouth Naval Memorial, Devon, England (Panel 9)

James Jamison was a son of Joseph and Elizabeth Jamison (nee Muckle) who lived in Millisle. They were married on 31 May 1855 in Carrowdore Presbyterian Church. Joseph Jamison worked as a blacksmith and he and Elizabeth had at least six children – William John (died 19 April 1878 aged 20), Maggie Jane (died 10 February 1883 aged 22), Armenia (died 15 February 1883 aged 19), Lizzie (died 15 May 1887 aged 20), David and James. Joseph Jamison died on 12 January 1912 and Elizabeth Jamison died on 6 December 1914

James Jamison married Jane Millar and they lived in Millisle. They had at least eight children – James, Alexander (died 2 April 1885 aged 1), Annie, David Joseph, Angus, Samuel, Robert and George. Jane Jamison died on 28 June 1929.

J

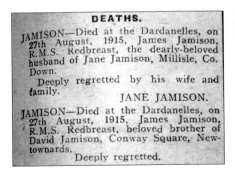

DEATHS.

JAMISON—Died at the Dardanelles, on 27th August, 1915, James Jamison, R.M.S. Redbreast, the dearly-beloved husband of Jane Jamison, Millisle, Co. Down.
Deeply regretted by his wife and family.
JANE JAMISON.

JAMISON—Died at the Dardanelles, on 27th August, 1915, James Jamison, R.M.S. Redbreast, beloved brother of David Jamison, Conway Square, Newtownards.
Deeply regretted.

James Jamison worked as a seaman and during the Great War he served as a greaser in the Mercantile Marine Reserve. He died of dysentery at the Dardanelles on 27 August 1915 and he was buried at sea. He is commemorated on Donaghadee and District War Memorial; in Millisle Presbyterian Church and on both the Jamison and Millar family grave headstones in Millisle Presbyterian Graveyard.

Four of James Jamison's sons were on active service in the Great War. Lieutenant Robert Jamison served in the Royal Air Force and was awarded the Distinguished Flying Cross; Lieutenant Samuel Jamison and Corporal George Jamison served in the Royal Irish Rifles and Corporal David Jamison served in the Canadian Mounted Rifles.

Jamison, William John (Willie) (served as Armour, William John)
Rifleman
No. 42558, 2nd Battalion, Royal Irish Rifles
Died on Tuesday 26 October 1920 (aged 21)
Baghdad (North Gate) War Cemetery, Iraq (Grave XIV. J. 14)

William John Jamison's great-niece contributed some of the family details that follow and she has asked for them to be included.

William John Armour was born on 3 May 1899 and he was a son of Sarah Jane Armour and William Jamison who at that time were not married. In 1901 Willie Armour and three siblings were living in the Newtownards workhouse with their mother Sarah Jane Armour. Sarah Jane worked as a farm servant and she stated that she belonged to the Irish Church. Willie Armour's father William Jamison (spelt Jameson in the 1901 census) worked as a weaver and he lived with his widowed mother Margaret at 1 Movilla Street, Newtownards. Margaret stated that her religious denomination was Roman Catholic and William stated that his was Church of England. There was family opposition to William Jamison and Sarah Jane Armour getting married.

In 1911 Sarah Jane Armour and her seven children (Maggie, Willie, James, Mary Katherine, Luezia, Jennie and Elizabeth) were living at 78 Movilla Street while their father William Jamison was still living at 1 Movilla Street with his widowed mother Margaret. William Jamison and Sarah Jane Armour were married on 21 November 1914 in Newtownards Parish Church of Ireland (St Mark) and they had at least eleven children.

Willie Armour was just 15 years old when he enlisted soon after the outbreak of the Great War and he was sent home again when his mother showed his birth certificate to the army authorities. A few weeks later Willie Armour enlisted again and his Medal Index Card shows that he served with the 8th and 1st Battalions Royal Irish Rifles (564) and the 9th Battalion Royal Irish Fusiliers (42558). His regimental number was 19/46093.

Willie Armour was 17 years old when he married Elizabeth McBlain on 16 September 1916 in Newtownards Parish Church of Ireland (St Mark) and it was while Willie was serving with the Royal Irish Fusiliers that their son William John was born on 6 November 1918. Six weeks later, on 19 December 1918, baby William John Armour died of acute bronchitis. His grandmother Sarah Jane Jamison (nee Armour) was present when he died and she registered his death. At the time of his son's death Willie Armour was on active service with the Royal Irish Rifles.

In the autumn of 1920 William John Armour was serving with the 2nd Battalion Royal Irish Rifles in Mesopotamia and it was there that he died on 26 October 1920. After Rifleman Willie Armour died his family was informed that he had been shot by a sniper whilst swimming.

The War Memorial in Newtownards was unveiled and dedicated on 26 May 1934 and during the deliberations that took place in the lead-up to the ceremony Willie Armour's family made representation to the Organising Committee for Willie's surname to be inscribed on the memorial as 'Jamison' rather than 'Armour'. The Committee agreed and so Rifleman Willie Armour is commemorated on Newtownards War Memorial as 'Jamison, WJ' whilst in the booklet produced for the unveiling and dedication ceremony he is listed as Rifleman William J Armour Royal Irish Rifles.

Johnston, Alfred
Rifleman
No. 20/498, 1st Battalion, Royal Irish Rifles
Died of wounds on Friday 4 October 1918 (aged 18)
Dadizeele New British Cemetery, Belgium (Grave III. E. 16)

J

Alfred Johnston was the only son of James and Agnes Johnston (nee Melville) who lived at 40 William Street, Newtownards. They were married on 16 January 1889 in Newtownards Roman Catholic Church. James Johnston worked as a general labourer and he died in the early 1900s. Alfred had five sisters – Lizzie, Amelia, Ethel, Florence and Madge. In his youth Alfred was a member of 1st Newtownards Boy Scouts. He enlisted on 5 July 1917 and after training at Newtownards Camp he went to the front on 3 April 1918. He served with the 1st Battalion Royal Irish Rifles.

Rifleman Alfred Johnston was wounded in action on 3 October 1918 during the Allied offensive against all sections of the German line and he died in a dressing station the following day as a result of shrapnel wounds to his right arm and leg. In a letter to Alfred's mother from 110th Field Ambulance the Wesleyan Chaplain, the Rev Ernest Gimblett, expressed his sympathy. He assured her that the doctors had done all they possibly could but they were unable to save him and Alfred died peacefully at 5.30 pm on 4 October 1918.

Alfred Johnston's mother and sisters placed a 'For King and Country' notice in the *Newtownards Chronicle* and it contained the verse:

> *'Sleep on my dear and only son*
> *While tears of sorrow fall:*
> *Eyes weep on earth, but thou art safe*
> *Where Christ is all in all.*
> *And this loved spot which saw thy birth,*
> *You never more shall see on earth;*
> *Yet Christ has made a home for thee*
> *To live through all eternity.'*

Rifleman Alfred Johnston is commemorated on Newtownards and District War Memorial (surname spelt Johnstone) and in Regent Street Methodist Church Newtownards.

Johnston, Andrew
Private
No. 14349, 9th Battalion, Princess Victoria's (Royal Irish Fusiliers)
Killed in action on Saturday 1 July 1916 (aged 21)
Thiepval Memorial, France (Pier and Face 15 A)

Andrew Johnston was born in Newtownards and he was a son of Robert and Anne Johnston. The Johnston family moved to Portadown where they lived at 149 West Street. Robert Johnston worked as a tinsmith and he and Anne had at least nine children including Esther, Daniel and Andrew.

Andrew Johnston worked as a carder of tow before the outbreak of the Great War and he enlisted in Portadown. He served with the 9th Battalion Royal Irish Fusiliers in 108th Brigade of the 36th (Ulster) Division and he was killed in action on the first day of the Battle of the Somme. Private Andrew Johnston is commemorated on Newtownards and District War Memorial (surname spelt Johnstone).

Johnston, Elliott
Military Cross
Captain
'B' Company, 13th Battalion, Royal Irish Rifles
Killed in action on Saturday 1 July 1916 (aged 28)
Thiepval Memorial, France (Pier and Face 15 A and 15 B)

Elliott Johnston was born in Newtownards on 12 May 1888 and he was the second son of Samuel and Isabella Johnston (nee Elliott) who lived in

Corporation North, Newtownards. They were married on 2 May 1884 in Elmwood Avenue Presbyterian Church Belfast. Samuel Johnston founded the Glen Printing and Finishing Works in Newtownards and he and Isabella had at least five children – William Petticrew, Edith Georgina, Elliott, Ernest Clifford (born 1890) and Irene Beatrice (born 1893). Elliott, Ernest and Irene Johnston were baptised in Strean Presbyterian Church Newtownards. The Johnston family moved to Belfast where they lived at 'Ardenza', King's Road and later at 1 Deramore Park.

Elliott Johnston attended Campbell College between 1903 and 1906 and Queen's University Belfast (Faculty of Commerce) from 1910 to 1913. He managed the stitching department in Glen Printing and Finishing Works before the outbreak of the Great War and he was Senior Half-Company Commander of Newtownards 'D' Company Ulster Volunteer Force.

Elliott Johnston served with the 13th Battalion Royal Irish Rifles in 108th Brigade of the 36th (Ulster) Division – as Second Lieutenant from 13 September 1914, Lieutenant from 1 Dec 1914 and Captain from February 1916. Elliott distinguished himself at the Dollymount School of Musketry in Dublin being graded 1st Class Instructor and he was appointed Assistant Adjutant to the 13th Battalion.

In June 1915, as a token of their esteem, the workers in the Glen Printing and Finishing Works presented Elliott Johnston with a service revolver, wristlet watch with a luminous dial, prismatic compass, map case, clasp knife and a combination knife, fork and spoon.

Initially Captain Johnston was reported as missing in action after the first day of the Battle of the Somme and there was little hope that he was still alive. Colonel Savage wrote to Elliott's father and in the letter he said, 'Captain Johnston was leading two platoons of his company in the advance of 1 July. The most I can discover about him is from Corporal Bailie of his company who was close to him near the second line of the German trenches when he was hit through the body above the hip and I regret to say he thinks he was killed. The heavy machine gun fire across the spot prevented any help being given to him'.

Colonel Savage went on to tell Elliott's father that on the night of 26/27 June Elliott had planned and executed a raid on the German trenches. With three other officers and 100 men he had brought back thirteen German prisoners, one of whom was an officer. Colonel Savage wrote, 'It was the most successful raid done by our Division'. During that raid Lance Corporal **John McCracken** from Newtownards was killed.

For this conspicuous gallantry during operations Captain Elliott Johnston was awarded the Military Cross and it was presented to Elliott's father by Brigadier-General Hacket Pain CB in a ceremony at Palace Barracks Holywood on Wednesday 25 April 1917. Elliott Johnston was the first officer in the 13th Battalion to be awarded a medal for gallantry.

The last letter sent home by Elliott Johnston was written on 30 June 1916 and it was delivered after he was killed in action. Captain Elliott Johnston is commemorated on Newtownards and District War Memorial; on the Memorial Plaque in Strean Presbyterian Church Newtownards; in the PCI Roll of Honour for Belmont Presbyterian Church Belfast; on the North of Ireland [Rugby] Football Club Memorial Plaque; in the Belfast Book of Honour (page 296); on the Campbell College and QUB War Memorials and in the QUB Book of Remembrance (Page 29).

Johnston, James Stevenson (James)
Rifleman
No. 17980, 'C' Company, 13th Battalion, Royal Irish Rifles
Killed in action on Saturday 1 July 1916 (aged 23)
Serre Road Cemetery No. 2, France (Grave VI. F. 10)

James Stevenson Johnston was born in Belfast and he was a son of Stevenson and Margaret Johnston (nee Thompson). They were married on 21 January 1887 in Ballygowan Presbyterian Church and their daughter Margaret was baptised in that church. Before the Great War James Johnston was employed as a farm servant by John Hamilton who farmed in the townland of Ballystockart, Comber.

COMBER HEROES.
Amongst the casualties reported in this week's lists are:—
. Rifleman J. Johnston (No. 17,980), previously reported missing, now reported killed.

James Johnston enlisted in Downpatrick and he served with the 13th Battalion Royal Irish Rifles in 108th Brigade of the 36th (Ulster) Division. After the first day of the Battle of the Somme Rifleman James Johnston was posted as missing in action and in February 1917 he was officially reported as killed in action. In the *Newtownards Chronicle* he was described as one of the 'Comber Heroes'. Rifleman James Stevenson Johnston is commemorated in the Belfast Book of Honour (Page 299).

Johnston, Robert
Rifleman
No. 6728, 1st Battalion, Royal Irish Rifles
Killed in action on Sunday 9 May 1915 (aged 19)
Ploegsteert Memorial, Belgium (Panel 9)

Robert Johnston is commemorated on Newtownards and District War Memorial as Robert Johnstone Jun. He was born on 19 May 1895 in Newtownards and he was a son of John and Agnes Johnston (nee Auld) who lived at 33 Mill Street. They were married on 3 December 1892 in Second Newtownards Presbyterian Church. John Johnston worked as a tinsmith and he and Agnes had at least seven children – William John, Robert, Maggie, James, Annie, Agnes Cahoon and Andrew. They were all baptised in Greenwell Street Presbyterian Church Newtownards.

Prior to the outbreak of the Great War Robert and his brother William John worked in a factory – Robert as a cage-carrier and William John as an oiler. Robert enlisted shortly after the outbreak of hostilities and after serving for a time with the Royal North Downs he was drafted to the 1st Battalion Royal Irish Rifles then in France.

J

During the time that Rifleman Robert Johnston was on active service he and his mother exchanged letters on a regular basis. She became anxious when one of her letters to Robert was returned by one of Robert's comrades. In a covering letter dated 12 May 1915 Lance Corporal Hoey informed Robert's mother that Robert had been wounded at Rouge Bancs and he did not know whether Robert had been taken to hospital or not. Agnes Johnston commissioned a letter to be written and sent to the Infantry Record Office in Dublin but they were unable to provide any information as to his whereabouts.

In June 1915 Rifleman Robert Johnston was posted as missing in action and in May 1916 it was officially confirmed that he had been killed in action. Robert's mother placed a 'For King and Country' notice in the *Newtownards Chronicle* and it contained the verse:

'Although he lies somewhere in France,
And his grave we cannot see,
As long as life and memory lasts
We will remember thee.

His warfare o'er, his battle fought;
His victory won, though dearly bought;
His fresh young life could not be saved,
He slumbers now in a soldier's grave.'

At the time of Robert's death his brother William John Johnston was serving with the 18th (Reserve) Battalion Royal Irish Rifles at Clandeboye having been invalided home from the 13th Battalion Royal Irish Rifles (17986).

Robert's father John Johnston (7347) having also been invalided home was serving with the 4th Battalion Royal Irish Rifles at Carrickfergus.

Robert's uncle William Auld – a brother of his mother – had also been invalided home after being wounded in the Dardanelles with the 6th Battalion Royal Irish Rifles (10859).

Three other uncles, brothers of his father, were on active service at the front and one of them, his uncle **Robert Johnston** (6359), was killed in action on the same day and in the same place that he died.

J
Johnston, Robert
Lance Corporal
No. 6359, 1st Battalion, Royal Irish Rifles
Killed in action on Sunday 9 May 1915
Ploegsteert Memorial, Belgium (Panel 9)

Robert Johnston is commemorated on Newtownards and District War Memorial as Robert Johnstone Sen. He was born in Newtownards, he lived in Belfast at 51 Urney Street and he enlisted in Newtownards. Lance Corporal Robert Johnston (6359) and his nephew Rifleman **Robert Johnston** (6728) both served in the 1st Battalion Royal Irish Rifles and they both died on the same day at Rouge Bancs. Their bodies were never recovered and they are both commemorated on the same panel of the Ploegsteert Memorial and on Newtownards and District War Memorial – as Robert Johnstone Sen and Robert Johnstone Jun respectively.

Robert Johnston Senior is also commemorated in the Belfast Book of Honour (Page 301) and Robert Johnston Junior is also commemorated in the PCI Roll of Honour for Greenwell Street Presbyterian Church Newtownards.

Johnston, Samuel
Able Seaman
No. 192792, HMS *Monmouth*, Royal Navy
Killed in action on Sunday 1 November 1914 (aged 32)
Plymouth Naval Memorial, Devon, England (Panel 1)

Samuel Johnston joined the Royal Navy in 1897 when he was 15 years old. He and Maria Brown Davidson were married on 3 January 1913 in Donaghadee Methodist Church. At that time Samuel was living in Primrose Street, Bangor and Maria was living in Edward Street, Donaghadee where her father James worked as a fisherman.

Samuel Johnston had 17 years of naval experience when he was killed in action at the Battle of Coronel in the Pacific Ocean off the coast of Chile. In this battle HMS *Monmouth* and HMS *Good Hope* both sank with a combined loss of some 1570 lives. There were no survivors from either ship. When Samuel Johnston died his wife Maria was living at 4 Victoria Terrace, Donaghadee.

Johnston, Stephen
The name Stephen Johnston is commemorated in Killinchy Parish Church of Ireland where he is described as '13th RIR, killed in action'. This name has not been found amongst the casualty lists for the 13th Battalion or for any other Battalion of the Royal Irish Rifles. Desk searches and public appeals to date have yielded no further information.

Johnston, Thomas (Tommy)
Rifleman
No. 19038, 'B' Company, 13th Battalion, Royal Irish Rifles
Killed in action on Thursday 16 August 1917 (aged 20)
Tyne Cot Cemetery, Belgium (Grave VII. E. 10)

Thomas Johnston was born on 14 March 1897 and he was the eldest son of Thomas and Mary Ann Johnston (nee Murphy) of The Warren, Springvale, Ballywalter. They were married on 31 December 1891 in Ballywalter Parish Church of Ireland. Both father and son worked as agricultural labourers.

Thomas and Mary Ann Johnston had at least twelve

children (including two sets of twins) – Elizabeth, Agnes, Thomas, Robert and Annie, William John and David, Hugh, David, James, Mary and Walter.

Tommy Johnston enlisted shortly after the outbreak of the Great War and he served with the 13th Battalion Royal Irish Rifles in 108th Brigade of the 36th (Ulster) Division. He was wounded in action during the Battle of the Somme.

Rifleman Tommy Johnston was posted as missing in action on 16 August 1917 at Langemarck during the Third Battle of Ypres and a year later his parents received official confirmation that he had been killed in action on or since that date. They placed a 'For King and Country' notice in the *Newtownards Chronicle* and it contained the verse:

'For his King and country well he stood,
Unknown to coward's fears;
In battle strife he shed his blood
With the Ulster Volunteers.
When alone in my sorrow and bitter tears flow,
There stealeth a dream of the sweet long ago,
Unknown to the world Tommy stands by my side,
And whispers: Dear mother, death cannot divide.'

At the time of Tommy's death one of his younger brothers was also on active service.

Rifleman Tommy Johnston is commemorated on Ballywalter and District War Memorial and in Ballywalter Parish Church of Ireland (Holy Trinity). He is also commemorated on the family grave headstone in Whitechurch Cemetery Ballywalter. Tommy's father died on 12 February 1941 and his mother died on 24 December 1942.

Johnston, William
Private
No. 27060, 9th Battalion, Royal Inniskilling Fusiliers
Killed in action on Saturday 1 July 1916
Thiepval Memorial, France (Pier and Face 4 D and 5 B)

William Johnston was born in Newtownards, he lived in Newtownards and he enlisted in Belfast. He served with the 9th Battalion Royal Inniskilling Fusiliers in 109th Brigade of the 36th (Ulster) Division and he was killed in action on the first day of the Battle of the Somme.

Initially he was posted as missing in action and in the 2 March 1918 edition

Officially Reported Killed.

The name of Private W. Johnston (No. 27,060), Royal Inniskilling Fusiliers, Newtownards, appears in this week's official casualty list as being killed instead of missing.

of the *Newtownards Chronicle* there was a report that 'the name of Private W Johnston (27060) Royal Inniskilling Fusiliers Newtownards appears in this week's official casualty list as being killed instead of missing'.

Johnston, William James
Private
No. 22152, 9th Battalion, Princess Victoria's (Royal Irish Fusiliers)
Killed in action on Thursday 16 August 1917 (aged 34)
Tyne Cot Memorial, Belgium (Panel 140 to 141)

William James Johnston was born on 11 May 1883 in Kircubbin and he was a son of William and Elizabeth Johnston (nee Blair) who were married in Ballywalter Parish Church of Ireland. William and Elizabeth had at least six children all of whom were baptised in Kircubbin Parish Church of Ireland – William James, Elizabeth, Hugh, Martha, Agnes Mary and Robert.

William James Johnston and Margaret McClements were married on 29 October 1902 in Glastry Presbyterian Church and they lived at 9 Upper Charleville Street, Belfast. William James enlisted in Belfast and he served with the 9th Battalion Royal Irish Fusiliers in 108th Brigade of the 36th (Ulster) Division.

Private William James Johnston was killed in action on 16 August 1917 at Langemarck during the Third Battle of Ypres and he is commemorated in the Belfast Book of Honour (Page 303).

J

Jones, James
Rifleman
No. 18/1102, 8th Battalion, Royal Irish Rifles
Killed in action on Tuesday 7 August 1917 (aged 19)
Ypres (Menin Gate) Memorial, Belgium (Panel 40)

James Jones was born in Portavogie and he was the only son of Robert and Agnes Jones (nee Bell). They were married on 22 April 1892 in Ballyhemlin Non-Subscribing Presbyterian Church. Robert Jones worked as an agricultural labourer and he and Agnes had at least four children – Mary, Maggie, James and Jinnie. Agnes Jones worked as a seamstress and she died in the early 1900s.

The Jones family moved to Newtownards and there they lived at 7 Mary Street, later 29 William Street.

Mr. Robert ones, 29 William Street, Newtownards (formerly of Portavogie), has been officially informed that his only son, Rifleman James Jones (No. 1,102), Royal Irish Rifles (Ulster Division), was killed in action on 7th August.

Rifleman James Jones served with the 8th Battalion Royal Irish Rifles in 107th Brigade of the 36th (Ulster) Division. He was killed in action on 7 August 1917 whilst his Battalion was holding the line during the Third Battle of Ypres. His father and sisters placed a 'For King and Country' notice in the *Newtownards Chronicle* and it contained the verse:

'He will answer no more the roll call,
Nor rush to the bugle sound;
But, Lord, when the roll is called in Heaven,
May his name in Thy book be found'

Rifleman James Jones is commemorated on Newtownards and District War Memorial and in Ballyhalbert Parish Church of Ireland (St Andrew) at Ballyeasborough.

J

Jordan, Lowry
Military Medal
Corporal
No. 4034, 2nd Battalion, Rifle Brigade, transferred to (129799), Royal Flying Corps (Royal Air Force from 1 April 1918)
Died on Monday 22 July 1918 (aged 28)
Ballygowan Presbyterian Churchyard, Co. Down (Grave 139)

Lowry Jordan was born on 27 August 1889 in Ballygowan and he was a son of James and Robina Jordan (nee Mills). They were married on 1 May 1874 in Gilnahirk Presbyterian Church. James Jordan worked as a quarry labourer and he and Robina had at least nine children – James, Jane (died), David, John (died), Lowry, John, Thomas, William and Jane.

Before the Great War Lowry Jordan was employed by the Prudential Assurance Company in Belfast and as a Reservist he rejoined the Army on mobilisation in August 1914. Previously he had served as a Driver with the Royal Field Artillery before being transferred to the Rifle Brigade and in 1913 he was placed on the reserve list.

In the Great War Lowry Jordan served as a Rifleman with the Rifle Brigade (4034) and he went to France on 7 November 1914. In November 1916 he was awarded the Military Medal 'for conspicuous gallantry during a raid on the enemy trench on 25 June 1916. As soon as he entered the enemy trench he was wounded by a bomb but continued with his work. He rescued a wounded comrade from some of the enemy who were pulling him down a dug-out and saw him to a place of safety. Returning to the same place he despatched the would-be captors and left the trench with Lieutenant Murray. He also refused to leave the officer after being twice ordered to do so'. Subsequently he was promoted to the rank of Lance Corporal.

Because of his wounds he was deemed unfit for further active service in the Army but in 1918 he was sufficiently recovered to join the Royal Flying Corps. Corporal Lowry Jordan died suddenly on 22 July 1918 at Blandford, Dorset and his remains were interred in the graveyard adjoining Ballygowan Presbyterian Church. After a memorial service conducted by the Rev WK McLernon a contingent of the Norfolks fired three volleys over his grave and sounded *The Last Post*. Corporal Lowry Jordan is commemorated in Ballygowan Presbyterian Church.

J

Jordan, Samuel Wallace (Wallace)
Rifleman
No. 19041, 'C' Company, 13th Battalion, Royal Irish Rifles
Killed in action on Saturday, 1 July 1916 (aged 20)
Tincourt New British Cemetery, France (Grave VIII. H. 17)

Samuel Wallace Jordan was born in Ballygowan on 27 December 1895 and he was a son of John and Elizabeth (Lizzie) Jordan (nee Dempster). They were married on 6 July 1894 in Gilnahirk Presbyterian Church. John Jordan worked as a farmer and he and Lizzie had at least eight children – Alexander, Samuel Wallace, Louisa Disney, William Hobson, Sarah Jane, Elizabeth, Thomas Shaw and Agnes Mills. Wallace Jordan was baptised in Ballygowan Presbyterian Church.

Ballygowan Rifleman Killed.

Reported missing on July 1, 1916, Rfm. Samuel Wallace Jordan, Royal Irish Rifles, is now officially returned as killed on that date. Previous to enlistment he was in the service of Mr. Robert Gilliland, Moneyrea. At the age of eighteen he heard his country's call. He was a member of L.O.L. 1207, Ballygowan, and the Ulster Volunteer Force. Two of his brothers are in the Army. Their parents reside at Ballygowan.

Wallace Jordan worked as a farm servant for Robert Gilliland who was a publican and farmer in the townland of Moneyreagh. Wallace was a member the Ulster Volunteer Force and also of LOL No. 1207 in Ballygowan. Wallace Jordan enlisted in Belfast, he served with the 13th Battalion Royal Irish

Rifles in 108th Brigade of the 36th (Ulster) Division and he was killed in action on the first day of the Battle of the Somme.

Rifleman Wallace Jordan is commemorated in Ballygowan Presbyterian Church and at the time of his death two of his brothers, Alexander (died 3 October 1958) and William, were also on active service.

Kane, Robert
Rifleman
No. 18/375, 12th Battalion, Royal Irish Rifles
Died on Sunday 28 March 1920 (aged 20)
Newtownards (Movilla) Cemetery, Co. Down, (Grave 1. 277)

K

Robert Kane was a son of Richard and Margaret Kane who lived in Roundhill Street, Belfast. Richard Kane worked as a labourer in the shipyard and he and Margaret had at least two children – Robert and Annie Wilson Kane. The Kane family moved to the townland of Ballymaconnell, Bangor and Robert enlisted in July 1915. He served with the 12th Battalion Royal Irish Rifles in 108th Brigade of the 36th (Ulster) Division and he died at Ballymaconnell, Bangor on 28 March 1920 after he had been discharged from the Army.

Rifleman Robert Kane is buried in Movilla Cemetery, Newtownards and he is commemorated on Bangor and District War Memorial; in the RBL Album in North Down Museum (Page 49) and on the Memorial Plaque in the RBL Bangor Branch.

Keeling, George B
Lieutenant
Royal Indian Marine
Drowned on Sunday 19 March 1916
Bombay (St. Thomas) Cathedral Memorial, Mumbai, India

George B Keeling was the third son of John Stamp Keeling who lived at 1 The Coastguards, Millisle and before that in South Parade, Belfast. John Stamp Keeling worked as a landscape artist (lithographic) and he had at least four children of his own. In 1911 he was 72 years old and he lived in the townland of Ballymacruise, Carrowdore with his wife Mary Anne and her daughter (his adopted daughter). John Stamp Keeling died on 9 January 1922.

After attending Methodist College Belfast, George Keeling worked as a seaman and he served his apprenticeship with the Lord Line (Messrs Thomas Dixon & Sons Belfast). He was with the company for 25 years and he rose step by step until he was in command of the SS *Lord Dufferin*. He relinquished that position in January 1916 when Messrs Dixon sold the SS *Lord Dufferin*. He applied for Admiralty employment and was given a commission in the Royal Indian Marine.

On 3 February 1916 George Keeling and Dorothy Webb were married in Cardiff and just over six weeks later Lieutenant George B Keeling was drowned when his ship sank during a voyage between Bombay and Karachi. His ship was in a convoy and it is thought that it may have struck a floating mine. His death was reported in the 1 April edition of the *Newtownards Chronicle* under the headline 'The Late Lieut. Keeling of Millisle' and he is commemorated on the Methodist College Belfast War Memorial. One of George Keeling's brothers had been killed some years earlier in a collision at sea.

Keilty, David John
Rifleman

K

No. 10117, 2nd Battalion, Royal Irish Rifles
Died of disease on Saturday 16 September 1916 (aged 22)
Belfast (Dundonald) Cemetery, Co. Down (Grave F6. 427)

There is significant variation in the spelling of his name and in CWGC records he is associated with the 1st Battalion Royal Irish Rifles:

William J Keilty	Newtownards and District War Memorial
D J Keilty	CWGC
D J Kielty	*Newtownards Chronicle*
David John Keilty	1901 & 1911 Census, 'Soldiers Died in the Great War'
David James Kielty	PCI Roll of Honour

David John Keilty was born on 16 March 1894 in Newtownards and he was the only child of David John and Maggie Keilty (nee Spears) who lived in East Street. They were married on 7 June 1889 in Greenwell Street Presbyterian Church Newtownards and it was there that baby David John was baptised. David John Senior worked as a general labourer and after his wife Maggie died he and Mary Ann Brown were married on 1 May 1908 in First Donaghadee Presbyterian Church. They had at least three children – Robert, Hugh and David John (born in 1917 after his step brother had died on active service).

David John Keilty Junior also worked as a general labourer and he lived for a time in Belfast. He enlisted in Newtownards, he served with the 2nd Battalion Royal Irish Rifles and he went to France on 16 August 1914.

Rifleman David John Keilty died of disease on 16 September 1916 and he is commemorated on Newtownards and District War Memorial; in the PCI Roll of Honour for Greenwell Street Presbyterian Church and in the Belfast Book of Honour (Page 310).

Keith, Daniel Maclean (Daniel)
Private
No. 9438, 1st Battalion, Royal Scots Fusiliers
Killed in action on Wednesday 16 June 1915
Ypres (Menin Gate) Memorial, Belgium (Panel 19 and 33)

K

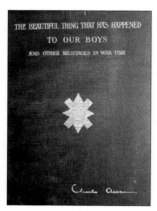

Daniel Maclean Keith was born in Paisley, he enlisted in Glasgow and he served as a Drummer with the 1st Battalion Royal Scots Fusiliers. His wife lived in Newtownards and after Private Daniel Keith was killed in action on 16 June 1915 she received a memorial sympathy card from Paisley Town Council. The card was surmounted by two wreaths with between them the words 'European War'. In the centre there was a figure of an angelic warrior holding a sword in one hand and in the other a large Union banner. The wording on the card was: 'The Provost, Magistrates and Councillors of the Borough of Paisley desire to convey to you their deep sympathy in your great bereavement in the death of Daniel Keith, your brave husband, who gave his life for King and Country'. A copy of the book entitled *The Beautiful Thing That Has Happened to Our Boys* accompanied the card.

Private Daniel Keith is commemorated on Newtownards and District War Memorial (as Duncan Keith) and also in Donaghadee Parish Church Graveyard on his wife's family grave headstone (Graham) along with the inscription:

'Until the day break and the shadows flee away'

Keith, Thomas Alexander (Thomas)
Private
No. 20639, 10th Battalion, Canadian Infantry (Alberta Regiment)
Died on Thursday 22 April 1915 (aged 24)
Ypres (Menin Gate) Memorial, Belgium (Panel 24-28-30)

Thomas Alexander Keith was born on 10 November 1890 and he was a son of Andrew and Harriett Keith (nee Robson) who lived in the townland of Ballyvester, Donaghadee. They were married on 30 April 1886 in First Donaghadee Presbyterian Church. Andrew Keith worked as an agricultural labourer and he and Harriett had at least ten children – Henry, William James, Thomas Alexander, Mary Emma, Andrew Hanna, Elizabeth, Joseph, Francis French, Harriett Arabella and John Robson. All of the children were baptised in First Donaghadee Presbyterian Church.

Thomas Keith moved to Canada where he worked as a carpenter before he enlisted on 24 September 1914 in Valcartier, Quebec. In his attestation papers it was noted that he was 5 feet 7½ inches tall. He served with the 10th Battalion Alberta Regiment and he died on 22 April 1915 some seven months after he enlisted. His brother Andrew served with the 13th Battalion Royal Irish Rifles, was awarded the Military Medal and survived the war.

Private Thomas Alexander Keith is commemorated on Donaghadee and District War Memorial and in First Donaghadee Presbyterian Church.

Kelly, Edward John (Edward)
Rifleman
No. 4/7074, 1st Battalion, Royal Irish Rifles
Killed in action on Sunday 9 May 1915 (aged 22)
Ploegsteert Memorial, France (Panel 9)

There is some variation in his Regimental number:

771 (CWGC)
1074 (newspaper report)
7074 ('Soldiers Died in the Great War 1914 – 1919').

Edward John Kelly was born on 12 February 1893 in Newtownards and he was a son of Alice Kelly who worked as an embroiderer. Edward and his sister Mary Ann lived with their mother, uncle and grandmother in Mill Street. Edward was baptised in Greenwell Street Presbyterian Church Newtownards.

K

Edward Kelly enlisted in Newtownards and he joined the 4th Battalion Royal Irish Rifles. He went to France on 28 December 1914 to replace casualties and he served with 'D' Company 1st Battalion Royal Irish Rifles. He was posted as missing in action after the action at Rouge Bancs on 9 May 1915 and his mother sought information about him through the pages of the *Newtownards Chronicle*. Later it was officially confirmed that he had been killed in action.

Rifleman Edward Kelly is commemorated on Newtownards and District War Memorial and in the PCI Roll of Honour for Greenwell Street Presbyterian Church Newtownards.

Kelly, Hugh
Rifleman
No. 266, 'B' Company, 13th Battalion, Royal Irish Rifles
Died of wounds on Thursday 16 August 1917 (aged 28)
Lijssenthoek Military Cemetery, Belgium (Grave XVII. AA. 14)

K

Hugh Kelly was born in Comber and he was a son of Henry and Margaret Kelly (nee Duff) who lived in Railway Street. They were married on 2 January 1880 in Newtownards Registry Office. Henry Kelly worked as a farm servant and he and Margaret had at least nine children including John, Henry, Thomas, Hugh, Mary, James and Samuel.

Prior to joining the army Hugh Kelly worked as a shipyard labourer and then for Mr Milling (Undertaker) in The Square, Comber. Hugh Kelly and Sarah Ringland were married on 5 November 1910 in St Anne's Church of Ireland Belfast. They lived in Bridge Street, Comber and they had at least two children – Henry and a daughter that he never saw. Hugh Kelly enlisted in Belfast and he served with the 13th Battalion Royal Irish Rifles in 108th Brigade of the 36th (Ulster) Division. He was wounded on 14 February 1917 and again during the Third Battle of Ypres. He died of wounds on 16 August 1917 and he is commemorated on Comber and District War Memorial and in Second Comber Presbyterian Church.

Kelly, James Armstrong (James)
Sergeant
No. 16393, 7th Service Battalion, Royal Inniskilling Fusiliers
Died in hospital on Monday 8 November 1915 (aged 45)
Brookwood Cemetery, Surrey, England (Grave Q. 176614)

James Armstrong Kelly was the youngest son of William and Mary A Kelly who lived at Downhill, Castlerock, Co Londonderry. James Kelly and Clarissa (Clara) Eleanor Blevings were married on 9 February 1907 in St Anne's Church of Ireland Belfast, they had one daughter and they lived at 36 Court Street, Newtownards. One of James's sisters and her family also lived in Court Street while another sister, Mrs Murphy, lived in Cobalt, Ontario in Canada.

Signalling Sergeant Kelly died suddenly in Inkerman Military Hospital, St John's, Woking in Surrey. Before being posted to the 7th Service Battalion he had served for 22 years with the 1st Battalion Royal Inniskilling Fusiliers. He saw foreign service in Canada, Crete, Malta, China, South Africa and India.

His discharge papers from the South African War contain the record of his gallant conduct and note that in that campaign he was awarded the Distinguished Conduct Medal. In addition he held the Queen's Medal with six clasps and the King's Medal with two clasps.

Sergeant Kelly retired from active service on 4 January 1913 but he rejoined the army at the outbreak of the Great War. He was attached to the 7th Battalion Royal Inniskilling Fusiliers as a signalling instructor. His sudden death resulted in an inquest. He had complained of pains on the evening of Saturday 6 November 1915 and was admitted to hospital the next day. He died around 7.00 am on Monday 8 November 1915. A post-mortem examination showed a 'diseased and enlarged heart' with other organs affected. The cause of death was stated to be 'dilation producing syncope'.

Sergeant Kelly was buried on Thursday 11 November 1915 with full military honours and he is commemorated on Newtownards and District War Memorial and in Newtownards Parish Church of Ireland (St Mark).

K

Kelly, William George (George)
Rifleman
**No. 18005, 'B' Company, 13th Battalion, Royal Irish Rifles
Killed in action on Saturday 1 July 1916 (aged 28)
Thiepval Memorial, France (Pier and Face 15 A and 15 B)**

William George Kelly was born on 18 October 1887 in Newtownards and he was the eldest son of John and Mary Ann Kelly (nee Dickson) who lived at 55 Wallace's Street No. 2. They were married on 11 July 1885 in Newtownards Parish Church of Ireland. John Kelly worked as a linen weaver and he and Mary Ann had at least five children – Richard, William George, Thomas, Lizzie and Agnes. William George Kelly was baptised in Fourth Newtownards Presbyterian Church.

George Kelly worked as a wool weaver before the Great War and after he died his looms still stood in the earthen-floored house where he had left them when he went to war. George Kelly enlisted in Newtownards and he served with the 13th Battalion Royal Irish Rifles in 108th Brigade of the 36th (Ulster) Division. He was posted as missing in action after the first day of the Battle of the Somme and a year later it was officially confirmed that he had been killed in action.

His father, mother, brother and sisters placed a 'For King and Country' notice in the *Newtownards Chronicle* and an 'In Memoriam' notice the following year contained the text:

'And how can man die better?'

Rifleman George Kelly is commemorated on Newtownards and District War Memorial and in the PCI Roll of Honour for Greenwell Street Presbyterian Church Newtownards.

Kemp, Robert
The name Robert Kemp is listed on Newtownards and District War Memorial and in the booklet produced for the Unveiling and Dedication Ceremony held on Saturday 26 May 1934 he is described as a Rifleman in the Royal Irish Rifles. Desk searches and public appeals to date have yielded no further information.

Kennedy, John
Rifleman
No. 7264, 1st Battalion, Royal Irish Rifles
Killed in action on Thursday 16 August 1917 (aged 20)
Hooge Crater Cemetery, Belgium (Grave XVI. D. 5)

John Kennedy was born in Comber, he lived in Dundonald and he enlisted in Newtownards. CWGC Debt of Honour records indicate that he was 20 years old when he died on 16 August 1917 and from that it may be concluded that he was around 14 years of age at the time of the 1911 Census. Census information provides unsubstantiated evidence about his family circumstances. In 1911 there was a 14-year old John Kennedy living in the townland of Ballyrogan, Newtownards. He boarded with and worked as an agricultural labourer for Isabella McMurry, a 69-year old widowed farmer.

Comber Rifleman Reported Killed.
Rifleman J. Kennedy (No. 7,246), R.I. Rifles, Comber, who was previously posted as missing, is now officially reported killed.

Rifleman John Kennedy was killed in action on 16 August 1917 at Langemarck during the Third Battle of Ypres and initially he was posted as missing in action. Under the headline 'Comber Rifleman Reported Killed' the 2 March 1918 edition of the *Newtownards Chronicle* carried a report which indicated that Rifleman J Kennedy (7246; note the sequence of digits) Royal Irish Rifles Comber who was previously posted as missing is now officially reported killed.

There are two John Kennedys with Newtownards connections who were Riflemen in the Royal Irish Rifles and only one of them is listed on Newtownards and District War Memorial – either Rifleman John Kennedy (7264) or Rifleman John Kennedy (17/1773).

Kennedy, John
Rifleman
No. 17/1773, 8th Battalion, Royal Irish Rifles
Died of wounds on Thursday 2 August 1917
Brandhoek New Military Cemetery, Belgium (Grave II. E. 7)

John Kennedy was born in the townland of Moneyreagh, he lived in Newtownards and in November 1915 he enlisted in Belfast. He joined the 17th Battalion Royal Irish Rifles and then was posted to the 8th Battalion in 107th Brigade of the 36th (Ulster) Division. Rifleman John Kennedy died of wounds on 2 August 1917 during the Third Battle of Ypres.

There are two John Kennedys with Newtownards connections who were

Riflemen in the Royal Irish Rifles and only one of them is listed on Newtownards and District War Memorial – either Rifleman John Kennedy (7264) or Rifleman John Kennedy (17/1773).

Kennedy, Samuel
Rifleman
No. 12983, 8th Battalion, Royal Irish Rifles
Killed in action on Sunday 2 July 1916
Thiepval Memorial, France (Pier and Face 15 A and 15 B)

In 'Soldiers Died in the Great War 1914 – 1919' it is recorded that Samuel Kennedy was born in Cavan, he lived in Newtownards and he enlisted in Belfast. He served with the 8th Battalion Royal Irish Rifles in 107th Brigade of the 36th (Ulster) Division and in the CWGC Debt of Honour it is recorded that Rifleman Samuel Kennedy died on 2 July 1916. In the heat of battle the 8th Battalion Royal Irish Rifles did not make a casualty return on 1 July 1916 and many military historians agree that those 8th Battalion casualties listed on the 2 July return were killed in action on 1 July.

Kenny, William David (William)
Victoria Cross
Lieutenant
4th Battalion, 39th Garhwal Rifles
Killed in action on Friday, 2 January 1920 (aged 20)
Jandola Cemetery, India (Grave 5)
Delhi Memorial (India Gate), India (Face 31)

K

William David Kenny was born on 1 February 1899 in Saintfield and he was the eldest child of John Joseph and Miriam Martha Kenny (nee Newton). They were married on 11 November 1896 in St Nicholas's Parish Church of Ireland Carrickfergus and they had at least two other children – Georgina Martha and Gerald Henry. John Joseph Kenny was a Constable in the Royal Irish Constabulary and for a time he was stationed in Donaghadee. Before that the family lived in the townland of Glenloughan, Scarva, Co Down.

William David Kenny was commissioned into the Indian Army as a Second Lieutenant on 31 August 1918 and he was posted to the 4th Battalion 39th Garhwal Rifles. A year later he was promoted Lieutenant, he was killed in action on 2 January 1920 during the Waziristan campaign and he was posthumously awarded the Victoria Cross.

An extract from the Third Supplement to the *London Gazette* dated 7 September 1920 records the following: 'For most conspicuous bravery and devotion to duty near Kot Kai (Waziristan) on the 2nd January 1920, when in command of a company holding an advanced covering position, which was repeatedly attacked by Mahsuds in greatly superior numbers. For over four hours this officer maintained his position, repulsing three determined attacks, being foremost in the hand-to-hand fighting which took place, and repeatedly engaging the enemy with bomb and bayonet. His gallant leadership undoubtedly saved the situation and kept intact the right flank, on which depended the success of the operations and the safety of the troops in rear. In the subsequent withdrawal, recognising that a diversion was necessary to enable the withdrawal of the company, which was impeded by their wounded, with a handful of his men he turned back and counter-attacked the pursuing enemy, and with the rest of his party, was killed fighting to the last. This very gallant act of self-sacrifice not only enabled the wounded to be withdrawn but also averted a situation which must have resulted in considerable loss of life.'

Lieutenant William David Kenny is commemorated on Donaghadee and District War Memorial and in Donaghadee Parish Church of Ireland. His Victoria Cross is on display in the National Army Museum, Chelsea.

K

Kerr, Andrew
Private
No. 8845, 1st/4th Battalion, Royal Scots Fusiliers
Died on Monday 12 July 1915
Helles Memorial, Gallipoli, Turkey (Panel 72 to 75)

In 'Soldiers Died in the Great War 1914 – 1919' it is recorded that Andrew Kerr was born in Newtownards, he lived in Barassie, Ayrshire and he enlisted in Kilmarnock. Private Andrew Kerr served with the Royal Scots Fusiliers and he died at the Dardanelles on 12 July 1915.

Kerr, Bernard *
Private
No. 3652, Connaught Rangers, transferred to (20949), 9th Battalion, Princess Victoria's (Royal Irish Fusiliers)
Killed in action on Friday 12 April 1918
Tyne Cot Memorial, Belgium (Panel 140 to 141)

In 'Soldiers Died in the Great War 1914 – 1919' it is recorded that Bernard Kerr was born in Belfast and he enlisted in Belfast. Private Bernard Kerr served with the Connaught Rangers (3652) and subsequently with the 9th Battalion Royal Irish Fusiliers. He was killed in action on 12 April 1918 and his death was reported in the *Newtownards Chronicle* under the headline 'Portaferry Fusilier Killed'.

Bernard Kerr and Bella Lennon were married on 7 October 1915 in Portaferry Roman Catholic Church and when Bernard died Bella was living in High Street, Portaferry. Private Bernard Kerr is commemorated in the Belfast Book of Honour (Page 317).

Kerr, Hugh
Lance Corporal
No. 64156, 150th Field Company, transferred to 'G' Depot Company, Royal Engineers, 36th (Ulster) Division
Died of dysentery on 2 October 1918 (aged 43)
Newtownards (Movilla) Cemetery, Co. Down (Grave 1. 48)

K

64156 LANCE CPL.
H.KERR
ROYAL ENGINEERS
2ND OCTOBER 1918 AGE 43

Hugh Kerr was born in the townland of Ballyhay, Newtownards and he was a son of Andrew and Jane Kerr (nee McClune). They were married on 23 September 1870 in Bangor Abbey. Andrew Kerr worked as a farmer and he and Jane had at least four children – Hugh, John Francis, Joseph and Sarah Jane.

Hugh Kerr worked as a carpenter before the Great War and he and his wife Agnes lived at 14 Kimberley Buildings, Newtownards. They had at least one child, a son named Andrew. Hugh Kerr enlisted in Belfast, he served with the Royal Engineers and he went to France on 5 October 1915 with the 150th Field Company.

Lance Corporal Hugh Kerr died of dysentery on 2 October 1918 at Stepping Hill Hospital, Stockport in England. His remains were brought home and then taken from there for burial in Movilla Cemetery Newtownards. He is commemorated on Newtownards and District War

Memorial; in the PCI Roll of Honour for Greenwell Street Presbyterian Church Newtownards and on the family grave headstone in Movilla Cemetery.

Kerr, James
Rifleman
No. 19048, 'B' Company, 13th Battalion, Royal Irish Rifles
Died of disease on Monday 13 June 1921 (aged 24)
Greyabbey Old Cemetery, Greyabbey, Co. Down

James Kerr was born in Ballywalter and he was a son of Hugh and Jane Kerr (nee Beckett) who lived in the townland of Springvale. They were married on 11 May 1885 in Greyabbey Parish Church of Ireland. Hugh Kerr worked as a labourer, Jane worked as an embroiderer and they had at least nine children – William Thomas, Edward, Jane, Agnes, Bessie, James, Henry, Robert and George. Jane Kerr died on 9 November 1904 aged 38.

James Kerr first worked as a dog boy when he left school. He enlisted on 17 September 1914 and he served with the 13th Battalion Royal Irish Rifles in 108th Brigade of the 36th (Ulster) Division. Rifleman James Kerr was wounded on the first day of the Battle of the Somme and he was discharged from the Army on 24 October 1919 because of 'abscesses'. He died on 13 June 1921 and he was buried in Greyabbey Old Cemetery.

K

Rifleman James Kerr is commemorated on Ballywalter and District War Memorial.

Kinlay, James Aloysius
Private
No. 436, 4th Regiment, South African Infantry
Died of wounds on Friday 21 July 1916 (aged 38)
Wimereux Communal Cemetery, France (Grave I. O. 15)

James Aloysius Kinlay was a son of James and Catherine Kinlay (nee Breen) of 37 Synge Street, Dublin and formerly of Portaferry, Co Down. They were married on 24 September 1871 in Portaferry Roman Catholic Church. James's connection with Portaferry was noted in the report of his death in the 5 August 1916 edition of the *Newtownards Chronicle*. James Kinlay Senior worked as a printer and he and Catherine had at least four children – James Aloysius, Hugh Joseph, Mary Catherine and Sarah Agatha.

James Aloysius Kinlay served for a year in the Royal Irish Rifles before he and his brother Hugh Joseph moved to South Africa. They lived in Capetown where James Aloysius Kinlay worked as a Civil Servant in the Department of Agriculture before he enlisted on 17 August 1915 at Potchefstroom. It was noted in his attestation papers that he was 5 feet 9½ inches tall and that he had a naevus above his umbilicus.

PORTAFERRY.
Pte. J. A. Kinlay, South African Infantry, son of Mr. James Kinlay, formerly of Portaferry, died of wounds.

Private Kinlay sailed from South Africa to England and from there he sailed to Alexandria in Egypt before he went to France. He disembarked at Marseilles on 20 April 1916 and he was seriously wounded on 17 July 1916 at Wimereux. He sustained gunshot wounds to his left shoulder and hand. Private James Aloysius Kinlay died four days later in hospital at Boulogne.

Kinnaird, John (Jack)
Private
No. 2680, 4th Battalion, Australian Infantry, AIF
Died of wounds on Friday 2 March 1917 (aged 27)
Warlencourt British Cemetery, France (Grave IV. B. 8)

K

John Kinnaird was born on 4 August 1889 and he was a son of William and Sarah Ann Kinnaird (nee Hodgins) who lived in East Street, then John Street and later at 41 South Street, Newtownards. They were married on 15 June 1885 in First Newtownards Presbyterian Church. William Kinnaird worked as a foreman in the municipal gas works and he and Sarah Ann had at least eleven children – William, Jane, John, Robert, Sarah Ann (died), Hugh, Elizabeth, David Hedley, Margaret Crawford, Sarah Ann and Ronald Orr. Jack Kinnaird worked as a plumber before he moved to Australia and there he worked as a miner before he enlisted on 29 July 1915 in Newcastle, New South Wales. In his attestation papers it was noted that he was 5 feet 6¼ inches tall and he cited his father as his next-of-kin.

He was posted to Egypt for a short period and from Alexandria he sailed to France. He disembarked in Marseilles on 30 March 1916 and in July that year he was wounded in action. He was hospitalised suffering from shell shock. Jack was wounded in action again on the morning of 2 March 1917 during an enemy attack at Le Barque and he died later that day. First news of his death came in a letter to his father from Private HG Brown, one of his comrades. After Jack Kinnaird's death was officially confirmed his personal effects comprising a tobacco pouch, unit colours, letters, cards, photos, wallet, pocket book, money belt, shell and scarf were sent to his father who was living at 41 South Street, Newtownards.

There were three 'For King and Country' notices in the 31 March 1917 edition of the *Newtownards Chronicle*, one from his parents, one from his brother Robert serving with the Canadians and one from his brother Hugh serving with the Royal Irish Rifles. Private Jack Kinnaird is commemorated on Newtownards and District War Memorial and in Newtownards Parish Church of Ireland (St Mark).

Knox, George
Second Lieutenant
8th Battalion, King's Own (Royal Lancaster Regiment)
Killed in action on Sunday 9 April 1916 (aged 34)
Ypres (Menin Gate) Memorial, Belgium (Panel 12)

Newtownards Family Bereaved.

Official word was received on 17th inst. that Second-Lieuteneant Geo. Knox, King's Own Royal Lancaster Regiment, who was formerly reported missing, was killed in action on 9th April. Lieutenant Knox, who was a young man of fine physique, and only aged 34, was, it appears, wounded by a bullet in the leg. After lying for some time he struggled up, and gallantly entered into the battle again, encouraging his men, when a shell terminated the existence of this young hero. Second-Lieutenant Knox was the second son of the late Mr. Geo. Knox, of Granshaw. Streatham Hill, London, S.W., a grandson of the late Mr. John Taylor, one of the leading merchants in his time in Newtownards, and a nephew of Mrs. R. B. Caughey, Saraville, Newtownards.

George Knox was the second son of George Knox of 'Granshaw', Streatham Hill in London and he was a grandson of the late John Taylor who had been one of the leading merchants in Newtownards. He was a nephew of Mrs R B Caughey of 'Saraville', Newtownards. In the 25 November 1916 edition of the *Newtownards Chronicle* Second Lieutenant George Knox's death was reported under the headline 'Newtownards Family Bereaved'. In the same edition there was a 'For King and Country' death notice.

K
L

Initially posted as missing in action his death on 9 April 1916 was officially confirmed six months later. He had been wounded in the leg and then killed by shellfire whilst leading his men during a German attack.

Laidlaw, George
Private
No. S/20127, 5th Battalion, Cameron Highlanders
Killed in action on Tuesday 18 July 1916 (aged 25)
Thiepval Memorial, France (Pier and Face 15 B)

In 'Soldiers Died in the Great War 1914 – 1919' it is recorded that George

Laidlaw was born in Barony, Glasgow and in the CWGC Debt of Honour it is recorded that he was a son of William Laidlaw who lived in the townland of Ballyeasborough, Ballyhalbert. He enlisted in Glasgow, he served with the Cameron Highlanders and he was killed in action on 18 July 1916 during the Battle of the Somme.

His family placed a 'Killed in Action' notice in the 26 August 1916 edition of the *Newtownards Chronicle* and, one year after Private George Laidlaw died, his sister and brother-in-law Nellie and William Palmer from Ballyeasborough placed an 'Our Heroes – In Memoriam' notice which contained the verse:

'Sleep on, dear brother, in your foreign grave,
A grave we may never see;
But as long as life and memory last
We will remember thee.'

Lamont, David
Lance Corporal
No. 11619, 9th Battalion, Royal Inniskilling Fusiliers
Killed in action on Saturday 1 July 1916
Mill Road Cemetery, France (Grave I. A. 29)

In 'Soldiers Died in the Great War 1914 – 1919' it is recorded that David Lamont was born in Newtownards and he enlisted in Belfast. He served with the 9th Battalion Royal Inniskilling Fusiliers in 109th Brigade of the 36th (Ulster) Division and he was killed in action on the first day of the Battle of the Somme.

Lane, Sidney
Lance Corporal
No. 3526, 1st Battalion, Irish Guards
Died of wounds on Saturday 29 May 1915
Boulogne Eastern Cemetery, France (Grave VIII. A. 56)

> **Former Newtownards Man Killed.**
> The relatives of Lance-Corporal Sydney Lane, Irish Guards, who resides at 11 Coolderry Street, Belfast, have been notified that he died on May 30 in France of wounds received in action. Deceased was the fourth son of the late Captain T. H. Lane, 3rd Battalion Royal Irish Rifles, who was Quarter-master of the Royal North Downs at Newtownards.

The death of Lance Corporal Sidney Lane was reported in the 5 June 1915 edition of the *Newtownards Chronicle* under the headline 'Former Newtownards Man Killed'. In the article his forename was spelt Sydney.

Sidney Lane was the fourth son of the late Captain TH Lane 3rd Battalion Royal Irish Rifles and he was born in Newtownards when his father was Quartermaster of the Royal North Downs. He enlisted in Belfast and he served with the 1st Battalion Irish Guards. When Lance Corporal Sidney Lane died of wounds on 29 May 1915 his family was living at 11 Coolderry Street in Belfast and he is commemorated in the Belfast Book of Honour (Page 326).

Laverty, Joseph
Second Lieutenant

13th Battalion, Royal Irish Rifles
Killed in action on Thursday 16 August 1917
Tyne Cot Memorial, Belgium (Panel 138 to 140 & 162 to 162A & 163A)

> **Former Newtownards School Teacher Killed.**
> Amongst the casualties reported this week is that of Second-Lieutenant Joseph Laverty, Royal Irish Rifles, who was killed in action on 16th inst. He was an assistant in Newtownards Model School prior to being appointed principal of Castlerobin N.S., Derriaghy. His parents live at Tobermore, County Derry.

Joseph Laverty worked as a teacher in Newtownards Model School prior to being appointed principal of Castlerobin National School in Derriaghy. His parents lived in Tobermore, Co Londonderry.

Second Lieutenant Joseph Laverty served with the 13th Battalion Royal Irish Rifles in 108th Brigade of the 36th (Ulster) Division and he was killed in action on 16 August 1917 at Langemarck during the Third Battle of Ypres. He is commemorated on the QUB War Memorial and in the QUB Book of Remembrance (Page 31).

Lawson, Hugh
The name Hugh Lawson is listed on Newtownards and District War Memorial and in the booklet produced for the Unveiling and Dedication Ceremony held on Saturday 26 May 1934 he is described as a Corporal in the Royal Irish Rifles. Desk searches and public appeals to date have yielded no further information.

Ledgerwood Brothers: John and Samuel
John and Samuel Ledgerwood were born in Newtownards and they were sons of William and Agnes Ledgerwood (nee Brown) who lived in East Street. William and Agnes were married on 22 May 1875 in Newtownards Parish Church of Ireland. Later the Ledgerwood family moved to 11 Upper Court

Street. William Ledgerwood worked as a wool weaver and he and Agnes had at least seven children including Mary, Letitia, John, Agnes, Margaret (Maggie) and Samuel.

Samuel Ledgerwood was the first of the two brothers to die on active service in the Great War. However, official confirmation that Samuel had been killed in action did not reach his family until after they heard officially that John had died:

Ledgerwood, Samuel Hugh (Samuel)
Rifleman
No. 18079, 'B' Company, 13th Battalion, Royal Irish Rifles
Killed in action on Saturday 1 July 1916 (aged 23)
Thiepval Memorial, France (Pier and Face 15 A and 15 B)

Samuel Ledgerwood was born on 10 May 1893 and prior to the outbreak of the Great War he worked as a cotton weaver. He enlisted in Newtownards and he served with the 13th Battalion Royal Irish Rifles in 108th Brigade of the 36th (Ulster) Division. Rifleman Samuel Ledgerwood was posted as missing in action after the first day of the Battle of the Somme and his family in Newtownards anxiously awaited further news.

Ledgerwood, John
Rifleman
No. 18/1284, 9th Battalion, Royal Irish Rifles
Died of wounds on Saturday 6 January 1917 (aged 33)
Bailleul Communal Cemetery Extension (Nord), France (Grave III. A. 134)

Prior to the outbreak of the Great War John Ledgerwood worked as a cotton weaver and he enlisted in Newtownards. Rifleman John Ledgerwood served with the 9th Battalion Royal Irish Rifles in 107th Brigade of the 36th (Ulster) Division. On 11 December 1916 he sustained severe gunshot wounds to his right arm and right leg and he was admitted to No. 2 Casualty Clearing Station. The following day the Sister-in-Charge wrote to inform his mother that he was 'going on as well as could be expected under the circumstances'. On New Year's Day 1917 John wrote a letter to his mother telling her that he had had to have his leg amputated:

'My Dear Mother – During the last two days my knee has given me a little further trouble and at the suggestion of the doctor I had my leg taken off above the knee last evening. This had to be in order to save my life so that I begin the New Year 1917 with the highest and best prospects. Even now the pain is less than formerly and everyone in hospital is pleased with me. Of my ultimate restoration to health there seems no doubt'.

Rifleman John Ledgerwood Dies from Wounds.

Rifleman John Ledgerwood, son of Mrs. Ledgerwood, at present residing at 11 Upper Court Street, Newtownards, has made the supreme sacrifice after undergoing an operation which promised to be successful.

Then, on 6 January 1917 Sister D McPherson wrote to John's mother to tell her that he had died that morning and to express sympathy on behalf of all the hospital staff. She said, 'Although everything was done for him that could possibly be done he passed away peacefully at 2.30 o'clock. He did not leave any message but yesterday he expressed a wish that he would have liked to have seen his mother before he died and that he was always thinking of her. I have saved you a lock of his hair which I now enclose as I thought you would like to have it'.

The Ledgerwood family placed four 'For King and Country' notices in the 13 January 1917 edition of the *Newtownards Chronicle*. The one from his widowed mother and his sister Maggie contained the verse:

> 'We prayed that God would keep him,
> And shield him in the fray;
> But alas! Our hopes were blighted
> When the sad news came that day,
> Short was thy life my darling son,
> But peaceful is thy rest;
> Mother misses you most of all,
> Because she loved you best'

The other notices were from his sister Agnes and brother-in-law James McClean of 5 Lower Mary Street; his widowed sister Mary Warden of 34 Upper Movilla Street and his sister Letitia and brother-in-law Private John Dogherty of 51 Pound Street, Newtownards.

Within four weeks of John's death Agnes Ledgerwood received official notification that her son Samuel had also been killed in action and so the Ledgerwood family placed a further series of four 'For King and Country' notices in the 10 February 1917 edition of the *Newtownards Chronicle*. This time the one from his widowed mother and his sister Maggie contained the verse:

'I often think of days gone by,
When we were all together;
A shadow o'er our life is cast,
Two loved sons gone for ever.
Friends may forget them, but mother will never,
They will dwell in our hearts till life's journey is done;
Lord, teach us to live, that when our days are ended,
We'll be met at the gates by our dear hero sons'

Riflemen John and Samuel Ledgerwood are both commemorated on Newtownards and District War Memorial and in Newtownards Parish Church of Ireland (St Mark).

Ledlie, George

Corporal George Ledlie Royal Irish Rifles is commemorated on the Memorial Plaque in Ballyhalbert Parish Church of Ireland (St Andrew) at Ballyeasborough. In the 1901 Census there is an Episcopalian Ledlie family living at 35 Ballyeasborough, Ballyhalbert. William and Maggie Ledlie had at least eight children – Jane, William James, Robert, Joseph, George (aged 9), David, Thomas and John.

Desk searches and public appeals to date have not confirmed a connection between these 1901 census data and the soldier commemorated in Ballyhalbert Parish Church of Ireland (St Andrew) at Ballyeasborough.

Lennon, Robert
Private
No. 2482, 29th Division Cyclist Corps, transferred to (25195), 2nd Battalion, South Wales Borderers
Died on Sunday 28 May 1916 (aged 24)
Auchonvillers Military Cemetery, France (Grave II. A. 24)

Robert Lennon was born in Shankill, Belfast and he lived at 11 John Street, later 25 Hillview Terrace, in Newtownards with his sister Lizzie and his grandparents James and Rachael Kinghan (spelt Kingham in a newspaper notice). Before the Great War James Kinghan worked as a fireman in a saw-mill and Robert Lennon worked as a packer in a linen warehouse.

Robert Lennon enlisted in Belfast and he served with the 1st Battalion Royal Inniskilling Fusiliers (10195) and the 29th Divisional Cyclist Corps. Later he was transferred to the 2nd Battalion South Wales Borderers. Private Robert Lennon was killed accidentally in France on 28 May 1916 and his sister

L

Elizabeth Finlay, together with his grandmother Rachael Kinghan and his uncle Robert Kinghan, placed a 'For King and Country' notice in the 15 July edition of the *Newtownards Chronicle*.

The following year his sister Lizzie and his brother-in-law William James Finlay (on active service) from Rubane, Kircubbin placed an 'Our Heroes – In Memoriam' notice in the *Newtownards Chronicle* and it contained the verse:

'Peaceful be your rest, dear brother,
Tis sweet to breathe your name;
In life we loved you very dear,
In death we do the same'

Private Robert Lennon is commemorated on Newtownards and District War Memorial (in the booklet produced for the Unveiling and Dedication Ceremony held on 26 May 1934 he is described as a Rifleman in the Royal Irish Rifles). He is also commemorated in the Belfast Book of Honour (Page 338).

L

Lightbody, Robert John (Robert)
Private
No. 23664, 1st Battalion, Royal Inniskilling Fusiliers
Killed in action on Wednesday 10 November 1915 (aged 21)
Skew Bridge Cemetery, Gallipoli, Turkey (Special Memorial A. 51)

Robert John Lightbody was a son of Samuel and Jane Lightbody (nee Rea) who lived at 8 Front Shuttlefield, Newtownards. They were married on 9 March 1897 in Newtownards Registry Office. Samuel Lightbody worked as a general labourer and he and Jane had at least eight children/step-children – James, Thomas Andrew, Mary Elizabeth, Jane, Robert John, Samuel, Alexander and Agnes

Robert Lightbody enlisted in Newtownards and he served with the Royal Inniskilling Fusiliers in Omagh before being transferred to Londonderry. He left there on 16 October 1915 bound for Gallipoli. Less than a month later he was dead, another Ardsman killed in the Dardanelles.

Robert's father received the official news of his son's death from the Record

Office in Dublin. He also received a letter from a Military Chaplain, the Rev SH Semple of the 7th Royal Scots. In his letter the Chaplain expressed his sympathy and conveyed the news that Robert had been shot and killed instantaneously by a stray bullet near 'Brown House'. The shooting happened during the night when Private Robert Lightbody was working with a fatigue party about 800 yards behind the firing line. The Rev Semple conducted the burial service at 4.00 pm the following day.

The Rev Semple went on to describe the terrain. He wrote, 'The ground all over this peninsula is at present brown after summer heat. Winter rains are beginning and spring flowers grow profusely. At Eastertide they will be fresh and beautiful and each year they are renewed.'

When Robert Lightbody was killed in action his brother Samuel, also a Private in the Royal Inniskilling Fusiliers, was being held as a prisoner of war in Germany where he had been since August 1914.

After his death Robert Lightbody's family placed a 'Killed in Action' notice in the *Newtownards Chronicle* and it contained the verse:

L

'We oftimes sit and think of him,
We cannot think he's dead;
We little thought when he left home,
It was our last farewell.'

Private Robert Lightbody is commemorated on Newtownards and District War Memorial and in Second Newtownards Presbyterian Church.

Logan, Samuel
Private
No. 8866, 2nd Battalion, Royal Inniskilling Fusiliers
Killed in action on Sunday 29 September 1918
Dadizeele New British Cemetery, Belgium (Grave VI. F. 33)

Samuel Logan was born in Shankill, Belfast and he enlisted in Newtownards. He served with the 2nd Battalion Royal Inniskilling Fusiliers and he was killed in action on 29 September 1918, by then with 109th Brigade in the 36th (Ulster) Division during the Allied offensive against all sections of the German line. Private Samuel Logan is commemorated on Newtownards and District War Memorial.

Logan, William Edwin
Lance Corporal
No. 3943, 16th Battalion, Australian Infantry, AIF
Killed in action on Tuesday 6 February 1917 (aged 38)
Villers-Bretonneux Memorial, France

William Edwin Logan was born in Gilford, Co Down and he was a son of Samuel and Mary Logan (nee McKee). They were married on 1 June 1876 in Gilford Presbyterian Church. Samuel Logan was a Sergeant in the Royal Irish Constabulary and for a time he was stationed in Comber.

William Edwin Logan moved to Australia and, prior to the outbreak of the Great War, he worked as a butcher. In August 1915 William Edwin Logan enlisted in Perth and it was noted in his attestation papers that he was 5 feet 6¼ inches tall. He was promoted in the field to the rank of Lance Corporal in October 1916.

Lance Corporal William Edwin Logan was killed in action by an exploding shell at Gueudecourt on 6 February 1917. It was reported that his death was instantaneous and that he was buried by his comrades in the trench where he fell. When Lance Corporal Logan died he was unmarried, both of his parents were dead and he had no brothers. Mrs Florence Porter, his eldest sister, was his next-of-kin and she received his medals.

Lowry, Andrew
Private
No. 23767, 8th Battalion, Royal Scots Fusiliers
Killed in action on Thursday 19 September 1918 (aged 32)
Doiran Military Cemetery, Greece (Grave III. C. 2)

Andrew Lowry was born in the townland of Tullynakill, Killinchy and he was a son of Robert and Elizabeth (Eliza) Lowry (nee Sloan) who lived in the townland of Lisbane. They were married on 11 August 1868 in Tullynakill Parish Church of Ireland. Robert Lowry worked as a thatcher and he and Eliza had at least ten children including John, Andrew, Eliza and Nannie.

Before he moved to Scotland Andrew Lowry worked first as an apprentice thatcher with his father and then as a tailor. Andrew Lowry and his wife Annabella lived at 139 Hillhouse Street, Springburn, Glasgow and he enlisted in Glasgow. He served with the 8th Battalion Royal Scots Fusiliers and he was killed in action on 19 September 1918 during the Allied offensive against all sections of the German line. Private Andrew Lowry is commemorated on Comber and District War Memorial and in Killinchy Presbyterian Church.

Lowry, Henry Cooke
Captain
Army Veterinary Corps
Died of disease on Tuesday 11 July 1916 (aged 32)
Basra War Cemetery, Iraq (Grave III. M. 20)

Henry Cooke Lowry was born in Belfast and he was the only son of James and Susanna (Susie) Lowry (nee Lowry). James Lowry worked as a draper in Belfast and he and Susanna Lowry who came from the townland of Ballyblack were married in Ballyblack Presbyterian Church on 13 October 1880. James and Susie Lowry had at least three children – Henry Cooke, Susie and Lillie. Lillie died aged two and Susie died aged 17.

Susanna Lowry died on 25 March 1890 aged 29 and James married Elizabeth Humphreys. They had at least two children – Madge and Mary Eliza Grant (Marion), both born in 1893. Madge died in 1893 and Marion died in 1899.

When James Lowry died on 13 May 1909 he was a JP and he was living in Magheramorne, Co Antrim. Both James and Susanna Lowry are commemorated in Greyabbey Old Graveyard. The grave has a large obelisk with inscriptions on four sides and on one side 'Captain Henry Cooke Lowry who died on active service at Mesopotamia 11 July 1916' is commemorated.

Henry Cooke Lowry served with the Army Veterinary Corps and he went to Egypt on 30 March 1915. He died of disease on 11 July 1916 and at the time of his death his aunt, Miss Susanna Milliken Warden Lowry, was living in Candahar Street, Belfast. Captain Lowry is commemorated in the PCI Roll of Honour for Rosemary Street Presbyterian Church Belfast and in the Belfast Book of Honour (Page 347).

Lowry, Robert
Rifleman
No. 18111, 'B' Company, 13th Battalion, Royal Irish Rifles
Killed in action on Saturday 1 July 1916 (aged 21)
Thiepval Memorial, France (Pier and Face 15 A and 15 B)

Robert Lowry was born on 27 October 1894 and he was the eldest son of Robert and Mary Elizabeth Lowry (nee McDowell) who lived in the townland of Ballywatticock, Newtownards. They were married on 1 December 1893

L

in Killinchy Non-Subscribing Presbyterian Church. Robert Lowry Senior worked as an agricultural labourer and he and Mary has at least twelve children – Robert, William, John, Susannah, Thomas, Mary Elizabeth, Samuel, Jane, Alexander, David, Agnes McKnight and George. The four eldest children were baptised in Killinchy Presbyterian Church and the eight youngest in Greenwell Street Presbyterian Church Newtownards.

Prior to the outbreak of the Great War Robert Lowry Junior worked as an agricultural labourer. He was a member of the Guild and Bible class at Ballyblack Presbyterian Chuch and he was secretary of both Loughries True Blues LOL No.1948 and the local contingent of the Ulster Volunteer Force.

As soon as hostilities began Robert joined the 13th Battalion Royal Irish Rifles and he served in 108th Brigade of the 36th (Ulster) Division. During the evening before the start of the Battle of the Somme he wrote a letter to his parents. In the letter his main concern was not for what he and his comrades would have to face the following day but rather for those back at home. Rifleman Robert Lowry was posted as missing in action after the first day of the Battle of the Somme.

Like every other family that received such news the Lowry family lived in hope that Robert might have survived. But it was not to be; in February 1917 Robert's family received the official news that extinguished all hope – 'missing since first of July, now reported killed in action, place unknown.' Robert's parents, brothers and sisters placed a 'For King and Country' notice in the *Newtownards Chronicle* and it contained the verse:

'His warfare o'er, his battle fought,
His victory won, though dearly bought;
Dear is the spot where our loved one is laid,
Dear is the memory that shall never fade.
A little while and we shall meet
The loved one gone before,
And we shall clasp his hands again
On yonder golden shore'

At the time of Robert's death his brother William was at home having been wounded whilst on active service with the 9th Argyll and Sutherland Highlanders. Rifleman Robert Lowry is commemorated on Newtownards and District War Memorial and in the PCI Roll of Honour for Greenwell Street Presbyterian Church Newtownards.

Lundy, James
Rifleman
No. 5856, 1st Battalion, Royal Irish Rifles
Killed in action on Sunday 18 November 1917
Tyne Cot Memorial, Belgium (Panel 138 to 140 & 162 to 162A & 163A)

In 'Soldiers Died in the Great War 1914 – 1919' it is recorded that James Lundy was born in Ballygowan, he lived in Carlisle and he enlisted in Lisburn. He served with the 1st Battalion Royal Irish Rifles and he was killed in action on 18 November 1917 while transporting supplies to the front line.

Lynch, John
Private
No. 3304, 1st Battalion, Irish Guards
Killed in action on Friday 6 November 1914 (aged 24)
Ypres (Menin Gate) Memorial, Belgium (Panel 11)

John Lynch was born in Comber and he was a son of Philip and Kate Lynch who lived at 22 Castle Street when Philip Lynch was a police constable in the Royal Irish Constabulary stationed in Comber. Philip and Kate Lynch had at least six children – John, Mary, Edward, Frederick, Robert James and Annie.

John Lynch lived in Kilmessan, Co Meath and he enlisted in Newry. He served with the 1st Battalion Irish Guards and he was killed in action on 6 November 1914. At that time his parents were living in Main Street, Clonmellon, Co Westmeath.

Lyttle, Andrew
Private
No. 907411, 5th Battalion, Canadian Infantry (Saskatchewan Regiment)
Died of wounds on Wednesday 11 April 1917 (aged 21)
Barlin Communal Cemetery Extension, France (Grave I. H. 40)

Andrew Lyttle was born on 12 August 1895 and he was a son of Robert and Margaret Lyttle who lived in the townland of Ballymartin, Killinchy. Robert Lyttle worked as a farmer and he and Margaret had at least eleven children – Robert, Hamilton, Elizabeth, Andrew, William, Anna, David, Mary, James, Samuel and Alexander.

Andrew Lyttle worked as a labourer before he moved to Canada where he lived in Cupar, Saskatchewan and worked as a farmer. He enlisted in Regina, Saskatchewan on 11 March 1916 and it was noted in his attestation papers that he was 5 feet 11 inches tall. He served with the 5th Battalion Canadian Infantry (Saskatchewan Regiment) and he died of wounds on 11 April 1917.

Killinchy-Canadian Killed.

Mr. Robert Lyttle, Shaw's Bridge, Belfast (late of Killinchy), has been notified of the death from wounds of his youngest son, Private Andrew Lyttle, Canadian Infantry. Deceased was one of four brothers in the Canadians, William, Robert, and Hamilton, all of whom have been wounded. Robert has been four times wounded, and is now in hospital in London.

In the 2 June 1917 edition of the *Newtownards Chronicle* Private Andrew Lyttle's death was reported under the headline 'Killinchy-Canadian Killed'. The report indicated that Robert Lyttle of Shaw's Bridge Belfast (late of Killinchy) had been notified of the death from wounds of his son Private Andrew Lyttle, Canadian Infantry. The report continued, 'Deceased was one of four brothers in the Canadians, William, Robert and Hamilton, all of whom have been wounded. Robert has been four times wounded and is now in hospital in London'.

Private Andrew Lyttle is commemorated in Killinchy Parish Church of Ireland as Andrew Little; in Killinchy Presbyterian Church as A Little and in the PCI Roll of Honour for Killinchy Presbyterian Church as Andrew Lyttle. Hamilton, Robert and William Lyttle are listed in the PCI Roll of Honour as having survived the Great War although in Killinchy Parish Church of Ireland all four brothers are listed as having been killed in action.

Mackey, James Glover (James)
Rifleman
No. 7342, 2nd Battalion, Royal Irish Rifles
Died of wounds on Friday 28 April 1916 (aged 20)
Aubigny Communal Cemetery Extension, France (Grave I. B. 5)

James Glover Mackey was born on 10 April 1896 in the townland of Whitespots, Newtownards. He was the second son of William and Elizabeth (Lizzie) Mackey (nee Glover). He had three sisters, Sarah Ann, Mary Agnes and Margaret (Maggie) and two brothers, Robert and John. Four of the children including James were baptised in Greenwell Street Presbyterian Church Newtownards. The Mackey family moved to live at the Floodgates, Newtownards. The children were orphaned when their mother

Ma

Lizzie died in 1911 aged 39 and their father William died in 1912 aged 44. James was 16.

James Mackey was 18 years old when he enlisted in Holywood on 20 November 1914 and he signed up for a period of six years. On 31 August 1915 he was posted to the 2nd Battalion Royal Irish Rifles and he went to France. He died of wounds on 28 April 1916 while his Battalion was holding the line.

James's sister Maggie married M Malone and they lived at 99 Mill Street, Newtownards. When James died Maggie and her brother John placed a 'For King and Country' notice in the 13 May 1916 edition of the *Newtownards Chronicle* and it contained the verse:

'Sleep on, dear brother, your troubles are over,
Your duty on earth is done,
You fought for liberty and honour,
And the prize of life you won.'

A year later Maggie and John placed an 'Our Heroes – In Memoriam' notice in the *Newtownards Chronicle* and it contained the verse:

Ma

'No loved ones stood around him,
To bid a last farewell;
No word of comfort could we give
The one we loved so well.'

Rifleman James Glover Mackey is commemorated on Newtownards and District War Memorial; in the PCI Roll of Honour for Greenwell Street Presbyterian Church Newtownards and in Newtownards Parish Church of Ireland (St Mark).

MacMahon, Herbert Henry (Herbert)
Lance Corporal
No. 26424, 10th Battalion, Royal Dublin Fusiliers
Killed in action on Monday 13 November 1916 (aged 24)
Thiepval Memorial, France (Pier and Face 16C)

The death on active service of Lance Corporal Herbert Henry MacMahon was reported in the 9 December 1916 edition of the *Newtownards Chronicle* under the headline, 'Former Newtownards Minister's Son Killed'. The report made reference to his father's ministry in Newtownards. The Rev Herbert Henry MacMahon was a Methodist minister who ministered in several counties in Ireland including Wicklow, Down and Tipperary. He and his

wife Emily (nee Cronhelm) had at least four children – Lillie Aikin, Henry Herbert, Violet Cronhelm and Fanny Louisa.

Herbert MacMahon Junior was born on 3 February 1892 in Bray, Co Wicklow. He was educated at Wesley College and he obtained a BA Degree from Trinity College Dublin. When war began he was living in Holywood. He was an accepted candidate for the Methodist ministry and he was a divinity student in Methodist College Belfast.

Lance Corporal Herbert Henry MacMahon enlisted in Belfast, he served with the 10th Battalion Royal Dublin Fusiliers and he was killed in action on 13 November 1916 at Beaumont Hamel during the Battle of the Ancre while making an attack on the enemy trenches. He is commemorated on the Memorial Plaque in Methodist College Belfast.

Maddock, William
Private   Ma
No. 1594, 7th (Blythswood) Battalion, Highland Light Infantry
Died of wounds on Tuesday 13 July 1915 (aged 20)
Lancashire Landing Cemetery, Gallipoli, Turkey (Grave D. 67)

William Maddock was born in Belfast (according to the 1911 census) and he was a son of William and Mary Jane Maddock (nee McCreight) who lived at 59 Medway Street in Belfast. They were married on 3 July 1885 in Newtownards Parish Church of Ireland. William Maddock Senior worked as a general labourer and he and Mary Jane had at least four children – Samuel (born in America), Mary, Elizabeth (born in County Down) and William (born in Belfast). The death on active service of Private William Maddock was reported in the 9 October 1915 edition of the *Newtownards Chronicle* and there it was stated that William had been born in James Street, Newtownards.

William Maddock enlisted in Glasgow, he served with the Highland Light Infantry and on 13 July 1915 he died of wounds sustained in action at Gallipoli the previous day. William's father was dead and so it was his uncle Thomas Maddock living in Balfour Street, Newtownards who received the official notification about his death. During the Great War Thomas Maddock's two sons along with 19 nephews and two sons-in-law were on active service. Private William Maddock is commemorated on Newtownards and District War Memorial and in the Belfast Book of Honour (Page 356).

Magee, David
Stoker First Class
No. SS/109577, HMS *Indefatigable*, Royal Navy
Killed in action on Wednesday 31 May 1916 (aged 23)
Plymouth Naval Memorial, Devon, England (Panel 16)

David Magee was born in the townland of Glastry, Ballyhalbert and he was a son of James and Agnes Magee (nee Caughey). They were married on 9 February 1885 in Portaferry Roman Catholic Church. James Magee worked as an agricultural labourer and he and Agnes had at least ten children – Minnie, James, Lizzie, Cassie, David, Agnes, Sarah, Maggie, Bernard and Hugh. The Magee family moved to Newtownards where they lived at 24 William Street and by 1911 David Magee was serving in the Royal Navy.

Stoker First Class David Magee was killed in action aboard HMS *Indefatigable* on 31 May 1916 during the Battle of Jutland. Commissioned in 1911, this British battle-cruiser was hit by shellfire from the German battle-cruiser SMS *Von der Tann* that caused two massive explosions. More than 1000 crew members were killed. At the time of David's death his parents were living at 2 Iris Street, Belfast and he is commemorated in the Belfast Book of Honour (Page 356). SMS *Von der Tann* was scuttled in June 1919 at Scapa Flow and then raised in the 1930s for scrap.

Magill, John
Rifleman
No. 19684, 'C' Company, 13th Battalion, Royal Irish Rifles
Killed in action on Saturday 1 July 1916 (aged 20)
Thiepval Memorial, France (Pier and Face 15 A and 15 B)

John Magill was born in Belfast and he was a son of John Magill. He lived in the townland of Moneyreagh and he enlisted in Belfast. Rifleman John Magill served with the 13th Battalion Royal Irish Rifles in 108th Brigade of the 36th (Ulster) Division and he was killed in action on the first day of the Battle of the Somme. He is commemorated on Comber and District War Memorial and in the Belfast Book of Honour (Page 360).

Magrath, Meyrick Myles
Distinguished Service Order
Major
291st Brigade, Royal Horse Artillery and Royal Field Artillery
Killed in action on Friday 2 August 1918 (aged 29)
Montigny Communal Cemetery, France (Grave C. 13)

Meyrick Myles Magrath was born on 24 May 1889 in Bareilly, Uttar Pradesh, India and he was the only son of Lieutenant Colonel Charles William Stanford Magrath (Royal Army Medical Corps) and Laura Katherine Magrath who lived in Ivy House, Ballycastle, Co Antrim. He was educated at Wellington College and he got his first commission from the Royal Military Academy at Woolwich on 18 December 1908. He was promoted to the rank of Lieutenant on 18 December 1911 and then Captain on 18 December 1914. He was killed in action on 2 August 1918, some four months after the birth of his son Meyrick James Magrath. In the CWGC Debt of Honour it is recorded that Major Meyrick Myles Magrath was the 'husband of Rose Austin Worsley (formerly Magrath), of Breamore House, Ballywalter, Co Down'. Major Magrath's father died on 19 May 1924.

Ma

Mahaffy, George (served as Mahaffey, George)
Lance Corporal
No. 13/18402, 'B' Company, 13th Battalion, Royal Irish Rifles
Killed in action on Saturday 1 July 1916 (aged 35)
Thiepval Memorial, France (Pier and Face 15 A and 15 B)

George Mahaffy was born in Detroit in the United States of America and his wife Isabella was born in Scotland. George Mahaffy worked as a plasterer and the Mahaffy family lived in Belfast for a time before moving to 3 Ella's Villas, Bangor Road, Newtownards. George and Isabella had eight children including Maggie, Georgina, Jennie, Herbert and Elizabeth. In the CWGC Debt of Honour his surname is spelt Mahaffey.

Before the war George Mahaffy was a member of the Ulster Volunteer Force. He enlisted in Newtownards on 17 September 1914 and he served with the

13th Battalion Royal Irish Rifles in 108th Brigade of the 36th (Ulster) Division. He went to France in October 1915 and he was home on leave in February 1916. Rifleman George Mahaffy was killed in action on the first day of the Battle of the Somme. Initially he was posted as missing in action and in June 1917 his death was officially confirmed.

Isabella and her eight children, along with George's sister Jane who was a nurse in Baltimore USA, placed a 'For King and Country' notice in the 16 June 1917 edition of the *Newtownards Chronicle*. Rifleman George Mahaffy is commemorated on Newtownards and District War Memorial and as George Mahaffey in Newtownards Parish Church of Ireland (St Mark).

Maidens, John
Military Medal
Private
No. 3335, 1st Battalion, Princess Victoria's (Royal Irish Fusiliers)
Killed in action on Saturday 26 August 1916 (aged 28)
Poelcapelle British Cemetery, Belgium (Grave LVI. C. 7)

Ma

John Maidens was born in 1888 in Doncaster, Yorkshire and he was a son of Charles and Alice Maidens. They lived at 91 Catherine Street, Doncaster and they had at least eight children – Arthur, Alice, John, Fred, Florrie, Willie, Edgar and Nellie.

Private J. Maidens (No. 3,335), who enlisted in the R. I. Fusiliers at Newtownards, is officially reported killed.

According to a report in the 30 September 1916 edition of the *Newtownards Chronicle* John enlisted in Newtownards (in 'Soldiers Died in the Great War 1914 – 1919' it is recorded that he enlisted in Carrickfergus). He served with the 1st Battalion Royal Irish Fusiliers, he was awarded the Military Medal and he was killed in action on 26 August 1916.

Majury, James
The name James Majury is listed on Donaghadee and District War Memorial and also in Donaghadee Parish Church of Ireland where it is recorded that he served with the Royal Naval Reserve.

Desk searches and public appeals to date have yielded no further information.

Majury, William John (William) (served as McJury, William John)
Rifleman
No. 7165, 2nd Battalion, Royal Irish Rifles
Died of wounds on Friday 18 December 1914 (aged 21)
Bailleul Communal Cemetery (Nord), France (Grave E. 13)

Ma

William John Majury was born in Dundonald and he was a son of William J and Jane Majury (nee Wilson) who lived in the townland of Killarn, Newtownards. They were married on 19 May 1893 in Dundonald Presbyterian Church. In the CWGC Debt of Honour and in 'Soldiers Died in the Great War 1914 – 1919' his surname is spelt McJury.

Rifleman William John Majury enlisted in Newtownards and he served with the 4th Battalion and then the 2nd Battalion Royal Irish Rifles. He died of wounds on 18 December 1914 in a Casualty Clearance Station at Bailleul.

MAJURY—In loving memory of Rifleman Wm. John Majury, 4th Batt., attached to 2nd R. I. Rifles, who died in hospital in France, 18th December, 1914, and was buried in Belluel Cemetery.
Inserted by his sorrowing Father, Mother, and Brothers.
WILLIAM and J. MAJURY.
Killarn, Newtownards.

William John Majury was a member of the Purple Vine LOL No. 1056 in Dundonald and after he died there were two 'Killed in Action' notices in the Newtownards Chronicle – one placed by his family and one placed by George Wightman and Charles McIlwaine on behalf of the Lodge. Rifleman William John Majury is commemorated on

Newtownards and District War Memorial and in the PCI Roll of Honour for Dundonald Presbyterian Church.

Mallon, George

The name George Mallon is listed on Newtownards and District War Memorial and in the booklet produced for the Unveiling and Dedication Ceremony held on Saturday 26 May 1934 he is described as a Rifleman in the Royal Irish Rifles. Desk searches and public appeals to date have yielded no further information.

Marsh, Hector Claude
Lance Corporal
No. 8486, 'D' Company, 2nd Battalion, Royal Irish Rifles
Killed in action on Tuesday 27 October 1914 (aged 22)
Le Touret Memorial, France (Panel 42 and 43)

Ma

> **R. I. Rifles Officer Missing.**
> Second-Lieutenant A. G. V. Marsh, Royal Irish Rifles, attached Yorkshire Regiment, missing, is one of the seven soldier sons of Lieutenant and Quarter-master E. H. Marsh, late 19th Battalion Royal Irish Rifles, who served for 25 years in the Army prior to rejoining the war. Most of his seven sons went into the Rifles. Two of them were taken prisoner at Mons and another was killed at Neuve Chapelle. Mrs. Marsh and family are at present residing in Newtownards.

Lance Corporal Hector Claude Marsh was born in St John's, Malta and he was one of the seven soldier sons of Captain Edward Henry Marsh and Alice Marsh (nee Telling). Captain Marsh, late 19th Battalion Royal Irish Rifles, had served for 25 years in the Army and he rejoined at the outbreak of the Great War. Captain Marsh had an address in Folkestone and his wife and family lived in Newtownards. Most of the seven Marsh brothers joined the Royal Irish Rifles and Lance Corporal Hector Claude Marsh enlisted in Dundalk. He served with the 2nd Battalion and he was killed in action on 27 October 1914 at Neuve Chapelle.

Marshall, Andrew
Rifleman
No. 6028, 11th Battalion, Royal Irish Rifles
Killed in action on Saturday 1 July 1916
Thiepval Memorial, France (Pier and Face 15 A and 15 B)

Andrew Marshall was born in Dunbarton, Scotland and on 23 September 1915 he and Martha Smyth were married in Newtownards Parish Church of Ireland. His address was Bordon Army Camp, Hampshire and Martha lived at 111 Mill Street, Newtownards. Andrew served with the 11th Battalion

Mrs. Marshall, of 111 Mill Street, has been officially informed that her husband, Pte. Andrew Marshall, of the 11th Royal Irish Irish Rifles (the South Antrims), was wounded at the Front on the 23rd of October. This soldier reads the "Chronicle" each week, and we can assure him of the wishes of ourselves and all his fellow-townsmen for his speedy recovery.

Royal Irish Rifles in 108th Brigade of the 36th (Ulster) Division and he was wounded on 23 October 1915. When he recovered he went to the Western Front and he was killed in action on the first day of the Battle of the Somme. Rifleman Andrew Marshall is commemorated on Newtownards and District War Memorial and in Newtownards Parish Church of Ireland (St Mark).

Marshall, Robert
Private
No. 9691, 1st Battalion, Royal Inniskilling Fusiliers
Killed in action on Saturday 21 August 1915 (aged 25)
Helles Memorial, Gallipoli, Turkey (Panel 97 to 101)

Robert Marshall was born in Newtownards and he was a son of Robert and Susannah Marshall (nee Wallace) who lived in Movilla Street before they moved to 33 Greenwell Street. Robert Marshall Senior worked as a general labourer and he and Susannah had at least nine children including Mary Jean, Robert, Agnes, James and Isabella. James and Isabella were baptised in Greenwell Street Presbyterian Church Newtownards.

Ma

NEWTOWNARDS SOLDIER MISSING AT THE DARDANELLES.

Official intimation was received on Friday morning by the parents of Private Robert Marshall, 1st Bn. Royal Inniskilling Fusiliers, formerly of Market St., but now residing at 33 Greenwell Street, that Private Marshall had been posted as missing since 21st August. Private Marshall had seven years service in the army and came home from India for the Front. Any information regarding him will be gratefully received by his parents.

Robert Marshall joined the army around 1907 and he served in India before the war. He went to the front and served with the 1st Battalion Royal Inniskilling Fusiliers. Initially he was posted as missing in action and later it was officially confirmed that he had been killed in action at Gallipoli on 21 August 1915. Private Robert Marshall is commemorated on Newtownards and District War Memorial and in the PCI Roll of Honour for Greenwell Street Presbyterian Church Newtownards.

Marshall, Robert (Bobby)
Private
No. 700864, 43rd Battalion, Canadian Infantry (Manitoba Regiment)
Died of wounds on Thursday 8 August 1918 (aged 26)
Crouy British Cemetery, France (Grave IV. C. 2)

Robert Marshall was born on 6 October 1891 and he was a son of Robert and Anna Marshall (nee Marshall) who lived in the townland of Ballystockart,

Comber. They were married on 29 March 1878 in Ballygowan Presbyterian Church. Robert Marshall Senior worked as a carrier in Belfast before moving to Ballystockart where he worked as a farmer. He and Anna had at least seven children – Catherine, Thomas, Anna, Martha, Robert, William, and David John (died of rheumatic fever aged 17). Robert was baptised in First Comber Presbyterian Church.

Robert Marshall Junior also worked as a farmer both before and after he moved to Canada. On 14 April 1913 he sailed on the *Letitia* from Glasgow to St John in New Brunswick. In Canada he lived at 667 Simcoe Street, Winnipeg. Robert enlisted in Winnipeg on 18 January 1916 and in his attestation papers it was noted that he was 5 feet 6½ inches tall.

Ma

Private Robert Marshall served with the 43rd Battalion Canadian Infantry (Manitoba Regiment) and he died of wounds on 8 August 1918. He is commemorated on Comber and District War Memorial and in First Comber Presbyterian Church.

Marshall, Robert H
Lance Corporal
No. 18434, 'B' Company, 13th Battalion, Royal Irish Rifles
Killed in action on Wednesday 14 February 1917 (aged 22)
St. Quentin Cabaret Military Cemetery, Belgium (Grave II. A. 14)

Robert H Marshall was born in Ballyclare and he was the eldest son of Adam and Isabella Marshall (nee McQuillan). They were married on 10 January 1891 in Trinity Parish Church of Ireland Belfast. The Marshall family moved to Comber where they lived at 28 Brownlow Street and later at 26 Brae Side. Adam Marshall worked as a mechanic and he and Isabella had at least ten children including Jinnie, Robert, Sarah, John, Maggie, William, Arthur and Isabella.

Before the war Robert Marshall was employed by Messrs John Andrews &

Company in Comber. He enlisted in September 1914 and he served with the 13th Battalion Royal Irish Rifles in 108th Brigade of the 36th (Ulster) Division. In late December 1916 he was home on leave, just seven weeks before he was killed in action at around 6.00 pm on 14 February 1917. He and his comrades repelled an attack on their line by a German patrol and as the attackers retreated under fire Robert Marshall was killed by their retaliatory bombardment. In an attack earlier that day Rifleman **William McKittrick** was killed and Rifleman **Robert Robinson** was wounded; Robert Robinson died the following day.

The Presbyterian Chaplain of the Battalion wrote a letter of condolence to Robert Marshall's mother in which he described Lance Corporal Robert Marshall as 'a brave and loyal man'. He is commemorated on Comber and District War Memorial; on the Andrews Mill Memorial Plaque and in Second Comber Presbyterian Church.

Ma

Martin, Alexander (Alex)
Private
No. 12/800, Auckland Regiment, NZEF
Killed in action on Sunday 25 April 1915 (aged 20)
Lone Pine Memorial, Gallipoli, Turkey (Panel 72)

Alexander Martin was born in County Antrim and he was a son of John and Isabella Martin (nee Mayes) who lived in the townland of Magheraliskmisk, Lisburn. They were married on 26 December 1890 in Magheragall Parish Church of Ireland Lisburn. John Martin was a farmer and he and Isabella had at least nine children – Thomas, William Robert, Alexander, Sarah, John, James, Elizabeth Isabella, Samuel and Joseph.

Alexander Martin moved to Australia in 1913, then to New Zealand and during the Great War he served with the Auckland Regiment NZEF. Private Alexander Martin was killed in action on 25 April 1915 at Gallipoli. In the CWGC Debt of Honour the family address is on record as 'Moor Farm Donaghadee' but this is not substantiated by information from other sources which give the address as 'Moor Farm Magheragall'. Alex's father served as a rural councillor in Magheragall and the Rev Dundas, Rector of Magheragall Parish Church, paid tribute to Private Martin from the pulpit on Sunday 20 June 1915.

Private Alexander Martin is commemorated on the family grave headstone in Magheragall Parish Church graveyard and in Lisburn's Dead 1914 – 1919 (Friends' School Lisburn WW1 Research Project).

Martin, James
Private
No. 17423, 8th Battalion, Royal Inniskilling Fusiliers
Killed in action on Friday 18 May 1917 (aged 24)
Kemmel Chateau Military Cemetery, Belgium (Grave N. 66)

Ma

James Martin was born on 9 June 1892 in Greyabbey and he was a son of Robert and Ellenor (Ellen) McGowan Martin (nee George) who lived in Greyabbey before they moved to 23 Little Frances Street, Newtownards. They were married in Greyabbey Presbyterian Church. Robert Martin worked as a blacksmith and he and Ellen had at least eight children – James (1892), Jane (1894), Agnes (1897), David John (1901), Samuel George (1903), Henry King (1905), Hugh William (1907) and Flora George (1910). James and Jane were baptised in Greyabbey Presbyterian Church and the other children were baptised in Greenwell Street Presbyterian Church Newtownards. James Martin worked first with his father as a smith's helper and then as a block printer in the Ulster Print Works, Newtownards.

On 1 September 1914 James Martin enlisted in Dublin, he joined the Royal Inniskilling Fusiliers and in July 1915 he went with the 10th (Irish) Division to the Dardanelles. The following month he took part in the landing at Suvla Bay Gallipoli. After a period of service he contracted dysentery and was taken to England where he was in hospital for some time. When he recovered he was attached to the 8th Battalion Royal Inniskilling Fusiliers in 49th Brigade of the 16th (Irish) Division and he left Londonderry for France on 12 April 1916.

After Private James Martin was killed by shellfire on 18 May 1917 the Rev CF McConnell, the Presbyterian Chaplain who conducted his funeral, wrote to James's father to express his sympathy. The Rev McConnell wrote, 'His body rests in peace. The shells still scream over that quiet little spot but his soul is now in higher service.'

One of James Martin's brothers was also on active service and the Martin family placed a 'For King and Country' notice in the *Newtownards Chronicle*. It contained the verse:

'The shock was great, the loss severe,
We little thought the end was near;
It's only those who have lost can tell
The pain of parting, not saying farewell'

Private James Martin is commemorated on Newtownards and District War Memorial and in the PCI Roll of Honour for Greenwell Street Presbyterian Church Newtownards.

Martin, John
Rifleman
No. 7616, 4th & 1st Battalions, Royal Irish Rifles
Killed in action on Saturday 1 July 1916 (aged 29)
Thiepval Memorial, France (Pier and Face 15 A and 15 B)

Ma

John Martin was born in Newtownards and he was a son of John and Mary Martin (nee Malcolmson) who lived in John Street Lane. They were married on 7 July 1879 in First Lurgan Presbyterian Church. John Martin Senior worked as an agricultural labourer and he and Mary had at least four children – Mary Jane, Francis Russell, David and John. They also had a two-year old adopted daughter called Mary Frances Malcolmson Martin. Francis Russell was baptised in Regent Street Presbyterian Church and David was baptised in Greenwell Street Presbyterian Church.

John Martin Junior worked first as a tailor's apprentice and then as a garden labourer. He and Elizabeth Morris were married on 24 November 1904 in Newtownards Parish Church of Ireland and they lived at 45a East Street, Newtownards with their five children, Mary (1905), John (1906), Maggie (1908), William (1910) and Frank (1911), the eldest of whom was eleven when their father was killed in action.

John Martin enlisted in Newtownards, he joined the 4th Battalion Royal Irish Rifles and was then posted to the Western Front to reinforce the 1st Battalion.

He was attached to the Machine Gun Section and he was killed in action on the first day of the Battle of the Somme. His wife Lizzie placed a 'For King and Country' notice in the *Newtownards Chronicle* and it contained the verse:

> 'Away in a nameless grave in France,
> My loving husband doth lie;
> He gave his life for his country,
> What nobler death could he die?
> Sleep on, dear husband, your battle's o'er,
> Your duty on earth is done;
> You fought for liberty and honour,
> And the prize of life you won.
> Only in form we both are parted,
> But our hearts will true remain;
> And one day we'll be united,
> Never more to part again'

Ma

Rifleman John Martin is commemorated on Newtownards and District War Memorial; in Newtownards Parish Church of Ireland (St Mark) and on the PCI Roll of Honour for Greenwell Street Presbyterian Church Newtownards.

Martin, Richard Henry
Sergeant
No. 9056, 2nd Battalion, Royal Irish Rifles
Killed in action on Monday 26 October 1914 (aged 23)
Le Touret Memorial, France (Panel 42 and 43)

Richard Henry Martin was the elder son of Colour Sergeant Richard Martin and Alice Martin and theirs was a much-travelled family. Richard Martin Senior was born in County Antrim and he was a career soldier. Alice Martin was born in Gibraltar. Richard Martin Junior was born in Fermoy, Co Cork and his younger brother William was born in County Armagh.

When Colour Sergeant Richard Martin was attached to the Permanent Staff of the Royal North Downs in Newtownards the family lived in Mary Street. Both sons followed in their father's footsteps and joined the army. Richard Henry Martin served with the 2nd Battalion Royal Irish Rifles and rose to the non-commissioned rank of Sergeant. Shortly after the outbreak of the Great War he went from Tidworth Camp in Wiltshire to the Western Front and he was killed by an enemy bullet at Neuve Chapelle on 26 October 1914.

At that time his widowed mother was living in Dublin. His last letter to her

KILLED IN ACTION.

MARTIN—October 26th, 1914, at Neuve Chapelle, Sergeant Richard Henry Martin, 2nd Battalion Royal Irish Rifles, eldest son of the late Col. Sergt. Richard Martin, Royal North Downs.

was dated 20 October 1914 and she received it on the day that he was killed. However it wasn't until 24 January 1915 that she received official notification from the War Office that Sergeant Richard Henry Martin had been killed in action. His brother Lance Corporal William Martin also served with the Royal Irish Rifles and he was wounded and taken prisoner in 1917. Sergeant Richard Henry Martin is commemorated on Newtownards and District War Memorial and on Page 345 in the Cork Book of Honour (*A Great Sacrifice*).

Martin, William
Private
No. 841683, 24th Battalion, Canadian Infantry (Quebec Regiment)
Killed in action on Wednesday 10 January 1917 (aged 29)
Tranchee de Mecknes Cemetery, France (Grave L. 6)

William Martin was born in Newtownards on 17 March 1887. He moved to Canada and he worked there as an ammunition worker and driver. When he enlisted in Montreal on 4 March 1916 he was living at 221 Colborne Street. He was unmarried and he cited as his next-of-kin his sister Elizabeth McNeely who lived at 12 Main Street, Stevenston, Ayr in Scotland.

Ma

It was noted in his attestation papers that he was 5 feet 7 inches tall and that he had extensive scarring from burns on both arms and all over his back. He had a tattoo on his left arm in the form of a girl's head and the words 'Love Maggie'. Sometime between 4 March 1916 and William's death on 10 January 1917 William Martin and Margaret J Watson got married. Maggie's address in Canada was 52 Appleton Avenue, Toronto.

When Maggie Martin moved back to Newtownards she lived at 129 Mill Street and after her husband was killed in action on 10 January 1917 she placed a 'For King and Country' notice in the *Newtownards Chronicle*. It contained the verse:

'Little I thought when we said good-bye,
It should be the last parting between you and I;

I loved you in life, you are dear to me still,
But in grief we must bend to God's holy will.'

> **OUR HEROES—IN MEMORIAM.**
> MARTIN—In loving memory of my dear husband, Private Wm. Martin, Canadian Infantry, killed in action on January 10, 1917.
> Safe from the world's alluring harms,
>   Beneath His watchful eye;
> Thus in the circle of His arms
>   May he for ever lie.
>   MARGARET J. MARTIN.
> 129 Mill St., Newtownards.

In January 1918 Maggie placed an 'Our Heroes – In Memoriam' notice in the *Newtownards Chronicle* and Private William Martin is commemorated on Newtownards and District War Memorial and in Newtownards Parish Church of Ireland (St Mark).

Mason, Roland Hugh
Private
No. 15190, 2nd Battalion, Royal Irish Regiment
Died of spinal fever on Saturday 7 July 1917 (aged 22)
Longuenesse (St. Omer) Souvenir Cemetery, France (Grave IV. C. 46)

Roland Hugh Mason was born in February 1895 in the townland of Tieveshilly, Portaferry and he was a son of James and Catherine Mason (nee Savage). They were married on 16 April 1884 in Portaferry Roman Catholic Church. James Mason was a farmer and he and Catherine had at least seven children – Margaret Isabella (died aged 18), Mary Anne, Catherine Jane, James Joseph, Roland Hugh, Patrick Edward and John Gerard.

> **Portaferry Fusilier Succumbs to Fever.**
> Mr. James Mason, Tieveshilly, Portaferry, has been notified that his son, Corporal Roland H. A. Mason, Royal Irish Fusiliers, died on the 7th inst. from spinal fever.

Roland Hugh Mason enlisted in Portaferry and he served with the 2nd Battalion Royal Irish Regiment. He died of spinal fever on 7 July 1917.

Matear, Robert
Private
No. 10/1290, Wellington Regiment, NZEF
Killed in action on Thursday 29 April 1915 (aged 24)
Lone Pine Memorial, Gallipoli, Turkey (Panel 76)

Robert Matear was born on 8 February 1891 and he was the second son of Charles and Annie Matear (nee Robinson). They were married on 14 August 1889 in Ballycopeland Presbyterian Church Millisle. Charles Matear was a farmer in the townland of Ballywilliam, Donaghadee and he and Annie had at least seven children including Thomas, Robert, Isabella, Agnes, Martha

Ma

(died 1896 aged 1) and William. Robert's mother died in childbirth on 26 September 1899 aged 43 and she was buried with her infant child. The children were baptised in Shore Street Presbyterian Church Donaghadee.

KILLED IN ACTION.

MATEER—Killed in action on June the 8th, in Gallipoli, Turkey, Private Robt. Mateer, aged 24, 17th Ruahines, Wellington Infantry, New Zealand Force, second and dearly beloved son of Charles Mateer, Ballywilliam, Donaghadee, Co. Down.

Robert Matear moved to New Zealand and during the Great War he served with the Wellington Regiment (17th Ruahines) NZEF. Private Robert Matear was killed in action at Gallipoli on 29 April 1915 and he is commemorated on Donaghadee and District War Memorial and in Shore Street Presbyterian Church Donaghadee. He is also commemorated on the family grave headstone in Donaghadee Parish Church of Ireland Graveyard where the date of death is inscribed as 8 June 1915. Robert's father Charles died on 13 November 1935.

Mathers, Thompson
Rifleman
No. 2450, 2nd Battalion, Royal Irish Rifles
Killed in action on Tuesday 22 October 1918 (aged 30)
Harlebeke New British Cemetery, Belgium (Grave VIII. A. 11)

Ma

Thompson Mathers was born in Newtownards and he worked as an agricultural labourer. He and Agnes McClure were married on 6 May 1910 in Second Newtownards Presbyterian Church and they lived at 163 Greenwell Street Newtownards.

Thompson Mathers enlisted in Newtownards on 14 December 1914 and he joined the Royal North Downs. After training at Carrickfergus he went to France on 29 July 1915 and he joined the 2nd Battalion Royal Irish Rifles.

After more than a year in the fighting line he was wounded on 8 August 1916 and invalided home for seven months. In March 1917 he resumed duty in the trenches. He was posted as wounded and missing in action on 22 October 1918 during the Allied offensive against all sections of the German line and in July 1919 it was officially confirmed that he had been killed in action. His wife placed a 'For King and Country' notice in the *Newtownards Chronicle* and it contained the verse:

'I pictured your safe homecoming,
And longed to clasp your hand,
But God has postponed the meeting,
Which will be in a better land'

Rifleman Thompson Mathers is commemorated on Newtownards and District War Memorial and in the PCI Roll of Honour for Greenwell Street Presbyterian Church Newtownards.

Matier, Daniel
Corporal
No. 7659, 1st Battalion, Royal Irish Rifles
Killed in action on Sunday 9 May 1915 (aged 28)
Ploegsteert Memorial, Belgium (Panel 9)

Ma

Daniel Matier (Mateer in the 1901 census) was born in Newtownards and he was a son of Isabella Matier who worked as a seamstress and lived at 78 East Street. Daniel Matier lived in Rangoon in India, he enlisted in Belfast and he served with the 1st Battalion Royal Irish Rifles. He was killed in action on 9 May 1915 during the Allied attack at Rouge Bancs.

Corporal Daniel Matier is commemorated on Newtownards and District War Memorial and in the PCI Roll of Honour for Greenwell Street Presbyterian Church Newtownards. In the CWGC Debt of Honour his forename is recorded as David.

Mawhinney, William John (see McWhinney, William John)

Mayne, Andrew McCutcheon (Andrew)
Private
No. 810, 2nd Battalion, Rhodesia Regiment
Died of Blackwater Fever on Friday 9 February 1917 (aged 37)
Morogoro Cemetery, Tanzania, Africa (Grave VIII. E. 13)

Andrew McCutcheon Mayne was born on 23 June 1879 and he was the second son of Thomas and Frances (Fanny) Mayne (nee McCutcheon) who lived in Mill Street and later in 'Mount Pleasant', Newtownards. They were married on 31 December 1874 in Belmont Presbyterian Church. Thomas Mayne worked as a provision merchant and he and Fanny had at least six children – William, Frances Elizabeth, Andrew McCutcheon, Catherine

McCutcheon, Jane Swan and James. The children were baptised in Regent Street Presbyterian Church Newtownards. Andrew's mother died on 7 May 1903 and his father died on 26 April 1908.

Andrew Mayne was a member of the Ards Lacrosse Club and he worked in the family grocery business before he moved to South Africa in 1902. There he was in business with Hugh Robert Hastings who later died of Blackwater Fever. Andrew Mayne took up farming at Umtali in Rhodesia where he grew maize – the staple food of the region. When war broke out he sold his farm and joined the Rhodesia Regiment. He served under General Jan Smuts in the East African campaign and in 1916 he was shot in the leg. He was hospitalised in Capetown for six weeks before he was able to rejoin his Regiment. Private Mayne continued on active service until he died of Blackwater Fever on 9 February 1917.

> **FOR KING AND COUNTRY.**
>
> MAYNE—February 9, 1917, in East Africa (of Blackwater fever) Private Andrew Mayne, 2nd Rhodesian Regiment, late of Mountpleasant, Newtownards.

It was his brother Councillor William Mayne who received official confirmation of Andrew's death from the Colonial Office in Downing Street, London. William had his business in High Street, Newtownards, he lived in 'Mount Pleasant', Newtownards and the Mayne family placed a 'For King and Country' notice in the 3 March 1917 edition of the *Newtownards Chronicle*. Private Andrew McCutcheon Mayne is commemorated in Melsetter War Memorial Hall Zimbabwe and on Newtownards and District War Memorial. He is also commemorated on the family grave headstone in Movilla Old Cemetery, as is his nephew Lieutenant Colonel Robert Blair (Paddy) Mayne who fought in the Second World War and who died on 14 December 1955.

McA

McAlpine, Francis (Frank)*
Corporal
No. 28854, 126th Siege Battery, Royal Garrison Artillery
Killed in action on Saturday 7 July 1917 (aged 32)
Belgian Battery Corner Cemetery, Belgium (Grave I. A. 16)

Corporal Frank McAlpine was born in Newtownards and he was the only son of Mary McAlpine who lived at 180 Mill Street. Frank McAlpine enlisted in Glasgow, he served with the Royal Garrison Artillery and he was killed in action on 7 July 1917 during heavy enemy shelling.

On 15 July Second Lieutenant JS Henderson wrote to

Frank's mother to express his condolences. He wrote, 'It is my sorrowful duty to inform you that Corporal McAlpine was killed on 7 July 1917. He was an excellent soldier, trusted by the officers and idolised by his men. His last words were ordering them to a place of safety. Death was instantaneous and he lies buried in a small graveyard somewhere in Belgium. We all miss him and his cheerful ways and send our deepest sympathy in your great loss. His personal effects which I am sending to you were collected from his kit. His jacket, for which he turned back, was destroyed by a shell.'

Mary McAlpine placed a 'For King and Country' notice in the 11 August 1917 edition of the *Newtownards Chronicle* and it contained the verse:

McA

> '*He sleeps beneath foreign soil,*
> *A soldier brave was he;*
> *His noble life he freely gave*
> *To keep his country free.*
> *I little thought when he left home*
> *That he would ne'er return;*
> *That he so soon in death would sleep,*
> *And leave me here to mourn.*'

Corporal Frank McAlpine is commemorated on Newtownards and District War Memorial and in the PCI Roll of Honour for Greenwell Street Presbyterian Church Newtownards.

McAlpine, George Turner (George)
Private
No. 2528, 4th Regiment, South African Infantry
Killed in action on Wednesday 10 April 1918 (aged 28)
Ypres (Menin Gate) Memorial, Belgium (Panel 15 – 16 and 16A)

There is some variation in the spelling of his surname – McAlpine (his signature, CWGC, Greenwell Street Presbyterian Church and Newtownards War Memorial), Macalpine (First Bangor Presbyterian Church) and MacAlpine (RBL and Bangor War Memorials).

George Turner McAlpine was the youngest son of Robert McAlpine who lived at 24 Wallace's Street,

Newtownards. George lived at 19 Beatrice Avenue in Bangor for a time before he moved to South Africa. He enlisted in Potchefstroom on 26 August 1915 and in his attestation papers it was noted that he was 5 feet 8 inches tall.

He served in both the 3rd and 4th Regiments of the South African Infantry and he was wounded on five occasions before he was killed in action on 10 April 1918. Private George Turner McAlpine is commemorated on Newtownards and District War Memorial; on Bangor and District War Memorial; in the RBL Album in North Down Museum (Page 35); on the Memorial Plaque in RBL Bangor Branch and in First Bangor Presbyterian Church. He is commemorated in the PCI Roll of Honour for Greenwell Street Presbyterian Church Newtownards.

McAvoy Brothers: Edward and John

Edward and John McAvoy were born in Newtownards and they were sons of Daniel and Ellen Jane McAvoy (nee McAlpin) who were married on 31 October 1877 in Greenwell Street Presbyterian Church Newtownards and who lived at 140 Mill Street. Daniel McAvoy worked as a general labourer and he and Ellen Jane had at least eight children – Edward Ferguson (died), William, Maggie, Eliza (Lizzie), Edward Ferguson McCalpin, Eleanor, Anna Isabella and John Magilton. The children were baptised in Greenwell Street Presbyterian Church Newtownards. John McAvoy was the first of the two brothers to die, 11 days before Edward, but Edward's death was the first to be officially confirmed:

McA

McAvoy, Edward Ferguson McCalpin (Edward)
Rifleman
No. 18125, 'B' Company, 13th Battalion, Royal Irish Rifles
Died of wounds on Wednesday 12 July 1916 (aged 27)
Etaples Military Cemetery, France (Grave II. B. 81A)

Edward Ferguson McCalpin McAvoy was born on 5 August 1888 and prior to the outbreak of the Great War he worked as a garden labourer. Edward McAvoy and Jane (Jean) Dorrian were married on 22 February 1912 in Greenwell Street Presbyterian Church Newtownards and they had two children – Mary Margaret (1912) and Eleanor Maud (1916). Edward enlisted in Newtownards, he joined the 13th Battalion, Royal Irish Rifles (1st County Down Volunteers) and he went to France in October 1915. He served in 108th Brigade of the 36th (Ulster) Division.

Rifleman Edward McAvoy received a gunshot wound in the chest on 1 July 1916 and his wounds were so severe that he died eleven days later on 12 July 1916 in 26 General Hospital Etaples. His younger daughter Eleanor Maud was just five months old (born on 8 February 1916).

Edward's wife Jane and their two daughters lived at 4 Talbot Street Newtownards with Jane's parents. Edward's parents and his sister and brother-in-law Lizzie and James Cargo placed separate 'For King and Country' notices in the 22 July 1916 edition of the *Newtownards Chronicle*. In the years that followed they placed 'Our Heroes – In Memoriam' notices and the one from Lizzie in 1917 contained the verse:

'How a sister's heart is aching
For a brother she loved well;
He gave his all for his country,
In honour's cause he fell.'

McAvoy, John Magilton (John)
Rifleman

McA

No. 18183, 'B' Company, 13th Battalion, Royal Irish Rifles
Killed in action on Saturday 1 July 1916 (aged 19)
Thiepval Memorial, France (Pier and Face 15 A and 15 B)

John Magilton McAvoy was born on 4 March 1897 and prior to the outbreak of the Great War he worked as a garden labourer. He enlisted in Newtownards, he joined the 13th Battalion Royal Irish Rifles (1st County Down Volunteers) and he went to France in October 1915. He served in 108th Brigade of the 36th (Ulster) Division.

> **Missing, but Prisoner of War.**
> Mrs. E. J. M'Avoy, 140, Mill Street, has been officially informed that her son (No. 18,183), Rifleman J. M'Avoy, R. I. Rifles, who was previously reported as missing, is now reported as a prisoner of war in Dulmen Camp, Germany. Mrs. M'Avoy's eldest son, Rifleman E. M'Avoy, R.I.R., died of wounds received in action on 3rd July, 1916.

Rifleman John McAvoy was killed in action on the first day of the Battle of the Somme but it was some time before this was officially confirmed. Initially he was posted as missing in action and then in September 1916, two months after they were notified about Edward's death, his family received news that John was being held as a prisoner of war in Dulmen Camp Germany. Later it was officially confirmed that he had been killed in action on 1 July 1916.

Rifleman Edward McAvoy and Rifleman John McAvoy are both commemorated on Newtownards and District War Memorial and in the PCI Roll of Honour for Greenwell Street Presbyterian Church.

Three Newtownards families related by marriage suffered bereavement during the first two weeks of the Battle of the Somme when four men who are commemorated in this book died:

- **James Dorrian** (16420)
- His sister Susanna's husband **Robert McCartney** (13/343)
- His sister Jane's husband **Edward McAvoy** (18125)
- Edward's brother **John McAvoy** (18183)

Three women living at 4 Talbot Street were widowed.

McBlain, James
Private
No. 3/6756, 1st Battalion, Gordon Highlanders
Killed in action on Sunday 15 November 1914 (aged 38)
Le Touret Memorial, France (Panel 39 to 41)

The name James McBlain is listed on Newtownards and District War Memorial but it is not listed in the booklet produced for the Unveiling and Dedication Ceremony held on Saturday 26 May 1934. In 'Soldiers Died in the Great War 1914 – 1919' it is recorded that Private James McBlain (3/6756) who served with the 1st Battalion Gordon Highlanders was born in Newtownards and he enlisted in Hamilton. He was 38 years old when he died on 15 November 1914.

McB

James McBlain was born on 13 February 1876 in William Street, Newtownards and he was a son of Stewart and Mary McBlain (nee Dowling) who lived at 38 Movilla Street, Newtownards. Stewart McBlain worked as a bleach-works labourer, Mary worked as a sewer and they had at least eight children – Stewart, Agnes, Mary, James, Elizabeth, John, Margaret and Jane.

James Blain served in the South African War and in civilian life he worked as a labourer. James McBlain and Minnie White were married on 24 December 1902 in Greenwell Street Presbyterian Church Newtownards and they had at least eight children – James, Stewart, Henry, Mary, Duncan, John, David and Elizabeth.

At the beginning of the Great War James McBlain rejoined the colours in Hamilton, Scotland and he served with the 1st Battalion Gordon Highlanders. His brother Stewart served with the Royal Corps of Signals. James McBlain was killed in action on 15 November 1914 and he is commemorated on Newtownards and District War Memorial.

McBratney, John Henry
Rifleman
No. 2907, 14th Battalion, Royal Irish Rifles
Killed in action on Saturday 6 May 1916 (aged 24)
Authuile Military Cemetery, France (Grave D. 52)

McB

John Henry McBratney was born in the townland of Drumaness, Ballynahinch and he was a son of Samuel William and Annabel McBratney (nee Healy) who lived at 28 Brownlow Street, Comber. They were married on 2 April 1888 in Killinchy Presbyterian Church. Later the McBratney family moved to the townland of Toye between Killinchy and Killyleagh. John Henry McBratney's brother served in France with the Royal Engineers.

Rifleman John Henry McBratney served with the 14th Battalion Royal Irish Rifles in 109th Brigade of the 36th (Ulster) Division and he was killed in action on 6 May 1916 whilst defending the Allied line against a German attack. In a letter to the bereaved parents Captain Mulholland wrote 'Your boy fell during a heavy bombardment of the trenches. The platoon he belonged to suffered severely, losing their officer and many men. Their names will go down in the history of this regiment for their pluck and courage. They stuck to their trenches and carried out their dead officer's orders which he had given to them before he was hit.'

Lieutenant Monard, officer commanding 'D' Company wrote, 'Despite the fact that men were falling all around him your son stuck nobly to his post......he would not desert his post though certain death awaited him.'

Private **James Healy**, who was John Henry McBratney's uncle and his mother Annabel's brother, was killed in action on 27 April 1916 just nine days before his nephew was killed in action. Rifleman John Henry McBratney is commemorated on Comber and District War Memorial and in Second Comber Presbyterian Church.

McBride, John
Private
No. 5108, 1st Battalion, Scots Guards
Killed in action on Monday 25 January 1915 (aged 30)
Le Touret Memorial, France (Panel 3 and 4)

John McBride was born in Kircubbin and he was a son of John and Margaret (Martha) McBride (nee McMaster) who lived in the townland of Innishargie. They were married on 24 December 1882 in Nunsquarter Roman Catholic Church Kircubbin. John McBride Senior worked as an agricultural labourer and he and Martha had at least nine children including John, James Joseph, William, Thomas, Eliza Ann and Selena.

John McBride Junior was a Reservist and he too worked as an agricultural labourer. He rejoined the colours in Glasgow, he served with the 1st Battalion Scots Guards and he was killed in action on 25 January 1915.

Initially Private John McBride was reported by the War Office as missing in action on 25 January 1915 and subsequently it was officially confirmed that he had been killed in action on or since that date.

McB

McBride, William
Rifleman
No. 19/794, 'B' Company, 13th Battalion, Royal Irish Rifles
Killed in action on Thursday 16 August 1917 (aged 27)
Tyne Cot Memorial, Belgium (Panel 138 to 140 & 162 to 162 A & 163 A)

William McBride was born in Belfast and he and his wife Eliza Jane and their children lived at 33 Movilla Street, Newtownards. Prior to the outbreak of the Great War William McBride worked in the shipyard at Queen's Island, Belfast. He enlisted on 6 December 1916 in Belfast and he served with the 13th Battalion Royal Irish Rifles in 108th Brigade of the 36th (Ulster) Division. He had only been in the trenches for a few months when he was killed in action on 16 August 1917 at Langemarck during the Third Battle of Ypres. Initially Rifleman William McBride was reported as missing in action and in August 1918 Eliza Jane McBride received official notification that her husband was presumed to have been killed in action. She placed an 'In Memoriam' notice in the *Newtownards Chronicle*.

Rifleman William McBride is commemorated in the Belfast Book of Honour (Page 384).

McBride, William Thomas (William)
Private
No. 208545, Royal Engineers, transferred to (141019), 37th Company, Machine Gun Corps (Infantry)
Died of wounds on Sunday 24 March 1918 (aged 24)
St. Sever Cemetery Extension, France (Grave P. VI. D. 11A)

McB

William Thomas McBride was born on 11 September 1893 in Newtownards and he was a son of James and Eliza McBride (nee Wallace) who lived in Sunbeam Cottage, 2 Corry's Quarter Street. They were married on 3 September 1872 in Newtownards Zion Methodist Church. James McBride worked as a farm servant, Eliza worked as a seamstress and they had at least six children – Margaret Ann, Alexander, James, Agnes Rankin, William Thomas and Nathaniel Ditty. The children were baptised in First Newtownards Presbyterian Church.

Prior to the outbreak of the Great War William McBride worked as a carpenter. He enlisted in Belfast and he served with the Royal Engineers (208545) before being transferred to the Machine Gun Corps.

Private William McBride died of wounds on 24 March 1918 and he is commemorated on Newtownards and District War Memorial.

McBurney Brothers: Edward and James

Edward and James McBurney were sons of Thomas and Anna McBurney (nee Wilson) of 'Moatville', 17 Ballyrickard, Comber. They were married on 14 November 1890 in First Newtownards Presbyterian Church. Thomas McBurney was a farmer and he and Anna had at least ten children including Edward (Teddy), Nan, Bessie, Jeannie, James (Jim), Harriette and Marjorie. The McBurney family built 'Moatville' in 1903. Jeannie McBurney was engaged to be married to Lieutenant **Sam Geddis** who died on active service on 19 September 1918. Jeannie never married. On 15 April 1919 Nan McBurney married Lieutenant Robin Wilson by special licence. The ceremony was conducted by the Rev JKL McKean and took place at 'Moatville'. James McBurney was the first of the two brothers to die:

McBurney, James Wilson (Jim)
Second Lieutenant
14th Battalion, Royal Irish Rifles
Killed in action on Thursday 16 August 1917 (aged 19)
Tyne Cot Memorial, Belgium (Panel 138 to 140 & 162 to 162 A & 163 A)

Jim McBurney was born on 12 August 1898 and he was educated at RBAI. He was a member of the QUB Officers' Training Corps and in June 1915, at the age of 16 years 10 months, he joined the 17th Battalion Royal Irish Rifles. He was sent to Drogheda during the Easter Rising in 1916 and then spent some time at the Curragh. He finished his training at Fermoy in the 7th Cadet Battalion. He obtained his commission in September 1916 and he was posted to the 20th Battalion Royal Irish Rifles at Newtownards. He went to France as a Platoon Commander with the 14th Battalion in December that year. Jim fought at the Battle of Messines in June 1917 and survived.

McB

Second Lieutenant James McBurney was killed in action on 16 August 1917, the first day of the Battle of Langemarck. In a letter to Jim's parents Second Lieutenant J Riddy wrote 'He was a brave and good comrade and most cheerful under all circumstances. Since I joined the regiment we were the closest friends and a truer friend I never wish to have. Jim and I slept in the same tent before the attack and he seemed to know something would happen to him for he asked me to write and, if I could, to bring him back to a dressing station in case he was hurt but I thought he was joking. He was in good form before the attack. I was on his right flank. He went forward at the head of his men and did splendid work and showed a fine example of Irish pluck, leading and cheering his men on against fearful odds and machine gun fire. He was first at the enemy strongpoint but got shot in the chest before getting in. Although dying fast he urged the men on and his last words were, 'Tell my father and mother I died at the head of my men fighting for my country.' After the attack his body was not recovered.

Lieutenant McGhie wrote to Jim's parents and said that Jim was one of the finest boys he had ever known. He sought to give them reassurance by telling them that Jim was shot through the heart 'dying almost without pain.'

The Rev John Knowles, Presbyterian Chaplain said that just as Jim had given the order for his men to rush the enemy position he was shot. In spite of the loss of their leader his men carried out his last command. They captured the position and took ten prisoners.

Second Lieutenant James McBurney is commemorated on Comber and District War Memorial; in First Comber Presbyterian Church; on the family headstone in Comber Cemetery; on the QUB War Memorial; in the QUB Book of Remembrance (Page 34) and on the RBAI War Memorial.

McBurney, Edward Wilson (Teddy)
Engineer Lieutenant
Transport Service, Royal Navy
Died on Wednesday 2 July 1919 (aged 28)

McB
McC

Teddy McBurney was born on 29 December 1890, the eldest son of Thomas and Anna McBurney, and for a time he worked as an apprentice engine fitter in the Harland & Wolff Shipyard Belfast. During his apprenticeship he made a stained glass window which was installed in 'Moatville' at the back of the house.

Teddy joined the Royal Naval Reserve and became a career seaman. During the Great War he served in the Royal Navy Transport Service and he died on 2 July 1919 during a trans-Atlantic trip. He was buried at sea. His family commissioned a stained glass window from Clokey Stained Glass in Belfast and this was installed in 'Moatville' at the front of the house.

Engineer Lieutenant Edward McBurney is commemorated in First Comber Presbyterian Church and on the family grave headstone in Comber Cemetery.

McCallum, Hugh
Company Sergeant Major
No. 15/9241, Cyclist Corps, 36th (Ulster Division), transferred to 15th Battalion, then 12th Battalion, Royal Irish Rifles
Killed in action on Saturday 1 December 1917 (aged 23)
Grevillers British Cemetery, France (Grave IX. B. 5)

Hugh McCallum was born on 16 December 1893 and he was the eldest son of John and Charlotte McCallum (nee Dornan) who were married in Greyabbey Presbyterian Church. They lived in Greyabbey where John

McCallum worked as a blacksmith and he and Charlotte had at least four children – Hugh, Agnes Jane, Catherine and Eleanor Martha. Hugh was baptised in Greyabbey Presbyterian Church. Later John and Charlotte McCallum moved to Scotland where they lived at 1 Blacklands Row, Kilwinning in Ayrshire.

On leaving school Hugh McCallum served his apprenticeship in gardening when he worked in Rosemount Gardens, Greyabbey for the Montgomery family. He went from there to Charleston Gardens in County Roscommon where he worked for Sir Gilbert King. After that he went to work in the Flood Hall Gardens in County Kilkenny. From there he secured a position in Belle Vue Park Dublin which was owned by Mr MVB Douglas DL. After that Hugh McCallum moved to Scotland where he was employed for a year by the Marquis of Tweeddale at Haddington, Edinburgh.

Shortly after the outbreak of the Great War, Hugh McCallum joined the Cyclist Corps of the 36th (Ulster) Division. He was transferred to the 15th and then the 12th Battalion Royal Irish Rifles (Central Antrim Volunteers) and he served in 108th Brigade of the 36th (Ulster) Division. In April 1917 he had a short period of home leave before returning to the fighting line and on 1 December 1917 Company Sergeant Major Hugh McCallum was killed in action.

McC

When he died Hugh McCallum was a married man and he had relatives living in Greyabbey. His uncle and aunt Mr and Mrs Samuel Bell placed an 'Our Heroes – In Memoriam' notice in the *Newtownards Chronicle* and it contained the verse:

> *'Some time we hope to meet him:*
> *Some time, we know not when,*
> *We shall clasp his hand in a better land*
> *And never part again.'*

Company Sergeant Major Hugh McCallum is commemorated on Greyabbey and District War Memorial located on the outside wall of Greyabbey Parish Church of Ireland (St Saviour); in the PCI Roll of Honour for Trinity Presbyterian Church Greyabbey and on the family grave headstone in Greyabbey Old Cemetery.

McCandless, James
Rifleman
No. 11364, 2nd Battalion, Royal Irish Rifles
Killed in action on Friday 6 September 1918 (aged 18)
Messines Ridge British Cemetery, Belgium (Grave I. D. 5)

James McCandless was the eldest son of Thomas and Elizabeth McCandless (nee Minnis) who were married in Second Comber Presbyterian Church and who lived at 9 Queen Street, Newtownards. Thomas McCandless worked as a dealer and he and Lizzie had at least ten children including James, Thomas, Robert, Mary, Lizzie, William, Alexander and David. Prior to the outbreak of the Great War James McCandless worked in the Ulster Print Works, Newtownards.

James McCandless enlisted on 26 July 1917 in Newtownards and after training at Clandeboye, Holywood and Ballykinlar Camps he went to France at the end of March 1918. He served with the 2nd Battalion Royal Irish Rifles and less than six months later, on 6 September 1918, Rifleman James McCandless was killed in action during the Allied offensive against all sections of the German line.

McC

> **FOR KING AND COUNTRY.**
> M'CANDLESS—September 6th, 1918, killed in action in France (11364) Rifleman James' M'Candless, Royal Irish Rifles, eldest son of Elizabeth and Thos. M'Candless, 9 Queen Street, Newtownards.
> The news was sad, the blow was hard: God's will, it shall be done; With a manly heart he did his part, And a crown of victory won.
> Deeply regretted by his Mother, Father, Sisters and Brothers.

His parents placed a 'For King and Country' notice in the 14 December 1918 edition of the *Newtownards Chronicle* and it contained the verse:

'The news was sad, the blow was hard;
God's will, it shall be done;
With a manly heart he did his part,
And a crown of victory won.'

Rifleman James McCandless is commemorated on Newtownards and District War Memorial and in the PCI Roll of Honour for Greenwell Street Presbyterian Church Newtownards.

McCann, Frederick (Fred)
Lance Corporal
No. 1524, 15th Battalion, Australian Infantry, AIF
Died of wounds on 9 June 1918 (aged 26)
Crouy British Cemetery, France (Grave III. A. 21)

Frederick McCann was born on 31 October 1891 and he was a son of Samuel and Ellen Jane McCann (nee McCormick) who lived in the townland of

Ballycullen, Newtownards. They were married on 23 July 1889 in Donegall Pass Presbyterian Church Belfast. Samuel McCann worked as a general labourer and he and Ellen had at least five children – John, Robert, Frederick, James and Helen. Fred was baptised in Regent Street Presbyterian Church Newtownards. Samuel McCann died in 1906 and Robert, Frederick and James McCann moved to Australia. Ellen McCann went to live at 41 Hatfield Street, Belfast and Fred McCann's cousins, the Misses McDowell, lived in Wyndham Terrace, Belfast.

Fred McCann worked in Australia as a labourer and he enlisted at Enoggera in Queensland on 16 December 1914. He cited his brother Robert as his next-of-kin and in his attestation papers it was noted that he was 5 feet 8½ inches tall.

In September 1917 Lance Corporal Fred McCann suffered severe gunshot wounds to his leg and shoulder and he was transferred to the First Southern General Hospital in Birmingham for treatment. He recovered sufficiently to be able to rejoin his Battalion on 9 March 1918.

McC

In June 1918 Lance Corporal Fred McCann was wounded again, this time fatally. He suffered gunshot wounds to his left arm and his right thigh and a bullet had penetrated his abdomen. He died at the 47th Casualty Clearing Station on 9 June 1918.

Everything that Fred McCann possessed when he died was listed – one Testament, three notebooks, one letter, one fountain pen, one pencil, one mirror, cards, one matchbox and one silk scarf. His possessions were sent to his brother Robert in Bundaberg, Queensland in Australia and his memorial scroll and his memorial plaque were sent to his mother Ellen in Belfast. Lance Corporal Fred McCann is commemorated on Newtownards and District War Memorial and in the Belfast Book of Honour (Page 388).

McCann, James
Lance Corporal
No. 2943, 1st Battalion, Royal Inniskilling Fusiliers
Killed in action on Saturday 1 July 1916 (aged 21)
Thiepval Memorial, France (Pier and Face 4 D and 5 B)

James McCann was a son of William and Mary McCann (nee Bunting) who lived in Donaghadee. They were married on 10 March 1877 in Shore Street

Presbyterian Church Donaghadee. William McCann worked as a seaman and he and Mary had at least ten children including Andrew, Jane, William, Annie (died 1882), Robert (died 1900), Francis Ernest, James, Annie and Elizabeth. The four eldest of the McCann children were baptised in Shore Street Presbyterian Church Donaghadee before the family moved to Belfast where they lived in Seaview Street, Glasgow Street and Ritchie Street. William McCann Senior died on 24 November 1926 aged 72 and Mary died on 18 March 1950 aged 94.

Prior to enlisting in the Army James McCann worked as a rivetter's boy in the shipyard. He served with the 1st Battalion Royal Inniskilling Fusiliers in 87th Brigade of the 29th Division and he was killed in action on the first day of the Battle of the Somme. Lance Corporal James McCann is commemorated on the family grave headstone in Donaghadee Parish Church of Ireland Graveyard and in the Belfast Book of Honour (Page 388).

McCann, Thomas (Tom)
Corporal
No. 18307, 9th Battalion, Royal Inniskilling Fusiliers
Killed in action on Thursday 21 March 1918 (aged 21)
Pozieres Memorial, France (Panel 38 to 40)

McC

Thomas McCann was born on 31 January 1897 in Newtownards and he was a son of Thomas and Margaret Jane McCann (nee Galloway). They were married on 3 October 1891 in Fourth Newtownards Presbyterian Church. Thomas and his brother Robert James were baptised in that same church. When their mother died Thomas and Robert James lived at 59 Church Street, Newtownards with their maternal grandparents John and Maggie Galloway.

Thomas McCann Senior worked as a bleach works labourer and, after he married Elizabeth (Lizzie) Allen on 27 December 1903 in Second Newtownards Presbyterian Church, Thomas and Robert lived with them and Lizzie's daughter Nellie at 37 Church Street, Newtownards. Thomas and Lizzie had at least eight children – David Allen, Mary, Owen, Samuel, Elizabeth, William, Ruth and Thomas (born in 1919 and named after Thomas who was killed in action in 1918). The six youngest children were baptised in Greenwell Street Presbyterian Church Newtownards.

Prior to the outbreak of the Great War Thomas McCann worked as a grocer's labourer. He enlisted in Newtownards and he went to France in October 1915. He served with the 9th Battalion Royal Inniskilling Fusiliers in 109th Brigade of the 36th (Ulster) Division and he was wounded during the Battle of the Somme and again at the Battle of Messines. Corporal Thomas McCann was killed in action on 21 March 1918 during the opening battle of the German 'Michael' offensive on the Western Front. Captain TD Morrison, adjutant of the Battalion and son of the principal of the Londonderry Schools in Newtownards wrote to Thomas McCann's father.

In the letter he described the circumstances of Thomas's death, 'During the attack he went forward with some of his men to drive out a party of the enemy who had entered our line. He succeeded in his task but unfortunately was killed just as he completed it. He was buried where he fell. Your son was one our most promising non-commissioned officers.'

After Tom was killed in action his family placed a 'For King and Country' notice in the *Newtownards Chronicle* and it contained the verse:

'He fell at his post like a soldier brave,
He answered his Master's call;
He sleeps far away in a hero's grave,
For his country's cause he did fall.
In the bloom of life death claimed him,
In the pride of his manhood days;
None knew him but to love him,
None mentioned his name but with praise.'

McC

Corporal Tom McCann is commemorated on Newtownards and District War Memorial and in the PCI Roll of Honour for Greenwell Street Presbyterian Church Newtownards.

McCartan, John
Rifleman
Royal Irish Rifles
Died on Friday 12 April 1918 (aged 31)

The name John McCartan is listed on Newtownards and District War Memorial and in the booklet produced for the Unveiling and Dedication Ceremony held on Saturday 26 May 1934 he is described as a Rifleman in the Royal Irish Rifles. John McCartan was the eldest son of John and Elizabeth (Lizzie) McCartan who were associated with three addresses in Newtownards between 1911 and 1918 – 32 West Street, 32 John Street Lane and 32 Wyndham Terrace.

John and Lizzie McCartan (nee Dorrian) were married on 5 April 1885 in Downpatrick Roman Catholic Church and they had at least eight children including John, Hugh, Anna, James, Theresa and Catherine. Prior to the outbreak of the Great War John McCartan Junior worked as an agricultural labourer. Rifleman McCartan served with the Royal Irish Rifles and he died in Newcastle-upon-Tyne on 12 April 1918. His funeral was accorded military honours.

> M'CARTAN—April 12th, 1918, at New-castle-on-Tyne, John, eldest son of John and Elizabeth M'Cartan, 32 John Street Lane, Newtownards. (Funeral accorded full military honours).
> Deeply regretted by his Father, Mother, Brothers, and Sisters.

After John died his family placed a notice in the 20 April 1918 edition of the *Newtownards Chronicle* and Rifleman John McCartan is commemorated on Newtownards and District War Memorial. Although desk searches and public appeals to date have not confirmed a connection, there is evidence to suggest that this soldier's number was 4/7178. He enlisted on 27 August 1914 and joined the 4th Battalion Royal Irish Rifles. He went to France on 29 December 1914 to join one of the regular battalions and he was discharged on 10 July 1915 due to sickness.

McC

McCartney, Robert
Rifleman
No. 13/343, 'B' Company, 13th Battalion, Royal Irish Rifles
Killed in action on Saturday 1 July 1916 (aged 23)
Thiepval Memorial, France (Pier and Face 15 A and 15 B)

Robert McCartney was born in Glasgow and he was the eldest son of William John and Mary McCartney (nee Lindsay) who were married on 1 January 1890 in Second Newtownards Presbyterian Church. They lived in Donaghadee Road, Newtownards when they returned from Scotland after their first two children were born. William John McCartney worked as a wool weaver and he and Mary had at least eleven children including Elizabeth, Robert, Mary, James, Jane, William, John Lindsay, Ethel and Eleanor. Six of the children were baptised in Greenwell Street Presbyterian Church Newtownards.

Like his father, Robert McCartney worked as a wool weaver and he and Susanna Dorrian were married on 29 January 1915 in Newtownards Parish Church of Ireland. Susanna and their son Robert who was baptised in

Greenwell Street Presbyterian Church lived at 4 Talbot Street, Newtownards with Susanna's parents William John and Ellen Dorrian. Robert McCartney enlisted in Belfast, he served with the 13th Battalion Royal Irish Rifles in 108th Brigade of the 36th (Ulster) Division and he was killed in action on the first day of the Battle of the Somme. Initially he was posted as missing in action and in June 1917 it was officially confirmed that he had been killed. Susanna placed a 'For King and Country' notice in the 9 June 1917 edition of the *Newtownards Chronicle* and it contained the verse:

> *'One by one the links are slipping,*
> *One by one our heroes fall;*
> *And you, my darling husband,*
> *Have answered the great Roll Call'*

Robert's father, mother, brother and sisters also placed a 'For King and Country' notice and it contained the verse:

> *'No mother's care did him attend,*
> *Nor o'er him did a father bend;*
> *No sisters by to shed a tear,*
> *No brother by his words to hear.*
> *Sick, dying in a foreign land,*
> *No father by to take his hand;*
> *No mother near to close his eyes,*
> *Far from his native land he lies.*
> *If the grave should open*
> *What changes you would see,*
> *But the Lord knew best*
> *To take you home to rest'*

McC

Rifleman Robert McCartney is commemorated on Newtownards and District War Memorial and in the PCI Roll of Honour for Greenwell Street Presbyterian Church Newtownards.

Three Newtownards families related by marriage suffered bereavement during the first two weeks of the Battle of the Somme when four men who are commemorated in this book died:

- **James Dorrian** (16420)
- His sister Susanna's husband **Robert McCartney** (13/343)
- His sister Jane's husband **Edward McAvoy** (18125)
- Edward's brother **John McAvoy** (18183)

Three women living at 4 Talbot Street were widowed.

McChesney, John
Rifleman
No. 18215, 'B' Company, 13th Battalion, Royal Irish Rifles
Died on Friday 29 November 1918 (aged 41)
Newtownards (Movilla) Cemetery, Co. Down (Grave 1. 195)

John McChesney was born on 1 June 1877 and he was a son of John and Rachel McChesney (nee Gibson) who lived in Victoria Avenue and later East Street, Newtownards. They were married on 31 October 1868 in Newtownards Parish Church of Ireland and they had at least five children – Ellen Jane, Charles (died), Mary Catherine, John and Robert James all of whom were baptised in Greenwell Street Presbyterian Church.

John McChesney worked as a heckler (flax comber) and general labourer before the Great War. He was 37 years old when he enlisted on 17 September 1914 in Newtownards but he declared his age to be 30 years 3 months. He was posted to the 13th Battalion Royal Irish Rifles on 17 September 1914 and he was discharged from the Army on 16 March 1915 because of Valvular Disease of the Heart (VDH).

McC

Rifleman John McChesney died of heart failure on 29 November 1918 and he was buried in Movilla Cemetery. He is commemorated on Newtownards and District War Memorial and in the PCI Roll of Honour for Greenwell Street Presbyterian Church Newtownards.

McClean, Alexander (Alex)
Private
No. 32697, 2nd Battalion, Otago Regiment, NZEF
Died of wounds on Sunday 17 June 1917 (aged 28)
Trois Arbres Cemetery, France (Grave I. R. 10)

Alexander McClean was born on 7 November 1888 and he was a son of John and Mary Ann McClean (nee Barbour) who lived in Donaghadee. They were married in Fourth Newtownards Presbyterian Church. John McClean worked as a gardener and he and Mary Ann had a son called Alexander who was born on 24 March 1887. Alexander died and their next child was born on 7 November 1888. They called him Alexander too. Both

Alexanders were baptised in Donaghadee Parish Church of Ireland.

Alexander McClean and Hilda Bunting were married on 23 September 1910 in St Anne's Church of Ireland Belfast. They lived in Donaghadee where Alex worked on the County Down Railway before they moved to New Zealand around 1913.

Donaghadee-New Zealander Dies of Wounds.

Intimation is to hand that Private Alex. M'Clean, New Zealand Forces, has died of wounds received in action. Deceased, who formerly resided at Donaghadee, and worked on the County Down Railway, emigrated four years ago. He leaves a widow and two children in Dunedin.

Private Alex McClean served with the 2nd Battalion Otago Regiment NZEF and he died of wounds on 17 June 1917. At the time of his death his wife Hilda and their two children lived in St Kilda, Dunedin, New Zealand and his parents lived at 2 Greenville Street, Belfast. Private Alex McClean is commemorated in the Belfast Book of Honour (Page 394).

McClelland, Alexander (Sandy)
Rifleman
No. 7610, 4th Battalion, Royal Irish Rifles
Killed on Thursday 27 April 1916 (aged 18)
Greyabbey Old Cemetery, Co. Down (Grave about middle of cemetery)

McC

Alexander McClelland was born on 26 August 1897 and he was the fourth son of James and Agnes McClelland (nee Ledlie) who lived in the townland of Balligan, Kircubbin. They were married on 26 April 1881 in Balligan Church of Ireland. James McClelland worked as a stone mason and he and Agnes had at least ten children including Jane, Agnes, Robert (died), Robert James (died), Grace, Ellen, James, Mary, Alexander and Robert. They were baptised in Kircubbin Parish Church of Ireland.

Sandy McClelland served with the 4th Battalion Royal Irish Rifles (Machine Gun Section) and he was killed in Dublin on 27 April 1916. His funeral was on 1 May 1916 to the family burying ground in Greyabbey. The following year the McClelland family placed an 'Our Heroes – In Memoriam' notice in the 28 April 1917 edition of the *Newtownards Chronicle*. In it Sandy McClelland was 'Ever remembered by his loving Father, Mother, Sisters and Brothers' and it contained the verse:

'The news was sad, the blow was hard,
God's will, it shall be done;

With a manly heart he did his part,
Our dear beloved son'

On 29 April 1917, the day after the notice was published and two days after the first anniversary of Sandy's death, Sandy's father James McClelland died and he was interred beside his son. Rifleman Sandy McClelland is commemorated in Kircubbin Parish Church of Ireland (Holy Trinity) and on the family grave headstone in Greyabbey Old Cemetery.

McClelland, James
Rifleman
No. 10528, 2nd Battalion, Royal Irish Rifles
Killed in action on Monday 6 August 1917 (aged 17)
Ypres (Menin Gate) Memorial, Belgium (Panel 40)

McC

James McClelland was born in Bangor on 28 February 1900 and he was the eldest son of James and Annabella (Eliza) McClelland (nee Gordon). They were married in Second Newtownards Presbyterian Church. James had five brothers and sisters – Eliza, Thomas George and Isabella who were baptised in Ballygrainey Presbyterian Church and John and Annie who were baptised in Greenwell Street Presbyterian Church Newtownards.

James McClelland was underage when he enlisted in Newtownards and he was just 17 years of age when he died. He served with the 2nd Battalion Royal Irish Rifles and he was killed in action on Monday 6 August 1917 during the Third Battle of Ypres. His body was never recovered. The 2nd Battalion of the Royal Irish Rifles was in action at Westhoek Ridge on the night of 5 August 1917 and there was an intense German barrage at Chateau Wood. Heavy intermittent shelling continued over the next three days and there were many casualties.

At the time of Rifleman James McClelland's death the McClelland family was living at 9 Ann Street, Newtownards and he is commemorated on Newtownards and District War Memorial; in the annals of Ballygrainey Presbyterian Church and in the PCI Roll of Honour for Greenwell Street Presbyterian Church Newtownards.

McClement, John
Seaman
SS *Lord Ormonde*, Mercantile Marine
Drowned on Tuesday 30 January 1917 (aged 38)
Buried at sea

In response to public appeals for information the name John McClement from Kircubbin was put forward. His name is not included in the CWGC Debt of Honour and research has shown that John McClement died when he was washed overboard and drowned on 30 January 1917 during a voyage aboard the SS *Lord Ormonde* from the United States of America.

John McClement was a son of James and Agnes McClement (nee Mahood) who were married on 24 August 1865 in St Anne's Church of Ireland Belfast and they had at least eight children – Tom, Agnes, Samuel, Robert, Mary Ann, John, Lizzie and Hugh. Agnes was baptised in Ballyhemlin Non-Subscribing Presbyterian Church Ballyhalbert and five of the children (Samuel, Robert, Mary Ann, Lizzie and Hugh) were baptised in Kircubbin Presbyterian Church. John's brother Samuel was lost at sea in 1890 aged 16, his father James died in 1898 aged 58 and his mother Agnes died in 1899 aged 56.

McC

The SS *Lord Ormonde* was built in 1889 and was one of the Lord Line ships. The Lord Line (Irish Shipowners Company) was founded by Thomas Dixon in 1879 and, amongst other routes, operated services between Belfast and Baltimore. The company went into liquidation in 1917 and the SS *Lord Ormonde* was sold to Davie SB & Repair Company Quebec. Other Lord Line ships were sold to the Head Line (Ulster Steamship Company). In March 1918 the SS *Lord Ormonde* was damaged in a U-boat attack.

John McClement is commemorated on the family grave headstone in Kircubbin Presbyterian Church graveyard – as is his brother Captain Tom McClement (retired) who served in the Mercantile Marine during the Great War and who died on 11 October 1921 aged 53.

McClements, Robert
Rifleman
No. 17/489, 8th Battalion, Royal Irish Rifles
Killed in action on Sunday 2 July 1916 (aged 37)
Thiepval Memorial, France (Pier and Face 15 A and 15 B)

Robert McClements was born in Killinchy and he was a son of William (died 27 February 1913) and Martha (died 10 December 1901) McClements. Robert

lived at 7 Martin Street, Belfast and he enlisted in Belfast in May 1915. He served with the 8th Battalion Royal Irish Rifles in 107th Brigade of the 36th (Ulster Division) and in the CWGC Debt of Honour he is listed as having died on the second day of the Battle of the Somme. In the heat of battle the 8th Battalion Royal Irish Rifles did not make a casualty return on 1 July 1916 and many military historians agree that those 8th Battalion casualties listed on the 2 July return were killed in action on 1 July.

Robert McClements is commemorated in the Belfast Book of Honour (Page 397) and on the family grave headstone in Killinchy Non-Subscribing Presbyterian Churchyard.

McCloone, Bryan
Corporal
No. 9682, 13th Battalion, Cheshire Regiment
Killed in action on Friday 7 July 1916
Thiepval Memorial, France (Pier and Face 3 C and 4 A)0

In 'Soldiers Died in the Great War 1914 – 1919' it is recorded that Bryan McCloone was born in Portaferry, he lived in Narin, Co Donegal and he enlisted in Chester. He served with the 13th Battalion Cheshire Regiment and he was killed in action on 7 July 1916 during the Battle of the Somme.

McClure Brothers, Hugh and James
Hugh and James McClure were sons of Thomas and Margaret McClure who lived at 6 Talbot Street, Newtownards. Thomas McClure worked as a stone mason and he and Margaret had at least eight children – Elizabeth, William, Margaret, Hugh, James, Agnes, Mary and Annie. Hugh was the first of the two brothers to die:

McClure, Hugh
Rifleman
No. 18231, 'B' Company, 13th Battalion, Royal Irish Rifles
Died on Sunday 22 October 1916 (aged 23)
Newtownards (Movilla) Cemetery, Co. Down (Grave I. 91)

Prior to the outbreak of the Great War Hugh McClure worked as a cloth soaper. He was a member of the Newtownards contingent of the Ulster Volunteer Force and at the outbreak of hostilities he joined the 13th Battalion

Royal Irish Rifles (1st County Down Volunteers). He went to France in October 1915 and he served in 108th Brigade of the 36th (Ulster) Division, fighting in the trenches through the winter months. On 7 February 1916 he narrowly escaped death when he was in the same dug-out as four Ardsmen who were killed by a German shell (**James Calvert, David McConnell, Charlie Newell and Jack Tate**). Trench warfare took its toll on his health and in June 1916 he was invalided home. He returned to 6 Talbot Street, Newtownards to live with his parents.

FOR KING AND COUNTRY.

McCLURE—October 22, 1916, at his residence, 6, Talbot Street, Newtownards, Private Hugh M'Clure, 13th Batt. Royal Irish Rifles. The remains of our beloved son were interred in the family burying-ground, Movilla, on 24th inst.
THOS. and MAGGIE M'CLURE.

Rifleman Hugh McClure died of bronchitis on Sunday 22 October 1916 and he was buried with full military honours the following Tuesday. The bands of the 20th Battalion Royal Irish Rifles under Bugle-Major Hammerton and the 10th Battalion Royal Irish Fusiliers under Bandmaster May played funeral marches on the way to Movilla Cemetery. The members of the firing party under Sergeant Brown wore stripes of gold lace on their sleeves signifying that they had been wounded in action. All had belonged to the 13th Battalion Royal Irish Rifles and were subsequently attached to the 20th Battalion.

A large contingent of soldiers under the command of Second Lieutenant JK Farrow followed the remains. Many soldiers who had fought alongside Hugh McClure on the battlefields in France and had been wounded in action turned out to pay their respects. At the request of his parents Hugh's coffin, enshrouded in the Union Jack, was borne through Newtownards on the shoulders of his brother, Rifleman James McClure (who had been wounded in action on 1 July 1916), and three of his comrades.

The service at the graveside was conducted by the Rev WLT Whatham Rector of Newtownards and Chaplain to the local military forces. After the customary three volleys over the open grave the buglers sounded the 'Last Post'. Rifleman Hugh McClure is commemorated on Newtownards and District War Memorial and in Newtownards Parish Church of Ireland (St Mark).

McC

McClure, James
Rifleman
No. 18230, 'B' Company, 13th Battalion, Royal Irish Rifles

Prior to the outbreak of the Great War James McClure worked as a winding master. He was a member of the Newtownards contingent of the Ulster Volunteer Force and at the outbreak of hostilities he joined the 13th Battalion Royal Irish Rifles (1st County Down Volunteers). He went to France in October 1915 and he served in 108th Brigade of the 36th (Ulster) Division, fighting in the trenches through the winter months.

> Rfm. James M'Clure (No. 18,230) is at present in Townley's Military Hospital, Farnworth, Bolton, Lancs., suffering from a bullet wound in the right foot and shrapnel wounds in the leg, sustained in the action of 1st July. He is a son of Thomas and Maggie M'Clure, 6 Talbot Street, and joined the 1st Co. Downs at the beginning of the war, proceeding to the front in October, 1915.

Rifleman James McClure was wounded in action on the first day of the Battle of the Somme. He sustained a bullet wound in the right foot and shrapnel wounds in the leg. He was transferred to Townley's Military Hospital, Farnworth, Bolton in Lancashire and he was at home in Newtownards to carry the coffin at his brother's funeral on 24 October 1916.

McC

Rifleman James McClure is commemorated on Newtownards and District War Memorial; desk searches and public appeals to date have yielded no further information about his death.

McClure, Joseph (Joe)
Petty Officer
Royal Navy
Died on Monday 21 January 1924 (aged 48)
Newtownards (Movilla) Cemetery, Co. Down

The name Joseph McClure is listed on Newtownards and District War Memorial and in the booklet produced for the Unveiling and Dedication Ceremony held on Saturday 26 May 1934 he is described as a Petty Officer in the Royal Navy.

Petty Officer Joseph McClure died on 21 January 1924 and his death was reported in the 26 January 1924 edition of the *Newtownards Chronicle*. It was reported that, as a boy, he had worked for a time in the Glen Printing and Finishing Works and then in the Castle Gardens Spinning Mill. He joined the Royal Navy at the age of 16 years and he had 27 years of service when he was demobilised in England in July 1919. He had served aboard HMS *Superb*, HMS *Tribune* and HMS *Royal Sovereign* and during the Great War he had fought in the Battle of Jutland. He had also served for a time in the submarine service.

After demobilisation Joseph McClure lived in James Street, Newtownards and he worked for the postal service. He died on 21 January 1924 and at his funeral Captain Rayner and Staff-Sergeant Cooper represented the military. As the hearse passed Army Headquarters in Regent Street Newtownards the guard presented arms. There were many floral tributes, among them one from his sisters Sarah and Margaret.

McCluskey, William James (William)
Rifleman
No. 19096, 'A' Company, 13th Battalion, Royal Irish Rifles
Died of disease on Sunday 18 April 1915 (aged 21)
Ballymanish Presbyterian Cemetery, Portaferry, Co. Down

William James McCluskey was born in Portaferry and he was a son of James and Ellen McCluskey who lived in the townland of Ballycam. James McCluskey worked as an agricultural labourer and he and Ellen had at least nine children including Cynthia, Samuel, Jane Ellen, William James, Hugh and Minnie.

McC

William James McCluskey enlisted in Ballywalter shortly after the outbreak of the Great War and he joined the 13th Battalion Royal Irish Rifles. When he was in Clandeboye Training Camp he contracted a cold, complications arose and he was taken home to Portaferry where he was attended by members of the Portaferry Branch of the Medical Nursing Staff.

Rifleman McCluskey died at home on Sunday 18 April 1915 and his funeral took place the following Tuesday. Wreaths were sent by his comrades in Clandeboye Camp, his comrades in the Portaferry contingent of the Ulster Volunteer Force, members of LOL No. 673 and the nurses who attended during his illness. His nurses added a message:

> 'We nursed him with our tenderest care,
> Until the Master came
> And took him to that land of bliss,
> Where he is free from pain'

Rifleman William James McCluskey is commemorated in Portaferry Presbyterian Church. His brother Hugh served in the Great War and survived.

McConnell Brothers: David and Robert

David and Robert McConnell were born in Donaghadee and they were sons of David and Mary Ellen McConnell (nee Strain) who moved from Donaghadee to Bangor where they lived in the townland of Corporation, Bangor and then at 53 Church Street. They were married on 8 September 1890 in Newtownards Registry Office. David McConnell Senior worked as a farm labourer after serving for seven years in the Royal Garrison Artillery and he and Mary had at least ten children including Jane (Jenny), David, Robert, Stephen, Samuel, Mary, Joseph and Maggie. Jane, David and Robert were baptised in Donaghadee Parish Church of Ireland.

At the age of 40 years and 2 months David McConnell Senior enlisted in Bangor on 14 September 1914 and he joined the Royal Irish Rifles (18141). His wife Mary was ill for several weeks and she died on 22 October 1914. A report in the 23 October 1914 edition of the *Newtownards Chronicle* stated that six of her ten children 'were totally unfit to look after themselves'. In relation to their mother's death, the report writer expressed the opinion that 'a woman in humble circumstances could not, with the delay in the Government remittances, have received nourishment requisite to her delicate condition'. In the circumstances her husband David was discharged from the army on 25 November 1914. David was the first of the two brothers to die in the Great War:

McConnell, David
Rifleman
No. 16737, 'A' Company, 13th Battalion, Royal Irish Rifles
Killed in action on Saturday 1 July 1916 (aged 19)
Serre Road Cemetery No. 2, France (Grave VII. A. 1)

David McConnell was born on 24 September 1896 and before the Great War he worked as a general servant for William and Jane Shanks who farmed in the townland of Ballyfotherly, Donaghadee. David McConnell enlisted in Donaghadee and he served with the 13th Battalion Royal Irish Rifles in 108th Brigade of the 36th (Ulster Division). He was posted as missing in action after the first day of the Battle of the Somme and his father appealed for news concerning his son.

Later it was officially confirmed that Rifleman David McConnell had been killed in action and he is commemorated on Donaghadee and District War

McC

Memorial; on Bangor and District War Memorial; in the RBL Album in North Down Museum (Page 18) and on the Memorial Plaques in the RBL Bangor Branch, Conlig Orange Hall, Donaghadee Parish Church of Ireland and Bangor Parish Church of Ireland (St Comgall).

McConnell, Robert (Bertie)
Rifleman
No. 2313, 'A' Company, 13th Battalion Royal Irish Rifles
Died of disease on Friday 8 March 1918 (aged 20)
Bangor New Cemetery, Newtownards Road, Bangor, Co. Down (Grave 5S. 70)

Robert McConnell was born on 26 February 1898 and he was educated at Bangor Endowed School. Prior to the outbreak of the Great War he worked as a van-man. He enlisted on 20 November 1914 in Belfast and he was posted to the 13th Battalion Royal Irish Rifles. In late 1916 Rifleman Bertie McConnell was hospitalised in the Canadian General Hospital Boulogne after contracting bronchitis and on 21 January 1917 he was transferred to a hospital in England and from there he went to Forster Green Hospital in Belfast. On 7 April 1917 he was discharged from the Army when he was deemed no longer physically fit for war service.

McC

Rifleman Bertie McConnell died in Belfast on 8 March 1918 (5 March 1918 in the RBL Album) and he is commemorated on Bangor and District War Memorial; in the RBL Album in North Down Museum (Page 18) and on the Memorial Plaques in RBL Bangor Branch, Bangor Parish Church of Ireland (St Comgall) and Bangor Grammar School.

McConnell, David
Rifleman
No. 18238, 'B' Company, 13th Battalion, Royal Irish Rifles
Killed in action on Monday 7 February 1916 (aged 22)
Mesnil Ridge Cemetery, France (Grave G. 4)

David McConnell was born on 6 February 1894 in Newtownards and he was a son of Robert and Mary Elizabeth McConnell (nee Cassidy) who lived at 22

Wallace's Street No. 2. They were married on 12 July 1892 in Newtownards Parish Church of Ireland. Robert McConnell worked as a hand loom weaver and he and Mary Elizabeth had at least seven children – Maria, David, Annie, Robert, William John, Mary Elizabeth and Eveline.

Prior to the outbreak of the Great War David McConnell worked as a cloth lifter. He was a member of the Ulster Volunteer Force, he enlisted in Newtownards and he served with the 13th Battalion Royal Irish Rifles in 108th Brigade of the 36th (Ulster) Division. David's father Robert who served in the South African War also enlisted and he served as a Corporal with the Royal Irish Rifles (18143).

McC

Rifleman David McConnell was one of four Ardsmen who were killed in action together on 7 February 1916. They were all members of the 13th (Service) Battalion of the Royal Irish Rifles (1st Co Down Volunteers). The others were Rifleman **James Calvert** from the townland of Tullycore Killinchy, Bandsman **Charlie Newell** of 54 South Street Newtownards and Rifleman **Jack Tate** of Frances Street and North Street, Newtownards. Rifleman **Hugh McClure** from Newtownards survived but died at home on 22 October 1916 after being invalided out of the army. David McConnell had been a member of the No. 5 Platoon football team and a short time before his death he had played in a match in the platoon competition.

The officer in charge of the platoon was Lieutenant **Elliott Johnston**, a son of Samuel Johnston JP, Glen Printing and Finishing Works in Newtownards. He described the circumstances of their deaths. He said that during a heavy bombardment a shell from the German lines exploded in the midst of a party of men killing three and wounding three. James Calvert, David McConnell and Charlie Newell were killed outright; Jack Tate died later from his injuries. The three men who died immediately were laid to rest together and the burial service was conducted by one of the brigade chaplains, the Rev Charles Campbell Manning, Rector of Comber.

On that occasion Lieutenant Johnston escaped injury but he was killed in action five months later on the first day of the Battle of the Somme. After David's death the McConnell family placed a 'For King and Country' notice in the *Newtownards Chronicle*. Rifleman David McConnell is commemorated on Newtownards and District War Memorial and in Newtownards Parish Church of Ireland (St Mark).

McConnell, Hugh
Died on Sunday 4 March 1917
Newtownards (Movilla) Cemetery, Co. Down (Section 4)

Hugh McConnell is listed in the burial register for Movilla Old Cemetery Newtownards where he is described as a soldier who died of bronchitis on 4 March 1917. He is commemorated in the PCI Roll of Honour for Second Newtownards Presbyterian Church where he is described as a Private in the Royal Irish Fusiliers who was wounded and died. Desk searches and public appeals to date have yielded no further information.

McConnell, Joseph
Rifleman
No. 18/996, 12th Battalion, Royal Irish Rifles
Killed in action on Sunday 12 August 1917 (aged 31)
Ypres (Menin Gate) Memorial, Belgium (Panel 40)

McC

Joseph McConnell was born on 13 September 1885 in Donaghadee and he was a son of Joseph and Mary McConnell (nee McGaughy) who lived at 27 Moat Street. They were married on 11 December 1867 in Newtownards Registry Office. Joseph and Mary had at least eight children – Alexander, Joseph (died), Charlotte (died), Sarah, Charlotte, Joseph, Ellen and James. The first six were baptised in Donaghadee Parish Church of Ireland. Mary McConnell was widowed on 29 January 1891 and she worked as an embroiderer. Mary died on 31 July 1913.

Joseph McConnell worked as a farm labourer before the outbreak of the Great War, he enlisted in Belfast and he served with the 12th Battalion Royal Irish Rifles in 108th Brigade of the 36th (Ulster) Division.

Rifleman Joseph McConnell was killed in action on 12 August 1917 whilst holding the line during the Third Battle of Ypres and he is commemorated on Donaghadee and District War Memorial and in Donaghadee Parish

Church of Ireland. He is also commemorated on the family grave headstone in Donaghadee Parish Church Graveyard.

McConnell, Patrick (see Moore, Patrick)

McConnell, Robert
Died of disease on Tuesday 13 June 1916 (aged 24)

amongst the Donaghadee soldiers.—Deep regret was **Young Soldier Dies.**—Deep regret was occasioned in Donaghadee at the death of Mr. Robert M'Connell, a well-known Donaghadee resident, which took place at the residence of his uncle (Mr. Robert Simpson) on Tuesday last. The deceased who was only some 24 years of age had been in failing health for some time. He joined the Army after the formation of the Ulster Division and served for some time, but failing health necessitated a discharge. He afterwards served in the coast watchers. The funeral took place on Thursday, and the large and representative attendance fully testified to the esteem in which the deceased was held.

In the 16 and 17 June 1916 editions of the *County Down Spectator* and *Newtownards Chronicle* respectively the death of Robert McConnell was reported. Described in the reports as 'a young soldier' and 'a well-known Donaghadee resident' he died on 13 June 1916 at his uncle's residence.

Robert McConnell lived at 12 Shore Street, Donaghadee with his uncle and aunt Robert and Maggie Simpson and their children Maggie and Robert Simpson. Prior to the outbreak of the Great War Robert McConnell and Robert Simpson Senior both worked as general labourers.

Robert McConnell joined the army after the formation of the 36th (Ulster) Division but he was discharged on medical grounds. After that he served with the Coastguard but once again failing health necessitated his discharge. His health continued to decline and he died on 13 June 1916.

McCoy, William James (William)
Lance Corporal
No. 2734, 'B' Company, 13th Battalion, Royal Irish Rifles
Killed in action on Saturday 1 July 1916 (aged 19)
Pozieres British Cemetery, France (Grave IV. U. 9)

William James McCoy was born in Monaghan and he was a son of James and Ellen McCoy (nee Pearson). They were married on 26 September 1887 in Grange Church of Ireland, Armagh. James McCoy worked as an agricultural labourer and he and Ellen had at least nine children including Lily, Ellen, Margaret, William James, Martha (Meta), Sadie, Thomas and Mary Elizabeth who was baptised in Greenwell Street Presbyterian Church

McC

Newtownards. The McCoy family lived in Ballybarnes Cottages, Newtownards and William James worked as a quarry labourer. He enlisted in Belfast, he served with the 13th Battalion Royal Irish Rifles in 108th Brigade of the 36th (Ulster) Division and he was killed in action on the first day of the Battle of the Somme.

Lance Corporal William James McCoy is commemorated on Newtownards and District War Memorial and in the PCI Roll of Honour for Greenwell Street Presbyterian Church Newtownards.

McCracken, John
Lance Corporal
No. 18146, 'B' Company, 13th Battalion, Royal Irish Rifles
Killed in action on Tuesday 27 June 1916 (aged 36)
Authuile Military Cemetery, France (Sp. Mem. B. 2)

John McCracken was born in the townland of Ballyblack and in 1901 he was living at 154 Greenwell Street, Newtownards with his widowed father James and his widowed grandmother Margaret McCracken. John McCracken worked as a fowl butcher, James McCracken worked as a general labourer and Margaret McCracken worked as a seamstress. John McCracken and Elizabeth (Lizzie) McCullough were married on 5 August 1904 in Newtownards Parish Church of Ireland and they had at least three children including a daughter called Maggie. They lived at 163 Greenwell Street, 12 Windmill Row and 83 East Street in Newtownards.

McC

John McCracken was a member of the Ulster Volunteer Force before the war and he enlisted in Newtownards. He joined the 1st Co Down Volunteers and he went to the front in October 1915 with the 13th Battalion Royal Irish Rifles in 108th Brigade of the 36th (Ulster) Division. He was a bass drummer in the 13th Battalion Band. John McCracken was killed in action on 27 June 1916 and in letter of condolence to John's wife Captain Charles Murland outlined the circumstances of John's death, 'He was out with a [raiding] party on special duty and had done splendid work. He had just completed bandaging a wounded man and was going over to attend another one when he was instantaneously killed by a shell'. This was the raid led by Captain **Elliott Johnston** who was awarded the Military Cross for his conspicuous gallantry.

John McCracken had also been a bass drummer in Lord Londonderry's Own

Church Lads Brigade (CLB) Flute Band and the members placed a 'Killed in Action' notice in the *Newtownards Chronicle*, as did his wife Lizzie. Hers contained the verse:

'A loving husband, true and kind,
Missed by those he left behind.
Forget him! No, I never will,
As time rolls on I love him still,
He gave his life for his country.
What more could he do'

Lance Corporal John McCracken is commemorated on Newtownards and District War Memorial and in Newtownards Parish Church of Ireland (St Mark). His CWGC headstone in Authuile Military Cemetery bears two inscriptions:

'Known to be buried in this cemetery'

'Their glory shall not be blotted out'

McC

McCready, James Morrison (James)
Rifleman
No. 16740, 'A' Company, 13th Battalion, then 11th/13th Battalion, then 12th Battalion, Royal Irish Rifles
Died of wounds on Sunday 25 August 1918 (aged 19)
Arneke British Cemetery, France (Grave III. E. 26)

James Morrison McCready was born in Saltcoats, Ayrshire in Scotland and he was a son of James and Ellen McCready (nee Little) who lived at 12 Harbour Street. James McCready worked as a general labourer and he and Ellen had at least seven children including Catherine, James and Sarah (all born in Scotland) and William, Alexander and Isabella (all born in County Down).

James McCready enlisted in Donaghadee and he served with the 13th Battalion Royal Irish Rifles in 108th Brigade of the 36th (Ulster) Division. In November 1917 the 11th and 13th Battalions were amalgamated and when they were disbanded in February 1918 James was transferred to the 12th Battalion. Rifleman James McCready died of wounds on 25 August 1918 during the Allied offensive against all sections of the German line and he is commemorated on Donaghadee and District War Memorial and in Donaghadee Parish Church of Ireland.

McCready, John*

The name John McCready is listed on Newtownards and District War Memorial and in the booklet produced for the Unveiling and Dedication Ceremony held on Saturday 26 May 1934 he is described as a Rifleman in the Royal Irish Rifles. In the 4 January 1919 edition of the *Newtownards Chronicle* it was reported that Rifleman J McCready (18/1351) Royal Irish Rifles was home in Greyabbey after having been released from a German Prisoner of War camp. Desk searches and public appeals to date have not confirmed a connection between this soldier and the one who is commemorated on Newtownards and District War Memorial.

McCulloch, John

Rifleman
No. 1378, 8th Battalion, Royal Irish Rifles
Killed in action on Sunday 2 July 1916 (aged 18)
Thiepval Memorial, France (Pier and Face 15 A and 15 B)

John McCulloch was born on 30 October 1897 in Comber and he was the only child of James McCulloch JP and Mary Leathem McCulloch (nee Orr). They were married on 11 January 1897 in Gilnahirk Presbyterian Church. James McCulloch was a farmer and the family lived in the townland of Gransha, Moneyreagh.

McC

John McCulloch enlisted in Belfast and he served with the 8th Battalion Royal Irish Rifles. On 2 July 1916 he was posted as missing in action and in April 1917 it was officially confirmed that he had been killed in action 'on that date or since'. In the heat of battle the 8th Battalion Royal Irish Rifles did not make a casualty return on 1 July 1916 and many military historians agree that those 8th Battalion casualties listed on the 2 July return were killed in action on 1 July.

John's father placed a 'For King and Country' notice in the 21 April 1917 edition of the *Newtownards Chronicle*. John had been a member of the Central Presbyterian Association in Belfast and at the May 1917 meeting of its Governing Body reference was made to the fact that Rifleman John McCulloch had 'died a hero's death' and sympathy was extended to his parents.

Rifleman John McCulloch is commemorated on Comber and District War Memorial and in First Comber Presbyterian Church. John's parents paid for the erection of a memorial pulpit 'to the glory of God and in memory of their only son, John McCulloch, and 22 other members of First Comber Presbyterian Church who died in the Great War 1914 – 1919'. The pulpit design incorporates a memorial plaque listing the names and it has twenty three arched sections, one for each life lost. A story handed down by word of mouth is that the central section of the pulpit was transported by train to Comber station in a large crate and it was taken from there to the church by horse-drawn cart. While the driver was waiting for help to lift the crate off the back of the cart, the horse suddenly shunted backwards, the front of the cart lifted and the crate slid off the back of the cart and landed upright and undamaged on the ground. John's mother died on 31 March 1925 and his father died on 17 February 1928.

McCullough, Hugh
Private
No. 3/5735, 5th Battalion, Cameron Highlanders
Died of wounds on Saturday 27 April 1918 (aged 27)
Arneke British Cemetery, France (Grave I. E. 5)

McC

Hugh McCullough was the second son of Alexander and Margaret (Maggie) McCullough (nee Shanks) who lived in the townland of Ballycastle, Mountstewart, Newtownards. They were married on 23 October 1885 in Greyabbey Parish Church of Ireland (St Saviour) and they had at least seven children – Alexander, Annie, Francis Shanks, Hugh, William John, Jane and James. Alexander McCullough died on 28 March 1910 aged 45 and Maggie worked as an embroiderer.

Hugh McCullough enlisted in Inverness in August 1914 and he went to France on 1 May 1915. He served with the Cameron Highlanders and at the Battle of Loos in September 1915 he suffered a gunshot wound in his left thigh. He was admitted to hospital in Rouen and when he recovered he returned to the line. He had two spells of home leave, the last being in August 1917. Private Hugh McCullough died of multiple gunshot wounds in No. 13 Casualty Clearing Station on 27 April 1918 and the sister-in-charge wrote a letter of sympathy to Hugh's mother. In the letter she wrote, 'He had been admitted during the day suffering from a very severe wound of the abdomen and his case was practically hopeless from the first. However, it will comfort you to know that although we could not save his life we were able to relieve his sufferings. He did not leave any message'.

On behalf of all members of the McCullough family Maggie placed a notice in the 11 May 1918 edition of the *Newtownards Chronicle*. The verse that it

M'CULLOUGH—April 27, 1918, died of wounds at No. 13 Casualty Clearing Station, France, Private Hugh M'Cullough (No. 5,735), Cameron Highlanders, aged 27 years, second and dearly-beloved son of the late Sandy and Maggie M'Cullough, Ballycastle, Mountstewart. His remains were interred in a cemetery in Flanders on 28th April.

The blow was hard, the shock severe,
To part with one I loved so dear;
It was God's will it should be so,
At His command we all must go.

Had I but seen him at the last,
Or raised his drooping head,
My heart would not have felt so sore,
The bitter tears I shed.

One by one the links are slipping,
One by one they're called away;
How the circle has been broken,
Will it be complete some day?

But God is good. He will give me grace
To bear my heavy cross;
He is the only one who knows
How bitter is my loss.

Brave to the last.
Father, in Thy gracious keeping,
Leave I now my dear Hugh sleeping.

Deeply regretted by his sorrowing Mother, Sister, and Brothers (one of the latter wounded, and in hospital); also his Brother and Sister-in-law, Toronto, Canada.
MAGGIE M'CULLOUGH.

contained concluded with the lines:

'Brave to the last
Father, in Thy gracious keeping,
Leave I now my dear Hugh sleeping'

Hugh's brother Alexander served with the Royal Irish Rifles during the Great War and he was also wounded in April 1918. At the time of Hugh's death Alexander was recuperating in hospital in England.

Rifleman Hugh McCullough is commemorated on Newtownards and District War Memorial; on Greyabbey and District War Memorial located on the outside wall of Greyabbey Parish Church of Ireland (St Saviour) and on the family grave headstone in Greyabbey Old Graveyard.

McC

McCullough, James (father) and James (son)

James McCullough Senior was the first of the two men to die:

McCullough, James
Rifleman
No. 3728, 8th Battalion attached 17th Battalion, Royal Irish Rifles
Died of wounds on Tuesday 2 May 1916 (aged 54)
Grangegorman Military Cemetery, Co. Dublin (Grave CE. 810)

Rifleman James McCullough (3728) was born in Poona in India on 8 October 1861. He was a son of Private Francis McCullough, 95th Foot Regiment and Mary Ann McCullough (nee Wallace). Both of James's parents came originally from Newtownards.

James McCullough and Sarah Ann Reid were married on 10 December 1888 in St Mary's Parish Church of Ireland Belfast and sometime after 1912 they moved to Donaghadee where they lived at 29 Manor Street.

During the Great War James McCullough was posted to Dublin. He was shot in the right arm on 27 April 1916 during the Easter Rising and he died on 2 May 1916 as a result of the wound. Initially he was buried in the grounds of the King George V Hospital in Dublin and then in 1920 his body was exhumed and re-interred in Grangegorman Military Cemetery. Rifleman James McCullough is commemorated in Donaghadee Parish Church of Ireland. In the CWGC Debt of Honour his age at death is recorded as 38.

McCullough, James
Rifleman
No. 6846, 2nd Battalion, Royal Irish Rifles
Killed in action on Tuesday 17 July 1917 (aged 22)
St. Quentin Cabaret Military Cemetery, Belgium (Grave II. F. 1)

McC

James McCullough was born on 29 March 1895 in Finmore Street, Belfast and he was a son of James and Sarah Ann McCullough (nee Reid). When James was about 17 years of age the family moved to Donaghadee and they lived at 29 Manor Street.

James McCullough was wounded in May 1915 and his mother received a letter from the Matron of No. 13 General Hospital in Boulogne informing her that her son was being transferred by hospital ship to England.

On 10 January 1917 James McCullough and Elizabeth (Lizzie) Strain were married in Ballygrainey Presbyterian Church. At the time of their marriage Lizzie was living in the townland of Ballyfotherly and James's address was given as Carrickfergus (where his Battalion was stationed). After they got married their address was 22 East Street, Donaghadee. Six months after he was married Rifleman James McCullough was killed in action on 17 July 1917 during road construction in a forward area of the battlefield. He is commemorated on Donaghadee and District War Memorial and in First Donaghadee Presbyterian Church.

McCullough, John
The name John McCullough is listed in the PCI Roll of Honour for Shore Street Presbyterian Church Donaghadee as having died and he is described

as a Rifleman in the 'RIR'. This abbreviation could represent the Royal Irish Rifles or the Royal Irish Regiment. Desk searches and public appeals to date have yielded no further information.

McCully, James
Private
No. 17321, 1st/5th Battalion, Alexandra Princess of Wales's Own (Yorkshire Regiment)
Died on Monday 11 November 1918 (aged 21)
Liege (Robermont) Cemetery, Belgium (Grave 38)

James McCully was born in 1897 in Coxhoe, Co Durham and he was a son of William and Charlotte McCully who lived in Church Street, Coxhoe. William McCully came from Newtownards and he worked as a coalminer in County Durham. He and Charlotte had at least four children – David, James, Margaret and Sarah.

James McCully lived in Kelloe, Co Durham and he enlisted at Deaf Hill Colliery. He served with the Yorkshire Regiment and he died on Armistice Day, 11 November 1918.

McC

James McCully's father William lived at 2 Ella's Villas, Bangor Road, Newtownards and James is commemorated on Newtownards and District War Memorial where his surname is spelt McCulley and it is listed out of alphabetical order.

McCutcheon, Daniel
Rifleman
No. 16711, 'A' Company, 13th Battalion, Royal Irish Rifles
Killed in action on Saturday 1 July 1916 (aged 21)
Thiepval Memorial, France (Pier and Face 15 A and 15 B)

Daniel McCutcheon was born in Donaghadee and he was a son of John and Mary McCutcheon. He worked as an agricultural labourer and he lived in Meetinghouse Street, Donaghadee with members of his extended family. He and Margaret Henry were married on 20 August 1912 in Donaghadee Parish Church of Ireland.

Daniel McCutcheon enlisted in Donaghadee, he served with the 13th Battalion Royal Irish Rifles in 108th Brigade of the 36th (Ulster) Division and he was killed in action on the first day of the Battle of the Somme. Initially posted as missing in action it was officially confirmed in June 1917 that he was presumed dead.

Rifleman Daniel McCutcheon was survived by his widow Margaret and their three children who lived at 25 Union Street, Donaghadee. He is commemorated on Donaghadee and District War Memorial and in Donaghadee Parish Church of Ireland.

McCutcheon, James
Private
No. 42692, New Zealand Rifle Brigade, NZEF
Died of wounds on Tuesday 18 September 1917 (aged 35)
Etaples Military Cemetery, France (Grave XXVI. B. 9A)

McC

James McCutcheon was the eldest son of Andrew McCutcheon who lived at 'Edenvale' in the townland of Cunningburn, Newtownards. Andrew McCutcheon worked as a farmer and, after James's mother died, Andrew married Mary Clegg (a widow, nee Dalzell) on 7 November 1893 in Regent Street Presbyterian Church Newtownards. Andrew and Mary had no children. James McCutcheon was the eldest of at least six children – James, Jane, George, Andrew, Mary and John.

James McCutcheon moved to New Zealand around 1909 and he enlisted there on 4 January 1917. He left Wellington on 2 April 1917 aboard the Troopship *Corinthic* and he arrived in Plymouth, England in June that year to complete his training. Before going to France in July, James was granted two-day's leave to visit his father in Newtownards. Working conditions in France were harsh for the dangerous work of laying communications cables at night. On 17 September 1917 Andrew McCutcheon received a telegram from the Officer in Charge of New Zealand Records in London informing him that his son was dangerously ill in the 56th General Hospital at Etaples and 'might be visited if desired'.

Andrew McCutcheon requested further details and the following day he received another telegram with the message, 'Very much regret to inform you that information has just been received that your son, Rifleman James McCutcheon, died 12.15 this morning (18th September) from shell wound in left shoulder'. Further information came later from Nurse KM Smith, Matron in the hospital 'He was very seriously ill when admitted to this hospital and there was little hope of his recovery, although everything possible was done for him. There was a change for the worse in his condition yesterday and he was unconscious from then until the time of his death. He was unable to leave any messages'.

Private James McCutcheon is commemorated on Newtownards and District War Memorial and in First Newtownards Presbyterian Church.

McCutcheon, John
Rifleman
No. 16743, 'B' Company, 13th Battalion, Royal Irish Rifles
Killed in action on Saturday 1 July 1916 (aged 35)
Thiepval Memorial, France (Pier and Face 15 A and 15 B)

John McCutcheon was born in Dundonald and he was a son of Catherine McCutcheon. John and his mother lived at 7 The Square, Comber and in 1911 his married sister Mary Tompsett, her husband William Tompsett and their two children John and George Tompsett were living there too. John McCutcheon worked as a labourer before the outbreak of the Great War and he enlisted in Belfast. His brother-in-law **William Tompsett** was killed in action on 30 October 1914 during the First Battle of Ypres.

McC
McD

John McCutcheon joined the 13th Battalion (1st Co Down) Royal Irish Rifles and he went to Seaford, Sussex in July 1915. The Battalion came under the orders of 108th Brigade in the 36th (Ulster Division) and they landed at Boulogne in October 1915.

Rifleman John McCutcheon was killed in action on the first day of the Battle of the Somme and he is commemorated on Comber and District War Memorial and in Second Comber Presbyterian Church.

McDermott, Robert
Private
No. 830179, 144th Battalion, Canadian Infantry (Quebec Regiment)
Died on Saturday 25 January 1919 (aged 43)
Brandon Cemetery, Manitoba, Canada (Grave L. 35. B. 'A'. S. 17)

Robert McDermott was born on 13 November 1875 and he was a son of Thomas and Margaret McDermott who lived in Ballywalter. They had at least seven children – Robert, James, Henry, Margaret Ann and three who died in infancy. Robert's mother Margaret died on 28 May 1880 aged 25.

Robert McDermott worked as a bread server and he and Agnes Martha Taylor were married on 15 May 1896 in Carrowdore Presbyterian Church. They had two children, Thomas James and Annie Jeanetta, and they lived in Carrowdore. Later the family moved to Castlereagh Street, Newtownards.

Robert McDermott moved to Canada where he worked as a labourer. He enlisted in Winnipeg, Manitoba on 20 December 1915 and in his attestation papers it was noted that he was 5 feet 8 inches tall. Private Robert McDermott served with the 144th Battalion Canadian Infantry (Quebec Regiment) and he died on 25 January 1919 in Brandon Hospital, Manitoba.

> M'DERMOTT—In loving memory of my dear husband, Robert, who departed this life at Brandon, Manitoba, on the 25th of January, 1919, and was interred in the City Cemetery, Brandon.
> Yet again we hope to meet thee,
> When the strife of life is fled,
> And with joy in heaven to greet thee,
> Where no farewell tears are shed.
> Inserted by his sorrowing Wife and Daughter.
> AGNES and ANNIE M'DERMOTT.
> Carrowdore.

McD

Robert McDermott is commemorated in Carrowdore Presbyterian Church and on a family grave headstone in Whitechurch Cemetery Ballywalter. This headstone was erected by his widow Agnes and also commemorated thereon are their two children, Thomas who died on 5 May 1912 aged 15 and Annie who died on 12 May 1926 aged 22. In 1923 Agnes and Annie placed an 'In Memoriam' notice in the *Newtownards Chronicle* and it contained the verse:

'Yet again we hope to meet thee,
Where the strife of life is fled,
And with joy in heaven to greet thee,
Where no farewell tears are shed'

McDonagh, John

The name John McDonagh is listed on Newtownards and District War Memorial and in the booklet produced for the Unveiling and Dedication Ceremony held on Saturday 26 May 1934 he is described as a Gunner in the Royal Garrison Artillery. Desk searches and public appeals to date have yielded no further information.

McDonald, Andrew
Rifleman
No. S/12900, 9th Battalion, Rifle Brigade
Killed in action on Thursday 6 January 1916 (aged 24)
Ypres (Menin Gate) Memorial, Belgium (Panel 46 – 48 and 50)

Andrew McDonald was born on 23 March 1891 in Newtownards and he was the eldest son of John and Anna McDonald (nee Welsh) who lived at 4 Forde Street. They were married on 27 March 1889 in First Newtownards Presbyterian Church. John McDonald worked as a tweed weaver and he and Anna had three children – Andrew and twins Hugh and Martha (born 25 May 1895). Hugh died in infancy. Andrew McDonald was baptised in Regent Street Methodist Church Newtownards.

In 1907 when Andrew was 16 years of age he and his father sailed to the USA to visit relatives in Philadelphia. After Andrew's mother Anna died his father John married Margaret Byers on 1 December 1908 in Wesley Centenary Methodist Church Bangor. They had eight children – Dinah, Min, Charlie (killed aged 18 years when his bike crashed into a horse on Bradshaw's Brae), Andrew (born on 24 June 1916, and named after his half-brother Andrew who had been killed in action five months earlier), John (proprietor of McDonald's Flower Shop in Newtownards), Sam (who continued to live in the family home in Forde Street until it was demolished in the early 1980s), Bob and Neil.

McD

Andrew McDonald worked as a hand-loom weaver, as did his father John and his paternal grandfather Andrew after whom he was named. Both Andrew's paternal and maternal grandparents lived in Corry's Street Newtownards (known locally as Corry's Deed or Corry's Quarter). In 1912 Andrew signed the Ulster Covenant. He enlisted in Newtownards on 7 June 1915 and he went to France in November 1915 with the Rifle Brigade. The last letter that Andrew's family received from him was dated 27 December 1915 and in it he said that he was well. He was killed in action ten days later on 6 January 1916.

Andrew McDonald died while endeavouring to save the life of a comrade. In a letter to Andrew's father Second Lieutenant AF Willmer, Officer Commanding 'A' Company, described the circumstances. Andrew had gone out from the trenches under cover of darkness with a group of other men to bring in a wounded comrade. While he was carrying the stretcher Andrew was shot and couldn't walk. Dawn was breaking and in the gathering light it was impossible to get him back to the trenches. As Andrew lay wounded he was killed outright by a sniper's bullet. The following night his comrades buried him where he had died.

The McDonald family placed a 'Killed in Action' notice in the 5 February 1916 edition of the *Newtownards Chronicle*. In 1917 and in subsequent years they placed 'Our Heroes – In Memoriam' notices. One in 1917 contained the verse:

'One year has passed, but still we miss him,
Some may think the wound is healed;
But they little know the sorrow
That lies within our hearts concealed.'

Rifleman Andrew McDonald is commemorated on Newtownards and District War Memorial and in Regent Street Methodist Church Newtownards.

McDonald, Mark William (Mark)
Second Lieutenant
4th Battalion, Royal Inniskilling Fusiliers
Drowned on Monday 2 August 1915 (aged 19)
Glenarm New Cemetery, Co. Antrim (Grave A. 24)

McD

Mark William McDonald was born on 30 July 1896 in West Derby, Lancashire and he was a son of Mark and Mary Ethel McDonald who lived in Ferry Street, Portaferry. Mark McDonald Senior who came from County Antrim was a medical practitioner and he and Mary (who came from County Wicklow) had at least three children – John A (died), Mark William and Mary Elizabeth.

Mark McDonald was educated at Campbell College and there he was a member of the Officers' Training Corps (OTC). He was also a member of the Ulster Volunteer Force. He entered Trinity College Dublin in the autumn of 1914 and joined Trinity OTC. He obtained a commission in the 4th Battalion Royal Inniskilling Fusiliers some two months before he was drowned on 2 August 1915 in Tullagh Bay, Co Donegal. That afternoon two young officers, Wycomb and McDonald, went for a swim in the sea. Mark McDonald was seized with cramp and before his comrade could reach him he was swept away by an outgoing current.

Lieutenant Wycomb raised the alarm and military personnel, constabulary officers and civilians hurried to the scene. A rowing boat was launched and six Tullagh fishermen along with Sergeant Golden from the Royal Irish Constabulary in Clonmany, Inishowen scoured the bay with drag-nets. As darkness deepened the operation was called off and then resumed at 5.00 am the following day. Half an hour later the body of Second Lieutenant Mark

McDonald was recovered and taken to the nearby military camp. Mark McDonald's parents had lost their second son. An intercessory service was held in Ardkeen Parish Church of Ireland where Mark had been a regular communicant.

McDonald, Robert
Farrier Sergeant
No. 8005, 18th Div. Artillery, Royal Field Artillery
Died on Thursday 29 April 1915 (aged 49)
Ipswich Old Cemetery, Suffolk, England (Grave S. 4. 2)

Robert McDonald was born around 1866 in Scotland and he was a son of Hamilton and Mary Ann McDonald who lived in the townland of Ballystockart, Comber. Hamilton McDonald worked as a farm labourer and he and Mary Ann had at least eight children including Robert and Mary Ann.

Robert McDonald worked as a carter and he and Jane Patterson were married on 6 January 1902 in St Anne's Church of Ireland Belfast. Jane already had five daughters – Maggie, Sarah, Rebecca, Mary and Susan. Robert and Jane McDonald had at least four children including Jennie, Maud and Annette. Robert and his wife, daughters and step-daughters lived at 47 Thorndyke Street in Belfast.

McD

—The death is reported from Ipswich of Farrier-Sergeant Robert M'Donald, D Battery, 85th Brigade, R.F.A., as the result of an accident. Deceased was the eldest son of the late Mr. Hamilton M'Donald, Ballystockart, Dundonald, and his wife and four children live at 47 Thorndyke Street, Belfast. Deceased was an old soldier, and he enlisted after the war broke out. He was about to shoe a mule when the animal kicked him in the stomach, rupturing the small intestine and causing death in a few hours. The interment took place at Ipswich.

After the outbreak of the Great War Robert McDonald enlisted and he served with the Royal Field Artillery. On 29 April 1915 he was about to shoe a mule when the animal kicked him in the stomach and ruptured his small intestine. Farrier Sergeant Robert McDonald died a few hours later and he is commemorated in the Belfast Book of Honour (Page 417).

McDonnell, Alexander
Gunner
No. 166671, 214th Siege Battery, Royal Garrison Artillery
Killed in action on Wednesday 5 September 1917 (aged 37)
Vlamertinghe New Military Cemetery, Belgium (Grave VII. G. 11)

Alexander McDonnell was born on 26 January 1880 in Portaferry. He was a son of John and Ellen McDonnell (nee Moore) who lived in the townland

of Ballyspurge, Quintin, Portaferry. They were married on 19 October 1866 in Glastry Presbyterian Church. John McDonnell was a farmer and he and Ellen had at least seven children – William (died 3 September 1913), John (died 4 August 1915), Annie, Jane Isabella, Alexander, Samuel and James. The children were baptised in Portaferry Presbyterian Church. Their father John died on 15 June 1915 just a few weeks before his son John. Their mother Ellen died on 12 February 1921.

Before moving to England Alexander McDonnell worked as a draper's assistant. He and his wife lived at 5 Park Road, St Anne's-on-Sea in Lancashire. Alexander enlisted in Southport and he served during the Great War with the Royal Garrison Artillery. Gunner Alexander McDonnell was killed in action on 2 September 1917 and he is commemorated in Portaferry Presbyterian Church and on the family grave headstone in Ballymanish Cemetery Portaferry.

McDonnell, David John (David)
McD
Rifleman
No. 18/1191, 'B' Company, 13th Battalion, Royal Irish Rifles, then 11th/13th Battalion, then 22nd Entrenching Battalion
Killed in action on Thursday 28 March 1918 (aged 23)
Pozieres Memorial, France (Panel 74 to 76)

David John McDonnell was born on 15 April 1895 and he was the eldest son of David John and Mary McDonnell (nee Bailie) who lived in the townland of Ballyfinragh and later Ballygalget, Portaferry. They were married on 12 June 1894 in Glastry Presbyterian Church. David John McDonnell Senior worked as a farmer and he and Mary had at least five children – David John, Martha, Isabella Jane (Ginnie), Thomas James and Mary. The children were baptised in Portaferry Presbyterian Church and their father David John McDonnell died on 29 November 1916. Their mother Mary died on 7 August 1946.

The following details have been provided by David John McDonnell's great-niece. David McDonnell worked with his father on the family farm and after a disagreement with his father about a horse he left home and enlisted. Some time later he asked his father to buy him out of the army, which his father did. There still were tensions in the relationship and one day David left the farm in his working clothes and never returned. He borrowed a suit from a neighbour, he enlisted in Newtownards and he served with the Royal Irish Rifles.

David McDonnell enlisted in December 1915 in Newtownards and joined the 18th Battalion Royal Irish Rifles. He was posted to the 13th Battalion in 108th Brigade of the 36th (Ulster) Division and in November 1917 the 11th and 13th Battalions were amalgamated. When they were disbanded in February 1918 David was transferred to the 22nd Entrenching Battalion and he was killed by shellfire on 28 March 1918 during the German 'Michael' offensive. Rifleman David McDonnell is commemorated on the Memorial Window in Portaferry Presbyterian Church and on the family grave headstone in Ballymanish Cemetery Portaferry where his date of death is inscribed as 20 March 1918.

McDonnell, John
Private
No. 827085, 24th Battalion, Canadian Infantry (Quebec Regiment)
Died on Wednesday 15 August 1917 (aged 34)
Vimy Memorial, France

McD

John McDonnell was born on 2 December 1882 in Ballycastle, Co Antrim and he was a son of Daniel and Annie McDonnell (nee Patterson). John's mother came from Kircubbin and the McDonnell family moved to Canada.

John McDonnell worked as a rancher and he enlisted in Kamloops, British Columbia on 31 October 1916. It was noted in his attestation papers that he was 5 feet 10½ inches tall. He served with the 24th Battalion Canadian Infantry (Quebec Regiment) and he died on 15 August 1917.

McDowell, Alexander
Private
No. 332021, 1st/6th Battalion, King's (Liverpool Regiment)
Killed in action in France on Tuesday 9 April 1918
Loos Memorial, France (Panel 27 to 30)

In 'Soldiers Died in the Great War 1914 – 1919' it is recorded that Alexander McDowell was born in Newtownards and he enlisted in Liverpool. He served with the King's (Liverpool Regiment) and he was killed in action on 9 April 1918. Private Alexander McDowell is commemorated in Second Newtownards Presbyterian Church.

McDowell Brothers: Joseph and William

Joseph and William McDowell were born in Newtownards and they were sons of Joseph and Jane McDowell who lived in Queen Street and later in Wallace's Street No. 2, Newtownards. Joseph and Jane had at least seven children – Elizabeth, John, James, Andrew, Joseph, Mary Jane and William. Joseph McDowell Senior died before 1901 and Jane worked as an embroiderer. Joseph was the first of the two brothers to die in the Great War:

McDowell, Joseph
Rifleman
No. 1819, 7th Battalion, Royal Irish Rifles
Killed in action on Friday 16 June 1916 (aged 28)
St. Patrick's Cemetery, Loos, France (Grave III. B. 28)

McD

Joseph McDowell served with the Royal North Downs and worked as a general labourer before the outbreak of the Great War. He rejoined the colours in Newtownards on 23 October 1914 and he served with the 7th Battalion Royal Irish Rifles. Rifleman Joseph McDowell went to the front on 22 December 1915 and he was killed in action on 16 June 1916. Two of his brothers were also on active service and both were wounded, one in France and one in Egypt.

The McDowell family placed a 'Killed in Action' notice in the 15 July edition of the *Newtownards Chronicle* and they placed 'Our Heroes – In Memoriam' notices each year thereafter. The 1917 and 1918 notices contained the verses:

'Although we're in a far-off land,
And your grave we cannot see,
As long as life and memory last,
We shall remember thee'

'God knows the way; He holds the key,
He guides us with unerring hand;
Some time with tearless eyes we'll see,
Yes, there, up there we'll understand'

McDowell, William
Lance Corporal
No. 10169, 1st Battalion, Royal Irish Rifles
Died of wounds on Tuesday 29 August 1916 (aged 25)
Vermelles British Cemetery, France (Grave V. B. 3)

Prior to the outbreak of the Great War William McDowell worked as a general labourer. He enlisted in Newtownards, he served with the 1st Battalion Royal Irish Rifles and he died of wounds on 29 August 1916 during the Battle of the Somme. Each year thereafter his mother, his brothers and his sister Mary placed 'Our Heroes – In Memoriam' notices in the *Newtownards Chronicle*. The 1917 and 1918 insertions contained the verses:

'Had I but got one last fond look into your loving face,
Or had I got the chance to kneel down in that place
To hold your hand, dear William, while your life blood ebbed away,
My heart would not have felt so much the tears I shed today.'

'You have answered, dear brother, the call of the brave;
And somewhere you rest in a hero's grave
What more or what better could any lad give
Than his life for his country that others might live?'

McD

Both Rifleman Joseph McDowell and Lance Corporal William McDowell are commemorated on Newtownards and District War Memorial and in Newtownards Parish Church of Ireland (St Mark).

McDowell, James W
The name James W McDowell is listed on the War Memorial Plaque in Ballygowan Presbyterian Church. Desk searches and public appeals to date have yielded no further information.

McDowell, John Taggart (John)
Rifleman
No. 18272, 'B' Company, 13th Battalion, Royal Irish Rifles

John Taggart McDowell was born on 29 December 1895 in Ballywalter and he was a son of William and Elizabeth McDowell (nee Cheal) who were married on 1 April 1894 in Ballyculter Parish Church of Ireland Downpatrick. William McDowell worked as an agricultural labourer and he and Elizabeth had three children all of whom were baptised in Ballywalter Parish Church of Ireland – John Taggart, James (born 1898) and William Henry (born 1900). Their mother Elizabeth died in 1900.

Prior to the outbreak of the Great War John McDowell worked as a labourer. He enlisted in Belfast on 24 September 1914 and he served with the 13th Battalion Royal Irish Rifles in 108th Brigade of the 36th (Ulster) Division. On 2 February 1915 he was discharged from the Army because he was deemed to be medically unfit for active service due to pulmonary tuberculosis.

Rifleman John McDowell is commemorated on Ballywalter and District War Memorial and on the War Memorial in Ballywalter Parish Church of Ireland (Holy Trinity). Because Ballywalter and District War Memorial was unveiled on 25 October 1922 it may be assumed that he died sometime between 2 February 1915 and 25 October 1922.

McDowell, Robert John (Robert)
Lance Corporal
No. 154577, 1st Battalion, Canadian Pioneers
Killed in action on Friday 23 June 1916 (aged 25)
Ypres (Menin Gate) Memorial, Belgium (Panel 32)

Robert John McDowell was born on 8 May 1891 and he was a son of Samuel and Jane McDowell (nee Bowman) who lived in Ballygowan. They were married on 26 May 1882 in Ballygowan Presbyterian Church. Samuel and Jane McDowell had at least seven children – Mary Elizabeth, James, Eliza Jane, Margaret Ann, Henry, Robert John and Samuel.

Robert McDowell worked as a conductor on the Belfast trams before he moved to Canada around 1913. There he worked as a motorman before he enlisted in Vancouver on 12 October 1915. In his attestation papers it was noted that he was 5 feet 8½ inches tall.

Lance Corporal Robert McDowell was killed in action on 23 June 1916 and he is commemorated in Ballygowan Presbyterian Church.

McGaffin Brothers: James and Robert
James and Robert McGaffin were sons of James and Ellen McGaffin (nee

Sloan) who lived in the townland of Annaghbane, Newry. They were married on 25 April 1877 in Warrenpoint Presbyterian Church. James McGaffin Senior worked as a farmer and a labourer and he and Ellen had at least nine children – George, James, Thomas, Ellen, William, Joseph, Robert, Isabella and Maggie. James McGaffin Junior worked as a farm servant for Robert McComb who farmed in the townland of Lisnatierny, Banbridge. After Ellen died James McGaffin Senior married Sarah Hendry on 4 February 1902 in Warrenpoint Presbyterian Church and he and Sarah had at least two children – Tillie and Hugh. James and Sarah moved to Camlough, Newry and then to Belfast where they lived at 131 Matilda Street.

Brothers James and Robert McGaffin moved to Donaghadee where they worked for a time before moving to Canada. They lived in Toronto and both worked as labourers. James and Robert enlisted in Toronto on 26 July 1915 along with their brother Joseph who worked as a brass finisher. The three brothers were allocated consecutive service numbers – James 136088, Joseph 136089 and Robert 136090. Joseph survived but James and Robert were both killed in action on the same day – 15 September 1916:

McGaffin, James

McG

Private
No. 136088, 1st Canadian Mounted Rifles Battalion
Killed in action on Friday 15 September 1916 (aged 33)
Vimy Memorial, France

James McGaffin was born on 7 July 1883 and on 2 September 1904 he and Emily Strain were married in Shore Street Presbyterian Church Donaghadee. Their son George was baptised there. When they moved to Toronto they lived at 263 Harvie Avenue. In James's attestation papers it was noted that he was 5 feet 7 inches tall. He served with the 1st Canadian Mounted Rifles and he was killed in action on 15 September 1916.

Private James McGaffin is commemorated on Donaghadee and District War Memorial and as W McGaffin in Shore Street Presbyterian Church Donaghadee.

McGaffin, Robert Sloane (Robert)

Private
No. 136090, 1st Canadian Mounted Rifles Battalion
Killed in action on Friday 15 September 1916 (aged 26)
Vimy Memorial, France

Robert Sloane McGaffin was born on 6 June 1890 and in his attestation papers it was noted that he was 5 feet 7 inches tall. He served with the 1st Canadian Mounted Rifles Battalion and he was killed in action on 15 September 1916.

> **"NO SURRENDER" L.O.L. 241, DONAGHADEE.**
> GAFFIN — PATTON — STRAIN — The Officers and Members of above Lodge desire to express their deep regret at the loss of their highly-respected brethren—Private Robt. Gaffin, Ballyhay, 74th C.M.R. (Canadians), killed in action 15th September, 1916; Rifleman Wm. Patton, Ballyfotherly, 13th Royal Irish Rifles, killed in action 1st July, 1916; and Rifleman Saml. Strain, Donaghadee, 13th Royal Irish Rifles, killed in action 1st July, 1916.
> WM. ROBERT M'CAULEY, W.M.
> ROBERT JOHN REA, Secretary.

Robert McGaffin had been a member of No Surrender LOL No. 241 in Donaghadee and the officers and members placed a 'For King and Country' notice in the 16 June 1917 edition of the *Newtownards Chronicle*. They expressed 'their deep regret at the loss of their highly respected brethren'. The notice commemorated the deaths of Robert McGaffin (surname spelt Gaffin) Ballyhay; **William Patton** Ballyfotherly and **Samuel Strain** Donaghadee. It was signed by William Robert McCauley and Robert John Rea.

Private Robert McGaffin is commemorated on Donaghadee and District War Memorial and in Shore Street Presbyterian Church Donaghadee.

McG

McGimpsey, James
Private
No. 351053, 9th Battalion, Royal Scots
Killed in action on Monday 23 April 1917 (aged 21)
Arras Memorial, France (Bay 1 and 2)

James McGimpsey was born on 5 March 1896 and he was the only son of James and Mary McGimpsey (nee Regan) who lived in Main Street, Greyabbey. They were married on 14 May 1894 in Newtownards Parish Church of Ireland and they had at least three children – James, Maria and Agnes. James McGimpsey Senior died on 17 May 1902 aged 33 and Mary worked as an embroiderer.

James McGimpsey enlisted in Edinburgh, he served with the Royal Scots and he was killed in action on 23 April 1917. In May 1917 his mother Mary heard officially about his death in a letter from the Territorial Force Record Office in Hamilton, Scotland.

Private James McGimpsey is commemorated on Greyabbey and District War Memorial located on the outside wall of Greyabbey Parish Church of Ireland

(St Saviour); in the PCI Roll of Honour for Trinity Presbyterian Church Greyabbey and also on the family grave headstone in Movilla Cemetery Newtownards.

McGimpsey, James
Rifleman
No. 18/206, 'D' Company, 11th Battalion, Royal Irish Rifles
Killed in action on Saturday 1 July 1916 (aged 19)
Mill Road Cemetery, France (Grave VI. C. 4)

James McGimpsey was a grandson of Martin and Eleanor (Ellen) McGimpsey (nee McGimpsey) who lived in the townland of Loughries Newtownards. They were married on 7 October 1870 in First Newtownards Presbyterian Church. Martin McGimpsey was a farmer and he and Ellen had at least seven children. Ellen died before 1901 and James McGimpsey grew up on his widowed grandfather's farm along with his uncle and aunts James, Mary, Elizabeth and Eleanor McGimpsey.

McG

James McGimpsey trained at Clandeboye and in July 1915 he went to Seaford in Sussex. In October he landed at Boulogne and went to the front with the 11th Battalion Royal Irish Rifles in 108th Brigade of the 36th (Ulster) Division. He was killed in action on the first day of the Battle of the Somme.

James McGimpsey's grandfather, uncle and aunts placed 'Our Heroes – In Memoriam' notices in the *Newtownards Chronicle* and the one in the 30 June 1917 edition contained the verse:

'For his King and country well he stood,
Unknown to coward's fears;
In battle strife he shed his blood
With the Ulster Volunteers'

Rifleman James McGimpsey is commemorated on Newtownards and District War Memorial.

McGimpsey, James Campbell (James)
Private
No. 21395, 8th Battalion, Canadian Infantry (Manitoba Regiment)
Died of wounds on Saturday 13 April 1918 (aged 27)
Etaples Military Cemetery, France (Grave XXIX. B. 11A)

James Campbell McGimpsey was born on 28 March 1891 and he was the second son of Robert and Grace McGimpsey (nee Campbell) who lived in the Teacher's Residence, East Street, Newtownards. They were married on 4 February 1887 in Carrowdore Presbyterian Church. For more than 40 years Robert McGimpsey was the Principal of East Street No. 2 National School (known locally as 'McGimpsey's School') and he and Grace had ten children – David, Jeannie (died of peritonitis aged 6), Edward Bruce, James Campbell, Robert (Bertie), William (Billy), Hugh Campbell, John Gilbert (known as Albert), Agnes Jane and Marian Elizabeth. Eight of the children, including James, were baptised in First Newtownards Presbyterian Church.

McG

James McGimpsey moved to Canada where he worked as a dry goods clerk in the T Eaton Company (founded in 1869 by Timothy Eaton and employing in excess of 30,000 people). On 23 September 1914 he enlisted in Valcartier, Quebec where there was a large military training camp with space for some 32,000 men in tents and 8,000 horses. In his attestation papers it was noted that he was 5 feet 7 inches tall. He went to France in February 1915 and that year he suffered gas poisoning. On 26 September 1916 he suffered multiple gunshot wounds and he was hospitalised in England for nine months before he was pronounced fit to return to the front line. He was granted two weeks leave which he spent in Newtownards. At that time four of his brothers were also on active service – David, James, Bertie (who worked on the building of the Titanic) and Billy (who grew up on an adjoining farm owned by Martin McGimpsey, an uncle by marriage and whose grandson **James McGimpsey** was also killed in action). Another brother, Hugh, had been injured in a weight-lifting accident and was unable to serve.

David McGimpsey moved to Australia, served in the Australian forces and was taken prisoner of war. Private Albert McGimpsey Machine Gun Corps was wounded by shrapnel on 6 September 1916 and Lance Corporal Billy McGimpsey was taken prisoner on 1 July 1916. After the war Billy moved to Canada and he worked for the T Eaton Company.

Private James McGimpsey died at 9.00 pm on 13 April 1918 in 24 General Hospital Etaples as a result of multiple head injuries sustained three days earlier. Captain JW Williams, Chaplain, wrote to James's mother to express his condolences and he outlined the circumstances in which James sustained his fatal injuries, 'On the morning of 10 April an enemy raiding party came over and during the fight that ensued your son behaved very gallantly. He fired the machine-gun until the pans were empty and then he flung the pans at the enemy and went at them afterwards with the empty gun. Finally he was wounded by a hand-grenade thrown by the enemy. He was taken out that day and died in hospital on 13 April'.

Captain Williams went on to say that James Campbell was being recommended for some honour and he also quoted the orders that had been issued by Lieutenant-General AW Currie who commanded the Canadian Corps, 'In the coming battle you will advance or fall where you stand, facing the enemy'.

The President of the T Eaton Company wrote to Robert McGimpsey to express his sympathy. The family placed 'Our Heroes – In Memoriam' notices in the *Newtownards Chronicle* and the one in the 19 April 1919 edition contained the verse:

McG

> 'In the graveyard sweetly sleeping,
> Where the flowers gently wave,
> Lies the one we loved so dearly
> In a lonely, far off grave'

Private James McGimpsey is commemorated on Newtownards and District War Memorial and in First Newtownards Presbyterian Church. He is also commemorated on the War Memorial in the grounds of the Legislative Building in Winnipeg; on the memorial in what was Eaton's store (now a sports complex) and in the Book of Remembrance in Ottawa where a page is turned every day.

McGimpsey, Robert (Bob)
Rifleman
No. 18/1594, 14th Battalion, Royal Irish Rifles
Killed in action on Friday 3 August 1917 (aged 36)
Ypres (Menin Gate) Memorial, Belgium (Panel 40)

Robert McGimpsey was born in America and he and his wife Annie (Anna) lived in Scotland for a time. Robert McGimpsey worked as a general labourer and it was in Scotland that Lillie, their first child, was born. The McGimpsey family moved to the townland of Ballycopeland, Millisle where they had two more children – Robert and Mary Ann.

> Mrs. Anna M'Gimpsey, who resides at Ballycopeland, Millisle, with her three children, has received the dread news that her husband, Rifleman Robert M'Gimpsey, Royal Irish Rifles (Ulster Division), popularly known as "Bob" M'Gimpsey, was killed in action on 3rd August.

Bob McGimpsey enlisted in Newtownards and served with the 14th Battalion Royal Irish Rifles in 109th Brigade of the 36th (Ulster) Division. He was killed in action on 3 August 1917 while holding the line at the beginning of the Third Battle of Ypres. At the time of his death his children were eleven, nine and seven years of age. After Bob was killed in action Annie McGimpsey placed a 'For King and Country' notice in the *Newtownards Chronicle* and it contained the verse:

'My home is so lonely, my heart is so sad,
My children are calling for their soldier dad.
I mourn for you, my husband dear,
Who for King and country fell;
With a manly heart you did your part,
And sent me your last farewell'

McG

Rifleman Bob McGimpsey is commemorated on Donaghadee and District War Memorial and in Millisle Presbyterian Church.

McGimpsey, Thomas

The name Thomas McGimpsey is listed on Newtownards and District War Memorial and in the booklet produced for the Unveiling and Dedication Ceremony held on Saturday 26 May 1934 he is described as a Private in the Royal Irish Regiment.

The death on active service of Thomas McGimpsey Royal Irish Regiment (2768) was reported on page 91 of the 1917 Newtownards Almanac beside the date 14 October 1916.

> 14...This week's fatal casualty lists include :—Newtownards—Pte. T. M'Gimpsey (No. 2,768), Royal Irish Regiment, killed.

This Regimental Number is the same as that reported in the 14 October 1916 edition of the *Newtownards Chronicle* for **Thomas Guiney** from Portaferry who served with the Royal Irish Regiment and who was killed in action on 9 September 1916.

> **Newtownards Casualties.**
> Killed.
> Private T. Guiney (No. 2,768), Royal Irish Regiment, is officially reported killed.

Desk searches and public appeals to date have yielded no further information about Thomas McGimpsey.

McGinn, Hugh
Rifleman
No. 9776, 2nd Battalion, Royal Irish Rifles
Killed in action on Sunday 24 March 1918
Pozieres Memorial, France (Panel 74 to 76)

In 'Soldiers Died in the Great War 1914 – 1919' it is recorded that Hugh McGinn lived in Belfast and he enlisted in Newtownards. He served with the 2nd Battalion Royal Irish Rifles and he was killed in action on 24 March 1918 at Cugny during the German 'Michael' offensive which began on 21 March.

Rifleman Hugh McGinn is commemorated on Newtownards and District War Memorial and in the Belfast Book of Honour (Page 427).

McGreechan, Robert James (James)
Lance Corporal
No. 7605, 2nd Battalion, Royal Irish Rifles
Killed in action on Friday 7 July 1916 (aged 30)
Thiepval Memorial, France (Pier and Face 15 A and 15 B.

McG

Robert James McGreechan was born on 16 November 1885 in Newtownards and he was a son of Robert James and Mary McGreechan (nee Johnston) who lived in Church Street and later in Forde Street, Newtownards. They were married on 5 December 1883 in Regent Street Presbyterian Church Newtownards. Robert James McGreechan Senior worked as a labourer and he and Mary had at least nine children – Maggie, Robert James, John Todd, Agnes, Henry, Daniel, Hugh Todd, William and Minnie. Some of the children (including Robert James) were baptised in Regent Street Presbyterian Church Newtownards, others in First Newtownards Presbyterian Church and the spelling of the surname in church records was Magrehan, Magreehan and McGreehan. Robert James McGreechan Junior worked as a labourer in Alex Dickson's Nurseries and on 11 October 1915 he and Catherine Mawhinney were married in First Newtownards Presbyterian Church.

James McGreechan enlisted in Newtownards in 1915, he served with the 2nd Battalion Royal Irish Rifles and he was killed in action on 7 July 1916 during the Battle of the Somme. James McGreechan and his wife Catherine had lived for a time at Sullatober, Carrickfergus and when James died Catherine was living in the townland of Dunadry in County Antrim. One of James's brothers was also on active service.

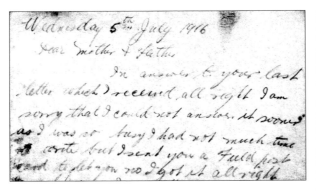

Lance Corporal Robert James McGreechan penned his last letter to his mother and father on 5 July 1916, just two days before he was killed in action. In the letter he apologised for not writing sooner and he said, 'I was so busy I had not much time to write'. He expressed the hope that everyone at home was well and he asked specifically about his mother's headaches. He asked her to write to Catherine from time to time, if she was well enough to do so and, if she wasn't, to get wee Willie to write to Catherine.

McG

James told his parents about the very heavy showers of rain they'd been having and he said that he had been suffering from very bad blisters on his feet. They were a bit better and he went on, 'I hope by God's Help pulling me through that I will be spared to see the old town again'. He sent his love to all the family and he drew two rows of kisses 'for wee Minnie and wee Ellen and all the rest'. By the time his family received the letter Lance Corporal Robert James McGreechan was dead. He is commemorated on Newtownards and District War Memorial (as Magreechan). In 'Soldiers Died in the Great War 1914 – 1919' his surname is spelt McGreeghan and in the CWGC Debt of Honour his age is recorded as 32.

In 2003 after reading in his letter about how soldiers' feet were affected in the trenches Margaret Graham was inspired to pen the following lines in alliterative style:

FLANDERS
Flowers flutter freely
Fierce frenzied fighting
Frozen frost-bitten feet
Friendships formed fraternities
Frayed flags flying
Fanaticism finally felled
Flowers fallen for freedom

McGreeghan, Hugh
Driver
No. 261264, 321st Brigade, Royal Field Artillery
Died of pneumonia on Tuesday 19 November 1918 (aged 18)
Comber New Cemetery, Co. Down (Grave 2.58)

Hugh McGreeghan was born on 3 December 1899 in the townland of Unicarval, Ballymaglaff, Comber and he was a son of Hugh and Jane McGreeghan (nee Black) who lived in Maxwell Court, Comber. They were married on 17 June 1892 in First Newtownards Presbyterian Church and they had at least two children, Samuel (1897) and Hugh (1899), both of whom were baptised in First Newtownards Presbyterian Church. Their mother died when the children were very young.

During the Great War Hugh McGreeghan served as a Driver in the Royal Field Artillery. He died of pneumonia on 19 November 1918 in Tower Close Hospital in Norwich and he was buried in Comber New Cemetery.

McG

McGreevy Brothers: Hugh and Patrick
Hugh and Patrick McGreevy were born in Killinchy and they were sons of Patrick and Alicia (Alice) McGreevy who lived in the townland of Barnamaghery, Derryboye. Hugh was the first of the two brothers to die in the Great War:

McGreevy, Hugh
Private
No. 8819, 6th Battalion, Royal Irish Regiment
Killed in action on Saturday 9 September 1916 (aged 38)
Thiepval Memorial, France (Pier and Face 3 A)

Hugh McGreevy enlisted in Newtownards and he served with the 6th Battalion Royal Irish Regiment in 47th Brigade of the 16th (Irish) Division. He was killed in action at Ginchy on 9 September 1916.

McGreevy, Patrick
Private
No. 12177, 6th Battalion, Royal Inniskilling Fusiliers
Killed in action on Thursday 3 October 1918
Templeux-le-Guerard British Cemetery, France (Grave I. K. 17)

Patrick McGreevy enlisted in Clydebank and he served in Gallipoli, Macedonia and Palestine with the 6th Battalion Royal Inniskilling Fusiliers in 31st Brigade of the 10th (Irish) Division. He was killed in action in France on 3 October 1918 during the Allied offensive against all sections of the German line. In 'Soldiers Died in the Great War 1914 – 1919' his surname is spelt McGreavey.

McHugh, William (see Boal, William)

McIlveen Brothers: John and William

John and William Hewitt McIlveen were born in Comber and they were sons of Joseph and Ellen Jane McIlveen (nee Crowe) who lived at Hillhead and later in Railway Street, Comber. They were married on 29 April 1893 in Gilnahirk Presbyterian Church. Joseph McIlveen worked as a general labourer and he and Ellen had three children – John, William and Harriet. After Ellen died Joseph McIlveen remarried. He and Jane Lowry were married on 1 May 1903 in Dundonald Presbyterian Church and they had at least three children – Jane, Robert and Joseph.

McH
McI

Both John and William McIlveen worked in Andrew's Mill before the Great War. They enlisted together in Comber and were allocated consecutive numbers. John was the first of the two brothers to die in the Great War:

McIlveen, John
Rifleman
No. 18302, 'B' Company, 13th Battalion, Royal Irish Rifles
Killed in action on Saturday 1 July 1916 (aged 22)
Cerisy-Gailly Military Cemetery, France (Grave III. C. 13)

John McIlveen served with the 13th Battalion Royal Irish Rifles in 108th Brigade of the 36th (Ulster) Division and he was killed in action on the first day of the Battle of the Somme.

McIlveen, William Hewitt (William)
Rifleman
No. 18303, 'B' Company, 13th Battalion, Royal Irish Rifles, then
11th/13th Battalion, then 22nd Entrenching Battalion
Killed in action on Friday 29 March 1918 (aged 22)
Pozieres Memorial, France (Panel 74 to 76)

William McIlveen served with the 13th Battalion Royal Irish Rifles in 108th Brigade of the 36th (Ulster) Division and he survived the Battle of the Somme. In November 1917 the 11th and 13th Battalions were amalgamated and when they were disbanded in February 1918 William McIlveen was transferred to the 22nd Entrenching Battalion. He was killed in action on 29 March 1918 one day after Rifleman **David John McDonnell** from Portaferry was killed.

Riflemen John and William McIlveen are both commemorated on Comber and District War Memorial; on the Andrew's Mill Memorial Plaque and in Second Comber Presbyterian Church.

McIlwrath, Alexander (served as McIlwraith, Alexander)
Rifleman
No. 18/950, 12th Battalion, Royal Irish Rifles
Died of wounds on Monday 13 August 1917 (aged 21)
Lijssenthoek Military Cemetery, Belgium (Grave XVII. F. 12A)

McI

There is some variation in the spelling of the surname (McIlwraith in the CWGC Debt of Honour and in the 1911 census).

Alexander McIlwrath was born in Comber and he was a son of James and Elizabeth McIlwrath (nee Rodgers) who lived in the townland of Cherryvalley. They were married in Ballymacarrett Parish Church of Ireland (St Patrick). James McIlwrath worked as an agricultural labourer and he and Elizabeth had at least three children – Isabella, Alexander and James Corbett.

Prior to the outbreak of the Great War Alexander McIlwrath worked as an apprentice shoemaker and he lived in Comber. He enlisted in November 1915 in Newtownards and joined the 18th Battalion Royal Irish Rifles. Rifleman Alexander McIlwrath was posted to the 12th Battalion Royal Irish Rifles in 108th Brigade of the 36th (Ulster) Division and he died of wounds on 13 August 1917 when his Battalion was holding the line during the Third Battle of Ypres. He is commemorated on Comber and District War Memorial and in Comber Parish Church of Ireland (St Mary).

McIlwrath, James (see Harris, James)

McJury, William John (William) (see Majury, William John)

McKay, Robert
Rifleman
No. 19107, 'A' Company, 13th & 12th Battalions, Royal Irish Rifles
Killed in action on Monday 15 April 1918 (aged 34)
Tyne Cot Memorial, Belgium (Panel 138 to 140 & 162 to 162A & 163A)

Robert McKay was born in Greyabbey and he was a son of Robert and Jane McKay (nee Reid) who lived in the townland of Kilnatierney, Greyabbey. They were married on 7 July 1866 in Newtownards Registry Office. Robert McKay Senior came from Scotland, he worked as a farm labourer and he and Jane had at least six children – Catherine, John, Grace, Harriet Jane, Robert and James. Robert McKay Senior died before 1911 and Jane worked as an embroiderer.

Robert McKay Junior lived in Greyabbey where he worked as an agricultural labourer. He enlisted in Ballywalter and served with the 13th Battalion Royal Irish Rifles in 108th Brigade of the 36th (Ulster) Division. In November 1917 the 11th and 13th Battalions were amalgamated and when they were disbanded in February 1918 Robert was posted to the 12th Battalion Royal Irish Rifles.

Rifleman Robert McKay was killed in action on 15 April 1918 during the German 'Michael' offensive and he is commemorated on Greyabbey and District War Memorial located on the outside wall of Greyabbey Parish Church of Ireland (St Saviour) and on the family grave headstone in Greyabbey Old Graveyard. Robert's sister Harriet Jane McKay married Thomas Henry Regan on 8 January 1897 in Greyabbey Parish Church and their son **Robert Regan** (Robert McKay's nephew) was killed in action in the Great War on 1 October 1918 – some six months after his uncle was killed.

McKee, Alexander
Lieutenant
10th Battalion, Royal Irish Rifles
Killed in action on Thursday 22 November 1917 (aged 35)
Cambrai Memorial, France (Panel 10)

Alexander McKee was born in Belfast and he was the only son of Alexander McKee of the Ulster Spinning Company Ltd and Agnes McKee who lived at 20 Madison Avenue, Antrim Road, Belfast.

McI
McJ
McK

Alexander McKee Junior worked as a draper's assistant before the Great War and he was a member of the Young Citizen Volunteers. When war was declared he joined the Black Watch and subsequently obtained a commission in the Royal Irish Rifles. In 1916 he was stationed in Dublin and then he went to France. Lieutenant Alexander McKee was killed in action on 22 November 1917 during the Battle of Cambrai and with family connections in Newtownards his death was reported in the *Newtownards Chronicle* under the headline 'Newtownards Resident Bereaved'. He is commemorated in the Belfast Book of Honour (Page 439).

McKee Brothers: Frederick and Robert

Frederick and Robert McKee were sons of James and Mary Ann McKee (nee McCormick) who lived in the townland of Drumfad, Carrowdore and then at 77 Greenwell Street, Newtownards. They were married on 25 November 1876 in Greenwell Street Presbyterian Church and they had at least ten children including William James (died 3 January 1908), Eliza, Robert, Grace (died 1886 aged 8 months), Frederick, Margaret Jane (died 15 March 1894 aged 4), David Henry, Margaret Jane and Alexander Fulton (died). James McKee died on 9 July 1911 aged 54. Robert was the first of the two brothers to die in the Great War:

McK

McKee, Robert
Lance Corporal
No. 6766, 2nd Battalion, Royal Irish Rifles
Killed in action on Monday 24 May 1915 (aged 31)
Dickebusch New Military Cemetery, Belgium (Grave L. 26)

Robert McKee was born on 28 May 1883 in Carrowdore and he was the second son and the fourth child of James and Mary Ann McKee. He was baptised in Carrowdore Presbyterian Church.

Robert McKee was an ex-soldier who had served in South Africa with the Royal Army Medical Corps. He served for three years with the colours and for nine years in the reserve. He and Mary Kelly were married on 9 January 1907 in Newtownards Parish Church of Ireland. They had four children, William James, Edward, Maggie and Winifred, all of whom were baptised in Greenwell Street Presbyterian

Church. Robert was a member of the local branch of the Ulster Volunteer Force and when war broke out he joined the Royal North Downs. On 3 December 1914 he went to the front and soon afterwards he was promoted to the rank of Lance Corporal.

Lance Corporal Robert McKee was killed by enemy shellfire on 24 May 1915. At the time of his death Robert's wife Mary and their children were living at 101 Mill Street, Newtownards. When Mary heard officially on 7 June 1915 that Robert had been killed in action she already knew that he was dead. Two days earlier she had heard the news from an uncle who had received a letter from one of Robert's comrades in arms. The news came less than a week after Mary McKee had received a field postcard from her husband intimating that he was quite well.

Robert McKee's youngest child, Winifred, whom he never saw, was only six months old when he died. Robert's younger brother Frederick McKee was killed in action on 7 June 1917, two years to the day after the news of Robert's death was officially conveyed to his family.

McK

There were three 'Killed in Action' notices in the 12 June 1915 edition of the *Newtownards Chronicle*, one from his sorrowing wife and family, one from his sorrowing mother, brothers and sisters and one from his sister and brother-in-law Lizzie and Alexander Andrews then living at 78 Greenwell Street, Newtownards. The one from his wife and family contained the verse:

'No scream of shells disturb his rest,
No tramp of charging feet;
The Commander above has said, "Well Done;"
Need we grudge him the rest so sweet.
Some day, some time, my eyes shall see
Thy face I loved so well;
Some day I'll clasp his loving hand,
And never say farewell.
Thine a hero's grave'

McKee, Frederick (Fred)
Rifleman
No. 18/1542, 14th Battalion, Royal Irish Rifles
Killed in action on Thursday 7 June 1917 (aged 29)
Spanbroekmolen British Cemetery, Belgium (Grave D. 8)

Frederick McKee was born on 16 April 1888 in Carrowdore and he was the sixth child and the third son of James and Mary Ann McKee. He was

baptised in Carrowdore Presbyterian Church.

Fred McKee enlisted on 29 August 1916, he trained with the 18th Battalion Royal Irish Rifles and he went to the Western Front. Some seven weeks before he was killed in action on 7 June 1917 he was attached to the 14th Battalion Royal Irish Rifles in 109th Brigade of the 36th (Ulster) Division. In a letter of sympathy to Fred's mother the Rev John Knowles, Presbyterian Chaplain, told her that Fred had been killed in action at Messines Ridge during the attack on 7 June. He said, 'We found his body on the battlefield and buried him the next day.' He told her that a service was held at the graveside and the spot was marked with a cross.

There were two 'For King and Country' notices in the 23 June 1917 edition of the *Newtownards Chronicle* and the one from his sorrowing mother contained the verse:

'Had we but seen him at the last,
Or raised his drooping head,
Our hearts would not have felt so sore,
The bitter tears we shed.'

McK

The second was from his loving sister and brother-in-law Lizzie and Alexander Andrews then living at 81 Greenwell Street, Newtownards and it contained the verse:

'We little thought when he left home
That he would ne'er return;
That he so soon in death would sleep,
And leave us here to mourn.'

Lance Corporal Robert McKee and Rifleman Fred McKee are both commemorated on Newtownards and District War Memorial and in the PCI Roll of Honour for Greenwell Street Presbyterian Church Newtownards.

McKee, Hugh Andrew (Hugh)
Driver
No. T4/123760, 3rd Company (Bradford), Army Service Corps
Died of pneumonia on Wednesday 27 October 1915 (aged 45)
Carrowdore (Christ Church) Churchyard, Co. Down (Old Ground. 59A close to road)

In 'Soldiers Died in the Great War 1914 – 1919' Driver McKee's number is T4/023650.

Hugh Andrew McKee was a son of Edward and Elizabeth McKee (nee Johnston) who lived in the townland of Ballyfrenis, Carrowdore. They were married on 24 November 1868 in Newtownards Registry Office. Hugh McKee worked as an agricultural labourer and he and Elizabeth Johnston were married on 11 November 1889 in Carrowdore Parish Church of Ireland. They lived in the townland of Ballyrawer, Carrowdore and they had at least seven children – William Edward, Anna Jane Johnston, Sarah Ellen, Mary Eliza, Margaret, David Wallace and Agnes.

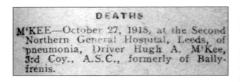

Hugh Andrew McKee enlisted in Donaghadee and he served with the Army Service Corps. Driver Hugh McKee died of pneumonia on 27 October 1915 in the Second Northern General Hospital in Leeds and he is commemorated on Donaghadee and District War Memorial and in Carrowdore Parish Church of Ireland (Christ Church).

McK

McKee, James
Sergeant
No. 21392, 8th Battalion, Canadian Infantry (Manitoba Regiment)
Killed in action on Saturday 14 April 1917 (aged 20)
Vimy Memorial, France

James McKee was born on 20 June 1896 and he was a son of John and Margaret McKee (nee Walker) who lived in the townland of Grangee, Carrowdore. They were married on 29 April 1890 in Millisle Presbyterian Church. John McKee was a farmer and he and Margaret had at least eight children – David, Jane (Jeanie), Nellie, James, Robert, William, Samuel and Annie. Seven of these children including James were baptised in Millisle Presbyterian Church. Jeanie McKee died on 15 August 1912 aged 20.

James McKee moved to Canada where he worked in the grocery trade before he enlisted in Valcartier, Quebec on 23 September 1914. He declared 20 January 1894 as his date of birth although church records indicate that he was just 18 years old when he enlisted. It was noted in his attestation papers that he was 5 feet 7½ inches tall. James McKee served with the 8th Battalion Canadian Infantry and he was killed in action on 14 April 1917.

Sergeant James McKee is commemorated on Donaghadee and District War Memorial; in Millisle Presbyterian Church and on the family grave headstone in the adjoining graveyard.

McKee, John (Jack)
Lance Corporal
No. 4637, 1st Battalion, Royal Irish Rifles
Died of wounds on Monday 29 April 1918 (aged 18)
New Irish Farm Cemetery, Belgium (Grave II. E. 6)

John McKee was a son of Bernard and Mary McKee (nee Hughes) who lived in Loughgall, Co Armagh. They were married on 17 June 1894 in Armagh Roman Catholic Church. John's mother died when he was very young and he and his widowed father lived with John's widowed grandmother Ann McKee.

John McKee and Cecilia (Cissie) Maxwell were married on 28 March 1918 in Newtownards Roman Catholic Church and one month later John died during the German 'Michael' offensive. When Lance Corporal John McKee died of wounds on 29 April 1918 Cissie was living at 87 Movilla Street, Newtownards. Captain WH Hutchison, Chaplain to the Forces, wrote to express his sympathy and to tell her that her husband was a brave soldier.

McK

He explained that most of the Battalion records, including the next-of-kin lists, had been lost during the retreat from St Quentin and that he had only been able to trace her because of a letter from her that was found in Jack's pocket. Cissie placed a 'For King and Country' notice in the *Newtownards Chronicle* and it contained the verse:

'I hope he rests in Heaven,
A member of the fold;
My loving prayer will ever be,
Have mercy on his soul.'

Lance Corporal Jack McKee is commemorated on Newtownards and District War Memorial.

McKee, Samuel
Private
No. 4261, 28th Battalion, Australian Infantry, AIF
Died of wounds on Thursday 1 November 1917 (aged 27)
Lijssenthoek Military Cemetery, Belgium (Grave XXI. CC. 18)

Samuel McKee was born on 23 October 1890 and he was a son of James and Rebecca (Helena) McKee (nee McConnell) who lived in the townland of Gransha, Ballymaglaff. They were married on 12 April 1880 in Dundela Presbyterian Church. James McKee worked as a farm servant and he and Rebecca had at least seven children – Mary, David, Bella, James, Samuel, Rebecca and Henry. All of these children were baptised in Granshaw Presbyterian Church.

McK

Samuel McKee moved to Australia where he worked as a farm labourer before he enlisted in Perth on 7 February 1916. He cited Comber as his place of birth and his mother Rebecca as his next-of-kin. It was noted in his attestation papers that he was 5 feet 2½ inches tall. He made his will on 6 March 1916.

He served with the 28th Battalion Australian Infantry and went to France in August 1916. He was wounded in action on 3 May 1917 and again on 31 October 1917. He died of his wounds in the 3rd Canadian Casualty Clearing Station the following day. His sole legatee was Miss Perla White who lived at 100 Brown Street East, Perth.

Private Samuel McKee is commemorated in the PCI Roll of Honour for Granshaw Presbyterian Church Moneyreagh.

McKendry, Samuel
The name Samuel McKendry is listed on Newtownards and District War Memorial and in the booklet produced for the Unveiling and Dedication Ceremony held on Saturday 26 May 1934 he is described as a Gunner in the Royal Garrison Artillery. Gunner Samuel McKendry (5552) Royal Garrison Artillery went to France on 10 July 1915 and he survived the Great War. Desk searches and public appeals to date have not confirmed a connection between these service data and the soldier who is commemorated on Newtownards and District War Memorial.

McKenna, John

The name John McKenna is listed on Newtownards and District War Memorial and in the booklet produced for the Unveiling and Dedication Ceremony held on Saturday 26 May 1934 he is described as a Private in the Royal Irish Fusiliers. Desk searches and public appeals to date have yielded no further information.

McKeown, Arthur
Sapper
No. 41043, 63rd Field Company, Royal Engineers
Killed in action on Friday 5 November 1915
Railway Dugouts Burial Ground, Belgium (Grave I. D. 4)

In 'Soldiers Died in the Great War 1914 – 1919' it is recorded that Arthur McKeown was born in Newtownards and he enlisted in Belfast. He served with the 63rd Field Company Royal Engineers. Sapper Arthur McKeown was killed in action at Passchendaele on 5 November 1915.

McK

McKeown, Charles
Rifleman
No. 11395, 6th Battalion, Royal Irish Rifles
Killed in action on Sunday 30 December 1917 (aged 23)
Chatby Memorial, Egypt

Charles McKeown was born in Newtownards and he was a son of William and Elizabeth McKeown (nee Pennington) who lived in Mill Street. They were married on 30 June 1884 in Newtownards Registry Office. William McKeown worked as a carter and he and Elizabeth had at least six children including William John, James, Charles and Ellen. Charles McKeown worked as a labourer and he enlisted in Newtownards. He served with the 6th Battalion Royal Irish Rifles in 29th Brigade of the 36th (Ulster) Division and he fought at Gallipoli, in Salonika and in Palestine.

Newtownards Rifleman Believed Drowned
Last week-end's casualty list officially reported that (No. 11,395) Rifleman C. M'Keown, Royal Irish Rifles, of Newtownards, is missing, believed drowned.

It was reported in the 23 February 1918 edition of the *Newtownards Chronicle* that Rifleman Charles

McKeown was 'missing believed drowned' and later it was officially confirmed that he had been killed in action. He is commemorated on Newtownards and District War Memorial and in the PCI Roll of Honour for Greenwell Street Presbyterian Church Newtownards.

McKibben, Hamilton
Rifleman
No. 25772, 2nd Battalion, Royal Irish Rifles
Killed in action on Tuesday 16 December 1919
Basra War Cemetery, Iraq (Grave II. G. 1)

The name Hamilton McKibben is listed on the Memorial Plaque in Second Newtownards Presbyterian Church and in the PCI Roll of Honour for that church he is described as a Rifleman in the Royal Irish Rifles.

Information has been provided that a father and son from that congregation, both named Hamilton McKibben, served in the Great War. There is evidence that Hamilton McKibben Senior served with the 7th Battalion Royal Irish Rifles (19926) before being transferred to the Labour Corps (606504) and that he was discharged from the Army on 10 March 1919.

Hamilton McKibben Junior served with the 2nd Battalion Royal Irish Rifles and he was killed in action on 16 December 1919 in Iraq.

McKibbin, John Hill (John)
Corporal
No. 6079, 1st Battalion, Royal Irish Rifles
Killed in action on Sunday 9 May 1915 (aged 24)
Ploegsteert Memorial, Belgium (Panel 9)

John Hill McKibbin was born on 14 October 1890 in Newtownards and he was the elder son of James and Mary McKibbin (nee Scott) who lived in Mark Street, later in Robert Street (47 Front Shuttlefield). They were married on 26 December 1889 in Newtownards Parish Church of Ireland. James McKibbin worked as a labourer and he and Mary had at least eight children including John Hill, Mary Jane, William James, Mary, Sarah,

McK

Reubina and Elizabeth. The children were baptised in Greenwell Street Presbyterian Church.

John McKibbin worked as a labourer before joining the Royal North Downs (4th Battalion Royal Irish Rifles). He was called up on mobilisation and he went to the front in November 1914. He fell victim to the severe weather that prevailed in the fighting line during the month of December 1914 and he returned home suffering from frostbite to his feet.

 He recovered and returned to the front in March 1915 and was in the fighting line continuously until he was killed in action on 9 May 1915 during the battle of Fromelles. The first news of Corporal John McKibbin's death reached Newtownards in a letter to David Cahoon from Rifleman Alfred McKimm (one of John's comrades). The news was soon confirmed in an official notice from the Infantry Record Office.

Alfred McKimm wrote, 'I am very sorry to have to tell you that your old chum got killed on Sunday 9 May so I want you to tell his father. I would tell him myself only I don't know his address. John was killed while he was going up to the German trenches. He had a letter in his pocket for his mother. I could not get near him owing to the heavy fire, so you can remember him to the rest of his chums, and don't forget to tell his father.'

McK

In May 1916 the McKibbin family placed an 'Our Heroes – In Memoriam' notice in the *Newtownards Chronicle* and it contained the verse:

> *'One long and dreary year has passed*
> *Since this great sorrow fell;*
> *The shock that we received that day*
> *We still remember well.*
> *His warfare o'er, his battles fought,*
> *His victory won, though dearly bought,*
> *His fresh young life could not be saved,*
> *He slumbers now somewhere in a hero's grave.'*

Corporal John McKibbin is commemorated on Newtownards and District War Memorial and in the PCI Roll of Honour for Greenwell Street Presbyterian Church Newtownards.

McKibbin, Robert
Rifleman
No. 2314, 'A' Company, 13th Battalion, Royal Irish Rifles
Killed in action on Saturday 1 July 1916 (aged 26)
Thiepval Memorial, France (Pier and Face 15 A and 15 B)

In some records the surname is spelt McKibben.

Robert McKibbin was born on 10 January 1890 in Donaghadee and he was a son of Andrew and Elizabeth McKibbin (nee Fullerton) who lived at 9 Shore Street. They were married on 8 April 1889 in Donaghadee Parish Church of Ireland. Andrew McKibbin worked as a tailor and he and Elizabeth had at least six children – Robert, William Thompson, David, Andrew, Mary Jane and Elizabeth. The children were baptised in Donaghadee Parish Church of Ireland. Robert's mother died on 25 June 1899 aged 30 and his sister Elizabeth died on 24 September 1900 aged one year.

McK

Robert McKibbin enlisted in Belfast and he served with the 13th Battalion Royal Irish Rifles in 108th Brigade of the 36th (Ulster) Division. He named as his next-of-kin his brother David who lived at 6 Shore Street, Donaghadee. Rifleman Robert McKibbin was killed in action on the first day of the Battle of the Somme and he is commemorated on Donaghadee and District War Memorial and in Donaghadee Parish Church of Ireland.

McKimm, David
The name David McKimm is listed on Newtownards and District War Memorial and in the booklet produced for the Unveiling and Dedication Ceremony held on Saturday 26 May 1934 he is described as a Rifleman in the Royal Irish Rifles. Two Riflemen named David McKimm with Newtownards connections have been identified:

- David McKimm (1461) son of William who lived at 2 Wallace's Street Newtownards enlisted in Belfast in October 1885. Aged 18 he was a baker by trade.

- David McKimm (1806) of 29 George's Street Newtownards aged 45 years 9 months enlisted in Belfast on 23 November 1914. A general labourer, he had previous service with the 2nd Battalion Royal Irish Rifles and he was posted to the Depot Battalion; he did not serve overseas. He was married to Margaret and they had six children – Margaret, Isobel, Mary, Alice, Grace and David. He was discharged from the Army on 28 January 1920.

Desk searches and public appeals to date have not confirmed a positive connection between either of these sets of these service data and the David McKimm who is commemorated on Newtownards and District War Memorial.

McKimm, James
Private
No. 193, 1st Battalion, Irish Guards, transferred to (M2/193481), 52nd M.T. Company, Army Service Corps
Died on Thursday 12 October 1916 (aged 38)
Newtownards (Movilla) Cemetery, Co. Down (Grave 11. 33)

James McKimm was born in Newtownards and he and Margaret Sherrit who came from Aberdeen were married in Hammersmith, London. They lived for a time in Aberdeen before moving to Belfast where they lived at 18 Parker Street and later 6 Methuen Street. James and Margaret had at least seven children including Thomas James (1903), Maria Annie (1907), Louisa (1909), William (1911), Richard (1913) and Samuel (22 January 1916). Thomas James was born in Aberdeen and their other children were born in Belfast.

McK

James McKimm worked as a steam traction engine driver before he enlisted on 27 June 1916 in Belfast. At attestation he declared his age to be 35 although in 1911 he had declared it to be 33. He served with the 1st Battalion Irish Guards (193) before being transferred to the Mechanical Transport Company of the Army Service Corps. Two of his brothers served with the King's Royal Rifle Corps and he applied for a transfer to that Regiment. Private James McKimm was found dead at Thornhill Camp, Aldershot and he is commemorated on Newtownards and District War Memorial and in the Belfast Book of Honour (Page 445).

McKimm, Robert
Rifleman
No. 18/63, Royal Irish Rifles, transferred to (32739), East Lancashire Regiment, transferred to (614826), Labour Corps, transferred to (3/25599), Royal Irish Rifles
Died of endocarditis on Wednesday 22 November 1922 (aged 51)
Newtownards (Movilla) Cemetery, Co. Down

Robert McKimm and his wife Martha (nee McWhinney) lived at 4 Windmill

Row, Newtownards and they were married on 4 April 1893 in Second Newtownards Presbyterian Church. Robert McKimm worked as a labourer and he and Martha had at least nine children including Rachel, Robert, Edward, Maggie Eleanor, Martha Ann, Andrew and Mary Jane. The children were baptised in Greenwell Street Presbyterian Church Newtownards.

Robert McKimm enlisted in May 1915 when he was 44 years old and he served with the Royal Irish Rifles (18/63), the East Lancashire Regiment (32739) and the Labour Corps (614826) before returning to the Royal Irish Rifles (3/25599).

Robert McKimm died on 22 November 1922 at 4 Windmill Road, Newtownards and his son Robert and his widow Martha and family placed two separate death notices in the 25 November 1922 edition of the *Newtownards Chronicle*. The following year Martha placed an 'Our Heroes – In Memoriam' notice and it contained the verse:

McK

'Oh happy day that fixed my choice
On Thee my Saviour and my God
He is gone to the Lord who redeemed him
It was Jesus who called him away;
He is gone to the loved ones in glory,
From night to the splendour of day'

The name Robert McKimm is listed on Newtownards and District War Memorial and in the booklet produced for the Unveiling and Dedication Ceremony held on Saturday 26 May 1934 he is described as a Rifleman in the Royal Irish Rifles.

McKittrick, David
Private
No. 437974, 44th Battalion, Canadian Infantry (New Brunswick Regiment)
Died on Sunday 19 November 1916 (aged 30)
Vimy Memorial, France

There is some variation in how the surname is spelt – McKittrick (attestation papers and newspaper report) and McKitterick (census and CWGC Debt of Honour). The date of birth declared at attestation was 15 June 1886 although his age at death in the CWGC Debt of Honour is recorded as 23.

David McKittrick was born on 15 June 1886 and he was the eldest son of Alexander and Lizzie McKittrick who lived in the townland of Carrowreagh and later Ballybeen. Alexander McKittrick worked as an agricultural labourer and he and Lizzie had ten children including David, Alfred, Maggie, Lizzie, William and Samuel.

David McKittrick moved to Canada in 1906 where he worked as a labourer before he enlisted at Edmonton on 19 November 1915. It was noted in his attestation papers that he was 5 feet 3 inches tall. He served with the 44th Battalion Canadian Infantry (New Brunswick Regiment) and he went to the front in August 1916. Private David McKittrick died on 19 November 1916, exactly one year after he enlisted. He is commemorated in the PCI Roll of Honour for Dundonald Presbyterian Church.

McKittrick, William
Rifleman
No. 18/160, 'B' Company, 13th Battalion, Royal Irish Rifles
Killed in action on Wednesday 14 February 1917 (aged 28)
St. Quentin Cabaret Military Cemetery, Belgium (Grave II. A. 13)

McK

William McKittrick was born in Newtownards and prior to the outbreak of the Great War he was employed by Mrs William Gill of Church Street Newtownards. He worked as a labourer and he and Jean (Jennie) Johnston were married on 14 November 1910 in St Anne's Church of Ireland Belfast. Jennie worked as a factory hand before their sons were born – Robert Hugh in 1913 and William in 1915. Both were baptised in Greenwell Street Presbyterian Church and the McKittrick family lived at 6 Church Street Newtownards.

William McKittrick enlisted in Belfast, he joined the 1st County Down Volunteers in June 1915 and he went to the front the following October with the 13th Battalion Royal Irish Rifles in 108th Brigade of the 36th (Ulster) Division. His father-in-law Sergeant John Johnston also served with the 13th Battalion Royal Irish Rifles.

Rifleman McKittrick was killed in action on 14 February 1917 and the Battalion War Diary shows that he died during a German bombardment which began at 1.00 am. Afterwards Captain GJ Apperson wrote in a letter of sympathy to William's widow, 'He was a splendid soldier and one of the most useful men in the company. No matter how hard things were he never grumbled and always he did more than his share of the work'. In that same attack Rifleman **Robert Robinson** was wounded and he died the following day. At 6.00 pm that day there was another enemy attack during which Lance Corporal **Robert H Marshall** was killed.

William's family placed a 'For King and Country' notice in the *Newtownards Chronicle* and 'Our Heroes – In Memoriam' notices in the years thereafter. His death was deeply regretted by his wife, son, father-in-law, mother, brother Richard and sister-in-law. His widow Jennie inserted the verse:

'Too far away thy grave to see,
But not too far to think of thee;
When days are dark and friends are few,
Dear husband how I think and long for you.
I often think of days gone by,
When we were all together;
A shadow o'er our life is cast,
A husband gone forever'

McK
McL

Rifleman William McKittrick's widow and son moved to 8 Short Street, Newtownards. He is commemorated on Newtownards and District War Memorial and in the PCI Roll of Honour for Greenwell Street Presbyterian Church Newtownards.

McKnight, George
The name George McKnight is listed on Newtownards and District War Memorial and in the booklet produced for the Unveiling and Dedication Ceremony held on Saturday 26 May 1934 he is described as a Private in the Royal Irish Regiment. Desk searches and public appeals to date have yielded no further information.

McLaughlin, William
Private (Trooper)
No. 7072, 1st South African Mounted Brigade
Died of cerebral-malarial fever on Monday 5 March 1917 (aged 23)
Thaba Tshwane (Old No.1) Military Cemetery, South Africa (Grave A. 15)

William McLaughlin was the only son of Daniel and Catherine (Kate) McLaughlin (nee Hendron) who lived in Church Street, Newtownards. They were married on 15 January 1883 in Newtownards Roman Catholic Church. Daniel McLaughlin worked as a wool weaver and he and Kate had five children – Isabella, Annie J, Agnes, Maggie and William. Kate McLaughlin died before 1911 and Daniel and his family moved to 5 Balfour Street, Newtownards.

FOR KING AND COUNTRY.

M'LAUGHLIN—5th March, 1917, at Roberts Heights, Pretoria, South Africa, from cerebral-malarial fever, Trooper William M'Laughlin, 1st South African Mounted Brigade, only son of Daniel M'Laughlin, 5 Balfour Street, Newtownards. R.I.P. Deeply regretted by his sorrowing Father and four Sisters.

William McLaughlin moved to South Africa and during the Great War he served with the 1st South African Mounted Brigade. Private William McLaughlin died of cerebral-malarial fever at Roberts Heights, Pretoria, South Africa on 5 March 1917 and he is commemorated on Newtownards and District War Memorial (as William McLoughlin).

McLean Brothers: Charles and Duncan

Four McLean brothers served in the Great War. Duncan who was the eldest served with the Royal Irish Rifles, Norman served with the Royal Engineers, Peter served with the Canadian Highlanders and Charlie who was the youngest served with the Argyll & Sutherland Highlanders.

They were sons of Peter and Mary McLean (nee Hutchinson) who lived at 13 Mark Street, Newtownards. Peter McLean held a directorship in the Glen Printing and Finishing Works. The McLean family moved to Newtownards from Scotland (where at least two of their children, Mary and Duncan, were born). Peter and Mary McLean had at least nine children – Mary, Duncan, Maggie, John, Peter, Norman, Hugh Charles Hutchinson, Flora and Annie. Charles was the first of the two brothers to die on active service during the Great War:

McLean, Hugh Charles Hutchinson (Charlie)
Private
No. 301278, 'B' Company, 1st/8th Battalion, Princess Louise's (Argyll & Sutherland Highlanders)
Killed in action on Saturday 17 March 1917 (aged 18)
Roclincourt Military Cemetery, France (Grave I. B. 20)

Charles McLean was born on 30 July 1898 in Newtownards and he was baptised in Strean Presbyterian Church Newtownards. Prior to the outbreak of the Great War Charlie worked as an apprentice in motor car engineering with Messrs Morrison Brothers Newtownards and then as an apprentice in the Sirocco Works Belfast. He enlisted in Belfast in September 1916.

McL

In a letter dated 30 March 1917 to Private McLean's mother, Second Lieutenant George M Warnock of the 8th Argyll and Sutherland Highlanders informed her that her youngest son Private Charles McLean was missing in action. He described the circumstances. During a British advance on the morning of 17 March Charlie took part in a very successful bombing raid on the enemy's trenches and since then he had not been seen or heard of. During the raid he was seen doing good work but at roll-call he was found to be missing. His platoon officer and many comrades were killed during the raid and none of the survivors saw him fall. Later his body was found by the party detailed to clear the battlefield.

McLean, Duncan
Rifleman
No. 18162, 'B' Company, 13th Battalion, Royal Irish Rifles
Killed in action on Thursday 16 August 1917 (aged 30)
Tyne Cot Memorial, Belgium (Panel 138 to 140 & 162 to 162A & 163A)

Duncan McLean was born in Scotland and he moved to Newtownards with his parents. Prior to the outbreak of the Great War he worked as an engineer-fitter in the Glen Printing and Finishing Works. He and Maggie Finlay were married on 19 April 1907 in Dundonald Presbyterian Church and they had six children all of whom were baptised in Strean Presbyterian Church Newtownards – Mary Hutchinson, Agnes Finlay, Peter, Martha Finlay, Duncan (in 1915) and Andrew Finlay (in 1916).

In September 1914 Duncan McLean joined the 1st County Down Volunteers when he enlisted in Newtownards and he went to the front in October 1915. Duncan served with the 13th Battalion Royal Irish Rifles in 108th Brigade of the 36th (Ulster) Division and five months after his brother Charlie was killed in action Duncan was also killed in action. Initially he was posted as missing in action on 16 August 1917 and in July 1918 it was officially confirmed that he had been killed in action at the Battle of Langemarck. These were anxious times for the McLean family in Newtownards. Lance Corporal

Norman McLean serving with the Royal Engineers was in York Hospital being treated for wounds sustained in action. These wounds were so severe that Norman was given his discharge papers from the army. Corporal Peter McLean serving with the Canadians was in a military hospital in England suffering from the effects of gas poisoning. Peter recovered sufficiently to be sent back to the front.

> **FOR KING AND COUNTRY.**
> M'LEAN—Previously reported missing, now officially reported killed on 16th August, 1917, No. 18162, Rifleman Duncan M'Lean, R.I. Rifles (1st Co. Down Volunteers), dearly beloved husband of Maggie M'Lean.
> 13 Balfour Street, Newtownards.

When Rifleman Duncan McLean died his wife Maggie and their children were living at 13 Balfour Street, Newtownards.

Private Charles McLean and Rifleman Duncan McLean are both commemorated on Newtownards and District War Memorial and in the PCI Roll of Honour for Strean Presbyterian Church Newtownards. Duncan is also commemorated in Greyabbey Masonic Lodge No. 183.

McMaster, David
Rifleman
No. 18330, 'B' Company, 13th Battalion, Royal Irish Rifles
Killed in action on Friday 23 November 1917 (aged 20)
Moeuvres Communal Cemetery Extension, France (Grave I. D. 23)

McM

David McMaster was born on 11 September 1897 in Portaferry and he was the youngest son of David and Annie McMaster (nee McMaster) who lived in the townland of Ballycranbeg, Kircubbin. They were married on 22 November 1877 in Kircubbin Presbyterian Church. David McMaster Senior was a farmer and he and Annie had at least thirteen children including Charlotte Jane, Anna Eliza, Agnes, Lucy (died 20 August 1914), Ellen, Thomas (died 28 July 1908), Sarah, Fanny Forde, William Arbuthnot, Charles, William John and David. The children were baptised in Kircubbin Presbyterian Church. One of David's sisters was married to Joseph McDowell and they lived in High Street, Newtownards.

Rifleman David McMaster enlisted in Newtownards, he served with the 13th Battalion Royal Irish Rifles in 108th Brigade of the 36th (Ulster) Division and he was killed in action on 23 November 1917 during the Battle of Cambrai. He is commemorated in Kircubbin Presbyterian Church and on the family grave headstone in the adjoining graveyard. David's mother died on 17 May 1930 and his father died on 5 May 1937 aged 95.

McMath, Francis
Company Sergeant Major
No. 57550, 122nd Field Company, Royal Engineers, 36th (Ulster) Division
Died of wounds on Saturday 11 December 1915 (aged 41)
Louvencourt Military Cemetery, France (Plot 1. Row C. Grave 20)

Francis McMath was born on 22 February 1874 in Donaghadee and he was a son of James and Margaret McMath (nee Fulton) who lived in the townland of Drumfad, Carrowdore. They were married on 29 June 1861 in Millisle Presbyterian Church and they had at least three children – Francis, Jane and Agnes. The children were baptised in Carrowdore Parish Church of Ireland.

McM

Records show that Francis McMath lived in Dublin for a time. He enlisted in Belfast and served with the 122nd Field Company Royal Engineers. He went to France with the 36th (Ulster) Division in October 1915. Two months later, on 11 December 1915, Company Sergeant Major Francis McMath died of wounds at Louvencourt.

McMath, John (Jack)
Officer of the Order of the British Empire
Captain
SS *Manitou*, Mercantile Marine
Died on Tuesday 16 July 1918 following an operation (aged 46)
Port Said War Memorial Cemetery, Egypt (Grave D. 2)

John (known as Jack) McMath was born in Portaferry on 8 June 1872. He was a son of John and Mary McMath (nee Kirkpatrick) and he had a brother named Edward. Jack's father worked as a mariner and was lost at sea in 1875 when the ship *Rathfern* foundered in the China Sea. Jack's mother and his brother both died in 1916. Jack went to sea at an early age and he attained the rank of Captain.

Jack McMath and Sara Elliott Hill were married on 3 June 1907 in Edinburgh and they had two children – John Charles McMath and Mary Moray McMath. John Charles McMath became a geologist and he served in the Second World War during which he attained the rank of Major. He was a member of the War Crimes Commission in Norway and also the War Crimes Commission in Singapore for the Burma to Siam Railway.

During the Great War Jack McMath served as Captain aboard the SS *Manitou*. This ship was built originally for the Wilson and Furness-Leyland Line and had accommodation for 120 first class passengers. After conversion in Liverpool SS *Manitou* served as a British Military Transport ship and had capacity for 1100 people. In October 1914 the ship left Gaspe Bay in Quebec bound for Devonport and the story goes that the bear cub in London Zoo which inspired the Winnie the Pooh stories travelled from Canada to England on this crossing.

The SS *Manitou* was attacked by enemy submarines on a number of occasions during the Great War and on one voyage to Egypt Captain McMath's gallant actions aboard the lead ship in the convoy led to him being decorated – an Officer of the Order of the British Empire. This was awarded posthumously on 14 September 1918 because Captain Jack McMath died on 16 July 1918 following an operation to remove his appendix. He was recovering well after the operation but developed peritonitis.

McM

Captain Jack McMath is commemorated on the Memorial Plaque in Ballyphilip Parish Church of Ireland (St James) Portaferry.

McMillan, David H
Private
**No. 17271, Highland Light Infantry, transferred to (15092), Leinster Regiment, transferred to (40048), 2nd Battalion, Royal Dublin Fusiliers
Died of wounds on Friday 21 December 1917 (aged 19)
Tincourt New British Cemetery, France (Grave III. G. 25)**

David H McMillan was an orphan who was placed in Newtownards Workhouse and subsequently boarded out in 1902 by the Newtownards Board of Governors. He was four years of age when he was placed with Margaret and James McDowell who farmed near Kircubbin. James and Margaret McDowell were in their mid 50s without any children of their own.

David McMillan was educated in Kircubbin and he

won a silver medal for good conduct and drill proficiency as a member of the Boys' Brigade. After leaving school David went to sea for two years and then he was engaged in railway work in Glasgow. He enlisted and joined the Highland Light Infantry (17271). Later he was transferred to the Leinster Regiment (15092) and then to the Royal Dublin Fusiliers (40048).

Private David McMillan died on 21 December 1917 from the effects of gunshot wounds to the chest. David's foster parents James and Margaret McDowell who lived in Rowantree Cottage, Kircubbin placed a 'For King and Country' notice in the *Newtownards Chronicle*. David was also remembered by his sister Mrs Toomath who lived in Strandtown, Belfast.

In the December 1917 and January 1918 editions of the *Newtownards Chronicle* it was reported that Private David McMillan had been 'wounded at the Battle of Loos in December 1915 and again at Ypres in August 1917 when he was awarded the Military Medal for conspicuous gallantry in the field'. It was reported in the press that, 'for gallantry on the same occasion his officer won the Victoria Cross'. Neither in David's army records nor on his CWGC headstone is there any reference to the award of a Military Medal (MM) and his service medal entitlement indicates that he did not serve overseas in 1915.

The misinformation in the newspaper reports may have arisen because of the fact that in 1917 'his officer' in the Royal Dublin Fusiliers was Sergeant James Ockendon who was awarded the Victoria Cross east of Langemarck on 4 October 1917 during the Third Battle of Ypres and who himself had been awarded the Military Medal in August 1917. One of nine children Sergeant James Ockendon VC MM was born on 10 December 1890 in Portsmouth and he joined the Royal Dublin Fusiliers in 1909. When he was awarded the Victoria Cross Sergeant Ockendon was acting as Company Sergeant-Major and, regardless of his own safety, he attacked an enemy machine-gun position capturing the gun and killing the crew. Then he led an attack on another enemy position, killing four of the enemy and capturing 16 prisoners. In 1918 Sergeant Ockendon was awarded the Belgian Croix de Guerre and he died on 29 August 1966 aged 75.

Private David McMillan is commemorated on Newtownards and District War Memorial (with MM inscribed) and on the Memorial Plaque in Kircubbin Presbyterian Church (without MM inscribed).

McM

McMillan, John
Private
No. 799083, 19th Battalion, Canadian Infantry (Central Ontario Regiment)
Killed in action on Tuesday 8 May 1917 (aged 25)
Vimy Memorial, France

John McMillan was born on 30 December 1891 and he was the eldest son of William and Maggie McMillan (nee Andrews) who lived at 45 William Street, Newtownards. They were married on 16 February 1891 in Newtownards Parish Church of Ireland. William McMillan worked as a quarry labourer and before moving to Canada John worked as a labourer in a bleach works. John had a younger brother called Willie and a younger sister called Maggie.

In Canada John McMillan worked as a motorman and he lived at 129 Seaton Street, Toronto. He enlisted on 12 January 1916 in Toronto and it was noted in his attestation papers that he was unmarried, he was 5 feet 6½ inches tall and he had the initials J M tattooed on his left forearm.

McM

Private John McMillan served with the 19th Battalion Canadian Infantry (Central Ontario Regiment) and he was killed in action on 8 May 1917. There were two 'For King and Country' notices in the 26 May 1917 edition of the *Newtownards Chronicle*. The first was from his sorrowing father, mother, sister and brother and it included the verse:

'God is good, He'll give us grace
To bear our heavy cross;
He is the only one Who knows
How bitter is our loss.'

The second was from Lord Londonderry's Own CLB Flute Band Newtownards of which Private McMillan had been a member. He is commemorated on Newtownards and District War Memorial and in Regent Street Methodist Church Newtownards.

McMillan, Michael
Private
No. 11599, Royal Inniskilling Fusiliers, transferred to (48141), 8th Battalion, Machine Gun Corps (Infantry)
Killed in action on Thursday 26 June 1919 (aged 26)
Archangel Allied Cemetery, Russian Federation (Sp. Mem. B91), buried Ust-Vaga Burial Ground

Michael McMillan was born in Newtownards and he was a son of Andrew and Mary Colville McMillan (nee Brown) who moved to 30 Greenville Street, Connswater in Belfast. They were married on 2 November 1886 in First Newtownards Presbyterian Church and they had at least three children – James, William Scott and Michael. James and William were baptised in First Newtownards Presbyterian Church. Michael enlisted in Belfast and he served with the Royal Inniskilling Fusiliers (11599) and subsequently with the 8th Battalion Machine Gun Corps.

Private Michael McMillan was killed in action on 26 June 1919 during the civil war in Russia and he is commemorated in the Belfast Book of Honour (Page 454).

McM

McMillan, Robert Watson (Robert)
Private
No. A/20091, 19th Battalion, Canadian Infantry (Central Ontario Regiment)
Died of wounds on Friday 30 June 1916 (aged 23)
Lijssenthoek Military Cemetery, Belgium (Grave VIII. B. 33)

Robert McMillan was born on 29 August 1892 in Newtownards and he was the eldest son of Alexander and Annie McMillan (nee Watson). They were married on 22 August 1891 in Newtownards Zion Methodist Church and they lived at 93 Greenwell Street Newtownards. Alexander worked as a general labourer, Annie worked as a wool weaver and they had at least seven children all of whom were baptised in Greenwell Street Presbyterian Church – Robert Watson, Mary Elizabeth Bennett, Alexander, Mary, John Watson, Albert and William.

Robert McMillan moved to Canada around 1912 and he worked there as a labourer before he enlisted in Winnipeg on 18 December 1914. In his attestation papers it was noted that he was 5 feet 11 inches tall and he had a tattoo (part of a flag) on his left arm. Private Robert McMillan served with the 19th Battalion Canadian Infantry (Central Ontario Regiment) and he went to the front in the summer of 1915. Robert was wounded in action on 16 June 1916 and he died of his injuries two weeks later.

Private Robert McMillan is commemorated on Newtownards and District War Memorial and in the PCI Roll of Honour for Greenwell Street Presbyterian Church Newtownards.

McMillan, Samuel
Rifleman
No. 13171, 8th Battalion, Royal Irish Rifles
Killed in action on Sunday 2 July 1916
Thiepval Memorial, France (Pier and Face 15 A and 15 B)

In 'Soldiers Died in the Great War 1914 – 1919' it is recorded that Samuel McMillan was born in Newtownards and he enlisted in Belfast. He served with the 8th Battalion Royal Irish Rifles in 107th Brigade of the 36th (Ulster) Division. In the CWGC Debt of Honour Private Samuel McMillan is recorded as having died on the second day of the Battle of the Somme. In the heat of battle the 8th Battalion Royal Irish Rifles did not make a casualty return on 1 July 1916 and many military historians agree that those 8th Battalion casualties listed on the 2 July return were killed in action on 1 July.

McM

McMullan, Edward*
Private
No. 2601, Royal Irish Regiment, transferred to (21947), 8th Battalion, Princess Victoria's (Royal Irish Fusiliers)
Died of wounds on Tuesday 25 April 1916 (aged 24)
Vermelles British Cemetery, France (Sp. Mem. 6)

Edward McMullan was a son of Richard and Sarah McMullan who lived in Shore Street, Portaferry. Richard McMullan worked as a sailor and he and Sarah had at least eleven children including Sarah, Jinnie, Thomas, Richard, Edward, Catherine, Nellie, James, Hugh and Eliza Ann.

Before the Great War Edward McMullan worked as a fisherman and he enlisted in Belfast. He served with the Royal Irish Regiment (2601) and subsequently with the 8th Battalion Royal Irish Fusiliers in 49th Brigade of the 16th (Irish) Division.

Private Edward McMullan died of wounds on 25 April 1916 and it was

A BRAVE PORTAFERRY VOLUNTEER.

The Nationalist Volunteers of Portaferry are pleased to learn that Edward M'Mullan, of Shore Street, has by his gallant conduct and deeds of heroism gained marks of distinction from his commanding officers in the field of battle in France. Private M'Mullan was a member of the National Volunteers, Portaferry Company, 1st Batt. East Down Regiment, and was one of the first of the company to join after Mr. Redmond's appeal. He has received the following letter from Major-General Hickie:

The Irish Brigade.

No. 21,947 Private Edward M'Mullan, 8th Batt. Royal Irish Fusiliers.

I have read with much pleasure the reports of your Regimental Commander and Brigade Commander regarding your gallant conduct and devotion to duty in the field on April 10th, 1916, and have ordered your name and deed to be entered in the record of the Irish Division.

W. B. HICKIE, Major-Gen.,
Commanding 16th Irish Division.

reported in the 29 April 1916 edition of the *Newtownards Chronicle* that he had been commended for his gallantry by WB Hickie, Major-General Commanding 16th (Irish) Division. Major-General Hickie ordered his name and deed to be entered in the record of the 16th (Irish) Division.

McMullan, John Joseph (John)*
Private
No. 4152, Royal Irish Regiment, transferred to (21941), 8th Battalion, Princess Victoria's (Royal Irish Fusiliers)
Killed in action on Wednesday 6 September 1916 (aged 20)
Quarry Cemetery, France (Grave IV. J. 4)

John Joseph McMullan was born in the townland of Ballyphillip, Portaferry and he was a son of James and Rebecca McMullan (nee Boomer) who lived in Little Back Lane, Portaferry. They were married on 18 January 1893 in Portaferry Roman Catholic Church and they had at least four children – James, John Joseph, Sarah and William. Rebecca McMullan was widowed before 1911

Before the Great War John McMullan lived in Portaferry and he was a member of the Irish National Volunteers. He enlisted in Newtownards, he served with the Royal Irish Regiment (4152)

PORTAFERRY.

Official intimation has reached Portaferry that Private John M'Mullan, Royal Irish Fusiliers, was killed on the 6th ult., and Private Thomas Guiney, of the same regiment, was killed on the 9th ult. Both were members of the I.N.V.

and subsequently with the 8th Battalion Royal Irish Fusiliers in 49th Brigade of the 16th (Irish) Division. Private John McMullan was killed in action at Guillemont on 6 September 1916.

McM

McMullan, Patrick

The name Patrick McMullan is listed on Newtownards and District War Memorial and in the booklet produced for the Unveiling and Dedication Ceremony held on Saturday 26 May 1934 he is described as a Rifleman in the Royal Irish Rifles. Desk searches and public appeals to date have yielded no further information.

McMullan, Thomas
Rifleman
No. 19/340, 15th Battalion, Royal Irish Rifles
Died of wounds on Sunday 18 August 1918 (aged 26)
Arneke British Cemetery, France (Grave III. E. 4)

In 'Soldiers Died in the Great War 1914 – 1919' it is recorded that Thomas McMullan was born in Killinchy. He was a son of Thomas and Sarah McMullan (nee Jamison) who lived in the townland of Clay, Derryboye and later in the townland of Ballynacraig, Inch. They were married on 16 October 1883 in Ballygowan Presbyterian Church. Thomas McMullan Senior worked as an agricultural labourer and he and Sarah had at least nine children including Mary, David, Thomas, Robert, Alexander, Lizzie and Annie.

McM
McN

Thomas McMullan Junior worked as a farm servant for Samuel McCormick who farmed in the townland of Rathcunningham, Killyleagh. On 23 October 1913 he and Letitia Breen were married in Inch Parish Church of Ireland and they lived at Pikestone, Downpatrick. He enlisted in Belfast and he served with the 15th Battalion Royal Irish Rifles in 107th Brigade of the 36th (Ulster) Division. Rifleman Thomas McMullan died of wounds on 18 August 1918 during the Allied offensive against all sections of the German line.

McMullan, William

The name William McMullan is listed on Newtownards and District War Memorial and in the booklet produced for the Unveiling and Dedication Ceremony held on Saturday 26 May 1934 he is described as a Rifleman in the Royal Irish Rifles. Desk searches and public appeals to date have yielded no further information.

McNally, Hugh Francis DeSalle (Hugh)*
Surgeon
HMS _Hampshire_, Royal Navy
Killed by a mine explosion on Monday 5 June 1916 (aged 24)
Portsmouth Naval Memorial, Hampshire, England (Panel 11)

Hugh Francis McNally was born in Belfast and he was a son of Nicholas and Elizabeth McNally who lived in Raglan Street, Belfast. Nicholas McNally worked as a National School Teacher and he and Elizabeth had at least five children – John, Hugh, Rose, Mary Ann and Nicholas. Later they moved to 'The Shore', Portaferry.

Hugh McNally served as a surgeon aboard HMS *Hampshire* and he was killed around 7.40 pm on 5 June 1916 when the ship struck a mine off the Orkneys. HMS *Hampshire* was on route to Russia and the principal passenger aboard was Lord Kitchener who was travelling there to participate in strategic discussions. Lord Kitchener also perished.

McN

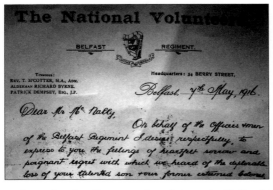

William J McCann, Secretary of The National Volunteers Belfast Regiment, wrote to Hugh's father to express sympathy on behalf of the officers and men of the Belfast Regiment in which Hugh had been a Colonel. Surgeon Hugh McNally is commemorated in the Belfast Book of Honour (Page 458) and on the family grave headstone in Ballyphilip Roman Catholic Graveyard Portaferry. Hugh's father Nicholas died on 28 November 1927 and his mother Elizabeth died on 19 July 1931.

McNeice, Daniel
Gunner
No. 275556, Royal Garrison Artillery
Died on Saturday 20 July 1918 (aged 36)
Shankill Cemetery, Lurgan, Co. Armagh (Grave 710A in North-East part)

Daniel McNeice was born in the townland of Shankill, Lurgan and he was a son of Daniel and Annie McNeice (nee Nesbitt). They were married on 6 December 1868 in Shankill Parish Church of Ireland and they lived in Lurgan. The McNeice family moved to Belfast where they lived in Balfour Avenue and Daniel Junior worked as a clerk in an income tax office.

In 'Soldiers Died in the Great War 1914 – 1919' it is recorded that Daniel

McNiece (note spelling) lived in Donaghadee and he enlisted in Belfast. Gunner Daniel McNeice served with the Royal Garrison Artillery and he died on 20 July 1918. After the war his medals were sent to Mrs Marion MacBride who lived at Woodlands, Donaghadee. Daniel's father died on 23 August 1924.

McNeilly, James
Lance Corporal
No. 18375, 'B' Company, 13th Battalion, Royal Irish Rifles
Killed in action on Saturday 1 July 1916 (aged 21)
Thiepval Memorial, France (Pier and Face 15 A and 15 B)

James McNeilly was born in Newtownards and he was the only son of James and Elizabeth (Lizzie) McNeilly (nee McFall) who were married on 13 July 1900 in Greenwell Street Presbyterian Church Newtownards. When Lizzie McNeilly was widowed on 27 July 1909 she worked in a factory and she and her son James lived with her mother Margaret McFall in Frederick Place. They moved to Mark Street and then to 61 North Street, Newtownards.

Prior to the outbreak of the Great War James McNeilly worked as a tenter for Messrs Ross Brothers in their Bloomfield factory in Belfast. He served his time with the Ards Weaving Company and he was an original member of First Newtownards Boy Scouts Company which he joined at the inauguration of the Boy Scouts movement in Newtownards by the Rev WLT Whatham. James was an Assistant Scoutmaster of the Troop and he was also Captain of the Ards Parochial Football Team.

McN

James McNeilly enlisted in Newtownards and he served with the 13th Battalion Royal Irish Rifles in 108th Brigade of the 36th (Ulster) Division. In September 1915 he was accidentally injured and hospitalised in England. He went to the front and he was posted as missing in action after the first day of the Battle of the Somme. In February 1917 it was officially confirmed that he had been killed in action.

FOR KING AND COUNTRY.
M'NEILLY—Previously reported missing on the 1st July, 1916, now reported killed in action on that date, (18,375) Lance-Corporal James M'Neilly, 13th Batt. Royal Irish Rifles (1st Co. Down Volunteers), the only and dearly-loved son of Elizabeth and the late James M'Neilly.
I have given my all to Jesus.
Deeply regretted by his sorrowing Mother.
E. M'NEILLY.
61 North Street, Newtownards.
Dublin and American papers please copy.

His mother placed a 'For King and Country' notice in the 17 February 1917 edition of the *Newtownards Chronicle* with a request for the Dublin and American papers to copy. It contained the text:

'I have given my all to Jesus'

Lance Corporal James McNeilly is

commemorated on Newtownards and District War Memorial and in Newtownards Parish Church of Ireland (St Mark). He is also commemorated on the family grave headstone in Movilla Cemetery Newtownards. His mother Lizzie died on 9 February 1954.

McPhillips, John
Rifleman
No. 9273, 2nd Battalion, Royal Irish Rifles
Died of wounds on Saturday 11 August 1917 (aged 20)
Brandhoek New Military Cemetery, Belgium (Grave VI. B. 1)

John McPhillips was born in Donaghadee and he was a son of Jane McPhillips who lodged at 40 Ballyhay. Jane McPhillips was widowed before 1901 and she worked as a general servant. She had two children – John and Eveline.

McP
McQ

John McPhillips enlisted in Clonmel, Co Tipperary and he served with the 2nd Battalion Royal Irish Rifles. Rifleman John McPhillips died of wounds on 11 August 1917 during the fighting at Westhoek Ridge and he is commemorated on Newtownards and District War Memorial.

McQuiston, William Dalzell (William)
Rifleman
No. 18168, 'B' Company, 13th Battalion, Royal Irish Rifles
Killed in action in France on Saturday 1 July 1916 (aged 27)
Thiepval Memorial, France (Pier and Face 15 A and 15 B)

William McQuiston was born on 23 October 1888 in Newtownards and he was a son of John and Sarah McQuiston (nee Crothers) who lived in Wallace's Street No. 2. They were married on 13 February 1879 in Fourth Newtownards Presbyterian Church. John McQuiston worked as a cotton weaver and he and Sarah had at least five children – Robert John, Sarah, Andrew, Edward Stevenson and William Dalzell. John McQuiston Senior died on 19 January 1911.

William McQuiston worked as a house painter before the Great War and he and Eleanor (Ellen) Dempster were married on 11 May 1912 in First Donaghadee

Presbyterian Church. He was a member of the Ulster Volunteer Force and of LOL No. 1054 in Newtownards. William enlisted in Newtownards and he served with the 13th Battalion Royal Irish Rifles in 108th Brigade of the 36th (Ulster) Division. Rifleman William McQuiston was posted as missing in action after the first day of the Battle of the Somme and in June 1917 it was officially confirmed that he had been killed in action. His wife Eleanor was living at 76 Upper Movilla Street, Newtownards and she placed a 'For King and Country' notice in the 23 June edition of the *Newtownards Chronicle*. It was on behalf of herself and her two little children, Elizabeth born in 1913 and Letitia Boyce born in 1915 (both baptised in Greenwell Street Presbyterian Church Newtownards), and it contained the verse:

> *'The news was sad, the blow was hard,*
> *God's will, it shall be done;*
> *With a manly heart he did his part*
> *And a crown of victory won'*

Rifleman William McQuiston is commemorated on Newtownards and District War Memorial and in the PCI Roll of Honour for Greenwell Street Presbyterian Church Newtownards.

McR

McRoberts, Thomas
Second Lieutenant
20th Battalion, Royal Irish Rifles
Killed in action on Monday 13 August 1917 (aged 28)
Tyne Cot Cemetery, Belgium (Grave LXV. E. 4)

Thomas McRoberts was the younger son of Thomas McRoberts who lived in Castle Street, Comber. Thomas McRoberts Senior worked as a draper and house furnisher and Thomas Junior assisted him. Thomas and Jane McRoberts had at least eleven children including Jane, Thomas, Margaret, Susanna and Nellie. Thomas Senior died on 19 December 1912.

Prior to the outbreak of the Great War Thomas McRoberts was a member of the North Down Regiment of the Ulster Volunteer Force and he joined the ranks of a reserve battalion of the 36th (Ulster) Division. From there he was sent to a Cadet Unit from which he qualified for a commission. He left for the Western Front on 30 April 1917 and less than four months later he was killed in action. His widowed mother

placed a 'For King and Country' notice in the 1 September edition of the *Newtownards Chronicle*.

Second Lieutenant Thomas McRoberts is commemorated on Comber and District War Memorial; in Comber Masonic Lodge No. 46 and in Comber Parish Church of Ireland (St Mary). He is named with **Captain GJ Bruce** and **Second Lieutenant E De Wind** on the Banner of LOL No. 100 (Comber Ulster Defenders).

McTaggart, Andrew

The name Andrew McTaggart is listed on Newtownards and District War Memorial and in the booklet produced for the Unveiling and Dedication Ceremony held on Saturday 26 May 1934 he is described as a Private in the Colonials.

McT

Andrew McTaggart was one of four brothers on active service in the Great War and his brother Thomas had a military funeral in Newtownards after he died at home on 23 January 1916. Whilst Thomas McTaggart is commemorated in Newtownards Parish Church of Ireland (St Mark), Andrew McTaggart is not. Desk studies and public appeals to date have yielded no further information as to when Andrew McTaggart died.

McTaggart, Thomas
Rifleman
No. 6565, 4th Battalion, Royal Irish Rifles (Royal North Downs) attached to 2nd Battalion, Royal Irish Rifles
Died of consumption on Sunday 23 January 1916
Newtownards (Movilla) Cemetery, Co. Down (Grave 5. 18)

In some newspaper reports the surname is spelt McTeggart.

In the 29 January 1916 edition of the *Newtownards Chronicle* the funeral of Rifleman Thomas McTaggart was reported under the headline 'Military Funeral in Newtownards'. It was reported that Thomas McTaggart who had ten years military service had been wounded when fighting at the front and, 'owing to the exposure to which he was subjected at the time, contracted consumption'.

Thomas was discharged and for several months his mother cared for him in her home at 37 Frederick Street, Newtownards. The Rev WLT Whatham communicated details of Thomas McTaggart's service to the Adjutant of the 10th (Reserve) Battalion Royal Irish Fusiliers stationed in Newtownards and Colonel Fitzgerald agreed to provide for a military funeral. The brass band of the Fusiliers with draped drums played on the way to the cemetery. The coffin was covered with the Union Jack on which was placed the deceased's cap, belt and side-arms.

Rifleman Thomas McTaggart had three brothers on active service in the Great War – Pte John McTaggart, 2nd Battalion Royal Inniskilling Fusiliers attached to the 3rd Battalion; Rifleman Watson McTaggart, 4th Battalion Royal Irish Rifles and Andrew McTaggart serving with the Canadians.

> **OUR HEROES—IN MEMORIAM.**
>
> M'TAGGART—In loving memory of my dear son, Rifleman Thomas M'Taggart, who died, through wounds received in action, on 23rd January, 1916, and interred in the family burying-ground, Movilla.
>
> Death came stealing o'er his pillow,
>   Ere the dawning of the day;
> Without a sigh, without a struggle,
>   Peacefully he passed away.
> Love cannot die, we love you still,
>   For memory's golden chain
> Doth link our hearts to yours on high,
>   Until we meet again.
> Inserted by his sorrowing Mother, Father, Sister, and Brothers.
>
> 37 Frederick Street,
>   Newtownards.

Thomas's family placed an 'Our Heroes – In Memoriam' notice in the 20 January 1917 edition of the *Newtownards Chronicle* and it contained the verse:

McT

'Death came stealing o'er his pillow,
Ere the dawning of the day;
Without a sigh, without a struggle
Peacefully he passed away.
Love cannot die, we love you still,
For memory's golden chain
Doth link our hearts to yours on high,
Until we meet again'

Rifleman Thomas McTaggart is commemorated on Newtownards and District War Memorial and in Newtownards Parish Church of Ireland (St Mark).

McTear, Hugh
Private
No. 12013, 1st Battalion, Highland Light Infantry
Died of wounds on Monday 17 May 1915 (aged 20)
Le Touret Memorial, France (Panel 37 and 38)

Hugh McTear was born in Glasgow and he was a son of Daniel McTear. The McTear family moved to Newtownards where they lived at 4 Kennel Lane. Hugh McTear enlisted in Glasgow, he served with the 1st Battalion Highland Light Infantry and he died of wounds on 17 May 1915.

McVea, Robert
Rifleman
No. 249, 2nd Battalion, Royal Irish Rifles
Killed in action in France on Sunday 24 March 1918 (aged 19)
Pozieres Memorial, France (Panel 74 to 76)

The surname is spelt McVea on the family grave headstone in Cloughey Presbyterian Churchyard, McVey in the CWGC Debt of Honour, McVeigh in Church records and McVeagh in both the 1901 and 1911 census.

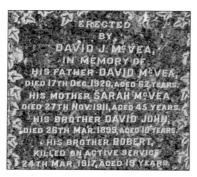

Robert McVea was born on 14 August 1898 in Portavogie and he was a son of David and Sarah McVea (nee Palmer). They were married on 23 June 1888 in Glastry Presbyterian Church near Ballyhalbert. David McVea worked as a fisherman and he and Sarah had at least nine children – David John (1 April 1889, died on 26 March 1899), Eliza Ann, Henry (3 June 1892), Thomas James (8 August 1893), Maggie Ellen (17 August 1895), Robert (14 August 1898), David John (named after his brother who died), Agnes Palmer and Adam (27 June 1909). The children were baptised in Cloughey Presbyterian Church. Sarah McVea died on 27 November 1911 aged 45.

McV
McW

Robert McVea enlisted in Newtownards and he served with the 2nd Battalion Royal Irish Rifles. Rifleman Robert McVea was killed in action on 24 March 1918 when the Battalion came under violent attack by the enemy in 'overwhelming numbers'. Many men were killed that day.

Rifleman Robert McVea is commemorated on the family grave headstone in Cloughey Presbyterian Churchyard.

McWha, Dupree William
Private
No. 6/3394, Canterbury Regiment, NZEF
Killed in action on Thursday 18 April 1918 (aged 25)
Sucrerie Military Cemetery, France (Grave IV. E. 3)

The McWha family farmed in the townland of Ballyrolly, Carrowdore and Dupree William McWha was a son of Francis (Frank) and Alice Annie Ellen McWha (nee Parsons) who lived in Murchison, Nelson in the South Island when they moved to New Zealand. They had four children – Francis Robert,

Dupree William (born 16 November 1892), Robert John and David Leslie – all born in Murchison.

> M'WHA—In loving memory of Private Dupree William M'Wha (63394), New Zealand Expeditionary Force, killed in action in France on April 18, 1918, second son of Frank M'Wha, Matakitaki, Murchison, Nelson, New Zealand. Ever remembered by his Cousins, ISABEL M'WHA and ISABEL FINLAY.

Dupree William McWha was killed in action on 18 April 1918 and one year later his cousins Isabel McWha and Isabel Finlay placed an 'Our Heroes – In Memoriam' notice in the 19 April 1919 edition of the *Newtownards Chronicle*. Isabel McWha's father James McWha and her uncle Dupree McWha both worked as farmers in Ballyrolly, Carrowdore.

McWhinney Brothers: Hamilton and William John

Hamilton and William John McWhinney were born in Newtownards and they were sons of Maggie McWhinney who lived in Mill Street. Maggie McWhinney worked as charwoman and she had at least four children – William John, Hamilton, Samuel and Jane. All three brothers were on active service during the Great War and their surname is spelt Mawhinney in some official records and in some newspaper reports. William John McWhinney was the first of the two brothers to die in the Great War:

McW

McWhinney, William John (served as Mawhinney, William John)
Private
No. 7544, 1st Battalion, Royal Irish Rifles
Died of wounds on Thursday 11 March 1915 (aged 31)
Merville Communal Cemetery, France (Grave I. B. 16)

William John McWhinney worked as an apprentice butcher before he enlisted and he served in India for 12 years with the 1st Battalion Royal Irish Rifles. At the outbreak of the Great War he came home with his Battalion and proceeded to the front line. Bugler McWhinney (spelt Mawhinney in the CWGC Debt of Honour) was wounded in action on 5 March 1915 and the War Office conveyed this news to his sister Jane who was living in William Street Newtownards. Later she was informed that William John had died of his wounds on 11 March 1915.

William John's brother Hamilton placed a 'Killed in Action' notice in the 17 April 1915 edition of the *Newtownards Chronicle* and it contained the verse:

'Though my heart may break with sorrow,
By the grief so hard to bear,
I shall meet him some bright morrow
In our Father's mansion fair'

Five months after William John died Hamilton McWhinney was killed in action on 15 August 1915. Private (Bugler) William John McWhinney is commemorated on Newtownards and District War Memorial.

McWhinney, Hamilton
Private
No. 12576, 6th Battalion, Princess Victoria's (Royal Irish Fusiliers)
Killed in action on Sunday 15 August 1915 (aged 28)
Helles Memorial, Gallipoli, Turkey (Panel 178 to 180)

Prior to the outbreak of the Great War Hamilton McWhinney worked as a general labourer and on 18 July 1906 he and Martha Reid Conway were married in Newtownards Registry Office. He enlisted in Newtownards, he served with the 6th Battalion Royal Irish Fusiliers in 31st Brigade of the 10th (Irish) Division and he was killed in action at Kirich Tepe in the Dardanelles on 15 August 1915.

McW

A peculiar pathos attaches to the death of Private Hamilton Mawhinney, 12,576, Royal Irish Fusiliers, which occurred at the Dardanelles on 15th August, 1915. Only four days before his gallant sacrifice of life for his King and country's honour, his wife was buried in Movilla Cemetery. He has left four motherless children, the youngest a baby. The Rector of the Parish is acting as guardian for these orphans meanwhile, and will be glad to receive articles of clothing, of which they are still in need.

The report of his death in the 18 September 1915 edition of the *Newtownards Chronicle* pointed up another tragic aspect. Just four days before Hamilton McWhinney was killed in action his wife Martha was buried in Movilla Cemetery. She died of consumption and the newspaper report pointed out that Hamilton's death had 'left four motherless children, the youngest a baby'. The report went on 'The Rector of the Parish is acting as guardian for these orphans meanwhile, and will be glad to receive articles of clothing, of which they are in need'. Three of the children were Maggie (born 1906), Mary Jane Conway (born 1908) and David Conway (born 1912).

Private (Bugler) Hamilton McWhinney is commemorated on Newtownards and District War Memorial and in Newtownards Parish Church of Ireland (St Mark).

McWilliams, Andrew
Rifleman
No. 19/26, 1st Battalion, Royal Irish Rifles
Killed in action on Sunday 24 March 1918 (aged 20)
Pozieres Memorial, France (Panel 74 to 76)

Andrew McWilliams was born on 17 March 1898 and he was a son of Ben and Ellen McWilliams (nee Thompson) who lived at 42 Manor Street, Donaghadee. They were married on 30 September 1890 in Ballycopeland Presbyterian Church. Ben McWilliams was a mariner and he and Ellen had at least eight children including Mary, John, Andrew, Benjamin, Robert, Alfred and Elizabeth. Andrew was baptised in Donaghadee Parish Church of Ireland.

Andrew McWilliams enlisted in November 1915 in Belfast and he served with the 1st Battalion Royal Irish Rifles. When Andrew was posted as missing in action his mother appealed for information as to her son's fate. Later it was officially confirmed that Rifleman Andrew McWilliams had been killed in action on 24 March 1918 during the retreat from St Quentin and he is commemorated on Donaghadee and District War Memorial and in Donaghadee Parish Church of Ireland.

McW
Me

Medland, Wilfred Harold (Harold)
Company Sergeant Major
No. 9259, 9th Battalion, Princess Victoria's (Royal Irish Fusiliers)
Killed in action on Thursday 16 August 1917
Tyne Cot Cemetery, Belgium (Grave IV. H. 16)

For a time Harold Medland was stationed in Newtownards. He was the youngest son of Mr and Mrs James Medland who lived in Chertsey in Surrey and he served with the 9th Battalion Royal Irish Fusiliers in 108th Brigade of the 36th (Ulster) Division.

MARRIAGE.
MEDLAND—DAWSON—June 28, 1916, at the 1st Newtownards Presbyterian Church, by the Rev. Dr. Wright, D.D., Company Sergeant-Major W. Medland, Royal Irish Fusiliers, youngest son of James Medland, Chertsey, Surrey, to Margaret, eldest daughter of Joseph Dawson, and granddaughter of the late Samuel and Mrs. Dawson, Castle St., Newtownards.

On 28 June 1916 Harold Medland and Margaret Dawson were married in First Newtownards Presbyterian Church. Margaret was the eldest daughter of Joseph Dawson and grand-daughter of the late Samuel Dawson of Castle Street, Newtownards. The Rev Dr Wright conducted the wedding ceremony and three days later the Rev Wright's son **Matthew John Wright** was killed in action on the first day of the Battle of the Somme.

FOR KING AND COUNTRY.

MEDLAND—Killed in action, 15th August, 1917, Company-Sergeant-Major Harold Medland, Royal Irish Fusiliers, youngest son of Mr. and Mrs. James Medland, Chertsey, Surrey, and dearly-loved husband of Margaret Medland, Castle Street, Newtownards.

Company Sergeant Major Medland was killed in action at Langemarck on 16 August 1917 and at that time his wife Margaret was living in Castle Street, Newtownards. She placed a 'For King and Country' notice in the 8 September 1917 edition of the *Newtownards Chronicle*. Company Sergeant Major Harold Medland is commemorated on Newtownards and District War Memorial.

Mellefont, Thomas Gray (Thomas)
Lance Corporal
No. 9887, 2nd Battalion, Royal Irish Rifles
Killed in action on Monday 26 October 1914 (aged 19)
Le Touret Memorial, France (Panel 42 and 43)

Me

Thomas Gray Mellefont was born in Millisle and he was a son of Robert and Susan Mellefont. In 1901 Robert Mellefont was a Royal Navy pensioner and he and his family had moved from Millisle to Wexford which was Robert's home county. His wife Susan was born in Dublin. Robert and Susan Mellefont had at least five children – Sarah, Frances, Gilbert, Susan and Thomas. Baby Susan was baptised in Carrowdore Parish Church of Ireland.

Thomas Mellefont enlisted in Dublin and he served with the 2nd Battalion Royal Irish Rifles. He was killed on 26 October 1914 in a German attack at Neuve Chapelle during the Battle of La Bassee.

Melville, William John (William)
Private
No. 26726, 10th Battalion, Royal Inniskilling Fusiliers
Killed in action on Saturday 1 July 1916 (aged 34)
Thiepval Memorial, France (Pier and Face 4 D and 5 B)

William John Melville was born on 24 May 1882 and he was a son of Hugh and Elizabeth (Lizzie) Melville who lived in the townland of Ballycross, Donaghadee. William John was baptised in Donaghadee Parish

Church of Ireland. Lizzie Melville worked as a domestic servant and William worked as a painter.

William Melville and Sarah Campbell were married on 9 June 1910 in Ballygrainey Presbyterian Church and they had at least two children, Hugh Campbell and Nancy, both of whom were baptised in Shore Street Presbyterian Church Donaghadee.

William Melville enlisted in Donaghadee, he served with the 10th Battalion Royal Inniskilling Fusiliers in 109th Brigade of the 36th (Ulster) Division and he was killed in action on the first day of the Battle of the Somme. Private William Melville is commemorated on Donaghadee and District War Memorial and in Shore Street Presbyterian Church Donaghadee.

Menown, William
Corporal
No. 129419, 'A' Company, 72nd Battalion, Canadian Infantry (British Columbia Regiment)
Killed in action on Thursday 1 March 1917 (aged 26)
Villers Station Cemetery, France (Grave VI. D. 8)

Me
Mi

> **PORTAFERRY.**
> Information has been received by Mr. John Menown, Church Street, Portaferry, of the death in action of his youngest son, Corporal William Menown, Canadian Infantry. Deceased, who was 26 years of age, was in Vancouver when he volunteered for service shortly after the outbreak of war. He is survived by his young wife.

William Menown was born on 5 June 1890 and he was the youngest son of John and Elizabeth Menown who lived in Church Street, Portaferry. John Menown worked as an engine driver and he and Elizabeth had at least three children – May, Joseph and William. William moved to Canada where he worked as a steam fitter before he enlisted in Vancouver, British Columbia on 11 August 1915. In his attestation papers it was noted that he was 5 feet 6½ inches tall and that his 'teeth need fixing'. He served with the 72nd Battalion Canadian Infantry (British Columbia Regiment) and he was killed in action on 1 March 1917. In the CWGC Debt of Honour his surname is spelt Manown. Corporal William Menown was survived by his wife, parents, brother and sister.

Millar, Thomas
Sergeant
No. 15499, 8th Battalion, Royal Irish Rifles
Died on Wednesday 12 July 1916
Thiepval Memorial, France (Pier and Face 15 A and 15 B)

In 'Soldiers Died in the Great War 1914 – 1919' it is recorded that Thomas Millar was born in Ballygowan and he enlisted in Belfast. He died on 12 July 1916 whilst serving with the 8th Battalion Royal Irish Rifles in 107th Brigade of the 36th (Ulster) Division. Sergeant Thomas Millar is commemorated in the Belfast Book of Honour (Page 469).

Millar, Thomas
Rifleman
No. 18471, 12th Battalion, Royal Irish Rifles
Died of heart failure on Tuesday 9 November 1920
Newtownards (Movilla) Cemetery, Co. Down (Grave 13. 30)

Mi

Rifleman Thomas Millar enlisted in September 1914, he served with the 12th Battalion Royal Irish Rifles in 108th Brigade of the 36th (Ulster) Division and he was discharged from the Army on 23 August 1918 because he was no longer physically fit for war service. He was suffering from 'Valvular Disorder of the Heart' (VDH). Thomas Millar died of heart failure on 9 November 1920 and he is commemorated on Newtownards and District War Memorial.

Millar, William Barry Ritchie (Barry)
Corporal
No. 2653, 45th Battalion, Australian Infantry, AIF
Killed in action on Thursday 7 June 1917 (aged 25)
Ypres (Menin Gate) Memorial, Belgium (Panel 7-17-23-25-27-29-31)

William Barry Ritchie Millar was born on 15 November 1891 and he was a son of John and Mary Millar (nee Rainey) who lived at 'Rockmount', Ballygowan. They were married on 19 August 1890 in Second Comber Presbyterian Church. John Millar was a farmer and he and Mary had at least six children – William Barry Ritchie, Jane Rainey, Alexander Rainey, James, Samuel Abernethy and Margaret.

Barry Millar worked for Riddels Ltd in Belfast and his colleagues there presented him with a gold watch before he left for Australia in August 1913. in Australia he worked as a commercial traveller before he enlisted on 4

July 1915 in Liverpool, New South Wales. In his attestation papers it was noted that he was 5 feet 11 inches tall. He was promoted to the rank of Lance Corporal on 29 April 1916 and Corporal on 18 August 1916. Corporal Barry Millar was killed in action on 7 June 1917.

On 1 July 1917 a memorial service was held for him in Ballygowan Presbyterian Church. The Rev William K McLernon paid tribute to his memory by recalling the fact that Barry was 'one of the first two members of the Sunday school to gain the gold medal for ten successive years of attendance without being once absent and that his attendance was maintained until he became a member of the teaching staff of the Sunday school'.

Ballygowan-Australian Killed.

Intimation has been received by Mr. and Mrs. Millar, of Rockmount, Ballygowan, that their son, Corporal W. Barry Millar, of the Australians, was killed in action. On last Sunday evening a memorial service was held for him in Ballygowan Presbyterian Church. The Rev. Wm. K. M'Lernon, paying a tribute to his memory, recalled the fact that he was one of the two first members of the Sunday-school to gain the gold medal for ten successive years' attendance without being once absent, and that his attendance was maintained until he became a member of the teaching staff of the school.

Corporal William Barry Ritchie Millar is commemorated in Ballygowan Presbyterian Church and on the family grave headstone in the adjoining graveyard.

Mi

Miller, Joseph
Private
No. 26766, 9th Battalion, Royal Inniskilling Fusiliers
Killed in action in France on Saturday 1 July 1916
Mill Road Cemetery, France (Grave I. D. 19)

In 'Soldiers Died in the Great War 1914 – 1919' it is recorded that Joseph Miller was born in Comber and he enlisted in Londonderry. Research has shown that this soldier was born in the townland of Cumber, Claudy and he lived in the townland of Ervey, Cross – both in County Londonderry. Private Joseph Miller served with the 9th Battalion Royal Inniskilling Fusiliers in 109th Brigade of the 36th (Ulster) Division and he was killed in action on the first day of the Battle of the Somme.

Miller, William Thomas (William)
Rifleman
**No. 18/562, 8th Battalion, Royal Irish Rifles
Died of wounds on Friday 17 August 1917 (aged 19)
Mont Huon Military Cemetery, France (Grave III. M. 7A)**

In some records, including the CWGC Debt of Honour, the family surname is spelt Millar.

William Thomas Miller was born on 21 February 1898 in Newtownards and he was the third surviving son of Thomas James and Mary Ann Miller (nee Ferguson) who lived in Scrabo Road. They were married on 3 November 1885 in First Newtownards Presbyterian Church. Thomas James Miller worked as a quarry labourer and he and Mary Ann had at least eleven children – Joseph (died), Ellenor Boyd, George, David John Ferguson, Lizzie, Agnes Beattie, William Thomas, Nellie, Jane Martin, Mary Annie and Joseph. William was baptised in First Newtownards Presbyterian Church.

Mi

Prior to the outbreak of the Great War William Miller worked in the Royal Nurseries Newtownards for Messrs Alex Dickson & Sons Ltd. He enlisted in October 1915 and did his training at the Clandeboye Camp. Having been allocated to the Signalling Section of a Belfast Battalion he went to the front in January 1917.

MILLER—August 17th, died of wounds received in action on 7th August, Rifleman Wm. Miller, Signalling Section Royal Irish Rifles (Ulster Division), third son of Thomas James Miller, 44 Church Street, Newtownards.

On 17 August 1917 Rifleman William Miller died of the wounds he had received in action on 7 August 1917 during the Third Battle of Ypres. His father and his sister Nellie who lived at 44 Church Street, Newtownards placed a 'For King and Country' notice in the *Newtownards Chronicle*.

Rifleman William Miller is commemorated (as Millar) on Newtownards and District War Memorial and in the PCI Roll of Honour for First Newtownards Presbyterian Church.

Milligan, John
Rifleman
**No. 18/1106, 11th & 12th Battalions, Royal Irish Rifles
Died on Tuesday 7 June 1921 (aged 26)
Ballyhalbert (St. Andrew) Church of Ireland Churchyard, Co. Down**

MILLIGAN—In fond and loving memory of my dear son, John Milligan, who departed this life on 5th June, 1921, and was interred in the family burying-ground, Ballyeasboro.
There is a link death cannot sever; Love and remembrance last for ever. Ever remembered by his loving Mother and Sister.
MARGET and NANNIE MORELAND Ballygraffin, Kircubbin.

John Milligan was born in the townland of Ballygraffan, Kircubbin and he was a grandson of James and Margaret Milligan. Both John and his grandfather worked as farm labourers. John worked for Thomas Warnock of Ballygraffan.

John Milligan enlisted in Kircubbin on 22 November 1915 aged 20 years 11 months and he joined the 18th Battalion Royal Irish Rifles. From 7 June 1916 he served in France with the 11th Battalion in 108th Brigade of the 36th (Ulster) Division. He was gassed on 13 August 1917. He was transferred to the 12th Battalion on 29 November 1917, then to the 3rd Battalion and then back to the 12th Battalion. He was discharged from the Army on 13 March 1919 and on 26 August 1920 he was awarded a disability pension. His level of disability was recorded as '100%' and it was attributed to the effects of gas poisoning. He died on 7 June 1921 and was buried in the graveyard beside Ballyhalbert Parish Church of Ireland (St Andrew) at Ballyeasborough.

Rifleman John Milligan is commemorated in Kircubbin Parish Church of Ireland (Holy Trinity).

Mi

Mills, John
Rifleman
No. 17/1810, 10th Battalion, Royal Irish Rifles
Killed in action on Saturday 1 July 1916 (aged 19)
Thiepval Memorial, France (Pier and Face 15 A and 15 B)

John Mills was born in Ballygowan and in November 1915 he enlisted in Belfast. He joined the 17th Battalion Royal Irish Rifles and he went to the front with the 10th Battalion Royal Irish Rifles in 107th Brigade of the 36th (Ulster) Division. Rifleman John Mills was killed in action on the first day of the Battle of the Somme. He is commemorated in Ballygowan Presbyterian Church and in the Belfast Book of Honour (Page 471) where his address is given as 91 Ardenvohr Street, Belfast. Evidence from one source suggests that he was a son of Robert John and Martha Mills (nee McVeigh) who were married on 21 December 1888 in Ballygowan Presbyterian Church. They had at least eleven children all of whom were baptised in Ballygowan Presbyterian Church – Elizabeth (1889), Margaret (1890), Martha (1891), William (1894), John (1896; died), John (1897), Thomas (1899), Sarah Jane (1902), Robert (1905), Samuel (1908) and David (1912).

Miskelly, Samuel
Rifleman
No. 15602, 8th Battalion, Royal Irish Rifles
Killed in action on Sunday 2 July 1916 (aged 22)
Thiepval Memorial, France (Pier and Face 15 A and 15 B)

Samuel Miskelly was born on 8 June 1894 in Newtownards and he was a son of John and Mary Bella Miskelly (nee Strain). They were married on 16 November 1891 in Greenwell Street Presbyterian Church Newtownards. John Miskelly worked as a tailor and he and Mary had at least ten children including Margaret, Samuel, John, Henry, Jane and Robert. Margaret, Samuel, John and Henry Miskelly were baptised in Greenwell Street Presbyterian Church. After John Miskelly died Mary Miskelly married Samuel Norris and they had at least three children – Robert, Elizabeth and David. Samuel Norris worked as a labourer and he, Mary, their children and his step-children lived at 7 Bangor Street, Belfast.

Mi

Samuel Miskelly enlisted in Belfast, he served with the 8th Battalion Royal Irish Rifles in 107th Brigade of the 36th (Ulster) Division and in the CWGC Debt of Honour it is recorded that he was killed in action on the second day of the Battle of the Somme. In the heat of battle the 8th Battalion Royal Irish Rifles did not make a casualty return on 1 July 1916 and many military historians agree that those 8th Battalion casualties listed on the 2 July return were killed in action on 1 July. Rifleman Samuel Miskelly is commemorated in the Belfast Book of Honour (Page 472).

Miskimmin, Joseph (served as Miskimmins, Joseph)
Rifleman
No. 6832, 2nd Battalion, Royal Irish Rifles
Killed in action in France on Sunday 9 July 1916 (aged 17)
Pozieres British Cemetery, France (Grave III. B. 19)

In the CWGC Debt of Honour the surname is spelt Miskimmins. Joseph Miskimmin was born on 2 October 1898 in the townland of Herdstown, Donaghadee. He was a son of George and Elizabeth Miskimmin (nee Tierney) who were married on 27 May 1878 in Donaghadee Parish Church of Ireland. They had at least ten children all of whom were baptised in Donaghadee Parish Church of Ireland – Margaret Jane,

Essie McWilliams, James (died), James, Hugh, John, William Robert, Mary Hastings, Annie Jane and Joseph. Joseph enlisted in Newtownards and he served with the 2nd Battalion Royal Irish Rifles. Rifleman Joseph Miskimmin was killed in action on 9 July 1916. That day the Battalion was in a forward position and took some casualties under 'friendly fire' from the Allied artillery barrage. Later in the day there were further casualties when the Germans attacked from Contalmaison Wood.

Rifleman Joseph Miskimmin is commemorated on Donaghadee and District War Memorial and in Donaghadee Parish Church of Ireland (in both cases the surname is spelt Miskimmin).

Miskimmin, Samuel George (Samuel)
Sergeant
No. 18413, 'C' Company, 13th Battalion, Royal Irish Rifles, transferred to (17756), 108th Company, Machine Gun Corps (Infantry), 36th (Ulster) Division
Died of wounds on Sunday 25 November 1917 (aged 23)
Hermies British Cemetery, France (Grave C. 9)

Mi

Samuel George Miskimmin was born in Killyleagh and he was a son of David and Annie Miskimmin (nee Woods) who lived in the townland of Ballybundon, Killinchy. They were married on 2 May 1877 in Second Saintfield Presbyterian Church. David Miskimmin was a farmer and he and Annie had at least twelve children including Sarah, Mary (died aged about 20), Robert, Agnes, David, Thomas, Meta (died of TB aged about 30), William (died aged about 19) and Samuel.

Killinchy Rifleman Dies of Wounds.
Sergt. Samuel Geo. Miskimmin, Machine Gun Corps, son of Mr. David Miskimmin, Ballybundon, Killinchy, died of wounds received in action on 22nd November. Prior to the outbreak of war he was in Messrs. Coombe, Barbour, & Coombe's, joining the Royal Irish Rifles shortly after hostilities commenced.

Prior to the outbreak of the Great War Samuel George Miskimmin worked for the firm of Messrs Coombe, Barbour & Coombe in Belfast. He enlisted in Downpatrick and he served in 'C' Company 13th Battalion Royal Irish Rifles (18413) in 108th Brigade of the 36th (Ulster) Division.

Samuel was transferred to the Machine Gun Corps and on 10 June 1916 he was wounded when an enemy shell exploded close by. Private **John Price** was killed in the attack and Samuel wrote a letter of sympathy to John's mother.

In the letter he said, 'I cannot express in words how I felt when I came to myself and saw before me, in such a condition, poor John. I could hardly realise that it was he, as we were speaking to each other so soon before. He, being so much bigger than I, saved me from being perhaps killed. I don't know how I escaped at all, I had been knocked below him. When I came to myself and saw what had happened, I wished it had been the other way, it was heartbreaking.' Samuel went on, 'I am now in hospital, I wanted to stop as I would have liked to be at the burial, but I had to come for a few days rest until my nerves got settled. God knows I would gladly have gone in his place as I think he will be more missed than I would.'

Some 17 months later, on 25 November 1917, Samuel died of wounds received in action on 22 November 1917 at Cambrai. Sergeant Samuel George Miskimmin is commemorated in Raffrey Presbyterian Church and Killinchy Parish Church of Ireland. He is listed on Comber and District War Memorial (surname spelt Miskimmon) as having served and survived. His father David died on 12 February 1934.

Mitchell, David
Captain
Royal Army Medical Corps
Died of disease on 31 October 1920 (aged 26)
Tullynakill Graveyard, Co. Down

David Mitchell was born on 14 December 1893 and he was the youngest son of James and Elizabeth (Lizzie) Mitchell (nee Patterson) who lived in the townland of Ringneal, Killinchy and later in Railway Street, Comber. They were married in First Killyleagh Presbyterian Church. James Mitchell was a farmer and he and Lizzie had at least eight children – Robert, Anna, Martha, Minnie, Jane, William, Thomas and David. When James Mitchell died on 23 August 1895 at the age of 63 Robert took over the role of Head of Family.

David Mitchell studied medicine and after he qualified in 1914 he joined the Royal Army Medical Corps. While he was serving in No. 1 General Hospital in India he contracted malaria and after his war service he came home to take up a medical appointment in Birmingham. He contracted scarlet fever and with his already impaired state of health as a contributory factor he died on 31 October 1920. Captain David Mitchell is commemorated in First Comber Presbyterian Church and on the family grave headstone in Tullynakill Graveyard.

Mitchell, William Hamilton
Lieutenant
8th Battalion, Canadian Infantry (Manitoba Regiment)
Died on Monday 27 November 1916 (aged 30)
Villers Station Cemetery, France (Grave III. B. 19)

William Hamilton Mitchell was born on 28 November 1885 in Belfast and he became a career soldier. He served in the Royal Inniskilling Fusiliers before moving to Canada in 1905. He served for three years on the Permanent Force in Canada and, on 23 September 1914, he volunteered for the first Expeditionary Force and enlisted in Valcartier, Quebec. In his attestation papers it was noted that he was 5 feet 7½ inches tall. He attained the rank of Company Sergeant Major and in August 1915 he obtained a commission for service in the field.

Mi
Mo

Lieutenant Mitchell was wounded at St Julien in August 1915 and he was wounded again in 1916 before he died on 27 November 1916, the day before his 31st birthday. His next-of-kin in Ireland was his brother John who lived in Brownlow Street, Comber. Lieutenant William Hamilton Mitchell is commemorated in the Belfast Book of Honour (Page 474).

Monks, James
The name James Monks is listed on Newtownards and District War Memorial and in the booklet produced for the Unveiling and Dedication Ceremony held on Saturday 26 May 1934 he is described as a Sergeant in the Royal Irish Rifles. Sergeant John Monks (6339) 7th Battalion Royal Irish Rifles died on Thursday 16 August 1917 and he is commemorated on Tyne Cot Memorial. Desk searches and public appeals to date have not conclusively confirmed a connection between these service data and the soldier who is commemorated on Newtownards and District War Memorial.

Montgomery, James
Rifleman
No. 9/3778, 9th Battalion, Royal Irish Rifles, transferred to (333801),
421st Agricultural Company, Labour Corps
Died of pneumonia on Thursday 31 October 1918 (aged 49)
Carnmoney Cemetery, Co. Antrim (Grave X. 94)

James Montgomery was born in Newtownards and he was a son of Alexander and Jane Montgomery who moved to Belfast. James Montgomery enlisted in Belfast and he went to France on 2 October 1915. He served with the 9th Battalion Royal Irish Rifles in 107th Brigade of the 36th (Ulster) Division before being transferred to the 421st Agricultural Company Labour Corps. Rifleman James Montgomery died of pneumonia on 31 October 1918 and he is commemorated in the Belfast Book of Honour (Page 476).

Montgomery, Samuel
Rifleman
No. 18/977, 12th Battalion, Royal Irish Rifles
Killed in action on Thursday 21 March 1918 (aged 20)
Pozieres Memorial, France (Panel 74 to 76)

Mo

MONTGOMERY—In loving memory of my dear son, Rifleman Samuel Montgomery, No. 977, 12th Royal Irish Rifles, reported missing on 21st March, 1918, now reported killed on that date.

Taken away in his early youth,
Taken from those he loved,
From serving his King on earth below
To serve his Great King above.

Ever remembered by his loving Father, Mother, Sisters and Brothers.
GEORGE AND ELLEN SMYTH. Ballyrickard, Comber.

MONTGOMERY—In loving memory of my dear brother, Rifleman Samuel Montgomery, No. 977, 12th Royal Irish Rifles reported missing on 21st March, 1918, now reported killed on that date.

True hearts that loved you
With sweetest affection,
Always shall love you
In death just the same.

Ever remembered by his loving Brother,
DAVID MONTGOMERY.
Ballyrickard, Comber.

Samuel Montgomery was a son of David and Ellen Montgomery (nee Kennedy) who were married on 31 October 1889 in Newtownards Parish Church of Ireland. They lived in the townland of Ballyalton, Comber and they had at least three children, Sarah, David and Samuel. After David Montgomery Senior died, the family lived in the townland of Greengraves, Newtownards. They lived with Ellen's father Henry Kennedy who worked as an agricultural labourer.

Ellen Montgomery married George Smyth on 6 November 1901 in Comber Parish Church of Ireland and Samuel Montgomery lived with them in the townland of Ballyrickard. George Smyth worked as a labourer and he and Ellen had at least four children – Maggie Jane, Mary, William and George.

Samuel Montgomery enlisted on 15 November 1915 in Newtownards and he joined the 18th Battalion Royal Irish Rifles. He went to the front with the 12th Battalion Royal Irish Rifles in 108th Brigade of the 36th (Ulster Division) and he was killed in action on 21 March 1918 at the beginning of the German 'Michael' offensive. Rifleman Samuel Montgomery is commemorated on Comber and District War Memorial as having served and survived.

Montgomery, William
Private
No. 21917, Scots Rifles, transferred to (40674), 6th Battalion, King's Own Scottish Borderers
Died of wounds on Tuesday 10 April 1917 (aged 24)
Aubigny Communal Cemetery Extension, France (Grave I. L. 2)

William Montgomery was born in Newtownards and he was a son of Jane Montgomery. Jane Montgomery worked as a washerwoman and they lived in Mark Street. Later William and his brother Andrew and his sister Mary boarded with John and Jane Cargo and their three children in Little Francis Street. John Cargo worked as a blacksmith and William Montgomery worked in a print works before he moved to Scotland. He lived in Rutherglen, Lanark and he enlisted there. He served initially with the Scots Rifles (21917) before being transferred to the 6th Battalion King's Own Scottish Borderers.

Private William Montgomery died of wounds at the 42nd Casualty Clearing Station in France on 10 April 1917 and his brother and sister placed a 'For King and Country' notice in the 28 April 1917 edition of the *Newtownards Chronicle*. It contained the text:

'For ever with the Lord'

At the time of William's death Driver Andrew Montgomery was on active service with the Royal Engineers and Mary was living at 6 Greenwell Street Newtownards. Private William Montgomery is commemorated on Newtownards and District War Memorial and in Second Newtownards Presbyterian Church.

Montgomery, William Savage (William)
Private
No. 790294, 29th Battalion, Canadian Infantry (British Columbia Regiment)
Killed in action on Wednesday 11 April 1917 (aged 19)
Vimy Memorial, France

William Savage Montgomery was born on 4 December 1897 in Killinchy and he was the eldest son of David Alexander and Anna Montgomery (nee Savage) who lived on Sketrick Island. They were married on 24 December 1896 in Killinchy Presbyterian Church. David Montgomery worked as a farm labourer and he and Anna had at least six children – William, Hugh, James, Thomas, David and Rosina. William was baptised in Killinchy Presbyterian Church.

William Montgomery moved to Canada where he worked as a farmer before he enlisted on 5 January 1916 in New Westminster, British Columbia. In his attestation papers it was noted that he was 5 feet 6 inches tall and he cited his father as his next-of-kin. He served with the 29th Battalion Canadian Infantry (British Columbia Regiment) and he was killed in action at Vimy Ridge on 11 April 1917. Private William Savage Montgomery is commemorated in Killinchy Presbyterian Church.

Mooney, Edward
Rifleman
No. 7525, 14th Battalion, Royal Irish Rifles
Killed in action on Saturday 23 March 1918
Ham British Cemetery, France (Grave II. B. 12)

In 'Soldiers Died in the Great War 1914 – 1919' it is recorded that Edward Mooney was born in Newtownards and he enlisted in Belfast. Rifleman Edward Mooney served with the 14th Battalion Royal Irish Rifles in 109th Brigade of the 36th (Ulster) Division and he was killed in action on 23 March 1918.

Mo

Moore, Catherwood
Private
No. 13627, 2nd Battalion, Royal Scots Fusiliers
Died on Tuesday 31 July 1917 (aged 23)
Ypres (Menin Gate) Memorial, Belgium (Panel 19 and 33)

Catherwood Moore was born on 12 October 1893 in Donaghadee and he was a son of William and Mary Moore (nee Gaw) who lived in Castle Square, Bangor. They were married on 29 April 1890 in Ballycopeland Presbyterian Church. William Moore worked as a railway labourer, Mary worked as a charwoman and they had at least six children – Robert, Samuel, Catherwood, Maggie Agnes, Isabella and Helen Georgina. They were baptised in Shore Street Presbyterian Church Donaghadee.

Catherwood Moore worked as a farm labourer and in 1911 he was employed by Sarah Jane Kerr, a widow who farmed in the townland of Ballycrochan. Catherwood moved to Scotland where he lived in Stevenston, Ayrshire. He enlisted in Kilwinning, Ayrshire and he served with the Royal Scots Fusiliers. Private Catherwood Moore died on 31 July 1917.

Mo

Moore, Hamilton (Hammy)
Corporal
No. G/153, 1st Garrison Battalion, Royal Irish Rifles
Died of cholera on Wednesday 3 October 1917 (aged 48)
Karachi 1914 – 1918 War Memorial, Pakistan

Hamilton Moore was a son of Mr and Mrs William John Moore who lived at 35 Victoria Avenue, Newtownards. Hamilton worked as a tailor and his father William John was a career soldier. Hamilton Moore and Elizabeth Gunning McGimpsey were married on 3 June 1912 in Ballygilbert Presbyterian Church and at the time of Hammy's death Elizabeth and their two children were living at 37 Pound Street, Newtownards.

> **FOR KING AND COUNTRY.**
>
> MOORE—3rd October, 1917, died of cholera at the Army Clothing Factory, Old Fort, Multan City, India, Sergeant Hamilton Moore (Hammy), dearly-beloved husband of Elizabeth Moore. Deeply regretted by his sorrowing Wife and two little Children.
> 37 Pound St., Newtownards.
>
> MOORE—3rd October, 1917, died from cholera at Multan, India, Sergeant Hamilton (Hammy) Moore, Royal Irish Rifles.
> Deeply regretted.
> WM. J. MOORE.
> South St., Newtownards.

Corporal Hammy Moore served with the 1st Garrison Battalion Royal Irish Rifles and he died of cholera at the Army Clothing Factory, Old Fort, Multan City in India. His widow Elizabeth placed a 'For King and Country' notice in the 20 October 1917 edition of the *Newtownards Chronicle* and Hammy is commemorated on Newtownards and

District War Memorial and in Second Newtownards Presbyterian Church.

Moore, Hugh
Private
No. 437255, 46th Battalion, Canadian Infantry (Saskatchewan Regiment)
Died of wounds on Wednesday 25 October 1916 (aged 36)
Adanac Military Cemetery, France (Grave VI. C. 5)

Hugh Moore was born on 16 August 1880 in Newtownards and he was the only son of Hugh and Mary Moore who lived at 12 Greenwell Street. Hugh Moore Senior worked as a master blacksmith and he and Mary had at least four children before Mary died – Hugh, Agnes Jane, Eleanor Anne and Mary. A newspaper report of the day described Hugh Moore Senior as 'a blacksmith and horse-shoer of more than ordinary cleverness'.

Mo

Hugh Moore Junior worked as a joiner before he moved to Canada and there he worked as a farmer. He enlisted on 17 May 1915 in Edmonton, Alberta and it was noted in his attestation papers that he was 5 feet 8½ inches tall. Private Hugh Moore served with the Canadian Infantry and he died of wounds on 25 October 1916. Initially he was reported as wounded and missing in an area known as 'Death Valley' and his death 'on or since that date' was officially confirmed in June 1917. By then his father was dead and his sisters placed a 'For King and Country' notice in the 30 June 1917 edition of the *Newtownards Chronicle*. Two eye-witness reports from his comrades clarified the circumstances of his death:

- 'He was in 13th Platoon. Near Courcellette we were attacking on 25 October. We only got part of the way when we had to retire back to our trenches which we held. I saw Moore lying badly wounded in a shell-hole near our trench. I stopped and dressed his wounds. Stretcher bearers took him to the dressing station'.

- 'When he was struck his entrenching tools were on his back; the bullet passed through them. I saw him lifted and taken to the dressing station and I am told he died there'.

Private Hugh Moore's isolated battlefield grave was located in 1924 and he was re-interred in Adanac (Canada spelt backwards) Military Cemetery. He is commemorated on Newtownards and District War Memorial and in the

PCI Roll of Honour for Greenwell Street Presbyterian Church Newtownards.

Moore, John Ross (John)
Second Lieutenant
3rd Battalion, Connaught Rangers attached 7th Battalion, Royal Inniskilling Fusiliers
Killed in action on Saturday 9 September 1916 (aged 20)
Thiepval Memorial, France (Pier and Face 15 A)

John Ross Moore was a son of Samuel and Annie Moore and at the time of John's death his father was manager of the Ulster Bank in Ballina, Co Mayo. John's grandfather had been a Unitarian minister in Newtownards.

> **Newtownards Man Killed.**—Second-Lieut. John R. Moore, Connaught Rangers (attached Royal Inniskilling Fusiliers), killed on 9th inst., was the elder son of Mr. S. Moore, of the Ulster Bank, Ballina, who was formerly pro-manager of the branch in Londonderry. Mr. Moore is a native of Newtownards, where his father was a Unitarian minister, and Mrs. Moore is a daughter of Mr. John Ross, Lurgan. The deceased officer was 21 years of age.

Second Lieutenant John Moore served with the 3rd Battalion Connaught Rangers attached to the 7th Battalion Royal Inniskilling Fusiliers in 49th Brigade of the 16th (Irish) Division. When he was killed in action at Ginchy on 9 September 1916 his death was reported in the *County Down Spectator* under the headline 'Newtownards Man Killed'.

Mo

Moore, Patrick (served as McConnell, Patrick)
Private
No. 505421, Royal Engineers, transferred to (85487), 1st/8th Battalion, Durham Light Infantry
Killed in action on Monday 27 May 1918
Soissons Memorial, France

In 'Soldiers Died in the Great War 1914 – 1919' it is recorded that Patrick Moore was born in Newtownards, he lived in Berwick-on-Tweed and he enlisted in Belfast. He served with the 1st/8th Battalion Durham Light Infantry and before that the Royal Engineers (505421). He served under the alias Patrick McConnell and he was killed in action on 27 May 1918 during the German spring offensive.

Moore, William (Willie)
Second Lieutenant
10th Battalion, Princess Victoria's (Royal Irish Fusiliers)
Killed in action on Thursday 16 August 1917 (aged 25)
Tyne Cot Memorial, Belgium (Panel 140 to 141)

Second Lieutenant William Moore was born on 16 June 1892 and he was a son of Dr Archibald and Mrs Elizabeth Rogers Moore (nee Stevenson). They were married on 10 April 1889 in Maghera Presbyterian Church and they lived in 'Ashley House', Mountpottinger, Belfast. William Moore attended Campbell College from 1905 to 1912.

William Moore enlisted and he obtained a commission as Second Lieutenant with the 10th Battalion Royal Irish Fusiliers. Until May 1917 he served as a bombing instructor and was stationed in Newtownards where he was well known in the local community. He went to France and on 15 June 1917 he wrote a letter to his mother from the 36th (Ulster) Division Base Depot at Le Havre and he intimated that he was going to the front with the 9th Battalion Royal Irish Fusiliers in 108th Brigade of the 36th (Ulster) Division. The last letter that he wrote was to his father and it was dated 14 August 1917. In it he said that he was soon to be in action again and that he might not be able to write very much for a while. 'Whatever happens, don't worry', he wrote. Second Lieutenant William Moore was killed in action on 16 August 1917 during the Battle of Langemarck and he is commemorated on the Campbell College War Memorial; on the QUB War Memorial and in the QUB Book of Remembrance (Page 42). William's father died on 30 May 1922.

Moore, William
Lance Corporal
No. 14985, 6th Battalion, Royal Irish Rifles
Killed in action on Wednesday 11 August 1915 (aged 44)
Helles Memorial, Gallipoli, Turkey (Panel 177 and 178)

William Moore was born in the townland of Loughries, Newtownards and he was a career soldier. His father Thomas was a farmer. William Moore served for twelve years in the Royal Artillery, for four years in the Royal Garrison Artillery and for three years as a Special Reservist in the Royal Irish Rifles. In civilian life he worked as a quarryman in Gill's Quarries at Scrabo, Newtownards.

William Moore and Ann Jane Robinson were married on 12 July 1894 in Ballyblack Presbyterian Church. They lived at 154 Greenwell Street, Newtownards and they had at least eleven children including Agnes Mary, Ellen Jane, Anna Elizabeth, Emma, Maggie, Maud, James Tomlinson, Isabella and Wilhelmina. Eight of the children were baptised in Greenwell Street Presbyterian Church.

After the outbreak of the Great War William Moore re-enlisted in Newtownards and he was attached to the 6th Battalion Royal Irish Rifles in 29th Brigade of the 10th (Irish) Division. He was killed in action at the Dardanelles on 11 August 1915 and he left behind a widow and eight daughters, the youngest of whom he never saw. A comrade who witnessed William's death said that he met with 'an instantaneous and painless call'. He went on 'The huge shell which caused havoc of slaughter made a hole in the ground as large as one of Gill's quarries on Scrabo'.

William's widow Ann placed a 'Killed in Action' notice in the 11 September 1915 edition of the *Newtownards Chronicle* and it contained the verse:

> *'Sleep in peace, O dearest husband,*
> *Thou art happy, thou art blest;*
> *Earthly cares and sorrows ended,*
> *Nought can break thy holy rest.*
> *Yet again we hope to meet him*
> *When the day of life is fled,*
> *And in heaven with joy to greet him,*
> *Where no farewell tear is shed'*

On 27 March 1916 it was reported in the *Newtownards Chronicle* that his daughter Maud aged 6 had sustained serious burns after her clothes caught fire while her mother was cooking. Lance Corporal William Moore is commemorated on Newtownards and District War Memorial and in the PCI Roll of Honour for Greenwell Street Presbyterian Church Newtownards.

Moreland, J

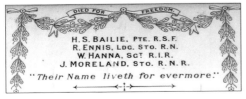

The name J Moreland is listed in Glastry Presbyterian Church and in the PCI Roll of Honour he is described as a Stoker in the Royal Naval Reserve. In the CWGC Debt of Honour only one casualty in the Royal Navy named J Moreland is listed for the designated war years:

Stoker First Class John Moreland (SS/114522) served aboard HMS *Invincible* in the Royal Navy and he died on Wednesday 31 May 1916 aged 21. He was a son of James and Louisa Moreland of 66 West Street, Glasgow and he is commemorated on Portsmouth Naval Memorial, Hampshire, England (Panel 19). Desk searches and public appeals to date have not confirmed a connection between these service data and the seaman who is commemorated in Glastry Presbyterian Church.

Morgan Brothers: John Joseph Leo and Samuel Valentine

John Joseph Leo and Samuel Valentine Morgan were sons of the late Colour Sergeant John Morgan, Instructor of Musketry in the Royal North Downs, Newtownards – a position he had held for some 23 years – and Elizabeth Morgan (nee Calwell). In civilian life John Morgan Senior had been a shoemaker and he and Elizabeth had at least eight children – Samuel Valentine, May, John Joseph Leo, Bridgetta, Sydney, Patrick Herbert, Violet and Beatrice. John Joseph Leo was the first of the two brothers to die in the Great War:

Morgan, John Joseph Leo
Mentioned in Despatches
Company Quartermaster Sergeant
No. 6668, 1st Battalion, Royal Irish Rifles
Lieutenant
2nd Battalion, Royal Inniskilling Fusiliers
Died of wounds on Sunday 16 May 1915
Bethune Town Cemetery, France (Grave II. G. 16)

Mo

John Joseph Leo Morgan was born in Newtownards and he received his education in the Ann Street and Model Schools in the town. For about two years he was employed as a Law Clerk with John McKee, Solicitor. Around 1904 he joined the Royal Irish Rifles and served for a time on the Permanent Staff of the local Battalion before joining the Depot at Belfast. There he served as Orderly Room Sergeant for the 83rd Regimental District and as Clerk in the No.11 District Office. After Belfast he joined the 2nd Battalion Royal Irish Rifles at Dover and then the 1st Battalion Royal Irish Rifles in India. He served for five years in India and then returned to England at the end of October 1914. He was promoted to commissioned rank on 3 November 1914 and he was posted to the Royal Inniskilling Fusiliers. He went to France on 28 November 1914. It was reported in the press that 'he married Miss Saintry who had been a schoolmistress at Victoria Barracks for some years'.

Percival Phillips, an eminent journalist stationed at the British Headquarters in the Field described the beginning of the Battle of Festubert: The 2nd Battalion of the Royal Inniskilling Fusiliers took part in the first attack at 11.30 pm on the evening of Saturday 15 May 1915. The Battalion advanced along both sides of what was known as the 'Cinder Track' in order to attack the German trenches which were at an angle. The Germans turned heavy and sustained machine-gun fire on the left of the Inniskilling's line and held it back. The two Companies on the right made a successful advance across open ground and took the trench. The Battalion sustained heavy losses and was shelled all day on Sunday 16 May as it held the captured position.

After the assault Lieutenant JJL Morgan helped to reorganise his men in the captured German trenches and he went back to his own lines repeatedly with messages and to bring up reinforcements. During one of these journeys he fell mortally wounded. Lieutenant JJL Morgan was a younger brother of Lieutenant Samuel Valentine Morgan. At that time Lieutenant SV Morgan was Adjutant of the 3rd Battalion Royal Irish Rifles in Dublin and it was reported in the press that 'he had the distinction of being the only non-commissioned officer of the British Army ever appointed to an adjutancy'.

Mo

Captain CAM Alexander, Adjutant 2nd Battalion Royal Inniskilling Fusiliers attached to the 5th Infantry Brigade wrote to Lieutenant SV Morgan: 'Your brother died a hero. On the night of 15/16 May we made an attack on the German line commencing at 11.30 pm. Morgan's Company was the leading Company on the right. This Company advanced with great dash and carried the German trenches. Your brother went back for reinforcements and while returning with them fell mortally wounded. He was one of the first officers to be taken away early on the morning of the 16 May by motor ambulance to the Officer's Hospital at Bethune but he died there about mid-day. He was buried in the Town Cemetery by a military chaplain. Captain Hewitt commanding the company wrote to me to say how well Morgan had done'.

At the time of Lieutenant JJL Morgan's death his widow, Mrs MM Morgan, lived at 37 York Road, Aldershot. Through the War Office she received an appreciative letter from the King informing her that her late husband had been Mentioned in Despatches from Field-Marshal Sir John French. The Field-Marshal's letter to the Secretary of State for War was dated 30 November 1915 and it was published in the *London Gazette* on Saturday 1 January 1916:

Morgan, Samuel Valentine
Long Service and Good Conduct Medal
Lieutenant
2nd Battalion, Royal Irish Rifles
Killed in action on Friday 10 August 1917 (aged 37)
Ypres (Menin Gate) Memorial, Belgium (Panel 40)

Samuel Valentine Morgan was born on 5 June 1880 in Church Street Newtownards and he became a career soldier. He enlisted on 28 January 1896 as Boy No. 4717 and was posted to the 3rd Battalion Royal Irish Rifles as a Bugler. He was appointed Lance Corporal on 1 June 1901, promoted Corporal 1 October 1901, Lance Sergeant 23 September 1902 and Sergeant 4 January 1903. He served as Orderly Room Sergeant with the Louth Rifles (6th Royal Irish Rifles Militia) and on 28 June 1908 he was posted to the 3rd Battalion, appointed Orderly Room Sergeant and promoted Colour-Sergeant, then Quartermaster Sergeant on 28 June 1911. He was awarded the Long Service and Good Conduct Medal for 18 years service. He received his commission as Second Lieutenant on 1 October 1914 and at the same time was appointed acting Adjutant of the 3rd Battalion Royal Irish Rifles under Lieutenant Colonel WEC McCammond. When the Long Service and Good Conduct Medal was being presented, the officer performing the ceremony referred to Second Lieutenant Morgan as 'a shining example to others who had joined the ranks'. He pointed out that 'with ability, perseverance and a high sense of duty every soldier had the opportunity of receiving commissioned rank'.

Samuel Valentine Morgan was promoted to the rank of Lieutenant on 8 June 1915 and he was appointed Adjutant of the Battalion. He held that position in Dublin and Belfast until the spring of 1917 when he went to the front. During the Easter Rising in 1916 his Battalion had been stationed in Portobello Barracks in Dublin. Later he gave evidence before the Royal Commission which investigated the case surrounding Captain JC Bowen-Colthurst and the shooting of Messrs Francis Sheehy-Skeffington, Patrick McIntyre and Thomas Dickson in the Barracks.

Lieutenant SV Morgan went to the front in May 1917 and he joined the 2nd Battalion Royal Irish Rifles. He was appointed to the rank of Acting-Captain with effect from 1 August 1917 and he was killed in action ten days later. During the week preceding his death at Westhoek on 10 August 1917

Mo

he experienced very heavy fighting and two days before his death a high explosive shell that burst close to him destroyed his revolver. At first he was reported officially as having been wounded in action but a subsequent telegram from the War Office stated that he had died on the same day.

Lieutenant Morgan married Rose Gertrude Marquess on 21 August 1911 in the Roman Catholic Church of St Malachy in Belfast. She had been Lady Principal of the Ann Street National School in Newtownards and they had two children – John Leo born on 6 August 1912 and Gertrude Elizabeth born on 23 January 1917. The family lived at 9 Court Street, Belfast and subsequently moved to 3 Southwell Road, Bangor before going to Southampton. Writing to Lieutenant SV Morgan's widow, the Commanding Officer of the Battalion said that Lieutenant SV Morgan had been killed 'while very gallantly leading his company in an attack'. He said that Lieutenant Morgan had been shot through the head and his death was instantaneous.

There can be little doubt that the deaths of two of her brothers, one of them so very recently, cast a shadow over the wedding of Margaret Bridgetta (Jetty) Hermione Morgan to Stewart Spencer Churchill Henry on 24 October 1917. The wedding took place in Fountainville Presbyterian Church Belfast and the groom was the youngest son of the late William Henry, founder of the *Newtownards Chronicle*. At the time of the wedding the bride's mother lived at 24 St Alban's Gardens, Belfast.

Mo

Both Lieutenant John Joseph Leo Morgan and Lieutenant Samuel Valentine Morgan are commemorated on Newtownards and District War Memorial.

Morris, William
Private
No. 10166, 1st Battalion, Royal Inniskilling Fusiliers
Killed in action on Saturday 22 May 1915 (aged 24)
Twelve Tree Copse Cemetery, Gallipoli, Turkey (Sp. Mem. C. 166)

William Morris was born in Newtownards and he was a son of William and Margaret (Maggie) Morris who lived at 30 Little Francis Street, Newtownards. William Morris Senior worked as a bricklayer's labourer and he and Maggie had at least ten children including Jane, Mary, Lizzie, William. At least six of their children died in infancy.

William Morris Junior worked as a labourer in a bleach works before he joined the Royal Inniskilling Fusiliers around 1911. He served in India and was transferred to the front in 1915. Private William Morris was killed in action at Gallipoli on 22 May 1915 and a memorial service for him was held in Newtownards Parish Church of Ireland on Saturday 26 June 1915. It was reported that Private William Morris was the first member of the congregation to be killed in the Great War. Subsequently another 75 members of the congregation died.

His family placed an 'Our Heroes – In Memoriam' notice in the 17 June 1916 edition of the Newtownards Chronicle and it contained the verse:

'Too far away thy grave to see,
But not too far to think of thee;
No morning dawns, no night returns,
But what we think of thee'

Private William Morris is commemorated on Newtownards and District War Memorial and as William Morriss in Newtownards Parish Church of Ireland (St Mark).

Mo

Morrison, James
Rifleman
No. 6321, 16th Battalion, Royal Irish Rifles
Killed in action on Thursday 29 June 1916 (aged 18)
Thiepval Memorial, France (Pier and Face 15 A and 15 B)

James Morrison was born in Comber and he was a son of George and Eliza Jane Morrison (nee Donnan) who lived in the townland of Lisbane. They were married on 18 April 1881 in First Killyleagh Presbyterian Church. George Morrison was a farmer and he and Eliza Jane had at least eleven children including Mary Anna Charlotte, Ellen, Robert George, Martha, Eliza Jane, Sarah Donnan, William Thomas, James, Catherine and Agnes.

James Morrison worked as a clerk in the flax spinning mill of Messrs Andrews & Co in Comber and he was a member of the Comber Company of the North Down Ulster Volunteer Force. He joined the Young Citizen Volunteers at Randalstown in May 1915 and then transferred to the 16th Battalion Royal Irish Rifles (Pioneers). He went to France with the first draft of the 36th (Ulster) Division in 1915 and he was killed in action on 29 June 1916. Captain WR Whyte wrote to James's father to express his condolences and in the letter he described the circumstances of James's death. 'He was in the trenches with the rest of the company working when a shell exploded near him and killed him instantly'.

Rifleman James Morrison is commemorated on Comber and District War Memorial; on the Andrew's Mill Memorial Plaque and in both Killinchy Parish Church of Ireland and Killinchy Presbyterian Church.

Morrison, Robert
Sapper
No. 100645, 134th Army Troops Company, Corps of Royal Engineers
Died of wounds on Wednesday 5 September 1917 (aged 37)
Dozinghem Military Cemetery, Belgium (Grave V. A. 16)

Robert Morrison was born in Dundonald, he lived in Newtownards and in July 1915 he enlisted in Belfast. He was the only surviving son of John and Elizabeth Morrison who lived in 'Lindsay's Cottage' in the townland of Whitespots, Newtownards. Before the war Robert Morrison worked as a wheelwright and he enlisted on 20 May 1915 in Belfast. Sapper Robert Morrison served with the Corps of Royal Engineers on the Home Front before going to France on 1 February 1916 to work on road and rail construction there. He died of wounds on 5 September 1917 at a Casualty Clearing Station in France and his family placed a 'For King and Country' notice in the *Newtownards Chronicle*. William's death was deeply regretted by 'his aged father and mother and his only sister.'

Mo

Sapper Robert Morrison is commemorated on Newtownards and District War Memorial and it was his mother who signed the receipt for his medals on 16 September 1921.

Morrison, Walter
The name Walter Morrison is listed on Newtownards and District War Memorial and in the booklet produced for the Unveiling and Dedication Ceremony held on Saturday 26 May 1934 he is described as a Private in the Colonials. Desk searches and public appeals to date have yielded no further information.

Morrow, George
Private
No. 23606, 9th Battalion, Princess Victoria's (Royal Irish Fusiliers)
Killed in action on Thursday 16 August 1917 (aged 20)
Tyne Cot Memorial, Belgium (Panel 140 to 141)

George Morrow was born in the townland of Shankill in County Armagh and he was a son of James H Morrow who had addresses in both Newtownards (22 Church Street) and Lurgan (23 Victoria Street). George Morrow enlisted in Lurgan and he served with the 9th Battalion Royal Irish Fusiliers in 108th Brigade of the 36th (Ulster) Division.

SATURDAY, SEPTEMBER 22, 1917.

COUNTY DOWN AND THE WAR.

Private George Morrow was killed in action on 16 August 1917 at Langemarck although initially he was posted as missing in action.

Information Wanted.
Private George Morrow, Royal Irish Fusiliers, is missing since the 16th Aug., and is believed wounded and prisoner. Information will be very gratefully received by his father, 22 Church Street, Newtownards, or 23 Victoria Street, Lurgan.

There were rumours that he had been wounded and taken prisoner and his father appealed for information to be sent to either of his two addresses.

In July 1918 it was officially confirmed that Private George Morrow had been killed in action and he is commemorated on Newtownards and District War Memorial.

Mo

Morrow, James
Rifleman
No. 13/6013, 11th Battalion, Royal Irish Rifles
Killed in action on Saturday 1 July 1916 (aged 17)
Thiepval Memorial, France (Pier and Face 15 A and 15 B)

James Morrow was born on 20 November 1898 in Carrowdore and he was a son of James and Agnes Morrow (nee Coulter). They were married on 7 January 1898 in Ballycopeland Presbyterian Church. James enlisted at Clandeboye and he joined 13th Battalion Royal Irish Rifles. A short time later he was one of a contingent of men transferred from the 13th to the 11th Battalion Royal Irish Rifles and he went to the front with the 11th Battalion in 108th Brigade of the 36th (Ulster) Division. Rifleman James Morrow was killed in action on the first day of the Battle of the Somme. The last letter that he wrote was dated 30 June 1916 and addressed to his aunt Mrs Mary McGivern in Carrowdore.

In August 1916 his two uncles Samuel and Thomas Morrow and his two aunts Mrs Mary McGivern and Mrs Jane Burch placed a 'For King and Country' notice in the *Newtownards Chronicle*. A year later his aunts placed an 'Our Heroes – In Memoriam' notice and it contained the verse:

> 'He never shunned his country's call,
> But gladly gave his life – his all;
> He died, the helpless to defend,
> An Ulster soldier's noble end
> We little thought when he left home
> That he would ne'er return;
> That he so soon in death would sleep,
> And leave us here to mourn.'

Rifleman James Morrow is commemorated in Carrowdore Presbyterian Church.

Muckle, Hugh

Mu

Horseman
SS *Cabotia* (Glasgow), Mercantile Marine
Killed in action on Friday 20 October 1916 (aged 38)
Tower Hill Memorial, London

Hugh Muckle was born on 12 May 1878 and he was a grandson of Thomas and Agnes Muckle (nee Magill) who lived in the townland of Ballycopeland. They were married on 8 March 1853 in Ballycopeland Presbyterian Church. Thomas Muckle was a farmer and he and Agnes had at least two children – Agnes and Mary. Thomas Muckle died on 31 May 1911.

Hugh Muckle was a son of Agnes Muckle and he was baptised in Ballycopeland Presbyterian Church. Hugh worked on the family farm before he went to sea. Horseman Hugh Muckle was killed in action whilst serving aboard SS *Cabotia*. The SS *Cabotia* was a British merchant ship and on 20 October 1916 she was intercepted by German submarine U-69 and sunk by gunfire when she was 120 miles West-North-West of Tory Island on route from Montreal to Liverpool. More than 30 seamen died including the Captain. At the time of Hugh Muckle's death his mother Agnes was living in the townland of Killaughey, Donaghadee.

Mulholland, Hon. Andrew Edward Somerset
Captain
1st Battalion, Irish Guards
Killed in action on Sunday 1 November 1914 (aged 32)
Ypres Town Cemetery, Belgium (Grave E2. 3)

Captain the Hon. Andrew Edward Somerset Mulholland was the eldest son of Henry Lyle Mulholland 2nd Baron Dunleath and Baroness Dunleath (Norah Louisa Fanny Ward) who were married on 28 July 1881 and who lived in Ballywalter Park, Ballywalter. They had five children – Andrew Edward Somerset, Eva Norah Helen, Charles Henry George (3rd Baron), Henry George Hill and Godfrey John Arthur Murray Lyle.

Mu

Captain the Hon. Andrew Edward Somerset Mulholland married Lady Hester Joan Byng on 10 June 1913 and they lived at 22 Great Cumberland Place in London. They had one child, Daphne Norah Mulholland born on 11 March 1915, some 4½ months after her father died. Captain Mulholland 1st Battalion Irish Guards was killed in action on 1 November 1914 at the Battle of Ypes. Members of Downpatrick Cricket Club wrote to Lord Dunleath to express their sympathy and in his reply Lord Dunleath said that his son had been 'fighting for the cause of Christ in the world and for the British Empire'.

Captain the Hon. Andrew Edward Somerset Mulholland's three brothers were also on active service. In 1916 it was reported that the Hon. Henry George Hill Mulholland, who had been serving at the front, had suffered a serious breakdown in health and as a result he resigned his commission. When he recovered he rejoined as a Private and attended a cavalry training school in Ireland. Subsequently he was appointed Second Lieutenant. In 1917 it was reported that Captain the Hon. Charles Henry George Mulholland DSO had been appointed Brigade Major attached to Headquarters units and that Captain the Hon. Godfrey John Arthur Murray Lyle Mulholland was home on leave from France. In July 1915 he had returned home from Australia where he had been private secretary to the Governor of South Australia and he joined the Army Service Corps.

Captain the Hon. Andrew Edward Somerset Mulholland is commemorated on Ballywalter and District War Memorial; in Ballywalter Parish Church of Ireland (Holy Trinity) and on the North of Ireland [Rugby] Football Club Memorial Plaque.

Mulholland, George Ellison
Acting Bombardier
No. 275974, 15th Heavy Battery, Royal Garrison Artillery
Died on Saturday 27 October 1917
Beirut War Cemetery, Lebanese Republic (Grave 16)

In 'Soldiers Died in the Great War 1914 – 1919' it is recorded that George Ellison Mulholland was born in Newtownards and he enlisted in Weymouth. He served with the Royal Garrison Artillery (375974 in the CWGC Debt of Honour) and he went to Egypt on 24 July 1915. He died on 27 October 1917.

In the 1901 census it is recorded that a Mulholland family who were Presbyterians lived in the townland of Drumhirk, Newtownards. Cornelius Mulholland (a grocer aged 80 and Head of the family) lived with his wife Sarah (aged 60), his son George (a grocer's assistant aged 20) and his daughter Maria (aged 19).

Mu

Cornelius Mulholland from Drumhirk and Sarah Patterson from Craigavad were married on 10 February 1880 in St Enoch's Presbyterian Church Belfast. Sarah died on 4 May 1910 and Cornelius died on 18 October 1915 aged 95.

Desk searches and public appeals to date have not confirmed a connection between these 1901 census data and the soldier who is buried in Beirut War Cemetery.

Mulholland, Neil McLean (Neil)
Rifleman
No. 11471, 6th Battalion, Royal Irish Rifles
Killed in action on Wednesday 11 August 1915 (aged 39)
Helles Memorial, Gallipoli, Turkey (Panel 177 and 178)

Neil Mulholland was born in 1876 in Dumfries and he was a son of Captain William Mulholland (Master Mariner) and Agnes Mulholland (nee Heron). Agnes died on 2 March 1890 and William died on 14 April 1899. Neil Mulholland and Mary Jane McDade were married on 5 February 1907 in St Anne's Church of Ireland Belfast.

Neil Mulholland enlisted in Belfast, he served with the 6th Battalion Royal

Irish Rifles in 29th Brigade of the 10th (Irish) Division and he was killed in action at Gallipoli on 11 August 1915.

Rifleman Neil Mulholland is commemorated on the family grave headstone in Whitechurch Cemetery Ballywalter as is his wife Mary Jane who died on 17 March 1918 aged 32.

Mulholland, Walter
Private
No. 3176, 1st Battalion, Royal Inniskilling Fusiliers
Killed in action on Saturday 1 July 1916
Y Ravine Cemetery, France (Grave D. 102)

In 'Soldiers Died in the Great War 1914 – 1919' it is recorded that Walter Mulholland was born in Newtownards and he enlisted in Belfast. He served with the 1st Battalion Royal Inniskilling Fusiliers in 87th Brigade of the 29th Division and he went to Gallipoli on 12 August 1915. After being evacuated from Gallipoli in January 1916 he went to France in March 1916 and he was killed in action on the first day of the Battle of the Somme.

Mu

Mullan, Alexander
Rifleman
No. 18521, 'B' Company, 13th Battalion, Royal Irish Rifles
Killed in action on Saturday 1 July 1916 (aged 20)
Thiepval Memorial, France (Pier and Face 15 A and 15 B)

In some records the surname is spelt Mullen.

Alexander Mullan was born in Comber and he was a son of James and Lizzie Mullan (nee Fisher) who lived in Mill Street. They were married on 6 October 1887 in Comber Parish Church of Ireland. James Mullan worked as a railway plate layer and he and Lizzie had at least seven children – Sarah, Jane, George, Charles, Alexander, Agnes and Minnie.

Alexander Mullan worked as a doffer before he enlisted in Comber. He served with the 13th Battalion Royal Irish Rifles in 108th Brigade of the 36th (Ulster) Division and he was killed in action on

Pte. Alexander Mullen, killed, Castle Street, Comber.

the first day of the Battle of the Somme. At that time the Mullan family lived in Castle Street, Comber.

Rifleman Alexander Mullan is commemorated on Comber and District War Memorial and in Comber Parish Church of Ireland (St Mary).

Mullan Brothers: David and Hugh

David and Hugh Mullan were sons of William and Mary Anne Mullan (nee McDowell) who lived in Movilla Street Newtownards and who were married on 23 October 1875 in Newtownards Parish Church of Ireland. William Mullan worked as a general labourer and he and Mary had at least five children – John, Hugh, William, David Swan and Margaret Jane. David and Hugh Mullan were baptised in Greenwell Street Presbyterian Church Newtownards. David was the first of the two brothers to die on active service in the Great War:

Mullan, David Swan (David)
Rifleman
No. 16855, 'B' Company, 13th Battalion, Royal Irish Rifles
Killed in action on Saturday 1 July 1916 (aged 29)
Thiepval Memorial, France (Pier and Face 15 A and 15 B)

Mu

David Swan Mullan was born on 6 April 1887 in Newtownards and he worked as a general labourer before he enlisted in Belfast. He served with the 13th Battalion Royal Irish Rifles in 108th Brigade of the 36th (Ulster) Division and he was killed in action on the first day of the Battle of the Somme.

Mullan, Hugh
Private
No. 30255, 11th Battalion, Royal Scots Fusiliers
Died of wounds on Sunday 22 October 1916 (aged 33)
Thiepval Memorial, France (Pier and Face 6 D and 7 D)

His surname is spelt McMullan in the CWGC Debt of Honour.

Hugh Mullan was born on 24 September 1883 in Newtownards and he enlisted in Alloa, Clackmannanshire. He served with the 11th Battalion Royal Scots Fusiliers and he died of wounds on 22 October 1916. His family placed a 'For King and Country' notice in the 2 December 1916 edition of the *Newtownards Chronicle* and it included the lines:

'For his country nobly he died,
We grieve, yet dark sorrow is lit by pride.
God's will be done.'

Both Rifleman David Mullan and Private Hugh Mullan are commemorated on Newtownards and District War Memorial and in the PCI Roll of Honour for Greenwell Street Presbyterian Church Newtownards.

Mullan, James
Lance Sergeant
No. 6637, 'G' Company, 2nd Battalion, Royal Irish Rifles
Died of wounds on Sunday 28 November 1915 (aged 39)
Le Bizet Cemetery, France (Grave B. 4)

Mu

James Mullan was born in the townland of Ballyblack, Newtownards. He worked as a farm labourer and he and his wife Mary Elizabeth had at least five children including Sarah, Thomas John, Hugh and William David (born 1911). Having previously been a Reservist with the 4th Battalion Royal Irish Rifles (Royal North Downs) James rejoined the colours in Newtownards at the outbreak of the Great War. He was attached to the 2nd Battalion Royal Irish Rifles and he was posted to the Western Front in October 1914.

Lance Sergeant James Mullan was granted a week's home leave in September 1915 and he was only back in the firing line for about two months when he died on 28 November 1915 of wounds sustained while he was with a working party repairing communication trenches. At that time his wife and family were living at 6 Darragh's Lane, Church Street, Newtownards.

Lance Sergeant James Mullan is commemorated on Newtownards and District War Memorial and in the PCI Roll of Honour for Greenwell Street Presbyterian Church Newtownards.

Mullen, Patrick
Rifleman
No. 6694, 'B' Company, 1st Battalion, Royal Irish Rifles
Killed in action on Tuesday 11 April 1916 (aged 30)
Becourt Military Cemetery, France (Grave I. H. 2)

Patrick Mullen was born in Newtownards and he was a son of John and Grace Mullen. Information from one source suggests that Grace's maiden name was Busby and that she and John were married on 10 August 1865 in

Newtownards Registry Office. Patrick was described in the press as 'an all-round athlete'. He moved to Belfast where he lived at 31 English Street. He was a special Reservist who was called up at the outbreak of war and he served with the 1st Battalion Royal Irish Rifles.

Rifleman Patrick Mullen was killed in action on 11 April 1916 during heavy enemy bombardment of the trenches and at that time his wife Ellen and their two children were living at 22 Tun Street, Belfast. Patrick had three brothers on active service – Drum-Major John Mullen (Connaught Rangers), Private Hugh Mullen (Royal Inniskilling Fusiliers) and Rifleman William Mullen (Royal Irish Rifles, wounded at Neuve Chapelle). Rifleman Patrick Mullen is commemorated in the Belfast Book of Honour (Page 492).

Mu

Another Newtownards Soldier Killed in Action.

Bugler P. Mullen, Royal Irish Rifles, killed in action on the 11th ult., was 31 years of age. He was a native of Newtownards, resided at 31 English Street, Belfast, and as a special reservist was called up on the outbreak of war. Deceased was an all-round athlete. Three of his brothers are serving in the Army, viz., Drum-Major John Mullen, Connaught Rangers ; Private Hugh Mullen, Inniskilling Fusiliers ; and Rifleman Wm. Mullen, Royal Irish Rifles (wounded at Neuve Chapelle). Deceased is survived by his wife and two children.

Murphy, Joseph
Private
No. 20055, 8th Battalion, Royal Dublin Fusiliers
Killed in action on Saturday 9 September 1916
Thiepval Memorial, France (Pier and Face 16 C)

In 'Soldiers Died in the Great War 1914 – 1919' it is recorded that Joseph Murphy was born in Newtownards and he enlisted in Dundalk. He served with the 8th Battalion Royal Dublin Fusiliers in 48th Brigade of the 16th (Irish) Division. Private Joseph Murphy was killed in action at Ginchy on 9 September 1916.

Murphy, Robert
Master
SS *Lough Fisher*, Mercantile Marine
Killed on Saturday 30 March 1918 (aged 37)
Tower Hill Memorial, London, England

Robert Murphy was born on 18 March 1881 and he was a son of William John and Susanne Murphy (nee McClement) who lived in Ballywalter. They were married on 29 June 1869 in Ballywalter Parish Church of Ireland.

William John and Susanne had at least eight children – Hugh, Charles (died), Robert, Charles, David, Agnes, James and Andrew. Robert Murphy went to sea and he and his wife Jane (Jeannie) (nee Henry) lived at 1 Dunleath Terrace, Ballywalter. They were married on 20 November 1911 in Glastry Presbyterian Church and they had at least two children – Irena (born 30 August 1913) and Robert (born 12 August 1914). Both children were baptised in Ballywalter Presbyterian Church.

Captain Robert Murphy was killed when his ship, the SS *Lough Fisher*, was shelled and sunk by a German submarine 12 miles South East of Cork on 30 March 1918. He is commemorated on Ballywalter and District War Memorial and on the family grave headstone in Whitechurch Cemetery Ballywalter.

Murray, Henry Alan
Lance Corporal
No. 18/20311, 12th Battalion, Royal Irish Rifles
Killed in action on Monday 15 April 1918 (aged 19)
Tyne Cot Memorial, Belgium (Panel 138 to 140 & 162 to 162 A & 163 A)

Mu

Henry Alan Murray was born in 1899 and he was the only son of Dr John James Goodalatte Murray FRCS and Mrs Isabel Murray who lived at 112 Liscard Road, Liscard, Cheshire. His mother continued to live there after his father died.

In 'Soldiers Died in the Great War 1914 – 1919' it is recorded that Henry Alan Murray lived in Newtownards and he enlisted in Clandeboye. He joined the 18th Battalion Royal Irish Rifles and he went to the front with the 12th Battalion in 108th Brigade of the 36th (Ulster) Division. Lance Corporal Henry Alan Murray was killed in action during the German offensive on 15 April 1918 and he is commemorated on the QUB War Memorial and in the QUB Book of Remembrance (Page 17).

Murray, Joseph
Private
No. 5592, 6th Battalion, Connaught Rangers
Killed in action on Thursday 8 March 1917
Kemmel Chateau Military Cemetery, Belgium (Grave M. 75)

Joseph Murray was born in Newtownards, he lived in Newtownards, he enlisted in Lurgan and he served with the 6th Battalion Connaught Rangers in 47th Brigade of the 16th (Irish) Division. He went to Gallipoli on 3 October 1915 and from there via Salonika to the Western Front. Private Joseph

Murray was killed in action on 8 March 1917 and he is commemorated on Newtownards and District War Memorial and in Newtownards Parish Church of Ireland (St Mark).

In the booklet produced for the Unveiling and Dedication of Newtownards and District War Memorial held on Saturday 26 May 1934 Joseph Murray is described as a Rifleman in the Royal Irish Rifles.

Murray, Samuel
Rifleman
**No. 20/292, 14th Battalion, Royal Irish Rifles
Killed in action on Thursday 16 August 1917 (aged 23)
Tyne Cot Memorial, Belgium (Panel 138 to 140 & 162 to 162 A & 163 A)**

Samuel Murray was the fourth son of James and Elizabeth Murray (nee Cameron) who lived in the townland of Ballyblack, Newtownards. They were married on 28 April 1879 in Ballyblack Presbyterian Church. James Murray worked as a road contractor and farmer and he and Elizabeth had twelve children – William Hugh, James, John, Susanna, Maggie Elizabeth, Samuel, Isabella Boyd, David Sidney, Frederick, Lily, Cecil and Henry Campbell Bannerman. The children were all baptised in Ballyblack Presbyterian Church. Prior to the outbreak of the Great War Samuel lived with two of his sisters, Maggie and Bella, at 129 Greenwell Street in Newtownards. Samuel's father James died on 24 February 1929.

Mu

After the outbreak of the Great War Samuel Murray was engaged in munitions work and he joined the Army in May 1917. After three months training he was drafted to France in August 1917 and after two weeks at the Base he was sent up to the front line. It was reported that he went over the top at Langemarck on his 23rd birthday and that Rifleman Samuel Murray was killed in action that day.

Initially Rifleman Samuel Murray was posted as missing in action and in November 1917 it was officially confirmed that he had been killed in action.

At that time his brother Sidney was also on active service with the Royal Irish Rifles. Sidney Murray was shot in the eye, the bullet coming out through the back of his head. He survived the Great War but spent the remainder of his life in hospital at Downpatrick.

Samuel's father, mother, sisters and brothers placed a 'For King and Country' notice in the *Newtownards Chronicle* and it contained the verse:

> *'What'er we fondly call our own*
> *Belongs to Heaven's Great Lord;*
> *The blessings lent us for a day*
> *Are soon to be restored'*

At a morning service in Ballyblack Presbyterian Church the Rev R Graham conveyed sympathy to the Murray family on behalf of the congregation. He based his words on the text, 'Greater love hath no man than this that a man lay down his life for his friends' (St John 15:13). Speaking about Samuel, the Rev Graham said, 'like all good soldiers he hated war and loathed the very thought of having to kill a fellow-man yet he saw there was no other way of saving the world from the brutality and fiendishness of militarism and he went to do his duty like a man'.

In August 1918 Samuel's family placed an 'In Memoriam' notice in the *Newtownards Chronicle*, as did Annie Bell from Kilmarnock. Annie Bell's notice contained the verse:

> *'In dreams I see his dear sweet face*
> *And kiss his wounded brow,*
> *And whisper as I loved him then*
> *I love his memory now.'*

In 2011 the Murray family is continuing its efforts to trace the family of Annie Bell. Samuel Murray is commemorated on Newtownards and District War Memorial and in Ballyblack Presbyterian Church.

Neill, James

The name James Neill is listed on Newtownards and District War Memorial and in the booklet produced for the Unveiling and Dedication Ceremony held on Saturday 26 May 1934 he is described as a Rifleman in the Royal Irish Rifles. Desk searches and public appeals to date have yielded no further information.

Nelson, Albert Edward (Albert)
Rifleman
No. 18/827, 12th Battalion, Royal Irish Rifles
Killed in action on Thursday 22 November 1917 (aged 22)
Cambrai Memorial, France (Panel 10)

Albert Edward Nelson was a son of Hans and Sarah Nelson (nee Frame). Albert Edward and his sisters Martha and Anna lived with their uncles James and Robert Frame and their grandmother Isabella Frame in the townland of Carnesure, Comber. Both James and Robert Frame worked as flax dressers.

> **Comber Rifleman Killed.**
> Rifleman Albert Nelson, Royal Irish Rifles, killed in action on 22nd December, was a brother of Miss Martha Nelson, Carnesure, Comber, and nephew of Mr. James Frame, of Carnesure.

Albert Nelson enlisted in Newtownards in November 1915 and he joined the 18th Battalion Royal Irish Rifles. He went to the front with the 12th Battalion Royal Irish Rifles in 108th Brigade of the 36th (Ulster) Division and he was killed in action at Cambrai on 22 November 1917. Rifleman Albert Nelson is commemorated on Comber and District War Memorial and in Comber Non-Subscribing Presbyterian Church.

N

Nelson, Samuel Horace
Lance Corporal
No. 47497, Liverpool Regiment, transferred to (47645), 18th Battalion, Manchester Regiment
Killed in action on Wednesday 31 October 1917 (aged 20)
Messines Ridge British Cemetery, Belgium (Grave III. D. 25)

Samuel Horace Nelson was born in 1897 in Toxteth, Liverpool and he was a son of Samuel and Elizabeth Nelson (nee Parkinson) who lived at 52 Beaumont Street, Liverpool. They were married in 1891 in West Derby, Lancashire. Samuel Horace Nelson enlisted in Liverpool and he served with the Liverpool Regiment (47497) before being transferred to the Manchester Regiment.

> **FOR KING AND COUNTRY.**
> NELSON—October 31, 1917, killed in action, Lance-Corporal Samuel Horace, aged 20 years, youngest son of Mr. and Mrs. S. Nelson, 52 Beaumont Street, Liverpool.

Lance Corporal Nelson was killed in action on 31 October 1917 and his parents placed a 'For King and Country' notice in the 10 November 1917 edition of the *Newtownards Chronicle*.

Desk searches and public appeals to date have yielded no further information about his connection with the Ards area.

Newell Brothers: Charles and Thomas

Charles and Thomas Newell were born in Millisle and they were sons of Thomas and Eliza Newell (nee Kerr) who were married on 7 January 1889 in Ballycopeland Presbyterian Church. They lived in the townland of Ballymacruise, Carrowdore. Thomas Newell Senior worked as a labourer and he and Eliza had at least eight children including Lizzie, Thomas, Mary, Maggie Jane, Charlie, George and Alexander. Four of the children including Charles (but not Thomas) were baptised in Millisle Presbyterian Church. Later the Newell family moved to South Street, Newtownards. Charles was the first of the two brothers to be killed in action:

Newell, Charles (Charlie)
Rifleman (Bandsman)
No. 18559, 'B' Company, 13th Battalion, Royal Irish Rifles
Killed in action on Monday 7 February 1916 (aged 19)
Mesnil Ridge Cemetery, France (Grave G. 6)

N

Charles Newell was born on 12 April 1896. Prior to the outbreak of the Great War he worked as a rougher in the Castle Gardens Mill in Newtownards. He was a member of True Blues Loyal Orange Lodge No. 1055 in Newtownards and also of the North Down Regiment of the Ulster Volunteer Force.

Bandsman Charlie Newell was one of four Ardsmen who were killed in action together on 7 February 1916. They were all members of the 13th (Service) Battalion of the Royal Irish Rifles (1st Co Down Volunteers) serving with 108th Brigade in the 36th (Ulster) Division. The others were Rifleman **James Calvert** from the townland of Tullycore, Killinchy, Rifleman **David McConnell** of 22 Wallace's Street No. 2, Newtownards and Rifleman **Jack Tate** of Francis Street and North Street, Newtownards.

18559 RIFLEMAN
C. NEWELL
ROYAL IRISH RIFLES
7TH FEBRUARY 1916 AGE 19

The officer in charge of the platoon was Lieutenant **Elliott Johnston**, a son of Samuel Johnston JP, Glen Printing and Finishing Works in Newtownards. He described the circumstances of their deaths. During a heavy bombardment a shell from the German lines exploded in the midst of a party of men killing three and wounding three. James Calvert, David McConnell and Charlie Newell were killed outright; Jack Tate died later from his injuries. The three men who died immediately were laid to rest together and the burial service was conducted by one of the brigade chaplains, the Rev Charles Campbell Manning, Rector of Comber. On that occasion Lieutenant Johnston escaped injury but he was killed in action five months later on the first day of the Battle of the Somme. Charlie Newell's brother Thomas was also killed in action on 1 July 1916.

After the death of Rifleman Charlie Newell there were two notices in the 19 February 1916 edition of the *Newtownards Chronicle*. One was from his mother, sisters and brothers and one was from Lord Londonderry's Own CLB Flute Band of which Charlie had been a member.

Newell, Thomas
Rifleman (Bandsman)
No. 18/87, 11th Battalion, Royal Irish Rifles
Killed in action on Saturday 1 July 1916 (aged 26)
Thiepval Memorial, France (Pier and Face 15 A and 15 B)

Prior to the outbreak of the Great War Thomas Newell worked as a general labourer and like Charlie he was a member of Loyal Orange Lodge No. 1055. He enlisted in Belfast in May 1915 and he joined the 18th Battalion Royal Irish Rifles. He went to France on 5 October 1915 with the 11th Battalion Royal Irish Rifles in 108th Brigade of the 36th (Ulster) Division and he was killed in action on the first day of the Battle of the Somme while he was in the Lewis Gun Section of the Battalion. Initially he was reported as missing in action and the following May it was officially confirmed that he had been killed.

N

There were two 'For King and Country' notices in the 26 May 1917 edition of the *Newtownards Chronicle*, one from his mother, sisters and brothers and one from Lord Londonderry's Own CLB Flute Band of which Thomas, like Charlie, had been a member. The family notice included the verse:

> *'Forth into the dreadful battle*
> *The steadfast soldier goes'*
> *No friend when he lies dying*
> *His eyes to kiss and close;*
> *Yet never alone is the Christian,*
> *Who lives by faith and prayer,*

For God is a friend unchanging,
And God is everywhere.'

Brothers Charlie and Thomas Newell were killed in action within five months of each other and both are commemorated on Newtownards and District War Memorial and in Second Newtownards Presbyterian Church. Charles Newell is also commemorated in *Ballymoney Heroes 1914 – 1918* (Page 75).

Niblock, Robert Douglas
Private
No. 421, 8th Battalion, 2nd Infantry Brigade, AIF
Died of wounds Sunday 25 April / Monday 3 May 1915 (aged 32)
Alexandria (Chatby) Military and War Memorial Cemetery, Egypt
(Grave E. 94)

Robert Douglas Niblock was born in March 1883 and he was the fourth son of James and Agnes Niblock who lived in Comber. He moved to Australia in 1901 where he worked as a bricklayer. He enlisted on 22 August 1914 at Broadmeadows in the state of Victoria and he joined the Australian Imperial Force. In his attestation papers it was noted that Robert Douglas Niblock was 5 feet 7 inches tall and he cited his brother John as his next-of-kin. Robert's papers provide an example of how confusion concerning place-names can arise. In his papers it is recorded that Robert Douglas Niblock was born 'in the parish of Cumber near the town of Belfast in the county of Antram'.

Robert was wounded during the landings at Gallipoli and the date of his death is not known precisely. In his records it is stated that he died of wounds sometime between 25 April and 3 May 1915.

Comber-Australian Soldier Killed.

Mr. John Niblock, Bridge Street, Comber, has received information that his brother, Private Robert D. Niblock, 8th Battalion Australian Infantry, has died of wounds at the Dardanelles on 10th inst. Mr. Niblock left for Australia about fourteen years ago, and when war broke out he immediately volunteered for active service. He was the fourth son of the late Mr. James Niblock, of Comber, and a younger brother of Mr. James Niblock, the well-known North Down cricketer and hockey player. He leaves a wife and son in Australia.

At the time of Robert's death his wife Louisa Elizabeth Dickson Niblock lived at 275 Hyde Street, Yarraville, Victoria, Australia. They had one son – Ronald Stanley James Niblock. Robert's brother John lived in Bridge Street, Comber and after he was notified about Robert's death John placed a death notice in the *Newtownards Chronicle*.

Robert's widow was granted a war pension of £52 per annum and his son Ronald Stanley James Niblock was granted a war pension of £15 per annum, both with effect from 10 July 1915. The inventory of his effects shows that he had an identity disc, a note-book, a wrist-watch and a Testament. These belongings were sent to his widow in 'a brown paper parcel'.

Private Robert Douglas Niblock is commemorated on Comber and District War Memorial; in Comber Non-Subscribing Presbyterian Church and in the Belfast Book of Honour (Page 506).

Nicholas, Thomas Lewis
Second Mate
SS *Beatrice* (London), Mercantile Marine
Drowned on Friday 20 July 1917 (aged 26)
Tower Hill Memorial, London, England

Thomas Lewis Nicholas was born in the townland of Balligan and he was a son of Thomas Lewis Nicholas and Margaret (Maggie) Nicholas (nee Johnston) who were married on 9 February 1886 in Ballywalter Presbyterian Church. Thomas Lewis Nicholas Senior came from Newquay in Cardiganshire, Wales and, like his father before him, he worked as a sailor. Maggie Johnston came from Balligan where her father David was a farmer.

Thomas Lewis Nicholas drowned on 20 July 1917 when the SS *Beatrice* was torpedoed by the German submarine UC-47 and sank in the English Channel around ten miles from the Lizard. Built in 1890 and with a gross register tonnage (GRT) of 712 the SS *Beatrice* was on a voyage from Penarth in the Vale of Glamorgan to Rouen in France with a cargo of coal.

At the time of his death Second Mate Thomas Lewis Nicholas's parents were living at Caedelyn, Mount Pleasant in Swansea.

N

Nisbet, Archibald
Private
No. 25257, 3rd Battalion, Highland Light Infantry
Died of consumption on Monday 13 January 1919 (aged 29)
Newtownards (Movilla) Cemetery, (Grave 1. 104)

Archibald Nisbet was born in Galston, Ayr in Scotland and he was a son of Mr and Mrs James Nisbet. In civilian life he was employed by the firm of Edward Watson in Argyll Street, Glasgow.

Archibald Nisbet and Jane (Jeannie) Maddock were married on 14 January 1916 in Newtownards Parish Church of Ireland and they lived at 25 Balfour Street, Newtownards with Jeannie's father Thomas Maddock. Thomas Maddock was head of the engineering department at the Ards Weaving

Company and it was reported in the 22 February 1919 edition of the *Newtownards Chronicle* that he had 23 near relatives who had served or were serving in the war – two sons, two sons-in-law and nineteen nephews. Six of them died including Archibald Nisbet (son-in-law) and **William Maddock** (nephew).

NISBET—January 13th, 1919, at the residence of his father-in-law (Thomas Maddock, 25 Balfour Street, Newtownards), Archibald Nisbet, formerly employed by Mr. Edward Watson, Argyll Street, Glasgow, and late of 14th Highland Light Infantry. His remains were interred in Movilla Cemetery on Wednesday afternoon, 15th inst.

His weary hours and days of pain,
His troubled nights are past:
His ever patient wornout frame
Has found sweet rest at last.

Deeply regretted by his sorrowing Wife and Child,
JEANNIE NISBET.
(Glasgow papers please copy.)

Archibald and Jeannie Nisbet had one child, a son named Thomas Archibald Maddock Nisbet. After Private Archibald Nisbet died Jeannie placed a notice in the *Newtownards Chronicle* and it contained the verse:

'His weary hours and days of pain,
His troubled nights are past;
His ever patient worn out frame
Has found sweet rest at last'

Private Archibald Nisbet is commemorated on Newtownards and District War Memorial.

Norris, Thomas
Private
No. 23066, 'D' Company, 9th Battalion, Royal Inniskilling Fusiliers
Killed in action on Saturday 1 July 1916 (aged 18)
Thiepval Memorial, France (Pier and Face 4 D and 5 B)

Thomas Norris was born in Newtownards and he was a son of Henry and Margaret Norris who lived at 23 Movilla Street. Henry Norris worked as a general dealer and he and Margaret had at least nine children including Jessie, Thomas, Elizabeth, Harry, Maggie, Edgar and John.

Thomas Norris enlisted in Newtownards, he served with the 9th Battalion Royal Inniskilling Fusiliers in 109th Brigade of the 36th (Ulster) Division and he was killed in action on the first day of the Battle of the Somme.

At the time of Thomas's death his parents were living at 9 Kingswood Street in Belfast and Private Thomas Norris is commemorated in the Belfast Book of Honour (Page 509).

O'Lone Brothers: Robert James and Walter Percy
Robert James and Walter Percy O'Lone were sons of Quartermaster Sergeant John O'Lone who was stationed at Victoria Barracks in Belfast. John O'Lone

was a native of Belfast and he and his wife Mary lived in Bog Road, Pottinger before they moved to Castleview Road, Knock. The O'Lone family moved to Victoria Road in Bangor and then to the townland of Loughriscouse between Newtownards and Donaghadee. John and Mary O'Lone had at least eleven children including Henrietta Eleanor, John Alexander, Edith Mary, Robert James, Harry Ralph, Walter Percy and Gertrude Caroline.

In the letters column of the 6 March 1915 edition of the *Newtownards Chronicle* there was a tribute to Quartermaster Sergeant John O'Lone who had rejoined the Royal Irish Rifles in October 1914. At 73 years of age he was still hale and hearty and 'felt fit for several more years of service'. Having first enlisted in 1859 he had served for 34 years in the Army and saw service in many places including India, China, Japan, South Africa and Mauritius. He was awarded the Meritorious Service Medal and the Long Service and Good Conduct Medal. John O'Lone lived to see two of his soldier sons killed in action in the Great War. Walter Percy O'Lone was the first of the two brothers to die:

O'Lone, Walter Percy
Distinguished Conduct Medal
Mentioned in Despatches
Captain
2nd Battalion, Royal Irish Rifles
Killed in action on Saturday 25 September 1915 (aged 25)
Ypres (Menin Gate) Memorial, Belgium (Panel 40)

O

Captain Walter Percy O'Lone was born in 1890 in Belfast and he enlisted on 20 May 1905. He served as a Rifleman in the 2nd Battalion Royal Irish Rifles and was promoted to the rank of Sergeant in February 1914. He was wounded at Aisne in September 1914 and then severely wounded at Ypres in November 1914. He had a toe amputated and was hospitalised in England.

Described as 'an exceptionally smart officer' Walter Percy O'Lone won his commission from the ranks in April 1915. He was awarded the DCM as a Sergeant (7511) for 'conspicuous gallantry on numerous occasions under the most difficult circumstances, especially at Illies, and also for gallantry in voluntarily conveying most important messages under heavy rifle fire and shell fire on two occasions.'

Captain Walter Percy O'Lone was killed in action during an attack at Hooge on 25 September 1915. Ground conditions were very muddy and this slowed progress as well as making the advancing soldiers easier targets for enemy gunfire. Captain Walter O'Lone did reach the German trenches but he was killed there. His brother Bob survived this action but Bob was killed in action two months later.

At the time of Walter Percy O'Lone's death his wife Annie was living at 'Belle Vista', Ballynahinch – they had been married for only six months. Walter Percy O'Lone and Annie Spence were married on 18 March 1915 in All Saints Parish Church of Ireland Belfast. Annie O'Lone died on 14 July 1945 aged 49 and she is buried in Movilla New Cemetery, Newtownards.

O'Lone, Robert James (Bob)
Mentioned in Despatches
Captain
2nd Battalion, Royal Irish Rifles
Killed in action on Thursday 11 November 1915 (aged 31)
Tancrez Farm Cemetery, Belgium (Grave I. G. 14)

O

Captain Robert James O'Lone was born in 1884 in Belfast and he enlisted on 29 March 1902. Like his brother he served with the 2nd Battalion Royal Irish Rifles and he won his commission from the ranks.

Robert James O'Lone and Gladys Louise Edwards were married on 22 August 1912 in the Wesleyan Chapel in Dover and they had at least two children – Robert John and Gladys Mary. Robert John O'Lone served in the Army and he rose to the rank of Colonel. He fought in Burma during the Second World War and he was awarded the DSO. In his turn, Robert John's son Brigadier Digby O'Lone also served in the Army.

Captain Robert James O'Lone was killed near Le Bizet at 9.30 pm on 11 November 1915 when he visited a listening post whilst engaged in reconnoitring duty. Captain O'Lone died soon after being shot in the stomach and his comrades laid him to rest. At the time of Robert James O'Lone's death his wife was living at 11 Grove Avenue, Twickenham, Middlesex.

Captain Robert James O'Lone and Captain Walter Percy O'Lone are both commemorated on Newtownards and District War Memorial; in First Newtownards Presbyterian Church and in the Belfast Book of Honour (Page

514). Captain Robert James O'Lone is also commemorated on Dover War Memorial.

O'Neill Brothers: John and William

John and William O'Neill were sons of Samuel and Sarah O'Neill (nee Bell) who lived at 34 William Street, Newtownards, and who were married on 11 May 1888 in Glastry Presbyterian Church. Samuel O'Neill worked as an agricultural labourer and he and Sarah had at least nine children – Martha, William, Mary, John, James Alexander, Ellen, Samuel, Thomas and David. The first three were baptised in Glastry Presbyterian Church and the rest in Greenwell Street Presbyterian Church Newtownards. James Alexander O'Neill (18577) served with the Royal Irish Rifles and before that he worked as an employee of the *Newtownards Chronicle*. John O'Neill was the first of the two brothers to be killed in action although William's death was the first to be confirmed:

O'Neill, John
Corporal
No. 18576, 'B' Company, 13th Battalion, Royal Irish Rifles
Killed in action on Saturday 1 July 1916 (aged 22)
Thiepval Memorial, France (Pier and Face 15 A and 15 B)

O

John O'Neill was born on 25 May 1894 and he was the second son of Samuel and Sarah O'Neill. Prior to the outbreak of the Great War John worked as a labourer in a factory.

John O'Neill enlisted in Newtownards and he joined the 13th Battalion Royal Irish Rifles (1st County Down Volunteers). He went to France with 108th Brigade of the 36th (Ulster) Division and he was posted as missing in action after the first day of the Battle of the Somme. Over the ensuing months his parents received a succession of bad news. John's brother William was posted as missing in action on 3 September 1916 and his brother James Alexander was wounded and in hospital.

In October 1916 it was officially confirmed that Corporal John O'Neill had been killed in action on 1 July 1916 but this confirmation came *after* the official confirmation that Private William O'Neill had been killed in action on 3 September 1916

Sarah O'Neill died within a year of her two sons being killed. She was in her late forties. In July 1917 the O'Neill family placed an 'Our Heroes – In Memoriam' notice in the *Newtownards Chronicle* and it contained the verse:

'We prayed that God would guard him,
And shield him in the fray;
But alas! our hopes were blighted
When the sad news came that day'

O'Neill, William
Private
No. 10395, 'D' Company, 2nd Battalion, King's Own Scottish Borderers
Killed in action on Sunday 3 September 1916 (aged 26)
Delville Wood Cemetery, France (Grave XXIII. K. 5)

William O'Neill was born on 26 May 1890 and he was the eldest son of Samuel and Sarah O'Neill. He served with the King's Own Scottish Borderers and he was killed in action on 3 September 1916.

In September 1917 the O'Neill family placed an 'Our Heroes – In Memoriam' notice in the *Newtownards Chronicle* and it contained the verse:

'He little thought when leaving home,
It would be his last good-bye;
But some day we hope to meet him
In that happy home on high'

Corporal John O'Neill and Private William O'Neill are both commemorated on Newtownards and District War Memorial and in the PCI Roll of Honour for Greenwell Street Presbyterian Church.

O'Neill, John
Rifleman
No. 19157, 'B' Company, 13th Battalion, Royal Irish Rifles
Killed in action on Saturday 1 July 1916 (aged 25)
Thiepval Memorial, France (Pier and Face 15 A and 15 B)

John O'Neill was born on 1 August 1890 in Ballywalter and he was a son of James and Eliza O'Neill (nee Bell). They were married on 17 January 1881 in Ballywalter Presbyterian Church. James O'Neill worked as an agricultural labourer and he and Eliza had at least nine children all of whom were baptised in Ballywalter Presbyterian Church – Mary Jane, James (died 1903 aged 19), Sarah, Eliza, John, Samuel, Maggie, Annie and William.

Prior to the outbreak of the Great War John worked as a general labourer. He enlisted in Ballywalter and served with the 13th Battalion Royal Irish Rifles in 108th Brigade of the 36th (Ulster) Division. Rifleman John O'Neill was killed in action on the first day of the Battle of the Somme and he is commemorated on Ballywalter and District War Memorial and in Ballywalter Presbyterian Church. He is also commemorated on the family grave headstone in Whitechurch Cemetery Ballywalter. John's mother died just four weeks after her son, on 29 July 1916 aged 58.

O

Oliver, Ellis
Private
No. 16322, 6th Battalion, Princess Victoria's (Royal Irish Fusiliers)
Killed in action on Friday 10 September 1915 (aged 26)
Helles Memorial, Gallipoli, Turkey (Panel 178 to 180)

Ellis Oliver was born in County Antrim and he was the eldest son of Andrew Johnston Oliver and Mary Oliver (nee Brown) who moved to Castle Street, Comber. They were married on 25 January 1887 in Kilbride Parish Church of Ireland Newtownabbey. Andrew Oliver worked as a merchant tailor and he and Mary had at least nine children including Ellis, William, Mary, John, Matilda and Mabel.

Ellis Oliver served with the 6th Battalion Royal Irish Fusiliers in 31st Brigade of the 10th (Irish) Division and he was killed in action on 10 September 1915 at the Dardanelles

Private Ellis Oliver is commemorated on Comber and District War Memorial and in First Comber Presbyterian Church.

Oliver, William
Fireman
No. 924181, HMS *Mechanician*, Royal Navy Reserve
Killed in action on Sunday 20 January 1918 (aged 33)
Plymouth Naval Memorial, Devon, England (Panel 31)

William Oliver was born in Newtownards and he was the fourth son of George and Jane Oliver (nee Harrison) who lived in East Street. They were married on 27 June 1874 in Newtownards Parish Church of Ireland. George Oliver worked as a weaver, Jane worked as an embroiderer and they had at least fourteen children including Jane, Lena, George, James, William, Lizzie, Hugh, Harry and Minnie.

Four of William's brothers served before and/or during the Great War. James served during the South African Campaign, he went to France in 1914 and was presented with a certificate for bravery under shell fire. Harry served with the 1st Leinster Regiment and was seriously wounded. It was reported that he was recommended for the Distinguished Conduct Medal. George was wounded in the South African Campaign and served with a Home Battalion during the Great War. Hugh served with the Royal Irish Rifles in India before moving to Canada where he worked in a munitions factory during the Great War.

William Oliver served as a Fireman aboard HMS *Mechanician* and he died when this ship was torpedoed by a submarine on 20 January 1918 to the west of St Catherine's Point, the southernmost point on the Isle of Wight.

William Oliver and Agnes Whitford were married on 18 January 1906 in Trinity Parish Church of Ireland Belfast and they had at least one child, a daughter named Ruth who was born in 1910. At the time of William's death Agnes and Ruth were living at 41 Linwood Street, Belfast and before that at 18 Byron Street with Agnes's widowed mother. William's parents, brothers, sisters, wife and daughter placed a joint 'For King and Country' notice in the *Newtownards Chronicle* and it contained the line:

'Gone but not forgotten'

Fireman William Oliver is commemorated on Newtownards and District War Memorial.

Orr Family: Andrew, Francis, Hugh and John

When Andrew Orr was killed in action on 31 July 1916 the patriotism of the Orr family was reported in the *Newtownards Chronicle*. The relationship of each family member to Andrew's father John was described:

John's son **Andrew Orr**, killed in action on 31 July 1916

John's son **John Orr**, serving with the Ulster Division at the front line (16 months later John was killed in action on 22 November 1917)

John's son Francis Orr serving with a Canadian Battalion

John's son Hugh Orr serving on H.M.S. *Illustrious*

John's son Nicholas Orr serving with the Machine Gun Corps

John's brother **Hugh Orr** killed in action on 17 May 1915

John's half-brother **Francis Orr** killed in action on 5 May 1915

John's half-brother James Orr serving with a Scottish Regiment

John's half-brother Robert Orr serving with a Scottish Regiment

In order to clarify these relationships it is useful to refer back to Andrew's and John's paternal grandfather Nicholas Orr:

Nicholas Orr and Margaret Kinney were married on 12 November 1859 in Ballywalter Presbyterian Church and they had five children all of whom were baptised in that church – John (born 12 May 1860), Francis (1862, died), Ellen (1864), Francis (1866) and **Hugh (born 11 November 1869 and killed in action 17 May 1915)**. After his wife Margaret died Nicholas Orr married Eliza Jane Mawhinney on 30 July 1877 in Newtownards Registry Office and they had ten children – Nicholas (1878), Maggie (1879), William (1881), Eliza Jane (1883), **Francis (born 8 August 1885 and killed in action 5 May 1915)**, James (1887), Sarah (1888), Edward (1890), Robert (1893) and Minnie McCaw (1895 died 1896).

John Orr, son of Nicholas and Margaret Orr, lived in the townland of Ballywhisken, Millisle. He worked as a labourer and he and Mary Baird were married on 22 December 1882 in Ballywalter Presbyterian Church. They had seven sons all of whom were baptised in that church – **John (born 18 March 1883 and killed in action 22 November 1917)**, James (1884), Francis (1887), Hugh (1889), Alexander (1891), **Andrew (born 17 August 1893 and killed in action 31 July 1916)** and Nicholas (1895). Mary Orr died on 29 July 1898 aged 40.

Francis was the first of the four family members to die, then Hugh, Andrew and John:

Orr, Francis (Frank)
Rifleman
No. 8298, 1st Battalion, Royal Irish Rifles
Killed in action on Wednesday 5 May 1915 (aged 29)
Royal Irish Rifles Graveyard, France (Grave I. C. 8)

Francis Orr was born on 8 August 1885 and he was baptised in Carrowdore Parish Church of Ireland. Francis was a half-brother of John Orr whose sons Andrew and John were also killed in action.

Frank Orr enlisted in Belfast and he served with the 1st Battalion Royal Irish Rifles. He was killed in action on 5 May 1915 and at the time of his death his mother Eliza Jane Orr was living at 278 Crimea Street, Belfast. Rifleman Frank Orr is commemorated in the Belfast Book of Honour (Page 519).

Orr, Hugh
Private
No. 9285, 2nd Battalion, Highland Light Infantry
Killed in action on Monday 17 May 1915 (aged 45)
Le Touret Memorial, France (Panel 37 and 38)

Hugh Orr was born on 11 November 1869 and he was baptised in Ballywalter Presbyterian Church. His nephews Andrew and John were killed in action in the Great War, as was his half-brother Francis. Private Hugh Orr served with the 2nd Battalion Highland Light Infantry, he was killed in action on 17 May 1915 and he is commemorated in Carrowdore Parish Church of Ireland (Christ Church) where his regiment is given as 'RIR'. He is also commemorated in the Belfast Book of Honour (Page 519).

Orr, Andrew
Rifleman
No. 55918, 19th Battalion, Canadian Infantry (Central Ontario Regiment)
Killed in action on Monday 31 July 1916 (aged 22)
Bedford House Cemetery, Belgium (Enclosure No. 4 I. G. 4)

Andrew Orr was born on 17 August 1893 and he was baptised in Ballywalter Presbyterian Church. He was the sixth of John Orr's seven sons and he moved to Canada where he worked as a labourer. He enlisted in Toronto

on 12 November 1914 and in his attestation papers it was noted that he was 5 feet 5 inches tall and he had a tattoo on his right arm. Andrew Orr was a bachelor and he cited his father John as his next-of-kin.

Rifleman Andrew Orr served with the 19th Battalion Canadian Infantry (Central Ontario Regiment) and after he was killed in action on 31 July 1916 Major GF Morrison, his Battalion commander, wrote to Andrew's father to express sympathy on behalf of the Battalion. Major Morrison outlined the circumstances of Andrew's death, 'He was on duty in the front line trenches and at 9.30 pm he was shot through the head and killed instantly by a German sniper'.

In July 1917 John Orr placed an 'Our Heroes – In Memoriam' notice in the *Newtownards Chronicle* and it contained the verse:

> *'When duty called he was there*
> *To do his bit and take his share;*
> *His heart was good, his spirit brave,*
> *His resting place a soldier's grave.*
> *We cannot tell the next to fall*
> *Beneath the chastening rod;*
> *One must be next, then let us all*
> *Prepare to meet our God.'*

Rifleman Andrew Orr is commemorated on Ballywalter and District War Memorial and in Ballywalter Presbyterian Church.

Orr, John
Rifleman
No. 18/774, 12th Battalion, Royal Irish Rifles
Killed in action on Thursday 22 November 1917 (aged 34)
Cambrai Memorial, France (Panel 10)

John Orr was born on 18 March 1883 in the townland of Kilbright, Carrowdore and he was baptised in Ballywalter Presbyterian Church. He was the eldest of John Orr's seven sons and prior to the outbreak of the Great War he worked as a labourer. John Orr Junior and Margaret Jane McLean were married in 1910 and they lived with Margaret Jane's widowed mother Margaret in the townland of Ballywhisken, Millisle.

John and Margaret Jane Orr had six children all of whom were baptised in Ballywalter Presbyterian Church – John Andrew and Francis (twins born 1911; both died), Elizabeth Mary (1912), Francis (1913), John Andrew (1915) and George born on 28 March 1917 just eight months before his father was killed in action.

> ORR—22nd November, 1917, killed in action in France, Rifleman John Orr (No. 774), R.I. Rifles, beloved husband of Margaret Jane Orr, Ballywhisken.
> Should your frail corpse be never found,
> Your loving soul to Heaven has fled,
>   Where Happiness abound.
> I am lonely, oh, so lonely,
>   And my heart with pain is sore,
> Till I grasp your hand in a better land,
>   On the great eternal shore.
> Deeply regretted by his loving Wife and
>   Family.
> Ballywhisken.

John Orr enlisted in Belfast in November 1915 and he joined the 18th Battalion Royal Irish Rifles. He went to the front with the 12th Battalion Royal Irish Rifles in 108th Brigade of the 36th (Ulster) Division and he was killed in action at Cambrai on 22 November 1917. After Rifleman John Orr died his widow Margaret Jane placed a 'For King and Country' notice in the *Newtownards Chronicle* and it contained the verse:

O

> *'Should your frail corpse be never found,*
> *Your loving soul to heaven has fled,*
> *Where happiness abound*
> *I am so lonely, oh, so lonely,*
> *And my heart with pain is sore,*
> *Till I grasp your hand in a better land,*
> *On the great eternal shore'*

Rifleman John Orr is commemorated on Ballywalter and District War Memorial and in Ballywalter Presbyterian Church.

Orr, Hamilton (Hammy)
Rifleman
No. 6795, 'B' Company, 1st Battalion, Royal Irish Rifles
Killed in action on Sunday 15 November 1914 (aged 29)
Rue-du-Bacquerot (13th London) Graveyard, France (Grave G. 2)

Hamilton Orr was born on 28 December 1884 and he was the second son of James and Lizzie Orr (nee Dickson) who lived at 50 James Street, Newtownards. They were married on 19 November 1880 in Newtownards Parish Church of Ireland. James Orr worked as a Sanitary Sub-Officer and he and Lizzie had at least eleven children including Francis, Ann Jane, Hamilton, David, Lizzie, Mary, Catherine, James, William and Sarah. Hamilton was one of seven of the children who were baptised in First Newtownards Presbyterian Church.

 James Orr was known locally as 'Brass Buttons Orr' (a reference to the brass buttons on his Sanitary Sub-Officer's uniform) and this distinguished him from his brother David who was known locally as 'Porch Orr' (he had added a porch to his house 'Kateville' in North Street, Newtownards). Both James and David had sons named Hamilton who were on active service in the Great War and both cousins died.

Hamilton Orr (son of James Orr) worked as an apprentice plumber before he enlisted in the army around 1902. He served in Belfast, Londonderry and Dublin before being posted to India with the 1st Battalion Royal Irish Rifles and he served there for about ten years.

After the outbreak of the Great War Hammy returned from India through Aden and he arrived in Liverpool on 22 October 1914. He was granted two day's leave of absence and he came home for a brief visit to Newtownards. He returned to England to rejoin his Battalion at Horsley Park Camp in Winchester and he left there on 5 November to go to the Western Front. On 10 November his mother received a postcard from him telling her that he was well.

The next communication that the family received was a letter from Company Sergeant Major CH Welsman informing them that Rifleman Hamilton Orr had been killed in the trenches at Rue Tilleloy on the night of 15 November 1914 (the Battalion had gone into the trenches for the first time that afternoon). He assured them that Hammy's death had been 'almost painless'. Official confirmation that Rifleman Hamilton Orr had died followed soon thereafter.

Hammy's father, mother, sisters and brothers placed a notice in the *Newtownards Chronicle* and it contained the verse:

> 'O God of Love, O King of Peace,
> Make wars throughout the world to cease,
> The wrath of sinful man restrain,
> Give Peace, O God, give Peace again.'

Rifleman Hamilton Orr is commemorated on Newtownards and District War Memorial and in Strean Presbyterian Church Newtownards.

Orr, Hamilton
Mentioned in Despatches (×2)
Captain
Royal Irish Rifles
Died of diabetes on Friday 8 April 1921 (aged 28)
Newtownards (Movilla) Cemetery, Co. Down (Grave 5. 137)

Hamilton Orr was born on 1 August 1892 and he was the fourth son of David and Catherine (Kate) Orr (nee Whalley) who lived at 'Kateville', North Street, Newtownards. They were married on 26 April 1886 in Ann Street Reformed Presbyterian Church Newtownards. David Orr worked as an auctioneer and he and Kate had at least ten children – James Whalley, John Stevenson, David, Hamilton, William, Andrew (died), Jane, Charles, Catherine May and Andrew. The eight eldest children were baptised in First Newtownards Presbyterian Church. David Orr was known locally as 'Porch Orr' (he had added a porch to his house 'Kateville') and this distinguished him from his brother James Orr who was known locally as 'Brass Buttons Orr' (a reference to the brass buttons on his Sanitary Sub-Officer's uniform). Both David and James had sons named Hamilton who were on active service in the Great War and both cousins died.

Prior to the outbreak of the Great War Hamilton Orr (son of David Orr) served his apprenticeship in Belfast Ropeworks and he became chief clerk in the dispatch department. Details of his active service during the Great War were published in the 12 April 1921 edition of the *Newtownards Chronicle*. On 15 March 1915 Hamilton joined the 18th Battalion Royal Irish Rifles under Colonel RG Sharman Crawford DL. As a Second Lieutenant he was selected for special training in Dublin as a 'Messing Officer' and when he returned he took charge of messing arrangements for the 18th Battalion. He was promoted Lieutenant and when the Battalion moved to Salisbury Plain he was transferred to the 52nd Battalion Devonshire Regiment at Cromer in Norfolk. He volunteered for service in Russia, he was promoted Captain and he was sent out to Murmansk. He was one of the last to leave Murmansk on the withdrawal of British troops in November 1919. Captain Orr was twice Mentioned in Despatches, first by Sir William Robertson on 28 August 1919 for services rendered in the Eastern Command and afterwards by Lord Rawlinson on 4 February 1920 for services rendered in North Russia during the period 1 March to 15 October 1919. It was further reported that 'the rigours of the Russian climate laid the foundation of the illness to which Captain Orr succumbed'.

On 21 May 1920 Captain Hamilton Orr made application for his medals and emblem (having been Mentioned in Despatches) and less than a year later he died. He had travelled to Bath for treatment for his illness and it was there that he died on 8 April 1921. His remains were brought back to Newtownards and there was a large representation of military personnel at his funeral. Hamilton's funeral was another sad occasion for the Orr family; the previous August one of Hamilton's sisters died. Captain Hamilton Orr is commemorated on Newtownards and District War Memorial.

Orr, Robert
Rifleman
No. 18/1688, 18th Battalion, Royal Irish Rifles
Died of pneumonia on Friday 28 June 1918 (aged 17)
Newtownards (Movilla) Cemetery (Grave 11. 26)

Robert Orr was born in March 1901 in Newtownards and he was a son of William John and Flora Orr (nee Boyd) who lived at 34 Mill Street. They were married on 5 May 1884 in Newtownards Parish Church of Ireland. William John Orr worked as a dealer and he and Flora had at least ten children including Maggie, Mary, James, William, Hugh, Rubina, Samuel, Isabella and Robert.

Robert Orr was a young child when his father died and it is on record that he joined the army twice. On the first occasion he was so young that he was 'claimed off'. Not to be denied he enlisted again on 26 February 1917 and joined the 18th Battalion Royal Irish Rifles. He declared that he was 18 years old, he was a labourer and he was unmarried. It was noted in his attestation papers that he was 5 feet 6¼ inches tall and he cited as his next-of-kin his mother Flora. On a couple

O

of occasions Robert Orr went absent without leave from the training camp at Clandeboye to visit friends and on 3 July 1917 he was transferred to the 20th Battalion Royal Irish Rifles.

On 14 September 1917 at Newtownards Robert Orr was discharged from the Army on the grounds of being underage; at that time he was aged 16 years 169 days. He obtained employment as an auxiliary postman in Newtownards and he died of pneumonia on 28 June 1918.

In the 6 July 1918 edition of the *Newtownards Chronicle* his funeral was reported under the headline 'Buried with Military Honours'. A contingent of military personnel under the charge of Company Quarter Master Sergeant Stevens attended the funeral and Lord Londonderry's Own Flute Band, of which Robert had been a member, played with the drums draped.

In the house of mourning and at the graveside the Rev Canon WLT Whatham, Rector of Newtownards Parish Church of Ireland (St Mark) conducted the services.

O

Orr, Robert James
Rifleman
No. 18580, 'B' Company, 13th Battalion, Royal Irish Rifles
Killed in action in France on Saturday 1 July 1916 (aged 20)
Thiepval Memorial, Somme, France (Pier and Face 15 A and 15 B)

Robert James Orr was born in Comber and he was a son of Washington and Margaret Jane (Maggie) Orr (nee Rea) who lived at 13 Hill Head. They were married on 8 March 1895 in Dundonald Presbyterian Church. Washington Orr worked as a labourer in a whiskey distillery and he and Maggie had at least seven children including Robert James, Margaret, Minnie, Washington, Samuel and Mona.

Prior to the outbreak of the Great War Robert James Orr worked in a mill and he lived at 40 Mill Street, Comber with his aunt Mary Graham and his cousins Robert, Minnie and John. He enlisted in Comber, he served with the 13th Battalion Royal Irish Rifles in 108th Brigade of the 36th (Ulster) Division and was killed in action on the first day of the Battle of the Somme.

Rifleman Robert James Orr is commemorated on Comber and District War Memorial as Robert J Orr and in Second Comber Presbyterian Church as Robert Orr. In the CWGC Debt of Honour he is commemorated as James Orr.

Orr, Samuel (Sam)
Lance Corporal
No. 64162, 121st Field Company, Royal Engineers
Died of wounds on Monday 27 March 1916 (aged 23)
Ste. Marie Cemetery, France (Div. 19. V. 3)

Samuel Orr was born in Portaferry and he was a son of Samuel and Mary Orr (nee Beck) who lived in Church Street. They were married on 29 June 1892 in Portaferry Presbyterian Church. Samuel Orr Senior worked as a seaman and he and Mary had at least five children – Samuel, Hugh, John, Margaret and Mary Isabella.

Samuel Orr Jnr was a member of the Ulster Volunteer Force and in 1915 he enlisted in Belfast. He served with the 121st Field Company Royal Engineers in the 36th (Ulster) Division and he died of wounds on 27 March 1916 in the Base Hospital at Le Havre in France. The report of his death in the 1 April 1916 edition of the *Newtownards Chronicle* paid tribute to his 'virtuous principles' and it contained the verse:

> *'He is not dead, the child of our affection,*
> *But gone into that school: where*
> *He no longer needs our poor protection,*
> *And Christ Himself doth rule'*

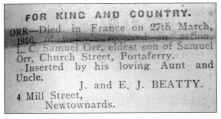

FOR KING AND COUNTRY.
ORR—Died in France on 27th March, 1916, of wounds received in action, L. C. Samuel Orr, eldest son of Samuel Orr, Church Street, Portaferry.
Inserted by his loving Aunt and Uncle.
J. and E. J. BEATTY.
4 Mill Street,
Newtownards.

His uncle and aunt Mr and Mrs James Beatty of 4 Mill Street Newtownards placed a 'For King and Country' notice in the same edition of the *Newtownards Chronicle*. Lance Corporal Sam Orr is commemorated in Portaferry (Ballyphilip) Parish Church of Ireland (St James). Two weeks after Sam died his brother Hugh, who was serving his apprenticeship in the Portaferry Medical Hall, heard that he had passed the Pharmaceutical Preliminary Examination held in Dublin. Hugh. Sam Orr's father Samuel died on 25 September 1935.

Oswald, Joseph
Rifleman
No. 13371, 8th Battalion, Royal Irish Rifles
Died of wounds on Tuesday 4 April 1916
Le Treport Military Cemetery, France (Plot 2. Row K. Grave 6)

In 'Soldiers Died in the Great War 1914 – 1919' it is recorded that Joseph

O

Oswald was born in Ballynahinch and he enlisted in Belfast. He served with the 8th Battalion Royal Irish Rifles in 107th Brigade of the 36th (Ulster) Division.

The death took place in the 16th General Hospital on 4th inst. of Rifleman Joseph Oswald, Royal Irish Rifles. Deceased was a brother of Miss Oswald, Auburn, Donaghadee.

Rifleman Joseph Oswald died of wounds in the 16th General Hospital on 4 April 1916 and at the time of his death one of his sisters was living at 'Auburn', Donaghadee and another sister was living in University Road, Belfast. Rifleman Joseph Oswald is commemorated in the Belfast Book of Honour (Page 520).

Paden, Gilbert (Bertie)
Lance Corporal
No. 18/90, 12th Battalion, Royal Irish Rifles
Killed in action on Thursday 22 November 1917 (aged 19)
Cambrai Memorial, France (Panel 10)

Gilbert Paden was born in 1898 and he was the second son of Samuel and Maggie Paden (nee Ross) who lived at 18 High Street, Newtownards. They were married on 17 February 1886 in Glastry Presbyterian Church. Samuel Paden was a watchmaker and he and Maggie had at least seven children – Samuel, Rebecca, Mary Jane, Beatrice, Gilbert (Bertie), Ernest and William Hugh Ross.

Bertie Paden enlisted in May 1915 and he joined the 18th Reserve Battalion of the Royal Irish Rifles. Bertie served in Dublin during the Easter Rising in 1916. He went to the Western Front with the 11th Battalion (South Antrim) Royal Irish Rifles and was there for five months. After a further period of home service he returned to France and served with the 12th Battalion (Mid Antrim) Royal Irish Rifles from May 1917 until he was killed in action on 22 November 1917 at Cambrai.

PADEN—November 22, killed in action in France, Lance-Corpl. W. H. R. G. (Bertie) Paden, Royal Irish Rifles, second son of Samuel Paden, High Street, Newtownards.

Lance Corporal Bertie Paden's family placed a 'For King and Country' notice in the *Newtownards Chronicle* and he is commemorated on Newtownards and District War Memorial and in Second Newtownards Presbyterian Church.

Pagan, Alexander
Rifleman
No. 18/678, 11th Battalion, Royal Irish Rifles
Killed in action on Wednesday 8 August 1917 (aged 31)
Ypres (Menin Gate) Memorial, Belgium (Panel 40)

Alexander Pagan was born on 17 November 1885 in Newtownards and he was the youngest son of Samuel and Catherine (sometimes Kathleen) Pagan (nee Mullen) who were married on 21 October 1876 in Newtownards Parish Church of Ireland. They lived in the townland of Ballyblack, Newtownards before moving to 39 Mill Street, Newtownards. Both Samuel and Alexander Pagan worked as agricultural labourers. Samuel and Catherine Pagan had at least nine children including Jane, John, Martha, Sarah and Alexander. Alexander was baptised in Greenwell Street Presbyterian Church Newtownards.

Alexander Pagan enlisted in Newtownards, he went to the front in June 1916 with the 11th Battalion Royal Irish Rifles in 108th Brigade of the 36th (Ulster) Division and he was killed in action on 8 August 1917 during the Third Battle of Ypres. Captain W Somers wrote to Alexander's parents to inform them that Alexander had been killed in action. On the day that Rifleman Alexander Pagan died his brother Rifleman John Pagan was wounded.

PAGAN—Killed in action on 8th August, 1917, Rifleman Alexander Pagan (No. 18,678), Royal Irish Rifles, youngest son of Saml. and Kathleen Pagan, 39 Mill Street, Newtownards.

He sleeps beside his comrades,
In a hallowed grave unknown;
But his name is written in letters of love
In the hearts he has left at home.

Inserted by his sorrowing Father, Mother, Sisters, and Brothers.

Alexander's father, mother, sisters and brothers placed a 'For King and Country' notice in the *Newtownards Chronicle* and it contained the verse:

'He sleeps beside his comrades,
In a hallowed grave unknown;
But his name is written in letters of love
In the hearts he has left at home.'

Rifleman Alexander Pagan is commemorated on Newtownards and District War Memorial and in the PCI Roll of Honour for Greenwell Street Presbyterian Church Newtownards.

Palmer, Alexander (Alex)
Rifleman
No. 3/8836, 15th Battalion, Royal Irish Rifles
Died of wounds on Sunday 2 July 1916 (aged 19)
Warloy-Baillon Communal Cemetery Extension, France (Grave I. B. 16)

Alexander Palmer was born on 13 August 1896 in Newtownards and he was the eldest son of William and Martha Palmer (nee Pollock) who lived at 18 Kimberley Buildings, Donaghadee Road, Newtownards. They were married on 20 March 1896 in Greenwell Street Presbyterian Church Newtownards (it was a double ceremony because Martha's brother William John Pollock was married on the same day). William Palmer was a farmer before he worked as a general labourer and he and Martha had at least seven children – Alexander, Adam Keag, Isabella, Samuel, Robert James, George Dalzell and David. The first four children were baptised in Ballyfrenis Presbyterian Church (when William farmed in the townland of Ballywhisken), Robert James was baptised in Kircubbin Presbyterian Church (the Palmer family was related to the Keag family who lived at Rubane) and the last two children were baptised in Greenwell Street Presbyterian Church Newtownards (after the Palmer family moved to Newtownards).

8836 RIFLEMAN
A. PALMER
ROYAL IRISH RIFLES
2ND JULY 1916 AGE 19

Prior to the outbreak of the Great War Alexander Palmer worked as a packer. In 'Soldiers Died in the Great War 1914 – 1919' it is recorded that he enlisted in Clydebank. He served with the 15th Battalion Royal Irish Rifles and he died of wounds on 2 July 1916. Rifleman Samuel Montgomery wrote a letter of sympathy to Alex Palmer's mother and in it he wrote 'After being wounded he was taken to hospital. He was up in the trenches with a few more of his chums on a working party two days before the advance came off and that is where he got wounded.' His parents also received a letter from the Rev Hugh F Kirker who lived in Ballyfrenis Manse, Donaghadee. He wrote 'I have felt it more than anything since I heard it. I baptised him; soon it will be 20 years ago…. it's hard on you both but you have reason to be proud of such a son.'

Rifleman Alex Palmer is commemorated on Newtownards and District War

P

Memorial and in the PCI Roll of Honour for Greenwell Street Presbyterian Church Newtownards.

Palmer, Robert

The name Robert Palmer is listed on Newtownards and District War Memorial and in the booklet produced for the Unveiling and Dedication Ceremony held on Saturday 26 May 1934 he is described as a Private in the Colonials.

Robert Palmer was born on 12 January 1896 in the townland of Ballyeasborough, Ballyhalbert and he was a son of Robert and Agnes Palmer (nee Coffey) who were married on 4 October 1878 in Glastry Presbyterian Church. They had at least six children, all of whom were baptised in Glastry Presbyterian Church – Elizabeth, Sarah, Mary Jane, Adam, William and Robert. Robert Palmer Junior moved to Langham, Saskatchewan in Canada where he worked as a banker before he enlisted on 2 March 1916 at Winnipeg. It was noted in his attestation papers that he was 5 feet 10 inches tall and he was allocated service number 871339. Desk searches and public appeals to date have not confirmed a connection between these service data and the soldier who is commemorated on Newtownards and District War Memorial.

P

Parker, Leonard Edward John (Leonard)
Corporal
No. 20/168, 13th Battalion, Royal Irish Rifles
Died in an accident on Monday 17 December 1917 (aged 20)
Newtownards (Movilla) Cemetery, Co. Down (Grave 11. 97)

Leonard Edward John Parker was born in Catford, Kent and he was a son of Edward Thomas and Lilian Parker who lived at 47E Dartmouth Road, Forest Hill in London. Prior to the outbreak of the Great War he worked as a cinematograph operator and, when his employer joined the Ulster Division, Leonard followed his lead. Leonard Parker enlisted in Kingston-on-Thames, Surrey in May 1916, he joined the 20th Battalion Royal Irish Rifles and subsequently he went to France with the 13th Battalion Royal Irish Rifles in 108th Brigade of the 36th (Ulster) Division. He was wounded in action and when he recovered he was attached to the 19th Battalion Royal Irish Rifles and stationed in Newtownards.

Unfortunate Occurrence in Newtownards Camp.

A FATAL BOMBING PRACTICE.

N.C.O. KILLED—OFFICER SUC-

On 17 December 1917 around thirty men were engaged in bombing practice with three officers observing from behind a partition of sandbags. At 3.00 pm Corporal Parker entered the bombing trench, took up his position and threw one bomb without incident. He pulled the pin from another bomb and raised his arm to throw it. When he was holding the bomb directly above his head ready for throwing, it exploded. Corporal Parker was killed instantly and several others were injured, including Major William Charles Hall who died at 11.00 pm that evening.

An inquiry held the following day found that Major William Charles Hall and Corporal Leonard Edward John Parker died 'from wounds accidentally received and caused by the premature explosion of a bomb while engaged at bombing practice at Newtownards Camp'.

The remains of Major Hall were removed to Narrow Water Castle, Warrenpoint and he was buried in Clonallon Parish Church of Ireland graveyard. Corporal Parker was buried with full military honours in Movilla Cemetery Newtownards.

Parkes, Frederick (Fred)
Rifleman
No. 18588, 1st Battalion, Royal Irish Rifles
Killed in action on Monday 14 October 1918 (aged 27)
Dadizeele New British Cemetery, Belgium (Grave II. B. 14)

Frederick Parkes was born in Newcastle-under-Lyme, Staffordshire. He moved to Newtownards and, prior to the outbreak of the Great War, Fred worked as a motor driver for the Ards Transport Company. He and his wife Elizabeth (nee Dalzell) lived at 46 Little Francis Street, Newtownards. They were married on 3 June 1914 in Helen's Bay Presbyterian Church. They had two children – Freda Cambrai born on 20 November 1917 and Elizabeth (Isabella) McCutcheon born on 6 December 1918, two months after her father died.

Fred Parkes enlisted in Belfast, he served as a Rifleman with the 1st Battalion Royal Irish Rifles and he was killed in action at Gulleghem on 14 October 1918.

PARKES—Killed in action on the 14th October, 1918, Rifleman Fred Parkes, Royal Irish Rifles (late Y.C.V.'s), dearly-beloved husband of Elizabeth Parkes.
Deeply regretted by his loving Wife and little Daughter.
46 Little Frances Street, Newtownards.

After Fred died his widow placed a 'For King and Country' notice in the 16 November edition of the *Newtownards Chronicle*. Rifleman Fred Parkes is commemorated on Newtownards and District War Memorial and in First Newtownards Presbyterian Church.

Parkhill, James*
Rifleman
No. 864, 12th Battalion, Royal Irish Rifles
Died of consumption on Monday 17 February 1919 (aged 28)
Newtownards (Movilla) Cemetery, Co. Down (Grave 11. 123)

James Parkhill was born in Ballycastle, Co Antrim and he was a son of Robert and Christina Parkhill who lived at 2 Wilson's Row and later in Castle Street, Ballycastle. Robert Parkhill worked as a general labourer and he and Christina had at least five children including James, John Munro, Elizabeth and Joseph. James Parkhill worked as a labourer and he was employed for a time by J Fulton in Armoy. James Parkhill and Mary McMullan were married on 11 November 1908 in Ramoan Parish Church of Ireland Ballycastle and they had one daughter named Christina who was born on 30 October 1909. After her mother Mary died Christina lived with James's parents, Robert and Christina, in Ballycastle.

James Parkhill enlisted in Belfast on 12 October 1914 and he declared his age to be 24 years 10 months. He declared that he was Church of Ireland, a labourer and a widower. In his attestation papers it was noted that he was 5 feet 3¼ inches tall and he cited his mother as his next-of-kin. He joined the 12th Battalion Royal Irish Rifles and was then posted to the 18th Battalion. On 19 July 1916 he went to France to the Base Depot and he went to the fighting line with the 9th Battalion in 107th Brigade of the 36th (Ulster) Division. James Parkhill returned to the Base Depot on 12 October 1916 and he went to the 18th Battalion on 31 October 1916. He went back to France on 5 January 1917

P

with the 12th Battalion and on 22 March 1917 he sustained serious gun-shot wounds – a compound fracture of the tibia and fibula in his right leg and flesh wounds in his left leg and chest. He was taken to a casualty clearing station and from there he was transported to York Military Hospital on 10 April 1917. He stayed there until 12 November 1917 and on 13 November 1917 he was discharged from the Army when he was deemed to be no longer physically fit for active service.

In November 1917 James Parkhill returned to Newtownards to live with his wife Margaret (on 11 February 1916 James Parkhill and Margaret Stritch, a widow, were married in Newtownards Parish Church of Ireland). Margaret lived at 1 Mary Street and later in Circular Road, Newtownards. James Parkhill died of consumption on 17 February 1919 and he was buried in Movilla Cemetery. It was his widow Margaret who received his medals on 16 June 1922. James Parkhill's brother Joseph also served with the 12th Battalion Royal Irish Rifles (1779) and he was killed in action on 1 July 1916. Joseph Parkhill is commemorated on the Thiepval Memorial (Panels 15A and 15B), in Ramoan Parish Church of Ireland in Ballycastle and in *Ballycastle Heroes 1914 – 1918* by Robert Thompson.

P

Paton, James
Private
No. 241244, 'A' Company, 1st/4th Battalion, Royal Scots Fusiliers
Died of wounds on Wednesday 25 April 1917 (aged 20)
Alexandria (Hadra) War Memorial Cemetery, Egypt (Grave A. 39)

James Paton was born on 26 April 1896 in Newtownards and he was the eldest son of Francis and Mary (Minnie) Paton (nee Gunning) who lived in the townland of Ballygrangee, Newtownards before they moved to Old Station House, Troon in Ayrshire. They were married in Greyabbey Parish Church of Ireland and they had at least three children all of whom were baptised in Carrowdore Parish Church of Ireland – James, Florence Wilson and Francis. James Paton's grandfather William Paton lived in the townland of Ballygrangee.

James Paton worked as a plate-layer on the railway before joining the colours in September 1915. He enlisted in Ayr and served with the Royal Scots Fusiliers. Private James Paton was wounded on 22 April 1917 during fighting at Gaza in Palestine and he died three days later (one day short of his 21st birthday).

After his death and each year thereafter his parents placed 'Our Heroes – In Memoriam' notices in the *Newtownards Chronicle*. His comrade Private John Watson Currie placed similar notices and one contained the verse:

'So ready to answer the call to the brave,
Although he now rests in a far distant grave;
What more or better could any man give
Than die for his country that others might live.'

Private James Paton is commemorated on Troon War Memorial.

Patterson, David Bell
Rifleman
No. 18589, 'B' Company, 13th Battalion, Royal Irish Rifles
Killed in action in France on Saturday 1 July 1916
Thiepval Memorial, France (Pier and Face 15 A and 15 B)

In 'Soldiers Died in the Great War 1914 – 1919' it is recorded that David Bell Patterson was born in Newtownards and he enlisted in Comber.

Rifleman David Bell Patterson went to France in October 1915, he served with the 13th Battalion Royal Irish Rifles in 108th Brigade of the 36th (Ulster) Division and he was killed in action on the first day of the Battle of the Somme.

P

Patterson, James
Lance Corporal
No. 18614, 'B' Company, 13th Battalion, Royal Irish Rifles
Killed in action in France on Saturday 1 July 1916 (aged 21)
Thiepval Memorial, France (Pier and Face 15 A and 15 B)

James Patterson was born in 1894 in Ballygowan and he was the eldest son of Samuel Kerr Patterson and Mary Jane Patterson (nee Magee) who lived in the townland of Ballyrush, Ballygowan. They were married on 18 June 1891 in Gilnahirk Presbyterian Church. Samuel Kerr Patterson worked as a farmer and he and Mary Jane had at least nine children including Mary Kerr, James, William John, David Taylor, Samuel Kerr, Andrew Magee, Maud and Margaret Kerr.

After leaving school James Patterson lived in Newtownards and he worked as an apprentice in the hardware trade. He was employed by Messrs Riddels

Ltd, Donegall Place, Belfast. He enlisted in Comber, he served with the 13th Battalion Royal Irish Rifles in 108th Brigade of the 36th (Ulster) Division and he was killed in action on the first day of the Battle of the Somme. Initially he was posted as wounded and missing in action and in August 1916 it was officially confirmed by the War Office that he had been killed in action.

James's Colonel wrote a letter of sympathy to James's father and in the letter he outlined the circumstances of James's death. James was in command of the Lewis Gun team attached to 'B' Company when it advanced towards the German trenches. Only three men of the team returned and all were wounded. Earlier James Patterson had been recommended for a commission and he was scheduled to go to a School for Cadets in October 1916.

Lance Corporal James Patterson is commemorated on Comber and District War Memorial (as Corporal) and in Second Comber Presbyterian Church. His father Samuel Kerr Patterson died on 27 May 1935.

Patterson, Robert
Rifleman

P

No. 18613, 'C' Company, 13th Battalion, Royal Irish Rifles
Killed in action on Saturday 1 July 1916
Thiepval Memorial, France (Pier and Face 15 A and 15 B)

In 'Soldiers Died in the Great War 1914 – 1919' it is recorded that Robert Patterson was born in Purdysburn, he lived in Belfast and he enlisted in Comber. There is evidence from one source that Robert Patterson was working in Comber when he enlisted. Desk searches and public appeals to date have yielded no further information.

Patterson, William James
Corporal

No. 18606, 'B' Company, 13th Battalion, Royal Irish Rifles
Killed in action on Saturday 1 July 1916
Thiepval Memorial, France (Pier and Face 15 A and 15 B)

William James Patterson was born in Moneyreagh, he enlisted on 19 September 1914 in Newtownards and he served with the 13th Battalion Royal Irish Rifles in 108th Brigade of the 36th (Ulster) Division. His address was 197 Mill Street, Newtownards and he had served in 'B' Company of the Newtownards Branch of the Ulster Volunteer Force. Corporal William James Patterson was killed in action on the first day of the Battle of the Somme and his wife Mary was living at 278A Newtownards Road, Belfast.

Corporal William James Patterson is commemorated on Newtownards and District War Memorial; in the PCI Roll of Honour for Regent Street Presbyterian Church Newtownards and in the Belfast Book of Honour (Page 526).

Patton, James
Rifleman
No. 18622, 'B' Company, 13th Battalion, Royal Irish Rifles attached 1st/1st Northumbrian Field Ambulance, Royal Army Medical Corps
Killed in action on Friday 29 March 1918 (aged 26)
Pozieres Memorial, France (Panel 74 to 76)

James Patton was born in Comber and he was a son of David and Jane Patton (nee Allen) who lived at 18 Brownlow Street, Comber. They were married on 11 July 1885 in Killinchy Presbyterian Church. David Patton worked as a general labourer and he and Jane had at least thirteen children including Agnes, David, Joseph, James, Isabella, Mary, Sarah, Susannah, Grace and Samuel.

P

Prior to the outbreak of the Great War James Patton was employed as a mill worker in Andrew's Mill, Comber. He enlisted in Comber, he served with the 13th Battalion Royal Irish Rifles and he was wounded on two occasions – on 26 February 1917 and on 16 August 1917 at the Battle of Langemarck. In November 1917 the 11th and 13th Battalions Royal Irish Rifles were amalgamated and then disbanded in February 1918. When James Patton recovered from his wounds he was attached to the 1st/1st Northumbrian Field Ambulance, Royal Army Medical Corps and he was killed in action in France on 29 March 1918 shortly after the commencement of the German 'Michael' offensive.

Rifleman James Patton is commemorated on Comber and District War Memorial; on the Andrews Mill Memorial Plaque and in First Comber Presbyterian Church.

Patton, Samuel Forbes (Samuel)
Driver
No. 13/600, 8th Battery, 2nd Brigade, New Zealand Field Artillery, NZEF
Died of illness on Wednesday 24 July 1918 (aged 27)
Newtownards (Movilla) Cemetery, Co. Down (Grave 4. 49)

 Samuel Forbes Patton was born on 3 December 1890 and he was the youngest son of Alexander and Mary Patton (nee Johnston) who were married on 7 February 1873 in Ballywalter Presbyterian Church. Alexander Patton was a farmer in the townland of Ballyrea, Newtownards. Alexander and Mary had at least nine children – David, Annie, William, Alexander, Lizzie, Minnie, John, Jennie and Samuel Forbes. Samuel was baptised in Strean Presbyterian Church Newtownards. Mary Patton died and the family moved to the townland of Crossnamuckley, Newtownards.

Two of Samuel Patton's brothers, David and Alexander, served in the South African War. David served in the Cape Mounted Rifles and he escaped after being taken prisoner by the Boers.

Samuel moved to Te Puke in North Island, New Zealand and he enlisted there a short time before the outbreak of the Great War. Initially he served as a Trooper in the Auckland Mounted Rifles in the New Zealand Expeditionary Force. He left Auckland on 16 October 1914 bound for Suez in Egypt.

Samuel was wounded in the Dardanelles campaign and although he recovered from his wounds he contracted an illness that ultimately caused his death. He was discharged from the army and it was reported in the press that he bore his illness stoically throughout. Samuel Patton died at his father's residence in Crossnamuckley and on Friday 26 July 1918 he was buried with military honours in the family burying ground in Movilla Cemetery.

The firing party and buglers from the Norfolk Regiment came from Clandeboye Camp, Bangor. The day after Samuel's funeral his father placed a death notice in the *Newtownards Chronicle*. At the morning service in Ballyblack Presbyterian Church on 28 July 1918 the Rev R Graham paid tribute to Samuel Patton and the congregation extended their sympathy to the Patton family.

Driver Samuel Patton is commemorated on Newtownards and District War Memorial and in Ballyblack Presbyterian Church.

Patton, Thomas
Private
No. 412821, 20th Battalion, Canadian Infantry (Central Ontario Regiment)
Killed in action on Tuesday 25 April 1916 (aged 32)
Ridge Wood Military Cemetery, Belgium (Grave I. T. 3)

Thomas Patton was born on 8 November 1883 in Newtownards and he was the fourth son of Thomas and Sarah Patton (nee Arnott) who were married on 22 December 1870 in First Newtownards Presbyterian Church and who lived at 104 Greenwell Street. Thomas Patton Senior worked as a carpenter and he and Sarah had at least ten children all of whom were baptised in First Newtownards Presbyterian Church – James (1872), Eliza (1875), John (1877), Agnes Mary (1879), William (1881), Thomas (1883), Henry (1885), Samuel (1888), Robert (1890) and Sarah (1895).

> PATTON—Killed in action in Belgium, on 25th April, 1916, Private Thomas Patton, of the 20th Battalion 2nd Contingent Canadians, fourth son of Thomas and Sarah Patton, 104 Greenwell Street, Newtownards.

Thomas Patton worked as a bricklayer both before and after he moved to Canada. He enlisted on 2 March 1915 in Lindsay, Ontario and in his attestation papers it was noted that he was 5 feet 5 inches tall. He served with the 20th Battalion Canadian Infantry (Central Ontario Regiment) and he was killed in action on 25 April 1916. Private Thomas Patton is commemorated on Newtownards and District War Memorial.

Patton, Thomas McBride (Thomas)
Rifleman
No. 4/7846, 6th Battalion, Royal Irish Rifles
Died of wounds on Sunday 10 December 1916 (aged 21)
Alexandria (Hadra) War Memorial Cemetery, Egypt (Grave A. 22)

Thomas McBride Patton was born on 15 October 1895 and he was a son of Henry and Mary Elizabeth Patton (nee McBride) who were married on 19 January 1894 in Ballycopeland Presbyterian Church and who lived with Henry's parents William and Ann Patton in the townland of Ballywilliam, Donaghadee. Theirs was a farming family and Henry and Elizabeth had at least four children – Thomas McBride, Annie Catherine, William and Sophia. Thomas and Annie were baptised in First Donaghadee Presbyterian Church. Thomas's grandfather William and his father Henry were both widowed in the early 1900s.

> DONAGHADEE.
> Rifleman T. Patton (No. 7,846) is officially reported to have died of wounds.

Thomas Patton enlisted in Donaghadee, he served with the 6th Battalion Royal Irish Rifles in 29th Brigade of the 10th (Irish) Division and he died on 10 December 1916 as a result of wounds sustained in the Balkans.

Rifleman Thomas McBride Patton is commemorated on Donaghadee and District War Memorial and in First Donaghadee Presbyterian Church.

Patton, William
Rifleman
No. 16934, 'A' Company, 13th Battalion, Royal Irish Rifles
Killed in action on Saturday 1 July 1916 (aged 25)
Thiepval Memorial, France (Pier and Face 15 A and 15 B)

William Patton was born on 31 August 1890 in the townland of Herdstown, Donaghadee and he was a son of William John and Martha Patton (nee Conway) who were married on 9 June 1884 in St Anne's Church of Ireland Belfast and who lived in the townland of Ballyfotherly, Donaghadee. William John Patton worked as an agricultural labourer and he had at least six children all of whom were baptised in Shore Street Presbyterian Church Donaghadee – Hugh, Jane, William, Robert, Mary and Isabella. William's mother died when William was a teenager.

Prior to the outbreak of the Great War William Patton worked as an agricultural labourer. He enlisted in Donaghadee, he served with the 13th Battalion Royal Irish Rifles in 108th Brigade of the 36th (Ulster) Division and he was killed in action on the first day of the Battle of the Somme.

P

William Patton had been a member of No Surrender LOL No. 241 in Donaghadee and the officers and members placed a 'For King and Country' notice in the 16 June 1917 edition of the *Newtownards Chronicle*. They expressed 'their deep regret at the loss of their highly respected brethren'. The notice commemorated the deaths of **Robert McGaffin** (spelt Gaffin), Ballyhay; William Patton, Ballyfotherly and **Samuel Strain**, Donaghadee. It was signed by William Robert McCauley and Robert John Rea.

Rifleman William Patton is commemorated on Donaghadee and District War Memorial and in Shore Street Presbyterian Church Donaghadee.

Peacock, John Luddington
Lieutenant
150th Field Company, Royal Engineers, 36th (Ulster) Division
Killed in action on Saturday 1 July 1916 (aged 35)
Connaught Cemetery, France (Grave XI. L. 3)

John Luddington Peacock was the youngest son of John Luddington Peacock and Mary G Peacock who lived in Southery Manor, Downham Market, Norfolk. He came to Newtownards in 1910 to take up the duties of clerk of works and resident engineer on behalf of the Urban Council in connection with the town's sewerage scheme; prior to that he had been in charge of similar schemes in England. When the vacancy occurred for the post of

LIEUTENANT
J. L. PEACOCK
ROYAL ENGINEERS
1ST JULY 1916 AGE 35

PEACOCK—In remembrance of Lieut. John L. Peacock, R.E., Town Surveyor of Newtownards, who fell in the gallant charge of the Ulster Division at Thiepval on 1st July, 1916.
Inserted by a Friend.

Town Surveyor in Newtownards he was elected to the position in December 1912. In January 1915 he 'offered his services to his King and country' and joined the Ulster Division. He served with the 150th Field Company (formerly with the 224th Field Company) Royal Engineers and he came home to Newtownards for a short period of leave in early June 1916.

Lieutenant John Luddington Peacock was killed in action on the first day of the Battle of the Somme and he is commemorated on Newtownards and District War Memorial and in Newtownards Parish Church of Ireland (St Mark).

In the May 1917 issue of the *Southery Parish Magazine* it was reported that a stained glass window in memory of John Luddington Peacock had been unveiled in Little Ouse, Littleport (the church where his father was a churchwarden). The window comprised two lights with St Michael on the right side and St George on the left side. The window bore the inscription:

'To the Glory of God and in loving memory of John Luddington Peacock, Lieutenant RE, the youngest son of John Luddington and Mary G Peacock who laid down his life for his country in France on 1 July 1916. RIP'.

Lieutenant Peacock is also commemorated on Southery War Memorial.

Peake Brothers: Reuben Henry and William John

Reuben Henry (Herbert) and William John Peake were sons of John and Elizabeth Peake (nee Hall) who moved from Downpatrick to the townland of Ballyatwood, Ballywalter. John was born in Scotland and Elizabeth was born in County Cavan. John Peake was employed by Lord Dunleath of Ballywalter Park where he worked for more than 22 years. He was head carpenter (he was a skilled cabinet maker and French polisher) and he and Elizabeth had eight children – William John (Jack), Dorothea (Dora), Mabel Elizabeth, Reuben Henry, Edmund Lewingdon (Eddie; died 1 March 1918), twins Robert Nyman (Bobbie) and Joseph Haddon (Joe), and Kathleen Florence.

Reuben and William John Peake were grandsons of the late John Peake of Church Street, Downpatrick and also of Mr and Mrs Joseph Hall of Drumcrow, Arva in County Cavan. William John Peake was the first of the two brothers to die on active service in the Great War.

P

Peake, William John (Jack)
Military Medal
Corporal
No. 19168, 'B' Company, 13th Battalion, Royal Irish Rifles
Killed in action on Saturday 1 July 1916 (aged 24)
Thiepval Memorial, France (Pier and Face 15 A and 15 B)

William John Peake was born in 1892 in Downpatrick and he was the eldest son of John and Elizabeth Peake. He was a member of LOL No.1076 in Ballywalter and Elijah RBP No.130 in Downpatrick.

William John Peake was a member of the Ballywalter Company of the Ulster Volunteer Force and, when the Ulster Division was formed, he enlisted in Ballywalter. He served with the 13th Battalion Royal Irish Rifles in 108th Brigade of the 36th (Ulster) Division and he was killed in action on the first day of the Battle of the Somme. Initially he was reported as missing in action as he had been seen to fall wounded about twenty yards from the German front line. In a letter to his parents his commanding officer informed them that Corporal William John Peake had been awarded the Military Medal for his excellent conduct on 26/27 June 1916 when he commanded a blocking party in the German trench and searched several dugouts getting two prisoners. When he returned to the Sunken Road he displayed great coolness under shell fire and led his party back successfully to the British lines.

In January 1917 it was officially reported that Corporal Peake had been killed in action. His Military Medal was handed over to his mother in June 1917 at the Newtownards Camp by Lieutenant Colonel SW Blacker DSO. In his address Lieutenant Colonel Blacker paid tribute to Corporal Peake and he described how the party of four officers and about 100 men of the 13th Royal Irish Rifles had penetrated the enemy trenches and brought back a captured machine-gun, 13 prisoners and, most importantly, 'information of the utmost importance which enabled the bringing to perfection of the arrangements for the big Somme push'. This was the raid led by Captain **Elliott Johnston** who was also killed in action on 1 July 1916.

William John's medal was presented to his mother and afterwards William John's father said a few words of thanks. Lady Dunleath also attended the ceremony. In addition to the medal, William John's mother received a parchment certificate from the Commander of the Division relating the circumstances of her son's gallant deed.

Peake Reuben Henry (Reuben)
Rifleman
No. 7611, 2nd & 7th Battalions, Royal Irish Rifles
Killed in action on Wednesday 8 August 1917 (aged 18)
Ypres (Menin Gate) Memorial, Belgium (Panel 40)

Reuben Peake was born on 11 September 1898 in Ballywalter and he was the second son of John and Elizabeth Peake. He enlisted in Newtownards and he served initially with the 2nd Battalion Royal Irish Rifles, later with the 7th Battalion.

Rifleman Reuben Peake was severely wounded on 9 July 1916 and was hospitalised in England but he recovered sufficiently to return to the fighting line and he served with the 7th Battalion Royal Irish Rifles in 48th Brigade of the 16th (Irish) Division. He was killed in action on 8 August 1917 whilst holding the line prior to the Battle of Langemarck.

Reuben Peake was killed in action just over one year after his elder brother William John was killed in action and at that time two of his uncles were also on active service in France. His brother Joe was serving with the Royal Engineers and, after Jack and Reuben were killed in action, Lord Dunleath made representation that Joe would not be posted overseas.

P

Corporal William John Peake and Rifleman Reuben Peake are both commemorated on Ballywalter and District War Memorial and in Ballywalter Parish Church of Ireland (Holy Trinity). They are also commemorated on the family grave headstone in Whitechurch Cemetery Ballywalter. William John Peake is commemorated on Downpatrick War Memorial. Their mother Elizabeth died on 20 June 1937 and their father John died on 25 June 1954 aged 93.

Pegg, Charles
Sergeant
No. 4361, Royal Irish Rifles, transferred to (52089), Princess Victoria's (Royal Irish Fusiliers)

The name Charles Pegg is listed on Newtownards and District War Memorial and in the booklet produced for the Unveiling and Dedication Ceremony held on Saturday 26 May 1934 he is described as a Sergeant in the Royal Irish Rifles.

Sergeant Charles Pegg served with the Royal Irish Rifles (4631) in Gallipoli before being transferred to the Royal Irish Fusiliers (52089). At a later date he was discharged from the Army. Desk searches and public appeals to date have yielded no further information.

Poag, James Stevenson (James)
Lance Corporal
No. 7170, 2nd Battalion, Royal Irish Rifles
Killed in action on Friday 23 October 1914 (aged 27)
Le Touret Memorial, France (Panel 42 and 43)

P

James Stevenson Poag was born in Belfast and he was a son of Robert and Rachel Poag (nee Stevenson) who lived at 64 Upper Meadow Street in Belfast. They were married on 22 April 1887 in Berry Street Presbyterian Church in Belfast. Robert Poag worked as a tailor and he and Rachel had at least seven children – James Stevenson, Helena, Robert, Mary Jane, Ellen Stevenson, William and Isaac Walker. Rachel Poag died on 8 September 1913.

When James Poag left school he worked as a messenger and later he worked for the Belfast City Tramway. He and Mary Killen were married on 9 December 1912 in Cregagh Presbyterian Church.

James Poag enlisted in Belfast, he served with the 2nd Battalion Royal Irish Rifles in 7th Brigade of the 3rd Division and he was killed in action at Neuve Chapelle on 23 October 1914 during heavy bombardment by the enemy. At that time his wife Mary was living at 3 William Street, Donaghadee.

Lance Corporal James Stevenson Poag is commemorated in the Belfast Book of Honour (Page 431) as is his brother Robert who served as a Bombardier (32049) in the Royal Garrison Artillery and who was killed in action on 5 September 1916. James Poag is also commemorated on the Belfast

Corporation Memorial Plaque (in Belfast City Hall) listing employees who lost their lives in the Great War.

Pollock, Charles
Rifleman
No. 4/7581, 2nd Battalion, Royal Irish Rifles
Killed in action on Wednesday 17 May 1916 (aged 18)
Arras Memorial, France (Bay 9)

Charles Pollock was born on 10 April 1898 in the townland of Cronstown, Newtownards and he was a son of Robert and Ellen Pollock (nee Beatty). The Pollock family lived in Donaghadee before they moved to Newtownards. Charles's brother Robert was baptised in Shore Street Presbyterian Church Donaghadee and Thomas, Hugh, Elizabeth, Charles, Maggie and John were baptised in Greenwell Street Presbyterian Church Newtownards.

Charles Pollock enlisted in Belfast, he joined the 4th Battalion Royal Irish Rifles and in 1916 he was transferred to the 2nd Battalion. Rifleman Charles Pollock was killed in action on 17 May 1916 during a sustained enemy attack with shells and trench mortars.

P

OUR HEROES—IN MEMORIAM.

POLLOCK—In sad and loving memory of my dear brother, Rifleman Charles Pollock, No. 7,581, Royal Irish Rifles, killed in action on May 17th, 1916.

Duty called, and he was there,
To do his bit and take his share;
His heart was good, his spirit brave,
His resting place a soldier's grave.

Ever remembered by his loving Brother and Sister-in-law.
ROBT. and MARTHA POLLOCK.
Cottown.

Charles's brother and sister-in-law Robert and Martha Pollock (nee Miskimmins) who lived in the townland of Cottown placed an 'Our Heroes – In Memoriam' notice in the 25 May 1918 edition of the *Newtownards Chronicle* and it contained the verse:

'Duty called, and he was there,
To do his bit and take his share;
His heart was good, his spirit brave,
His resting place a soldier's grave.'

Rifleman Charles Pollock is commemorated on Donaghadee and District War Memorial.

Pollock, James
Private
No. 2333, 6th & 2nd Battalions, Royal Irish Rifles, transferred to
(42467), 9th Battalion, Princess Victoria's (Royal Irish Fusiliers)
Died of influenza on Saturday 7 December 1918 (aged 29)
Tourcoing (Pont-Neuville) Communal Cemetery, France (Grave H. 6)

James Pollock was born on 1 July 1889 in the townland of Ballyhay, Donaghadee and he was a son of James and Ellen Pollock who were married in Newtownards Registry Office and who moved to the townland of Drumhirk, Newtownards. James Pollock Senior worked as an agricultural labourer and he and Ellen had at least thirteen children – Anna, Eliza, Christina, Robert, James, Richard, William, Hugh, Maggie, John, Thomas, Lizzie and Charles. The seven eldest were baptised in Shore Street Presbyterian Church Donaghadee and the six youngest in Greenwell Presbyterian Church Newtownards. James Jnr worked as an agricultural labourer before he enlisted on 2 December 1914. He was posted to the 6th Battalion Royal Irish Rifles on 21 December 1914 and to the 4th Battalion on 11 March 1915. He joined the 2nd Battalion on 3 January 1916 and was hospitalised in February because of 'a sebaceous cyst'. He rejoined his unit and his family was informed later that he had been killed in action on 17 May 1916. It was in fact Rifleman **Charles Pollock** who had been killed and when the mistake was realised James Pollock's family received a written apology. James suffered a gunshot wound to his left hand on 7 July 1916 and he had to have his forefinger amputated. James was hospitalised in Lancashire before rejoining the 4th Battalion. He was transferred to the 2nd Battalion and on 14 June 1917 he suffered a gunshot wound to his right foot.

Reflecting this error in communication, the 10 June 1916 edition of the *Newtownards Chronicle* carried a report under the headline 'This Week's Casualty Lists' which stated that Rifleman J Pollock (2333) from Donaghadee had been killed. Then in the 28 July 1917 edition of the same paper it was reported under the headline 'Donaghadee Rifleman Wounded' that Rifleman J Pollock (2333) from Donaghadee 'is officially reported wounded.'

James Pollock was hospitalised for a month after the injury to his right foot and a month after rejoining his unit he was gassed on 6 August 1917. He was posted to the Command Depot at Ballykinlar and then to the 4th Battalion. He spent a short period with the Machine Gun Corps. On 14 September 1918 he was transferred to the 9th Battalion Royal Irish Fusiliers (42467) and he returned to the Western Front. On 25 November 1918 he was admitted to the 10th Stationary Hospital at Arneke. His family was advised that he was dangerously ill and at 8.35 am on 7 December 1918 he died of influenza 'probably aggravated by exposure on military duty'. Private James Pollock is commemorated on Donaghadee and District War Memorial.

P

Pollock, John
Private
No. 29545, Royal Inniskilling Fusiliers, transferred to (3447), 8th Battalion, Royal Irish Regiment
Killed in action on Monday 12 August 1918 (aged 39)
Le Grand Hasard Military Cemetery, France (Plot 2. Row D. Grave 3)

John Pollock was born in Newtownards and he was a son of David and Mary Pollock who lived in Robert Street. David Pollock was a Private in the Lincolnshire Regiment and he and Mary had at least two children – John and Edward.

Prior to the outbreak of the Great War John Pollock worked as a general labourer in the spinning mills of Messrs George Walker & Co Ltd. He and Mary Jane Johnston were married on 12 October 1907 in Newtownards Parish Church of Ireland and they had three children – John (born 9 May 1908), Moses (born 16 March 1910) and Edward (born 5 June 1911). They lived in Front Shuttlefield Street, Newtownards. Aged 33, Mary Jane Pollock died of dropsy on 28 July 1914 and she is buried in Movilla New Cemetery.

John Pollock served with Royal Inniskilling Fusiliers (29545) and then with the 8th Battalion Royal Irish Regiment (3447). He was wounded twice in France and he was killed in action on 12 August 1918. Lieutenant O Patterson wrote to the bereaved family to express sympathy on behalf of the officers, NCOs and men in Private John Pollock's company. He wrote, 'I regret to inform you that your father was killed in action by shell fire'. John Pollock was buried on 13 August and Lieutenant Patterson continued, 'Your father was a good soldier and was popular among his comrades.'

POLLOCK—Killed in action, on 12-13th August, 1918, No. 3447, Private John Pollock, Royal Irish Regiment, dearly beloved father of Moses and John Pollock, 13 Ann Street, Newtownards,
Dearest children, I have left you
To the care of God above;
Do not let my absence grieve you,
For my sake each other love.
Deeply regretted by his Sons and Friends

Private John Pollock's sons John aged ten and Moses aged eight who were then living at 13 Ann Street in Newtownards placed a 'For King and Country' notice in the 7 September 1918 edition of the *Newtownards Chronicle*. It contained the verse:

'Dearest children, I have left you
To the care of God above;
Do not let my absence grieve you,
For my sake each other love.'

There was another notice in the paper and it was placed by his aunt and uncle Ellen and William John Dorrian who lived at 4 Talbot Street, Newtownards.

Private John Pollock is commemorated on Newtownards and District War Memorial and in Newtownards Parish Church of Ireland (St Mark).

Poole Brothers: Robert James and William Haire

Robert James Poole and William Haire Poole were born in Newtownards and they were sons of James and Sarah Jane Poole (nee Orme) who lived at 110 Greenwell Street. James and Sarah were married on 16 March 1878 in St John's Laganbank Church of Ireland in Belfast and they had at least nine children – Isabella, Sarah Jane, Robert James, Hugh Larmour, Samuel, John O'Haire, William Haire, Eliza Orme and Minnie Stratton. At least seven of the children were baptised in Greenwell Street Presbyterian Church Newtownards. Both parents died before their two sons died in the Great War. William Haire Poole was the first of the two brothers to die:

Poole, William Haire (William)
Rifleman
No. 18634, 'B' Company, 13th Battalion, Royal Irish Rifles
Killed in action on Saturday 1 July 1916 (aged 20)
Thiepval Memorial, France (Pier and Face 15 A and 15 B)

P

William Haire Poole was born on 29 November 1895 and he was the youngest son. He was baptised in Greenwell Street Presbyterian Church and prior to the outbreak of the Great War he worked as a cutter in a factory. He was a member of 'A' Company in the Ulster Volunteer Force in Newtownards. He enlisted in Newtownards, he served with the 13th Battalion Royal Irish Rifles in 108th Brigade of the 36th (Ulster) Division and he was killed in action on the first day of the Battle of the Somme. Initially he was posted as missing in action and in June 1917 it was officially confirmed that he had been killed.

POOLE—Missing since July 1st, 1916, now officially reported killed on that date or since, Rifleman William Poole (No. 18,634), Royal Irish Rifles, youngest and dearly-beloved son of the late James and Sarah Jane Poole.

One by one their seats have emptied,
One by one they went away;
How the circle has been broken,
Will it be complete one day?

Deeply regretted by his sorrowing Sisters and Brothers.
American papers please copy.

His sorrowing sisters and brothers placed a 'For King and Country' notice in the 23 June 1917 edition of the *Newtownards Chronicle* and they asked for the American papers to copy it. It contained the verse:

'One by one their seats have emptied,
One by one they went away;
How the circle has been broken,
Will it be complete one day?'

Poole, Robert James (Robert)
Rifleman
No. 7544, 4th Battalion, Royal Irish Rifles, transferred to (683942), 1st Reserve Garrison Battalion, Worcestershire Regiment, transferred to Labour Corps

Robert James Poole was born on 10 May 1880 and he was the eldest son. When Robert enlisted on 26 March 1915 in Belfast he gave his address as 5 Greenwell Street, Newtownards. He declared that he was aged 35, he was Presbyterian and he worked as a hairdresser. He cited his wife Elizabeth Poole (nee Cargo) as his next-of-kin. Robert and Elizabeth were married in Ballyblack Presbyterian Church and they had at least eight children – Jane Cargo (1904), Hugh (1907), Sarah (1909), Elizabeth (1913), Robert James (1915), Sarah (1916) and William John (1920).

Robert Poole joined the 4th Battalion Royal Irish Rifles (7544) and he was rated first class in musketry. On 14 May 1918 he was transferred to 'D' Company 1st Reserve Garrison Battalion Worcestershire Regiment (683942) and it is noted in his records that he was sick in September 1918. Subsequently he was transferred to the Labour Corps and on 21 March 1919 he went to the Army Reserve. Robert Poole did not serve overseas.

P

Both Rifleman William Poole and Rifleman Robert Poole are commemorated on Newtownards and District War Memorial. Desk searches and public appeals to date have not confirmed a date of death for Robert Poole.

Porter, James
Rifleman
No. 1463, 'B' Company, 13th Battalion, Royal Irish Rifles
Killed in action on Saturday 1 July 1916 (aged 23)
Thiepval Memorial, France (Pier and Face 15 A and 15 B)

James Porter was born on 6 January 1893 in Dundonald and he was a son of Joseph and Maggie Porter (nee Thompson) who moved to 'Ballyskeagh Cottage', Newtownards. Joseph Porter worked as an agricultural labourer and he and Maggie had at least six children including Maggie, Robert, James, Minnie and Lizzie. James was baptised in Ballygilbert Presbyterian Church.

Prior to the outbreak of the Great War James Porter worked as an agricultural labourer. He enlisted in Belfast, he joined the 13th Battalion Royal Irish

Rifles (1st County Down Volunteers) and he went to France in October 1915. He served in 108th Brigade of the 36th (Ulster) Division.

Rifleman James Porter was killed on the first day of the Battle of the Somme. Initially he was reported as missing in action and in June 1917 it was officially confirmed that he had been killed in action 'on or since that date'.

His brother and sisters placed a 'For King and Country' notice in the 7 July 1917 edition of the *Newtownards Chronicle* and it contained the verse:

'Peace, perfect peace, the future all unknown,
Jesus we know, and He is on the Throne;
It is enough, earth's struggles soon shall cease
And Jesus calls us to Heaven's perfect peace.'

Rifleman James Porter is commemorated on Newtownards and District War Memorial.

P

Porter, Joseph
Rifleman
No. 15785, 9th Battalion, Royal Irish Rifles
Died of wounds on Saturday 27 November 1915 (aged 20)
Miraumont Communal Cemetery, France (Grave B. 5)

Joseph Porter was born in Newtownards and he was the eldest son of James and Mary Porter (nee Courteney) who lived in the townland of Carrowreagh, Dundonald. They were married on 26 April 1893 in Agnes Street Presbyterian Church in Belfast. James Porter worked as an agricultural labourer and he and Mary had at least six children – Ellen Jane, Joseph, Sarah, Mary, James and William. The three youngest were baptised in Dundonald Parish Church of Ireland (St Elizabeth).

Prior to the outbreak of the Great War Joseph Porter worked as a pawnbroker's assistant, he enlisted in Belfast and he served with the 9th Battalion Royal Irish Rifles in 107th Brigade of the 36th (Ulster) Division. In the press it was reported that he died of wounds on 27 November 1915 while he was being held as a prisoner of war. In the CWGC Debt of Honour his date of death is recorded as 27 November 1915 whilst in 'Soldiers Died in the Great War 1914 – 1919' it is recorded that he died on 27 December 1915. He is commemorated in Dundonald Parish Church of Ireland (St Elizabeth).

Price, John
Private
No. 18638, 'B' Company, 13th Battalion, Royal Irish Rifles, transferred to (17765), 108th Machine Gun Company (Infantry), 36th (Ulster) Division
Killed in action on Saturday 10 June 1916 (aged 22)
Hamel Military Cemetery, France (Grave I. F. 15)

John Price was born in Ardmillan, Killinchy and he was the eldest son of William James and Sarah Price (nee McKee) who lived at 'Ashview', Lisbarnett, Comber. They were married on 28 April 1893 in Killinchy Presbyterian Church. William James Price was a farmer and he and Sarah had at least eight children – John, Samuel, Mary Elizabeth, Hugh McKee, William James, Sarah, Emily and Mabel Isabella. John worked on the family farm.

P

John Price was a signatory of the Ulster Covenant and prior to enlisting in Comber in September 1914 he was a member of the North Down (Comber) Ulster Volunteer Force. He served with the 13th Battalion Royal Irish Rifles (18638) before being transferred to the Machine Gun Company in 108th Brigade of the 36th (Ulster) Division. Private John Price was killed in action on 10 June 1916 when an enemy shell exploded close to him. After he died his companions penned a tribute. They remembered his 'gentle, brave and straightforward character together with his readiness to help the weak or timid.' They noted that he was not only 'a soldier of the King but a good soldier of Jesus Christ' and they extended sympathy to his parents, brothers and sisters.

A year later John's companions placed an 'Our Heroes – In Memoriam' notice in the *Newtownards Chronicle* and it contained the verse:

'No mother's care did him attend,
Nor o'er him did a father bend;
No sister by to shed a tear
No brother by his words to hear.

May the heavenly winds blow softly
O'er that sweet and hallowed spot;
Though the sea divides us from your grave,
You will never be forgot.'

 Captain JS Davidson who commanded 108th Brigade Machine Gun Company wrote a letter of condolence to John's mother. In the letter he paid glowing tribute to Private Price whom he said he had known since the early days of the war when they were at Clandeboye. A week before he was killed John had shown great bravery and coolness by going back across a most dangerous area and under intense fire bringing up a fresh supply of ammunition. John's death was said to be instantaneous and he was laid to rest in a little cemetery behind the trenches. The Rev Paton, Presbyterian Chaplain, took the service. Captain Davidson said that all of John's personal belongings would be sent on to her as soon as possible.

P Captain Davidson also wrote a letter to his own mother in Bangor in which he expressed his profound sadness and he said that John's death was like 'parting from a brother'. He asked his mother to visit John Price's mother and to convey to her verbally what a personal loss Captain Davidson felt. Less than three weeks after writing the letter to John's mother Captain **James Samuel Davidson** was killed in action on the first day of the Battle of the Somme.

At the time of the explosion on 16 June 1916 Sergeant Samuel George Miskimmin was standing close to John Price and was protected from the full force of the blast by John's body. Samuel suffered shell shock but survived the explosion and he wrote a letter of condolence to John's mother. **Samuel George Miskimmin** died of wounds some 17 months later, on 25 November 1917.

Private John Price is commemorated on Comber and District War Memorial and in both First Comber Presbyterian Church and Killinchy Parish Church of Ireland.

Pritchard, William John
Rifleman
No. 19171, 'A' Company, 13th Battalion, Royal Irish Rifles
Died on Monday 26 October 1914 (aged 19)
Greyabbey Old Cemetery, Co. Down (about middle of cemetery)

In some records the surname is spelt Prichard.

William John Pritchard was born on 22 August 1895 in Greyabbey and he was a son of William and Mary Ann Pritchard (nee Bell) who lived in the townland of Springvale, Ballywalter. They were married on 3 May 1895 in Greyabbey Parish Church of Ireland. William Pritchard worked as an agricultural labourer and he and Mary Ann had at least three children, all of whom were baptised in Greyabbey Parish Church of Ireland – William John, Mary Jane and Anna Elizabeth. William John's mother Mary Ann Pritchard died on 23 February 1912. His father William remarried twice thereafter and he died on 1 April 1934. He is interred in Greyabbey Old Graveyard.

Prior to the outbreak of the Great War William John Pritchard worked as an agricultural labourer. He enlisted in Ballywalter, he joined the 13th Battalion Royal Irish Rifles and he died on 26 October 1914. He took ill at Clandeboye Camp on Friday 23 October and he was transferred immediately to Holywood Hospital where he died of pneumonia three days later. A firing party of 12 men, together with the men of his own district, attended his funeral on 28 October 1914. Captain **George James Bruce** and William John Pritchard's platoon officer, Second Lieutenant K Morrow, also attended. Captain Bruce was killed in action on 2 October 1918.

P

Rifleman William John Pritchard is commemorated on Ballywalter and District War Memorial and in Ballywalter Parish Church of Ireland (Holy Trinity). He is also commemorated on the family grave headstone in Greyabbey Old Cemetery: 'WJ Pritchard, Rifleman, RIR, 13th Battalion, killed in action 26 October 1914, interred here, son of Mr and Mrs Wm Pritchard, Ballywalter'.

It is worth noting as a footnote to this tribute that a second William Pritchard from Greyabbey served with the Royal Irish Rifles (19170) in the Great War. He was a son of John Pritchard and while he was on active service he married Annie Brown on 22 January 1917 in Greyabbey Parish Church of Ireland. William Pritchard died on 10 June 1939 aged 46 and he is buried in Greyabbey Old Graveyard in the Brown family grave. It is this William Pritchard whose photograph appears in a montage of pictures entitled 'Ulster Division RIR Heroes Greyabbey 1914 – 1918 who fought in the great European War'.

P

Proctor, James
Sergeant
No. 18594, 'B' Company, 13th Battalion, Royal Irish Rifles
Killed in action on Thursday 16 August 1917 (aged 34)
Tyne Cot Cemetery, Belgium (Grave IV. B. 20)

James Proctor was born in Dingwall, Ross-shire in Scotland and he was a son of John and Barbara Proctor. John Proctor worked as a whiskey distillery manager and he and Barbara had at least thirteen children including Maggie, Mary Sinclair, James, Alexander, Stella, John, Barbara, Bella, Hugh, George William and Christina. The Proctor family moved to Ireland and they lived in County Antrim and in Dublin before moving to Comber where they lived in Killinchy Street. Reflecting their Scottish roots the name of their house was 'Dalvourne'.

James Proctor and Mary Niblock were married

on 17 December 1910 in Comber Non-Subscribing Presbyterian Church and they had at least one child, a son named John who was born in 1911.

James Proctor worked as a commercial clerk and then as a brewer before he enlisted in Comber. He served with the 13th Battalion Royal Irish Rifles in 108th Brigade of the 36th (Ulster) Division and he was wounded in action on 7 February 1916. He returned to active service and he was killed in action on 16 August 1917 at the Battle of Langemarck. His brother Hugh also served with the 13th Battalion Royal Irish Rifles.

Sergeant James Proctor is commemorated on Comber and District War Memorial; on the Roll of Honour for Comber Masonic Lodge No. 46 and in First Comber Presbyterian Church.

Pyper Brothers: David and Robert James

David and Robert James Pyper were sons of Maggie Pyper who lived in the townland of Glastry, Kircubbin. Maggie worked as a washerwoman and she had at least six children – Robert James, David, Minnie, Sarah, John and Adam.

Pyper, David
Rifleman
No. 18/1121, 11th Battalion, Royal Irish Rifles
Killed in action on Friday 1 September 1916 (aged 20)
Ration Farm (La Plus Douve) Annexe, Belgium (Grave II. C. 24)

David Pyper was born in Newtownards, he lived in Glastry and he enlisted in Newtownards. Rifleman David Pyper served with the 11th Battalion Royal Irish Rifles in 108th Brigade of the 36th (Ulster) Division and he was killed in action on 1 September 1916. He was one of many casualties when the Battalion came under sustained mortar attack by the enemy while they were holding the line.

Pyper, Robert James
Rifleman
No. 16948, 'B' Company, 13th Battalion Royal Irish Rifles, then 11th/13th Battalion, Royal Irish Rifles, then 22nd Entrenching Battalion
Killed in action on Sunday 31 March 1918 (aged 23)
Pozieres Memorial, France (Panel 74 to 76)

Robert James Pyper was born in Kircubbin, he lived in Glastry and prior to the outbreak of the Great War he worked as a farm servant.

When he enlisted in Belfast he joined the 1st County Down Volunteers and he served with the 13th Battalion Royal Irish Rifles in 108th Brigade of the 36th (Ulster) Division. In November 1917 the 11th and 13th Battalions Royal Irish Rifles were amalgamated and when they were disbanded in February 1918 Robert James was transferred to the 22nd Entrenching Battalion.

Rifleman Jas. Pyper, Glastry, Killed in Action.

Official news has been received by Mrs. Margaret Pyper, Glastry, Kircubbin, stating that her son, Rifleman Robert Jas. Pyper (No. 16,948), Royal Irish Rifles, was killed in action at the front on 31st March. Rifleman R. J. Pyper, like a good many other gallant lads of the Ards, joined the Ulster Division, and belonged to the 1st Co. Down Volunteers. The sincere sympathy of the many friends of the family goes out to Mrs. Pyper in her great sorrow, as this is her second boy who has made the supreme sacrifice for King and country.

Robert James was killed in action in France on 31 March 1918 and after he died his mother placed a 'For King and Country' notice in the *Newtownards Chronicle*. It contained the verse:

'The news was sad, the blow was hard,
God's will, it shall be done;
With a manly heart he did his part,
My dearly-beloved son'

Rifleman David Pyper and Rifleman Robert James Pyper are both commemorated on Newtownards and District War Memorial. Their names were added later at the end of the alphabetical list of names.

Quail, James Henry (Henry)
Lance Corporal
No. 18/1791, 12th Battalion, Royal Irish Rifles
Killed in action on Monday 15 April 1918 (aged 19)
Tyne Cot Memorial, Belgium (Panel 138 to 140 & 162 to 162 A & 163 A)

James Henry Quail was born in 1899 in County Monaghan and he was a son of Hugh Alexander and Josephine Quail. Hugh Alexander Quail (born in County Down) worked as a bank official and he and Josephine (born in

County Mayo) had at least five children including David, Hugh Herbert and James Henry. David and Hugh Herbert Quail were born in County Mayo.

The Quail family moved to the townland of Clontivrin, Newtownbutler and from there to Portadown before they came to Newtownards where they lived in Bank of Ireland House at 2 Regent Street.

Information Wanted—Lance-Cpl. Quail Missing.

If any soldier returning from Germany can give information regarding the fate of Lance-Corporal James H, Quail, 18/1791, 12th Royal Irish Rifles, his mother, Mrs. Quail, of 2 Regent Street, Newtownards, will be extremely grateful. He is officially reported as missing since the 15th April, 1918, when he was last seen "in a shell-hole near Messines, where he held out to the last moment, firing on the enemy who had practically surrounded the position."

James Henry Quail enlisted at Clandeboye in July 1917 and he trained with the 18th Battalion Royal Irish Rifles. He went to France on 29 March 1918 where he served with the 12th Battalion in 108th Brigade of the 36th (Ulster) Division. Less than three weeks later he was killed in action on 15 April 1918 at Messines while holding the line during the German 'Michael' offensive. Initially he was reported as missing in action; he was last seen 'in a shell-hole near Messines, where he held out to the last moment, firing on the enemy who had practically surrounded the position.' In January 1919 the Quail family appealed for information about him from any returning soldiers who had survived the battle. Later it was officially confirmed that Henry had been killed in action

At the time that Henry was killed both of his brothers were recovering from severe wounds. Private David Quail served with the Canadians and Second Lieutenant Hugh Herbert Quail served with the Tank Corps.

Lance Corporal James Henry Quail is commemorated on Newtownards and District War Memorial.

Quail, William James
Lance Corporal
No. 20/189, Royal Irish Rifles, transferred to (593781), 404th Agricultural Company, Labour Corps
Died of pneumonia on Saturday 22 February 1919 (aged 29)
Dunsford (St. Mary) Church of Ireland Churchyard, Downpatrick, Co. Down (near main door of church)

William James Quail was a son of WJ and Margaret Jane Quail. After his father died his mother married Samuel McCormick on 6 December 1895 in Dundrum Methodist Church and they lived in the townland of Ballywarren,

Downpatrick before they moved to 'Ballyrickard House', Comber. Samuel McCormick was a farmer and he and Margaret Jane had at least two children – Florence Mary and Samuel Henry. William James Quail and his sister Maggie Jane Quail lived with their mother, stepfather, half-sister and half-brother.

William James Quail enlisted and he served with the Royal Irish Rifles. He was wounded on 7 June 1917 and hospitalised in Dublin. After that he was transferred to the Labour Corps. His mother and stepfather moved to Twynholm, Kirkcudbright in Scotland and it was there that Lance Corporal Quail died on 22 February 1919. The cause of death was 'pneumonia following bronchitis'. He was interred in the family burying ground at Dunsford, Downpatrick on 24 February 1919.

Lance Corporal William James Quail is commemorated on Comber and District War Memorial and in Regent Street Methodist Church Newtownards.

Q Quigley, Charles Henry (Charles)
Private
No. 25212, 14ᵗʰ Battalion, Highland Light Infantry

Prior to the outbreak of the Great War Charles Quigley worked as a labourer. He and Maria Vallely were married on 3 March 1896 in St Anne's Church of Ireland Belfast and they lived at 88 Movilla Street, Newtownards. They had no children.

Charles Quigley enlisted on 11 November 1915 and in his attestation papers it was noted that he was 37 years of age. On 17 November 1915 he joined the 14ᵗʰ Battalion Highland Light Infantry and on 16 December 1915 he was transferred to the 3ʳᵈ Battalion. After serving for 224 days he was discharged from the Army at Hamilton in Scotland on 22 June 1916 when it was determined that he was no longer fit for war service because of 'inflammation of the dura mater'. It was noted that this illness had commenced with pains in his shoulders about two years previously and that his condition had steadily worsened. It was further determined that his disability was permanent and it was 'not the result of nor aggravated by service'. His application for a war pension was finally turned down in April 1919 by a Pensions Appeal Tribunal. When he was discharged from the Army his intended place of residence was 126 East Street, Newtownards. Desk searches and public appeals to date have yielded no information about his death.

Private Charles Quigley is commemorated on Newtownards and District War Memorial.

Quigley, Henry
Military Medal and Bar
Rifleman
No. 9583, 2nd Battalion, Royal Irish Rifles
Killed in action on Saturday 23 March 1918 (aged 21)
Pozieres Memorial, France (Panel 74 to 76)

Henry Quigley was a son of Samuel and Agnes Quigley (nee Cromie) who lived in the townland of Balloo, Killinchy. They were married on 19 May 1891 in Killinchy Non-Subscribing Presbyterian Church. Samuel Quigley worked as a kilnman and he and Agnes had at least five children – Hugh, Jane, Henry, James and Susanna.

Agnes Quigley died and on 24 April 1906 Samuel Quigley and Margaret (Maggie) Thompson were married in Killinchy Non-Subscribing Presbyterian Church. After Samuel died Maggie, her children and her step-children lived in the townland of Tullycore, Killinchy where Henry worked as a farm labourer.

Q

Henry Quigley enlisted in Newtownards and he was posted to the 2nd Battalion Royal Irish Rifles. He was awarded the Military Medal (Supplement to the *London Gazette* 18 October 1917) and a Bar to the Military Medal on 13 March 1918. Lance Corporal Henry Quigley was killed in action on 23 March 1918.

Quinn, John
Sergeant
No. PLY/14226, 2nd RM Battalion RN Div, Royal Marine Light Infantry
Killed in action on Saturday 28 April 1917 (aged 28)
Arras Memorial, France (Bay 1)

John Quinn was a son of David and Jane Quinn (nee Anderson) who lived with John Quinn (David's widowed father) in the townland of Cattogs, Comber. David and Jane were married on 11 February 1886 in St Anne's Church of Ireland Belfast. David Quinn was a farmer and he and Jane had at least ten children including John, David, Jane, Susanna, Hugh, William James, Sarah, Samuel Robert and Arthur Lowry.

 John Quinn enlisted around 1907 and he served with the Royal Marine Light Infantry. During the Great War Sergeant Quinn survived both the siege of Antwerp and the Dardanelles campaign and he was killed in action on 28 April 1917. At that time he had a brother on active service in the 36th (Ulster) Division.

Sergeant John Quinn is commemorated on Comber and District War Memorial and in First Comber Presbyterian Church.

Quinn, John Patrick
Corporal
No. 5780, 'A' Company, 1st Battalion, Royal Irish Rifles
Killed in action on Sunday 9 May 1915 (aged 29)
Ration Farm Military Cemetery, France (Grave VI. H. 26)

In some records the surname is spelt Quin.

John Patrick Quinn was born in Newtownards and he was a son of Hugh and Sarah Quinn who lived in Balfour Street and later at 72 East Street, Newtownards. Hugh Quinn worked as a labourer and he and Sarah had at least six children – Hugh, Agnes, John Patrick, Edward, Richard and Cathleen.

John Patrick Quinn lived in Newtownards, he enlisted in Ballykinlar, he served with the 1st Battalion Royal Irish Rifles and he was killed in action on 9 May 1915 at Rouge Bancs.

Corporal John Quinn is commemorated on Newtownards and District War Memorial.

Quinn, Thomas (Tommy)
Rifleman
No. 13411, 8th Battalion, Royal Irish Rifles
Killed in action on Sunday 2 July 1916 (aged 21)
Thiepval Memorial, France (Pier and Face 15 A and 15 B)

Thomas Quinn was baptised on 20 May 1895 in First Newtownards Presbyterian Church and he was a son of Robert and Margaret Quinn (nee Welsh) who lived in the townland of Killarn, Newtownards. They were married on 15 November 1882 in First Newtownards Presbyterian Church. Robert Quinn worked as an agricultural labourer and he and Margaret had at least twelve children including John, David, William, Jane, Mary Elizabeth,

Thomas, Andrew (died), Robert, Agnes and Andrew. Prior to the outbreak of the Great War Thomas Quinn worked as a painter.

Thomas Quinn enlisted in Belfast and went to France with the 8th Battalion Royal Irish Rifles in 107th Brigade of the 36th (Ulster) Division. Initially Rifleman Thomas Quinn was posted as missing in action on the second day of the Battle of the Somme and then in August 1917 it was officially confirmed that he had been killed. In the heat of battle the 8th Battalion Royal Irish Rifles did not make a casualty return on 1 July 1916 and many military historians agree that those 8th Battalion casualties listed on the 2 July return were killed in action on 1 July.

Tommy Quinn's parents placed a 'For King and Country' notice in the 11 August 1917 edition of the *Newtownards Chronicle* and it contained the verse:

> 'Friends may forget him, but father and mother will never,
> He will dwell in our hearts till life's journey is done;
> Lord, teach us to live that when our days are ended
> We'll be met at the gates by our dear hero son.
> When days are dark, and friends are few,
> Oh, Tommy, how we'll long for you'

There were two other notices, one from his brother and sister-in-law William and Ena Quinn and one from his sister and niece Jane and Mary Russell.

When Tommy Quinn's death was confirmed his brother William Quinn and his brother-in-law John Russell were also on active service. **John Russell** (13322) was killed in action on 31 July 1917 and so, two weeks after Jane Russell placed the death notice for her brother Tommy Quinn she placed another one for her husband John.

Rifleman Tommy Quinn is commemorated on Newtownards and District War Memorial and in First Newtownards Presbyterian Church.

Rae, Richard
Private
No. 15910, 12th Battalion, Royal Scots (Lothian Regiment)
Killed in action on Saturday 15 July 1916
Quarry Cemetery, France (Grave II. L. 10)

In some records the surname is spelt Rea.

REMEMBERING THEIR SACRIFICE

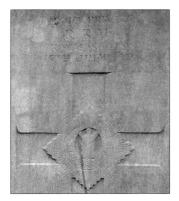

Richard Rae was born in Ballymena, Co Antrim and he was a son of James and Sarah Rae who lived in Greenvale Street, Ballymena. James Rae worked as a general labourer and he and Sarah had at least three children – Richard, David and James Hoy. Richard's father died in the early 1900s and his mother went to live with relatives – Samuel and Agnes Leetch (nee Rea) in Galgorm Street, Ballymena.

For a time Richard Rae worked for Messrs William McConnell & Sons (Provision Curers and Lard Refiners) in Hill Street, Ballymena. His brother James moved to Scotland where he and his wife Agnes lived in Kirkcaldy, Fifeshire. It was in Kirkcaldy that both brothers enlisted and they served with the 12th Battalion Royal Scots. James Rae was killed in action on 28 September 1915.

Private Richard Rae was killed in action on 15 July 1916, the day after the 12th Battalion Royal Scots launched an attack at Longueval during the Battle of the Somme. The 12th Battalion suffered very heavy casualties. At the time of Richard's death his mother was living at 12 Waverley Avenue, Ballymena and his wife was living in Newtownards.

> Private Richard Rea, Royal Scots, killed in action on 18th July, was for a number of years in the employment of Messrs. William M'Connell & Sons, Hill Street, Ballymena. His wife resides at Newtownards, and his mother at 12, Waveney Avenue, Ballymena.

Richard's death was reported in both the *Newtownards Chronicle* and the *Ballymena Observer*. Both brothers are commemorated on Ballymena War Memorial.

Rainey, David
Rifleman
No. 18/949, 12th Battalion, Royal Irish Rifles
Killed in action on Saturday 1 July 1916 (aged 27)
Thiepval Memorial, France (Pier and Face 15 A and 15 B)

David Rainey was born in Ballygowan and he was a son of Annie Stewart who lived in the townland of Tullyhubbert, Moneyreagh. Annie Stewart worked as a seamstress and David worked as a farm servant for the Jamison

> **Tullygirvan Rifleman Killed.**
> Mrs. Annie Stewart, Tullygirvan, Ballygowan, has received intimation that her son, Rifleman David Rainey, Royal Irish Rifles, missing since 1st July, is now reported killed.

family in the townland of Ballycreely, Moneyreagh

David Rainey lived in Comber, he enlisted in Newtownards and he served in France with the 12th Battalion Royal Irish Rifles in 108th Brigade of the 36th (Ulster) Division. He was killed in action on the first day of the Battle of the Somme although initially he was reported as missing in action. In May 1917 it was officially confirmed that he had been killed in action and at that time his mother was living in the townland of Tullygirvan, Ballygowan.

Rifleman David Rainey is commemorated in Ballygowan Presbyterian Church.

Rainey, Robert Boyd
Corporal
No. 12/23295, 9th Battalion, Royal Inniskilling Fusiliers
Killed in action on Thursday 7 June 1917 (aged 38)
Wytschaete Military Cemetery, Belgium (Grave II. E. 15)

In 'Soldiers Died in the Great War 1914 – 1919' it is recorded that Robert Boyd Rainey was born in Newtownards and he enlisted in Belfast. He was a son of William and Agnes Rainey. Corporal Robert Boyd Rainey served with the 9th Battalion Royal Inniskilling Fusiliers in 109th Brigade of the 36th (Ulster) Division and he was killed in action on 7 June 1917, the first day of the Battle of Messines.

R

Ravey, William
Rifleman
No. 17/853, 'D' Company, 8th Battalion, Royal Irish Rifles
Killed in action on Sunday 2 July 1916 (aged 26)
Thiepval Memorial, France (Pier and Face 15 A and 15 B)

William Ravey was born in Belfast and he was a son of John and Lizzie Ravey (nee Hughes) who lived at 133 Parkgate Avenue, Belfast. They were married on 7 June 1889 in Knock Methodist Church. John Ravey worked as a riveter in the shipyard and he and Lizzie had at least six children – William, John, David, Martha, Elizabeth and Alfred.

William Ravey worked as a plumber and he and Agnes Glenn were married on 9 July 1912 in Cregagh Presbyterian Church. They lived at 34 Glenvarlock Street, Belfast and they had one son named John. William enlisted in Belfast, he served with the 8th Battalion Royal Irish Rifles in 107th Brigade of the 36th (Ulster) Division and in the CWGC Debt of Honour it is recorded that he died on the second day of the Battle of the Somme. In the heat of battle the 8th Battalion Royal Irish Rifles did not make a casualty return on 1 July 1916 and many military historians agree that those 8th Battalion casualties listed on the 2 July return were killed in action on 1 July.

At the time of William's death his widow was living in Greyabbey and Rifleman William Ravey is commemorated on a headstone in Greyabbey Old Graveyard and in the Belfast Book of Honour (Page 546).

Rea, Daniel
Corporal
No. 10135, 10th Battalion, Hampshire Regiment
Killed in action on Saturday 21 August 1915 (aged 28)
Helles Memorial, Gallipoli, Turkey (Panel 125-134 or 223-226 228-229 & 328)

Daniel Rea was born on 21 November 1886 in Newtownards and he was a son of James and Margaret Rea (nee Savage) who were married on 13 April 1875 in First Newtownards Presbyterian Church. They had at least three children – James Savage (baptised in First Newtownards Presbyterian Church) and William John and Daniel (both baptised in Greenwell Street Presbyterian Church).

Daniel Rea enlisted in Southampton and he served with the 10th Battalion Hampshire Regiment. Between March 1915 and November 1916 this Battalion served in 29th Brigade of the 10th (Irish) Division and he was killed in action on 21 August 1915 at Gallipoli. Rifleman Daniel Rea is commemorated in the Belfast Book of Honour (Page 547).

Reains, William John (William)
Chief Stoker
No. 169665, HMS *Vivid*, Royal Navy
Died on Wednesday 12 January 1916 (aged 40)
Plymouth (Weston Mill) Cemetery, Devon (Naval Con. C. 3894)

William John Reains was born on 24 April 1875 in Donaghadee and he was a son of William John and Margaret Reains (nee Stewart). He was baptised in Shore Street Presbyterian Church Donaghadee.

William joined the Royal Navy when he was 18 years old and in 1901 he and Alice Maud Snell were married in Plymouth. Chief Stoker William John

R

Reains had more than 23 years service in the Royal Navy when he died on 12 January 1916. His death followed a prolonged illness and an operation in the Naval Hospital Devonport. During his naval career William saw service all over the world and he held the Somali and long service medals.

At the time of his death William's wife was living at 5 Herbert Street in Devonport. His sister and brother-in-law Alice Louisa and William McGimpsey (married on 21 October 1908 in First Newtownards Presbyterian Church) were living in Victoria Terrace, Donaghadee. His brother Henry and Jane Anna Hill were married on 4 January 1905 in Ballymacarrett Parish Church of Ireland (St Patrick's).

Regan Brothers: Robert and Samuel Hugh

Robert and Samuel Hugh Regan were born in the townland of Tullykevin, (Tullycavey) Ballywalter and they were sons of John and Catherine Regan (nee Reid) who lived in the townland of Springvale, Ballywalter. John and Catherine were married on 3 October 1884 in Ballywalter Presbyterian Church. John Regan worked as an agricultural labourer and he and Catherine had three children – Samuel Hugh, Annie Eliza and Robert. Catherine Regan died when Robert was very young and his father John married Elizabeth (Eliza) Thompson from Ballyhalbert on 26 February 1909 in Glastry Presbyterian Church. John and Eliza had at least two children, Isabella (born 19 November 1910) and John (born 24 October 1913). Both were baptised in Ballywalter Parish Church of Ireland. Robert was the first of the two brothers to die during the Great War:

R

Regan, Robert (Robbie)
Rifleman
No. 19183, 'B' Company, 13th Battalion, Royal Irish Rifles
Killed in action on Saturday 1 July 1916 (aged 21)
A.I.F. Burial Ground, France (Grave X. A. 2)

Robert Regan was born on 11 March 1895 and he was the second son of John and Catherine Regan. He was baptised in Ballywalter Parish Church of Ireland and he was very young when his mother died.

Prior to the outbreak of the Great War Robert Regan worked as an agricultural labourer. He enlisted in Ballywalter, he served with the 13th Battalion Royal Irish Rifles in 108th

Brigade of the 36th (Ulster) Division and he was killed in action on the first day of the Battle of the Somme.

Regan, Samuel Hugh (Samuel)
Rifleman
No. 19177, 'B' Company, 13th Battalion, Royal Irish Rifles
Died of pulmonary tuberculosis on Thursday 28 February 1918 (aged 32)
Whitechurch Cemetery, Ballywalter, Co. Down

Samuel Hugh Regan was born on 14 July 1885 and he was baptised in Ballywalter Presbyterian Church. He was the eldest child of John and Catherine Regan.

Prior to the outbreak of the Great War, Samuel Hugh Regan worked as a general labourer and he was employed by Lord Dunleath in Ballywalter Park. He and Elizabeth (Lizzie) Johnston were married on 29 April 1910 in Ballywalter Parish Church of Ireland. Lizzie worked as an embroiderer and they lived in the townland of Springvale, Ballywalter. Samuel and Lizzie had three children all of whom were baptised in Ballywalter Parish Church of Ireland – Kathleen born 1 February 1912, Mary Ann born 19 December 1913 and Samuel born 30 April 1917. Mary Ann was killed on 1 October 1916 when an army vehicle knocked her down on the Springvale Road. She was less than three years old. The vehicle was being driven by Lieutenant Leo McCormick 12th Battalion Royal Irish Rifles and at an inquest a verdict of accidental death was returned with no blame attached to anyone.

Samuel Hugh Regan enlisted in Ballywalter on 17 September 1914 and he joined the 13th Battalion Royal Irish Rifles. In his attestation papers it was noted that he was 5 feet 6¾ inches tall and he had a star and anchor tattoo on his left hand. He went to Clandeboye Camp for training and it was from there that he was discharged from the Army on 16 March 1915. He was considered unfit for further military service due to 'pulmonary tuberculosis attributable to service'. It was noted that his condition originated on 15 February 1915 in Clandeboye Camp and it was as a result of 'ordinary military service attributable to cold, damp and exposure'. He qualified for a pension with effect from 19 September 1917 (Chelsea No. 107782) and he died on 28 February 1918. He was buried in Whitechurch Cemetery Ballywalter on Sunday 3 March 1918 when his son Samuel was less than a year old. Samuel Hugh Regan is commemorated on the family grave headstone:

R

Erected by Samuel Regan in loving memory of his daughter Mary Ann Regan
killed in motor accident 1st Oct. 1916 aged 3 years
'Asleep in Jesus'
Also the above Samuel Regan who died 28th Feb. 1918 aged 32 years
'He giveth his beloved sleep'
Also his wife Elizabeth Regan died 21st Feb. 1980 aged 87 years.

Elizabeth Regan had been a widow for almost 62 years.

Both Rifleman Robert Regan and Rifleman Samuel Hugh Regan are commemorated on Ballywalter and District War Memorial and in Ballywalter Parish Church of Ireland (Holy Trinity).

Regan, Robert
Rifleman
No. 19/488, 'C' Company, 12th Battalion, Royal Irish Rifles
Killed in action on Tuesday 1 October 1918 (aged 19)
Dadizeele New British Cemetery, Belgium (Grave II. C. 20)

Robert Regan was born in the townland of Gordonall, Greyabbey and he was the eldest son of Thomas Henry and Harriet Jane Regan (nee McKay) who lived in the townland of Bootown, Greyabbey. They were married on 8 January 1897 in Greyabbey Parish Church of Ireland. Thomas Henry Regan worked as an agricultural labourer and he and Harriet had at least five children – Robert, Frederick, Edward, Ernest and John. Frederick, Ernest and John were baptised in Greyabbey Parish Church of Ireland.

R

On 23 May 1916 Robert Regan enlisted in Newtownards and he joined the Young Citizens' Volunteers. He spent three months training in Donard Camp, Newcastle before proceeding to France. He returned to Ireland for a time before going back to France on 29 March 1918. Shortly afterwards he was wounded in the leg and he spent time in an Australian field hospital before returning to the front line.

The last letter that he wrote to his father arrived on 3 October 1918 and in it he expressed the hope that he would soon be home again. By then Robert Regan was already dead but his family did not know it. On 24 October 1918 his family received official notification that Robert had been killed in action on 1 October 1918 during the Allied offensive against all sections of the German line.

In a letter to Robert's mother the Rev Hubert Orr said that Robert's Company had been ordered to attack a position which was strongly held by the enemy. In the advance Robert was hit in the chest by machine-gun fire and death was instantaneous.

Robert's father, mother and brothers placed a death notice in the 9 November 1918 edition of the *Newtownards Chronicle* and it contained the verse:

'In the bloom of life death claimed him,
In the pride of his manhood days,
Somewhere in France, we cannot tell,
The spot in which our dear son fell'

Rifleman Robert Regan is commemorated on Greyabbey and District War Memorial located on the outside wall of Greyabbey Parish Church of Ireland (St Saviour). Less than six months before Robert Regan died, his uncle **Robert McKay** was killed in action on 15 April 1918.

R

Regan, William
Rifleman
No. 19/730, 10th Battalion, Royal Irish Rifles
Killed in action on Tuesday 26 June 1917 (aged 19)
Derry House Cemetery No. 2, Belgium (Grave I. B. 5)

William Regan was born in Newtownards and he was a son of William and Margaret Regan who lived at 21 Wallace's Street. William Regan Senior worked as a tailor and he and Margaret had at least ten children including Robert, Jane, Maria, Maggie, Sarah, William, Andrew and John.

Described in the *Newtownards Chronicle* as a 'slip of a youth' William Regan enlisted in Belfast and he trained with the 19th Battalion Royal Irish Rifles before being transferred to the 10th Battalion in 107th Brigade of the 36th (Ulster) Division. He was killed by shellfire on 26 June 1917 and his comrades placed a 'For King and Country' notice in the *Newtownards Chronicle*. It contained the verse:

'No longer must the mourners weep,
Nor call departed Christians dead;
For death is hallowed into sleep,
And every grave becomes a bed.'

His widowed father, brothers and sisters placed a notice which contained the verse:

'He was a brother truly fond,
A friend both kind and true;
A better brother never lived,
His equals were but few.
He never shunned his country's call,
But gladly gave his life – his all;
He died, the helpless to defend,
An Ulster soldier's noble end'

The Rev DR Mitchell, Chaplain attached to the 10th Royal Irish Rifles, wrote to William's father to express his sympathy. In the letter he explained how William had been killed by shell fire when he was at his post of duty in a trench. His death had been instantaneous and under cover of darkness his body was recovered and buried the following day with 'as full military honours as the circumstances would permit. Because he was held in great esteem the commanding officer himself and all the headquarters officers were present at the funeral'. Rifleman William Regan is commemorated on Newtownards and District War Memorial and in Newtownards Parish Church of Ireland (St Mark).

Regan, W

The name Regan, W is listed once on Newtownards and District War Memorial; the name Regan W is listed twice on the War Memorial Plaque in Newtownards Parish Church of Ireland (St Mark).

Rifleman William Regan (19/730) who served with the 10th Battalion Royal Irish Rifles and who died on 26 June 1917 has been accounted for. Desk searches and public appeals to date have yielded no further information about the second Regan W who lived in Zion Place, Newtownards, and who is commemorated in Newtownards Parish Church of Ireland (St Mark).

Reid, James
Private
312th Infantry Regiment, 78th Infantry Division, US Army
Died on Friday 7 March 1919 (aged 29)
St. Mihiel American Cemetery, France (Plot A Row 9 Grave 10)

James Reid was born on 15 April 1889 and he was a son of John and Hester (Essie) Reid (nee Orr) who lived in Carrowdore. They were married on 17 October 1879 in Carrowdore Presbyterian Church. John Reid worked as an agricultural labourer and he and Essie had at least six children – James Bryans, Matilda, James, Maggie, Nevin and Robert John. All of the children were baptised in Carrowdore Presbyterian Church.

James Reid worked as a labourer both before and after he moved to the United States of America. He and Niven Stewart, also from Carrowdore, lived in Chicago, Illinois and it was there that both men enlisted on 5 June 1917.

James Reid served with the 312th Infantry Regiment 78th Infantry Division US Army and he died on 7 March 1919. **Niven Boyd Stewart** was killed in action on 10 November 1918.

Private James Reid and Corporal Niven Boyd Stewart are both commemorated in Carrowdore Presbyterian Church. James's mother Essie died in 1930 and his father John died in 1935.

Reid, Samuel James (Samuel)
Private
No. 9869, 1st Battalion, Royal Inniskilling Fusiliers
Killed in action on Saturday 22 May 1915 (aged 24)
Pink Farm Cemetery, Helles, Gallipoli, Turkey (Sp. Mem. 83)

Samuel James Reid was born on 22 April 1891 and he was a son of Samuel James and Matilda Reid (nee Burch) who were married on 23 March 1891 in Carrowdore Parish Church of Ireland. Samuel James Senior worked as an agricultural labourer and he and Matilda had seven children all of whom were baptised in Carrowdore Parish Church of Ireland – Samuel James, Hugh, Margaret, Anna, Eliza Jane, Agnes Burch and Mary Matilda who was born on 7 April 1900 just nine days before her mother died at the age of 29.

R

At that time the Reid family was living in Carrowdore with Ann Reid the children's paternal grandmother. Samuel James Senior married Ellen Campbell on 3 July 1901 in Ballyfrenis Free Church of Scotland (Presbyterian), Carrowdore and they had at least two children including John who was born on 19 May 1902 and baptised in Carrowdore Parish Church of Ireland. The Reid family moved from Carrowdore to Newtownards where Samuel James worked as a quarryman and they lived at 26 Front Shuttlefield before moving to 30 James Street, Newtownards.

Samuel James Junior served for seven years in the Army with the Royal Inniskilling Fusiliers, four of them in India. He went with the Expeditionary Force to Gallipoli and he died there on 22 May 1915. This is the date of death in official records although the date of death in some newspaper reports is 13 June 1915. His death was reported in the 26 June edition of the *Newtownards Chronicle* under the headline 'Killed at the Dardanelles' and in the words of the newspaper report 'When our troops forced a landing in Gallipoli they did so under a murderous hail of fire and at a severe cost. Private Reid and another comrade were the only two of 'H' Company of the Inniskillings left after a landing had been affected. At one period Private Reid had to practically bury himself in the sand for 48 hours to save himself.'

At the time of Samuel's death his brother Hugh was in hospital in France.

Private Samuel Reid's family placed an 'Our Heroes – In Memoriam' notice in the 23 June 1917 edition of the *Newtownards Chronicle* and it contained the verse:

> *'Two years have passed, but still we miss him,*
> *Some may think the wound is healed;*
> *But they little know the sorrow*
> *That lies beneath a smile concealed'*

At that time the Reid family was living at 45 Frederick Street, Newtownards. Private Samuel Reid is commemorated on Newtownards and District War Memorial and in Newtownards Parish Church of Ireland (St Mark).

Reilly, Thomas
Private
No. 6307, 13th Battalion, Australian Infantry, AIF
Died of wounds on Tuesday 6 February 1917 (aged 38)
Dernancourt Communal Cemetery Extension, France (Grave V. A. 2)

Thomas Reilly was born in Donaghadee and he was a son of Charles and

Elizabeth Reilly (nee McMeekin) who were married on 6 June 1869 in Ballycopeland Presbyterian Church. Charles Reilly worked as a policeman and he and Elizabeth had five children including William, Thomas and John. They moved to Belfast and then, after Charles died, Elizabeth worked as an embroiderer and the family moved back to Donaghadee (where Elizabeth was born). They lived at 7 Bow Street and Thomas Reilly worked as a railway fireman and then as an engine driver. Thomas got married around 1907 and he and his wife had one child, a daughter named Anne Maria. A short time later Thomas's wife died. Thomas moved to Australia where he worked as an engine driver and he enlisted on 1 May 1916 in Sydney. In his attestation papers it was noted that he was a widower, he was 38 years 4 months old and he was 6 feet 1½ inches tall. He left Sydney on 9 September 1916 aboard the *Euripides* and after a seven-week voyage he arrived in Plymouth on 26 October 1916.

Private Thomas Reilly went to France in mid-January 1917, he served with the 13th Battalion, Australian Infantry and he was wounded in action a few days later on 4 February 1917. He was taken to 1/1 South Midland Casualty Clearing Station in France and two days later he died of a fractured skull.

R

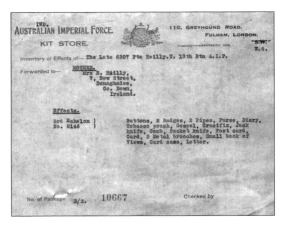

In his will he had written 'In the event of my death I give the whole of my property and effects to my mother Elizabeth Reilly'. His personal effects were gathered together and the following items were sent to his mother – buttons, 2 badges, 2 pipes, purse, diary, tobacco pouch, gospel, crucifix, jack knife, comb, pocket knife, post card, card, 3 metal brooches, small book of views, card case and letter.

At the time of Thomas's death his daughter Anne Maria was living in Point Road, Dundalk, Co Louth with Anne Lennon her widowed grandmother.

Private Thomas Reilly is commemorated on Donaghadee and District War Memorial.

Rice, Alfred James (Alfred)
Junior Second Engineer Officer
No. SS *Hungerford* (London), Mercantile Marine
Drowned on Tuesday 16 April 1918 (aged 26)
Tower Hill Memorial, London

Alfred James Rice was born in Newtownards and he was a son of Laurence and Agnes Rice (nee Edmonds) who were married on 16 August 1878 in Nunsquarter Roman Catholic Church, Kircubbin. They went to live at 107 Ogilvie Street in Belfast. Laurence Rice worked as a baker and he and Agnes had at least ten children including Henry, Robert, Laurence, Alfred James and Patrick Joseph.

Alfred James Rice worked as an engine fitter before he went to sea. He was drowned on 16 April 1918 after his ship, the SS *Hungerford* (London), was torpedoed and sunk in the English Channel by the German submarine UC-75 whilst on a voyage from Le Havre to New York. Eight lives were lost and Junior Second Engineer Officer Alfred James Rice is commemorated in the Belfast Book of Honour (Page 554).

R

Rice, William
It is recorded in the annals of Cloughey Presbyterian Church that William Rice, a member of the congregation, was killed in action in 1917. Research has shown that William Rice was born in County Antrim and he was a son of William Rice who worked as a carter. In 1911 William Rice Junior was working as a postman in Portaferry and he lived at 37 Market Square, Portaferry where he boarded with Robert and Minnie Lemon. Robert Lennon was as a master carpenter.

William Rice and Margaret McNamara were married on 14 April 1911 in Cloughey Presbyterian Church and afterwards their address was Post Office, Cloughey. William and Margaret had two children – Marjorie Jeanetta who was born on 17 February 1912 and William John who was born on 17 December 1913, became a seaman and was drowned at sea.

Six servicemen named W Rice who died in 1917 are listed in the CWGC Debt of Honour. Four can be eliminated by virtue of the family details provided. The service details for the most likely soldier are as follows:

Gunner William Rice served in 'A' Battery, 190th Brigade, Royal Field Artillery (195981), he died on 26 September 1917 and he is buried in Larch Wood (Railway Cutting) Cemetery (Special Memorial A 6) in Belgium. Desk searches and public appeals to date have not confirmed a connection between these service data and the serviceman who is commemorated in the annals of Cloughey Presbyterian Church.

Richardson, Mervyn Stronge (Mervyn)
Mentioned in Despatches
Captain
1st Battalion, Royal Welsh Fusiliers
Killed in action on Sunday 19 March 1916 (aged 21)
Point 110 New Military Cemetery, France (Grave D. 4)

Mervyn Stronge Richardson came from fighting stock that included General Sir Rollo Gillespie whose statue stands in Comber (a cousin of his great-grandfather) and Sir James Stronge of Tynan Abbey (his maternal great-grandfather).

Mervyn Richardson was born on 21 June 1894 in Killynether Castle Newtownards and he was the youngest son of Captain Arthur Percy Richardson and Ethel Mary Richardson (nee Stronge) who lived in Purton House, Purton in Wiltshire. Mervyn was educated at Bilton Grange, Rugby, Radley College and the Royal Military College Sandhurst. At Radley he was Captain of the Boats and he was a member of the Leander Club (a prestigious rowing club established in 1818).

Mervyn Richardson was commissioned on 15 August 1914 and in September 1914 he went to France with a draft, joined the 2nd Battalion on the Aisne and was in action continually till he sustained a gunshot wound in the back on 10 April 1915 and was admitted to No. 3 General Hospital at Treport. He was injured again in September 1915 by an enemy grenade and he was killed in action at Fricourt on 19 March 1916 when he died after being blown into a water-filled shell-hole by an exploding shell.

In the records it is noted that when he was in France Mervyn Richardson acted as Captain of the Regimental Rugby Team and that he was one of five officers selected to meet King George V on the King's first visit to the army in the field. Mervyn recorded details of 'the extraordinary day' he spent on Christmas Day 1914 when German and British soldiers met in no man's land, shook hands, exchanged gifts and agreed to cease hostilities for the day.

Captain Mervyn Stronge Richardson is commemorated on Newtownards and District War Memorial (in the War Memorial Booklet he is listed as having served in the Border Regiment) and on the Purton War Memorial in Wiltshire.

Rilley, James Henry*
Private
No. 18/1429, Royal Irish Rifles, transferred to (109545), 2nd Labour Company, Royal Irish Regiment, transferred to (2/L/517), 183rd Company, Labour Corps
Killed in action on Thursday 14 February 1918 (aged 37)
Boyelles Communal Cemetery Extension, France (Grave II. B. 3)

In some records the surname is spelt Riley (Newtownards and District War Memorial) and in other records it is spelt Reilly (1911 Census).

James Henry Rilley was born in Ballynahinch and later his mother lived in Killyleagh. James Rilley worked as a labourer for Robert McBurney in the townland of Ballyhenry, Comber and prior to the outbreak of the Great War James and his wife Mary (nee Courtney) lived at 114 Mill Street, Newtownards. They were married on 11 October 1901 in Raffrey Presbyterian Church and they had at least nine children including Samuel J, Minnie, Annie, William H, John Francis, Robert Sidney, Sarah Ellen and Eileen. The last four were baptised in Greenwell Street Presbyterian Church Newtownards.

James Henry Rilley enlisted in May 1916 in Newtownards and according to 'Soldiers Died in the Great War 1914 – 1919' he served with the Royal Irish Rifles (1429) before transferring to the Labour Corps. He was killed in action on 14 February 1918.

Mary Rilley first heard about her husband's death when she received a letter from the Rev Roland H Streatfield. He told her that the Labour Company had come under heavy shellfire on 14 February and that her husband was among the casualties. He assured her that James's death had been instantaneous. For the burial his coffin was draped with the Union Jack and at the graveside his comrades sang the hymns 'Abide with me' and 'Sun of my soul'.

Mary Rilley placed a 'For King and Country' notice in the 20 April 1918 edition of the *Newtownards Chronicle* and it contained the verse:

'One by one the links are slipping,
One by one our heroes fall;
And you my darling husband,
Have answered the great Roll-call.
A loving father, true and kind,
Loved by those he left behind;
Forget him, no, we never will,
As time goes on we love him still.'

Private James Henry Rilley is commemorated on Newtownards and District War Memorial and in Newtownards Parish Church of Ireland (St Mark).

Ritchie, Francis Michael (Frank)
Lance Corporal
No. 26839, 9th Battalion, Royal Inniskilling Fusiliers
Killed in action on Friday 29 March 1918 (aged 34)
Pozieres Memorial, Somme, France (Panel 38 to 40)

R

Francis Michael Ritchie was born in 1884 and he was a son of Francis Ritchie who lived in the townland of Ballyminstra, Killinchy. Francis Michael Ritchie worked as an agricultural labourer and he and Annie Maria Middleton were married on 25 March 1905 in Kilmood Church of Ireland. They had at least four children – Henry, Francis, Eliza Jane and James – and they lived in the townland of Ballymaglaff, Comber and later in the townland of Corporation South, Newtownards.

Frank Ritchie enlisted in Newtownards and he served with the 9th Battalion Royal Inniskilling Fusiliers in 109th Brigade of the 36th Ulster Division. He was killed in action on 29 March 1918 during the early stages of the German 'Michael' offensive. In the CWGC Debt of Honour his age is recorded as 28.

Ritchie, Henry Douglas (Henry)
Private
No. 7854, 4th Regiment, South African Infantry
Killed in action on Monday 9 April 1917 (aged 36)
Highland Cemetery, Roclincourt, France (Grave I. B. 5)

Henry Douglas Ritchie was born on 22 March 1881 and he was a son of John Whitla Ritchie and Mary Alice Ritchie (nee McDowell) who were married on 25 June 1874 in Gilnahirk Presbyterian Church. John Whitla Ritchie worked as a merchant in Comber and he and Mary had at least four children – Amy Whitla, James McDowell, Henry Douglas and Elizabeth (Lillie) Victoria. After Mary died John married Josephine McDowell on 15 April 1896 in Second Comber Presbyterian Church and they lived in High Street, Comber. They had at least one son – John Arnold.

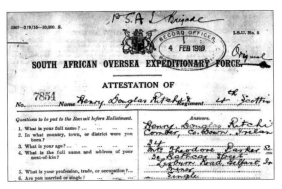

Henry Douglas Ritchie worked as a shop assistant and he lived in Bridge Street, Comber with his widowed maternal grandmother Jane McDowell (aged 89 in 1901). He moved to South Africa where he worked as a miner. He enlisted at Potchefstroom on 3 December 1915 and in his attestation papers it was noted that he was 34 years old and that he was 5 feet 11 inches tall. He cited as his next-of-kin his sister Elizabeth who was married to Joshua Theodore Parker and who lived at 30 Rathcar Street, Lisburn Road, Belfast. He joined the 4th Regiment South African Infantry and after his initial training he travelled from Capetown via Southampton to France.

Private Henry Douglas Ritchie went to the front on 23 November 1916 and he was killed in action on 9 April 1917. He is commemorated on Comber and District War Memorial and in First Comber Presbyterian Church. In the CWGC Debt of Honour his age is recorded as 33.

Ritchie, Hugh Graham (Hugh)
Private
No. 138207, 75th Battalion, Canadian Infantry (Central Ontario Regiment)
Died of disease (phthisis) on Friday 6 May 1921 (aged 26)
Toronto (Prospect) Cemetery, Canada (Veterans. Sec. 7. 976)

Hugh Graham Ritchie was born on 18 January 1895 and he was a son of Hugh and Cynthia Ritchie (nee Frame) who lived in Ballyhalbert. They were married on 5 July 1890 in May Street Presbyterian Church in Belfast. Hugh and Cynthia both worked as National School teachers and they had at least ten children all of whom were baptised in Glastry Presbyterian Church – Ethel, Arthur Frame, James Colville, Hugh Graham, Robert Workman,

John Andrew, Margaret Glover, Alexandrina and Albert Edward (twins) and Cynthia Gertrude.

Hugh Graham Ritchie moved to Canada where he worked as a cutter before the outbreak of the Great War. He enlisted on 20 July 1915 in Toronto and in his attestation papers it was noted that he was 5 feet 7 inches tall.

Private Hugh Ritchie served with the 75th Battalion Canadian Infantry and he died of phthisis (pulmonary tuberculosis) on 6 May 1921. He was buried in Toronto. Hugh Ritchie's mother died on 26 January 1930 and his father Hugh died on 31 January 1938.

Ritchie, Samuel
Private
No. 9088, 2nd Battalion, Royal Inniskilling Fusiliers
Killed in action on Wednesday 26 August 1914
La Ferte-Sous-Jouarre Memorial, France

In 'Soldiers Died in the Great War 1914 – 1919' it is recorded that Samuel Ritchie was born in Newtownards and he enlisted in Belfast. Private Samuel Ritchie served with the 2nd Battalion Royal Inniskilling Fusiliers and he was killed in action on 26 August 1914 just three days after he arrived in France.

Robinson, Alexander (Alex)
Rifleman
No. 18687, 'B' Company, 13th Battalion, Royal Irish Rifles
Killed in action on Saturday 1 July 1916 (aged 18)
Thiepval Memorial, France (Pier and Face 15 A and 15 B)

Alexander Robinson was born in Newtownards and he was a son of William Alexander and Grace Robinson (nee Rainey) who lived at 3 Lower Mary Street. Previous addresses in Newtownards included Mill Street and William Street Place. They were married on 23 September 1890 in Greenwell Street Presbyterian Church Newtownards. William Alexander Robinson worked as an agricultural labourer, Grace was a laundry worker and they had at least six children – James, Grace, Wilhelmina, Alexander, Jane and David.

Alexander Robinson worked as a message boy before the outbreak of the Great War and he served in 'B' Company of the local contingent of the Ulster Volunteer Force. He was underage when he enlisted in Newtownards on 17 September 1914 and he served with the 13th Battalion Royal Irish Rifles in 108th Brigade of the 36th (Ulster) Division.

R

ANOTHER NEWTOWNARDS MAN KILLED.

This week's casualty lists includes the name of (No. 18,687) Rifleman A. Robinson, Newtownards, who was previously reported missing, and is now reported killed.

Rifleman Alexander Robinson was killed in action on the first day of the Battle of the Somme. Initially he was posted as missing in action and it was officially confirmed in February 1917 that he had been killed in action. The Officers and Members of Total Abstainers Loyal Orange Lodge No. 991 expressed their regret in a 'For King and Country' notice that they placed in the 3 March 1917 edition of the *Newtownards Chronicle*. He is commemorated on Newtownards and District War Memorial and in the PCI Roll of Honour for Greenwell Street Presbyterian Church Newtownards.

Robinson, David
Rifleman
No. 18/20677, 2nd Battalion, Royal Irish Rifles
Killed in action on Sunday 24 March 1918 (aged 26)
Pozieres Memorial, France (Panel 74 to 76)

David Robinson was born on 20 January 1892 in Newtownards and he was the third son of Hugh and Alice Robinson (nee McCullough) who lived in East Street, Newtownards. They were married on 27 April 1883 Newtownards

Parish Church of Ireland and they had at least thirteen children including Hugh (1885), Mary, Agnes Jane (1887), David (1892), Alice, Andrew (1895), Annabelle (1897) and Maggie (1899). David's father Hugh died in the early 1900s and his mother worked as a general dealer. The family moved to 3 Castle Place in Newtownards.

Prior to the outbreak of the Great War David Robinson worked as a butcher. He enlisted in Belfast and joined the 18th Battalion Royal Irish Rifles. He was posted to the 2nd Battalion Royal Irish Rifles and when he was killed in action on 24 March 1918 at the beginning of the German 'Michael' offensive his Battalion was part of 108th Brigade in the 36th (Ulster) Division. Initially it was reported that David was missing in action and some six months later it was confirmed that he had been killed in action. His widowed mother placed a 'For King and Country' notice in the 21 September 1918 edition of the *Newtownards Chronicle* and it contained the verse:

R

> 'He sleeps not in his native land,
> But under foreign skies;
> He sleeps far from those he loved;
> In a hero's grave he lies.
> Friends may forget him, but his mother will never;
> He will dwell in my heart till life's journey is done.
> Lord! Teach me to live, and when my days are ended,
> I may meet at the gates, my dear hero son.'

The following week there were notices from his sister and brother-in-law Mary and Andrew McDowell of 4 Queen Street, Newtownards, his sister and brother-in-law Maggie and William Robson of 3 Castle Place, Newtownards, his two sisters in Canada and his brothers on active service. His two sisters in Canada lived in Winnipeg; Agnes was married to William Moorecroft and Alice was married to Samuel Kells.

Rifleman David Robinson is commemorated on Newtownards and District War Memorial and in Newtownards Parish Church of Ireland (St Mark).

Robinson, James
Rifleman
No. 18/1087, 12th Battalion, Royal Irish Rifles
Died of wounds on Tuesday 4 July 1916 (aged 22)
Puchevillers British Cemetery, France (Grave I. B. 36)

James Robinson was born in the townland of Cannyreagh, Donaghadee and he was a son of Mrs Agnes Robinson who lived in the townland of Ballyvester, Donaghadee. Agnes Robinson worked as a domestic servant and she had at least three children – Aggie, James and Minnie.

Prior to the outbreak of the Great War James Robinson worked as a farm servant on the farm belonging to his maternal grandparents James and Eliza Taylor who lived in Cannyreagh.

In November 1915 James Robinson enlisted in Donaghadee and joined the 18th Battalion Royal Irish Rifles. He was posted to the 12th Battalion Royal Irish Rifles and he served overseas in 108th Brigade of the 36th (Ulster) Division. On 4 July 1916 he died of wounds received during the Battle of the Somme.

After Rifleman James Robinson died three 'For King and Country' notices were placed in the *Newtownards Chronicle*, one from the Blue Banner Total Abstinence Loyal Orange Lodge No. 781 in Donaghadee, one from the Blue Banner Total Abstinence Royal Arch Purple Chapter No. 781 in Donaghadee and one from his mother, sister, grandparents and friends. The latter contained the verse:

> '*We do not know what pain he bore,*
> *We did not see him die,*
> *We only knew he passed away,*
> *And could not say good-bye*'

Rifleman James Robinson is commemorated on Donaghadee and District War Memorial and in First Donaghadee Presbyterian Church.

Robinson, John Singleton Henry (Jack)
Captain
13th Battalion attached 12th Battalion, Welsh Regiment
Died on Tuesday 24 September 1918 (aged 26)
Marteville Communal Cemetery, France (Grave C. 9)

R

R

John Singleton Henry (Jack) Robinson was born on 19 March 1892 and he was the third son of James and Elizabeth Robinson (nee McCullough) who lived in West Street and later in North Street, Newtownards. They were married on 12 July 1871 in Newtownards Parish Church of Ireland. James Robinson worked as a barber and he and Elizabeth had at least ten children including Margaret (1884), William James (1887), Elizabeth, Joseph, Ruth, Mary (1889), John (1892), Robert (1894) and Hugh. Jack's father James died on 27 December 1896. Prior to the outbreak of the Great War Jack Robinson worked as a teacher in the Model School Newtownards and then in St Barnabas's and St Enoch's in Belfast.

Jack joined the Queen's University Belfast Officers' Training Corps and he obtained his commission as Second Lieutenant in October 1915. He went to France on 26 June 1916 as a Lieutenant in the Welsh Regiment. His brother, Corporal William James Robinson, served at the front with the Engineers, US Army.

In July 1916 Jack was wounded at the Somme when he was buried by a bursting shell. After treatment Lieutenant Robinson had a period of home leave and when he returned to duty he was posted to the 3rd Battalion at Cardiff. He returned to the front line and in March 1917 he was admitted to hospital in Boulogne suffering from shell shock. In May 1917 he came home on convalescent leave for three weeks. Then he was posted for light duty with a battalion of his regiment stationed at Rhyl in Wales. He was promoted to the rank of Captain in February 1918.

Two weeks after a period of home leave in September 1918 Captain John Robinson (Robbie as he was known affectionately throughout the battalion) was killed by a sniper's bullet which passed straight through his head. Lieutenant Ivor Ajax wrote a letter of sympathy to Jack Robinson's mother who was then living at 7308 Race Street, Homewood, Pittsburgh, USA and with it he enclosed a letter which Jack had asked him to send in the event of him being killed. Jack wrote the letter on 24 September 1918, the day he died:

'Mother Darling, Brothers and Sisters
I am going into action again with my company and feel very proud indeed as
I know it will do well. We all know that it is for a good cause, and as it is all
in good hands we leave it at that. For myself, I trust in God as I have always
done, and am prepared for anything that might happen. If we don't meet again
in this world we will meet in His glorious Kingdom, where struggles all cease.

All I possess belongs to you, mother darling, and may God bless you all, and all my good friends. Au Revoir, your big loving son, Jack.'

Captain John Singleton Henry Robinson is commemorated on Newtownards and District War Memorial; in Newtownards Parish Church of Ireland (St Mark); on the QUB War Memorial; in the QUB Book of Remembrance (Page 47) and on the family grave headstone in Movilla Cemetery Newtownards.

Robinson, Robert
Rifleman
No. 460, 'A' Company, 13th Battalion, Royal Irish Rifles
Died of wounds on Thursday 15 February 1917 (aged 42)
Bailleul Communal Cemetery Extension (Nord), France (Grave III. A. 46)

Robert Robinson was born on 10 June 1874 in Donaghadee and he was a son of Abel and Margaret Robinson (nee Andrews) who lived in Bow Street. They were married on 4 January 1872 in Shore Street Presbyterian Church Donaghadee. Abel Robinson worked as a seaman, Margaret worked as an embroiderer and they had at least four children – Robert, Mary Matilda, Jane and Frances, all of whom were baptised in Shore Street Presbyterian Church. Robert Robinson's father Abel died on 4 August 1910 and his mother Margaret died on 11 December 1920.

R

Prior to the Great War Robert Robinson worked as a tailor. He and Hannah Kennedy were married on 28 March 1904 in Ballycopeland Presbyterian Church and they had two children – Margaret and Thomas Kennedy. Hannah Robinson died in 1909 aged 29. The Robinson family lived in Donaghadee and Robert was a member of the Ulster Volunteer Force. Robert Robinson enlisted in Belfast and he served with the 13th Battalion Royal Irish Rifles in 108th Brigade of the 36th (Ulster) Division. Due to illness he was invalided home in February 1916 for a short time before he returned to active service.

Rifleman R. Robinson (No. 460), Royal Irish Rifles, died of wounds. Deceased was connected with the U.V.F.

On 15 February 1917 Rifleman Robert Robinson died of wounds sustained around 1.00 am the previous day when there was a heavy enemy bombardment followed up by a raid. Rifleman **William McKittrick** was also killed during that bombardment on 14 February and then at 6.00 pm on 14 February there was another enemy attack during which Lance Corporal **Robert H Marshall** was killed.

Rifleman Robert Robinson is commemorated on Donaghadee and District

War Memorial; in Shore Street Presbyterian Church Donaghadee and on the family grave headstone in Donaghadee Parish Church of Ireland Graveyard.

Robinson, Robert Davidson (Rob)
Driver
**No. 14821, 1st Siege Battery Ammunitions Column, Australian Army
Service Corps, AIF
Died on Wednesday 6 April 1921 (aged 23)
South Brisbane Cemetery, Queensland, Australia
(Gen. 2. 3A. 1L. GRM/4*)**

Robert Davidson Robinson was born on 29 October 1897 in Killinchy and he was a son of James and Mary Robinson (nee Davidson). James Robinson was a farmer and he owned the Corn and Flax Mill at Balloo.

He and Mary had two children – Robert and James, both baptised in Killinchy Presbyterian Church. Mary's parents, Robert and Jane Davidson, lived with them as did Rob's half-brother Thomas (born 23 May 1885 and James Robinson's son from his earlier marriage to Anna Jane Graham).

Rob Davidson owned a motor-bike and he enjoyed riding along the country roads in County Down, often with his mother in the sidecar. He was 16 years old when the war began and he wanted to enlist. In order to distract him from this idea his mother sent him out to Australia in the autumn of 1915 to stay with her brother Jim, Jim's wife Louie and their four sons. Rob tried to enlist in Australia but he was rejected at his first attempt because he did not meet the minimum physical requirements of the AIF. He tried again on 2 January 1917 in Brisbane and this time he was accepted. It was noted in his attestation papers that he was 5 feet 6 inches tall. Around the same time all

R

four of his Davidson cousins in Australia enlisted – Robert, Eric, Walker and Peter.

Initially Rob was sent to the Motor Transport Unit at Enoggera Army Base near Brisbane and, after training as a Driver/Mechanic, his Unit arrived in England in late 1917 and they were stationed at the main AIF base in Salisbury. Rob went to France in February 1918 and was assigned to the 4th Motorised Transport Company. A month later, after the Germans launched a major offensive against the Allies in France, Rob was assigned to the 1st Siege Battery Ammunitions Column transporting equipment and munitions to the troops on the front line. In April 1918 Rob contracted trench fever, a disease transmitted by body lice, and he was hospitalised in Etaples before being taken to England. After four months recuperation, including a period of leave in Killinchy, he rejoined his unit in France in August 1918.

Following the Armistice Rob returned to England and was stationed in Salisbury. In June 1919 he was granted home leave for his half-brother's wedding and again during the summer to help with the flax harvest. He brought two of his Australian comrades with him.

Rob applied to be discharged in England rather than in Australia and the Australian Military Authorities required written evidence that he had guaranteed employment. Rob's father sent a letter to confirm that this was the case but somehow the letter did not arrive and Rob's application was turned down. In December 1919 Rob was sent back to Australia aboard the troop ship *Konign Luise*.

Rob suffered another relapse of trench fever and on 3 July 1920 he was honourably discharged from the AIF. He stayed with the Davidson family and was reunited with his four cousins, all of whom had survived the war. Rob established a small business as a meal and animal feed salesman but he missed his family and so he encouraged his parents to travel out to Australia to see him.

James and Mary Robinson set sail in March 1921 on a round-the-world voyage and after weeks at sea their first port of call in Australia was on 21 April at Freemantle near Perth. There they were met by a messenger bearing the terrible news that Rob had died on 6 April 1921.

When James and Mary Robinson reached Queensland they visited their son's grave and

Mary brought home a small box of mementoes – his cap and unit badges, service ribbons and buttons from his uniform along with white pebbles and dried white flowers from his grave. She found most touching of all, the brooch given by the AIF to mothers whose sons were in the war. The brooch was inscribed with the words 'To women of Australia for duty done'.

In her diary Mary Robinson wrote these words:

'I will not bind my soul to grief
As though death did divide
For 'tis as though the rose upon my garden wall
Had blossomed on the other side
Death doth hide
But not divide
Thou art but on the other side
Thou art with Christ
And Christ with me
In Christ united still are we'

R

Robinson, Samuel (Sammy)
Rifleman
No. 13/18686, 'B' Company, 13th Battalion, Royal Irish Rifles
Sunday 14 March 1920 (aged 31)
Killysuggan Graveyard, Newtownards, Co. Down (Grave 2. 2. 25)

Samuel Robinson was born on 13 February 1889 and he was the second son of David and Jane Robinson (nee South) who lived at 14 John Street, Newtownards. They were married on 14 July 1884 in Newtownards Parish Church of Ireland. David Robinson worked as a dealer and he and Jane had four sons – John, Samuel, David and Richard. Prior to the outbreak of the Great War Samuel Robinson also worked as a dealer and he was a member of 'B' Company in the local contingent of the Ulster Volunteer Force.

Samuel Robinson enlisted on 17 September 1914 and he served with the 13th Battalion Royal Irish Rifles in 108th Brigade of the 36th (Ulster) Division. On 14 February 1916 when he was in a front line trench north of the River Ancre he was seriously wounded in the head, chest and shoulder by a shell fired from the German trenches. Private **Hugh Shanks** from Newtownards was killed instantly by the same shell. In a letter to Samuel's mother the Rev Charles Campbell Manning, Chaplain to the Forces, assured her that Samuel was doing well and was quite cheerful. However, one week later Samuel was reported to be 'dangerously ill'. He was transferred to Queen Mary's Military Hospital in Whalley, Lancashire and from there on 20 June 1916 to the hospital in Victoria Barracks, Belfast. On 9 July 1916 he was posted to the 20th Battalion Royal Irish Rifles but he was no longer fit for war service so he was discharged from the army on 13 October 1916.

Samuel Robinson and Catherine (Kate) Coughlin were married on 21 October 1917 in a Belfast Roman Catholic Church and they lived at 42 South Street in Newtownards. It was there that Rifleman Samuel Robinson died on 14 March 1920 and he was buried the following day in Killysuggan Graveyard Newtownards. Kate placed a death notice in the 20 March 1920 edition of the *Newtownards Chronicle* and it contained the verse:

'He is gone to rest, his troubles are o'er;
He is free from all sorrow and pain;
The ills of this life he so patiently bore
Shall never distress him again'

In the same edition there were five other death notices: one from his mother and brothers David and Richard who lived at 14 John Street, one from his father at 17 Greenwell Street, one from his brother and sister-in-law John and Mary who lived at 9 Circular Street, one from his uncle, aunt and cousins who lived at 17 Greenwell Street and one from the Shanks family who lived at 21 John Street Lane. It was Samuel's father David who signed for his son's medals on 10 November 1921 and at that time David's address was 14 John Street, Newtownards.

Samuel Robinson is commemorated on Newtownards and District War Memorial.

Robinson, Samuel
Rifleman
No. 18699, 12th Battalion, Royal Irish Rifles
Killed in action on Saturday 1 July 1916 (aged 23)
Ancre British Cemetery, France (Grave II. F. 6)

Samuel Robinson was born in the townland of Ballyduff in County Antrim, he enlisted in Mossley and he went to France on 6 October 1915. He served with the 12th Battalion Royal Irish Rifles in 108th Brigade of the 36th (Ulster) Division.

Rfm. S. Robinson (No. 18,699), Bally-vester, is reported killed in action.

Rifleman Samuel Robinson was killed in action on the first day of the Battle of the Somme and in the 29 July 1916 edition of the *Newtownards Chronicle* it was reported under the headline 'Donaghadee' that he had been living in the townland of Ballyvester, Donaghadee.

Robinson, William (Willie)
Private
Seaforth Highlanders

Killed in Action.

Mr. and Mrs. Wm. Robinson, of 61 Dawson Street, Parkhead, Glasgow, have received intimation of the death of their son, William, killed in action at Hill 60 on 2nd April. Enlisting in the Seaforth Highlanders at the end of August he was sent to France after a short spell of training at Fort George. He was a pastry baker by trade, and was only 22 years of age. The late " Willie " Robinson was well known and highly esteemed and popular in Donaghadee and district, where he made hosts of friends when some 2 years ago he was employed in Mr. Stanner's bakery. His many friends in Donaghadee will deeply and sincerely regret the death of such a popular and promising young man and will extend their deepest sympathy to the sorrowing relatives in their sad bereavement. The feelings of sorrow will be tinged with pride at the fact that the young man has met his death in the honourable discharge of his duty and fighting for his King and country.

The death of William (Willie) Robinson was reported in the 28 May 1915 edition of the *County Down Spectator* under the headline 'Killed in Action'. The report stated that:

• Willie Robinson was a son of Mr and Mrs William Robinson who lived at 61 Dawson Street, Parkhead in Glasgow.

• Willie was a pastry baker by trade and he was 'well known and highly esteemed and popular in Donaghadee and district' from the time that he was employed in Stanner's bakery.

• Willie enlisted in August 1914, he served with the Seaforth Highlanders and after a short spell of training at Fort George he was sent to France

• Willie was killed in action on 2 April 1915 at Hill 60 (aged 22).

The *best fit* casualty recorded in the CWGC Debt of Honour is:

Private W Robinson
No. S/5413, 2nd Battalion, Seaforth Highlanders
Died on Sunday 25 April 1915
Seaforth Cemetery, Cheddar Villa, Belgium (Grave B. 1 Headstone 'A' 12)

In 'Soldiers Died in the Great War 1914 – 1919' it is recorded that this soldier was born in Barony, Lanarkshire and he enlisted in Glasgow.

Desk searches and public appeals to date have not confirmed conclusively that this soldier is the person who worked in Stanner's Bakery, Donaghadee.

Robinson, William Wadham
Private
No. 25300, 10th Battalion, Royal Dublin Fusiliers
Killed in action on Monday 13 November 1916 (aged 41)
Ancre British Cemetery, France (Grave I. C. 36)

William Wadham Robinson was born in Strabane, Co Tyrone and he was a son of James and Rose Robinson who lived in Patrick Street, Strabane.

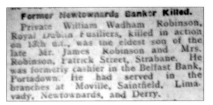

Former Newtownards Banker Killed.
Private William Wadham Robinson, Royal Dublin Fusiliers, killed in action on 13th inst., was the eldest son of the late Mr. James Robinson and Mrs. Robinson, Patrick Street, Strabane. He was formerly cashier in the Belfast Bank, Portadown. He had served in the branches at Moville, Saintfield, Limavady, Newtownards, and Derry.

William Wadham Robinson worked for the Belfast Banking Company Ltd and his death was reported in the 9 December 1916 edition of the *Newtownards Chronicle* under the headline 'Former Newtownards Banker Killed'. He worked in the Bank's Portadown branch as a cashier and it was in Portadown that he enlisted. He served with the Royal Dublin Fusiliers and he was killed in action on 13 November 1916 during the last days of the Battle of the Somme.

R

Robson, Robert
Private
No. T/4/128737, Army Service Corps, transferred to (41865), 1st Battalion, Princess Victoria's (Royal Irish Fusiliers)
Killed in action on Thursday 21 March 1918 (aged 42)
Pozieres Memorial, France (Panel 76 and 77)

Robert Robson was born on 8 August 1875 in the townland of Ballygrainey and he was a son of Robert and Catherine Robson (nee McCutcheon) who lived in the townland of Ballyboley, Greyabbey. They were married on 30 September 1862 in Ballyblack Presbyterian Church. Robert Robson Senior worked as a farmer and he and Catherine had at least eight children – Mary, Samuel, Sarah Elizabeth, Hugh, Robert (died), Robert, Margaret and John.

Prior to the outbreak of the Great War Robert Robson worked as a horse trainer and on 13 November 1906 he and Ellen Jane McGowan were married in Ballyfrenis Presbyterian Church, Carrowdore.

Robert Robson enlisted in August 1915 at Clandeboye and after training at Seaford in Sussex he proceeded to France. He served with the Army Service Corps (T/4/128737) before being transferred to the Royal Irish Fusiliers (41865). Private Robert Robson was killed in action on 21 March 1918, the first day of the German 'Michael' offensive. Initially he was reported as missing in action and on 1 May 1919 it was officially confirmed that he had been killed.

At the time of his death his wife and their two children were living at 52 Frederick Street in Newtownards and she placed an 'Our Heroes – In Memoriam' notice in the 17 May 1919 edition of the *Newtownards Chronicle*. It contained the verse:

'No loving hand clasped his that day,
No home voice said good-bye:
He fell in battle's dread affray,
But God Himself was nigh.
God knows how much I miss him,
And He counts the tears I shed,
And whispers Hush! he only sleeps
Your loved one is not dead'

R

Private Robert Robson is commemorated on Newtownards and District War Memorial (in the booklet produced for the Unveiling and Dedication Ceremony held on Saturday 26 May 1934 he is described as a Private in the Royal Inniskilling Fusiliers) and in the PCI Roll of Honour for Greenwell Street Presbyterian Church Newtownards (where he is described as a Private in the Army Service Corps).

Roseman, William
Private
No. 16573, 14th Battalion, Durham Light Infantry
Killed in action on Monday 27 September 1915 (aged 29)
Loos Memorial, France (Panel 106 and 107)

In 'Soldiers Died in the Great War 1914 – 1919' it is recorded that William Roseman was born in Newtownards. He was a son of Ross and Mary Roseman (nee Anderson) who were married on 8 September 1879 in Belfast Registry Office. The Roseman family moved to Gateshead-on-Tyne and in 1913 William Roseman married Edith Armes in Easington, Co Durham and they lived in Spennymoor, Co Durham. William Roseman enlisted in Durham and he served with the 14th Battalion Durham Light Infantry.

Private William Roseman was killed in action on 27 September 1915 and he is commemorated on Spennymoor War Memorial and in the Spennymoor Urban District Book of Remembrance 1914 – 1919.

Runaghan, James (Cha)
Private
No. 2499, 7th Battalion, Prince of Wales's Leinster Regiment (Royal Canadians)
Killed in action on Sunday 3 September 1916 (aged 39)
Thiepval Memorial, France (Pier and Face 16C)

In some records and reports the surname is spelt Runningan.

James Runaghan was born in Belfast and he and Elizabeth Kelly were married on 23 November 1907 in a Roman Catholic Church in Belfast. They lived in Ross Street, Belfast. James worked as a general labourer and they had at least two children including a daughter called Sarah.

Well-Known Footballer Killed.

The death is unofficially announced of Private James ("Cha") Runningan, Connaught Rangers, who is reported to have been killed on the 3rd inst. He was a well-known footballer, and will be remembered as a dashing centre-forward for Belfast Celtic a few years ago. He was for a time on the staff of the Royal North Downs, and during his stay in Newtownards played for the Ards Football Club. His wife resides at 3, Milton Street, Belfast. A brother of deceased was killed in action a short time ago, while a third brother is still on active service. The news of the casualty has been sent by the latter.

James Runaghan enlisted in Belfast and during the Great War he served with the Leinster Regiment. He was a well-known footballer having played centre forward for Belfast Celtic and it was reported in the *Newtownards Chronicle* that, when he was on the staff of the Royal North Downs and living in Newtownards, he played for the Ards Football Club.

Private James Runaghan was killed in action at Guillemont on 3 September 1916, less than six months after his brother John had been killed in action. John served with the Connaught Rangers (2329) and died on 28 March 1916. Two other brothers, Alexander and Owen, served in the Great War and survived.

Both James and John Runaghan are commemorated in the Belfast Book of Honour (Page 567).

R

Russell Brothers: Alexander and John

Alexander and John Russell were born in Newtownards and they were sons of John and Jane Russell (nee Miller) who lived in Greenwell Street and Wallace's Street No. 2 before moving to 56 Upper Movilla Street, Newtownards. They were married on 17 April 1876 in Newtownards Parish Church of Ireland. John Russell worked as a woollen weaver and he and Jane had at least ten children including Jane, Esther, Mary (1884), David (1886), John (1888), Sarah (1890) and Alexander (1896). They were baptised in Newtownards Parish Church of Ireland. Alexander was the first of the two brothers to be killed in action:

Russell, Alexander
Rifleman
No. 18713, 'B' Company, 13th Battalion, Royal Irish Rifles
Killed in action on Saturday 1 July 1916 (aged 20)
Thiepval Memorial, France (Pier and Face 15 A and 15 B)

Alexander Russell was born on 6 June 1896 and prior to the outbreak of the Great War he worked in a mill. He enlisted in Newtownards and served with the 13th Battalion Royal Irish Rifles in 108th Brigade of the 36th (Ulster) Division. Rifleman Alexander Russell was killed in action on the first day of the Battle of the Somme.

Russell, John
Corporal
No. 3/13322, 16th Battalion, Royal Irish Rifles
Killed in action on Tuesday 31 July 1917 (aged 28)
Ypres (Menin Gate) Memorial, Belgium (Panel 40)

John Russell was born on 13 December 1888 and prior to the outbreak of the Great War he worked as a painter. He and Jane Quinn were married on 1 May 1915 in First Newtownards Presbyterian Church. He enlisted in Newtownards, he joined the 3rd Battalion Royal Irish Rifles and was then transferred to either the 1st or 2nd Battalion. He went to France on 17 June 1915 and was transferred to the 16th Battalion Royal Irish Rifles in 36th (Ulster) Division. He was killed by enemy artillery fire on 31 July 1917 while at his post in a trench taken that day from the Germans. On 3 August 1917 Corporal John Russell was buried on the battlefield. At the time of his death John's

R

wife Jane and their daughter Mary lived in the townland of Killarn, Newtownards.

Jane Russell placed a 'For King and Country' notice in the 25 August 1917 edition of the *Newtownards Chronicle* – just two weeks after she had placed a similar notice for her brother **Tommy Quinn** (13411). Jane's notice for her husband contained the verse:

> 'How little I thought when I said good-bye
> It would be the last parting between you and I;
> I loved you in life, you are dear to me still,
> But in grief I must bend to God's holy will.'

Rifleman Alexander Russell and Rifleman John Russell are both commemorated on Newtownards and District War Memorial and in Newtownards Parish Church of Ireland (St Mark).

Russell Brothers: Andrew and Thomas

Andrew and Thomas Russell were sons of Andrew and Eliza Russell (nee Bell) who lived in Robert Street and later at 18 Mark Street, Newtownards. They were married on 24 June 1875 in Newtownards Parish Church of Ireland. Andrew Russell Senior worked as a general labourer and before that he had been a soldier in the South African War. He died in the early 1900s. Andrew and Eliza Russell had at least nine children – Joseph, John, Lizzie, Andrew, Samuel, Agnes, Jane, Thomas and William. At the outset of the Great War five of Eliza's sons were on active service:

Joseph Russell, Royal Irish Rifles, formerly Royal Irish Fusiliers

John Russell, Royal Irish Rifles

Andrew Russell, Cameron Highlanders

Samuel Russell, Royal Irish Rifles

Thomas Russell, Highland Light Infantry

Andrew was the first of the two brothers to die:

Russell, Andrew (Andy)
Private
No. 6693, 1st Battalion, Queen's Own Cameron Highlanders
Died of wounds on Tuesday 22 September 1914 (aged 30)
Netley Military Cemetery, Hampshire, England (Grave C. E. 1587)

Andrew Russell was the third son of Andrew and Eliza Russell and he was

an army reservist. Andrew got married towards the end of 1913 and he and his wife Mary lived at 56 Templemore Street in Belfast. Less than a year later Mary was widowed when Andy died of wounds on 22 September 1914. Andy Russell never saw his only daughter who was born two days before he died. Private Andrew Russell died in Netley Hospital, Southampton as a result of a bullet wound in the chest. He is commemorated on Newtownards and District War Memorial; in Newtownards Parish Church of Ireland (St Mark) and in the Belfast Book of Honour (Page 568). The inscription on his headstone reads:

'Peace perfect peace
Until the day dawn'

Andy Russell's twin sister Lizzie was married to Thomas Clarke who was serving with the North Irish Horse (794). They lived in West Street Newtownards and at the end of September 1914 Lizzie Clarke was informed that her husband was in hospital in France. Later Thomas Clarke was transferred to Netley Hospital – the same hospital where Lizzie's twin brother died. Just over one month after Private Andrew Russell died of wounds, his brother Thomas Russell was killed in action in France on 28 October 1914.

Russell, Thomas
Private
No. 12167, 2nd Battalion, Highland Light Infantry
Killed in action on Wednesday 28 October 1914 (aged 19)
Boulogne Eastern Cemetery, France (Grave III. A. 18)

Thomas Russell was the fifth son of Andrew and Eliza Russell and prior to the outbreak of the Great War he worked as an apprentice. He enlisted in 1913 and shortly after the outbreak of the Great War he was wounded in the cheek. Private Thomas Russell returned to the fighting line and it was reported in the press that he had been killed in action at Saint Julia on 28 October 1914. He is commemorated on Newtownards and District War Memorial and in Newtownards Parish Church of Ireland (St Mark).

In the 7 November 1914 edition of the *Newtownards Chronicle* the Editor published a letter from Thomas Russell's brother, Rifleman Samuel Russell, to his mother. At the time Samuel was in No. 2 Military Hospital, Beckett's Park, Leeds recovering from severe gunshot wounds to his shoulder and he was not aware that Thomas had been killed. Samuel Russell was wounded on 25 October 1914 during fighting in the trenches at La Bassee. Many of his comrades lost their lives or were very severely wounded. At the same time his brother John was in hospital at Stobcross in Scotland and his brother Joseph was in hospital at Leicester.

Russell, John
Rifleman
No. 18/529, 'B' Company, 13th Battalion, Royal Irish Rifles
Killed in action on Saturday 1 July 1916 (aged 23)
Serre Road Cemetery No. 2, France (Grave VI. F. 14)

John Russell was born in Newtownards and he was a son of John and Maggie Russell (nee Bowers) who lived in Frederick Street. They were married on 27 January 1894 in Newtownards Registry Office. Prior to the outbreak of the Great War both father and son worked as agricultural labourers. John Russell Senior and Maggie had at least seven children some of whom were baptised in Greenwell Street Presbyterian Church – John, Jane, Maggie, Annie, James, William and Robert.

R

John Jnr and Mary Russell (nee Russell) were married on 27 December 1915 in First Donaghadee Presbyterian Church and their son John was born on 3 September 1916, two months after his father was killed in action. Baby John was baptised in Greenwell Street Presbyterian Church Newtownards.

Intimation has been received that Rifleman John Russell (No. 529), who was missing after 1st July, 1916, is now reported killed in action. He also joined the 1st County Down Volunteers, and did his duty with the Ulster Division at the front. His residence was 13 Circular Row, and a wife and little son are left behind to mourn his loss.

John Russell enlisted in Newtownards in September 1915 and he joined the 18th Battalion Royal Irish Rifles. He was posted overseas to the 13th Battalion Royal Irish Rifles in 108th Brigade of the 36th (Ulster) Division. Initially he was posted as missing in action after the first day of the Battle of the Somme and then, in July 1917, it was officially confirmed that he had been killed on that date or since.

Two 'For King and Country' notices were placed in the 14 July 1917 edition of the *Newtownards Chronicle*, one by his wife Mary and his son John who lived at 13 Circular Row Newtownards and one by his sister-in-law Susan Russell and his cousin Annie Wilson.

The notice placed by his widow and son contained the verse:

'Only in form we both are parted,
But my heart will true remain;
But some day we'll be united,
Never more to part again'

And the notice placed by his sister-in-law and cousin contained the verse:

'His pleasant face and kindly smile
Are pleasant to recall;
He had a kindly word for each,
And died beloved by all'

Rifleman John Russell's body was recovered from the battlefield and buried in June 1927. He is commemorated on Newtownards and District War Memorial and in the PCI Roll of Honour for Greenwell Street Presbyterian Church Newtownards.

R

Russell, John*

The name John Russell (Mark Street) is listed on Newtownards and District War Memorial and in the booklet produced for the Unveiling and Dedication Ceremony held on Saturday 26 May 1934 he is described as a Rifleman in the Royal Irish Rifles.

The 1911 Census records show that there was a Russell family living in Mark Street Newtownards. Head of the family was John aged 31, born in Scotland; his wife Jane aged 26 was born in County Down and they had two children, Alma and Andrew. Evidence from one source suggests that John Russell and Jane McCormick were married on 2 September 1908 in St Anne's Church of Ireland Belfast. Desk searches and public appeals to date have not confirmed a connection between the 1911 census data and the soldier who is commemorated on Newtownards and District War Memorial. Another single source of evidence suggests that John Russell (Mark Street) on Newtownards War Memorial may have been the father of John Russell (18/529).

Russell, Robert

The name Robert Russell is listed on Newtownards and District War Memorial and in the booklet produced for the Unveiling and Dedication Ceremony held on Saturday 26 May 1934 he is described as a Rifleman in the Royal Irish Rifles.

Robert Russell was born in 1891 in Newtownards, he worked as a weaver and he lived at 174B Greenwell Street. He was a member of 'A' Company of the Newtownards contingent of the Ulster Volunteer Force and he enlisted on 17 September 1914. It was noted in his attestation papers that he was single, he was Presbyterian, he was 6 feet tall and he cited his mother Maggie as his next-of-kin. He joined the 13th Battalion Royal Irish Rifles (18711) and he was discharged from the Army on 12 December 1914 after 87 days in service. The reason given was that 'he was not likely to become efficient'. He suffered from varicose veins and he declined the opportunity to have an operation. He was granted a gratuity of 7 pounds 10 shillings and a weekly pension of 7 shillings and 2 pence. A discharged soldier named Robert Russell who died of tuberculosis on 24 November 1924 was buried in Movilla New Cemetery, Newtownards (Grave 1.93). Desk searches and public appeals to date have not confirmed a connection between these service and burial data and the soldier who is commemorated on Newtownards and District War Memorial. Evidence from one source suggests that Robert Russell may have been a brother of John Russell (18/529).

Saunders, Robert
Private
No. 32696, Border Regiment, transferred to (51448), 1st/10th Battalion, Manchester Regiment
Died of wounds on Monday 29 October 1917 (aged 24)
Zuydcoote Military Cemetery, France (Grave II. C. 10)

S

Robert Saunders was born on 25 January 1893 in Donaghadee and he was the eldest son of William and Maggie Saunders (nee Kerr) who lived at 40 Manor Street. They were married in Donaghadee Parish Church of Ireland. William Saunders worked as a general labourer, Maggie worked as a muslin sewer and they had at least seven children – Robert, David, William, Mary, Agnes, Lizzie and Sarah. Robert was baptised in Donaghadee Parish Church of Ireland.

Prior to the outbreak of the Great War Robert Saunders worked as a railway porter in Donaghadee. He enlisted in Wigton, Cumberland and he served with the Border Regiment (32696) before being transferred to the 1st/10th Battalion Manchester Regiment. Private Robert Saunders died of wounds on 29 October 1917 and he is commemorated on Donaghadee and District War Memorial and in Donaghadee Parish Church of Ireland.

Savage-Armstrong, Francis Savage Nesbitt (Francis)
Distinguished Service Order
Mentioned in Despatches (twice)
Lieutenant Colonel
1st Battalion, South Staffordshire Regiment
Commanding 11th Battalion Royal Warwickshire Regiment
Killed in action on Monday 23 April 1917 (aged 36)
Point-du-Jour Military Cemetery, France (Grave II. E. 12)

Francis Savage Nesbitt Savage-Armstrong was born on 5 July 1880 and he was a son of George Francis and Marie Elizabeth Armstrong (nee Wrixon). They were married in 1879 and they had three children – Francis Savage Nesbitt, John Raymond Savage and Arabella Guendolen. George Francis Armstrong assumed the additional surname of Savage in 1891 and he died on 24 July 1906. He is buried in the graveyard of the now ruined St Mary's Church of Ireland at Ardkeen (situated in the townland of Kirkistown).

S

Francis Savage Nesbitt Savage-Armstrong was educated at Shrewsbury School and he joined the Army on 19 September 1900. He served with the 1st Battalion South Staffordshire Regiment and 4th Mounted Infantry during the South African War. He served both at home and abroad before the outbreak of the Great War. He went to the Western Front on 3 November 1914 where he fought at Ypres and at Neuve Chapelle. He was wounded at Festubert on 16 May 1915 and he was killed in action at Arras on 23 April 1917 while he was serving as Commander of the 11th Battalion Royal Warwickshire Regiment.

Lieutenant Colonel Francis Savage Nesbitt Savage-Armstrong is commemorated on the Armstong family memorial plaque in Ardkeen Parish Church of Ireland (Christ Church) situated at Ballygela Road, Ardkeen in the townland of Kirkistown. The memorial plaque reads:

To the Glory of God and in memory of

- Edmund John Armstrong, died 12 October 1870, buried Old Cemetery, Monkstown, Co. Dublin
- His wife Jane, daughter of Rev Henry Savage of Glastry, died 3 January 1880, buried Monkstown
- Their sons, Henry Savage, died an infant 31 July 1840, buried Mount Jerome

- Edmund John, died 24 February 1865, buried Monkstown
- Their daughter Ann Eliza, married Captain WT Croft, 65th Regiment, died 29 January 1930, buried Tonbridge
- Their son George Francis Savage-Armstrong (the Poet), died 24 July 1906, buried St. Mary's, Ardkeen
- Their sons, Francis Savage Nesbitt, 1st South Staffordshire Regiment, Lieutenant Colonel, DSO, South Africa 1901 – 1902, 1st Ypres 1914, Neuve Chapelle 1915, wounded Festubert 16 May 1915, killed Arras 23 April 1917; John Raymond, Captain Leinster Regiment, wounded Hill 60 near Ypres 21 April 1915
- Their daughter Arabella Guendolen, VAD 1914 – 1918 War, died 20 August 1952, buried St. Mary's, Ardkeen

'Port after stormy seas; rest after toil'
'My peace I give unto you'

During the Great War Francis Savage Nesbitt Savage-Armstrong's brother Raymond served as a Captain in the 4th Battalion Leinster Regiment and his sister Guendolen served as a VAD nurse at the Richmond Military Hospital in Dublin.

S

Scarr, Joseph M
Private
No. 16447, 9th Battalion, Royal Scots Fusiliers
Died on Sunday 30 July 1916 (aged 36)
Edinburgh (Comely Bank) Cemetery, Scotland (Grave D. 27)

Joseph M Scarr was born in 1880 in Downham Market, Norfolk and he was a son of Joseph and Harriet Scarr. Joseph Scarr Senior was born in County Armagh and he worked as a flax dresser. Joseph and Harriett had four children – William, Martha, Fanny and Joseph M. Harriet died and Joseph Senior remarried. He and Eliza had two children – Gertrude and Annie and the Scarr family moved to 23 Mark Street, Newtownards.

Joseph Scarr enlisted in Consett, Co Durham, he served with the 9th Battalion Royal Scots Fusiliers and he died on 30 July 1916. In the CWGC Debt of Honour his age is recorded as 40.

Scott, David
Rifleman
**No. G/732, 'C' Company, 1st Garrison Battalion, Royal Irish Rifles
Died of heat apoplexy on Saturday 27 May 1916 (aged 46)
Cawnpore Cantonment New Cemetery**

Madras 1914 – 1918 War Memorial, Chennai, India (Face 23)

David Scott was born in 1870 in Newtownards and he was a son of Thomas and Jane Scott. David Scott worked as a wool weaver and he and his wife Maggie lived at 31 William Street, Newtownards. They had at least eight children – Thomas, Anna (Annie), David, Samuel, Elizabeth, Maggie Jane (Jeannie), Ellen (Nellie) and George.

Rifleman David Scott served for 18 months with the Royal Irish Rifles in Dublin and Dundalk before being posted to Cawnpore in India in February 1916 with the 1st Garrison Battalion. That Battalion had been formed in Dublin in November 1915.

David Scott died of heat apoplexy on 27 May 1916 and he was buried in Cawnpore Cantonment New Cemetery. His name is commemorated on the Madras 1914 – 1918 War Memorial at Chennai in India and this memorial bears the inscription:

> 'The soldiers whose names are honoured here served and died during the 1914 – 1918 war and are buried elsewhere in India.'

> SCOTT—In loving memory of Rifleman David Scott, First Garrison Regiment Royal Irish Rifles, who died at Cawn-pore, India, on 27th May, 1916.
> Had I but seen him at the last,
> Or raised his drooping head,
> My heart would not have felt so sore,
> The bitter tears I shed.
> Ever remembered by his Wife and Family.
> MAGGIE SCOTT.
> 7 Forde Street, Newtownards.

At the time of David's death his wife and children were living at 7 Forde Street Newtownards and Maggie placed an 'Our Heroes – In Memoriam' notice in the 26 May 1917 edition of the *Newtownards Chronicle*. It contained the verse:

> 'Had I but seen him at the last,
> Or raised his drooping head,
> My heart would not have felt so sore,
> The bitter tears I shed'

Rifleman David Scott is commemorated on Newtownards and District War Memorial and in Regent Street Methodist Church Newtownards.

Scott, Herbert Vesey
Captain
3rd Battalion, Rifle Brigade
Died of wounds on Wednesday 1 September 1915 (aged 34)
Wimereux Communal Cemetery, France (Grave III. O. 2)

Herbert Vesey Scott was born in Portaferry and he was a son of the Rev Francis Montgomery Scott and Anna Matilda Scott (nee Vesey). The Rev Scott was Rector of Ardquin Parish Church of Ireland Portaferry and he and Anna Matilda Vesey, who was a daughter of the manager of the Portaferry branch of the Belfast Banking Company, were married on 17 August 1876 in Ballyphilip Parish Church of Ireland Portaferry.

Herbert Vesey Scott was educated at Eton, he became a career soldier and prior to the Great War he served in South Africa and India. He excelled at polo and won several trophies. During the Great War he served with the Rifle Brigade and he died of wounds at Wimereux on 1 September 1915. Captain Herbert Vesey Scott is commemorated on Farlington War Memorial in Hampshire and on a Memorial Plaque in St Andrew's Church Farlington.

S

Scott, Samuel (Sam)
Sergeant
No. 42746, Canadian Field Artillery, Brigade Ammunition Column
Died of influenza on Sunday 20 October 1918 (aged 35)
Mount Hope Cemetery, Brandford, Ontario, Canada

Samuel Scott was born on 1 April 1883 in Newtownards and he was a son of William and Jane Scott (nee Brown) who lived in Mill Street, Newtownards. They were married on 11 September 1877 in First Newtownards Presbyterian Church. William Scott worked as an agricultural labourer and he and Jane had at least ten children – George Brown, William James, Samuel, Margaret Mary (died), Margaret Mary, Thomas Stuart, Robert, Sarah Jane, John Andrew and Agnes. They were all baptised in First Newtownards Presbyterian Church.

Samuel Scott moved to Canada where he worked as a carpenter. He and his wife Elizabeth lived at 9 North Park Street, Brantford, Ontario and he enlisted on 24 September 1914 at Valcartier, Quebec. In his attestation papers it was noted that he was 5 feet 5½ inches tall and that he had served for 18 months in the 8th Hussars.

Samuel Scott served on the Western Front with the Brigade Ammunition Column of the Canadian Field Artillery before returning to Canada. He died of influenza on 20 October 1918 at his home in North Park Street and the following day it was reported in the *Brantford Expositor* that he left a sorrowing wife and three children.

Sergeant Samuel Scott is commemorated on Newtownards and District War Memorial and in First Newtownards Presbyterian Church. Evidence from one source suggests that Sam Scott was a cousin of David John Thompson (18831) who died of wounds sustained on the first day of the Battle of the Somme.

Scott, T

In addition to these the following have died from disease contracted on service:—

W. Boal.
S. A. Boyd.
John Harvey.
A. Heron.
J. Armstrong Kelly.
D. J. Kielty.
H. M'Clure.
T. M'Taggart.
T. Scott.
D. J. Stratton.

In the 6 January 1917 edition of the *Newtownards Chronicle* a 'Roll of Sacrifice' for the town was published. The names of those men who had been killed in action or who had died of wounds were listed and below those names there was a list of ten names of men who had died from disease contracted on service. The name T Scott was included in that section.

Thomas Scott (13/2369) enlisted in September 1914 and he was posted overseas on 5 October 1915 with the 13th Battalion Royal Irish Rifles in 108th Brigade of the 36th (Ulster) Division. He was discharged because of 'sickness' on 11 October 1916. Desk searches and public appeals to date have not confirmed a connection between these service data and the soldier whose name was listed in the Roll of Sacrifice published in the 6 January 1917 edition of the *Newtownards Chronicle*.

Semple Brothers: Robert James and William

Robert James and William Semple were sons of George and Eleanor Jane Semple (nee Niblock) who lived at 27 East Street, Donaghadee. They were married on 21 June 1882 in Shore Street Presbyterian Church Donaghadee. George Semple worked as a general labourer and he and Eleanor Jane had at least nine children including Samuel, William, Ellen, Mary Bell, Eliza Ann, George, Robert James and Lydia. William and Robert James were baptised in Shore Street Presbyterian Church Donaghadee. Eleanor Jane Semple died in April 1916. William was the first of the two brothers to be killed in action:

Semple, William
Rifleman
No. 16999, 'A' Company, 13th Battalion, Royal Irish Rifles
Killed in action on Saturday 1 July 1916 (aged 31)
Thiepval Memorial, France (Pier and Face 15 A and 15 B)

William Semple was born on 8 August 1884 in the townland of Ballywilliam, Donaghadee and he was the second son of George and Eleanor Jane Semple. Prior to the outbreak of the Great War he worked as a general labourer. He enlisted in Donaghadee, he served with the 13th Battalion Royal Irish Rifles in 108th Brigade of the 36th (Ulster) Division and he was killed in action on the first day of the Battle of the Somme.

Donaghadee Rifleman Killed.
Reported missing on 1st July, Rifleman Wm. Semple, Royal Irish Rifles, is now returned as killed in action. He was the second son of Mr. George Semple, 27 East Street, Donaghadee.

Initially William was reported as wounded in action and in August 1916 the Red Cross reported that he was in Holywood Military Convalescent Hospital suffering from shell shock. This proved not to be the case and he was reclassified as missing in action. After it was officially confirmed in June 1917 that Rifleman William Semple had been killed in action on or since 1 July 1916, his friend Nan Bennett who lived in Hunter's Lane, Donaghadee placed a 'For King and Country' notice in the 16 June 1917 edition of the *Newtownards Chronicle*. It contained the verse:

> 'Too far away thy grave to see,
> But not too far to think of thee;
> When days are dark, and friends are few,
> How I'll think and long for you.
> I often think of days gone by,
> When we were all together;
> A shadow o'er our life is cast,
> A dear friend gone for ever'

Semple, Robert James (Robert)
Rifleman
No. 16998, 'A' Company, 13th Battalion, Royal Irish Rifles
Killed in action on Saturday 8 December 1917 (aged 20)
Thiepval Memorial, France (Pier and Face 15 A and 15 B)

Robert James Semple was born on 4 January 1897 in Donaghadee and he was the fourth son of George and Eleanor Jane Semple. He enlisted in Donaghadee and he joined the 13th Battalion Royal Irish Rifles. He served at the front in 108th Brigade of the 36th (Ulster) Division and he was home on a short leave in early May 1916. His mother had died and her funeral had taken place one week before he arrived.

THE SUPREME SACRIFICE.
Donaghadee Rifleman Killed.
Rifleman Robert James Semple, Royal Irish Rifles, killed in action on 8th Dec., was a son of Mr. George Semple and the late Mrs. Semple, 27 East Street, Donaghadee.

Rifleman Robert Semple was killed in action on 8 December 1917 shortly after the 13th and 11th Battalions of the Royal Irish Rifles were amalgamated.

Rifleman Robert Semple and Rifleman William Semple are both commemorated on Donaghadee and District War Memorial and in Shore Street Presbyterian Church Donaghadee. Robert and William Semple were cousins of Rifleman **William Semple** (18/775). Their father George and William's father Samuel were brothers.

Semple, William
Rifleman
No. 18/775, 11th Battalion, Royal Irish Rifles
Killed in action on Sunday 25 June 1916 (aged 26)
Thiepval Memorial, France (Pier and Face 15 A and 15 B)

William Semple was born on 19 September 1889 in Donaghadee and he was a son of Samuel and Mary Semple (nee Bell) who were married on 8 November 1877 in Millisle Presbyterian Church. They had at least six children all of whom were baptised in Shore Street Presbyterian Church Donaghadee – Hannah, Martha Ann, Hugh, Samuel, Mary and William. William Semple and Mary McWilliams were married on 25 April 1913 in Ballygrainey Presbyterian Church. They lived at 42 Manor Street Donaghadee and they had three children all of whom were baptised in Shore Street Presbyterian Church – Mary Eleanor (died), Walter and Mary Eleanor.

Rifleman W. Semple (No. 775), Royal Irish Rifles, previously reported wounded, is now reported wounded and missing.

William Semple enlisted in Belfast in November 1915 and he joined the 18th Battalion Royal Irish Rifles. In February 1916 he went to France where he served with the 11th Battalion Royal Irish Rifles in 108th Brigade of the 36th (Ulster) Division. He was killed by enemy shellfire whilst in the trenches on 25 June 1916 and official notification of his death was a three stage process. Initially he was reported as wounded in action and then in September 1916 this was updated to wounded and missing in action. Later it was officially confirmed that he had been killed in action.

Rifleman William Semple is commemorated on Donaghadee and District

War Memorial and in Shore Street Presbyterian Church Donaghadee. William Semple was a cousin of Rifleman **Robert James Semple** (16998) and Rifleman **William Semple** (16999). Their fathers were brothers.

Shanks, David
Rifleman
No. 13477, 10th Battalion, Royal Irish Rifles
Killed in action on Saturday 1 July 1916 (aged 35)
Thiepval Memorial, France (Pier and Face 15 A and 15 B)

David Shanks was born on 21 July 1880 in the townland of Ballyboley, Greyabbey and he was a son of George and Lizzie Ann Shanks (nee Johnston). They were married on 4 September 1877 in Second Newtownards Presbyterian Church. George Shanks worked as an agricultural labourer and he and Lizzie Ann had at least four children all of whom were baptised in Carrowdore Presbyterian Church – David, Jane, John and Lizzie.

David Shanks enlisted in Belfast, he served at the front with the 10th Battalion Royal Irish Rifles in 107th Brigade of the 36th (Ulster) Division and he was killed in action on the first day of the Battle of the Somme. After the war his wife Susan lived at 215 Chambers Avenue, Toronto, Ontario, Canada. Rifleman David Shanks is commemorated in Carrowdore Presbyterian Church.

S

Shanks, Hugh
Rifleman
No. 18748, 'B' Company, 13th Battalion, Royal Irish Rifles
Killed in action on Monday 14 February 1916 (aged 20)
Mesnil Ridge Cemetery, France (Grave I. 6)

Hugh Shanks was born in Glasgow and he was the second son of George and Eleanor Shanks (nee Smyth) who lived in the townland of Loughries, Newtownards. They were married on 1 January 1890 in Ballyblack Presbyterian Church. George Shanks was a farmer and he and Eleanor had at least six children – Sarah, George, Hugh, William, Margaret (Maggie) and David John. George was baptised in Ballyblack Presbyterian Church; Margaret and David John were baptised in Greenwell Street Presbyterian Church Newtownards.

18748 RIFLEMAN
H. SHANKS
ROYAL IRISH RIFLES
14TH FEBRUARY 1916 AGE 20

Prior to the outbreak of the Great War Hugh Shanks was a member of the Ballyblack contingent of the Ulster Volunteer Force which was connected with the 2nd Battalion of the North Down Regiment. Hugh's father George was a section sergeant in the same UVF Company. Hugh enlisted in Newtownards in September 1914 and he served with the 13th Battalion Royal Irish Rifles in 108th Brigade of the 36th (Ulster) Division. In early February the Division moved into the front line north of the River Ancre and on 14 February 1916 there was very heavy enemy shelling during the day. Rifleman Hugh Shanks was killed when a German shell exploded close to him in the trenches. At 6.00 pm that evening Colonel WH Savage conducted his funeral. Rifleman **Samuel Robinson** from Newtownards was seriously injured in the same explosion and Samuel died at home four years later on 14 March 1920.

Hugh's Testament, which he always carried with him, was returned to his family through the Rev Dr Wright, Newtownards. The Testament was perforated in four places and a piece of the shell that killed him was embedded in the book. When Hugh died his family placed a notice in the *Newtownards Chronicle* and it contained the verse:

> 'Short and sudden was the call,
> Not thinking death so near;
> No words of comfort could he leave
> To those he loved so dear
> At rest – all battles o'er
> The weary marching done
> Brave to the last, to his God he passed,
> And the victor's crown has won.'

On the Sunday after news of Hugh's death was received, the members of Ballyblack Presbyterian Church passed a resolution of sympathy to his family.

Hugh's elder sister Sarah was married to John Reid and they lived in Chicago. Each year after Hugh died they, and other family members, placed 'Our Heroes – In Memoriam' notices in the *Newtownards Chronicle*. One such notice included the verse:

> 'One year has passed since that sad day,
> When one we love was called away;

His memory is as dear today
As at the hour he passed away.
It is not the tears at the moment shed
That tell how beloved is the soul that has fled,
But the tears through many a long night wept,
And the sad remembrance so fondly kept.'

In addition to the family memorial notices there was always one from Driver Edward McBride, also on active service.

Rifleman Hugh Shanks is commemorated on Newtownards and District War Memorial and in Ballyblack Presbyterian Church. He is also commemorated on the family grave headstone in Ballyblack Presbyterian Churchyard.

Shanks, John Bassett (John)
Private
No. 123999, 5th Canadian Mounted Rifles Battalion
Died on Wednesday 28 August 1918 (aged 20)
Aubigny Communal Cemetery Extension, France (Grave IV. D. 58)

John Bassett Shanks was a son of John Bassett Shanks and Elizabeth Shanks (nee Reid) who lived in Portaferry. They were married on 14 December 1893 in Ballyphilip Parish Church of Ireland. John Bassett Shanks Senior was a farmer and he died on 5 January 1903. He and Elizabeth had at least four children – William, Mary Anne, John Bassett and James Henry.

John Shanks moved to Canada where he worked as a farm labourer before the outbreak of the Great War. He enlisted on 30 September 1915 in Lucan, Ontario and in his attestation papers it was noted that he was 5 feet 3 inches tall. As his next-of-kin he cited his elder brother William who was serving aboard HMS *Nelson*.

Private John Shanks served with the 5th Canadian Mounted Rifles Battalion and he died on 28 August 1918. Private Shanks is commemorated in Portaferry (Ballyphilip) Parish Church of Ireland (St James).

Shannon, John
Rifleman
No. 19197, 'B' Company, 13th Battalion, Royal Irish Rifles
Killed in action on Saturday 1 July 1916 (aged 27)
Thiepval Memorial, France (Pier and Face 15 A and 15 B)

John Shannon was born in Newtownards and he was the only child of Joseph

S

and Jane Shannon who lived in South Street and later at 23 East Street, Newtownards. Father and son both worked as agricultural labourers. John Shannon and Anna Johnston were married on 17 April 1908 in Newtownards Zion Methodist Church. Anna worked as a hem stitcher in a factory and they had at least one child – a son named Joseph. They lived in Court Street and later at 99 South Street, Newtownards.

John Shannon enlisted in Belfast in September 1914, he served with the 13th Battalion Royal Irish Rifles in 108th Brigade of the 36th (Ulster) Division and he was killed in action on the first day of the Battle of the Somme. Initially he was reported as missing in action and then in June 1917 it was officially confirmed that he had been killed in action. John and his father were members of True Blues LOL No.1055 in Newtownards and after John died, James Beale, who was secretary of the Lodge, sent a letter of sympathy to his parents. Joseph and Jane Shannon placed a 'For King and Country' notice in the 16 June 1917 edition of the *Newtownards Chronicle* and the following week John's widow Anna and their son Joseph did the same. The one from John's parents contained the verse:

S

> *'Short was his life, our darling son,*
> *But peaceful is his rest;*
> *Mother misses you most of all,*
> *Because she loves you best.*
> *The news was sad, the blow was hard,*
> *God's will, it shall be done;*
> *With a manly heart he did his part,*
> *Our dear beloved son'*

A year later his parents placed an 'Our Heroes – in Memoriam' notice and it contained the verse:

> *'When alone in my sorrow, and bitter tears flow,*
> *There stealeth a dream of the sweet long ago,*
> *Unknown to the world John stands by my side,*
> *And whispers, Dear Mother, death cannot divide'*

Rifleman John Shannon is commemorated on Newtownards and District War Memorial and in Regent Street Methodist Church Newtownards.

Shaw Brothers: James Rowan and William Maxwell

James Rowan and William Maxwell Shaw were sons of James Johnston Shaw (Professor of Metaphysics and Ethics) and Mary Elizabeth Shaw (nee Maxwell). They were married on 16 August 1870 in Greyabbey Presbyterian Church and they lived in Fishquarter House, Kircubbin. Rowan was the first of the two brothers to be killed in action:

Shaw, James Rowan (Rowan)
Second Lieutenant
9th Battalion, Cheshire Regiment
Killed in action on Tuesday 22 February 1916 (aged 35)
Pont-du-Hem Military Cemetery, France (Grave I. D. 5)

Second Lieutenant James Rowan Shaw was born in Belfast and he was the elder son. He served with the Cheshire Regiment and he was killed in action on 22 February 1916.

Shaw, William Maxwell
Distinguished Service Order
Mentioned in Despatches
Major
102nd Brigade, Royal Field Artillery
Killed in action on Monday 28 or Tuesday 29 May 1917 (aged 35)
Railway Dugouts Burial Ground, Belgium (Grave IV. C. 19)

S

Kircubbin Family Bereaved.

Major Wm. Maxwell Shaw, D.S.O., Royal Field Artillery, killed in action on 28th ult., was the younger son of the late Mr. James J. Shaw, K.C., Recorder of Belfast, and County Court Judge of Antrim (who succeeded Judge Fitzgibbon in 1909), and a grandson of the late Mr. John Maxwell Shaw, of Kircubbin. Maj. Shaw has been in the Army since 1900, and was at one time adjutant of the Cheshire Territorial Artillery Brigade. He had seen much service in the war, and had won the D.S.O. His elder brother, Second-Lieut. J. R. Shaw, Cheshire Regiment, was killed in February, 1916. Deceased's mother was a daughter of the late Mr. Wm. Maxwell, of Ballyherley, County Down. Judge Shaw was pro-Chancellor of the Queen's University of Belfast, and chairman of the University Commission. Deceased was a brother of Lady Woods, wife of Sir Robert Woods, the Dublin surgeon, who recently contested Trinity College.

The death of Major William Maxwell Shaw DSO was reported in the 9 June edition of the *Newtownards Chronicle* under the headline 'Kircubbin Family Bereaved'. It was reported that William Maxwell Shaw was the younger son of the late James J Shaw KC Recorder of Belfast and County Court Judge. He was a grandson of John Maxwell Shaw of Kircubbin and a brother of Lady Woods, wife of Sir Robert Woods who was a surgeon in Dublin.

In the same report there was reference to the death on active service of his brother Second Lieutenant Rowan Shaw.

William Maxwell Shaw was born on 19 April 1882 and he was educated at St Columba's College, Rathfarnham in Dublin. Commissioned on 19 December 1900, he was made Lieutenant on 19 December 1903, Captain on 13 November 1912 and Major on 27 July 1915. At different times he served with the 3rd Welsh Brigade, the 28th Cheshire Brigade and the 102nd Brigade Royal Field Artillery. He was awarded the DSO for gallantry at Martinpuich on 27 September 1915 and he was also Mentioned in Despatches (*London Gazette* of 4 January 1917 Page 209). Major William Maxwell Shaw was killed in action on 28/29 May 1917.

Shaw, Dennis de Courcey
Second Corporal
No. 51899, 'M' Depot Company, Royal Engineers
Died on Thursday 18 July 1918 (aged 35)
Manchester (Philips Park) Cemetery, England (Grave H. C.E. 487)

S

Dennis de Courcey Shaw was born on 10 January 1883 in Kircubbin and he was a son of Christopher and Catherine Shaw (nee Hughes). They were married on 26 July 1870 in Newtownhamilton Parish Church of Ireland in County Armagh and they had three children who were baptised in Kircubbin Parish Church of Ireland – Elizabeth, Dennis de Courcey and Joseph Stevenson.

Dennis de Courcey Shaw worked as a boilermaker and he and Annie Elizabeth Currie were married on 13 November 1906 in All Saints Church Newtown Heath. They had five children including John, Richard, de Courcey and Florence. Dennis enlisted on 4 September 1914 in Manchester and he served with the Royal Engineers. He went to France on 30 August 1915 and he was invalided home to England on 29 February 1916 after he sustained a gunshot wound to the neck. Thereafter he did munitions work for Grayson Ltd in Birkenhead and he died of pneumonia on 17 July 1918 at 45 Buckley Street, Newtown Heath, Manchester. It is interesting to note that Denis de Courcey Shaw died on 17 July and yet for official purposes thereafter the Army used the date 18 July – the date that they received notification of his death. After Second Corporal Dennis de Courcey Shaw died his widow asked for a military funeral and her request was granted.

Shaw, Frederick (Frew)
Rifleman
No. 19/345, Royal Irish Rifles
Died on Wednesday 7 January 1920 (aged 21)
Killinchy Non-Subscribing Presbyterian Churchyard, Co. Down (Grave in South-east part)

Frederick (Frew) Shaw was a son of Frew and Harriet Louisa Shaw (nee Valentine) who lived in the townland of Ballybundon, Killinchy. They were married on 8 December 1886 in Killinchy Non-Subscribing Presbyterian Church. Frew Shaw Senior was a farmer and he and Harriet had at least ten children including Jane A, Sarah, Harriet L, Margaret, William Russell, Frew, James Simpson, Christina and Robert. Frew Shaw Senior died on 7 December 1906 aged 39 and his wife Harriet Louisa died on 26 June 1952.

Frew Shaw enlisted in November 1915 and he joined the 19th Battalion, Royal Irish Rifles. He died at home and it is recorded on the family grave headstone in Killinchy Non-Subscribing Presbyterian Churchyard that he 'died of wounds received in action near Ypres'. On 23 November 1922 his mother Harriet Louisa applied for her late son's medals and at that time her address was 'c/o YWCA, Mildmay House, Blackburne Place, Liverpool'.

S

Shaw, Henry
Gunner
No. 253325, 'A' Battery, 50th Brigade, Royal Field Artillery
Killed in action on Wednesday 1 May 1918 (aged 29)
Lijssenthoek Military Cemetery, Belgium (Grave XXVIII. E. 15A)

There is some ambiguity as to Gunner Shaw's date of death. In the CWGC Debt of Honour his date of death is recorded as 29 April 1918. On the Crawford family grave headstone in Movilla Cemetery Newtownards it is inscribed as 1 May 1918 and this date is substantiated by the date stated in a letter of sympathy sent to Henry's mother by Captain Laidman.

Henry Shaw was born on 30 January 1889 in Newtownards and he was the second son of Robert and Letitia Shaw (nee Crawford) who lived at 8 Queen Street, Newtownards. They were married on 12 July 1886 in Greenwell Street Presbyterian Church

Newtownards. Robert Shaw worked as a wool weaver and he and Letitia had at least eleven children all of whom were baptised in Greenwell Street Presbyterian Church – James Crawford, Henry, Elizabeth, William John, Francis Crawford, Alexander, Robert, Letitia, Mary Anne, Margaret and Jane.

Prior to the outbreak of the Great War Henry Shaw worked as a painter and in 'Soldiers Died in the Great War 1914 – 1919' it is recorded that he enlisted in New York City, USA. He served with the Royal Field Artillery and he was killed in action on 1 May 1918. Captain JH Laidman wrote to Henry's mother to express sympathy on behalf of the whole Brigade and in the letter he related the circumstances of Henry's death. Around 5.00 pm on 1 May 1918 Gunner Henry Shaw was hit in the back by a splinter from a shell and he remained conscious for about three minutes before he died. Gunner Shaw had only been with 'A' Battery for a few days before he was killed in action.

S

Gunner Henry Shaw is commemorated on Newtownards and District War Memorial; in the PCI Roll of Honour for Greenwell Street Presbyterian Church and on the Crawford family grave headstone in Movilla Cemetery.

Sheals, John Joseph
Petty Officer First Class
No. 161948, HMS *Pembroke*, Royal Navy
Died on Saturday 27 January 1917 (aged 42)
Portaferry Roman Catholic Graveyard (West of Church)

In some census records and newspaper reports the surname is spelt Shiels.

John Joseph Sheals was baptised in Portaferry Roman Catholic Church on 2 July 1876 and he was a son of Thomas and Sarah Sheals (nee Smyth). They were married on 10 January 1875 in St Patrick's Roman Catholic Church, Ballyphilip. The death of Petty Officer First Class John Joseph Sheals was reported in the 3 February 1917 edition of the *Newtownards Chronicle* under the headline 'Portaferry Naval Officer's Death'. His address was given as Meeting-House Lane, Portaferry.

The report stated that an inquest had been held at St Pancras London. On 19 January 1917 John Joseph Sheals left his ship at the start of a period of leave

Portaferry Naval Officer's Death.

An inquest was held on Wednesday at St. Pancras, London, by Mr. P. Byrne, on John Joseph Shiels, 42, whose home was at Meeting-house Lane, Portaferry. Evidence given showed that the deceased was a first-class petty officer in the Royal Navy. On January 19th he left his ship on leave for the purpose of visiting his home in Ireland. On Saturday, whilst walking along Euston Road, he was seen to stagger and fall, striking his head on the pavement. He was removed to University College Hospital, where he became unconscious soon after his admission, and died in a couple of hours. Dr. Hickson stated that there was fracture of the skull, and a piece of the broken bone had lacerated the brain. Death was due to effusion of blood on the brain produced through the deceased having struck his head on the ground. The jury returned a verdict of accidental death.

and he intended to visit his home in Portaferry. On Saturday 27 January 1917 whilst walking along Euston Road in London he was seen to stagger and fall, striking his head on the pavement. He was taken to University College Hospital where he became unconscious soon after admission and he died two hours later.

At the inquest Dr Hickson stated that John Joseph Sheals's skull had been fractured and a piece of the broken bone had lacerated his brain. Death was due to effusion of blood on the brain and the jury returned a verdict of accidental death. John Joseph Sheals is commemorated on the family grave headstone in Portaferry Roman Catholic Church Graveyard:

'IHS In memory of John Joseph Sheals died 27 January 1917 aged 42 years, his mother Sarah Sheals died 1893 aged 60 years also his aunt Alice McNamara, died 16 April 1927 aged 83 years RIP'

S

Sheppard, John Meharry (John) (served as Shepherd, John)
Rifleman
No. 18/70, 13th Battalion, then 11th/13th Battalion, Royal Irish Rifles, then 22nd Entrenching Battalion
Died of wounds on Friday 29 March 1918 (aged 21)
Pozieres Memorial, France (Panel 74 to 76)

In some records the surname is spelt Shepherd (CWGC Debt of Honour) and in others Shepperd (Church Memorial). John Meharry Sheppard was born in Newtownards and he was a son of Robert and Jane Sheppard (nee Meharry) who lived at 52 Wallace's Street No. 2, Newtownards. They were married on 6 April 1885 in St Anne's Church of Ireland Belfast. Robert Sheppard worked as a bleach-works labourer and he and Jane had at least eight children including William, Maggie, Robert, Susan(ne), John Meharry and James Hutchinson. James was baptised in Greenwell Street Presbyterian Church Newtownards.

Prior to the outbreak of the Great War John Sheppard worked as a shoe-maker. He enlisted in Belfast and on 15 May 1915 he joined the 18th Battalion Royal Irish Rifles. He was transferred to the 13th Battalion Royal Irish Rifles (1st County Down Volunteers) and he went to the front on 8 December 1915. He served in 108th Brigade of the 36th (Ulster) Division. He was granted a ten-day period of home leave in August 1917 and in November 1917 the 11th and 13th Battalions Royal Irish Rifles were amalgamated. When they were disbanded in February 1918 John was posted to the 22nd Entrenching Battalion.

Rifleman John Sheppard died of wounds on 29 March 1918 and about a month later the circumstances surrounding his death emerged when John's father received a communication from Mrs AE Mygind who was Honorary Secretary of the Copenhagen Bureau of the British Red Cross Society in Denmark. John had been fatally wounded in action and as he lay dying he was found by a group of German soldiers. His last thoughts were of home.

Dated 30 April 1918, the letter from Mrs Mygind said:

'We have today received from the German Red Cross in Frankfurt the enclosed letter, to be forwarded to you at the request of a dying English soldier found by the Germans on the high road near Peronne. It was his last wish that his letter and photograph should be forwarded to you. We sincerely hope that these may be of some comfort to you in your grief.'

When John Sheppard died two of his brothers were on active service and his parents placed a 'For King and Country' notice in the *Newtownards Chronicle*. So too did his sister Maggie and her husband Hugh McMillan who lived at 54 Wallace's Street, Newtownards. The notice from his parents contained the verse:

'His cheery, sunny countenance shall ne'r from memory fade,
Nor yet will ever we forget the sacrifice he made.
And when we sit and mourn for him we seem to hear him say,
Keep up your hearts, we'll meet again, on that eternal day'

Rifleman John Meharry Sheppard is commemorated on Newtownards and District War Memorial and in the PCI Roll of Honour for Greenwell Street Presbyterian Church Newtownards.

Simms, John Sibbald (Jack)
Captain
12th Battalion, London Regiment (The Rangers)
Killed in action on Friday 26 October 1917 (aged 23)
Duhallow A.D.S. Cemetery, Belgium (Grave III. A. 2)

John Sibbald Simms was born on 15 July 1894 and he was the only son of Samuel Hugh and Mary Frances Sibbald Simms (nee Johnston) who lived in High Street, Newtownards. They were married on 22 February 1893 in Strean Presbyterian Church Newtownards. Samuel Simms worked as a draper and he and Mary had three children – John Sibbald, Eileen Mary and Kathleen Johnston. John Sibbald Simms was the only nephew of Major-General Rev Dr John M Simms CMG, Principal Chaplain to the British Armies in France.

Jack Simms was educated at Campbell College in Belfast and prior to the Great War he was serving his time with his uncle John Blow. John Blow was a principal in the firm of Messrs Blow & McKeag, Linen Merchants and they had premises in Clarence Place and Donegall Square North in Belfast.

Jack Simms was a keen golfer and he played in the Scrabo Club at Newtownards where his handicap was eight. He won several Club competitions including the President's Cup. He had success too in billiards competitions held in Newtownards.

In October 1914 Jack Simms enlisted as a Private in the Sportsmen's Battalion and he was promoted to a commission in June 1915 in the 2nd/12th London Rangers. He went to the front in February 1917 and he was promoted to the rank of Captain. Captain John Sibbald Simms was killed in action on 26 October 1917 and he is commemorated on Newtownards and District War Memorial; in Strean Presbyterian Church Newtownards and in Campbell College. Jack's father Samuel Hugh died on 13 January 1940 and his mother Mary Frances died on 19 December 1940.

Simonton, Mason
Private
No. 5634, 20th Battalion, Royal Fusiliers (City of London Regiment)
Died on Thursday 20 July 1916 (aged 21)
Serre Road Cemetery No. 2, France (Grave XIV. A. 13)

Mason Simonton was born in Ballymacarrett, Belfast and he was a son of William Davidson Simonton and Jenny Simonton (nee Mason) who lived at 1 Malone Park in Belfast. William Simonton worked as a packing case manufacturer and he and Jenny had at least three children – Mason, Ellen and William Brian. The Simonton family worshipped in Comber Non-Subscribing Presbyterian Church

Mason Simonton enlisted in Belfast, he served with the 20th Battalion, Royal Fusiliers and he died at High Wood on 20 July 1916. Private Mason Simonton is commemorated in Comber Non-Subscribing Presbyterian Church and on the family headstone in the adjoining graveyard; in Methodist College Belfast and in the Belfast Book of Honour (Page 586). Mason's father William died on 18 January 1929 and his mother Jenny died on 8 April 1946.

S

Simpson, James Francis (James)
Gunner
No. 3465, 9th Battalion, Royal Scots, transferred to (92343), 'C'
Battalion, Tank Corps
Died of wounds on Friday 30 November 1917 (aged 22)
Rocquigny-Equancourt Road British Cemetery, France (Grave IV. A. 22)

 James Francis Simpson was born on 10 April 1895 and he was a son of William and Mary Eliza Simpson (nee Dempster) who lived in the townland of Ganaway and later Ballywhisken, Millisle. They were married on 1 November 1878 in Carrowdore Parish Church of Ireland. William Simpson worked as an agricultural labourer, Mary Eliza worked as a sewer (embroiderer) and they had at least five children – William (1886), Margaret Anne (1892), James Francis (1895), Hugh Samuel (1897), and Robert Douglas (1900).

James enlisted early in 1915 in Edinburgh and he went to France on 13 October 1915 with the 9th Battalion Royal Scots (3465). He was wounded twice. At the beginning of 1917 he was transferred to the Tank Corps and

he died from wounds sustained during the Battle of Cambrai. At the time of James's death his younger brother Hugh was serving in Salonika.

After the War Office notified them that James had died his parents placed a 'For King and Country' notice in the *Newtownards Chronicle* and it contained the verse:

> *'Sleep on, dear son, in your foreign grave,*
> *A grave we may never see;*
> *But as long as life and memory last*
> *We will remember thee.'*

Gunner James Francis Simpson is commemorated in Carrowdore Parish Church of Ireland (Christ Church). James's father William died on 24 November 1940 and his mother Mary Eliza died on 12 April 1948.

Simpson, Thomas (served as Harvey, Thomas)
Gunner
No. 696399, 'Y' 57th Trench Mortar Battery, Royal Field Artillery
Killed in action on Tuesday 12 June 1917 (aged 25)
Rue-Petillon Military Cemetery, France (Grave I. N. 44)

Thomas Simpson was a son of William and Mary Simpson who lived at 3 Railway Street, Comber. William Simpson worked as a railway labourer and he and Mary had at least eight children – Joseph, William, Francis, Thomas, Minnie, James, Maria and John. Prior to the outbreak of the Great War Thomas Simpson worked as a farm labourer.

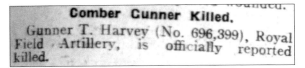

When Thomas Simpson enlisted in Bootle, Lancashire he used an alias and he served under the name of Thomas Harvey. He served with the Royal Field Artillery and Thomas Simpson, alias Thomas Harvey, was killed in action on 12 June 1917. At the time of Gunner Thomas Simpson's death all five of his brothers were on active service. Joseph Simpson conveyed their details by means of a letter which was published in the 15 September 1917 edition of the *Newtownards Chronicle*:

• Thomas killed

- Joseph served with the Royal Inniskilling Fusiliers (13795) and he was in the Military Convalescent Hospital in Holywood, Co Down recovering from wounds (this was Joseph's second time to be wounded and he was wounded for a third time in May 1918)

- James was in Salonika having previously been wounded

- Francis was in France where he had been since the outbreak of the Great War.

- William was in the American Army.

- John was in the Royal Irish Rifles.

GNR·THOMAS SIMPSON Gunner Thomas Simpson is commemorated on Comber and District War Memorial.

Simpson, William
Lance Corporal
No. 18767, 'B' Company, 13th Battalion, Royal Irish Rifles
Killed in action on Saturday 1 July 1916 (aged 25)
Thiepval Memorial, France (Pier and Face 15 A and 15 B)

S

William Simpson was born on 8 June 1891 in Newtownards and he was a son of William and Agnes Simpson (nee McGimpsey) who lived at 23 West Street. They were married on 22 June 1888 in First Newtownards Presbyterian Church. William Simpson worked as a stonecutter and he and Agnes had five children all of whom were baptised in First Newtownards Presbyterian Church – Margaret, William, Catherine, Agnes and Jane. When William's mother Agnes died in 1899 at the age of 32, Catherine and Agnes went to live with George and Catherine Bailie in East Street. William Simpson Senior married Sarah Paden on 25 July 1901 in First Newtownards Presbyterian Church and they had two children, Sarah and Robert. William Simpson died and his widow Sarah lived at 9 Pound Street, Newtownards.

Prior to the outbreak of the Great War William Simpson worked as a beetler in a linen factory. He enlisted in Newtownards and he served with the 13th Battalion Royal Irish Rifles in 108th Brigade of the 36th (Ulster) Division. Lance Corporal William Simpson was killed in action on the first day of the Battle of the Somme. Initially he was reported as missing in action and in June 1917 it was officially confirmed that he had been killed. His stepmother, brother and sisters placed a 'For King and Country' notice in the 16 June 1917 edition of the *Newtownards Chronicle*.

Lance Corporal William Simpson is commemorated on Newtownards and District War Memorial and in First Newtownards Presbyterian Church.

Sinclair, John
Rifleman
No. 2367, 'A' Company, 13th Battalion, Royal Irish Rifles
Killed in action on Saturday 1 July 1916 (aged 22)
Thiepval Memorial, France (Pier and Face 15 A and 15 B)

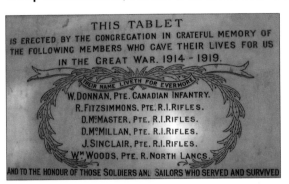

John Sinclair was born on 18 May 1894 in Kircubbin and he was a son of Margaret Sinclair who lived at 16 Back of Green. Margaret Sinclair worked as an embroiderer and she had at least five children including Margaret and John.

John Sinclair lived in Kircubbin, he enlisted in Belfast, he served with the 13th Battalion Royal Irish Rifles in 108th Brigade of the 36th (Ulster) Division and he was killed in action on the first day of the Battle of the Somme. Rifleman John Sinclair is commemorated in Kircubbin Presbyterian Church.

Skillen, Alexander
Rifleman
No. 12425, 1st Battalion, Royal Irish Rifles
Killed in action on Thursday 21 March 1918 (aged 36)
Grand-Seraucourt British Cemetery, France (Grave II. F. 17)

Alexander Skillen was born in Comber and he was a son of William James and Margaret Skillen who lived in High Street. William James Skillen worked as a blacksmith's helper and he and Margaret had at least thirteen children including Matthew, Alexander, Alice, Martha and Grace.

Alexander Skillen and Rachel Moore were married on 31 March 1902 in Belmont Presbyterian Church Belfast and they had at least five children including Mary, Margaret and William James. They lived in High Street, Comber before they moved to 15 Chater Street in Belfast. Alexander worked as a labourer in an engineering works before he got a job as a shipyard labourer on the Queen's Island in Belfast.

Comber Rifleman Killed.

Intimation has been received that Rifleman Alexander Skillen, Royal Irish Rifles, was killed in action in March. Deceased was the youngest son of Mr. William Jas. Skillen, High Street, Comber, and leaves a wife and four children, who reside at 15 Chater Street, Belfast. He was employed on the Queen's Island, and has two brothers on active service.

Alexander Skillen enlisted in Belfast and he served with the 1st Battalion Royal Irish Rifles. Rifleman Alexander Skillen was killed on 21 March 1918 during an intense enemy bombardment at the start of the German 'Michael' offensive and at that time two of his brothers were also on active service. He is commemorated on Comber and District War Memorial.

Skilling, James
Able Seaman
SS *Garron Head* (Belfast), Mercantile Marine
Killed on Friday 16 November 1917 (aged 45)
Tower Hill Memorial, London, England

In some records the surname is spelt Skillen.

James Skilling was born on 16 January 1872 in Donaghadee and he was a son of Alexander and Letitia Skilling (nee Morrison). They were married on 24 June 1854 in Donaghadee Parish Church of Ireland and they had at least four children who were all baptised in Donaghadee Parish Church of Ireland – Eliza Jane, Francis, Alexander and James. James's mother died on 19 May 1882 aged 53 and his father died on 29 September 1899.

James Skilling worked as a seaman and he and Mary Ann Jones were married on 7 October 1892 in Mountpottinger Methodist Church Belfast. They had at least three children – Alexander, James and Samuel.

James Skilling was one of 28 seamen who died when the SS *Garron Head* was torpedoed and sunk on 16 November 1917 by the German submarine U-103 in the Bay of Biscay. One of the Head Line ships, the SS *Garron Head* was on a voyage from Bilbao to Maryport with a cargo of iron ore.

At the time of James's death his family was living at 1 Auburn Terrace in Donaghadee. Able Seaman James Skilling is commemorated on Donaghadee and District War Memorial and in Donaghadee Methodist Church (as Skillen).

Sloan, George
Rifleman
No. 17004, 'B' Company, 13th Battalion, Royal Irish Rifles
Killed in action on Saturday 1 July 1916 (aged 30)
Thiepval Memorial, France (Pier and Face 15 A and 15 B)

George Sloan was born in Comber and he was a son of John and Elizabeth Sloan who lived at 9 Brae Side, Comber. Previously they had lived at Hill Head and also in High Street, Comber. John Sloan worked as a general labourer and he and Elizabeth had at least six children including Mary, George, Jane and Thomas.

Prior to the outbreak of the Great War George Sloan worked as a farm labourer. He enlisted in Belfast and he served in France with the 13th Battalion Royal Irish Rifles in 108th Brigade of the 36th (Ulster) Division.

> **Comber Rifleman Killed.**
> Official news has been received that Rifleman George Sloan, R.I. Rifles, who was posted as missing on 1st July, 1916, is now presumed to have been killed in action on that date. His folks live at 9 Braeside.

Rifleman George Sloan was posted as missing in action after the first day of the Battle of the Somme. A year later, in July 1917, it was officially confirmed that he had been killed in action on 1 July 1916. He is commemorated on Comber and District War Memorial and in Comber Non-Subscribing Presbyterian Church.

Sloan, William
Rifleman
No. 6791, 11th Battalion, Royal Irish Rifles
Killed in action on Saturday 1 July 1916 (aged 19)
Thiepval Memorial, France (Pier and Face 15 A and 15 B)

William Sloan was born in Newtownards and he was a son of Anthony and Lizzie Sloan (nee McCreedy) who lived in Roseneath Cottage, Main Street in Conlig. They were married on 24 August 1896 in Ballygilbert Presbyterian Church. Anthony Sloan worked as a general labourer and he and Lizzie had two children – William and Lillah.

At the age of 17, William Sloan enlisted at Clandeboye (without his parent's permission) and, along with other young men from Conlig, he came home wearing his uniform. He served with the 11th Battalion Royal Irish Rifles in 108th Brigade of the 36th (Ulster) Division and he was killed in action on the first day of the Battle of the Somme.

Initially he was posted as missing in action and after that his mother continued to set a place for him at table every mealtime in case he arrived home. Even after it was officially confirmed that Rifleman William Sloan had been killed in action his mother never accepted that he was dead. Until Lizzie Sloan died the front door of the house was never locked, day or night, in case William arrived home. Rifleman William Sloan is commemorated on Bangor and District War Memorial; in the RBL Album in North Down Museum (Page 62); on the RBL Bangor Branch Memorial Plaque and in Conlig Presbyterian Church. He is also commemorated on the family grave headstone in Bangor New Cemetery. His father Anthony died on 16 August 1931 and his mother Lizzie died on 24 January 1932.

Smith, James (see Smyth, James)

Smurthwaite, Donald Stuart Stirling
Second Lieutenant
'A' Company, 1st Battalion, Black Watch (Royal Highlanders)
Killed in action on Monday, 26 October 1914 (aged 20)
Ypres (Menin Gate) Memorial, Belgium (Panel 37)

S

Donald Stuart Stirling Smurthwaite was born on 12 June 1894 and he was a son of Baynes Wright and Charlotte Lillias Smurthwaite (nee Stirling) who had at least three children – Mary Duff, Donald Stuart Stirling and Jean Margaret Hamilton. Baynes Wright Smurthwaite was a solicitor and he died in 1912 aged 54. At the time of Donald Stuart Stirling Smurthwaite's death it was reported in the press that he was a nephew of Thomas A Warnock JP of Portaferry. Second Lieutenant Donald Stuart Stirling Smurthwaite served with the 1st Battalion Black Watch (Royal Highlanders) (commission reported on page 6304 of the *London Gazette*, 11 August 1914) and he was killed in action on 26 October 1914.

Smyth Brothers (Comber): David and John
David and John Smyth were born in Comber and they were sons of David and Elizabeth Smyth who lived in Mill Street, Comber. David was the first of the two brothers to be killed in action:

Smyth, David
Rifleman
No. 18802, 'B' Company, 13th Battalion, Royal Irish Rifles
Killed in action on Saturday 1 July 1916
Thiepval Memorial, France (Pier and Face 15 A and 15 B)

David Smyth enlisted in Comber, he served with the 13th Battalion Royal Irish Rifles in 108th Brigade of the 36th (Ulster) Division and he was killed in action on the first day of the Battle of the Somme. Initially he was reported as missing in action and in July 1917 it was officially confirmed that he had been killed in action. Less than one month later the Smyth family heard the news that their son John had also been killed in action.

Rifleman David Smyth is commemorated on Comber and District War Memorial.

Smyth, John
Rifleman
No. 18786, 'B' Company, 13th Battalion, Royal Irish Rifles
Killed in action on Monday 6 August 1917 (aged 21)
Potijze Chateau Grounds Cemetery, Belgium (Grave II. E. 21)

John Smyth enlisted in Comber, he served with the 13th Battalion Royal Irish Rifles in 108th Brigade of the 36th (Ulster) Division and he was wounded at the Battle of the Somme. He recovered and returned to the front and he was killed by enemy shellfire in the early morning of 6 August 1917 when the Battalion was holding the line prior to the Battle of Langemarck.

By the time John died the Smyth family had moved from Comber to 49 Beersbridge Road in Belfast and Rifleman John Smyth is commemorated on Comber and District War Memorial and in the Belfast Book of Honour (Page 598).

Smyth Brothers (Portaferry): David and John

David and John Smyth were born in Portaferry and they were sons of David and Isabella Smyth (nee Markey) who had five children – James (died on 11 October 1907), Samuel, John, David and Mary Isabella. They were grandsons of James and Ann Smyth. James Smyth died on 15 March 1902 and Ann Smyth died on 9 June 1917. Brothers David and John Smyth moved to Scotland where they lived in Kilmarnock, Ayrshire and that is where they both enlisted. John Smyth was the first of the two brothers to be killed in action:

Smyth, John
Private
No. 5416, 18th Battalion, Highland Light Infantry
Killed in action on Tuesday 18 July 1916 (aged 27)
Thiepval Memorial, France (Pier and Face 15 C)

S

John Smyth was baptised on 22 April 1889 in Portaferry Roman Catholic Church. In the Great War he served with the 18th Battalion Highland Light Infantry and he was killed in action on 18 July 1916 during the Battle of the Somme. In the CWGC Debt of Honour his surname is spelt Smith.

Smyth, David
Private
No. 11171, 2nd Battalion, King's Own Scottish Borderers
Killed in action on Sunday 3 September 1916 (aged 22)
Delville Wood Cemetery, France (Grave XXIII. D. 3)

David Smyth was baptised on 3 October 1893 in Portaferry Roman Catholic Church. In the Great War he served with the 2nd Battalion King's Own Scottish Borderers and he was killed in action on 3 September 1916 during the Battle of the Somme.

Both Private David Smyth and Private John Smyth are commemorated on the family grave headstone in Ballyphilip Roman Catholic Graveyard Portaferry.

Requisat in Pace

Smyth, David John
Rifleman
No. 18803, 'B' Company, 13th Battalion, Royal Irish Rifles
Killed in action on Saturday 1 July 1916 (aged 19)
Thiepval Memorial, France (Pier and Face 15 A and 15 B)

In some records the surname is spelt Smith, for example, 'Soldiers Died in the Great War 1914 – 1919', the 1901 and 1911 Census returns, Dundonald Presbyterian Church and Second Comber Presbyterian Church. In other records the surname is spelt Smyth, for example, CWGC Debt of Honour, Comber and District War Memorial and the *Newtownards Chronicle*.

David John Smyth was born in Comber and he was a son of Hugh and (Isa or Anna) Bella Smyth (nee Rea) who lived in Bridge Street, Comber. They were married on 5 September 1895 in Dundonald Presbyterian Church. Hugh Smyth worked as a distillery labourer and he and Bella had at least eight children including Mary Anne (Minnie), David John, James Martin, Margaret Jane, Isabella, Hugh and Elizabeth.

S

David John Smyth enlisted in Comber, he served with the 13th Battalion Royal Irish Rifles in 108th Brigade of the 36th (Ulster) Division and he was killed in action on the first day of the Battle of the Somme. Initially he was posted as missing in action and then in February 1917 it was officially confirmed that he had been killed in action. Rifleman David John Smyth is commemorated on Comber and District War Memorial (as Smyth) and in Second Comber Presbyterian Church (as Smith).

Smyth, David McCully (David)
Company Sergeant Major
No. 7741, Royal Irish Rifles attached 6th King's African Rifles
Died of disease on Wednesday 16 January 1918 (aged 31)
Dar Es Salaam War Cemetery, Tanzania (Grave 5. F. 16)

David McCully Smyth was born on 1 June 1886 in the townland of Ballyhay, Donaghadee and he was a son of Samuel and Maggie Smyth (nee Arnott) who lived at 87 Mill Street, Newtownards. They were married on 9 February 1878 in First Newtownards Presbyterian Church. Samuel Smyth worked as a general labourer and coal dealer and he and Maggie had at least eleven children – William James, Thomas, Samuel, James, David McCully, John, Hugh, Lizzie, Maggie, George and William Henry. The older children were baptised in Ballycopeland Presbyterian Church and the younger ones in First Newtownards Presbyterian Church.

Newtownards King's African Rifleman Makes the Supreme Sacrifice.
Information has been received by cable that Co.-Sergt.-Major David Smyth, King's African Rifles, has succumbed to malarial fever when doing his duty for King and country at Tabora with the British troops in conquering German East Africa. He was the gallant son of Mr. Samuel Smyth, 87 Mill Street, New-townards.

Prior to the outbreak of the Great War David Smyth worked as a painter. He enlisted in Belfast and he served with the Royal Irish Rifles. It was reported in the 26 January 1918 edition of the *Newtownards Chronicle* that Company-Sergeant-Major David Smyth had succumbed to malarial fever when doing his duty for King and country at Tabora during the fighting in German East Africa. He died on 16 January 1918 in Tabora Hospital.

A year after David's death his father, mother, brothers and sisters placed an 'Our Heroes – In Memoriam' notice in the 18 January 1919 edition of the *Newtownards Chronicle*. Company-Sergeant-Major David Smyth is commemorated on Newtownards and District War Memorial and in the PCI Roll of Honour for Greenwell Street Presbyterian Church.

S

Smyth, George
Rifleman
No. 9001, 1st Battalion, Royal Irish Rifles
Died on Wednesday 30 December 1914
Royal Irish Rifles Graveyard, France (Grave I. A. 2)

In the CWGC Debt of Honour it is recorded that Rifleman George Smyth was the husband of E Evans (formerly Smyth) of 6 George's Street, Newtownards. Rifleman George Smyth died on 30 December 1914 after the Christmas truce at a time when conditions in the waterlogged and muddy trenches were very bad. Desk searches and public appeals to date have yielded no further information.

Smyth, Irvine Johnston (Irvine)
Second Lieutenant
6th Battalion, Royal Inniskilling Fusiliers
Killed in action on Friday 3 September 1915 (aged 23)
Green Hill Cemetery, Gallipoli, Turkey (Grave I. C. 22)

Irvine Johnston Smyth was born in Lurgan and he was the eldest son of the Rev William Henry Smyth and Mary J Ruskell Smyth (nee Johnston). Mary was a daughter of the Rev Irvine Johnston and she and William Henry

Smyth were married on 11 September 1890 in Donaghadee Methodist Church where Mary's father ministered from 1890 until 1893. Later the Rev Irvine Johnston lived in Donaghadee Road, Bangor.

The Rev William Henry Smyth ministered in University Road and Carlisle Memorial Methodist Churches in Belfast and Wesley's Chapel Cork. Irvine Smyth's paternal grandfather, James Smyth, lived in Newtownards. Irvine Smyth was educated at Methodist College Belfast and at Wesley College Dublin and prior to the Great War he worked in the Civil Service in Dublin. He enlisted and served with the 6th Battalion Black Watch Territorials before obtaining a commission in the 6th Battalion Royal Inniskilling Fusiliers in December 1914. He served in 31st Brigade of the 10th (Irish) Division.

Second Lieutenant Irvine Smyth survived the landing at Suvla Bay in August 1915 but he was killed in action on 3 September 1915 when bringing the machine-gun section of the Battalion into action during a period of heavy shelling by the enemy. A brother officer wrote to Irvine's father to express his sympathy and in the letter he commended Irvine's skill in placing his guns and setting the range. He said that officers from other regiments would come to see how Irvine placed his guns and to check their ranges by Irvine's calculations. He also commended Irvine's coolness under fire and his bravery when going into the open to help comrades who had been wounded.

Second Lieutenant Irvine Smyth is commemorated on Newtownards and District War Memorial; in Methodist College, Belfast and Belfast Royal Academy; in the Belfast Book of Honour (Page 597) and on the family grave headstone in Bangor New Cemetery.

Smyth, James (served as Smith, James)
Rifleman
No. 18/690, 13th Battalion, Royal Irish Rifles
Killed in action on Wednesday 9 August 1916
Ration Farm (La Plus Douve) Annexe, Belgium (Grave III. A. 7)

In some official records the surname is spelt Smyth and in others, including the Commonwealth War Graves Commission, it is spelt Smith. It is recorded in the CWGC Debt of Honour that J Smith was the husband of Mrs Smith who lived in the townland of Scrabo, Newtownards. In 'Soldiers Died in the Great War 1914 – 1919' his forename is recorded as James and his surname is spelt Smyth.

18/690 RIFLEMAN J. SMITH ROYAL IRISH RIFLES 9TH AUGUST 1916

James Smyth was born in Killinchy and he was a son of Mary Smyth. He enlisted in Newtownards and he served with the 13th Battalion Royal Irish Rifles in 108th Brigade of the 36th (Ulster) Division. He was killed in action on 9 August 1916 by shellfire while holding the line in the Messines area. Rifleman James Smyth is commemorated in First Newtownards Presbyterian Church (as Smith) and on the family grave headstone in Killinchy Non-Subscribing Presbyterian Church graveyard.

KILLED.
Rifleman J. Smith (No. 690), Royal Irish Rifles, is officially reported killed.

Smyth, William

There are three William Smyths commemorated on Newtownards and District War Memorial, one from Greenwell Street, one from Mill Street and one from North Street. The Newtownards and District War Memorial was unveiled and dedicated on Saturday 26 May 1934 and it was reported in the 2 June 1934 edition of the *Newtownards Chronicle* that the North Street address inscribed for William Smyth was incorrect and should have been Regent Street instead of North Street.

Smyth, William (Greenwell Street)
Rifleman
No. 6823, 2nd Battalion, Royal Irish Rifles
Killed in action on Friday 19 May 1916 (aged 22)
Arras Memorial, France (Bay 9)

William Smyth was a son of George and Margaret Smyth who lived at 59 Greenwell Street in Newtownards. George Smyth worked as a general labourer and he and Margaret had at least four children George, William, Adam, Robert.

Prior to the outbreak of the Great War William Smyth worked as a general labourer. He was a member of the Ulster Volunteer Force and in August 1914 he enlisted

S

in Newtownards. He served with the 4th Battalion attached 2nd Battalion, Royal Irish Rifles.

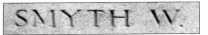 William went to the front in December 1914 and three months later he required hospital treatment after being wounded in the head during the Battle of Neuve Chapelle. He returned to the front and on 9 May 1915 he was severely wounded in the arm during the fighting around Hill 60. He was in hospital in England until August 1915 and, following rehabilitation, he returned to the Western Front. Rifleman William Smyth was killed in action on 19 May 1916 during heavy enemy bombardment of the trenches. At that time William's brother Adam was stationed at Holywood having been invalided home from the front six weeks previously. Adam Smyth, 13th Battalion Royal Irish Rifles (18809) was discharged from the Army on 4 July 1918 because of Valvular Disease of the Heart (VDH).

Members of Lord Londonderry's Own (CLB) Flute Band placed a 'For King and Country' notice in the 10 June 1916 edition of the *Newtownards Chronicle* and the following week his family and his loving friend Jessie Stevenson placed a 'For King and Country' notice which contained the verse:

S

'No more will the smile of his countenance brighten
The long, dreary days of the friends left behind;
For no one that knew him could ever forget him,
His ways were so loving, faithful and kind'

Rifleman William Smyth is commemorated on Newtownards and District War Memorial (as Wm Smyth Greenwell Street) and in Newtownards Parish Church of Ireland (St Mark).

Smyth, William John (William) (Mill Street)
Rifleman
No. 18/132, 11th Battalion, Royal Irish Rifles
Killed in action on Saturday 19 August 1916 (aged 24)
Ration Farm (La Plus Douve) Annexe, Belgium (Grave III. B. 8)

William John Smyth was born in Newtownards and he was a son of James and Eliza Jane Smyth (nee Whiteside) who lived at 131 Mill Street, Newtownards. James Smyth worked as a general labourer and he and Eliza Jane had at least seven children – William John, Maria, Agnes, Robert James, Charles, Francis and David. William John's paternal grandfather, also called William John Smyth, and his maternal grandmother Maria Whiteside were both widowed and they lived with James and Eliza Jane.

William John Smyth worked as a blacksmith before he moved to Canada where he worked as a tram conductor prior to the outbreak of the Great War. He returned home and on 1 May 1915 he enlisted in Belfast. He served with the 11th Battalion Royal Irish Rifles in 108th Brigade of the 36th (Ulster) Division and he was killed in action on 19 August 1916. At that time his wife was living at 43 McNeill Street in Glasgow and his father, Private James Smyth, was on active service in Salonika with the 6th Battalion Royal Irish Rifles.

Rifleman William John Smyth is commemorated on Newtownards and District War Memorial (as Wm Smyth Mill Street) and in Newtownards Parish Church of Ireland (St Mark) where his initials are inscribed as WT.

> SMYTH—Killed in action on August 19, 1916 (132) Private William J. Smyth, 11th Battalion Royal Irish Rifles, the beloved son of James and Eliza J. Smyth.
>
> No more will the smile of his countenance brighten
> The long dreary days of the friends left behind,
> For no one who knew him could ever forget him,
> His ways were so loving, faithful, and kind.
>
> Deeply regretted by his loving Father and Mother; also his Brothers and Sisters.
> 131, Mill Street,
> Newtownards.

S

Smyth, William (Willie) (Regent Street)
Rifleman
No. 18789, 'B' Company, 13th Battalion, Royal Irish Rifles, then 11th/13th Battalion, then 12th Battalion Royal Irish Rifles
Killed in action on Monday 2 September 1918 (aged 23)
Ploegsteert Memorial, Belgium (Panel 9)

William Smyth was born in Newtownards and he was a son of Hugh and Alice Smyth (nee McMorran) who lived in Mary Street, Newtownards. They were married on 27 June 1879 in Regent Street Presbyterian Church Newtownards. Hugh Smyth worked as a quarryman and he and Alice had at least six children – Jane, Agnes Chambers, Mary Elizabeth, Henrietta (Etta), Hugh Hamilton and William. Some of the children were baptised in Regent Street Presbyterian Church Newtownards. Alice Smyth died in 1896 aged 45. For a time William lived at 48 Regent Street, Newtownards with his uncle Thomas and aunt Agnes Chambers Irvine. Thomas Irvine worked as a picture framer.

Prior to the outbreak of the Great War, William Smyth was working as an apprentice block printer in the Glen Printing and Finishing Works in

Newtownards. In September 1914 he enlisted in Newtownards, he joined the 13th Battalion Royal Irish Rifles and in 1915 he went with 108th Brigade of the 36th (Ulster) Division to France. He was wounded in the Battle of the Somme. In November 1917 the 11th and 13th Battalions were amalgamated and when they were disbanded in February 1918 Willie was transferred to the 12th Battalion Royal Irish Rifles.

Rifleman William Smyth was killed in action on 2 September 1918 and the Rev J Herbert Orr wrote to Agnes Irvine to express his sympathy. He explained that in an advance to capture a town held by the Germans, William's company had been met by heavy machine-gun fire. William had been hit in the head by a bullet and he died 'almost instantaneously'. Rifleman Smyth was buried on the battlefield.

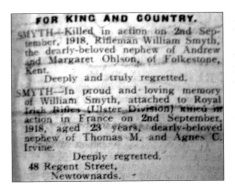

After William died there were three 'For King and Country' notices in the *Newtownards Chronicle*. One was from Thomas and Agnes Irvine, one was from Andrew and Margaret Ohlson of Folkestone Kent and the third was from the Officers and Brethren of Stuart's Volunteers Loyal Orange Lodge No. 872 of which he had been a member.

Rifleman William Smyth is commemorated on Newtownards and District War Memorial (as Wm Smyth North Street) and in the PCI Roll of Honour for Greenwell Street Presbyterian Church Newtownards.

Smythe, Francis (Frank)
Private
No. 1665, 5th Battalion, Highland Light Infantry
Killed in action on Monday 12 July 1915 (aged 29)
Helles Memorial, Gallipoli, Turkey (Panel 173 to 177)

> **Comber Soldier Killed at the Dardanelles.**
> News has been received that Private Frank Smythe, 5th Batt. Highland Light Infantry (Territorials), has been killed in action at the Dardanelles. Deceased was a son of the late Mr. E. Smythe, of Comber, and formerly lived in Upper Frank Street, Belfast. Before rejoining the Territorials, in which he formerly served, he was a driller in Halley's Motors, Ltd., Yoker, Glasgow. The day before his battalion left Methil for Gallipoli he attained his 29th birthday.

Francis Smythe was a son of Edward and Agnes Smythe who lived in Comber and then in Stormount Street, Belfast. Edward Smythe worked as a blacksmith and he and Agnes had at least four children – Francis, Mary, James and Ann.

Francis Smythe moved to Scotland where he worked as a driller in Halley's Motors Ltd, Yoker, Glasgow. He enlisted in Glasgow and he served with the 5th Battalion Highland Light Infantry. Just a few days before the Battalion left Methil in Fife for Gallipoli he celebrated his 29th birthday. Private Frank Smythe was killed in action on 12 July 1915 and his death was reported in the 4 September 1915 edition of the *Newtownards Chronicle* under the headline 'Comber Soldier Killed at the Dardanelles'.

Snodden, William John Stevenson (William)
Rifleman
No. 19837, 'C' Company, 13th Battalion, Royal Irish Rifles
Killed in action on Saturday 1 July 1916 (aged 19)
Thiepval Memorial, France (Pier and Face 15 A and 15 B)

In 'Soldiers Died in the Great War 1914 – 1919' it is recorded that William John Stevenson Snodden was born in Comber. He was born on 3 June 1897 and he was a son of Samuel and Jane Snodden (nee Stevenson) who were married on 2 January 1880 in Killinchy Presbyterian Church. Samuel Snodden was a farmer and he and Jane had at least nine children including Elizabeth, Henry, Roseanna, Samuel, Annie, Minnie and William John Stevenson who was baptised in Killinchy Presbyterian Church.

William Snodden lived in the townland of Ballymorran, Killinchy, he enlisted in Downpatrick and he served with the 13th Battalion Royal Irish Rifles in 108th Brigade of the 36th (Ulster) Division.

Rifleman William J Snodden was killed in action on the first day of the Battle of the Somme and he is commemorated in Killinchy Presbyterian Church. His father died on 11 March 1922 and his mother died on 31 January 1924.

Spain, Patrick P
Sergeant
No. 25947, 10th Battalion, Royal Dublin Fusiliers
Killed in action on Monday 13 November 1916 (aged 45)
Thiepval Memorial, France (Pier and Face 16C)

Patrick P Spain was born in County Donegal and when he was a member of the Royal Irish Constabulary he was stationed in Newtownards between periods of duty in Newry. His death was reported in the *Newtownards Chronicle* under the headline 'Former Newtownards Policeman Killed in Action' and in the report readers were reminded of his nickname when he was stationed in Newtownards – 'The Smiler' – because of his genial disposition. His death

S

was also reported in the *Newry Reporter* under the headline 'Well-Known Newry Boxer Killed'.

Patrick Spain was renowned as an all-round athlete, boxer and wrestler. He was a Reservist and at the outbreak of the Great War he went to France with the Irish Guards. He wrote a letter on 29 August 1914 from 4th Guards' Brigade and in it he said that they had been involved in three engagements. He described how they had arrived very tired at a small town 'about as big as Newry' with the intention of resting up. They were billeted in various houses in the town when word came through that the German Army was approaching. The people of the town began to flee with as many of their possessions as they could carry.

Field Artillery and Coldstream Guards went out to delay the advance of the enemy and amidst 'showers of shrapnel' Patrick Spain and his comrades tore up the square setts from the streets and built barricades at the ends of streets to keep back the foe. It was a dark evening and the attack was repulsed at the cost of many lives. Patrick went on, 'We retired in good order leaving behind us nothing but a scene of desolation in that once beautiful town, and of course our fallen comrades'.

Wounded this time.—Private T. P. Spain, of the Irish Guards, has been wounded, and lies in a hospital in France. Constable Spain was in the R.I.C. and was for some time stationed in Newtownards.

Patrick Spain was wounded at the Battle of the Marne and after treatment in hospital he returned to the front and served through the first winter of the Great War. Like so many others he suffered from the effects of frostbite. His spell of duty ended and he took his discharge from the Army. When he returned to Newry it was remarked that his jet-black hair had turned almost grey.

Patrick rejoined the police and he was stationed in Banbridge. It was there that he enlisted in response to the call for more recruits. He served with the Royal Dublin Fusiliers and was promoted to the rank of Sergeant. He returned to France and he was killed in action on 13 November 1916 in the Battle of The Ancre. Sergeant Patrick Spain is commemorated in *Newry's War Dead* (Pages 80 and 182) and in the County Donegal Book of Honour (Page 194).

Spence, John Milliken (Jack)
Lance Corporal
**No. 19845, 'B' Company, 13th Battalion, Royal Irish Rifles
Killed in action on Saturday 1 July 1916 (aged 20)
Thiepval Memorial, France (Pier and Face 15 A and 15 B)**

John Milliken Spence was born in Comber and he was a son of William Henry and Ann (Annie) Spence (nee Milliken) who were married on 19 April 1893 in Fitzroy Presbyterian Church Belfast and who lived at 21 Brownlow Street, Comber. William Spence worked as a National School teacher and he and Annie had at least five children – Olive, John Milliken, Maria Dorothy, Kathleen and William Gerald.

Jack Spence enlisted in Comber, he served with the 13th Battalion Royal Irish Rifles in 108th Brigade of the 36th (Ulster) Division and he was killed in action on the first day of the Battle of the Somme. Lance Corporal Jack Spence is commemorated on Comber and District War Memorial and in Comber Parish Church of Ireland (St Mary).

S

Spracklin, Edgar J
Leading Seaman
No. 1113X, Newfoundland Royal Naval Reserve, HMS *Bayano*
Died on Thursday 11 March 1915 (aged 36)
Ballyhalbert (St. Andrew) Church of Ireland Churchyard, Co Down (in North-East part)

Seven crew members from HMS *Bayano* are buried in graveyards on the Ards Peninsula.

Spracklin, Edgar J and one unidentified Royal Marine are buried in Ballyhalbert Church of Ireland (St Andrew) Graveyard Ballyeasborough.

Chater, Frederick William is buried in Whitechurch Graveyard Ballywalter.

Bain, AG; Wellstead, WA and two unidentified sailors are buried in Ballyphilip Church of Ireland Churchyard Portaferry.

Stannage, Robert
Lance Corporal
No. 6226, 2nd Battalion, Royal Irish Rifles
Killed in action on Monday 16 November 1914 (aged 33)
Pont-du-Hem Military Cemetery, France (Grave VIII. D. 6)

Robert Stannage was born in 1881 in Newtownards and he was a son of William John and Jane Stannage (nee Brown) who were married on 30 January 1877 in Newtownards Reformed Presbyterian Church. William John Stannage worked as a weaver and they lived in John Street, Newtownards. After Jane died William John moved to Bootle, Liverpool and Robert lived with his grandmother Sarah Stannage at 43 John Street, Newtownards. Robert's uncle Alex Ferguson also lived in John Street, Newtownards.

Robert Stannage was a career soldier with more than twelve years of service when he died. For a time he was a bugler in the 6th Militia Battalion Royal Irish Rifles (the Louth Rifles) and he was also attached to the staff of the Royal North Downs. He served in the South African War and for seven years in India. After the outbreak of the Great War Robert was attached to the 2nd Battalion Royal Irish Rifles and he was killed in the firing line on 16 November 1914.

After Robert died family members placed 'Killed in Action' notices in the *Newtownards Chronicle*. The one from his uncle and aunt Thomas and Sarah Stannage contained the verse:

'Though our hearts may break with sorrow
By the grief so hard to bear,
We shall meet him some bright morning
In our Father's mansion fair'

On each anniversary of Robert's death his father placed an 'Our Heroes – in Memoriam' notice in the *Newtownards Chronicle* and one contained the verse:

'He sleeps in death, far, far from home,
He owns a soldier's grave;
Proud Erin's sons o'er ocean foam
Have shown that he was brave

Place the old flag o'er his breast
Blackened, bloodstained in the fray
Leave him to his endless rest
Here in his cold bed of clay'

Lance Corporal Robert Stannage was married and when he died his widow and daughter Selina were living at 86 Mountjoy Street in Belfast. He is commemorated on Newtownards and District War Memorial; in Newtownards Parish Church of Ireland (St Mark) and in the Belfast Book of Honour (Page 605).

Stannage, Robert

On the War Memorial Plaque in Newtownards Parish Church of Ireland (St Mark) the name 'Stannage R' is listed twice. In a report published in the 6 August 1927 edition of the *Newtownards Chronicle* both were named Robert and their addresses were given as John Street Lane and William Street. Lance Corporal Robert Stannage from John Street who served with the 2nd Battalion Royal Irish Rifles (6226) and who was killed in action on 16 November 1914 has been identified but desk searches and public appeals to date have yielded no further information about Robert Stannage from William Street.

Stevenson, George
Private
No. 31897, 18th Battalion, Highland Light Infantry
Killed in action on Sunday 19 August 1917 (aged 38)
Thiepval Memorial, France (Pier and Face 15 C)

George Stevenson was born on 16 January 1879 in Newtownards and he was a son of Samuel and Rose Ann Stevenson (nee McMullen). They were married on 24 October 1866 in Newtownards Parish Church of Ireland. Samuel Stevenson worked as a labourer and he and Rose Ann had at least seven children – Samuel, John, Eliza Ann, William, Hugh, Ellen Jane and George.

When George Stevenson was in his late teens he went to Scotland where he worked as a stone-breaker. He and Agnes Dunn were married on 5 June 1908 and they lived in Carment Drive, Stevenston before moving to 27 Almswall Road in Kilwinning. George and Agnes had two sons – John and Robert Boyle.

George Stevenson enlisted in Kilwinning and he was posted to France at the beginning of 1917. Some eight months later, on 19 August 1917, he was killed in action.

George Stevenson's brother and sister-in-law John and Sarah Stevenson lived at 25 Mill Street, Newtownards. After George died they placed a 'For King and Country' notice in the *Newtownards Chronicle* and it contained the verse:

> *'His King and country called him,*
> *He died in a distant land;*
> *A loving mother waits in Heaven*
> *To take him by the hand'*

Private George Stevenson is commemorated on Newtownards and District War Memorial and on Kilwinning War Memorial.

Stevenson, Hugh
Gunner
No. 44222, 270th Siege Battery, Royal Garrison Artillery
Killed in action on Sunday 1 July 1917 (aged 25)
Ferme-Olivier Cemetery, Belgium (Grave Plot 3 Row C Grave 7)

S

Hugh Stevenson was born in Newtownards and he was a son of James and Catherine Stevenson (nee Harvey) who lived at 17 Frederick Street, Newtownards. They were married on 23 September 1887 in Ballygilbert Presbyterian Church and they had at least twelve children including Jessie, Hugh, Maggie, Sarah Jane, Catherine and Martha. Both Hugh and his father worked as labourers.

Hugh enlisted in Newtownards at the outbreak of the Great War and for a time he served with his unit in Malta. Hugh wrote letters home regularly to his mother Catherine and some of his letters arrived after she died on 22 June 1917. Just eight days later Hugh died.

Major HD Coleman who commanded the 270th Siege Battery didn't know that Catherine was dead when he wrote to her after Hugh's death to express his sympathy and in the letter he outlined the circumstances of Hugh's death.

Major Coleman said that Gunner Hugh Stevenson was killed instantly at his post 'serving the gun which was just about to be fired and he suffered no pain'. The Rev H A Norton, Chaplain to the Forces attached to the 2nd Anzac Corps of Heavy Artillery also wrote to Catherine Stevenson, 'On Sunday morning last his battery position was very heavily shelled by the enemy. All the men took cover, but in spite of this, as the result of a shell's explosion, your son, together with two other gunners were killed'.

After Gunner Hugh Stevenson was killed in action his father, sister, aunts and cousins on active service placed a 'For King and Country' notice in the 28 July 1917 edition of the *Newtownards Chronicle* and it contained the verse:

'A face still loved, so sadly missed,
His smile that was so bright;
He was so thoughtful, good and kind,
Time cannot blot him from my mind.
The hardest part is yet to come,
When the heroes do return;
And I miss among the cheering crowd
The face of my dear loved son'

S Gunner Hugh Stevenson is commemorated on Newtownards and District War Memorial.

Stevenson, James Croskery (James)
Rifleman
No. 7180, 2nd Battalion, Royal Irish Rifles
Killed in action on Saturday 8 July 1916 (aged 25)
Thiepval Memorial, France (Pier and Face 15 A and 15 B)

James Croskery Stevenson was born in Newtownards and he was a son of William and Sarah Stevenson (nee Croskery). They lived in Mill Street and they had at least seven children – Agnes, Anna, Ellen, Sarah, John, Maggie and James. John and Maggie were baptised in Granshaw Presbyterian Church, Moneyreagh.

James lived with his brother and sisters at 25 Church Street in Newtownards and prior to the outbreak of the Great War he worked in the Royal Nurseries Newtownards.

James enlisted in Newtownards, he joined the 4th Battalion Royal Irish Rifles (Royal North Downs) and he undertook his training at Holywood.

Subsequently he was drafted to the 2nd Battalion and he went to France where he served in 74th Brigade of the 25th Division.

Rifleman James Croskery Stevenson was killed while his Battalion was holding the line on 8 July 1916 during the Battle of the Somme. His brother and sisters placed a 'For King and Country' notice in the 5 August 1916 edition of the *Newtownards Chronicle*.

Rifleman James Croskery Stevenson is commemorated on Newtownards and District War Memorial and in First Newtownards Presbyterian Church.

Stevenson, Thomas
Lance Corporal
**No. 40847, 1st Battalion, Royal Irish Rifles
Killed in action on Thursday 16 August 1917 (aged 25)
Tyne Cot Memorial, Belgium (Panel 138 to 140 & 162 to 162 A & 163 A)**

Thomas Stevenson was a son of Thomas and Agnes Stevenson (nee McDowell) who lived at 67 South Street, Newtownards. They were married on 22 December 1888 in Regent Street Methodist Church Newtownards. Thomas Stevenson Senior worked as a woollen weaver and he and Agnes had four children – Robert, Thomas, Sarah and Martha. Thomas Stevenson Senior died in the early 1900s.

Prior to the outbreak of the Great War Thomas Stevenson worked as a grocer's assistant. When he enlisted in Antrim he joined the North Irish Horse as a Trooper and subsequently he was transferred to the 1st Battalion Royal Irish Rifles in 25th Brigade of the 8th Division.

Lance Corporal Thomas Stevenson was posted as missing in action at Westhoek Ridge on 16 August 1917 and one year later, in July 1918, it was officially confirmed that he had been killed in action. His brother and sister-in-law Robert and Ellen Stevenson who lived in Cleveland, Ohio placed a 'For King and Country' notice in the *Newtownards Chronicle*. So too did his widowed mother and his two sisters Sarah and Martha. Their notice contained the verse:

> *'Thou hast fought a noble battle,*
> *Bravely and nobly did thy best;*
> *All your troubles are now ended,*
> *Sleep, brave hero, sleep and rest*

No more we'll clasp thy loving hand
Nor hear thy voice now stilled,
Till we reach the land where you'll proudly stand
With earth's heroes – in action killed.'

Lance Corporal Thomas Stevenson is commemorated on Newtownards and District War Memorial and in Regent Street Methodist Church Newtownards.

Stewart Brothers: John and Niven Boyd

John and Niven Boyd Stewart were sons of James McGimpsey Stewart and Ann Jane Stewart (nee McKeag) who lived in Carrowdore and who were married on 24 March 1865 in Carrowdore Presbyterian Church. James Stewart worked as an agricultural labourer and he and Ann Jane had at least ten children including Anna Mary, James (died), John, James, Jane Hannah, Sarah, William Johnston and Niven Boyd. Both John and Niven were baptised in Carrowdore Presbyterian Church and John was the first of the two brothers to die:

Stewart, John
Private
No. 622464, 27th Battalion, Canadian Infantry (Manitoba Regiment)
Died on Friday 15 September 1916 (aged 35)
Vimy Memorial, France

John Stewart was born on 16 December 1880 and he worked as an agricultural labourer before he moved to Canada. He enlisted in Winnipeg on 19 May 1915 and in his attestation papers it was noted that he was 5 feet 9½ inches tall and that he was a farmer. John cited as his next-of-kin his wife Jane who was living in Carrowdore.

John Stewart served with the 27th Battalion Canadian Infantry (Manitoba Regiment) and he was killed in action on 15 September 1916.

Private John Stewart is commemorated in Carrowdore Presbyterian Church.

Stewart, Niven Boyd (Niven)
Corporal
56th Infantry Regiment, 7th Infantry Division, U S Army
Killed in action on Sunday 10 November 1918 (aged 27)
St Mihiel American Cemetery, France (Plot D Row 22 Grave 33)

In some records his first forename is spelt Nevin.

Niven Boyd Stewart was born on 4 January 1891 and he worked as a labourer both before and after he moved to the United States of America. He and James Reid, who was also from Carrowdore, lived in Chicago, Illinois and it was there that both men enlisted on 5 June 1917.

Niven Boyd Stewart served with the 56th Infantry Regiment 7th Infantry Division US Army and he was killed in action on 10 November 1918. **James Reid** died on 7 March 1919. Corporal Niven Boyd Stewart and Private James Reid are both commemorated in Carrowdore Presbyterian Church.

S

Stewart, James
Rifleman
No. 18/831, 12th Battalion, Royal Irish Rifles
Killed in action on Wednesday 15 August 1917 (aged 19)
Ypres (Menin Gate) Memorial, Belgium (Panel 40)

James Stewart was born on 20 February 1898 in Kircubbin and he was baptised in Kircubbin Parish Church of Ireland. He was a son of Jane Stewart who worked as a domestic servant and he lived in Kircubbin.

James Stewart enlisted in Newtownards in November 1915 and he joined the 18th Battalion Royal Irish Rifles. He went to the front where he served with the 12th Battalion Royal Irish Rifles in 108th Brigade of the 36th (Ulster) Division and he was killed in action on 15 August 1917, the day before the Battle of Langemarck.

Rifleman James Stewart is commemorated in Kircubbin Parish Church of Ireland (Holy Trinity).

Stewart, James

The name James Stewart is listed on Newtownards and District War Memorial and in the booklet produced for the Unveiling and Dedication Ceremony held on Saturday 26 May 1934 he is described as a Rifleman in the Royal Irish Rifles.

Desk searches and public appeals to date have not confirmed conclusively whether or not the James Stewart commemorated on Newtownards and District War Memorial is the same person who is commemorated in Kircubbin Parish Church of Ireland (Holy Trinity) or if they are two different soldiers.

Another Rifleman named James Stewart who joined the 13th Battalion Royal Irish Rifles (2366) was also born in Kircubbin. When he enlisted in Belfast on 2 December 1914 he was 19 years 4 months old and single, he worked as a labourer and he cited as his next-of-kin his mother Jane Armour. Although he was passed fit for service at attestation it was diagnosed soon thereafter that he had a congenital weakness in both arms and he was discharged from the Army on 17 February 1915. A link has not been confirmed between these service data and the soldier who is commemorated on Newtownards and District War Memorial.

Stewart, Robert (Donaghadee)

There are three Robert Stewarts commemorated on Donaghadee and District War Memorial and also in Donaghadee Parish Church of Ireland and one of them has the initial 'D'.

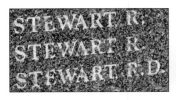

Research has identified four Robert Stewarts with Donaghadee connections:

Stewart, Robert
Rifleman
No. 17013, 'A' Company, 13th Battalion, Royal Irish Rifles, transferred to (17768), 108th Battalion, Machine Gun Corps (Infantry), 36th (Ulster) Division
Killed in action on Saturday 1 July 1916 (aged 21)
Thiepval Memorial, France (Pier and Face 5 C and 12 C)

Robert Stewart was born in Donaghadee and he was a son of James and Grace Stewart (nee Douglas) who lived at 97 Moat Street, Donaghadee. They were married on 17 April 1891 in Newtownards Parish Church of Ireland. James Stewart worked as a labourer and he and Grace had at least five children including Robert, Margaret Jane, George and William.

Robert Stewart enlisted in Donaghadee and he served with the 13th Battalion Royal Irish Rifles (17013) in 108th Brigade of the 36th (Ulster) Division before being transferred to the 108th Battalion Machine Gun Corps (Infantry). Rifleman Robert Stewart was killed in action on the first day of the Battle of the Somme and, along with two other soldiers named Robert Stewart, (one of them Robert D Stewart), he is commemorated on Donaghadee and District War Memorial and in Donaghadee Parish Church of Ireland.

Stewart, Robert
Rifleman
No. 17014, 'A' Company, 13th Battalion, Royal Irish Rifles
Killed in action on Saturday 1 July 1916 (aged 21)
A.I.F. Burial Ground, France (Grave X. A. 5)

S

Robert Stewart was born in 1895 in Donaghadee and he was a son of Alexander and a stepson of Annie Stewart who lived in Church Lane and later Manor Street, Donaghadee. Alexander Stewart worked as a general labourer and Annie was his second wife. Alexander Stewart had at least ten children – Alexander, Sarah, Elizabeth, Robert, Edith, John, William, Margaret, Henry and Samuel.

Robert Stewart worked as a general labourer before he enlisted in Donaghadee. He served with the 13th Battalion Royal Irish Rifles in 108th Brigade of the 36th (Ulster) Division and he was killed in action on the first day of the Battle of the Somme. Along with two other soldiers named Robert Stewart, (one of them Robert D Stewart), Rifleman Robert Stewart is commemorated on Donaghadee and District War Memorial; in Donaghadee Parish Church of Ireland and on the family grave headstone in the adjoining graveyard.

Stewart, Robert
Private
No. 8409, 2nd Battalion, Royal Inniskilling Fusiliers
Died of wounds on Monday 17 May 1915 (aged 30)
Lillers Communal Cemetery, France (Grave III. A. 41)

Robert Stewart was born in Donaghadee and he was a son of William and Elizabeth (Lizzie) Stewart (nee McMillan) who lived in Hunter's Lane, Donaghadee. They were married on 2 October 1869 in Newtownards Parish Church of Ireland. William Stewart worked as a general labourer and he and Lizzie had at least nine children including William, Lizzie, Robert, Mary and Jane.

Prior to the outbreak of the Great War Robert Stewart lived in Donaghadee. He was a Reservist and a member of the Ulster Volunteer Force before he was called to the colours. He served with the 2nd Battalion Royal Inniskilling Fusiliers and he died of wounds on 17 May 1915.

It was Robert's brother William who received the official notification about his death. William Stewart, his wife Anna and their children lived at 14 High Street in Donaghadee. Robert's sister Lizzie Fitzsimons lived in Hunter's Lane, Donaghadee. Lizzie placed a 'Killed in Action' notice in the 26 June 1915 edition of the *Newtownards Chronicle* and it contained the verse:

'The midnight stars are shining
Upon his silent grave,
The one we loved lies sleeping,
He lies in a hero's grave.'
'For ever with the Lord'

Desk searches and public appeals to date have not confirmed conclusively whether or not Private Robert Stewart (8409) is commemorated on Donaghadee and District War Memorial and/or in Donaghadee Parish Church of Ireland.

Stewart, Robert D

Research has identified a Robert D Stewart from Donaghadee who enlisted on 21 September 1914 in Belfast and at attestation he declared that he was Church of Ireland, a labourer, born in Donaghadee and 28 years 1 month old (he was in fact 32 years 4 months old). He joined the 13th Battalion Royal Irish Rifles (16977) and he was discharged 45 days later on 5 November 1914 as medically unfit because of a combination of kidney ailments – 'Bright's disease, Polyuria and Albuminuria'. It was noted in Robert's military file that his son Thomas was living in Bow Street, Donaghadee 'c/o Mrs Dempster'.

Robert D Stewart was born on 29 April 1882 and he was a son of Thomas John and Margaret (Maggie) Stewart (nee Adgey) who were married on 1 July

1872 in First Newtownards Presbyterian Church. They lived at 3 Hunter's Lane, Donaghadee and they had at least seven children – Anne (1874), Margaret (1879), Robert (1882), Esther (1884), Hugh, Byers (1889) and Finlay (1891). The children were baptised in Donaghadee Parish Church of Ireland. Thomas worked as a labourer and Maggie worked as an embroiderer. Maggie Stewart died in the early 1900s. Byers Stewart married James Dempster and they had at least two children – James (born in 1910) and Hugh Stewart (born on 30 April 1919 and baptised in Donaghadee Methodist Church).

Robert D Stewart married and he had two children – Thomas (1904) and Malvina (1907). After Robert's wife died his sister Maggie and his widowed father Thomas lived with them at 10 Hunter's Lane, Donaghadee. After Robert enlisted, his sister Byers Dempster looked after his son Thomas. Byers Dempster died on 2 April 1937 aged 48. Desk searches and public appeals to date have not confirmed a date of death for Robert D Stewart, nor have they conclusively confirmed whether or not Private Robert Stewart (16977) is commemorated on Donaghadee and District War Memorial and/or in Donaghadee Parish Church of Ireland.

Strain, Samuel

S

Rifleman
No. 17016, 'A' Company, 13th Battalion, Royal Irish Rifles
Killed in action on Saturday 1 July 1916 (aged 23)
A.I.F. Burial Ground, France (Grave X. A. 3)

Samuel Strain was a son of Alexander and Mary Ann Strain (nee Patty) who lived in townland of Hogstown, Donaghadee. They were married on 31 May 1884 in Newtownards Registry Office. Alexander Strain worked as a labourer and he and Mary Ann had at least eight children including Agnes, John, Elizabeth, Samuel, Maggie, Louisa and James. Some of the children were baptised in Donaghadee Parish Church of Ireland.

Prior to the outbreak of the Great War Samuel Strain worked as an agricultural labourer. He enlisted in Donaghadee, he served with the 13th Battalion Royal Irish Rifles in 108th Brigade of the 36th (Ulster) Division and he was killed in action on the first day of the Battle of the Somme.

Samuel Strain had been a member of No Surrender LOL No. 241 in Donaghadee and the officers and members placed a 'For King and Country' notice in the 16 June 1917 edition of the *Newtownards Chronicle*. They expressed 'their deep regret at the loss of their highly respected brethren'. The notice commemorated the deaths of **Robert McGaffin** (spelt Gaffin), Ballyhay; **William Patton**, Ballyfotherly and **Samuel Strain**, Donaghadee. It was signed by William Robert McCauley and Robert John Rea.

Rifleman Samuel Strain is commemorated on Donaghadee and District War Memorial and in Donaghadee Parish Church of Ireland.

Strain, William R

William R Strain served as a Rifleman (6769) with either the 1st or 2nd Battalion Royal Irish Rifles and he went to France on 30 April 1915. He died in the 1920s and he is commemorated on Newtownards and District War Memorial. Desk searches and public appeals to date have yielded no further information.

Stratton, David

In the 23 and 30 September 1933 editions of the Newtownards Chronicle two lists of names were published 'with the object of ensuring that all the names of men from Newtownards and District who were killed in the Great War or who died as the result of wounds received or disease contracted in the campaign are included'. Relatives were requested to report any omissions or mistakes. It was indicated that Rifleman David Stratton was from Church Street in Newtownards. A David Stratton served with the Royal Irish Rifles (18/111) and he went to France on 29 November 1915. Desk searches and public appeals to date have not confirmed a connection between these service data and the soldier named David Stratton who is commemorated on Newtownards and District War Memorial. Evidence from one source suggests that David may have been a twin brother of **George Stratton** who also died.

Stratton, David John (David)
Company Quartermaster Sergeant
No. 57842, 36th Signal Company, Royal Engineers
Died of pneumonia on Sunday 27 February 1916 (aged 39)
Newtownards (Movilla) Cemetery, Co. Down (Grave 2. 117)

David John Stratton was born on 19 July 1876 in Newtownards and he was a son of Joseph and Eliza Stratton (nee McGougan). They were married on 13 May 1875 in First Newtownards Presbyterian Church and David was

baptised in that church. A keen sportsman, David played football and he was a member of the Ards Air Gun Club. He was the Scoutmaster of 2nd Newtownards Troop of Boy Scouts. David Stratton worked as a despatch clerk and examiner in the block printing department of the Glen Printing and Finishing Works Ltd in Newtownards. For many years he took an interest in municipal affairs and at the election for Urban Councillors held in January 1914 he was returned as a member for Glen Ward.

David John Stratton and Edith Carter (born in England) were married on 25 July 1900 in St Anne's Church of Ireland Belfast and they had at least one child – a daughter named Eliza Jane who was born on 26 June 1901. They lived at 68 Balfour Street, Newtownards

David enlisted in September 1914 in Belfast and he joined the Ulster Division Engineers. For a time he was stationed for training with the signalling section at Downpatrick. He was promoted to the rank of Sergeant and on 3 October 1915 he went out from Borden Camp in England with the Ulster Division to the front. He was promoted to the rank of Company Quartermaster Sergeant and within a few weeks he contracted influenza. After treatment in hospital he resumed duty at the front. He suffered a relapse and was taken to St Luke's Hospital in Bradford, Yorkshire. Edith Stratton received a telegram on 7 February 1916 informing her that David's illness was serious and she crossed over that evening to be by his side. Three weeks later David Stratton died of pneumonia and his remains were brought home to Newtownards for burial.

Military and Boy Scout honours were accorded for the funeral which took place on Wednesday 1 March 1916. The Rev James Saulters conducted the service in the house and at the graveside. Representatives from the Army, the Boy Scout Movement and the Urban Council attended. The cortege moved from Balfour Street to Movilla Old Cemetery accompanied by the brass band of the Royal Irish Fusiliers. The firing party was provided by the 20th Battalion Royal Irish Rifles and Boy Scout buglers sounded the 'Last Post'.

FOR KING AND COUNTRY.

STRATTON—February 27th, 1916, at St. Luke's War Hospital, Bradford, Yorkshire, Company Q.M. Sergeant David J. Stratton, Royal Engineers (Ulster Division). His remains were interred in Movilla Cemetery, on Wednesday, 1st inst.
EDITH STRATTON.
68 Balfour Street,
Newtownards,

There were three 'For King and Country' notices in the 4 March 1916 edition of the *Newtownards*

Chronicle, one from his wife Edith, one from 2nd Newtownards Boy Scouts and one from members of Ards Air Gun Club. On 28 March 1916 Company Quartermaster Sergeant David John Stratton's remains were reinterred in Movilla New Cemetery and he is commemorated on Newtownards and District War Memorial and in the PCI Roll of Honour for Regent Street Presbyterian Church Newtownards. On the family grave headstone his age is inscribed as 41.

Stratton Family: Henry and Robert

Robert Stratton was born in Newtownards and he was a son of Henry (Harry) Stratton. Henry and Sarah McCullough were married on 7 November 1896 in Newtownards Parish Church of Ireland and they lived in Victoria Avenue and later at 66 East Street in Newtownards. Harry Stratton worked as a general labourer and he and Sarah had at least eight children including Robert, David, Isabella, Edith, Wilhelmina and Lizzie. Robert Stratton died on active service and his father Henry died on 10 November 1929:

Stratton, Robert
Rifleman
No. 4/7173, 1st Battalion, Royal Irish Rifles
Killed in action on Wednesday 23 August 1916 (aged 19)
Vermelles British Cemetery, France (Grave VI. D. 35)

Robert Stratton was the eldest son and prior to the outbreak of the Great War he worked in a mill. He enlisted in Newtownards, he went to France on 3 June 1915, he served with the 1st Battalion Royal Irish Rifles and he was killed in the trenches on 23 August 1916 during an enemy attack.

KILLED.
Rifleman R. Stratton (No. 7,123) is officially reported killed.

When Rifleman Robert Stratton was killed in action both his father Henry and his brother David were also on active service. Later David was taken prisoner of war. In September 1916 Robert's grandmother, aunts, uncles and immediate family placed 'For King and Country' notices in the *Newtownards Chronicle* and the one from his parents contained the verses:

'He marched away so bravely,
His young head proudly held;
His footsteps never faltered,
His courage never failed.
Short was thy life, my darling son,
But peaceful is thy rest;

Father and mother miss you most,
Because they loved you best
Now his earthly fight is o'er,
And in perfect peace he sleeps;
With the angels he is waiting
Till his loved ones he shall meet
The news was sad, the blow was hard,
God's will, it shall be done;
With manly heart he hath done his part,
My dear, beloved son'

In the 30 August 1919 edition of the *Newtownards Chronicle* there was an 'Our Heroes – In Memoriam' notice from Bella Boal who described Robert as her 'dear friend'. Rifleman Robert Stratton is commemorated on Newtownards and District War Memorial.

Stratton, Henry
Rifleman
No. 16980, 13th Battalion, Royal Irish Rifles, transferred to (231710) Labour Corps
Died in hospital on Sunday 10 November 1929 (aged 56)
Newtownards (Movilla) Cemetery, Co. Down

STRATTON—November 10, 1929, at the Hospital, Newtownards, Henry Stratton. The remains of my beloved husband were interred in Movilla Cemetery on Tuesday, 12th inst. Deeply regretted by his sorrowing Wife and Family.
SARAH STRATTON.
66, East Street, Newtownards.

Henry (Harry) Stratton served with the 13th Battalion Royal Irish Rifles (16980) and he went to France on 2 October 1915. After being severely wounded he was transferred to the Labour Corps (231710) and he was discharged from the Army on 30 May 1918. Henry Stratton died on Sunday 10 November 1929 in Newtownards Hospital and he is commemorated on Newtownards and District War Memorial. In 1931 his son David in the USA and his daughters Lily and Ina in Canada placed an 'In Memoriam' notice in the *Newtownards Chronicle* and it contained the verse:

'God knew that he was suffering,
And the hills were hard to climb,
So He closed his weary eyelids,
And whispered 'Peace be thine'

Stratton, George

The name George Stratton is listed on Newtownards and District War Memorial and in the booklet produced for the Unveiling and Dedication Ceremony held on Saturday 26 May 1934 he is described as a Rifleman in the Royal Irish Rifles.

Twins David and George Stratton were born on 31 October 1892 and they were sons of William John and Isabella Stratton (nee Thompson) who were married on 16 January 1892 in Greenwell Street Presbyterian Church Newtownards. A George Stratton who served with the Royal Irish Rifles (7206) enlisted on 31 August 1914 and was discharged on 19 April 1916 when he was deemed to be no longer physically fit for war service. He did not serve overseas. Desk searches and public appeals to date have not confirmed a connection between these family and service data and the soldier who is commemorated on Newtownards and District War Memorial. Evidence from one source suggests that George may have been a twin brother of **David Stratton** who also died.

Stratton, William
Private
No. 639185, 2nd Battalion, Canadian Infantry (Eastern Ontario Regiment)
Died on Friday 27 September 1918 (aged 25)
Quarry Wood Cemetery, France (Grave II. B. 38)

William Stratton was born on 14 August 1893 and he was a son of John and Mary Ann Stratton who lived in the townland of Nunsquarter, Kircubbin.

William Stratton worked as a labourer before he moved to Canada and there he lived at 12 Bennett Street, Brookville in Ontario. He enlisted on 5 January 1916 in Brookville and in his attestation papers it was noted that he was 5 feet 7 inches tall. He served with the 2nd Battalion Canadian Infantry (Eastern Ontario Regiment) and he died on 27 September 1918.

Strickland, Thomas
Rifleman
No. 19869, 'B' Company, 13th Battalion, Royal Irish Rifles
Died of wounds on Friday 16 February 1917 (aged 19)
Bailleul Communal Cemetery Extension (Nord), France (Grave III. A. 125)

Thomas Strickland was born in Comber and he was a son of Thomas and Jane Strickland (nee Gilliland) who lived at 7 Bridge Street, Comber. They were married on 17 September 1877 in Granshaw Presbyterian Church. Thomas Strickland Senior worked as a butcher and after he died Jane worked as a reeler in Andrew's mill. Thomas and Jane had at least seven children – Ellen, Sarah, Agnes, Robert, Charlotte, Thomas and John.

Rifleman T. Strickland (No. 19,869), Royal Irish Rifles, died of wounds. Prior to the outbreak of the Great War Thomas Strickland worked as a post-boy. He enlisted in Comber, he served with the 13th Battalion Royal Irish Rifles in 108th Brigade of the 36th (Ulster) Division and he was severely wounded on 14 February 1917. He died two days later and at the time of his death his sister, Mrs Sarah Burgess, was living in the townland of Carnasure, Comber. Rifleman Thomas Strickland is commemorated on Comber and District War Memorial.

Sumner, John David (John)
S

Chief Gunner
HMTB No. 96, Royal Navy
Drowned on Monday 1 November 1915 (aged 42)
Plymouth Naval Memorial, Devon, England (Panel 5)

The death of Chief Gunner John David Sumner was reported in the 6, 13 and 20 November 1915 editions of the *Newtownards Chronicle*. Under the headline 'Portaferry Officer on Lost Torpedo Boat' it was reported initially that Torpedo Boat No. 96 had sunk in the Straits of Gibraltar on 1 November 1915 after a collision and that two officers and nine men were missing. Then Chief Gunner John David Sumner's widow Jane who was living at 'Kildare', Devon Terrace in Plymouth received a telegram confirming that her husband had died (John D Sumner and Jane Rutherford were married on 12 December 1907 in Portaferry Presbyterian Church).

John D Sumner was well-known in Portaferry and he belonged to naval families on both his father's and his mother's side. He joined the Navy at the age of 14 and he had 28 years of service when he died. After his initial training he served aboard the cruiser *Raleigh* and in 1894 he saw active service in West Africa for which he received the Africa General Service Medal (Gambia Expedition). He next saw service in 1900 during the Boxer Uprising in North China and for that he received the China Medal. Later he served in the Persian Gulf and in home waters. He commanded Torpedo Boats and Destroyers continuously from March 1910 and he was made Commander of Torpedo Boat No. 96 in December 1914.

> **Memorial to Portaferry Hero.**—A handsome monument has been placed in Ballyphilip Churchyard, Portaferry, to the memory of Mr. John David Sumner, R.N., chief gunner- in command of a torpedo boat, who was drowned in a collision off Gibraltar on 1st November.

In the early morning of 1 November 1915 an auxiliary cruiser collided with and sank Torpedo Boat No. 96 in the Straits of Gibraltar. It was pitch dark at the time and neither vessel carried lights. Only eight men from the torpedo boat were saved. Chief Gunner John David Sumner was one of those who died and he is commemorated in Portaferry (Ballyphilip) Parish Church of Ireland (St James). He is also commemorated on a monument erected in the adjoining graveyard.

Swanger, Thomas Slade (Thomas)
Lance Corporal
No. 157563, Inland Water Transport, Royal Engineers
Drowned on Thursday 10 May 1917 (aged 43)
Newtownards (Movilla) Cemetery, Co. Down (Grave 11. 97)

Thomas Slade Swanger was born on 14 February 1874 in Bristol and he was a son of John and Sarah Ann Swanger.

Thomas Slade Swanger and Thursia Pocock were married on 21 July 1901 in St Clement's Church Bristol and they had at least nine children – Thomas George, Gladys Eveline, Hilda May, Arthur John, William Henry, Doris Lilian, Elsie Florence, Ivy Maude and Dorothy Grace who was born on 17 April 1915. Thomas Slade Swanger enlisted in Bristol and he served with Inland Water Transport in the Royal Engineers. Lance Corporal Thomas Swanger was found drowned at Ballyhalbert on 10 May 1917 and he is buried in Movilla New Cemetery.

Swindle, John
Rifleman
No. 18/908, 12th Battalion, Royal Irish Rifles
Killed in action on Tuesday 29 May 1917 (aged 24)
Pond Farm Cemetery, Belgium (Grave O. 12)

John Swindle was a son of George and Elizabeth (Lizzie) Swindle (nee McCullough) who lived at 26 Railway Street in Comber. They were married on 24 February 1885 in Comber Non-Subscribing Presbyterian Church. George Swindle worked as a railway watchman and he and Elizabeth had at least seven children including Margaret, Agnes, John, Martha and James.

Prior to the outbreak of the Great War John Swindle worked as a railway porter. He enlisted in Belfast, he joined the 18th Battalion Royal Irish Rifles, he served with the 12th Battalion Royal Irish Rifles in 108th Brigade of the 36th (Ulster) Division and he was killed in action on 29 May 1917 just before the start of the Battle of Messines. Rifleman John Swindle is commemorated on Comber and District War Memorial; in First Comber Presbyterian Church and in the Belfast Book of Honour (Page 617).

Tanner, William
Rifleman
No. 17/1039, 8th Battalion, Royal Irish Rifles
Died of wounds on Sunday 11 June 1916 (aged 18)
Authuile Military Cemetery, France (Grave D. 8)

William Tanner was born on 7 December 1897 in Donaghadee and he was a son of Samuel and Jane Tanner (nee Bell) who lived at 10 Castle Street, Donaghadee. They were married on 18 February 1897 in Ballycopeland Presbyterian Church. Samuel Tanner worked as a carpenter and he and Jane had at least three children – William, Hannah and Agnes. William was baptised in Shore Street Presbyterian Church Donaghadee.

William Tanner enlisted in Belfast, he went to France on 25 November 1915, he served with the 8th Battalion Royal Irish Rifles in 107th Brigade of the 36th (Ulster) Division and he died of wounds on 10 June 1916. At the time of his death it was reported in the press that Rifleman William Tanner was 'the first Donaghadee soldier of the Ulster Division to make the supreme sacrifice'.

In a letter to William's mother, William's commanding officer told her that 'William's last thoughts as he lay dying were of his mother'. Rifleman William Tanner is commemorated on Donaghadee and District War Memorial; in Shore Street Presbyterian Church Donaghadee and on the family grave headstone in Donaghadee Parish Church of Ireland Graveyard. William's father Samuel died on 26 July 1943 and his mother Jane died on 13 November 1949.

T

Tate, Hugh
Rifleman
No. 12443, 'A' Company, 8th Battalion, Royal Irish Rifles
Killed in action on Thursday 7 June 1917 (aged 30)
Lone Tree Cemetery, Belgium (Grave I. D. 5)

In 'Soldiers Died in the Great War 1914 – 1919' it is recorded that Hugh Tate was born in Donaghadee and he enlisted in Belfast. The 1901 census shows that a Hugh Tate aged 13 lived in Skipton Street, Belfast with his sister Martha and his parents William and Dora Tate. William Tate worked as a grocer.

Hugh Tate and Sarah Jane Atkinson were married on 3 November 1909 in St Anne's Church of Ireland Belfast and they lived in Chamberlain Street, Belfast. Hugh worked as a labourer in the shipyard and Sarah worked as a twister in the ropeworks. They attended St Clement's Parish Church of Ireland in Belfast.

Hugh Tate served with the 8th Battalion Royal Irish Rifles in 107th Brigade of the 36th (Ulster) Division and he was killed in action on the first day of the Battle of Messines. At that time Sarah Jane was living at 9 Mersey Street, Belfast and Rifleman Hugh Tate is commemorated in the Belfast Book of Honour (Page 618).

Tate, James
Sergeant
No. 19951, 'C' Company, 13th Battalion, Royal Irish Rifles
Killed in action on Saturday 1 July 1916 (aged 20)
Serre Road Cemetery No.1, France (Grave II. BB. 14)

James Tate was born in Ballynahinch and he was the eldest son of Joseph and Sarah Tate (nee Craig) who lived in the townland of Ballyminstra, Killinchy. They were married on 13 March 1896 in Second Ballynahinch Presbyterian Church. Joseph Tate was a farmer and he and Sarah had at least five children – James, John, Joseph, Margaret Jane and Sarah. The three youngest of these children were baptised in Killinchy Presbyterian Church. James received a gold medal from Killinchy Sabbath School for six years of unbroken attendance.

Prior to the outbreak of the Great War James Tate worked on the family farm and he was a member of the Ulster Volunteer Force. He was a married man with one child. He enlisted in Downpatrick and trained at Clandeboye Camp before going to Seaford in Sussex and then to the front in October 1915. He served with the 13th Battalion Royal Irish Rifles in 108th Brigade of the 36th Ulster Division and he was home for a short period of leave in May 1916. He was killed in action on the first day of the Battle of the Somme. His parents placed a 'For King and Country' notice in the 5 August 1916 edition of the *Newtownards Chronicle* and it contained the verse:

'The Lord breathed on the slain and led them home'

The newspaper report of his death focused on 'glory' rather than the horrors of that day: 'Great sympathy is felt with his father and mother, wife and child in his early death for King and country, but as his death was instantaneous a measure of consolation is afforded, as sudden death is sudden glory'.

His parents placed an 'Our Heroes – In Memoriam' notice in the 30 June 1917 edition of the *Newtownards Chronicle* and it contained the verse:

'Sleep on; there is nought now on earth that can wake thee,
No cruel guns' roar can disturb thy repose
Nor bursting of shells can now overtake thee
Save the call of the Trumpet when night draws to a close
Until that morn dawns we are patiently waiting,
While the past happy memories ever green shall remain;
And as years grow in number the anchor holds firmer,
Till hand shall clasp hand for to part ne'er again'

Rifleman James Tate is commemorated in Killinchy Parish Church of Ireland; in Killinchy Presbyterian Church and on the family grave headstone in Killinchy Presbyterian Church Graveyard. James Tate's mother Sarah died on 23 May 1927 and his father Joseph died on 31 January 1933.

Tate, John PK (Jack)
Rifleman
No. 19952, 'B' Company, 13th Battalion, Royal Irish Rifles
Died of wounds on Monday 7 February 1916 (aged 20)
Forceville Communal Cemetery and Extension, France (South boundary)

John PK Tate was born in Newtownards and he was a son of John and Sarah Jane Tate (nee Kirkpatrick) who lived at 12 Frances Street and had a business in North Street. They were married on 1 August 1884 in St Stephen's Church of Ireland Belfast. John Tate Senior was a wine and spirit merchant and he and Sarah had at least nine children including George, Janette, Agnes, John PK, Alfred WK and Alice Eileen. Jack Tate was educated at Newtownards Model School and Belfast Mercantile College and prior to the outbreak of the Great War he worked as an apprentice in the wholesale department of Messrs Riddel's Ltd in Donegall Place Belfast. He was a member of the Ulster Volunteer Force and he enlisted in Newtownards.

TATE—Killed in action in France on 7th February, 1916, John P. K. Tate, 13th R. I. Rifles (Ulster Division), dearly-beloved son of John Tate, Frances Street and North Street, Newtownards.
Deeply regretted.

Rifleman Jack Tate was one of four Ardsmen who were killed in action together on 7 February 1916. They were all members of the 13th (Service) Battalion of the Royal Irish Rifles (1st Co Down Volunteers). The others were Rifleman **James Calvert** of Tullycore Killinchy, Rifleman **David McConnell** of 22 Wallace's

Street No.2 Newtownards and Bandsman **Charlie Newell** of 54 South Street Newtownards.

The officer in charge of the platoon was Lieutenant **Elliott Johnston**, a son of Samuel Johnston JP, Glen Printing and Finishing Works in Newtownards. He described the circumstances of their deaths. During a heavy bombardment a shell from the German lines exploded in the midst of a party of men killing three and wounding three. James Calvert, David McConnell and Charlie Newell were killed outright and Jack Tate died later from his injuries. The three men who died immediately were laid to rest together and the burial service was conducted by one of the brigade chaplains, the Rev Charles Campbell Manning, Rector of Comber. On that occasion Lieutenant Johnston escaped injury but he was killed in action five months later on the first day of the Battle of the Somme.

Rifleman Jack Tate is commemorated on Newtownards and District War Memorial and in Newtownards Parish Church of Ireland (St Mark). On 8 February 1917 – one year and a day after Jack Tate died of wounds – his father John died.

Taylor, Alfred Squire
Captain
Royal Army Medical Corps attached 10th/11th Battalion, Highland Light Infantry
Killed in action on Tuesday 31 July 1917 (aged 29)
Ypres Town Cemetery Extension, Belgium (Grave III. B. 21)

Alfred Squire Taylor was a son of the Rev David Alexander Taylor and Dora Taylor who lived in Belfast at 'Eastbourne', 32 Windsor Avenue North and before that at 26 Malone Road. The Rev Taylor was a Presbyterian Clergyman and he and Dora had four children – David Robertson, Hugh Stowell, Alice Sirett and Alfred Squire. The Rev Taylor was living in Greyabbey when he died on 8 October 1941 aged 94. Both parents and two of their children are buried in Belfast City Cemetery.

Alfred Taylor studied medicine and during the Great War he served with the Royal Army Medical Corps attached to the 10th/11th Battalion Highland Light Infantry. He went to Mesopotamia on 18 March 1915 and he was killed in action on 31 July 1917 at the beginning of the Third Battle of Ypres.

Captain Alfred Squire Taylor is commemorated on Comber and District War Memorial; on the QUB War Memorial; in the QUB Book of Remembrance (Page 52) and in the Belfast Book of Honour (Page 618).

Taylor, David
Private
No. 12579, Princess Victoria's (Royal Irish Fusiliers), transferred to (18148), 2nd Battalion, Royal Irish Regiment
Died of wounds on Saturday 16 December 1916 (aged 33)
Kemmel Chateau Military Cemetery, Belgium (Grave X. 46)

David Taylor was born in Newtownards and he was the only son of Mrs Sarah Taylor who lived in George's Street, Newtownards, 82 Movilla Street, Newtownards and 34 The Butts, Kilwinning, Ayrshire. Sarah Taylor worked as a flowerer (embroiderer) and she and her children – David, Carol and Violet – lived for a time in Queen Street, Newtownards with Sarah's sister Elizabeth Crothers and her family.

Newtownards Soldier Succumbs to Wounds.

News has been received by Mrs. Sarah Taylor, 82 Movilla Street, Newtownards, that her only son, Private David Taylor, 2nd Battalion Royal Irish Regiment, has died from wounds received in action. Deceased had previously been wounded twice, and had gone out to the front for the third time when he met with his death.

Prior to the outbreak of the Great War David Taylor worked as a general labourer. He enlisted in Newtownards, he served initially with the 6th Battalion Royal Irish Fusiliers (12579) in 31st Brigade of the 10th (Irish) Division and he went to Gallipoli on 14 August 1915. After being wounded there he was transferred to the 2nd Battalion Royal Irish Regiment in 49th Brigade of the 16th (Irish) Division and he died of wounds on 16 December 1916.

Lieutenant Clifford CF Smith wrote to Sarah Taylor to express his sympathy and in his letter he told her that David had been 'wounded by a shell' and that he had died peacefully in hospital. Private David Taylor is commemorated on Newtownards and District War Memorial and in Newtownards Parish Church of Ireland (St Mark).

Taylor, Samuel (Sam)
Sergeant
No. 136240, 2nd Battalion, Canadian Mounted Rifles
Died of wounds on Saturday 5 October 1918 (aged 38)
St. Sever Cemetery Extension, France (Grave S. II. H. 20)

Samuel Taylor was born on 15 July 1880 and he was the eldest son of James Taylor who lived in the townland of Carryreagh, Donaghadee. James Taylor was a farmer and after Samuel's mother died James remarried. He and Elizabeth Martin were married on 21 January 1881 in First Newtownards Presbyterian Church and they had at least six children all of whom were baptised in First Donaghadee Presbyterian Church – William, Andrew, David, Elizabeth, John and Miriam.

Sam Taylor worked on the family farm before he moved to Toronto in Canada around 1905. There he worked as a teamster (driver) and he and his wife Maria lived at 548 King West and later at 1084 St Clarens Avenue in Toronto. They had four children. Sam Taylor enlisted in Toronto on 7 September 1915 when he was 35 years old and it was noted in his attestation papers that he was 5 feet 7¼ inches tall.

FOR KING AND COUNTRY.
TAYLOR—Died of wounds received in action on the 5th October, 1918, (136,240) Sergeant Sam Taylor, 2nd C.M.R., eldest and dearly loved son of James and Eliza Taylor, Cannyreagh, Donaghadee.
Deeply regretted.

It was the Rev Willis in Donaghadee who was informed by the Canadian Record Office that Sergeant Sam Taylor had died of wounds. At that time the Rev Willis was the County Director of the British Red Cross. Sam's family placed a 'For King and Country' notice in the *Newtownards Chronicle*. Sergeant Sam Taylor is commemorated on Donaghadee and District War Memorial and in First Donaghadee Presbyterian Church.

Taylor, William
Company Sergeant Major
No. 19223, 'D' Company 13th Battalion, Royal Irish Rifles
Killed in action on Saturday 1 July 1916 (aged 55)
Heath Cemetery, Harbonnieres, France (Grave VIII. K. 5)

Under the headline 'Portaferry' William Taylor's name was listed in the 2

September 1916 edition of the *Newtownards Chronicle* to correct an earlier erroneous report that Company Sergeant Major William Torney from Portaferry had been killed in action. The error may have occurred because of the similarity in their service numbers. William Torney was a son of Mary Torney who lived in Meetinghouse Lane, Portaferry and he served with the 13th Battalion Royal Irish Rifles (19233) before being transferred to the Northumberland Fusiliers (52290). Company Sergeant Major William Torney was discharged from the Army in 1919.

Desk studies and public appeals to date suggest that Company Sergeant Major William Taylor (19223) had no connection with the Ards area and his inclusion in this book is for interest only. He was born in Newry and prior to the outbreak of the Great War he worked as a general labourer. William and his wife Bridget lived in James Street, Newry and they had five children – John (Johnny), Mary Anne, Annie, William and George.

T

PORTAFERRY.
Co.-S.-M. Torney, R.I. Rifles, reported killed in a recent issue, should read Co.-S.-M. W. Taylor (No. 19,223).

William Taylor had previous service in the South African War, he enlisted in Newry, he served with the 13th Battalion Royal Irish Rifles in 108th Brigade of the 36th (Ulster) Division and he was killed in action on the first day of the Battle of the Somme. His son Johnny served with the 10th Company Machine Gun Corps (16495) and was killed in action on Thursday 4 October 1917 aged 25. Johnny's name is listed on Tyne Cot Memorial Belgium (Panel 154 to 159 and 163A).

David Martin, who served as a Private in the Royal Irish Fusiliers (7636) and who was a brother-in-law of William Taylor's brother George, was executed by the Germans on Saturday 27 May 1916. In 1914 David Martin with three other soldiers became separated from their unit and they were hidden by the villagers of Le Catelet in France. In May 1916 their hiding place was discovered and because they were in civilian clothes they were considered to be spies. They were executed by firing squad and buried in Le Catelet Churchyard. David Martin is commemorated in the Belfast Book of Honour (Page 368) and in *Newry's War Dead* (Pages 63 and 136). Company Sergeant Major William Taylor is commemorated in *Newry's War Dead* (Pages 82 and 136).

Taylor, William Robert (Robert)
Rifleman
**No. 17033, 'A' Company, 13th Battalion, Royal Irish Rifles
Killed in action on Saturday 1 July 1916 (aged 21)
Serre Road Cemetery No. 2, France (Grave XIII. A. 1)**

William Robert Taylor was born in the townland of Carryreagh, Donaghadee and he was a grandson of William and Charlotte Conway (nee Muckle) who lived in the townland of Killaughey, Donaghadee. William Conway was a farmer and he and Charlotte had at least eleven children including Mary, Jane, Thomas, Sarah, Hugh and Charlotte.

Prior to the outbreak of the Great War William Robert Taylor worked as a farm servant. He enlisted in Donaghadee, he went to France on 9 December 1915, he served with the 13th Battalion Royal Irish Rifles in 108th Brigade of the 36th (Ulster) Division and he was killed in action on the first day of the Battle of the Somme. Initially he was posted as missing in action and in June 1917 it was confirmed that he had been killed in action.

TAYLOR—Missing since 1st July, 1916 Rifleman William Robert (Robert) Taylor, Royal Irish Rifles, now reported killed, the dear grandson of William and C. Conway, Killaughey, and much-beloved nephew of Agnes Tollerton.

> Greater love hath no man,
> That he lay down his life,
> With all its promises,
> That other men might live.

Sadly mourned by his sorrowing Aunt.
AGNES TOLLERTON.
Canneyreagh, Donaghadee.
Deeply regretted by his many relatives.

Robert's aunt Agnes Tollerton placed a 'For King and Country' notice in the 16 June 1917 edition of the *Newtownards Chronicle* on behalf of his many relatives and it contained the verse:

> *'Greater love hath no man,*
> *That he lay down his life,*
> *With all its promises,*
> *That other men might live'*

Rifleman William Robert Taylor is commemorated on Donaghadee and District War Memorial.

Thomas, Basil Llewellyn Boyd (Basil)
Lieutenant
**15th Battalion, Royal Welsh Fusiliers attached 27th Company Machine Gun Corps
Killed in action on Monday 9 April 1917 (aged 21)
Roclincourt Valley Cemetery, France (Grave IV. H. 3)**

Ards Officer Killed.

Lieut. Basil Llewellyn Boyd Thomas, Machine Gun Corps, who was killed in action on Easter Monday, was the only son of Mr. and Mrs. W. J. Thomas, Penrallt, Herne Hill, London, and a grandson of the late Mr. James Boyd, of Ballyferris, Ards. He was 21 years of age.

The death of Lieutenant Basil Llewellyn Boyd Thomas was reported in the 21 April edition of the *Newtownards Chronicle* under the headline 'Ards Officer Killed'. He was the only son of William John and Eliza Jane Thomas (nee Boyd) who were married on 11 October 1894 in Ballywalter Presbyterian Church. The Thomas family moved to London where they lived at Penrallt, Herne Hill in London. Basil was a grandson of James Boyd who lived in the townland of Ballyferris, Ballywalter.

Lieutenant Basil Llewellyn Boyd Thomas served with the 15th Battalion Royal Welsh Fusiliers attached to the 27th Company Machine Gun Corps and he was killed in action on 9 April 1917.

Thompson, Charles
Rifleman
No. 7944, 13th Battalion, Royal Irish Rifles
Killed in action on Saturday 1 July 1916 (aged 29)
Thiepval Memorial, France (Pier and Face 15 A and 15 B)

In some records Charles Thompson's number is recorded as 7942.

Charles Thompson was born on 20 November 1886 in Donaghadee and he was a son of Charles and Catherine Thompson (nee Murray) who lived in Moat Street, Donaghadee. Charles's father died when Charles was a young boy and his mother Catherine worked as an embroiderer. Charles Thompson had two sisters – Sarah and Annie. Charles and Annie Thompson were baptised in Shore Street Presbyterian Church Donaghadee.

Prior to the outbreak of the Great War Charles Thompson worked as a gardener. He enlisted in Antrim, he served with the 13th Battalion Royal Irish Rifles in 108th Brigade of the 36th (Ulster) Division and he was killed in action on the first day of the Battle of the Somme.

Miss Thompson, 35. Grosvenor Road, Belfast, is anxious for news of her brother, Rifleman Charles Thompson (Co. Down Volunteers), unofficially reported killed on 1st inst. He was a native of Donaghadee. A comrade reports that he was killed by a bomb.

Initially it was reported that he was missing in action although there was an unofficial report from a comrade that he had been killed by a bomb. At the time of his death one of Charles's sisters was living at 35 Grosvenor Road in Belfast and she sought information as to what had happened to her brother.

Later it was officially confirmed that Rifleman Charles Thompson had been killed in action.

Rifleman Charles Thompson is commemorated on Donaghadee and District War Memorial; in Shore Street Presbyterian Church Donaghadee and in the Belfast Book of Honour (Page 622).

Thompson, Charles (Charlie)
Rifleman
No. 10302, 2nd Battalion, Royal Irish Rifles
Killed in action on Wednesday 25 August 1915 (aged 18)
Ramparts Cemetery, Belgium (Grave B. 24)

Charles Thompson was born on 19 May 1897 in Newtownards and he was the third son of Charles and Agnes Thompson (nee Kelly) who lived at 15 Back Shuttlefield (behind Robert Street), Newtownards. They were married on 11 July 1889 in First Newtownards Presbyterian Church. Charles Thompson Senior worked as a labourer and he and Agnes had at least seven children – William, Annie, John, Charles, Samuel, Agnes and Catherine.

Prior to the outbreak of the Great War Charlie Thompson worked as a smoother in a calico print-works. He enlisted in Newtownards, he joined the 2nd Battalion, Royal Irish Rifles and he was attached to the Machine Gun Section. Charlie had been in the fighting line for three months when he was killed by enemy shellfire on 25 August 1915.

After Rifleman Thompson was killed in action Rifleman Adam Tate (10345), one of Charlie's comrades in the Machine Gun Section, wrote to Charlie's father. Adam Tate was also from Newtownards and he and Charlie had worked together in the same print-works before the war. In his letter Adam Tate related how he had been talking to Charlie just before they both 'got hit at the same time'. Charlie Thompson was killed and Adam Tate was wounded. Rifleman Charles Thompson is commemorated on Newtownards and District War Memorial.

Thompson, David John (David)
Lance Corporal
No. 18831, 'B' Company, 13th Battalion, Royal Irish Rifles
Died of wounds on Saturday 1 July 1916 (aged 19)
Thiepval Memorial, France (Pier and Face 15 A and 15 B)

David John Thompson was born on 15 September 1896 in Newtownards and he was a son of Robert and Agnes Thompson (nee Brown) who were married on 7 November 1889 in First Newtownards Presbyterian Church. They lived at 21 Hillview Terrace, John Street, Newtownards. Robert Thompson worked as an agricultural labourer and he and Agnes had at least ten children – William Quinn, Eleanor (Nellie) Colville, Agnes Brown, David John, Samuel, Margaret Jane, Henrietta Crawford Orr, Robert (died), James (died) and Sarah Elizabeth (Sadie). The children were baptised in First Newtownards Presbyterian Church.

Prior to the outbreak of the Great War David Thompson worked as a message-boy. He enlisted on 17 September 1914, he served with the 13th Battalion Royal Irish Rifles in 108th Brigade of the 36th (Ulster) Division and he died in Thiepval Wood on 1 July 1916. He was hit by a sniper's bullet and he died four hours later from loss of blood. A fellow Ardsman named Eddie Crawford (13/100) stayed with him to the end and as David lay dying they sang together the hymn 'Abide With Me'. It was his sister Nellie, the eldest girl in the Thompson family, who had introduced David to the Christian Endeavour Group in Newtownards before the war.

Robert Doggart, another Ardsman, was one of the stretcher bearers and he reported afterwards that David had refused to drink any rum. In those days rum was the remedy given to wounded soldiers in an effort to numb their pain. It seems that David had a premonition that he was going to die. A few days before the battle, and knowing of its imminence, he wrote in a letter to his sister Nannie, 'Tell my mother and my sister Nellie….that I died an honourable death and went straight to heaven…'

Two months to the day before his death David Thompson and his friend William John Thompson (18829) wrote a letter to the Rev William Wright of First Newtownards Presbyterian Church asking him to convey their thanks to the members of the congregation for 'the splendid parcel which we received on Easter Monday'. They went on, 'It is very encouraging to know we are still remembered by the kind people at home, as it helps us to perform our duties more cheerfully under the sometimes trying circumstances. We would especially thank you for the little text card which is very helpful to us out here and reminds us of the Sabbaths spent in First Newtownards Presbyterian Church. We will now draw to a close, trusting this will find everyone in good health as it leaves us at present…'

William John Thompson and **Matthew Wright**, one of the Rev Wright's sons, were also killed in action on 1 July 1916 at the Battle of the Somme.

After David Thompson died his family placed a 'For King and Country' notice in the *Newtownards Chronicle*, as did one of his friends from Newtownards, Lance Corporal Jim Kelly who was serving with the Army Service Corps in France.

In July 1917 there were three 'Our Heroes – In Memoriam' notices in the *Newtownards Chronicle*. The first was from his father, mother, sisters and brothers and it contained the line:

> *'They miss him most who loved him best.'*

The second was from his uncle and aunt William and Maggie Quinn and the third was from his uncle, aunt and cousins (three of the latter on active service – Sam, Bob and John Scott) of 150 Mill Street, Newtownards. Evidence from one source suggests that this **Sam Scott** served with the Canadians and he died on 20 October 1918.

Lance Corporal David John Thompson is commemorated on Newtownards and District War Memorial and in First Newtownards Presbyterian Church.

Thompson, James
Rifleman
No. 19231, 'A' Company, 13th Battalion, Royal Irish Rifles
Killed in action on Saturday 1 July 1916 (aged 20)
Thiepval Memorial, France (Pier and Face 15 A and 15 B)

James Thompson was born on 11 December 1895 and he was a son of William and Margaret Thompson (nee Adair) who lived in the townland of Kirkistown, Kircubbin. They were married on 12 August 1886 in Glastry Presbyterian Church. William Thompson worked as a farm labourer and he and Margaret had at least seven children including Mary Isabella (27 September 1887), William (10 February 1889), Anna Eliza (3 April 1891), Margaret Jane (3 January 1893), James (11 December 1895) and Robert John (22 November 1900). The children were baptised in Cloughey Presbyterian Church.

Prior to the outbreak of the Great War James Thompson worked as an agricultural labourer on the farm of Hugh Bailie at Kirkistown. He enlisted in Ballywalter, he served with the 13th Battalion Royal Irish Rifles in 108th Brigade of the 36th (Ulster) Division and he was killed in action on the first day of the Battle of the Somme. Initially James was reported as missing in action and then in April 1917 it was officially confirmed that he had been killed in action. A family member wrote and published a poem in his memory:

In Loving Memory of

OUR DEAR SON

PRIVATE JAMES THOMPSON, R.I.R.

OF KIRKISTOWN,

WHO WAS KILLED IN ACTION AT THE BATTLE OF THE SOMME AT THIEPVAL
ON 1st JULY, 1916,

Aged 20 years.

"What I do thou knowest not now; but thou shalt know hereafter."—JOHN 13. 7.

A loved one has been called away,
  He's in our midst no more;
In a land afar his body lies
  Far from his native shore.

He bade us all a last farewell,
  A happy, brave "Good-bye";
And with the gallant few went forth
  To suffer and to die.

Upon the first day of July,
  Amidst the shot and shell,
'Twas in the battle of the Somme,
  He in the conflict fell.

What anguish fills each fainting heart,
  And many cheeks grow pale,
And in that sorrow-stricken home
  How many mourn and wail.

None in that home shall e'er forget,
  The one so bright and fair,
Who young in years was called away.
  Now sits a vacant chair.

No one was near when in that hour
  He breathed his latest breath;
But Jesus led him gently on
  Thro' the dark vale of death.

He answered not the roll call here
  But in that world so fair,
When Jesus calls the roll above
  He'll not be missing there.

We know 'twas in that solemn hour
  His spirit took its flight,
To dwell with God above the skies
  In realms of love and light.

Oh, sorrow not, but cast your care
  On Christ, the Unfailing One,
Who ever doeth all things well,
  And say "Thy will be done."

Let this a warning be to all
  To cease their sinful strife,
Thy soul may be required of thee,
  Escape thou for thy Life.

Oh, be prepared to meet thy God,
  This warning he doth give,
Consider now your latter end,
  Believe and thou shall live.

And then, where parting is unknown,
  All sorrow shall be o'er,
For strife and conflict never come
  On yonder happy shore.

Rifleman James Thompson is commemorated in the PCI Roll of Honour for Cloughey Presbyterian Church.

Thompson, John
Corporal
No. 17037, 'A' Company, 13th Battalion, Royal Irish Rifles
Killed in action on Thursday 16 August 1917 (aged 20)
Tyne Cot Memorial, Belgium (Panel 138 to 140 & 162 to 162A & 163A)

John Thompson was born on 19 October 1896 in Donaghadee and he was the eldest son and second child of Andrew and Elizabeth Thompson (nee Gunning) who lived at 99 Moat Street, Donaghadee. They were married on 12 April 1893 in Donaghadee Parish Church of Ireland. Andrew Thompson worked as a general labourer and he and Elizabeth had at least eight children including Catherine, John, Mary Jane, Andrew, James, Isabel and Robert. Catherine, John and Mary Jane were baptised in Donaghadee Parish Church of Ireland.

John Thompson enlisted in Donaghadee in 1914 and he served with the 13th Battalion Royal Irish Rifles in 108th Brigade of the 36th (Ulster) Division. In April 1916 he was home on short leave from the trenches and he was wounded in action on 1 July 1916. After he recovered Corporal John Thompson returned to the fighting line and he was killed in action on 16 August 1917 at the Battle of Langemarck. Initially John was reported as wounded and missing in action. Then in November 1917 it was officially confirmed that he had been killed in action on that date.

Corporal John Thompson is commemorated on Donaghadee and District War Memorial and in Donaghadee Parish Church of Ireland.

Thompson, John
Rifleman
No. 337, 16th Battalion, Royal Irish Rifles
Died of apoplexy on Friday 20 August 1920
Newtownards (Movilla) Cemetery, Co. Down (Grave 13. 36)

John Thompson served with the 16th Battalion Royal Irish Rifles, the Pioneer Battalion of the 36th (Ulster) Division and he died of apoplexy on 20 August 1920.

Rifleman John Thompson is buried in Movilla New Cemetery, Newtownards and in the cemetery records he is described as a labourer who was living in Belfast.

Thompson, John

The name John Thompson RIR is commemorated in Killinchy Parish Church of Ireland. Desk searches and public appeals to date have yielded no further information.

Thompson, Robert
Sergeant
No. 201703, 1st/4th Battalion, King's Own (Royal Lancaster Regiment)
Killed in action on Thursday 20 September 1917 (aged 24)
Tyne Cot Memorial, Belgium (Panel 18 to 19)

Robert Thompson's mother worked as housekeeper for John and Alice Wallace who lived in the townland of Ballyferris, Ballywalter. John Wallace was a farmer and his wife Alice died in 1912. Robert Thompson worked on the Wallace farm before he enlisted in 1911. Robert served at the Curragh for two years before being posted to India for a year. At the outbreak of the Great War he was posted to France and fought on the Western Front. He had two periods of home leave, the last one before he died being in March 1917.

Sergeant Robert Thompson served with the 1st/4th Battalion King's Own (Royal Lancaster Regiment) and he was killed in action on 20 September 1917. After Robert's death Captain Blain wrote to Mrs Thompson to express his sincere sympathy. In the letter he explained that Robert Thompson was killed 'while going forward with the company under heavy shell and machine-gun fire'.

Sergeant Robert Thompson is commemorated on Ballywalter and District War Memorial and in Ballywalter Presbyterian Church.

Thompson, Robert
Private
No. 18823, 'C' Company, 13th Battalion, Royal Irish Rifles, transferred to (17774), 108th Company, Machine Gun Corps, 36th (Ulster) Division
Died of wounds on Sunday 2 July 1916 (aged 21)
Warloy-Baillon Communal Cemetery Extension, France (Grave I. A. 2)

Robert Thompson was a son of Thomas and Matilda Thompson who lived in Dundonald, (before that in Killinchy and before that in County Londonderry). They were married on 23 March 1893 in Second Magherafelt Presbyterian Church. Thomas Thompson worked as a coachman and he and Matilda had at least three children including John and William. Robert enlisted in Downpatrick and he served with the 13th Battalion Royal Irish Rifles (18823) in 108th Brigade of the 36th (Ulster) Division before being transferred to the 108th Company Machine Gun Corps. Robert was wounded on the first day of the Battle of the Somme and died the following day. Private Robert Thompson is commemorated in Killinchy Parish Church of Ireland.

T

Thompson, William Henry
Private
No. 2978, 6th Battalion, Royal Munster Fusiliers

Newtownards Munster Fusilier Killed.
Official intimation has been received that No. 2978, Private Wm. Henry Thompson, 6th Batt. Royal Munster Fusiliers, has been killed in action at the Dardanelles, on August 9th. Deceased, who was just 19 years of age, enlisted about 10 months ago. In January last he was home on 7 days' leave, and in June was sent with his battalion to the Dardanelles. He was the son of William Henry and Mary Thompson, Greenwell Street, Newtownards, and grandson of Robert M'Cullough, Movilla Street, Newtownards.

In the 23 October 1915 edition of the *Newtownards Chronicle* it was reported that Private William Henry Thompson (2978) aged 19 and serving with the 6th Battalion Royal Munster Fusiliers had been killed in action at the Dardanelles on Monday 9 August 1915. Private William Henry Thompson is commemorated in Newtownards Parish Church of Ireland (St Mark) and in the Belfast Book of Honour (Page 627) where it is recorded that one of his sisters lived at 2 Matlock Street, Belfast.

William Henry Thompson was a son of William Henry and Mary Thompson who lived at 117 Greenwell Street, Newtownards. William Henry Thompson Senior worked as a general labourer and he and Mary had at least three children – Jane, Mary Anne and William Henry. William Henry's grandfather Robert McCullough lived in Movilla Street, Newtownards.

William Henry Thompson (2978) is not commemorated in the CWGC Debt of Honour. Research has shown that he enlisted shortly after the outbreak of the Great War. In January 1915 he enjoyed a short period of home leave and in June 1915 he went with the 6th Battalion Royal Munster Fusiliers in 30th Brigade of the 10th (Irish) Division to Gallipoli. Military records suggest that Private William Henry Thompson (2978) was transferred from the Royal Munster Fusiliers to the Labour Corps (489020).

Thompson, William James
Private
No. 14737, 9th Battalion, Princess Victoria's (Royal Irish Fusiliers)
Killed in action on Saturday 1 July 1916
Thiepval Memorial, France (Pier and Face 15 A)

William James Thompson was born in Bessbrook, Co Armagh and he was the eldest son of Samuel Thompson. After Samuel Thompson died William James's mother remarried (William James's step-father died a short time before William James was killed in action). In the CWGC Debt of Honour it is recorded that William James Thompson's wife Ellen lived at 35 West Street in Newtownards and evidence from one source suggests that they may have had a daughter named Mary Cordelia Thompson who was born on 26 February 1916.

There is evidence that, prior to the outbreak of the Great War, William James Thompson worked as an apprentice wood-turner in Bessbrook. He enlisted in Armagh, he served with the 9th Battalion Royal Irish Fusiliers in 108th Brigade of the 36th (Ulster) Division and he was killed in action on the first day of the Battle of the Somme. Initially he was reported as missing in action and later it was officially confirmed that he had been killed on 1 July 1916. Private William James Thompson is commemorated on Bessbrook War Memorial and in Bessbrook Parish Church of Ireland (Christ Church).

Thompson, William John
Rifleman
No. 18824, 'B' Company, 13th Battalion, Royal Irish Rifles
Died of wounds on Tuesday 30 May 1916 (aged 18)
Forceville Communal Cemetery and Extension, France
Plot 1 Row D Grave 12

William John Thompson was born in Comber and he was a son of John and Martha Thompson (nee Kielty) who were married on 15 March 1889 in First Comber Presbyterian Church. For a time they lived with Martha's parents William and Agnes Kielty in Killinchy Street, Comber. Later they moved to High Street, Comber. John Thompson worked as a general labourer and he and Martha had at least five children – Sarah, Agnes, William John, Martha and Annie.

Prior to the outbreak of the Great War William John Thompson was a member of the North Down Regiment of the Ulster Volunteer Force. He was underage when he enlisted in Comber, he served with the 13th Battalion Royal Irish Rifles in 108th Brigade of the 36th Ulster Division and he died of wounds on 30 May 1916. In the 10 June 1916 edition of the *Newtownards Chronicle* it was reported that he had been 'wounded by shrapnel in both legs and the injuries were so severe that he only lived a few hours'.

Rifleman William John Thompson is commemorated on Comber and District War Memorial and in First Comber Presbyterian Church. His age is recorded as 22 in the CWGC Debt of Honour (he exaggerated his age at enlistment).

Thompson, William John
Corporal
No. 18829, 'B' Company, 13th Battalion, Royal Irish Rifles
Killed in action on Saturday 1 July 1916 (aged 28)
Thiepval Memorial, France (Pier and Face 15 A and 15 B)

William John Thompson was born in Newtownards and he was a son of William John and Elizabeth Thompson (nee Baillie) who lived in the townland of Ballycullen, Newtownards. They were married on 7 May 1885 in First Newtownards Presbyterian Church. William John Thompson Senior worked as bleach-field linen labourer and he and Elizabeth had at least seven children – William John, Mary Jane, Walter, Norman, Andrew Mawhinney, Elizabeth and Anna. The children were baptised in First Newtownards Presbyterian Church. William John Thompson Senior died and the family moved to John Street and later to 161 Mill Street, Newtownards.

Prior to the outbreak of the Great War William John Thompson worked as hemstitch mechanic in a factory and he was a member of 'B' Company of the Newtownards contingent of the Ulster Volunteer Force. He enlisted in Newtownards, he served with the 13th Battalion Royal Irish Rifles in 108th Brigade of the 36th (Ulster) Division and he was killed in action on the first day of the Battle of the Somme. Initially he was reported as missing in action and in June 1917 it was officially confirmed that he had been killed in action. His family placed a 'For King and Country' notice in the 23 June 1917 edition of the *Newtownards Chronicle*.

Corporal William John Thompson is commemorated on Newtownards and District War Memorial and in First Newtownards Presbyterian Church.

Todd, Arthur
Private
No. 24573, 2nd Battalion, Grenadier Guards
Killed in action on Tuesday 27 August 1918 (aged 27)
Mory Abbey Military Cemetery, France (Grave V. C. 26)

T

Arthur Todd was born in Newtownards and he was a son of John and Maggie Todd (nee Holland) who lived in Church Street, Newtownards. They were married on 12 December 1889 in Regent Street Methodist Church Newtownards. John Todd worked as a labourer and he and Maggie had at least six children – Henry, Arthur, Samuel George, Agnes, Maggie and Rebecca. Arthur Todd had an older half-sister and half-brother – Sarah and John Todd. At least four of the children were baptised in Greenwell Street Presbyterian Church Newtownards.

Prior to the outbreak of the Great War Arthur Todd worked as a labourer. He enlisted in Belfast and he served with the 2nd Battalion Grenadier Guards. On 26 January 1918 Arthur Todd and Sarah Murphy were married in Newtownards Registry Office and Sarah lived at 12 Movilla Street, Newtownards. Private Arthur Todd was killed in action seven months later during an advance on 27 August 1918. The Rev CF Lyttleton, Chaplain, wrote to Sarah Todd to express his deepest sympathy and he assured her that Arthur's death had been 'quite painless and instantaneous'.

Sarah Todd had been married for just seven months when she was widowed and she placed a 'For King and Country' notice in the *Newtownards Chronicle*. It contained the verse:

'Taken away in his early youth,
Taken from those he loved,
From serving his King on earth below
To serve his great King above.
I little thought his time so short
When he on furlough came
When to the front again he went
Never to return again'

Private Arthur Todd is commemorated on Newtownards and District War Memorial.

Todd, George
Died of consumption on Thursday 29 August 1918 (aged 48)
Newtownards (Movilla) Cemetery, Co Down (Grave 11. 112)

In the records for Movilla New Cemetery there is an entry relating to the death of George Todd. He was a discharged soldier from Newtownards who died of consumption on 29 August 1918. Desk searches and public appeals to date have yielded no further information.

Tomelty, Charles
Private
No. 28777, Scottish Rifles, transferred to (48239), 13th Battalion, Royal Inniskilling Fusiliers
Killed in action on Tuesday 27 August 1918 (aged 27)
Outtersteene Communal Cemetery Extension, France (Grave II. H. 55)

Charles Tomelty was born in 1891 in Portaferry and he was baptised on 15 February 1891 in Portaferry Roman Catholic Church. Charles was a son of William and Sarah Tomelty (nee Convery) who had six children – Charles, Patrick, Robert, Sally, Billy and Jimmy. For a time Charles lived in New Row, Portaferry with his uncles Robert and John Convery and his aunt Eliza Convery. Both Robert and John Convery worked as carters and farmers.

Prior to the outbreak of the Great War Charles Tomelty worked as a carrier.

He enlisted in Ardrossan and he served with the Scottish Rifles (28777) before being transferred to the 13th Battalion Royal Inniskilling Fusiliers in 119th Brigade of the 40th Division.

Private Charles Tomelty was killed in action on 27 August 1918 during the Allied offensive against all sections of the German line and he is commemorated on the Convery family grave headstone in Ballyphilip Roman Catholic Cemetery Portaferry. Charles Tomelty's brother Patrick married Rose McNally, a sister of Surgeon **Hugh Francis McNally** who was killed when HMS *Hampshire* sank after striking a mine on 5 June 1916.

Tompsett, William
Private
No. L/6847, 2nd Battalion, Royal Sussex Regiment
Killed in action on Friday 30 October 1914 (aged 30)
Tyne Cot Cemetery, Belgium (Grave LXVII. H. I)

T

William Tompsett was born in 1884 in Eastbourne, Sussex. He was the only son of George and Mary Tompsett and he had five sisters – Mabel, Alice, Lucy, Ethel and Lizzie. He worked as a bricklayer all along the south coast of England until he joined the Royal Sussex Regiment at Lewes on 24 June 1902. He was posted to Ireland and on 5 November 1907 William Tompsett and Mary McCutcheon were married in St Anne's Church of Ireland Belfast.

William and Mary Tompsett lived with Mary's widowed mother Catherine McCutcheon in The Square, Comber and later in Glen Road, Comber. They had two sons, John and George, aged 6 and 4 at the outbreak of war.

Private William Tompsett was posted to France on 31 August 1914 and he was killed in action two months later on 30 October 1914 during the First Battle of Ypres. At the time of his death William's parents were living at 11 Marshall's Row in Brighton.

Private William Tompsett is commemorated on Comber and District War Memorial and on the Memorial Plaque in Comber Parish Church of Ireland (St Mary) (surname spelt Thompsett).

Mary McCutcheon Tompsett suffered bereavement again when her brother **John McCutcheon** was killed in action on the first day of the Battle of the Somme.

Trousdale, Frederick Hamilton (Frederick)
Rifleman
No. 18/608, 13th Battalion, Royal Irish Rifles
Died of disease on Monday 13 March 1916 (aged 25)
Le Treport Military Cemetery, France (Plot 1 Row N Grave 8)

Frederick Trousdale is included in this book as a further illustration of how townland names can sometimes lead to confusion. In 'Ireland's Memorial Records World War One 1914 – 1918' it is recorded that Frederick Hamilton Trousdale was born in the townland of Gransha. There are five townlands named Gransha in County Down with two of those in the Ards area (there are other townlands named Gransha in other counties). Research has shown that Frederick was a son of James and Matilda Trousdale (nee Hamilton) who were married on 17 May 1892 in First Dromore Presbyterian Church and that he has no apparent connection with either of the townlands named Gransha in the Ards area. Frederick Trousdale lived in Dromara, he enlisted in Clandeboye and he served with the 13th Battalion Royal Irish Rifles in 108th Brigade of the 36th (Ulster) Division. Rifleman Frederick Hamilton Trousdale was killed in action on 13 March 1916.

T
V

Vance Brothers: James and William
James and William Vance were born in Newtownards and they were sons of James and Annie Vance (nee McMillan) who lived at 19 Greenwell Street and before that at 12 George's Street, Newtownards. They were married on 14 April 1884 in Greenwell Street Presbyterian Church Newtownards. James Vance Senior fought in the South African War and then he worked as a labourer. He and Annie had at least eleven children – Robert, Mary (died), Mary, Isabella, William, Alexander, James, Eliza Jane, Patrick, John and Anna.

Three brothers served and only Alexander survived. He was discharged from the Army after suffering gas poisoning and being severely wounded – part of one foot was blown off in an explosion and he needed a series of operations to remove shrapnel from his leg. Alexander Vance died in 1965 and he is buried in Movilla Cemetery Newtownards alongside his father who died in 1937 and his mother who died in 1938. William Vance was the first of the two brothers to be killed during the Great War (five other siblings died of illness):

Vance, William
Rifleman
No. 6078, 2nd Battalion, Royal Irish Rifles
Died of wounds on Sunday 17 January 1915 (aged 24)
Loker Churchyard, Belgium (Grave II. E. 2)

William Vance was born in 1891 and prior to the outbreak of the Great War he worked in a factory. Before that he had served for nine years in the 4th Battalion Royal Irish Rifles (Royal North Downs). He and Mary Jane McCullough were married on 17 July 1914 in Second Newtownards Presbyterian Church and they had at least one child, a daughter named Mary Catherine. William Vance was a Reservist and at the outbreak of war he was recalled to the colours. He went to France on 9 November 1914, he served with the 2nd Battalion Royal Irish Rifles and he died of wounds on 17 February 1915. His widow Mary Jane and their daughter Mary Catherine lived at 8 West Street, Newtownards. Mary Jane placed a 'Killed in Action' notice in the *Newtownards Chronicle* as did his parents and theirs included the verse:

'We did not know what pain he bore,
We did not see him die;
We only knew he passed away,
And never said 'Good-bye'
Though our hearts may break with sorrow
By the grief so hard to bear,
We shall meet him some bright morning
In our Father's mansion fair'

Official notification about the death of Rifleman William Vance came in a letter addressed to his widow from the Infantry Record Office in Dublin. The Officer in Charge of No.11 District informed Mary Jane that William had died at 7 Field Ambulance in Locre after having been shot through the head. He expressed to her 'the sympathy and regret of the Army Council at her loss'.

Rifleman William Vance is commemorated on Newtownards and District War Memorial and in the PCI Roll of Honour for Greenwell Street Presbyterian Church. His widow Mary Jane Vance died one year later in February 1916.

Vance, James
Rifleman
No. 19236, 'B' Company 13th Battalion, Royal Irish Rifles
Killed in action on Thursday 16 August 1917 (aged 23)
Tyne Cot Memorial, Belgium (Panel 138 to 140 & 162 to 162 A & 163 A)

James Vance was born in 1894 and prior to the outbreak of the Great War he worked in a factory. He played inside forward for the Ards Football Club and in one newspaper report he was described as having outstanding ability. There was a prediction that James was destined for stardom on the football field. The report stated that 'his ability to shield and control the ball was legendary'.

James Vance enlisted in Newtownards and went to France on 6 October 1915. He served with the 13th Battalion Royal Irish Rifles in 108th Brigade of the 36th (Ulster) Division and he was killed in action on 16 August 1917 at the Battle of Langemarck. First official reports indicated that James had been wounded in action. Then he was listed as missing in action and later it was officially confirmed that he had been killed in action. Rifleman James Vance is commemorated on Newtownards and District War Memorial. In the CWGC Debt of Honour his age is recorded as 28.

Vance, William

The name William Vance is listed twice on Newtownards and District War Memorial and the two men are distinguished by the street that each was associated with – East Street and Greenwell Street. William Vance from Greenwell Street has been identified but not William Vance from East Street. In the booklet produced for the Unveiling and Dedication Ceremony held on Saturday 26 May 1934 William Vance (East Street) is described as a Rifleman in the Royal Irish Rifles. A discharged soldier named William Vance who died of bronchitis was buried in Movilla New Cemetery (10.120) on 23 October 1921. Desk searches and public appeals to date have yielded no further information.

Victor, Henry Edward
Lance Corporal
No. G/7574, 2nd Battalion, Duke of Cambridge's Own (Middlesex Regiment)
Killed in action on Saturday 1 July 1916 (aged 36)
Thiepval Memorial, France (Pier and Face 12 D and 13 B)

In 'Soldiers Died in the Great War 1914 – 1919' it is recorded that Henry Edward Victor was born in Belfast and he enlisted in Plymouth, Devon. He served with the 2nd Battalion Duke of Cambridge's Own (Middlesex Regiment) and he was killed in action on the first day of the Battle of the Somme.

DONAGHADEE.
Rifleman H. M'Gimpsey (No. 589), R.I. Rifles, is officially reported wounded.
Lance-Corporal H. E. Victor, Middlesex Regiment, previously missing, is now officially reported killed in action. He was the only son of Mr. J. George Victor, of Melbourne, formerly of Woodburn, Carrickfergus, and Donaghadee. He was a nephew of Mr. H. Blackburne, solicitor, Carrickfergus and Belfast, and came to England from Hong Kong to enlist.

His death was reported in the 23 September 1916 edition of the *Newtownards Chronicle* under the headline 'Donaghadee'. The report indicated that Lance Corporal Henry Edward Victor had been reported as missing in action initially and then it was officially confirmed that he had been killed in action. The report went on, 'He was the only son of Mr J George Victor of Melbourne, formerly of Woodburn, Carrickfergus and Donaghadee. He was a nephew of Mr H Blackburne, solicitor, Carrickfergus and Belfast and he came to England from Hong Kong to enlist'.

Henry Edward Victor was born on 8 June 1880 in Carrickfergus and he was a son of John George Victor (born on 20 May 1850 and baptised in Donaghadee Parish Church of Ireland) and Martha Jane Victor (nee Graham). John George Victor worked as a Harbour Master and he and Martha Jane were married on 10 March 1879 in Ballycarry Presbyterian Church. Lance Corporal Henry Edward Victor is commemorated in the Belfast Book of Honour (Page 638).

Walker, John
Private
No. 12451, 8th Battalion, Royal Irish Rifles, transferred to (19469), 107th Company, Machine Gun Corps (Infantry), 36th (Ulster) Division
Saturday 1 July 1916 (aged 32)
Serre Road Cemetery No. 2, France (Grave VI. J. 11)

John Walker was born in the townland of Ballyrogan, Newtownards and

V
W

he was a son of John and Mary Ann Walker (nee McGreeghan) who lived in the townland of Greengraves, Newtownards. They were married on 26 November 1883 in Newtownards Registry Office. John Walker Senior worked as an agricultural labourer and he and Mary Ann had at least eight children including John, Lizzie, James, Margaret, Rachel and Sarah.

Prior to the outbreak of the Great War John Walker worked as an agricultural labourer and he and his wife Ellen (nee Shaw) lived in the townland of Ballylisbredan, Ballymaglaff and later in Ballyoran, Ballymaglaff. They were married on 26 June 1904 in Dundonald Presbyterian Church and they had at least three children – Robert John, James and Mary Ann.

John Walker enlisted in Belfast and he served with the 8th Battalion Royal Irish Rifles (12451) in 107th Brigade of the 36th (Ulster) Division before being transferred to the Machine Gun Corps. Private John Walker was killed in action on the first day of the Battle of the Somme and he is commemorated on Comber and District War Memorial.

Walker, Samuel
Driver
No. 39071, 7th Battery, Royal Field Artillery
Died of wounds on Sunday 4 April 1915 (aged 32)
Ploegsteert Memorial, Belgium (Panel 1)

W

WALKER S.

THE LATE DRIVER S. WALKER.

The Last Newtownards Man Left in India.

Gunner T. M'Creadie, 38th Battery, R.F.A., Rawal Pindi, India, writes under date of 10th June:—Would you kindly allow me a small space in your weekly paper to convey my deepest sympathy to the relatives of the late Driver S. Walker, who died on the 5th April, 1915. We were great chums since I knew him about ten years ago; and being the last Newtownards man left in India, I was very sorry indeed when I received the sad news. I was waiting an answer to a letter which I sent him, but am sorry to say it reached there too late, and this grieved me more than I can say. The letter I received from his Sergt.-Major did not say where he died, and being a regular reader of your paper I did not see his name mentioned. I trust this will come to the notice of all who knew him in Newtownards. I shall be greatly indebted to you if you will grant me this favour.—Yours sincerely, Gunner T. M'Creadie.

Samuel Walker was born in Newtownards and he was a son of Samuel Walker and a stepson of Agnes Walker who lived at 77 Church Street and before that in West Street, Newtownards. Samuel had at least one brother (William) and two sisters (Agnes and Sarah Ann) and, after their mother died, their father Samuel married Agnes Gibson on 3 March 1894 in Greenwell Street Presbyterian Church Newtownards. Before he became a professional soldier Samuel Walker worked as an agricultural labourer on William Rankin's farm in the townland of Loughriscouse, Newtownards.

When the Great War began Samuel

Walker was serving in India. He was posted to Europe where he served with the Royal Field Artillery. Driver Samuel Walker died of wounds on 4 April 1915 and his death was reported in the 24 July 1915 edition of the *Newtownards Chronicle* by means of a letter written by Gunner T McCreadie who at that time was serving with the Royal Field Artillery in India. In the letter Gunner McCreadie described himself as 'the last Newtownards man left in India'.

Driver Samuel Walker is commemorated on Newtownards and District War Memorial and in the PCI Roll of Honour for Greenwell Street Presbyterian Church Newtownards.

Wallace, Robert H (Bob)
Company Sergeant Major
**No. 5619, 'C' Company, 2nd Battalion, Royal Irish Rifles
Died of wounds on Saturday 18 August 1917 (aged 34)
Calais Southern Cemetery, France (Plot H Row 3 Grave 4)**

W

Robert Wallace was a son of Robert and Mary Wallace (nee Boyd) who lived in Ballymena, Co Antrim. He served in the South African War and subsequently he was posted to the Royal North Downs at Newtownards.

Company Sergeant Major Bob Wallace was married twice. His first wife, Elizabeth, died on 12 March 1916 in Dublin. When Bob was serving with the Royal North Downs the family home was in John Street, Newtownards and when Company Sergeant Major Bob Wallace died of wounds his wife was living in Lancastrian Street, Carrickfergus. Company Sergeant Major Bob Wallace is commemorated on Newtownards and District War Memorial.

Walsh, James (Jimmy or Jamie)
Rifleman
**No. 19284, 'B' Company, 13th Battalion, Royal Irish Rifles
Killed in action on Saturday 1 July 1916 (aged 22)
Serre Road Cemetery No. 2, France (Grave VI. F. 13)**

James Walsh was born on 3 September 1893 in the townland of Ballylisbredan, Ballymaglaff and he was a son of John and Sarah Walsh who lived in the townland of Ballyaltikilligan, Comber. John Walsh worked as an agricultural labourer and he and Sarah had at least six children including Samuel, James, Henry, Ellen and Sarah. James was baptised in Dundonald Parish Church of Ireland (St Elizabeth).

Prior to the outbreak of the Great War James Walsh worked as an agricultural

labourer. He enlisted in Comber, he served with the 13th Battalion Royal Irish Rifles in 108th Brigade of the 36th (Ulster) Division and he was killed in action on the first day of the Battle of the Somme. Rifleman James Walsh is commemorated on Comber and District War Memorial and in Comber Parish Church of Ireland (St Mary).

Ward, GAC

The name GAC Ward is listed on Ballywalter and District War Memorial and he is described as a Captain in the Royal Navy. Desk searches and public appeals to date have yielded no further information.

W

Waring, John
Rifleman
No. 11/2255, 'D' Company, 11th Battalion, Royal Irish Rifles
Died of wounds on Thursday 26 October 1916 (aged 38)
Calais Southern Cemetery, France (Plot F Row 1 Grave 9)

John Waring was born in Blaris and he lived in Linenhall Street, Lisburn. He enlisted in Lisburn and served with the 11th Battalion Royal Irish Rifles in 108th Brigade of the 36th (Ulster) Division. In October 1915 he left Bordon Camp in Hampshire and went to France. One year later, on 26 October 1916, he died of wounds in the Millicent Sutherland Hospital at Calais.

Rifleman John Waring cited as his next-of-kin his sister Mary Waring who lived in Copeland, Donaghadee. He is commemorated on Lisburn War Memorial and in Lisburn's Dead 1914 – 1919 (Friends' School Lisburn WW1 Research Project).

Warnock, William
Private
No. 6699, 2nd Battalion, Royal Inniskilling Fusiliers
Killed in action on Wednesday 26 August 1914 (aged 33)
La Ferte-Sous-Jouarre Memorial, France

William Warnock was born on 27 July 1881 in Newtownards and he was a son of James and Sarah Warnock (nee Orr) who were married on 5 July 1875 in First Newtownards Presbyterian Church. They had at least fourteen children including John, James, Robert Alexander, William, Thomas, Annie & Samuel (twins), Jane & Samuel (twins), Thomas, Ellen and Hugh. Eight of the children including William were baptised in First Newtownards Presbyterian Church. The Warnock family moved to Belfast and William's father died in the 1890s. They lived in North Howard Street and at 1 Richmond Street in Belfast.

Prior to the outbreak of the Great War William Warnock worked as a labourer in the shipyard. He enlisted in Belfast, he served with the 2nd Battalion Royal Inniskilling Fusiliers in 12th Brigade of the 4th Division in the British Expeditionary Force and he arrived in France on 23 August 1914. Three days later he was killed in action on 26 August 1914. Private William Warnock is commemorated in the Belfast Book of Honour (Page 647).

Watters, James Campbell (James)
Second Lieutenant
71st Siege Battery, South African Heavy Artillery
Died of wounds on Friday 19 October 1917 (aged 27)
Nine Elms British Cemetery, Belgium (Grave VI. A. 2)

James Campbell Watters was born on 20 January 1890 in County Sligo and he was the elder son of the Rev Francis OM Watters MA and Mrs Kathleen Elizabeth Watters who lived at 17 Magheraboy, Sligo. The Rev Watters was a Presbyterian minister and he and Kathleen Elizabeth had at least four children – Annie, Francis, James Campbell and Thomas. James Watters's grandfather, the Rev Thomas Watters, was also a Presbyterian minister who for many years ministered in Regent Street Presbyterian Church Newtownards and it was in Newtownards that James's father Francis was born. The Rev Francis Watters and his family moved to South Africa where he ministered to the congregation of Wynberg, Cape Colony.

In 1913 James Watters graduated with a BA degree from Cape University and he was preparing to enter the Ordained Ministry in the Presbyterian

W

Church. He enlisted on 1 August 1915 at Rondebosch and in his attestation papers it was noted that he was 5 feet 10¼ inches tall. He cited his mother as his next-of-kin and her address was Craigroyston, Bissett Road, Wynberg.

WATTERS—Died of wounds, Second-Lieut. James Campbell Watters, South African Heavy Artillery, dearly-loved elder son of Rev. F. O. M. Watters, Wynberg, Cape Colony, South Africa.

James Watters served with the 73rd Battery South African Heavy Artillery and he was hospitalised for a period in 1916. On 20 February 1917 he was granted a commission in the field and posted to the 71st Battery. On 18 October 1917 he suffered severe wounds to both legs and he died in hospital the following day. His family placed a death notice in the 24 November 1917 edition of the *Newtownards Chronicle* and his connection with the town was reported under the headline 'The Supreme Sacrifice, Grandson of Late Rev Thomas Watters, Newtownards'.

At the time of James's death his parents were living in The Manse, Darling, Cape Province in South Africa and his younger brother, who was serving as a Gunner in German East Africa was in hospital. Second Lieutenant James Campbell Watters is commemorated on Newtownards and District War Memorial.

W

Waugh, John Brennan (John)
Private
No. 648945, 4th Canadian Mounted Rifles, Central Ontario Regiment
Died of bronchitis on Wednesday 29 September 1920 (aged 33)
Newtownards (Movilla) Cemetery, Co Down (Grave 4. 155)

John Brennan Waugh was born on 10 July 1887 in the townland of Mountstewart, Newtownards and he was a son of Elizabeth Jane Waugh. John moved to Canada where he lived in Notre Dame Street, Sudbury, Ontario and he worked as a druggist. He enlisted on 16 February 1916 at Sudbury and in his attestation papers it was noted that he was 5 feet 7½ inches tall and that he had served in the Canadian Militia. John cited his mother as his next-of-kin and at that time she was living in Ravenhill Road, Belfast. She had also lived at 81 High Street in Belfast.

After John Waugh was discharged from the army he returned to Ireland and he died of bronchitis on 29 September 1920. He was buried in Movilla Old Cemetery Newtownards and on his CWGC headstone his age is inscribed as

34. Private John Brennan Waugh is commemorated in the Belfast Book of Honour (Page 652).

Webb, Gilbert Watson (Gilbert)
Captain (Pilot)
22nd Squadron, Royal Flying Corps and Royal Irish Rifles
Killed in action on Saturday 1 July 1916 (aged 26)
Achiet-Le-Grand Communal Cemetery Extension, France (Grave IV. Q. 5)

Gilbert Watson Webb was born on 1 March 1890 and he was a son of Richard Thomas and Blanche Louise Webb (nee Stromeyer) who lived in Knock Avenue, Belfast. They were married in 1880 in Romford, Essex. Richard Webb was a linen manufacturer and he and Blanche had eight children – Melanie, Ethel, Richard Randall, William Henry, Hermann, Gilbert Watson, Karl and Blanche. Gilbert's father died on 5 May 1909 and at least three of Gilbert's brothers worked in the family linen manufacturing business – Messrs Webb,

W

Ards Weaving Co Ltd, Newtownards. Gilbert was educated at Campbell College and he was a member of the QUB Officers' Training Corps.

Gilbert Webb moved to Canada where he worked for a few years before returning to Ireland to enlist. On 9 October 1914 he obtained a commission in the 3rd Battalion Royal Irish Rifles. He served with the 2nd Battalion on the Western Front and he was wounded in the head on 8 May 1915. When he recovered he transferred to the Royal Flying Corps and on 4 May 1916 he flew his plane across the English Channel to France and was attached to a flying squadron. Aerial reconnaissance provided essential information about the layout of enemy trenches.

Brother of Messrs. Webb, Ards Weaving Co. (Ltd.), Killed.

Captain G. W. Webb, Royal Irish Rifles, attached Royal Flying Corps, killed in action on 1st July, was a son of the late Mr. R. T. Webb, and Mrs. Webb, Rath House, Knock, Belfast. He obtained a commission in the 3rd Battalion Royal Irish Rifles on 9th October, 1914, prior to which he had been for a few years in Canada, and hearing the call of his country, promptly responded.

Initially Captain Webb was reported as missing in action at the Somme on 1 July 1916. His death was confirmed in a letter written on 6 July by his observer Lieutenant WO Tudor-Hart of the Northumberland Fusiliers and Royal Flying Corps. Lieutenant Tudor-Hart was being held as a prisoner of war and in the letter he stated that Captain Webb and he were flying about six miles over the German lines when they were attacked by a number of German aeroplanes. Captain Webb was hit in the groin by a bullet and he died within two minutes. With great difficulty Lieutenant Tudor-Hart crash-landed the plane behind enemy lines and in the process suffered extensive injuries.

Captain Gilbert Watson Webb is commemorated in the Belfast Book of Honour (Page 652); on the North of Ireland [Rugby] Football Club Memorial Plaque; on the QUB War Memorial and in the QUB Book of Remembrance (Page 54).

Weir, John
Rifleman
No. 18/663, 'B' Company, 13th Battalion, Royal Irish Rifles
Killed in action on Saturday 1 July 1916 (aged 26)
Thiepval Memorial, France (Pier and Face 15 A and 15 B)

John Weir was born in Newtownards and he was a son of James and Elizabeth Weir (nee Johnston) who lived in George's Street and then Movilla Street, Newtownards. They were married on 30 April 1888 in St Anne's Church of Ireland Belfast. James Weir worked as a general labourer and he and Elizabeth had at least seven children – John, Mary, Elizabeth, Isabella, Ellen, Thomas and David James.

Prior to the outbreak of the Great War John Weir was a member of the Ulster Volunteer Force, he worked as a general labourer and he and his wife Mary Ann Weir lived at 65 Mill Street, Newtownards. John enlisted in Newtownards, he served with the 13th Battalion Royal Irish Rifles in 108th Brigade of the 36th (Ulster) Division and he was killed in action on the first day of the Battle of the Somme. Rifleman John Weir is commemorated on Newtownards and District War Memorial and in Newtownards Parish Church of Ireland (St Mark).

Wellstead, WA
Able Seaman
No. 179706, (R.F.R./P.O./B./797), HMS *Bayano*, Royal Navy
Died on Thursday, 11 March 1915
Ballyphilip Church of Ireland Churchyard, Co Down (Grave 198)

Seven crew members from HMS *Bayano* are buried in graveyards on the Ards Peninsula.

Spracklin, Edgar J and one unidentified Royal Marine are buried in Ballyhalbert Church of Ireland (St Andrew) Graveyard Ballyeasborough.

Chater, Frederick William is buried in Whitechurch Graveyard Ballywalter.

Bain, AG; Wellstead, WA and two unidentified sailors are buried in Ballyphilip Church of Ireland Churchyard Portaferry.

Wheeler, Albert (see Diver, Redmond Joseph)

White, Adam

The name Adam White is listed on the War Memorial Plaque in Kircubbin Parish Church of Ireland (Holy Trinity).

Adam White was born on 14 June 1891 in Kircubbin and he was a son of Adam and Susan White (nee Kelly) who lived in the townland of Gransha, Kircubbin. They were married on 11 August 1874 in Ballyhalbert Parish Church of Ireland at Ballyeasborough. Adam White worked as an agricultural labourer and he and Susan had at least eight children – John, Elizabeth, Mary, Ellen, James, William, Adam and Jane. Babies Adam and Jane were baptised in Kircubbin Parish Church of Ireland. Susan White died in 1899 aged 43. Desk searches and public appeals to date have yielded no information about Adam White's war service or his death.

White, Alexander (Sandy)
Private
No. 159754, 1st Battalion, Canadian Infantry (Western Ontario Regiment)
Died of wounds on Wednesday 11 April 1917 (aged 30)
Etaples Military Cemetery, France (Grave XXII. F. 9)

Alexander White was born on 7 April 1887 and he was the eldest son of Henry and Margaret White (nee Bennett) who lived in Mary Street, Newtownards. They were married on 16 January 1885 in Regent Street Methodist Church Newtownards. Henry White worked as an overseer in a spinning mill and he and Maggie had at least eleven children including Anna, Alexander, Jane, Matthew, John, James, Martha, Mary, Margaret and Margaret Eleanor.

W

When he left school Sandy White served his time with Messrs David O'Prey & Sons, Painters and Decorators and that was the trade that he followed when he moved to the United States of America. After the outbreak of the Great War Sandy travelled from the United States to Toronto and on 10 March 1916 he enlisted there and joined the 81st Battalion Canadian Infantry. In his attestation papers it was noted that Sandy was 5 feet 6 inches tall. He contracted a severe cold and as a result was unable to travel to England with his Battalion. He was transferred to the 9th Battalion and sailed with it to England. Sandy was granted a short leave during which he visited his parents in Newtownards. He went to France in August 1916 along with 400 others to make up the 1st Battalion.

During the advance on Vimy Ridge he and his whole platoon were completely wiped out by a bursting enemy shell. Sandy was picked up by the stretcher bearers and conveyed to the British Red Cross Hospital at Etaples but his spine was so severely fractured that he died the following day.

In his pocket there was a letter dated 6 April addressed to his mother. In the letter he thanked her for gifts from home and said that he would be in the line again on his birthday for the proposed 'big advance'. He expressed the hope that this advance would take them all the way to the Rhine.

W

> WHITE—April 11th, 1917, died of wounds at British Red Cross Hospital, Etaples, France, (No. 159,754) Private Alexander (Sandy) White, 1st Battalion Canadians, eldest son of Henry and Margaret White, 18 Mary Street, Newtownards.
> "He hath done what he could."
> Inserted by Father, Mother, Brothers, and Sisters.

When official news of Sandy White's death reached his family from the Canadian Record Office his father, mother, brothers and sisters placed a 'For King and Country' notice in the 21 April edition of the *Newtownards Chronicle* and it included the line:

'He hath done what he could'

Private Alexander White is commemorated on Newtownards and District War Memorial and in the PCI Roll of Honour for Greenwell Street Presbyterian Church Newtownards. His father Henry died on 19 May 1927 and his mother Margaret died on 19 October 1939.

Whiteside, Robert
Private
No. 27762, 2nd Battalion, Royal Inniskilling Fusiliers
Killed in action on Tuesday 15 October 1918
Dadizeele New British Cemetery, Belgium (Grave III. C. 11)

In 'Soldiers Died in the Great War 1914 – 1919' it is recorded that Robert Whiteside was born in County Tyrone, he lived in Newtownards and he enlisted in Londonderry. He served with the 2nd Battalion Royal Inniskilling Fusiliers in 12th Brigade of the 4th Division and when he was killed in action on 15 October 1918 during the Allied offensive against all sections of the German line the Battalion was in 109th Brigade of the 36th (Ulster) Division.

Whyte, James Gordon (Gordon)
Lance Corporal
No. 9265, 15th Battalion, Royal Irish Rifles
Killed in action on Friday 23 November 1917 (aged 20)
Thiepval Memorial, France (Pier and Face 15 A and 15 B)

James Gordon Whyte was born on 24 July 1897 and he was the third son of James and Mary Whyte (nee Mooney) who lived in Ballywalter. They were married on 25 May 1894 in Ballycopeland Presbyterian Church. James Whyte worked as an agricultural labourer and Mary worked at home as an embroiderer. James and Mary had five children – Joseph, Robert Lyttle, James Gordon, John and Hugh Alexander. All but Joseph were baptised in Ballywalter Presbyterian Church. Gordon's father died on 14 March 1907 aged 36. In both the 1901 and 1911 Census the family surname is spelt White.

W

Prior to the outbreak of the Great War Gordon Whyte was a member of the Ulster Volunteer Force and initially he joined the Cyclist Corps of the 36th (Ulster) Division. Subsequently he was transferred to the 15th Battalion Royal Irish Rifles in 107th Brigade of the 36th (Ulster) Division.

Lance Corporal Gordon Whyte was killed in action on 23 November 1917 in the Battle of Cambrai and he is commemorated on Ballywalter and District War Memorial and in Ballywalter Presbyterian Church. He is also commemorated on the family grave headstone in Whitechurch Cemetery Ballywalter. Gordon's mother Mary died on 9 July 1930.

Williamson, John Stanley
Second Lieutenant
1st Battalion, Lancashire Fusiliers
Died of wounds on Sunday 25 April 1915 (aged 28)
Helles Memorial, Gallipoli, Turkey (Panel 58 to 72 or 218 to 219)

Death of Lieutenant Williamson.

Lieutenant J. S. Williamson, 1st Battalion Lancashire Fusiliers, who has died in Alexandria, of wounds received in action at the Dardanelles, was a step-son of Rev. John Magill, formerly Methodist minister at Donaghadee, and subsequently at Clones, and who has been living in retirement in Somersetshire since last year. Of the deceased officer a friend writes that "he was a splendid Christian, unselfish, kind, a devoted son, who, when serving in India, and elsewhere abroad never missed a mail that could carry a letter to his mother."

In the CWGC Debt of Honour it is recorded that John Stanley Williamson was a son of Mrs Magill (formerly Williamson) of The Grove, Gilford and the late John Williamson.

In the 18 June 1915 edition of the *County Down Spectator* it was reported that Second Lieutenant John Stanley Williamson who had died of wounds on 25 April 1915 was a stepson of the Rev John Magill formerly Methodist minister at Donaghadee and subsequently Clones before he retired to Somerset. Second Lieutenant John Stanley Williamson served with the 1st Battalion Lancashire Fusiliers and he died of wounds at Gallipoli on 25 April 1915.

Wilson, Charles Hugh Parke (Charles)
Private
No. 30421, Canadian Army Service Corps
Died of influenza on Monday 4 November 1918 (aged 35)
Vancouver (Mountain View) Cemetery, Canada (Grave 2. 45. 14)

W

Charles Hugh Parke Wilson was born on 14 September 1883 in Portaferry and he was a son of Samuel and Annie Wilson (nee Parke) who lived in Market Square, Portaferry. They were married on 21 March 1879 in Cloughey Presbyterian Church. Samuel Wilson worked as a timber and hardware merchant and he and Annie had four children – James William Albert, Madeline Serita Elizabeth (died on 31 August 1906 aged 25), Charles Hugh Parke and Victor Samuel. They were all baptised in Portaferry Presbyterian Church. Samuel Wilson died on 2 May 1914 aged 73 and Annie Wilson died on 15 February 1919 aged 72.

Charles Wilson was a farmer before he moved to Canada and there he worked as a teamster (driver). He enlisted on 23 September 1914 at Valcartier, Quebec and it was noted in his attestation papers that he was 5 feet 9 inches tall and that he had previous service in the 15th Light Horse, Calgary. At attestation he declared his date of birth to be 14 September 1884 and he used Charles as his forename.

Private Charles Wilson served with the Canadian Army Service Corps and he died of influenza on 4 November 1918. He is commemorated in Portaferry Presbyterian Church and on the family grave headstone in Ballymanish

Cemetery Portaferry where the engraver inscribed Hugh Parke as his forenames.

Wilson, James

The name James Wilson is listed on Newtownards and District War Memorial and in the booklet produced for the Unveiling and Dedication Ceremony held on Saturday 26 May 1934 he is described as a Private in the Highland Light Infantry. Desk searches and public appeals to date have yielded no further information.

Wilson, William
Rifleman
No. 545, 'D' Company, 13th Battalion, Royal Irish Rifles
Killed in action on Saturday 1 July 1916
Thiepval Memorial, France (Pier and Face 15 A and 15 B)

BALLYMACASHEN.
Rifleman W. Wilson (No. 543), R.I. Rifles, previously reported missing, now reported killed.

W

William Wilson was born in Moira, he lived in Maralin and he enlisted in Banbridge. His address was stated to be Ballymacashen, Killinchy when his death was reported in the 25 November 1916 edition of the *Newtownards Chronicle*. He served with the 13th Battalion Royal Irish Rifles in 108th Brigade of the 36th (Ulster) Division (No. 543 in the newspaper article). Initially he was reported as missing in action and in November 1916 it was officially confirmed that he had been killed in action on the first day of the Battle of the Somme.

Woods, William
Private
No. 39040, 2nd Battalion, Loyal North Lancashire Regiment
Died of pneumonia on Thursday 4 July 1918 (aged 24)
Terlincthun British Cemetery, France (Grave I. D. 22)

William Woods was born on 11 April 1894 in Greyabbey and he was the second son of William John and Esther (Essie) Woods (nee McFadden) who lived in the townland of Blackabbey. They were married on 26 April 1891 in Kircubbin Presbyterian Church. William John Woods was a farmer and he and Essie had at least five children – Mary Jane, Hugh, William, James and Eileen. Essie Woods died on 2 February 1940 and her husband William John died the following day.

William Woods enlisted in Bradford, Yorkshire, he served with the 2nd Battalion Loyal North Lancashire Regiment and he died of pneumonia on 4 July 1918 in the Third Canadian General Hospital at Boulogne in France. His parents placed a 'For King and Country' notice in the 13 July 1918 edition of the *Newtownards Chronicle*. Private William Woods is commemorated on the War Memorial Plaque in Kircubbin Presbyterian Church and on the family grave headstone in the adjoining Graveyard.

Woodside, T

The name T Woodside was listed in a Roll of Honour for Newtownards published in the 6 January 1917 edition of the *Newtownards Chronicle*. Desk searches and public appeals to date have yielded no further information.

Wright, James
Rifleman
No. 19353, 'B' Company, 13th Battalion, Royal Irish Rifles
Killed in action on Thursday 16 August 1917 (aged 21)
Tyne Cot Memorial, Belgium (Panel 138 to 140 & 162 to 162A & 163A)

W

James Wright was born in Newtownards and his mother lived in Half Acre Lane, Newtownards. James Wright and Margaret (Maggie) McAvoy were married on 7 February 1916 in First Donaghadee Presbyterian Church (James's address was Clandeboye Camp). Maggie lived at 37 Wallace's Street in Newtownards and their son James was born on 26 July 1917 – less than a month before his father was killed. Baby James Wright was baptised in Greenwell Street Presbyterian Church Newtownards.

James Wright enlisted in Newtownards and he joined the 1st County Down Volunteers. He served with the 13th Battalion Royal Irish Rifles in 108th Brigade of the 36th (Ulster) Division.

After Rifleman James Wright was killed in action on 16 August 1917 at the Battle of Langemarck the Rev Robert Kelso, Chaplain to the Forces, wrote to James's widow. The chaplain expressed his sincere sympathy and told her that when the Ulster Division went over the top that morning her husband fell in the advance. James Wright's wife and mother both placed 'For King and Country' notices in the *Newtownards Chronicle* and the one from his wife contained the verse:

> 'A loving husband, true and kind,
> Missed by those he left behind;
> Forget him, no, we never will,
> As years roll on we love him still.
> He never shunned his country's call,
> But gladly gave his life – his all;
> He died the helpless to defend,
> An Ulster soldier's noble end'

The one from his mother contained the verse:

> 'He was the first to answer the sacrifice supreme,
> We cannot yet realise his death, it seems a hateful dream;
> Though we understand God's mercy in taking him to rest,
> The parting gave great anguish to those who loved him best.
> We never will forget you, James, nor your happy smiling face,
> You died for your King and country, and the honour of your race.'

Rifleman James Wright is commemorated on Newtownards and District War Memorial and in the PCI Roll of Honour for Greenwell Street Presbyterian Church Newtownards.

Wright, Matthew John (Matthew)
Second Lieutenant
'C' Company, 14th Battalion, Royal Irish Rifles
Killed in action on Saturday 1 July 1916 (aged 28)
Thiepval Memorial, France (Pier and Face 15 A and 15 B)

Matthew John Wright was born on 23 February 1888 and he was the fourth son of the Rev William Wright DD and Charlotte McW Wright (nee Robinson) who lived in Corporation South and later Circular Street in Newtownards. They were married on 9 December 1880 in First Broughshane Presbyterian Church, Co Antrim. The Rev Wright was the Minister in First Newtownards Presbyterian Church and he and Charlotte had eight children – Archibald Robinson (1881), Thomas (1882), William Martin (1884), Hannah Dunlop (1885), Charlotte McWilliams (1887), Matthew John (1888), Richard Ponsonby Maxwell (1890) and Alfred James (1897).

Prior to the outbreak of the Great War Matthew Wright worked as a timber merchant's assistant in the firm of Messrs James P Corry in Belfast and he was a member of one of the Newtownards companies of the North Down Regiment of the Ulster Volunteer Force. His brother William was a company commander in the UVF. Matthew joined the Young Citizen Volunteers as a Private and soon received a commission as Second Lieutenant in the same Battalion. He went to the front with 109th Brigade of the 36th (Ulster) Division in October 1915 and for a time he was an instructor in the bomb-throwing school.

Second Lieutenant Matthew Wright was wounded in May 1916 and he spent some time recuperating at home in Newtownards. At the same time his brother William was at home on leave and William was installed as Worshipful Master of Volunteers LOL No. 1501. Second Lieutenant Matthew Wright returned to duty and he was killed by an exploding shell on 1 July 1916. Three days earlier Matthew's brother William was seriously injured but William was able to return to active service. In all, four of the Wright brothers were on active service during the Great War. Matthew's father, the Rev William Wright, died of heart failure on 12 August 1919 and he was buried in Movilla New Cemetery Newtownards. Second Lieutenant Matthew John Wright is commemorated on Newtownards and District War Memorial and in First Newtownards Presbyterian Church.

Y

Young, Albert Edward (Albert)
Sergeant
No. 17175, 10th Battalion, Highland Light Infantry
Killed in action on Saturday 25 September 1915
Loos Memorial, France (Panel 108 to 112)

In some records, including the CWGC Debt of Honour, his first forename is Alfred. Albert Edward Young was a son of John and Martha Young who lived in Bridge Street, Comber. John Young worked as a distillery labourer and he and Martha had at least seven children including Albert Edward, Martha, James, Annie and a foster-son called David.

Comber-Highlander Killed.

Mr. John Young, Bridge Street, Comber, has been notified that his son, Sergt. Albert Young, 10th Battalion Highland Light Infantry, was killed in action on 25th September. Deceased enlisted in Scotland.

Albert Young moved to Scotland and he enlisted at Rutherglen in Lanarkshire. He served with the 10th Battalion Highland Light Infantry and he was killed in action on 25 September 1915. His death was reported in the 6 November 1915 edition of the *Newtownards Chronicle* in the form of a letter to the editor written by one of his comrades, A Carson of 97 McClure Street, Belfast. This letter pointed up the fact that Albert Young had written earlier in the year to the girls of Comber Mill asking them to send him a melodeon. The letter went on 'I am pleased to say the girls made a generous response as there was over £2 collected and the melodeon along with some 3000 cigarettes were sent to him to distribute amongst his company. Unfortunately Sergeant Young was killed on 25 September and as the parcel was only sent a few days before that date he, poor fellow, did not get time to acknowledge the gift'.

At the time James and David Young were also on active service and in 1917 Bombardier David Young Royal Garrison Artillery was awarded the Military Medal. Sergeant Albert Edward Young is commemorated on Comber and District War Memorial and in Comber Non-Subscribing Presbyterian Church.

Young Brothers: George and Henry

George and Henry Young were born in Ballygowan and they were sons of Hugh and Mary Young (nee Gardiner) who lived in the townland of Ravara, Ballygowan. Hugh Young worked as a labourer in a stone quarry and Mary Young worked as a seamstress. Hugh and Mary had at least thirteen children – Thomas Hugh, Sarah Jane, Mary, Agnes, George, William John, Henry (Harry), Elizabeth, Lucy Logan, Maggie, Mary, Barbara and James. Eleven of the children were baptised in Ballygowan Presbyterian Church and their mother died in the early 1900s. Henry Young was the first of the two brothers to die on active service:

Young, Henry (Harry)
Private
No. PO/1339 (S), 2nd Royal Marine Battalion, Royal Naval Division, Royal Marine Light Infantry
Killed in action on Saturday 6 April 1918 (aged 21)
Pozieres Memorial, France (Panel 1)

Henry Young was born on 14 August 1896 and prior to the outbreak of the Great War he worked as a tailor. He served with the Royal Marine Light Infantry and he was killed in action on 6 April 1918. A memorial service was held for him in Ballygowan Presbyterian Church on Sunday 28 April 1918, four days after his brother George was killed in action.

Y

Young, George
Private
No. T4/160141, 31st Division Transport, Army Service Corps,
transferred to (69289), Royal Fusiliers posted to 2nd/2nd Battalion
London Regiment (Royal Fusiliers)
Killed in action on Wednesday 24 April 1918 (aged 25)
Pozieres Memorial, France (Panel 19 to 21)

George Young was born on 16 June 1892 and prior to the outbreak of the Great War he worked as a farm labourer. He enlisted in Belfast and served initially with the 31st Division Transport Army Service Corps (T4/160141), then with the Royal Fusiliers posted to 2nd/2nd Battalion London Regiment (Royal Fusiliers) (69289).

Private George Young was killed in action on 24 April 1918, just 18 days after his brother Harry was killed in action. Private George Young and Private Harry Young are both commemorated in Ballygowan Presbyterian Church.

Y

Young, Charles

The name Charles Young is listed on Newtownards and District War Memorial and in the booklet produced for the Unveiling and Dedication Ceremony held on Saturday 26 May 1934 he is described as a Rifleman in the Royal Irish Rifles. Desk searches and public appeals to date have yielded no further information.

Young, James (Jim)
Rifleman
No. 582, 'B' Company, 13th Battalion, Royal Irish Rifles
Killed in action on Saturday 1 July 1916 (aged 29)
Thiepval Memorial, France (Pier and Face 15 A and 15 B)

James Young was born in Newtownards and he was a son of Mary Young who lived in the townland of Tullynagardy, Newtownards. James worked as a general labourer and he and Annie Wilson were married on 20 December 1907 in Greenwell Street Presbyterian Church Newtownards. They lived at 22 Corry Street, Newtownards and they had five sons – Andrew (1908), James, George Burch (1912), Robert (1914) and Elliott Thiepval who was born on 12 October 1916.

 James Young was a member of Apprentice Boys LOL No.128, he enlisted in Belfast and he joined the 1st County Down Volunteers. He went to France in October 1915, he served with the 13th Battalion Royal Irish Rifles in 108th Brigade of the 36th (Ulster) Division and he was killed in action on the first day of the Battle of the Somme. Initially James was posted as missing in action and then in September 1916 Annie was informed by the British Red Cross that he was being held as a prisoner of war in Germany.

Finally, in August 1917, it was officially confirmed that Rifleman James Young had been killed in action. Both his wife Annie and his mother Mary placed 'Our Heroes – In Memoriam' notices in the 25 August 1917 edition of the *Newtownards Chronicle* and the one from his wife contained the following verse:

'When alone in my sorrow, and bitter tears flow,
There stealeth a dream of the sweet long ago;
Unknown to the world, Jim stands by my side,
And whispers these words – Death cannot divide.
God is good, He will give me grace
To bear my heavy cross;
He is the only One Who knows
How bitter is my loss.'

Rifleman James Young is commemorated on Newtownards and District War Memorial and in the PCI Roll of Honour for Greenwell Street Presbyterian Church Newtownards.

Y

Names by Centre of Population

In this Section the names of servicemen with Ards connections who died in the Great War are presented alphabetically in relation to the centre of population they are associated with. Because people moved within the area, some of those who died had a demonstrable association with more than one population centre.

BALLYGOWAN AND DISTRICT

Private **James Bennett**
11th Battalion Royal Inniskilling Fusiliers

Sapper **Robert James Burrows**
150th Field Company Royal Engineers 36th (Ulster) Division

James Clarke
Ballygowan Presbyterian Church

Private **Albert Connolly**
Royal Army Service Corps attached 110th Field Ambulance RAMC

Rifleman **John Crossen**
6th Battalion Royal Irish Rifles

Rifleman **Robert Douglas**
11th Battalion Royal Irish Rifles

Rifleman **Samuel Gibson**
16th Battalion Royal Irish Rifles

Private **Samuel Grant**
29th Battalion Canadian Infantry (British Columbia Regiment)

Rifleman **Charles Francis Hill**
13th Battalion Royal Irish Rifles

Corporal **Lowry Jordan MM**
Royal Air Force

Rifleman **Samuel Wallace Jordan**
13th Battalion Royal Irish Rifles

Rifleman **James Lundy**
1st Battalion Royal Irish Rifles

Ballygowan and District continued…

James W McDowell
Ballygowan Presbyterian Church

Lance Corporal **Robert John McDowell**
1st Battalion Canadian Pioneers

Sergeant **Thomas Millar**
8th Battalion Royal Irish Rifles

Corporal **William Barry Ritchie Millar**
45th Battalion Australian Infantry AIF

Rifleman **John Mills**
10th Battalion Royal Irish Rifles

Rifleman **David Rainey**
12th Battalion Royal Irish Rifles

Private **George Young**
Royal Fusiliers posted to 2nd/2nd Battalion London Regiment (Royal Fusiliers)

Private **Henry Young**
2nd Royal Marine Battalion Royal Naval Division Royal Marine Light Infantry

BALLYHALBERT AND DISTRICT

Private **Beresford Addy**
27th Battalion Canadian Infantry (Manitoba Regiment)

Private **Hugh Samuel Bailie**
2nd Battalion Royal Scots Fusiliers

Rifleman **William John Dorman**
16th Battalion Royal Irish Rifles transferred to 459th Company Labour Corps

Stoker First Class **Robert Ennis**
HMS *Nottingham* Royal Navy

Sergeant **William Hanna**
1st Battalion Royal Irish Rifles

Ballyhalbert and District continued…

Private **George Laidlaw**
5th Battalion Cameron Highlanders

George Ledlie
Ballyhalbert Parish Church of Ireland (St Andrew)

Stoker First Class **David Magee**
HMS *Indefatigable* Royal Navy

Stoker **J Moreland**
Glastry Presbyterian Church

Rifleman **David Pyper**
11th Battalion Royal Irish Rifles

Rifleman **Robert James Pyper**
22nd Entrenching Battalion late 11th/13th Battalion Royal Irish Rifles

Private **Hugh Graham Ritchie**
75th Battalion Canadian Infantry (Central Ontario Regiment)

Leading Seaman **Edgar J Spracklin**
HMS *Bayano* Newfoundland Royal Naval Reserve

BALLYWALTER AND DISTRICT

Lance Corporal **John Adair**
10th Battalion Royal Irish Rifles

Private **William Blair**
12th Battalion Highland Light Infantry

Private **Alexander Boyle**
20th Battalion Australian Infantry AIF

Lance Corporal **William John Branch**
11th Battalion Essex Regiment

Rifleman **Robert Carpenter**
11th Battalion Royal Irish Rifles

Able Seaman **Frederick William Chater**
HMS *Bayano* Royal Naval Volunteer Reserve

Ballywalter and District continued...

Rifleman **Edward Corry**
13th Battalion Royal Irish Rifles

Rifleman **David Cromie**
13th Battalion Royal Irish Rifles

Private **James O'Neill Dorrian**
44th Battalion Canadian Infantry (New Brunswick Regiment)

Rifleman **George Edgar Edmonds**
7th Battalion Royal Irish Rifles

Rifleman (Bandsman) **George Coulter Gunning**
2nd Battalion Royal Irish Rifles

Lance Corporal **Walter Gunning**
13th Battalion Royal Irish Rifles

Rifleman **Thomas Johnston**
13th Battalion Royal Irish Rifles

Rifleman **James Kerr**
13th Battalion Royal Irish Rifles

Major **Meyrick Myles Magrath DSO**
291st Brigade Royal Horse and Field Artillery

Rifleman **John Taggart McDowell**
13th Battalion Royal Irish Rifles

Captain **The Hon Andrew Edward Somerset Mulholland**
1st Battalion Irish Guards

Rifleman **Neil McLean Mulholland**
6th Battalion Royal Irish Rifles

Master **Robert Murphy**
SS *Lough Fisher* Mercantile Marine

Second Mate **Thomas Lewis Nicholas**
SS *Beatrice* (London) Mercantile Marine

Rifleman **John O'Neill**
13th Battalion Royal Irish Rifles

Ballywalter and District continued…

Rifleman **Andrew Orr**
19th Battalion Canadian Infantry (Central Ontario Regiment)

Rifleman **John Orr**
12th Battalion Royal Irish Rifles

Rifleman **Reuben Peake**
2nd & 7th Battalions Royal Irish Rifles

Corporal **William John Peake MM**
13th Battalion Royal Irish Rifles

Rifleman **William John Pritchard**
13th Battalion Royal Irish Rifles

Rifleman **Robert Regan**
13th Battalion Royal Irish Rifles

Rifleman **Samuel Hugh Regan**
13th Battalion Royal Irish Rifles

Lieutenant **Basil Llewellyn Boyd Thomas**
15th Battalion Royal Welsh Fusiliers attd 27th Company Machine Gun Corps

Sergeant **Robert Thompson**
1st/4th Battalion King's Own (Royal Lancaster Regiment)

Captain **GAC Ward**
Ballywalter and District War Memorial

Lance Corporal **James Gordon Whyte**
15th Battalion Royal Irish Rifles

CARROWDORE AND DISTRICT

Sergeant **Alexander Colville MM**
1st/5th Battalion Royal Scots Fusiliers

Private **Samuel Blakely Dunn Donnan**
11th Battalion Royal Inniskilling Fusiliers

Samuel Hamilton
Carrowdore Parish Church of Ireland

Carrowdore and District continued…

Private **Robert McDermott**
144th Battalion Canadian Infantry (Quebec Regiment)

Private **Dupree William McWha**
Canterbury Regiment New Zealand Expeditionary Force

Rifleman **James Morrow**
11th Battalion Royal Irish Rifles

Rifleman **Francis Orr**
1st Battalion Royal Irish Rifles

Private **Hugh Orr**
2nd Battalion Highland Light Infantry

Private **James Reid**
312th Infantry Regiment 78th Infantry Division US Army

Rifleman **David Shanks**
10th Battalion Royal Irish Rifles

Gunner **James Francis Simpson**
'C' Battalion Tank Corps

Private **John Stewart**
27th Battalion Canadian Infantry (Manitoba Regiment)

Corporal **Niven Boyd Stewart**
56th Infantry Regiment 7th Infantry Division US Army

CLOUGHEY AND DISTRICT

Corporal **Edward Atkin**
Inland Water Transport Royal Engineers

Private **Thomas Donnan**
Canterbury Regiment NZEF

William Rice
Cloughey Presbyterian Church

Lt Colonel **Francis Savage Nesbitt Savage-Armstrong DSO and MID (x2)**
1st Bn South Staffordshire Rgt Commanding 11th Bn Royal Warwickshire Rgt

COMBER AND DISTRICT

Rifleman **John Allen**
13th & 12th Battalions Royal Irish Rifles

Rifleman **Robert Allen**
13th Battalion Royal Irish Rifles

Rifleman **James Auld**
13th Battalion Royal Irish Rifles

Rifleman **William Beers**
11th Battalion Royal Irish Rifles attached 108th Trench Mortar Battery

Private **John Arthur Bell**
1st Battalion Irish Guards

Rifleman **Robert John Black**
13th Battalion Royal Irish Rifles

Lance Corporal **George Taylor Boyd**
13th Battalion Royal Irish Rifles

Lance Sergeant **William John Brown**
13th Battalion Royal Irish Rifles

Captain (Brigade Major) **George James Bruce DSO MC (and Bar) MID (x3)**
109th Infantry Brigade 36th (Ulster) Division

Sergeant **Henry Burgess**
13th Battalion Royal Irish Rifles

Private **A Edward Campbell**
Comber and District War Memorial

Driver **George Casey**
251st Company Army Service Corps

Rifleman **James Casey**
Comber and District War Memorial

Rifleman **John Cathcart**
13th Battalion Royal Irish Rifles

Lance Corporal **Andrew Clarke**
1st Battalion Royal Irish Rifles

Comber and District continued…

Rifleman **William George Clifford**
10th Battalion Royal Irish Rifles

Rifleman **David Coey**
1st Battalion Royal Irish Rifles

Lance Corporal **Thomas Coey**
13th Battalion Royal Irish Rifles

Rifleman **William Coleman**
13th Battalion Royal Irish Rifles

Rifleman **Alexander Courtney**
1st Battalion Royal Irish Rifles

Second Lieutenant **Edmund De Wind VC**
15th Battalion Royal Irish Rifles

Rifleman **Andrew John Dempster**
13th Battalion Royal Irish Rifles

Private **DJ Dempster**
Royal Air Force

Rifleman **Robert Dempster**
14th Battalion Royal Irish Rifles

Rifleman **Robert James Dempster**
8th Battalion Royal Irish Rifles

Gunner **William Dickson**
5th Brigade Canadian Field Artillery

Rifleman **James Donaldson**
13th Battalion Royal Irish Rifles

Rifleman **John Donaldson**
13th Battalion Royal Irish Rifles

Rifleman **Samuel Donaldson**
13th Battalion Royal Irish Rifles

Private **James Edgar Drake**
43rd Battalion Canadian Infantry (Manitoba Regiment)

Comber and District continued…

Corporal James Munn Dugan
21st Entrenching Battalion late 10th Battalion Royal Irish Rifles

Corporal Henry Earney
7th/8th Battalion Royal Inniskilling Fusiliers

Private William Holland Kennedy Ellison
9th Battalion Princess Victoria's (Royal Irish Fusiliers)

Sapper Nathaniel Ferguson
Postal Section Corps of Royal Engineers

Sergeant James Finlay
13th Battalion Royal Irish Rifles

Rifleman James Fisher
11th Battalion Royal Irish Rifles

Rifleman Thomas James Fisher
13th Battalion Royal Irish Rifles

Private James Gabbey
9th Battalion Royal Inniskilling Fusiliers

Major John Campbell Galway
2nd Battalion Canadian Pioneers

Rifleman David John Gamble
12th Battalion Royal Irish Rifles

Corporal Francis Geddis
8th Battalion King's Own (Royal Lancaster Regiment)

Lieutenant Samuel McKee Geddis
1st Battalion Leicestershire Regiment

Rifleman Alexander Glover
16th Bn Royal Irish Rifles transfd to 889th Area Employment Coy Labour Corps

Lance Corporal John A Hare
13th Battalion Royal Irish Rifles

Sapper Joseph Hare
150th Field Company Royal Engineers 36th (Ulster) Division

Comber and District continued…

Rifleman **James Harris (served as James McIlwrath)**
8th Battalion Royal Irish Rifles

Captain **Cyril Gerrard Haselden**
Royal Engineers attached Australian Corps HQ

Private **James Healy**
2nd Battalion Royal Munster Fusiliers

Stoker First Class **Hector Hiles**
HMS *Goliath* Royal Navy

Lieutenant Colonel **Lawrence Arthur Hind MC MID (x2)**
1st/7th Battalion Sherwood Foresters (Notts and Derby Regiment)

Rifleman **James Hughes**
7th Battalion Royal Irish Rifles

Rifleman **Thomas Edward Ingram**
1st Battalion 3rd New Zealand Rifle Brigade NZEF

Private **Robert John Ireland**
325th Infantry Regiment 82nd Division American Expeditionary Force

Rifleman **James Stevenson Johnston**
13th Battalion Royal Irish Rifles

Rifleman **Hugh Kelly**
13th Battalion Royal Irish Rifles

Lance Corporal **William Edwin Logan**
16th Battalion Australian Infantry AIF

Private **John Lynch**
1st Battalion Irish Guards

Rifleman **John Magill**
13th Battalion Royal Irish Rifles

Private **Robert Marshall**
43rd Battalion Canadian Infantry (Manitoba Regiment)

Lance Corporal **Robert H Marshall**
13th Battalion Royal Irish Rifles

Comber and District continued…

Rifleman **John Henry McBratney**
14th Battalion Royal Irish Rifles

Engineer Lieutenant **Edward McBurney**
Transport Service Royal Navy

Second Lieutenant **James Wilson McBurney**
14th Battalion Royal Irish Rifles

Rifleman **John McCulloch**
8th Battalion Royal Irish Rifles

Rifleman **John McCutcheon**
13th Battalion Royal Irish Rifles

Driver **Hugh McGreeghan**
321st Brigade Royal Field Artillery

Rifleman **John McIlveen**
13th Battalion Royal Irish Rifles

Rifleman **William Hewitt McIlveen**
22nd Entrenching Battalion late 11th/13th Battalion Royal Irish Rifles

Rifleman **Alexander McIlwrath**
12th Battalion Royal Irish Rifles

Private **Samuel McKee**
28th Battalion Australian Infantry AIF

Second Lieutenant **Thomas McRoberts**
20th Battalion Royal Irish Rifles

Private **Joseph Miller**
9th Battalion Royal Inniskilling Fusiliers

Captain **David Mitchell**
Royal Army Medical Corps

Lieutenant **William Hamilton Mitchell**
8th Battalion Canadian Infantry (Manitoba Regiment)

Rifleman **Samuel Montgomery**
12th Battalion Royal Irish Rifles

Comber and District continued...

Rifleman **James Morrison**
16th Battalion Royal Irish Rifles

Rifleman **Alexander Mullan**
13th Battalion Royal Irish Rifles

Rifleman **Albert Edward Nelson**
12th Battalion Royal Irish Rifles

Private **Robert Douglas Niblock**
8th Battalion 2nd Infantry Brigade AIF

Private **Ellis Oliver**
6th Battalion Princess Victoria's (Royal Irish Fusiliers)

Rifleman **Robert James Orr**
13th Battalion Royal Irish Rifles

Lance Corporal **James Patterson**
13th Battalion Royal Irish Rifles

Rifleman **Robert Patterson**
13th Battalion Royal Irish Rifles

Rifleman **James Patton**
13th Bn Royal Irish Rifles attd 1st/1st Northumbrian Field Ambulance RAMC

Private **John Price**
108th Company Machine Gun Corps (Infantry) 36th (Ulster) Division

Sergeant **James Proctor**
13th Battalion Royal Irish Rifles

Lance Corporal **William James Quail**
404th Agricultural Company Labour Corps late Royal Irish Rifles

Sergeant **John Quinn**
2nd Royal Marine Battalion Royal Naval Division Royal Marine Light
Infantry

Private **Henry Douglas Ritchie**
4th Regiment South African Infantry

Private **Mason Simonton**
20th Battalion Royal Fusiliers (City of London Regiment)

Comber and District continued…

Gunner **Thomas Simpson (served as Thomas Harvey)**
'Y' 57th Trench Mortar Battery Royal Field Artillery

Rifleman **Alexander Skillen**
1st Battalion Royal Irish Rifles

Rifleman **George Sloan**
13th Battalion Royal Irish Rifles

Rifleman **David John Smyth**
13th Battalion Royal Irish Rifles

Rifleman **David Smyth**
13th Battalion Royal Irish Rifles

Rifleman **John Smyth**
13th Battalion Royal Irish Rifles

Private **Francis Smythe**
5th Battalion Highland Light Infantry

Lance Corporal **John Milliken Spence**
13th Battalion Royal Irish Rifles

Rifleman **Thomas Strickland**
13th Battalion Royal Irish Rifles

Rifleman **John Swindle**
12th Battalion Royal Irish Rifles

Captain **Alfred Squire Taylor**
Royal Army Medical Corps attached 10th/11th Battalion Highland Light
Infantry

Rifleman **William John Thompson**
13th Battalion Royal Irish Rifles

Private **William Tompsett**
2nd Battalion Royal Sussex Regiment

Rifleman **Frederick Hamilton Trousdale**
13th Battalion Royal Irish Rifles

Private **John Walker**
107th Company Machine Gun Corps (Infantry) 36th (Ulster) Division

Comber and District continued…

Rifleman **James Walsh**
13th Battalion Royal Irish Rifles

Sergeant **Albert Edward Young**
10th Battalion Highland Light Infantry

DONAGHADEE AND DISTRICT

Private **Maxwell Aiken**
11th (Lonsdale) Battalion Border Regiment

Private **James Angus**
29th Battalion Canadian Infantry (British Columbia Regiment)

Rifleman **John Blair Angus**
13th Battalion Royal Irish Rifles

Lance Corporal **Robert Angus**
2nd Battalion Royal Scots Fusiliers

Rifleman **William Angus**
13th Battalion Royal Irish Rifles

Private **Thomas Bailie**
4th Battalion Canadian Infantry (Central Ontario Regiment)

Lance Corporal **Alexander Campbell**
13th Battalion Royal Irish Rifles

Rifleman **James Campbell**
13th Battalion Royal Irish Rifles

Corporal **John Clark**
1st Battalion Royal Inniskilling Fusiliers

Thomas Clegg
Donaghadee Methodist Church

Private **Robert Coulter**
1st Battalion Royal Dublin Fusiliers

Rifleman **Thomas Davidson**
Royal Irish Rifles

Donaghadee and District continued…

Lance Corporal **William Drennan**
11th Battalion Royal Irish Rifles

Lieutenant **Samuel Gatensby**
15th Battalion Royal Irish Rifles

Private **James Gray**
2nd Battalion Scots Guards

Private **Albert Edward Gregory**
2nd Battalion Lincolnshire Regiment

Lance Corporal **William Charles Gregory**
2nd Battalion Lincolnshire Regiment

Lance Corporal **Thomas Griffin**
36th (Ulster) Division Signalling Company Royal Engineers

Private **Charles William Henry Hall**
2nd Battalion North Staffordshire Regiment

Rifleman **John Irvine Hamilton**
9th Battalion Royal Irish Rifles

Rifleman **George Hamilton**
12th Battalion Royal Irish Rifles

Rifleman **Hans Hamilton**
12th Battalion Royal Irish Rifles

Rifleman **Robert Hamilton**
12th Battalion Royal Irish Rifles

Able Seaman **Samuel Johnston**
HMS *Monmouth* Royal Navy

Private **Thomas Alexander Keith**
10th Battalion Canadian Infantry (Alberta Regiment)

Lieutenant **William David Kenny VC**
4th Battalion 39th Garhwal Rifles

James Majury
Donaghadee Parish Church of Ireland

Donaghadee and District continued...

Private **Alexander Martin**
Auckland Regiment NZEF

Private **Robert Matear**
Wellington Regiment NZEF

Lance Corporal **James McCann**
1st Battalion Royal Inniskilling Fusiliers

Private **Alexander McClean**
2nd Battalion Otago Regiment NZEF

Rifleman **David McConnell**
13th Battalion Royal Irish Rifles

Rifleman **Joseph McConnell**
12th Battalion Royal Irish Rifles

Rifleman **Robert McConnell**
13th Battalion Royal Irish Rifles

Robert McConnell
Newtownards Chronicle

Rifleman **James Morrison McCready**
12th Battalion Royal Irish Rifles

Rifleman **James McCullough**
8th Battalion attached 17th Battalion Royal Irish Rifles

Rifleman **James McCullough**
2nd Battalion Royal Irish Rifles

Rifleman **John McCullough**
Shore Street Presbyterian Church Donaghadee

Rifleman **Daniel McCutcheon**
13th Battalion Royal Irish Rifles

Private **James McGaffin**
1st Canadian Mounted Rifles Battalion

Private **Robert Sloane McGaffin**
1st Canadian Mounted Rifles Battalion

Donaghadee and District continued…

Rifleman **Robert McKibbin**
13th Battalion Royal Irish Rifles

Company Sergeant Major **Francis McMath**
122nd Field Company Royal Engineers 36th (Ulster) Division

Gunner **Daniel McNeice**
Royal Garrison Artillery

Rifleman **Andrew McWilliams**
1st Battalion Royal Irish Rifles

Private **William John Melville**
10th Battalion Royal Inniskilling Fusiliers

Rifleman **Joseph Miskimmin**
2nd Battalion Royal Irish Rifles

Private **Catherwood Moore**
2nd Battalion Royal Scots Fusiliers

Horseman **Hugh Muckle**
SS *Cabotia* (Glasgow) Mercantile Marine

Rifleman **Joseph Oswald**
8th Battalion Royal Irish Rifles

Rifleman **Thomas McBride Patton**
6th Battalion Royal Irish Rifles

Rifleman **William Patton**
13th Battalion Royal Irish Rifles

Lance Corporal **James Stevenson Poag**
2nd Battalion Royal Irish Rifles

Rifleman **Charles Pollock**
2nd Battalion Royal Irish Rifles

Private **James Pollock**
9th Battalion Princess Victoria's (Royal Irish Fusiliers)

Chief Stoker **William John Reains**
HMS *Vivid* Royal Navy

Donaghadee and District continued...

Private **Thomas Reilly**
13th Battalion Australian Infantry AIF

Rifleman **James Robinson**
12th Battalion Royal Irish Rifles

Rifleman **Robert Robinson**
13th Battalion Royal Irish Rifles

Rifleman **Samuel Robinson**
12th Battalion Royal Irish Rifles

Private **William Robinson**
2nd Battalion Seaforth Highlanders

Private **Robert Saunders**
1st/10th Battalion Manchester Regiment

Rifleman **Robert James Semple**
13th Battalion Royal Irish Rifles

Rifleman **William Semple**
11th Battalion Royal Irish Rifles

Rifleman **William Semple**
13th Battalion Royal Irish Rifles

Able Seaman **James Skilling**
SS *Garron Head* (Belfast) Mercantile Marine

Rifleman **Robert Stewart**
13th Battalion Royal Irish Rifles

Private **Robert Stewart**
108th Battalion Machine Gun Corps (Infantry) 36th (Ulster) Division

Private **Robert Stewart**
2nd Battalion Royal Inniskilling Fusiliers

Rifleman **Robert D Stewart**
Donaghadee and District War Memorial

Rifleman **Samuel Strain**
13th Battalion Royal Irish Rifles

Donaghadee and District continued…

Rifleman **William Tanner**
8th Battalion Royal Irish Rifles

Rifleman **Hugh Tate**
8th Battalion Royal Irish Rifles

Sergeant **Samuel Taylor**
2nd Battalion Canadian Mounted Rifles

Rifleman **William Robert Taylor**
13th Battalion Royal Irish Rifles

Rifleman **Charles Thompson**
13th Battalion Royal Irish Rifles

Corporal **John Thompson**
13th Battalion Royal Irish Rifles

Lance Corporal **Henry Edward Victor**
2nd Battalion Middlesex Regiment

Rifleman **John Waring**
11th Battalion Royal Irish Rifles

Second Lieutenant **John Stanley Williamson**
1st Battalion Lancashire Fusiliers

GREYABBEY AND DISTRICT

Rifleman **James Armour**
22nd Entrenching Battalion late 11th/13th Battalion Royal Irish Rifles

Private **James Bell**
2nd Battalion Argyll & Sutherland Highlanders

Rifleman **George Birney**
13th & 12th Battalions Royal Irish Rifles

Private **Joseph Craig**
2nd Battalion Canadian Infantry (Eastern Ontario Regiment)

Corporal **William Francis Cumming**
1st Battalion Royal Scots Fusiliers

Greyabbey and District continued…

Lieutenant Colonel **Charles William Reginald Duncombe**
21st Battalion King's Royal Rifle Corps

Private **James Hamilton**
58th Battalion Canadian Infantry (Central Ontario Regiment)

Private **Ernest Ludgate Hill**
26th Battalion Australian Infantry AIF

Lance Corporal **James Holland**
8th Battalion King's Royal Rifle Corps

Captain **Henry Cooke Lowry**
Army Veterinary Corps

Company Sergeant Major **Hugh McCallum**
12th Battalion Royal Irish Rifles

Private **James McGimpsey**
9th Battalion Royal Scots

Rifleman **Robert McKay**
12th Battalion Royal Irish Rifles

Rifleman **William Ravey**
8th Battalion Royal Irish Rifles

Rifleman **Robert Regan**
12th Battalion Royal Irish Rifles

KILLINCHY AND DISTRICT

Rifleman **James Calvert**
13th Battalion Royal Irish Rifles

Rifleman **William James Calvert**
13th Battalion Royal Irish Rifles

John Campbell
Killinchy Parish Church of Ireland

Rifleman **David Cromie**
8th Battalion Royal Irish Rifles

Killinchy and District continued…

Lance Corporal **William John Cromie**
13th Battalion Royal Irish Rifles

Rifleman **John Dynes**
9th Battalion Royal Irish Rifles

Lance Corporal **Robert Fitzsimons**
2nd Battalion Royal Irish Rifles

Captain **Archibald H Hamilton**
13th Battalion Royal Irish Rifles

Private **Robert Hewitt**
44th Battalion Canadian Infantry (New Brunswick Regiment)

Rifleman **Thomas Martin Horner**
8th Battalion Royal Irish Rifles

Corporal **Gerald Marcus Huston DCM**
7th Division Signal Company Royal Engineers

Stephen Johnston
Killinchy Parish Church of Ireland

Private **Andrew Lowry**
8th Battalion Royal Scots Fusiliers

Private **Andrew Lyttle**
5th Battalion Canadian Infantry (Saskatchewan Regiment)

Rifleman **Robert McClements**
8th Battalion Royal Irish Rifles

Private **Hugh McGreevy**
6th Battalion Royal Irish Regiment

Private **Patrick McGreevy**
6th Battalion Royal Inniskilling Fusiliers

Rifleman **Thomas McMullan**
15th Battalion Royal Irish Rifles

Sergeant **Samuel George Miskimmin**
108th Company Machine Gun Corps (Infantry) 36th (Ulster) Division

Killinchy and District continued…

Private William Savage Montgomery
29th Battalion Canadian Infantry (British Columbia Regiment)

Rifleman Henry Quigley MM (and Bar)
2nd Battalion Royal Irish Rifles

Lance Corporal Francis Michael Ritchie
9th Battalion Royal Inniskilling Fusiliers

Driver Robert Davidson Robinson
1st Siege Battery Ammunitions Column Australian Army Service Corps AIF

Rifleman Frew Shaw
Royal Irish Rifles

Rifleman William John Stevenson Snodden
13th Battalion Royal Irish Rifles

Sergeant James Tate
13th Battalion Royal Irish Rifles

John Thompson
Killinchy Parish Church of Ireland

Private Robert Thompson
108th Company Machine Gun Corps 36th (Ulster) Division

Rifleman William Wilson
13th Battalion Royal Irish Rifles

KIRCUBBIN AND DISTRICT

Lance Corporal Thomas John Ballance
13th Battalion Royal Irish Rifles

Rifleman William Bell
13th Battalion Royal Irish Rifles

Lieutenant William Angus Browne
53rd Squadron Royal Flying Corps

Robert Close
Kircubbin Parish Church of Ireland

Kircubbin and District continued...

Private **Patrick Docherty**
2nd Battalion Royal Scots Fusiliers

Private **John Donnan**
7th/8th Battalion Princess Victoria's (Royal Irish Fusiliers)

Private **William Donnan**
46th Battalion Canadian Infantry (Saskatchewan Regiment)

Lieutenant **Frederick St John Ford North Echlin**
70th Squadron Royal Flying Corps and Royal Fusiliers

Rifleman **John Ralston Fitzsimmons**
13th Battalion Royal Irish Rifles

Private **William James Johnston**
9th Battalion Princess Victoria's (Royal Irish Fusiliers)

Private **John McBride**
1st Battalion Scots Guards

Rifleman **Alexander McClelland**
4th Battalion Royal Irish Rifles

Seaman **John McClement**
Kircubbin Presbyterian Church Graveyard

Private **John McDonnell**
24th Battalion Canadian Infantry (Quebec Regiment)

Rifleman **David McMaster**
13th Battalion Royal Irish Rifles

Rifleman **John Milligan**
12th Battalion Royal Irish Rifles

Second Corporal **Dennis de Courcey Shaw**
'M' Depot Company Royal Engineers

Second Lieutenant **James Rowan Shaw**
9th Battalion Cheshire Regiment

Major **William Maxwell Shaw DSO MID**
102nd Brigade Royal Field Artillery

Kircubbin and District continued…

Rifleman **John Sinclair**
13th Battalion Royal Irish Rifles

Rifleman **James Stewart**
12th Battalion Royal Irish Rifles

Private **William Stratton**
2nd Battalion Canadian Infantry (Eastern Ontario Regiment)

Rifleman **James Thompson**
13th Battalion Royal Irish Rifles

Adam White
Kircubbin Parish Church of Ireland

Private **William Woods**
2nd Battalion Loyal North Lancashire Regiment

MILLISLE AND DISTRICT

Corporal **James Charles Burrows**
13th Battalion Royal Irish Rifles transferred to Labour Corps

Private **James Arthur Drennan**
1st Battalion Princess Victoria's (Royal Irish Fusiliers)

Greaser **James Jamison**
RMS *Redbreast* Mercantile Marine Reserve

Lieutenant **George B Keeling**
Royal Indian Marine

Rifleman **Robert McGimpsey**
14th Battalion Royal Irish Rifles

Driver **Hugh Andrew McKee**
3rd Company (Bradford) Army Service Corps

Sergeant **James McKee**
8th Battalion Canadian Infantry (Manitoba Regiment)

Lance Corporal **Thomas Gray Mellefont**
2nd Battalion Royal Irish Rifles

NEWTOWNARDS AND DISTRICT

Private **Edward Adair**
10th Battalion Royal Inniskilling Fusiliers

James Adair
Newtownards and District War Memorial

James Algie
Newtownards and District War Memorial

Able Seaman **Robert Algie**
HMS *Hawke* Royal Navy

Second Lieutenant **Hugh Charles Allen DCM**
1st/7th (Fife) Battalion (Territorial) Black Watch (Royal Highlanders)

Rifleman **Robert Hugh Allen**
13th Battalion Royal Irish Rifles

William J Allen
Newtownards and District War Memorial

Captain **Bertram Allgood**
1st Battalion Royal Irish Rifles

Rifleman **William Anderson**
1st Battalion Royal Irish Rifles

Private **Jonathan Ardill MID**
7th (South Irish Horse) Battalion Royal Irish Regiment

William Auld
Newtownards and District War Memorial

Private **Alexander Beattie**
9th Battalion Princess Victoria's (Royal Irish Fusiliers)

Private **James Davidson Beck**
Otago Regiment NZEF

David Bell
Newtownards and District War Memorial

Trooper **Herbert Alexander Bell**
10th Australian Light Horse Regiment AIF

Newtownards and District continued…

William Bell
Newtownards and District War Memorial

Rifleman **William Robert Bell**
1st Battalion Royal Irish Rifles

David Bennett
Durham Light Infantry

Corporal **Edward Bennett**
13th Battalion Royal Irish Rifles

Private **Hamilton Bennett**
213th Company Machine Gun Corps (Infantry)

Private **James Best**
2nd Battalion Scots Guards

Private **Thomas Best**
2nd Battalion Scots Guards

Rifleman **Thomas Blackadder**
9th Battalion Royal Irish Rifles

Sergeant **Alfred Blythe**
13th Battalion Royal Irish Rifles

Private **William Boal (served as William McHugh)**
1st Battalion Scots Guards

Rifleman **Alexander Boland**
10th Battalion Royal Irish Rifles

Private **Richard Boucher**
1st Battalion Royal Inniskilling Fusiliers

Rifleman **James Bowman**
8th Battalion Royal Irish Rifles

Quartermaster Sergeant **Andrew Boyd**
Canadian Military Authorities

Private **John Boyd**
47th Battalion Canadian Infantry (Western Ontario Regiment)

Newtownards and District continued…

Samuel Boyd
Newtownards and District War Memorial

Rifleman William Boyd
1st Battalion Royal Irish Rifles

Sergeant George Brankin
14th Battalion Royal Irish Rifles

James Brankin
Newtownards and District War Memorial

Private James McGilton Brett
13th Battalion Machine Gun Corps

Rifleman Arthur Rickwood Broderick
3rd Battalion Royal Irish Rifles

Hugh Brown
Newtownards and District War Memorial

Rifleman James Brown
2nd Battalion Royal Irish Rifles

Company Sergeant Major Martin Brown
17th Battalion Royal Irish Rifles

Rifleman Robert Buckley
11th Battalion Royal Irish Rifles

Rifleman George Burns
13th Battalion Royal Irish Rifles

Rifleman James Burns
Depot Royal Irish Rifles

Joseph Burns
Newtownards and District War Memorial

Lance Corporal Valentine Cairnduff
2nd Battalion Royal Inniskilling Fusiliers

Private Archibald Cairns
3rd Battalion Royal Inniskilling Fusiliers

Newtownards and District continued…

William John Cairns
Newtownards and District War Memorial

Rifleman **Thomas Calderwood**
13th Battalion Royal Irish Rifles

Rifleman **Archibald Thomas Campbell**
13th Battalion Royal Irish Rifles

Henry Campbell
Newtownards and District War Memorial

Company Sergeant Major **James Campbell**
7th Battalion Royal Irish Rifles

Gunner **James Campbell**
91st Heavy Battery Royal Garrison Artillery

Rifleman **John Campbell**
14th Battalion Royal Irish Rifles

Patrick Campbell
Newtownards and District War Memorial

William Campbell
Newtownards and District War Memorial

Lance Corporal **James Cardy**
6th Battalion Royal Irish Rifles

Rifleman **William Cardy**
2nd Battalion Royal Irish Rifles

Rifleman **Alexander Carlisle**
9th Battalion Royal Irish Rifles

Rifleman **James Carnduff**
1st Battalion Royal Irish Rifles

Rifleman **Robert Carnduff**
13th and 12th Battalions Royal Irish Rifles

Rifleman **Samuel Carnduff**
13th Battalion Royal Irish Rifles

Newtownards and District continued…

Private **James Carser**
6th (City of Glasgow) Battalion Highland Light Infantry

George Carson
Newtownards and District War Memorial

Lance Corporal **William James Caughey**
2nd Battalion Royal Scots Fusiliers

Rifleman **George Chambers**
2nd Battalion Royal Irish Rifles

Regimental Sergeant Major **Charles James Cherry**
1st Battalion Manchester Regiment

Lieutenant **Francis Cinnamond**
2nd Battalion Royal Inniskilling Fusiliers

William Clarke
Newtownards and District War Memorial

Lance Sergeant **James Clegg**
1st/6th Battalion North Staffordshire Regiment

Company Sergeant Major **David Condon**
Labour Corps

Private **Collins Alexander Cooke**
4th Battalion Canadian Mounted Rifles

Private **David Greer Cooke**
2nd Battalion Canadian Mounted Rifles

Private **William Cooper**
9th Battalion Border Regiment

Rifleman **Robert John Corry**
2nd Battalion and Depot Royal Irish Rifles

Rifleman **Thomas Corry**
8th Battalion Royal Irish Rifles

Lance Corporal **Joseph Croan**
1st/5th Battalion Seaforth Highlanders

Newtownards and District continued…

Joseph Crooks (MM unsubstantiated to date)
Newtownards and District War Memorial

Able Seaman Samuel Crooks
HMS *Thunderer* Royal Navy

Hugh Crowe
Newtownards and District War Memorial

Colour Sergeant John Isaac Cutler LS&GC
2nd (Garrison) Battalion Princess Victoria's (Royal Irish Fusiliers)

Private Patrick Daly
1st Battalion Irish Guards

Private Hugh Dalzell
9th Battalion Princess Victoria's (Royal Irish Fusiliers)

Private William John Dalzell
9th Battalion Royal Inniskilling Fusiliers

Lieutenant Robert Davison MC
12th Battalion King's (Liverpool Regiment)

Private Thomas Devlin
2nd Battalion Royal Irish Regiment

Sergeant Samuel DeVoy
13th Battalion Royal Irish Rifles

Rifleman John Dickson
12th Battalion Royal Irish Rifles

Rifleman Alexander Dines
1st Battalion Royal Irish Rifles attached 25th Light Trench Mortar Battery

Rifleman Thomas Dines
2nd Battalion Royal Irish Rifles

Private Redmond Joseph Diver (served as Albert Wheeler)
1st Battalion Black Watch (Royal Highlanders)

Rifleman Alexander Doggart
2nd Battalion Royal Irish Rifles

Newtownards and District continued…

Corporal **James Neil Doggart**
1st Battalion Royal Inniskilling Fusiliers

Rifleman **Thomas Maddock Doggart**
13th Battalion Royal Irish Rifles

Sergeant **William John Doherty LS&GC**
1st Battalion Royal Irish Rifles

Private **Adam Donaldson**
228th Company Machine Gun Corps (Infantry)

Private **John Dornan**
2nd Battalion Royal Inniskilling Fusiliers

Lance Corporal **James Dorrian**
13th Battalion Royal Irish Rifles

Rifleman **John Dorrian**
13th Battalion Royal Irish Rifles

Thomas Dorrian
Newtownards and District War Memorial

Rifleman **Thomas Dowdell**
3rd Battalion Royal Irish Rifles

Private **James Downes**
4th Battalion Canadian Infantry (Central Ontario Regiment)

Alfred Fenton
Newtownards and District War Memorial

Lance Corporal **Samuel Esler Fenton**
12th Battalion Royal Irish Rifles

Petty Officer **Hugh Ferguson**
Royal Navy

Company Sergeant Major **David Ferris LS&GC MID**
2nd Battalion Royal Irish Rifles

Captain **John William Field**
1st Battalion Royal Irish Rifles

Newtownards and District continued…

Rifleman **Robert Finlay**
8th Battalion Royal Irish Rifles

Rifleman **James Fisher**
1st Battalion Royal Irish Rifles

Sergeant **Henry Foster**
9th Battalion Royal Irish Rifles

Rifleman **John Foster**
2nd Battalion Royal Irish Rifles

Rifleman **William John Fowles**
13th Battalion Royal Irish Rifles

Private **William Francis**
2nd Battalion Royal Inniskilling Fusiliers

Rifleman **William Fryers**
2nd Battalion Royal Irish Rifles

Rifleman **John Fullerton**
14th Battalion Royal Irish Rifles

Boy First Class **Alfred Henry Victor Gadd**
HMS *Goliath* Royal Navy

Private **David Gamble**
1st Battalion Princess Victoria's (Royal Irish Fusiliers)

Driver **Alexander Gibson**
121st Field Company Royal Engineers 36th (Ulster) Division

Rifleman **Alexander Gibson**
1st Battalion Royal Irish Rifles

Rifleman **William James Gibson**
13th Battalion Royal Irish Rifles

Rifleman **Thomas Gilliland**
13th Battalion Royal Irish Rifles

Private **Patrick Gilmore**
8th Battalion Royal Dublin Fusiliers

Newtownards and District continued...

Private Samuel Gilmour
1st Battalion Royal Irish Rifles transferred to 194th Company Labour Corps

Thomas Girvin
Newtownards and District War Memorial

Rifleman **Thomas Glendinning**
3rd Battalion Royal Irish Rifles

Rifleman **Samuel Heslip Gordon**
13th Battalion Royal Irish Rifles

Rifleman **Charles Gorman**
1st Battalion Royal Irish Rifles

Private **James Gorman**
8th Battalion Cameronians (Scottish Rifles)

Private **Samuel Gourley**
25th Battalion Australian Infantry AIF

A Gracey
Newtownards Chronicle Roll of Sacrifice 6 January 1917

Sergeant **John Gracie**
1st Battalion Royal Irish Rifles

Rifleman **James Graham**
12th Battalion Royal Irish Rifles transferred to 311th Home Service Works
Company Labour Corps

Lance Corporal **Samuel John Gregg**
10th Battalion Royal Irish Rifles

Lance Corporal **James Gregory MM**
'C' Squadron 4th (Queen's Own) Hussars

Thomas Griffiths
Newtownards and District War Memorial

Rifleman **William Gunning**
13th Battalion Royal Irish Rifles

Private **Francis Haire**
1st Canadian Mounted Rifles Battalion

Newtownards and District continued…

Private **John Hall**
9th Battalion Royal Inniskilling Fusiliers

Rifleman **Alexander Hamill**
13th Battalion Royal Irish Rifles

Private **Patrick Hamill**
6th Battalion Princess Victoria's (Royal Irish Fusiliers)

Sergeant **George Hamilton**
1st Garrison Battalion Princess Victoria's (Royal Irish Fusiliers)

Private **John Hanna**
1st Battalion Royal Dublin Fusiliers

Lance Corporal **Thomas Harris**
1st Battalion Connaught Rangers

Lance Sergeant **Robert Bell Harrison**
1st Battalion Irish Guards

Rifleman **Thomas James Harrison MM**
13th Battalion Royal Irish Rifles

Private **David Harvey**
1st/5th Battalion Seaforth Highlanders

Rifleman **John Harvey**
13th Battalion Royal Irish Rifles

Rifleman **Robert Harvey**
18th Battalion Royal Irish Rifles transferred to Labour Corps

Rifleman **Albert Hawthorne**
12th Battalion Royal Irish Rifles

Rifleman **Robert Heaney**
London Regiment Royal Irish Rifles

Rifleman **Robert Henderson**
2nd Battalion Royal Irish Rifles

Private **Vincent Hendley**
7th/8th Battalion Princess Victoria's (Royal Irish Fusiliers)

Newtownards and District continued…

Sergeant Andrew Heron
4th Battalion Royal Irish Rifles

Rifleman James Heron
2nd Battalion Royal Irish Rifles

Driver Hugh Crouch Houston
64th Brigade Royal Field Artillery

Rifleman William Hurley
2nd Battalion Royal Irish Rifles

Sapper James Hutton
150th Field Company Royal Engineers 36th (Ulster) Division

Lance Corporal James Irvine
7th/8th Battalion King's Own Scottish Borderers

Rifleman John Irvine
2nd Battalion Royal Irish Rifles

Lance Corporal Robert Russell Irvine
7th Battalion Royal Irish Rifles

Rifleman James Mackenzie Irwin
2nd Battalion Royal Irish Rifles

Rifleman George Jamison
1st Battalion Royal Irish Rifles

Rifleman William John Jamison (served as William John Armour)
2nd Battalion Royal Irish Rifles

Rifleman Alfred Johnston
1st Battalion Royal Irish Rifles

Private Andrew Johnston
9th Battalion Princess Victoria's (Royal Irish Fusiliers)

Captain Elliott Johnston MC
13th Battalion Royal Irish Rifles

Rifleman Robert Johnston (Jnr)
1st Battalion Royal Irish Rifles

Newtownards and District continued...

Lance Corporal **Robert Johnston (Snr)**
1st Battalion Royal Irish Rifles

Private **William Johnston**
9th Battalion Royal Inniskilling Fusiliers

Rifleman **James Jones**
8th Battalion Royal Irish Rifles

Rifleman **Robert Kane**
12th Battalion Royal Irish Rifles

Rifleman **David John Keilty**
2nd Battalion Royal Irish Rifles

Private **Daniel Maclean Keith**
1st Battalion Royal Scots Fusiliers

Rifleman **Edward John Kelly**
1st Battalion Royal Irish Rifles

Sergeant **James Armstrong Kelly DCM**
7th Service Battalion Royal Inniskilling Fusiliers

Rifleman **William George Kelly**
13th Battalion Royal Irish Rifles

Robert Kemp
Newtownards and District War Memorial

Rifleman **John Kennedy**
1st Battalion Royal Irish Rifles

Rifleman **John Kennedy**
8th Battalion Royal Irish Rifles

Rifleman **Samuel Kennedy**
8th Battalion Royal Irish Rifles

Private **Andrew Kerr**
1st/4th Battalion Royal Scots Fusiliers

Lance Corporal **Hugh Kerr**
Depot Company Royal Engineers 36th (Ulster) Division

Newtownards and District continued…

Private **John Kinnaird**
4th Battalion Australian Infantry AIF

Second Lieutenant **George Knox**
8th Battalion King's Own (Royal Lancaster Regiment)

Lance Corporal **David Lamont**
9th Battalion Royal Inniskilling Fusiliers

Lance Corporal **Sidney Lane**
1st Battalion Irish Guards

Second Lieutenant **Joseph Laverty**
13th Battalion Royal Irish Rifles

Hugh Lawson
Newtownards and District War Memorial

Rifleman **John Ledgerwood**
9th Battalion Royal Irish Rifles

Rifleman **Samuel Hugh Ledgerwood**
13th Battalion Royal Irish Rifles

Private **Robert Lennon**
2nd Battalion South Wales Borderers

Private **Robert John Lightbody**
1st Battalion Royal Inniskilling Fusiliers

Private **Samuel Logan**
2nd Battalion Royal Inniskilling Fusiliers

Rifleman **Robert Lowry**
13th Battalion Royal Irish Rifles

Rifleman **James Glover Mackey**
2nd Battalion Royal Irish Rifles

Lance Corporal **Herbert Henry MacMahon**
10th Battalion Royal Dublin Fusiliers

Private **William Maddock**
7th Battalion Highland Light Infantry

Newtownards and District continued…

Lance Corporal George Mahaffy
13th Battalion Royal Irish Rifles

Private John Maidens MM
1st Battalion Princess Victoria's (Royal Irish Fusiliers)

Rifleman William John Majury
2nd Battalion Royal Irish Rifles

George Mallon
Newtownards and District War Memorial

Lance Corporal Hector Claude Marsh
2nd Battalion Royal Irish Rifles

Rifleman Andrew Marshall
11th Battalion Royal Irish Rifles

Private Robert Marshall
1st Battalion Royal Inniskilling Fusiliers

Private James Martin
8th Battalion Royal Inniskilling Fusiliers

Rifleman John Martin
1st Battalion formerly 4th Battalion Royal Irish Rifles

Sergeant Richard Henry Martin
2nd Battalion Royal Irish Rifles

Private William Martin
24th Battalion Canadian Infantry (Quebec Regiment)

Rifleman Thompson Mathers
2nd Battalion Royal Irish Rifles

Corporal Daniel Matier
1st Battalion Royal Irish Rifles

Private Andrew McCutcheon Mayne
2nd Battalion Rhodesia Regiment

Corporal Francis McAlpine
126th Siege Battery Royal Garrison Artillery

Newtownards and District continued...

Private **George Turner McAlpine**
4th Regiment South African Infantry

Rifleman **Edward Ferguson McCalpin McAvoy**
13th Battalion Royal Irish Rifles

Rifleman **John Magilton McAvoy**
13th Battalion Royal Irish Rifles

Private **James McBlain**
1st Battalion Gordon Highlanders

Rifleman **William McBride**
13th Battalion Royal Irish Rifles

Private **William Thomas McBride**
37th Company Machine Gun Corps (Infantry)

Rifleman **James McCandless**
2nd Battalion Royal Irish Rifles

Lance Corporal **Frederick McCann**
15th Battalion Australian Infantry AIF

Corporal **Thomas McCann**
9th Battalion Royal Inniskilling Fusiliers

John McCartan
Newtownards and District War Memorial

Rifleman **Robert McCartney**
13th Battalion Royal Irish Rifles

Rifleman **John McChesney**
13th Battalion Royal Irish Rifles

Rifleman **James McClelland**
2nd Battalion Royal Irish Rifles

Rifleman **Hugh McClure**
13th Battalion Royal Irish Rifles

James McClure
Newtownards and District War Memorial

Newtownards and District continued…

Petty Officer **Joseph McClure**
Royal Navy

Rifleman **David McConnell**
13th Battalion Royal Irish Rifles

Hugh McConnell
PCI Roll of Honour Second Newtownards Presbyterian Church

Lance Corporal **William James McCoy**
13th Battalion Royal Irish Rifles

Lance Corporal **John McCracken**
13th Battalion Royal Irish Rifles

John McCready
Newtownards and District War Memorial

Private **Hugh McCullough**
5th Battalion Cameron Highlanders

Private **James McCully**
1st/5th Battalion Yorkshire Regiment

Private **James McCutcheon**
New Zealand Rifle Brigade NZEF

John McDonagh
Newtownards and District War Memorial

Rifleman **Andrew McDonald**
9th Battalion Rifle Brigade

Farrier Sergeant **Robert McDonald**
18th Div Artillery Royal Field Artillery

Private **Alexander McDowell**
1st/6th Battalion King's (Liverpool Regiment)

Rifleman **Joseph McDowell**
7th Battalion Royal Irish Rifles

Lance Corporal **William McDowell**
1st Battalion Royal Irish Rifles

Newtownards and District continued...

Rifleman **James McGimpsey**
11th Battalion Royal Irish Rifles

Private **James Campbell McGimpsey**
8th Battalion Canadian Infantry (Manitoba Regiment)

Thomas McGimpsey
Newtownards and District War Memorial

Rifleman **Hugh McGinn**
2nd Battalion Royal Irish Rifles

Lance Corporal **Robert James McGreechan**
2nd Battalion Royal Irish Rifles

Lieutenant **Alexander McKee**
10th Battalion Royal Irish Rifles

Lance Corporal **John McKee**
1st Battalion Royal Irish Rifles

Rifleman **Frederick McKee**
14th Battalion Royal Irish Rifles

Lance Corporal **Robert McKee**
2nd Battalion Royal Irish Rifles

Samuel McKendry
Newtownards and District War Memorial

John McKenna
Newtownards and District War Memorial

Sapper **Arthur McKeown**
63rd Field Company Royal Engineers

Rifleman **Charles McKeown**
6th Battalion Royal Irish Rifles

Rifleman **Hamilton McKibben**
2nd Battalion Royal Irish Rifles

Corporal **John Hill McKibbin**
1st Battalion Royal Irish Rifles

Newtownards and District continued...

David McKimm
Newtownards and District War Memorial

Private James McKimm
52nd M.T. Company Army Service Corps

Rifleman Robert McKimm
Royal Irish Rifles

Private David McKittrick
44th Battalion Canadian Infantry (New Brunswick Regiment)

Rifleman William McKittrick
13th Battalion Royal Irish Rifles

George McKnight
Newtownards and District War Memorial

Private William McLaughlin
1st South African Mounted Brigade

Private Hugh Charles Hutchinson McLean
1st/8th Battalion Argyll & Sutherland Highlanders

Rifleman Duncan McLean
13th Battalion Royal Irish Rifles

Private David H McMillan (MM unsubstantiated to date)
2nd Battalion Royal Dublin Fusiliers

Private John McMillan
19th Battalion Canadian Infantry (Central Ontario Regiment)

Private Michael McMillan
8th Battalion Machine Gun Corps (Infantry)

Private Robert Watson McMillan
19th Battalion Canadian Infantry (Central Ontario Regiment)

Rifleman Samuel McMillan
8th Battalion Royal Irish Rifles

Patrick McMullan
Newtownards and District War Memorial

Newtownards and District continued…

William McMullan
Newtownards and District War Memorial

Lance Corporal James McNeilly
13th Battalion Royal Irish Rifles

Rifleman John McPhillips
2nd Battalion Royal Irish Rifles

Rifleman William McQuiston
13th Battalion Royal Irish Rifles

Andrew McTaggart
Newtownards and District War Memorial

Rifleman Thomas McTaggart
4th Battalion Royal Irish Rifles

Private Hugh McTear
1st Battalion Highland Light Infantry

Private Hamilton McWhinney
6th Battalion Princess Victoria's (Royal Irish Fusiliers)

Private (Bugler) William John McWhinney
1st Battalion Royal Irish Rifles

Company Sergeant Major Wilfred Harold Medland
9th Battalion Princess Victoria's (Royal Irish Fusiliers)

Rifleman Thomas Millar
12th Battalion Royal Irish Rifles

Rifleman William Thomas Miller
8th Battalion Royal Irish Rifles

Rifleman Samuel Miskelly
8th Battalion Royal Irish Rifles

James Monks
Newtownards and District War Memorial

Rifleman James Montgomery
9th Battalion 421st Agricultural Company Labour Corps

Newtownards and District continued…

Private William Montgomery
6th Battalion King's Own Scottish Borderers

Rifleman Edward Mooney
14th Battalion Royal Irish Rifles

Corporal Hamilton Moore
1st Garrison Battalion Royal Irish Rifles

Private Hugh Moore
46th Battalion Canadian Infantry (Saskatchewan Regiment)

Second Lieutenant John Ross Moore
3rd Battalion Connaught Rangers (attached 7th Bn Royal Inniskilling Fusiliers)

Second Lieutenant William Moore
10th Battalion Princess Victoria's (Royal Irish Fusiliers)

Lance Corporal William Moore
6th Battalion Royal Irish Rifles

Private Patrick Moore (served as McConnell)
1st/8th Battalion Durham Light Infantry

Lieutenant John Joseph Leo Morgan MID
2nd Battalion Royal Inniskilling Fusiliers

Lieutenant Samuel Valentine Morgan LS&GC
2nd Battalion Royal Irish Rifles

Private William Morris
1st Battalion Royal Inniskilling Fusiliers

Sapper Robert Morrison
134th Army Troops Company Royal Engineers

Walter Morrison
Newtownards and District War Memorial

Private George Morrow
9th Battalion Princess Victoria's (Royal Irish Fusiliers)

Acting Bombardier George Ellison Mulholland
15th Heavy Battery Royal Garrison Artillery

Newtownards and District continued…

Private **Walter Mulholland**
1st Battalion Royal Inniskilling Fusiliers

Lance Sergeant **James Mullan**
2nd Battalion Royal Irish Rifles

Rifleman **David Swan Mullan**
13th Battalion Royal Irish Rifles

Private **Hugh Mullan**
11th Battalion Royal Scots Fusiliers

Rifleman **Patrick Mullen**
1st Battalion Royal Irish Rifles

Private **Joseph Murphy**
8th Battalion Royal Dublin Fusiliers

Lance Corporal **Henry Alan Murray**
12th Battalion Royal Irish Rifles

Private **Joseph Murray**
6th Battalion Connaught Rangers

Rifleman **Samuel Murray**
14th Battalion Royal Irish Rifles

James Neill
Newtownards and District War Memorial

Lance Corporal **Samuel Horace Nelson**
18th Battalion Manchester Regiment

Rifleman (Bandsman) **Charles Newell**
13th Battalion Royal Irish Rifles

Rifleman (Bandsman) **Thomas Newell**
11th Battalion Royal Irish Rifles

Private **Archibald Nisbet**
3rd Battalion Highland Light Infantry

Private **Thomas Norris**
9th Battalion Royal Inniskilling Fusiliers

Newtownards and District continued…

Captain Robert James O'Lone MID
2nd Battalion Royal Irish Rifles

Captain Walter Percy O'Lone DCM MID
2nd Battalion Royal Irish Rifles

Corporal John O'Neill
13th Battalion Royal Irish Rifles

Private William O'Neill
2nd Battalion King's Own Scottish Borderers

Fireman William Oliver
HMS *Mechanician* Mercantile Marine Reserve

Rifleman Hamilton Orr (James Street)
1st Battalion Royal Irish Rifles

Captain Hamilton Orr MID (North Street)
Royal Irish Rifles

Rifleman Robert Orr
Royal Irish Rifles

Lance Corporal Gilbert Paden
12th Battalion Royal Irish Rifles

Rifleman Alexander Pagan
11th Battalion Royal Irish Rifles

Rifleman Alexander Palmer
15th Battalion Royal Irish Rifles

Robert Palmer
Newtownards and District War Memorial

Lance Corporal Henry J Parfitt
7th Battalion Rifle Brigade

Corporal Leonard Edward John Parker
13th Battalion Royal Irish Rifles

Rifleman Frederick Parkes
1st Battalion Royal Irish Rifles

Newtownards and District continued…

Rifleman James Parkhill
12th Battalion Royal Irish Rifles

Private James Paton
1st/4th Battalion Royal Scots Fusiliers

Rifleman David Bell Patterson
13th Battalion Royal Irish Rifles

Corporal William James Patterson
13th Battalion Royal Irish Rifles

Driver Samuel Forbes Patton
8th Battery 2nd Brigade New Zealand Field Artillery NZEF

Private Thomas Patton
20th Battalion Canadian Infantry (Central Ontario Regiment)

Lieutenant John Luddington Peacock
150th Field Company Royal Engineers 36th (Ulster) Division

Charles Pegg
Newtownards and District War Memorial

Private John Pollock
8th Battalion Royal Irish Regiment

Robert James Poole
Royal Irish Rifles transferred to Labour Corps

Rifleman William Haire Poole
13th Battalion Royal Irish Rifles

Rifleman James Porter
13th Battalion Royal Irish Rifles

Rifleman Joseph Porter
9th Battalion Royal Irish Rifles

Lance Corporal James Henry Quail
12th Battalion Royal Irish Rifles

Private Charles Henry Quigley
14th Battalion Highland Light Infantry

Newtownards and District continued…

Corporal **John Patrick Quinn**
1st Battalion Royal Irish Rifles

Rifleman **Thomas Quinn**
8th Battalion Royal Irish Rifles

Private **Richard Rae**
12th Battalion Royal Scots

Corporal **Robert Boyd Rainey**
9th Battalion Royal Inniskilling Fusiliers

Corporal **Daniel Rea**
10th Battalion Hampshire Regiment

Rifleman **William Regan**
10th Battalion Royal Irish Rifles

W Regan
Newtownards Parish Church of Ireland

Private **Samuel James Reid**
1st Battalion Royal Inniskilling Fusiliers

Junior Second Engineer Officer **Alfred James Rice**
SS *Hungerford* (London) Mercantile Marine

Captain **Mervyn Stronge Richardson MID**
1st Battalion Royal Welsh Fusiliers

Private **James Henry Rilley**
Royal Irish Regiment transferred to 183rd Company Labour Corps

Private **Samuel Ritchie**
2nd Battalion Royal Inniskilling Fusiliers

Rifleman **Alexander Robinson**
13th Battalion Royal Irish Rifles

Rifleman **David Robinson**
2nd Battalion Royal Irish Rifles

Captain **John Singleton Henry Robinson**
13th Battalion attached 12th Battalion Royal Welsh Regiment

Newtownards and District continued…

Rifleman **Samuel Robinson**
13th Battalion Royal Irish Rifles

Private **William Wadham Robinson**
10th Battalion Royal Dublin Fusiliers

Private **Robert Robson**
1st Battalion Princess Victoria's (Royal Irish Fusiliers)

Private **William Roseman**
14th Battalion Durham Light Infantry

Private **James Runaghan**
7th Battalion Prince of Wales's Leinster Regiment (Royal Canadians)

Rifleman **Alexander Russell**
13th Battalion Royal Irish Rifles

Private **Andrew Russell**
1st Battalion Queen's Own Cameron Highlanders

Corporal **John Russell**
16th Battalion Royal Irish Rifles

Rifleman **John Russell (Frederick St)**
13th Battalion Royal Irish Rifles

John Russell (Mark Street)
Newtownards and District War Memorial

Robert Russell (North Street)
Newtownards and District War Memorial

Private **Thomas Russell**
2nd Battalion Highland Light Infantry

Private **Joseph M Scarr**
9th Battalion Royal Scots Fusiliers

Rifleman **David Scott**
1st Garrison Battalion Royal Irish Rifles

Sergeant **Samuel Scott**
Canadian Field Artillery Brigade Ammunition Column

Newtownards and District continued…

T Scott
Newtownards Chronicle Roll of Sacrifice 6 January 1917

Rifleman **Hugh Shanks**
13th Battalion Royal Irish Rifles

Rifleman **John Shannon**
13th Battalion Royal Irish Rifles

Gunner **Henry Shaw**
50th Brigade Royal Field Artillery

Rifleman **John Meharry Sheppard**
22nd Entrenching Battalion late 11th/13th Battalion Royal Irish Rifles

Captain **John Sibbald Simms**
12th Battalion London Regiment (The Rangers)

Lance Corporal **William Simpson**
13th Battalion Royal Irish Rifles

Rifleman **William Sloan**
11th Battalion Royal Irish Rifles

Company Sergeant Major **David McCully Smyth**
16th Battalion Royal Irish Rifles attached 6th King's African Rifles

Rifleman **George Smyth**
1st Battalion Royal Irish Rifles

Rifleman **James Smyth**
13th Battalion Royal Irish Rifles

Second Lieutenant **Irvine Johnston Smyth**
6th Battalion Royal Inniskilling Fusiliers

Rifleman **William Smyth (Greenwell Street)**
2nd Battalion Royal Irish Rifles

Rifleman **William John Smyth (Mill Street)**
11th Battalion Royal Irish Rifles

Rifleman **William Smyth (North Street) (Regent Street)**
12th Battalion Royal Irish Rifles

Newtownards and District continued…

Sergeant Patrick P Spain
10th Battalion Royal Dublin Fusiliers

Lance Corporal Robert Stannage
2nd Battalion Royal Irish Rifles

Robert Stannage
Newtownards Parish Church of Ireland

Private George Stevenson
18th Battalion Highland Light Infantry

Gunner Hugh Stevenson
270th Siege Battery Royal Garrison Artillery

Rifleman James Croskery Stevenson
2nd Battalion Royal Irish Rifles

Lance Corporal Thomas Stevenson
1st Battalion Royal Irish Rifles

James Stewart
Newtownards and District War Memorial

William R Strain
Newtownards and District War Memorial

Company Quartermaster Sergeant David John Stratton
36th Signal Company Royal Engineers

George Stratton
Newtownards and District War Memorial

David Stratton
Newtownards and District War Memorial

Henry Stratton
Newtownards and District War Memorial

Rifleman Robert Stratton
1st Battalion Royal Irish Rifles

Lance Corporal Thomas Slade Swanger
Inland Water Transport Royal Engineers

Newtownards and District continued…

Rifleman **John PK Tate**
13th Battalion Royal Irish Rifles

Private **David Taylor**
2nd Battalion Royal Irish Regiment

Rifleman **Charles Thompson**
2nd Battalion Royal Irish Rifles

Lance Corporal **David John Thompson**
13th Battalion Royal Irish Rifles

Rifleman **John Thompson**
16th Battalion Royal Irish Rifles

Private **William Henry Thompson**
6th Battalion Royal Munster Fusiliers

Private **William James Thompson**
9th Battalion Princess Victoria's (Royal Irish Fusiliers)

Corporal **William John Thompson**
13th Battalion Royal Irish Rifles

Private **Arthur Todd**
2nd Battalion Grenadier Guards

George Todd
Movilla Burial Records

Rifleman **James Vance**
13th Battalion Royal Irish Rifles

Rifleman **William Vance**
2nd Battalion Royal Irish Rifles

William Vance (East Street)
Newtownards and District War Memorial

Driver **Samuel Walker**
7th Battery Royal Field Artillery

Company Sergeant Major **Robert H Wallace**
2nd Battalion Royal Irish Rifles

Newtownards and District continued...

Private **William Warnock**
2nd Battalion Royal Inniskilling Fusiliers

Second Lieutenant **James Campbell Watters**
71st Siege Battery South African Heavy Artillery

Private **John Brennan Waugh**
4th Battalion Canadian Mounted Rifles (Central Ontario Regiment)

Captain (Pilot) **Gilbert Watson Webb**
22nd Squadron Royal Flying Corps and Royal Irish Rifles

Rifleman **John Weir**
13th Battalion Royal Irish Rifles

Private **Alexander White**
1st Battalion Canadian Infantry (Western Ontario Regiment)

Private **Robert Whiteside**
2nd Battalion Royal Inniskilling Fusiliers

James Wilson
Newtownards and District War Memorial

T Woodside
Newtownards Chronicle Roll of Sacrifice 6 January 1917

Rifleman **James Wright**
13th Battalion Royal Irish Rifles

Second Lieutenant **Matthew John Wright**
14th Battalion Royal Irish Rifles

Charles Young
Newtownards and District War Memorial

Rifleman **James Young**
13th Battalion Royal Irish Rifles

PORTAFERRY AND DISTRICT

Lieutenant **Henry McDonnell Anderson MC**
5th Battalion Northumberland Fusiliers attd 63rd Battalion Machine Gun Corps

Portaferry and District continued...

Lance Corporal James Bailie
13th Battalion Royal Irish Rifles

Private AG Bain
HMS *Bayano* Royal Marine Light Infantry

Private Frederick G Beringer
87th Battalion Canadian Infantry (Quebec Regiment)

Stoker First Class William Ernest Beringer
HMS *Goliath* Royal Navy

Corporal John Norish Chasty
1st Battalion Royal Inniskilling Fusiliers

Lance Corporal Richard Christopher Chasty
1st Battalion Royal Inniskilling Fusiliers

First Mate Michael Collins
SS *Eveleen* (Belfast) Mercantile Marine

Private James J Corrigan
8th Battalion Royal Inniskilling Fusiliers

Petty Officer Stoker John Croskery
HMS *Arbutus* Royal Navy

Private John Joseph Delaney
1st Battalion Princess Victoria's (Royal Irish Fusiliers)

Rifleman Alexander Dodds
10th Battalion Royal Irish Rifles

Lance Corporal Andrew Donaldson
13th Battalion Royal Irish Rifles

Private William James Donnan
23rd Battalion Royal Fusiliers (City of London Regiment)

Private Hugh John M Dorrian
1st Battalion Royal Dublin Fusiliers

Private Thomas Emerson
1st Battalion Irish Guards

Portaferry and District continued…

Private **George Fisher**
38th Battalion Canadian Infantry (Eastern Ontario Regiment)

Stoker First Class **Hugh Fisher**
HMS *Vanguard* Royal Navy

Private **James Fitzsimmons**
7th/8th Battalion Princess Victoria's (Royal Irish Fusiliers)

Private **Thomas Guiney**
6th Battalion Royal Irish Regiment

Leading Boatman **John Hogan**
Tara War Signal Station Royal Navy

Private **Bernard Kerr**
9th Battalion Princess Victoria's (Royal Irish Fusiliers)

Private **James Aloysius Kinlay**
4th Regiment South African Infantry

Private **Roland Hugh Mason**
2nd Battalion Royal Irish Regiment

Corporal **Bryan McCloone**
13th Battalion Cheshire Regiment

Rifleman **William James McCluskey**
13th Battalion Royal Irish Rifles

Second Lieutenant **Mark William McDonald**
4th Battalion Royal Inniskilling Fusiliers

Gunner **Alexander McDonnell**
214th Siege Battery Royal Garrison Artillery

Rifleman **David John McDonnell**
22nd Entrenching Battalion late 11th/13th Battalion Royal Irish Rifles

Captain **John (Jack) McMath OBE**
SS *Manitou* Mercantile Marine

Private **Edward McMullan**
8th Battalion Princess Victoria's (Royal Irish Fusiliers)

Portaferry and District continued...

Private John Joseph McMullan
8th Battalion Princess Victoria's (Royal Irish Fusiliers)

Surgeon Hugh Francis DeSalle McNally
HMS *Hampshire* Royal Navy

Corporal William Menown
72nd Battalion Canadian Infantry (British Columbia Regiment)

Lance Corporal Samuel Orr
121st Field Company Royal Engineers

Captain Herbert Vesey Scott
3rd Battalion Rifle Brigade

Private John Bassett Shanks
5th Battalion Canadian Mounted Rifles

First Class Petty Officer John Joseph Sheals
HMS *Pembroke* Royal Navy

Second Lieutenant Donald Stuart Stirling Smurthwaite
1st Battalion Black Watch (Royal Highlanders)

Private David Smyth
2nd Battalion King's Own Scottish Borderers

Private John Smyth
18th Battalion Highland Light Infantry

Chief Gunner John David Sumner
HMTB *No. 96* Royal Navy

Company Sergeant Major William Taylor
13th Battalion Royal Irish Rifles

Private Charles Tomelty
13th Battalion Royal Inniskilling Fusiliers

Able Seaman WA Wellstead
HMS *Bayano* Royal Navy

Private Charles Hugh Park Wilson
Canadian Army Service Corps

PORTAVOGIE AND DISTRICT

Carpenter **Robert Hughes**
SS *Donegal* (Belfast) Mercantile Marine

Rifleman **Robert McVea**
2nd Battalion Royal Irish Rifles

Names by Cemetery and/or CWGC Memorial

In this Section the names of servicemen with Ards connections who died in the Great War are presented alphabetically by surname in relation to the Cemetery and/or CWGC Memorial where they are buried and/or commemorated. Where there is a specific CWGC grave or memorial reference this is shown beside the casualty's name.

A.I.F. Burial Ground, Flers, Somme, France
Rifleman William Angus	X. A. 4
Lt Col Charles William Reginald Duncombe	III. L. 29
Private James Gray	V. C. 30
Rifleman Robert Regan	X. A. 2
Rifleman Robert Stewart	X. A. 5
Rifleman Samuel Strain	X. A. 3

Abbeville Communal Cemetery Extension, Somme, France
Corporal James Charles Burrows	II. A. 30
Private John Hall	III. G. 1

Achiet-Le-Grand Communal Cemetery Extension, Pas de Calais, France
Lieutenant Frederick St John Ford North Echlin	IV. H. 7
Captain (Pilot) Gilbert Watson Webb	IV. Q. 5

Adanac Military Cemetery, Miraumont, Somme, France
Private Hugh Moore	VI. C. 5

Alexandria (Chatby) Military and War Memorial Cemetery, Egypt
Private Robert Douglas Niblock	E. 94

Alexandria (Hadra) War Memorial Cemetery, Egypt
Private James Paton	A. 39
Rifleman Thomas McBride Patton	A. 22

Ancre British Cemetery, Beaumont-Hamel, Somme, France
Rifleman Samuel Robinson	II. F. 6
Private William Wadham Robinson	I. C. 36

Archangel Allied Cemetery, (buried Ust-Vaga Burial Ground), Russian Federation
Private Michael McMillan	Sp. Mem. B91

Arneke British Cemetery, Nord, France

Rifleman James Morrison McCready	III. E. 26
Private Hugh McCullough	I. E. 5
Rifleman Thomas McMullan	III. E. 4

Arras Memorial, Pas de Calais France

Lance Sergeant James Clegg	Bay 7 and 8
Corporal William Francis Cumming	Bay 5
Private James McGimpsey	Bay 1 and 2
Rifleman Charles Pollock	Bay 9
Sergeant John Quinn	Bay 1
Rifleman William Smyth (Greenwell Street)	Bay 9

Aubers Ridge British Cemetery, Aubers, Nord, France

Private Thomas Best	V. B. 13

Aubigny Communal Cemetery Extension, Pas de Calais, France

Private John Joseph Delaney	II. E. 19
Rifleman James Glover Mackey	I.B.5
Private William Montgomery	I. L. 2
Private John Bassett Shanks	IV. D. 58

Auchonvillers Military Cemetery, Somme, France

Private Robert Lennon	II. A. 24

Authuile Military Cemetery, Somme, France

Lance Sergeant William John Brown	G. 8
Rifleman Charles Francis Hill	A. 12
Rifleman John Henry McBratney	D. 52
Lance Corporal John McCracken	Sp. Mem. B. 2
Rifleman William Tanner	D. 8

Baghdad (North Gate) War Cemetery, Iraq

Rifleman William John Jamison (served as Armour)	XIV. J. 14

Bagneux British Cemetery, Gezaincourt, Somme, France

Lieutenant Henry McDonnell Anderson MC	III. A. 9

Bailleul Communal Cemetery (Nord), Nord, France

Rifleman William John Majury	E. 13

Bailleul Communal Cemetery Extension (Nord), Nord, France

Rifleman Robert Carpenter	III. A. 152

Lance Corporal **Samuel John Gregg**	III. B. 189
Rifleman **William Gunning**	III. B. 24
Sapper **Joseph Hare**	III. B. 182
Rifleman **John Ledgerwood**	III. A. 134
Rifleman **Robert Robinson**	III. A. 46
Rifleman **Thomas Strickland**	III. A. 125

Bailleul Road East Cemetery, St. Laurent-Blangy, Pas de Calais, France

Rifleman **John Allen**	II. J. 11

Ballygowan Presbyterian Churchyard, Co. Down

Corporal **Lowry Jordan MM**	139

Ballyhalbert (St. Andrew) Church of Ireland Churchyard, Co.Down

Rifleman **John Milligan**	
Leading Seaman **Edgar J Spracklin**	North-East part

Ballymanish Presbyterian Cemetery, Portaferry, Co. Down

Rifleman **William James McCluskey**

Ballyphilip Church of Ireland Churchyard, Portaferry, Co. Down

Private **AG Bain**	197
Able Seaman **WA Wellstead**	198

Bangor New Cemetery, Newtownards Road, Bangor, Co. Down

Petty Officer **Hugh Ferguson**	4. R
Rifleman **Robert McConnell**	5S. 70

Bangor Old Abbey Churchyard, Co. Down

Rifleman **James Burns**	South-West part

Barlin Communal Cemetery Extension, Pas de Calais, France

Private **Andrew Lyttle**	I. H. 40

Basra War Cemetery, Iraq

Captain **Henry Cooke Lowry**	III. M. 20
Rifleman **Hamilton McKibben**	II. G. 1

Beauval Communal Cemetery, Somme, France

Driver **George Casey**	E. 13
Corporal **Gerald Marcus Huston DCM**	C. 31

Becourt Military Cemetery, Becordel-Becourt, Somme, France
Rifleman Patrick Mullen   I. H. 2

Bedford House Cemetery, Ieper, West-Vlaanderen, Belgium
Rifleman Andrew Orr   Enclosure No. 4 I. G. 4

Beirut War Cemetery, Lebanese Republic
Acting Bombardier George Ellison Mulholland   16

Belfast (Dundonald) Cemetery, Co. Down
Rifleman John Campbell   E5. 843
Private George Fisher   F5. 501
Rifleman David John Keilty   F6. 427

Belfast City Cemetery
Lieutenant Samuel Gatensby   Screen Wall. H3. 55
Captain Archibald H Hamilton   C. 617

Belgian Battery Corner Cemetery, Ieper, West-Vlaanderen, Belgium
Corporal Francis McAlpine   I. A. 16

Berlin South-Western Cemetery, Berlin, Brandenburg, Germany
Private Samuel Blakely Dunn Donnan   X. C. 5

Bethune Town Cemetery, Pas de Calais, France
Lance Sergeant Robert Bell Harrison   III. D. 87
Lieutenant John Joseph Leo Morgan MID   II. G. 16

Blaris Old Burial Ground, Co. Down
Company Sergeant Major Martin Brown   194A

Bombay (St. Thomas) Cathedral Memorial, Mumbai, India
Lieutenant George B Keeling

Boulogne Eastern Cemetery, Pas de Calais, France
Driver Alexander Gibson   IV. A. 12
Lance Corporal Sidney Lane   VIII. A. 56
Private Thomas Russell   III. A. 18

Boyelles Communal Cemetery Extension, Pas de Calais, France
Private James Henry Rilley   II. B. 3

Brandhoek Military Cemetery, Ieper, West-Vlaanderen, Belgium
Driver Hugh Crouch Houston   I. A. 14

Brandhoek New Military Cemetery, Ieper, West-Vlaanderen, Belgium
Rifleman John Kennedy   II. E. 7
Rifleman John McPhillips   VI. B. 1

Brandhoek New Military Cemetery No. 3, Ieper, West-Vlaanderen, Belgium
Corporal James Munn Dugan   I. O. 30

Brandon Cemetery, Manitoba, Canada
Private Robert McDermott   L. 35. B. 'A'. S. 17

Brookwood Cemetery, Surrey, England
Sergeant James Armstrong Kelly DCM   Q. 176614

Brown's Copse Cemetery, Roeux, Pas de Calais, France
Second Lieutenant Hugh Charles Allen DCM   II. B. 28

Bucquoy Road Cemetery, Ficheux, Pas de Calais, France
Private James Fitzsimmons   II. E. 12

Bully-Grenay Communal Cemetery, French Extension, Pas de Calais, France
Private James Healy   A. 81

Cabaret-Rouge British Cemetery, Souchez, Pas de Calais, France
Private Frederick G Beringer   VIII. E. 12
Captain John William Field   XXI. C. 6

Cairo War Memorial Cemetery, Egypt
Gunner James Campbell   F. 217

Calais Southern Cemetery, Pas de Calais, France
Company Sergeant Major Robert H Wallace   Plot H. Row 3. Grave 4
Rifleman John Waring   Plot F. Row 1. Grave 9

Cambrai Memorial, Louverval, Nord, France
Rifleman William George Clifford   Panel 10
Private William Donnan   Panel 3 and 4
Lieutenant Alexander McKee   Panel 10
Rifleman Albert Edward Nelson   Panel 10

Cambrai Memorial continued…

Rifleman **John Orr**	**Panel 10**
Lance Corporal **Gilbert (Bertie) Paden**	**Panel 10**

Cambrin Churchyard Extension, Pas de Calais, France

Private **James Bell**	**C. 5**

Carnmoney Cemetery, Co. Antrim

Rifleman **James Montgomery**	**X. 94**

Carrowdore (Christ Church) Churchyard, Co. Down

Driver **Hugh Andrew McKee**	**Old Ground 59A**

Caudry Old Communal Cemetery, Nord, France

Rifleman **David John Gamble**	**B. 4**

Cement House Cemetery, Langemark-Poelkapelle, West-Vlaanderen, Belgium

Private **Hugh John M Dorrian**	**XIV. C. 12**
Private **David Harvey**	**XI. D. 22**

Cerisy-Gailly Military Cemetery, Somme, France

Rifleman **Samuel Carnduff**	**III. C. 9**
Rifleman **John McIlveen**	**III. C. 13**

Chatby Memorial, Egypt

Rifleman **Charles McKeown**

Chatham Naval Memorial, Kent, England

Able Seaman **Robert Algie**	**Panel 1**
Stoker First Class **William Ernest Beringer**	**Panel 11**
Stoker First Class **Hugh Fisher**	**Panel 23**
Boy First Class **Alfred Henry Victor Gadd**	**Panel 10**
Stoker First Class **Hector Hiles**	**Panel 11**

City of London Cemetery and Crematorium, Manor Park, Essex, England

Rifleman **Robert Buckley**	**Screen Wall 235. 34A**

Cloughey Presbyterian Church Graveyard, Co. Down

Corporal **Edward Atkin**	**182 (at North end)**

Cologne Southern Cemetery, Cologne, Nordrhein-Westfal, Germany

Rifleman **Thomas Calderwood**	**XVII. B. 32**
Private **David Gamble**	**VIII. E. 20**

Comber New Cemetery, Co. Down

Private D J Dempster	5.305
Private James Finlay	5. 74
Rifleman Thomas James Fisher	8. 203
Rifleman Alexander Glover	5. 80
Driver Hugh McGreeghan	2.58

Connaught Cemetery, Thiepval, Somme, France

Private James Bennett	I. A. 20
Lieutenant John Luddington Peacock	XI. L. 3

Courcelette British Cemetery, Somme, France

Private James Edgar Drake	VIII. B. 9

Crouy British Cemetery, Crouy-sur-Somme, Somme, France

Private Robert Marshall	IV. C. 2
Lance Corporal Frederick McCann	III. A. 21

Dadizeele New British Cemetery, Moorslede, West-Vlaanderen, Belgium

Captain GJ Bruce DSO MC (and Bar) MID (x3)	III. E. 14
Rifleman David Coey	IV. D. 7
Lance Corporal Samuel Fenton	II. 1
Rifleman Alfred Johnston	III. E. 16
Private Samuel Logan	VI. F. 33
Rifleman Frederick Parkes	II. B. 14
Rifleman Robert Regan	II. C. 20
Private Robert Whiteside	III. C. 11

Dar Es Salaam War Cemetery, Tanzania, Africa

Company Sergeant Major David McCully Smyth	5. F. 16

Delhi Memorial (India Gate), India

Private Charles William Henry Hall	Face 23
Lieutenant William David Kenny VC	Face 31

Delville Wood Cemetery, Longueval, Somme, France

Private Thomas Guiney	XXIII. G. 4
Private William O'Neill	XXIII. K. 5
Private David Smyth	XXIII. D. 3

Dernancourt Communal Cemetery Extension, Somme, France

Private Thomas Reilly	V. A. 2

Rifleman Edward Ferguson McCalpin McAvoy   II. B. 81A
Private James McCutcheon   XXVI. B. 9A
Private James Campbell McGimpsey   XXIX. B. 11A
Private Alexander White   XXII. F. 9

Ferme-Olivier Cemetery, Ieper, West-Vlaanderen, Belgium
Gunner Hugh Stevenson   Plot 3 Row C Grave 7

Forceville Communal Cemetery and Extension, Somme, France
Rifleman John PK Tate   South boundary
Rifleman William John Thompson   Plot 1 Row D Grave 12

Ford Park Cemetery (formerly Plymouth Old Cemetery) (Pennycomequick), Devon, England
Able Seaman Samuel Crooks   General K. 26. 36

Fulham Palace Road Cemetery, London, England
Rifleman Arthur Rickwood Broderick   8B. D. 40

Glenarm New Cemetery, Co. Antrim
Second Lieutenant Mark William McDonald   A. 24

Grand-Seraucourt British Cemetery, Aisne, France
Rifleman George Chambers   Cugny German Cem. Mem. 30
Rifleman Alexander Skillen   II. F. 17

Grangegorman Military Cemetery, Co. Dublin
Sergeant George Hamilton   CE. 607
Rifleman James McCullough   CE. 810

Green Hill Cemetery, Gallipoli, Turkey
Second Lieutenant Irvine Johnston Smyth   I. C. 22

Grevillers British Cemetery, Pas de Calais, France
Lance Corporal Joseph Croan   X. E. 15
Company Sergeant Major Hugh McCallum   IX. B. 5

Greyabbey Old Cemetery, Co. Down
Rifleman James Kerr
Rifleman Alexander McClelland   middle of cemetery
Rifleman William John Prichard   middle of cemetery

Grove Town Cemetery, Meaulte, Somme, France
Lieutenant Robert Davison MC   I. O. 4

Ham British Cemetery, Muille-Villette, Somme, France
Rifleman Edward Mooney   II. B. 12

Hamel Military Cemetery, Beaumont-Hamel, Somme, France
Rifleman Alexander Dodds   I. B. 20
Private John Price   I. F. 15

Haringhe (Bandaghem) Military Cemetery, Poperinge, West-Vlaanderen, Belgium
Rifleman William Fryers   II. B. 3

Harlebeke New British Cemetery, Harlebeke, West-Vlaanderen, Belgium
Lance Corporal Thomas Coey   XII. A. 4
Private James Gabbey   VIII. D. 4
Sapper James Hutton   VII. A. 16
Rifleman Thompson Mathers   VIII. A. 11

Hautmont Communal Cemetery, Nord, France
Rifleman John Dickson   V. B. 4

Hawthorn Ridge Cemetery No. 1, Auchonvillers, Somme, France
Private Thomas Devlin   B. 59

Hazebrouck Communal Cemetery, Nord, France
Sergeant George Brankin   I. F. 11

Heath Cemetery, Harbonnieres, Somme, France
Company Sergeant Major William Taylor   VIII. K. 5

Hebuterne Military Cemetery, Pas de Calais, France
Rifleman Thomas Edward Ingram   I. L. 8

Helles Memorial, Gallipoli, Turkey
Rifleman John Crossen   Panel 177 & 178
Private Patrick Hamill   Panel 178-180
Private Andrew Kerr   Panel 72-75
Private Robert Marshall   Panel 97-101
Private Hamilton McWhinney   Panel 178-180

Lance Corporal **William Moore**	Panel 177 & 178
Rifleman **Neil McL Mulholland**	Panel 177 & 178
Private **Ellis Oliver**	Panel 178-180
Corporal **Daniel Rea**	Panel 125-134 or 223-226 228-229 & 328
Private **Francis Smythe**	Panel 173-177
2nd Lieutenant **John S Williamson**	Panel 58-72 or 218-219

Hermies British Cemetery, Pas de Calais, France
Sergeant **Samuel George Miskimmin**   C. 9

Highland Cemetery, Roclincourt, Pas de Calais, France
Private **Henry Douglas Ritchie**   I. B. 5

Hooge Crater Cemetery, Ieper, West-Vlaanderen, Belgium
Rifleman **John Kennedy**   XVI. D. 5

Ingoyghem Military Cemetery, Anzegem, West-Vlaanderen, Belgium
Rifleman **Alexander McBride**   C. 11

Ipswich Old Cemetery, Suffolk, England
Farrier Sergeant **Robert McDonald**   S. 4. 2

Jerusalem Memorial, Israel
Private **James Gorman**   Panel 25

Kantara War Memorial Cemetery, Egypt
Trooper **Herbert Alexander Bell**   B. 75

Karachi 1914-1918 War Memorial, Pakistan
Corporal **Hamilton Moore**

Kemmel Chateau Military Cemetery, Heuvelland, West-Vlaanderen, Belgium
Rifleman **William Beers**	M. 84
Rifleman **James Mackenzie Irwin**	B. 35
Private **James Martin**	N. 66
Private **Joseph Murray**	M. 75
Private **David Taylor**	X. 46

Kilclief Roman Catholic Churchyard, Co. Down
Private **James J Corrigan**   South-West of Church

Killinchy Non-Subscribing Presbyterian Churchyard, Co. Down
Rifleman **Frederick (Frew) Shaw**   South-East part

Killysuggan Graveyard, Newtownards, Co. Down
Company Quartermaster Sergeant David Condon
Joseph Crooks (MM unsubstantiated to date)
Rifleman Thomas Glendinning 1. 2. 23
Rifleman Samuel Robinson 2. 2. 25

La Ferte-Sous-Jouarre Memorial, Seine-et-Marne, France
Private John Arthur Bell
Private Samuel Ritchie
Private William Warnock

Lancashire Landing Cemetery, Gallipoli, Turkey
Private James Carser H. 38
Private William Maddock D. 67

Le Bizet Cemetery, Armentieres, Nord, France
Lance Sergeant James Mullan B. 4

Le Grand Hasard Military Cemetery, Morbecque, Nord, France
Private John Pollock Plot 2 Row D Grave 3

Le Touquet-Paris Plage Communal Cemetery, Pas de Calais, France
Rifleman James Brown II. A. 30

Le Touret Memorial, Pas de Calais, France
Rifleman William Robert Bell Panel 42 & 43
Rifleman James Carnduff Panel 42 & 43
Private Patrick Daly Panel 4
Rifleman James Fisher Panel 42 & 43
Private William Francis Panel 16 & 17
Rifleman Alexander Gibson Panel 42 & 43
Lance Corporal Thomas Harris Panel 43
Rifleman William Hurley Panel 42 & 43
Lance Corporal Hector Claude Marsh Panel 42 & 43
Sergeant Richard Henry Martin Panel 42 & 43
Private James McBlain Panel 39-41
Private John McBride Panel 3 & 4
Private Hugh McTear Panel 37 & 38
Lance Corporal Thomas Gray Mellefont Panel 42 & 43
Private Hugh Orr Panel 37 & 38
Lance Corporal James Stevenson Poag Panel 42 & 43

Le Treport Military Cemetery, Seine-Maritime, France

Rifleman Joseph Oswald	Plot 2 Row K Grave 6
Rifleman Frederick H Trousdale	Plot 1 Row N Grave 8

Liege (Robermont) Cemetery, Liege, Belgium

Private James McCully	38

Lijssenthoek Military Cemetery, Poperinge, West-Vlaanderen, Belgium

Corporal John Clark	VIII. D. 4
Private James Downes	VI. B. 6A
Rifleman Hugh Kelly	XVII. AA. 14
Rifleman Alexander McIlwrath (served as McIlwraith)	XVII. F. 12A
Private Samuel McKee	XXI. CC. 18
Private Robert Watson McMillan	VIII. B. 33
Gunner Henry Shaw	XXVIII. E. 15A

Lillers Communal Cemetery, Pas de Calais, France

Private Robert Stewart	III. A. 41

Loker Churchyard, Heuvelland, West-Vlaanderen, Belgium

Rifleman William Vance (Greenwell Street)	II. E. 2

Lone Pine Memorial, Gallipoli, Turkey

Private James Davidson Beck	Panel 75
Private Alexander Martin	Panel 72
Private Robert Matear	Panel 76

Lone Tree Cemetery, Heuvelland, West Vlaanderen, Belgium

Rifleman Hugh Tate	I. D. 5

Longuenesse (St. Omer) Souvenir Cemetery, Pas de Calais, France

Lance Corporal William John Branch	V. B. 62
Private Roland Hugh A Mason	IV. C. 46

Lonsdale Cemetery, Authuille, Somme, France

Sergeant John Gracie	II. D. 20

Loos Memorial, Pas de Calais, France

Private William Blair	Panel 108-112
Private Patrick Docherty	Panel 46-49
Private Patrick Gilmore	Panel 127-129
Private Alexander McDowell	Panel 27-30

Loos Memorial continued…

Private **William Roseman**	Panel 106 & 107
Sergeant **Albert Edward Young**	Panel 108-112

Louvencourt Military Cemetery, Somme, France

Corporal **John Norish Chasty**	Plot 1 Row C Grave 45
Company Sergeant Major **Francis McMath**	Plot 1 Row C Grave 20

Madras 1914-1918 War Memorial, Chennai, India

Regimental Sergeant Major **Charles James Cherry**	Face 21
Rifleman **David Scott**	Face 23

Manchester (Philips Park) Cemetery, Lancashire, England

2nd Corporal **Dennis de Courcey Shaw**	H. C.E. 487

Maroeuil British Cemetery, Pas de Calais, France

Private **James McGilton Brett**	IV. E. 15

Marteville Communal Cemetery, Attilly, Aisne, France

Captain **John Singleton Henry Robinson**	C. 9

Maubeuge (Sous-le-Bois) Cemetery, Nord, France

Captain **Cyril Gerrard Haselden**	DD. 7

Mendinghem Military Cemetery, Poperinge, West-Vlaanderen, Belgium

Rifleman **David Cromie**	IV. A. 3

Merville Communal Cemetery, Nord, France

Private (Bugler) **William John McWhinney**	I. B. 16

Mesnil Ridge Cemetery, Mesnil-Martinsart, Somme, France

Rifleman **James Calvert**	G. 5
Rifleman **David McConnell**	G. 4
Rifleman **Charles Newell**	G. 6
Rifleman **Hugh Shanks**	I. 6

Messines Ridge British Cemetery, Mesen, West-Vlaanderen, Belgium

Rifleman **Albert Hawthorne**	I. C. 41
Rifleman **James McCandless**	I. D. 5
Lance Corporal **Samuel Horace Nelson**	III. D. 25

Meuse-Argonne American Cemetery, Romagne-sur-Montfaucon, France

Private **Robert John Ireland**	Plot D Row 20 Grave 21

Mikra British Cemetery, Kalamaria, Greece
Private William Cooper   464

Mill Road Cemetery, Thiepval, Somme, France
Lance Corporal David Lamont   I. A. 29
Rifleman James McGimpsey   VI. C. 4
Private Joseph Miller   I. D. 19

Miraumont Communal Cemetery, Somme, France
Rifleman Joseph Porter   B. 5

Moeuvres Communal Cemetery Extension, Nord, France
Rifleman David McMaster   I. D. 23

Mont Huon Military Cemetery, Le Treport, Seine-Maritime, France
Rifleman William Thomas Millar   III. M. 7A

Montigny Communal Cemetery, Somme, France
Major Meyrick Myles Magrath DSO   C. 13

Morogoro Cemetery, Tanzania, Africa
Private Andrew McCutcheon Mayne   VIII. E. 13

Mory Abbey Military Cemetery, Mory, Pas de Calais, France
Private Arthur Todd   V. C. 26

Mount Hope Cemetery, Brandford, Ontario
Sergeant Samuel Scott

Netley Military Cemetery, Hampshire, England
Lance Corporal Richard Christopher Chasty   C. E. 1721
Private Andrew Russell   C. E. 1587

New Irish Farm Cemetery, Ieper, West-Vlaanderen, Belgium
Lance Corporal William John Cromie   XVIII. B. 9
Lance Corporal Andrew Donaldson   XIX. C. 12
Lance Corporal John McKee   II. E. 6

Newtownards (Movilla) Cemetery, Co. Down
James Adair
James Algie
William Bell
David Bennett   2. 25

Newtownards (Movilla) Cemetery continued...

William John Cairns	
Lance Corporal William James Caughey	11. 132
Rifleman Robert John Corry	11. 43
Rifleman James Graham	3. 30
Rifleman John Harvey	1. 279
Rifleman Robert Harvey	12. 89
Sergeant Andrew Heron	9. 111
Rifleman Robert Kane	1. 277
Lance Corporal Hugh Kerr	1. 48
Rifleman John McChesney	1. 195
Rifleman Hugh McClure	I. 91
Petty Officer Joseph McClure	
Hugh McConnell	Section 4
John McCready	
Private James McKimm	11. 33
Rifleman Robert McKimm	
Rifleman Thomas McTaggart	5. 18
Rifleman Thomas Millar	13. 30
Private Archibald Nisbet	1. 104
Captain Hamilton Orr MID	5. 137
Rifleman Robert Orr	11. 26
Corporal Leonard Edward John Parker	11. 97
Rifleman James Parkhill	11. 123
Driver Samuel Forbes Patton	4. 49
John Russell	
Company Quartermaster Sgt David John Stratton	2. 117
Henry Stratton	
Lance Corporal Thomas Slade Swanger	11. 97
Rifleman John Thompson	13. 36
George Todd	
Private John Brennan Waugh	4. 155

Niederzwehren Cemetery, Kassel, Hessen, Germany

Private William Boal (served as William McHugh)	IX. F. 8

Nine Elms British Cemetery, Poperinge, West-Vlaanderen, Belgium

Second Lieutenant James Campbell Watters	VI. A. 2

Outtersteene Communal Cemetery Extension, Bailleul, Nord, France

Private Charles Tomelty	II. H. 55

Peronne Communal Cemetery Extension, Somme, France

Rifleman Robert Heaney	V. H. 1

Pink Farm Cemetery, Helles, Turkey
Private Samuel James Reid — Sp. Mem. 83

Ploegsteert Memorial, Comines-Warneton, Hainaut, Belgium
Lance Corporal William Charles Gregory — Panel 3
Private Albert Edward Gregory — Panel 3
Sergeant William Hanna — Panel 9
Lance Corporal Robert Johnston — Panel 9
Rifleman Robert Johnston — Panel 9
Rifleman Edward John Kelly — Panel 9
Corporal Daniel Matier — Panel 9
Corporal John Hill McKibben — Panel 9
Rifleman William Smyth (Regent Street/North Street) — Panel 9
Driver Samuel Walker — Panel 1

Plymouth (Weston Mill) Cemetery, Devon, England
Chief Stoker William John Reains — Naval Con. C. 3894

Plymouth Naval Memorial, Devon, England
Stoker First Class Robert Ennis — Panel 15
Greaser James Jamison — Panel 9
Able Seaman Samuel Johnston — Panel 1
Stoker First Class David Magee — Panel 16
Fireman William Oliver — Panel 31
Chief Gunner John David Sumner — Panel 5

Poelcapelle British Cemetery, Langemark-Poelkapelle, Belgium
Private John Maidens MM — LVI. C. 7

Point 110 New Military Cemetery, Fricourt, Somme, France
Captain Mervyn Stronge Richardson MID — D. 4

Point-du-Jour Military Cemetery, Athies, Pas de Calais, France
Lt Col Francis SN Savage-Armstrong DSO MID (x2) — II. E. 12

Pond Farm Cemetery, Heuvelland, West-Vlaanderen, Belgium
Rifleman Thomas Blackadder — L. 13
Rifleman Thomas Martin Horner — M. 15
Rifleman John Swindle — O. 12

Pont-du-Hem Military Cemetery, La Gorgue, Nord, France
Lieutenant William Angus Browne — IV. G. 25

Pont-du-Hem Military Cemetery continued…

Second Lieutenant **James Rowan Shaw**	I. D. 5
Lance Corporal **Robert Stannage**	VIII. D. 6

Poperinghe Old Military Cemetery, Poperinge, West-Vlaanderen, Belgium

Rifleman **John Irvine**	I. M. 55

Port Said War Memorial Cemetery, Egypt

Captain **John (Jack) McMath OBE**	D. 2

Portaferry Roman Catholic Graveyard

Leading Boatman **John Hogan**	near South boundary
Petty Officer First Class **John Joseph Sheals**	West of Church

Portsmouth Naval Memorial, Hampshire, England

Petty Officer Stoker **John Croskery**	Panel 26
Surgeon **Hugh Francis DeSalle McNally**	Panel 11
Stoker First Class **John Moreland**	Panel 19

Potijze Chateau Grounds Cemetery, Ieper, West-Vlaanderen, Belgium

Rifleman **William James Gibson**	II. E. 23
Rifleman **John Smyth**	II. E. 21

Pozieres British Cemetery, Ovillers- La Boisselle, Somme, France

Gunner **William Dickson**	II. F. 35
Lance Corporal **William James McCoy**	IV. U. 9
Rifleman **Joseph Miskimmin**	III. B. 19

Pozieres Memorial, Somme, France

Rifleman **James Armour**	Panel 74-76
Rifleman **Robert Carnduff**	Panel 74-76
Rifleman **Alexander Courtney**	Panel 74-76
Second Lieutenant **Edmund De Wind VC**	Panel 74-76
Lance Corporal **Thomas Griffin**	Panel 10-13
Corporal **Thomas McCann**	Panel 38-40
Rifleman **David John McDonnell**	Panel 74-76
Rifleman **Hugh McGinn**	Panel 74-76
Rifleman **William Hewitt McIlveen**	Panel 74-76
Rifleman **Robert McVea**	Panel 74-76
Rifleman **Andrew McWilliams**	Panel 74-76
Rifleman **Samuel Montgomery**	Panel 74-76
Rifleman **James Patton**	Panel 74-76

Rifleman **Robert James Pyper**   Panel 74-76
Rifleman **Henry Quigley MM (and Bar)**   Panel 74-76
Lance Corporal **Francis Michael Ritchie**   Panel 38-40
Rifleman **David Robinson**   Panel 74-76
Private **Robert Robson**   Panel 76-77
Rifleman **John Meharry Sheppard**   Panel 74-76
Private **George Young**   Panel 19-21
Private **Henry Young**   Panel 1

Poznan Old Garrison Cemetery, Poland
Lieutenant **Francis Cinnamond**   II. B. 5

Premont British Cemetery, Aisne, France
Rifleman **Robert Hamilton**   IV. A. 26

Puchevillers British Cemetery, Somme, France
Rifleman **Samuel Heslip Gordon**   I. A. 26
Rifleman **James Robinson**   I. B. 36

Quarry Cemetery, Montauban, Somme, France
Private **John Joseph McMullan**   IV. J. 4
Private **Richard Rae**   II. L. 10

Quarry Wood Cemetery, Sains-les-Marquion, Pas de Calais, France
Private **William Stratton**   II. B. 38

Railway Dugouts Burial Ground, Ieper, West-Vlaanderen, Belgium
Private **David Greer Cooke**   VI. K. 18
Sapper **Arthur McKeown**   I. D. 4
Major **William Maxwell Shaw DSO MID**   IV. C. 19

Ramparts Cemetery, Lille Gate, Ieper, West-Vlaanderen, Belgium
Private **Charles Thompson**   B. 24

Ration Farm (La Plus Douve) Annexe, Comines-Warneton, Hainaut, Belgium
Rifleman **Robert Douglas**   II. C. 27
Rifleman **David Pyper**   II. C. 24
Rifleman **James Smyth (served as Smith)**   III. A. 7
Rifleman **William John Smyth (Mill Street)**   III. B. 8

Ration Farm Military Cemetery, La Chapelle-Darmentieres, Nord, France
Corporal **John Patrick Quinn**   VI. H. 26

Ridge Wood Military Cemetery, Ieper, West-Vlaanderen, Belgium
Private Thomas Patton   I. T. 3

Roclincourt Military Cemetery, Pas de Calais, France
Private Charles McLean   I. B. 20

Roclincourt Valley Cemetery, Pas de Calais, France
Lieutenant Basil Llewellyn Boyd Thomas   IV. H. 3

Rocquigny-Equancourt Road British Cemetery, Manancourt, Somme, France
Gunner James Francis Simpson   IV. A. 22

Roisel Communal Cemetery Extension, Somme, France
Private Jonathan (John) Ardill MID   Sp. Mem. 3

Royal Irish Rifles Graveyard, Laventie, Pas de Calais, France
Rifleman Francis Orr   I. C. 8
Rifleman George Smyth   I. A. 2

Rue-du-Bacquerot (13th London) Graveyard, Laventie, Pas de Calais, France
Rifleman Hamilton Orr (James Street)   G. 2

Rue-Petillon Military Cemetery, Fleurbaix, Pas de Calais, France
Gunner Thomas Simpson (served as Thomas Harvey)   I. N. 44

Salonika (Lembet Road) Military Cemetery, Greece
Colour Sergeant John Isaac Cutler LS&GCM   576

Sancourt British Cemetery, Nord, France
Private Thomas Bailie   I. D. 32

Serre Road Cemetery No. 1, Pas de Calais, France
Private Collins Alexander Cooke   IX. A. 19
Rifleman James Tate   II. BB. 14

Serre Road Cemetery No. 2, Somme, France
Rifleman James Stevenson Johnston   VI. F. 10
Rifleman David McConnell   VII. A. 1
Rifleman John Russell (Frederick St)   VI. F. 14
Private Mason Simonton   XIV. A. 13
Rifleman William Robert Taylor   XIII. A. 1

Private John Walker   VI. J. 11
Rifleman James Walsh   VI. F. 13

Shankill Cemetery, Lurgan, Co. Armagh
Gunner Daniel McNeice   710A (North-East part)

Skew Bridge Cemetery, Gallipoli, Turkey
Private Robert John Lightbody   Special Memorial A. 51

Soissons Memorial, Aisne, France
Private Patrick Moore (served as McConnell)

South Brisbane Cemetery, Queensland, Australia
Driver Robert Davidson Robinson   Gen 2. 3A. 1L(GRM/4*)

Spanbroekmolen British Cemetery, Heuvelland, West-Vlaanderen, Belgium
Rifleman Frederick McKee   D. 8

St. Mihiel American Cemetery, Thiaucourt, France
Private James Reid   Plot A Row 9 Grave 10
Corporal Niven Boyd Stewart   Plot D Row 22 Grave 33

St. Patrick's Cemetery, Loos, Pas de Calais, France
Rifleman Joseph McDowell   III. B. 28

St. Pol Communal Cemetery Extension, Pas de Calais, France
Private John Donnan   C. 15

St. Quentin Cabaret Military Cemetery, Heuvelland, West-Vlaanderen, Belgium
Lance Corporal John Adair   I.C. 35
Rifleman George Hamilton   II. B. 8
Lance Corporal Robert H Marshall   II. A. 14
Rifleman James McCullough   II. F. 1
Rifleman William McKittrick   II. A. 13

St. Sever Cemetery, Rouen, Seine-Maritime, France
Private Samuel Grant   B. 19. 14

St. Sever Cemetery Extension, Rouen, Seine-Maritime, France
Private Maxwell Aiken   P. IX. B. 1A
Lance Corporal James Gregory MM   P. IX. J. 7B

St. Sever Cemetery Extension continued…

Private **William Thomas McBride**	P. VI. D. 11A
Sergeant **Samuel Taylor**	S. II. H. 20

Ste. Marie Cemetery, Le Havre, Seine-Maritime, France

Rifleman **William Boyd**	Div. 19. N. 2
Sapper **Nathaniel Ferguson**	Div. 14. I. 2
Lance Corporal **Samuel Orr**	Div. 19. V. 3
Rifleman **William Boyd**	Div. 19. N. 2

Stirling (Mar Place) Cemetery, Stirlingshire, Scotland

Rifleman **William John Dorman**	YZ. 13

Strand Military Cemetery, Comines-Warneton, Hainaut, Belgium

Private **Hamilton Bennett**	IX. P. 2
Private **Thomas Donnan**	V. A. 16

Sucrerie Cemetery, Ablain-St. Nazaire, Pas de Calais, France

Private **James O'Neill Dorrian**	II. D. 4

Sucrerie Military Cemetery, Colinchamps, Somme, France

Private **Dupree William McWha**	IV. E. 3

Sunken Road Cemetery, Boisleux-St. Marc, Pas de Calais, France

Sergeant **Alexander Colville MM**	II. D. 24

Suzanne Communal Cemetery Extension, Somme, France

Lance Corporal **Valentine Cairnduff**	B. 10

Suzanne Military Cemetery No. 3, Somme, France

Lance Corporal **Alexander Campbell**	II. D. 12
Rifleman **Andrew John Dempster**	II. D. 11

Tancrez Farm Cemetery, Comines-Warneton, Hainaut, Belgium

Captain **Robert James O'Lone MID**	I. G. 14

Templeux-le-Guerard British Cemetery, Somme, France

Private **Patrick McGreevy**	I. K. 17

Terlincthun British Cemetery, Wimille, Pas de Calais, France

Rifleman **George Coulter Gunning**	X. A. B. 12
Private **William Woods**	I. D. 22

Thaba Tshwane (Old No.1) Military Cemetery, Gauteng, South Africa

Private **William McLaughlin**	A. 15.

Thiepval Memorial, Somme, France

Private Edward Adair	Pier and Face 4 D and 5 B
Rifleman Robert Hugh Allen	Pier and Face 15 A and 15 B
Rifleman William Anderson	Pier and Face 15 A and 15 B
Rifleman John Blair Angus	Pier and Face 15 A and 15 B
Lance Corporal Robert Angus	Pier and Face 3 C
Rifleman James Auld	Pier and Face 15 A and 15 B
Lance Corporal James Bailie	Pier and Face 15 A and 15 B
Lance Corporal Thomas John Ballance	Pier and Face 15 A and 15 B
Rifleman William Bell	Pier and Face 15 A and 15 B
Corporal Edward Bennett	Pier and Face 15 A and 15 B
Rifleman Robert John Black	Pier and Face 15 A and 15 B
Sergeant Alfred Blythe	Pier and Face 15 A and 15 B
Rifleman Alexander Boland	Pier and Face 15 A and 15 B
Private Richard Boucher	Pier and Face 4 D and 5 B
Rifleman James Bowman	Pier and Face 15 A and 15 B
Lance Corporal George Taylor Boyd	Pier and Face 15 A and 15 B
Sergeant Henry Burgess	Pier and Face 15 A and 15 B
Rifleman George Burns	Pier and Face 15 A and 15 B
Sapper Robert James Burrows	Pier and Face 8 A and 8 D
Rifleman William James Calvert	Pier and Face 15 A and 15 B
Rifleman Archibald Thomas Campbell	Pier and Face 15 A and 15 B
Rifleman Alexander Carlisle	Pier and Face 15 A and 15 B
Rifleman John Cathcart	Pier and Face 15 A and 15 B
Rifleman Edward Corry	Pier and Face 15 A and 15 B
Rifleman David Cromie	Pier and Face 15 A and 15 B
Private William John Dalzell	Pier and Face 4 D and 5 B
Rifleman Robert Dempster	Pier and Face 15 A and 15 B
Sergeant Samuel Devoy	Pier and Face 15 A and 15 B
Private Redmond Joseph Diver (Wheeler)	Pier and Face 10 A
Corporal James Neil Doggart	Pier and Face 4 D and 5 B
Rifleman Thomas Maddock Doggart	Pier and Face 15 A and 15 B
Rifleman James Donaldson	Pier and Face 15 A and 15 B
Rifleman John Donaldson	Pier and Face 15 A and 15 B
Rifleman Samuel Donaldson	Pier and Face 15 A and 15 B
Private John Dornan	Pier and Face 4 D and 5 B
Lance Corporal James Dorrian	Pier and Face 15 A and 15 B
Rifleman John Dorrian	Pier and Face 15 A and 15 B
Lance Corporal William Drennan	Pier and Face 15 A and 15 B
Rifleman John Dynes	Pier and Face 15 A and 15 B
Co Sgt Major David Ferris LS&GCM MID	Pier and Face 15 A and 15 B

Thiepval Memorial continued...

Rifleman **Robert Finlay**	Pier and Face 15 A and 15 B
Rifleman **James Fisher**	Pier and Face 15 A and 15 B
Rifleman **John Ralston Fitzsimmons**	Pier and Face 15 A and 15 B
Lance Corporal **Robert Fitzsimons**	Pier and Face 15 A and 15 B
Sergeant **Henry Foster**	Pier and Face 15 A and 15 B
Rifleman **William John Fowles**	Pier and Face 15 A and 15 B
Corporal **Francis Geddis**	Pier and Face 5 D and 12 B
Rifleman **Thomas Gilliland**	Pier and Face 15 A and 15 B
Rifleman **Charles Gorman**	Pier and Face 15 A and 15 B
Lance Corporal **Walter Gunning**	Pier and Face 15 A and 15 B
Rifleman **Alexander Hamill**	Pier and Face 15 A and 15 B
Rifleman **John Irvine Hamilton**	Pier and Face 15 A and 15 B
L/Cpl **Thomas James Harrison MM**	Pier and Face 15 A and 15 B
Rifleman **Robert Henderson**	Pier and Face 15 A and 15 B
Lt Col **Lawrence A Hind MC MID (x2)**	Pier and Face 10 C 10 D and 11 A
Rifleman **James Hughes**	Pier and Face 15 A and 15 B
Lance Corporal **Robert Russell Irvine**	Pier and Face 15 A and 15 B
Private **Andrew Johnston**	Pier and Face 15 A
Captain **Elliott Johnston MC**	Pier and Face 15 A and 15 B
Private **William Johnston**	Pier and Face 4 D and 5 B
Rifleman **William George Kelly**	Pier and Face 15 A and 15 B
Rifleman **Samuel Kennedy**	Pier and Face 15 A and 15 B
Private **George Laidlaw**	Pier and Face 15 B
Rifleman **Samuel Hugh Ledgerwood**	Pier and Face 15 A and 15 B
Rifleman **Robert Lowry**	Pier and Face 15 A and 15 B
L/Cpl **Herbert Henry MacMahon**	Pier and Face 16C
Rifleman **John Magill**	Pier and Face 15 A and 15 B
Lance Corporal **George Mahaffey**	Pier and Face 15 A and 15 B
Rifleman **Andrew Marshall**	Pier and Face 15 A and 15 B
Rifleman **John Martin**	Pier and Face 15 A and 15 B
Rifleman **John McGilton McAvoy**	Pier and Face 15 A and 15 B
Lance Corporal **James McCann**	Pier and Face 4 D and 5 B
Rifleman **Robert McCartney**	Pier and Face 15 A and 15 B
Rifleman **Robert McClements**	Pier and Face 15 A and 15 B
Corporal **Bryan McCloone**	Pier and Face 3 C and 4 A
Rifleman **John McCulloch**	Pier and Face 15 A and 15 B
Rifleman **Daniel McCutcheon**	Pier and Face 15 A and 15 B
Rifleman **John McCutcheon**	Pier and Face 15 A and 15 B
L/Corporal **Robert James McGreechan**	Pier and Face 15 A and 15 B
Private **Hugh McGreevy**	Pier and Face 3 A
Rifleman **James McIlwrath (Harris)**	Pier and Face 15 A and 15 B

Rifleman Robert McKibbin	Pier and Face 15 A and 15 B
Rifleman Samuel McMillan	Pier and Face 15 A and 15 B
Lance Corporal James McNeilly	Pier and Face 15 A and 15 B
Rifleman William McQuiston	Pier and Face 15 A and 15 B
Private William Melville	Pier and Face 4 D and 5 B
Sergeant Thomas Millar	Pier and Face 15 A and 15 B
Rifleman John Mills	Pier and Face 15 A and 15 B
Rifleman Samuel Miskelly	Pier and Face 15 A and 15 B
Second Lieutenant John Ross Moore	Pier and Face 15 A
Rifleman James Morrison	Pier and Face 15 A and 15 B
Rifleman James Morrow	Pier and Face 15 A and 15 B
Rifleman Alexander Mullan	Pier and Face 15 A and 15 B
Rifleman David Swan Mullan	Pier and Face 15 A and 15 B
Private Hugh Mullan (McMullan)	Pier and Face 6 D and 7 D
Private Joseph Murphy	Pier and Face 16C
Rifleman Thomas Newell	Pier and Face 15 A and 15 B
Private Thomas Norris	Pier and Face 4 D and 5 B
Corporal John O'Neill	Pier and Face 15 A and 15 B
Rifleman John O'Neill	Pier and Face 15 A and 15 B
Rifleman Robert James Orr	Pier and Face 15 A and 15 B
Lance Corporal Henry J Parfitt	Pier and Face 16 B and 16 C
Rifleman David Bell Patterson	Pier and Face 15 A and 15 B
Lance Corporal James Patterson	Pier and Face 15 A and 15 B
Rifleman Robert Patterson	Pier and Face 15 A and 15 B
Corporal William James Patterson	Pier and Face 15 A and 15 B
Rifleman William Patton	Pier and Face 15 A and 15 B
Corporal William John Peake MM	Pier and Face 15 A and 15 B
Rifleman William Haire Poole	Pier and Face 15 A and 15 B
Rifleman James Porter	Pier and Face 15 A and 15 B
Rifleman Thomas Quinn	Pier and Face 15 A and 15 B
Rifleman David Rainey	Pier and Face 15 A and 15 B
Rifleman William Ravey	Pier and Face 15 A and 15 B
Rifleman Alexander Robinson	Pier and Face 15 A and 15 B
Private James Runaghan	Pier and Face 16C
Rifleman Alexander Russell	Pier and Face 15 A and 15 B
Rifleman William Semple	Pier and Face 15 A and 15 B
Rifleman William Semple	Pier and Face 15 A and 15 B
Rifleman Robert James Semple	Pier and Face 15 A and 15 B
Rifleman David Shanks	Pier and Face 15 A and 15 B
Rifleman John Shannon	Pier and Face 15 A and 15 B
Lance Corporal William Simpson	Pier and Face 15 A and 15 B

Thiepval Memorial continued…

Rifleman **John Sinclair**	Pier and Face 15 A and 15 B
Rifleman **George Sloan**	Pier and Face 15 A and 15 B
Rifleman **William Sloan**	Pier and Face 15 A and 15 B
Private **John Smith**	Pier and Face 15 C
Rifleman **David Smyth**	Pier and Face 15 A and 15 B
Rifleman **David John Smyth**	Pier and Face 15 A and 15 B
Rifleman **William John S Snodden**	Pier and Face 15 A and 15 B
Sergeant **Patrick P Spain**	Pier and Face 16C
Lance Corporal **John Milliken Spence**	Pier and Face 15 A and 15 B
Private **George Stevenson**	Pier and Face 15 C
Rifleman **James Croskery Stevenson**	Pier and Face 15 A and 15 B.
Rifleman **Robert Stewart**	Pier and Face 5 C and 12 C
Rifleman **Charles Thompson**	Pier and Face 15 A and 15 B
Lance Corporal **David John Thompson**	Pier and Face 15 A and 15 B
Rifleman **James Thompson**	Pier and Face 15 A and 15 B
Private **William James Thompson**	Pier and Face 15 A
Corporal **William John Thompson**	Pier and Face 15 A and 15 B
Lance Corporal **Henry Edward Victor**	Pier and Face 12 D and 13 B
Rifleman **John Weir**	Pier and Face 15 A and 15 B
Lance Corporal **Gordon Whyte**	Pier and Face 15 A and 15 B
Rifleman **William Wilson**	Pier and Face 15 A and 15 B
2nd Lieutenant **Matthew John Wright**	Pier and Face 15 A and 15 B
Rifleman **James Young**	Pier and Face 15 A and 15 B

Tincourt New British Cemetery, Somme, France

Rifleman **Samuel Wallace Jordan**	VIII. H. 17
Private **David H McMillan (MM unsubstantiated to date)**	III. G. 25

Toronto (Prospect) Cemetery, Canada

Private **Hugh Graham Ritchie**	Veterans Sec. 7. 976

Tourcoing (Pont-Neuville) Communal Cemetery, Nord, France

Private **Albert Connolly**	M. 2
Private **James Pollock**	H. 6

Tower Hill Memorial, London, England

First Mate **Michael Collins**	SS *Eveleen* (**Belfast**)
Carpenter **Robert Hughes**	SS *Donegal* (**Belfast**)
Horseman **Hugh Muckle**	SS *Cabotia* (**Glasgow**)
Master **Robert Murphy**	SS *Lough Fisher*
Second Mate **Thomas Lewis Nicholas**	SS *Beatrice* (**London**)

Junior Second Engineer Officer **Alfred J Rice**	SS *Hungerford* (**London**)
Able Seaman **James Skilling**	SS *Garron Head* (**Belfast**)

Tranchee de Mecknes Cemetery, Aix-Noulette, Pas de Calais, France
Private **William Martin**	**L. 6**

Trefcon British Cemetery, Caulaincourt, Aisne, France
Lieutenant **Samuel McKee Geddis**	**C. 59**

Trois Arbres Cemetery, Steenwerck, Nord, France
Private **Alexander McClean**	**I. R. 10**

Tullynakill Graveyard, Killinchy, Co. Down
Captain **David Mitchell**

Twelve Tree Copse Cemetery, Gallipoli, Turkey
Private **John Hanna**	**XI. E. 14**
Private **William Morris**	**Sp. Mem. C. 166**

Tyne Cot Cemetery, Zonnebeke, West-Vlaanderen, Belgium
Rifleman **William Coleman**	**V. H. 14**
Rifleman **George Edgar Edmonds**	**LIV. D. 2**
Rifleman **Thomas Johnston**	**VII. E. 10**
Second Lieutenant **Thomas McRoberts**	**LXV. E. 4**
Company Sergeant Major **Wilfred Harold Medland**	**IV. H. 16**
Sergeant **James Proctor**	**IV. B. 20**
Private **William Tompsett**	**LXVII. H. I**

Tyne Cot Memorial, Zonnebeke, West-Vlaanderen, Belgium
Rifleman **George Birney**	**Panel 138-140 & 162-162A & 163A**
Rifleman **James Campbell**	**Panel 138-140 & 162-162A & 163A**
Private **Hugh Dalzell**	**Panel 140-141**
Sergeant **WJ Doherty LS&GCM**	**Panel 138-140 & 162-162A & 163A**
Private **Adam Donaldson**	**Panel 154-159 & 163A**
Private **William Holland K Ellison**	**Panel 140-141**
Private **Thomas Emerson**	**Panel 10-11**
Rifleman **John Fullerton**	**Panel 138-140 & 162-162A & 163A**
Private **Samuel Gilmour**	**Panel 160 & 162A & 163A**
Lance Corporal **John A Hare**	**Panel 138-140 & 162-162A & 163A**
Private **Vincent Hendley**	**Panel 140-141**
Private **William James Johnston**	**Panel 140-141**
Private **Bernard Kerr**	**Panel 140-141**
2nd Lieutenant **Joseph Laverty**	**Panel 138-140 & 162-162A & 163A**

Tyne Cot Memorial continued…

Rifleman **James Lundy**	Panel 138-140 & 162-162A & 163A
Rifleman **William McBride**	Panel 138-140 & 162-162A & 163A
2nd Lieutenant **James McBurney**	Panel 138-140 & 162-162A & 163A
Rifleman **Robert McKay**	Panel 138-140 & 162-162A & 163A
Rifleman **Duncan McLean**	Panel 138-140 & 162-162A & 163A
2nd Lieutenant **William Moore**	Panel 140-141
Private **George Morrow**	Panel 140-141
L/Corporal **Henry Alan Murray**	Panel 138-140 & 162-162A & 163A
Rifleman **Samuel Murray**	Panel 138-140 & 162-162A & 163A
L/Corporal **James Henry Quail**	Panel 138-140 & 162-162A & 163A
L/Corporal **Thomas Stevenson**	Panel 138-140 & 162-162A & 163A
Corporal **John Thompson**	Panel 138-140 & 162-162A & 163A
Sergeant **Robert Thompson**	Panel 18-19
Rifleman **James Vance**	Panel 138-140 & 162-162A & 163A
Rifleman **James Wright**	Panel 138-140 & 162-162A & 163A

V Beach Cemetery, Gallipoli, Turkey
Private **Robert Coulter**	Special Memorial A. 28

Vancouver (Mountain View) Cemetery, Canada
Private **Charles Hugh Parke Wilson**	2. 45. 14

Vermelles British Cemetery, Pas de Calais, France
Lance Corporal **Andrew Clarke**	III. O. 6
Rifleman **Alexander Dines**	VI. E. 5
Lance Corporal **William McDowell**	V. B. 3
Private **Edward McMullan**	Special Memorial 6
Rifleman **Robert Stratton**	VI. D. 35

Vevey (St. Martin's) Cemetery, Switzerland
Rifleman **Robert Allen**	65

Vignacourt British Cemetery, Somme, France
Private **Samuel Gourley**	III. A. 11

Villers Station Cemetery, Villers-au-Bois, Pas de Calais, France
Private **William Donnan**	V. G. 9
Corporal **William Menown**	VI. D. 8
Lieutenant **William Hamilton Mitchell**	III. B. 19

Villers-Bretonneux Memorial, Somme, France
Private **Ernest Ludgate Hill**
Lance Corporal **William Edwin Logan**

Villers-Bretonneux Military Cemetery, Somme, France
Private Alexander Boyle   X. F. 6

Villers-Faucon Communal Cemetery Extension, Somme, France
Corporal Henry Earney   I. C. 10

Vimy Memorial, Pas de Calais, France
Private Beresford Addy
Private James Angus
Private John Boyd
Private Francis Haire
Private Robert Hewitt
Private John McDonnell
Private James McGaffin
Private Robert Sloane McGaffin
Sergeant James McKee
Private David McKittrick
Private John McMillan
Private William Savage Montgomery
Private John Stewart

Vis-en-Artois British Cemetery, Haucourt, Pas de Calais, France
Private James Hamilton   X. A. 9

Vlamertinghe New Military Cemetery, Ieper, West Vlaanderen, Belgium
Gunner Alexander McDonnell   VII. G. 11

Warlencourt British Cemetery, Pas de Calais, France
Private John Kinnaird   IV. B. 8

Warloy-Baillon Communal Cemetery Extension, Somme, France
Rifleman Alexander Palmer   I. B. 16
Private Robert Thompson   I. A. 2

Whitechurch Graveyard, Ballywalter, Co. Down
Able Seaman Frederick William Chater   Middle S-E boundary
Rifleman Samuel Hugh Regan

Wimereux Communal Cemetery, Pas de Calais, France
Private James Aloysius Kinlay   I. O. 15
Captain Herbert Vesey Scott   III. O. 2

Woods Cemetery, Ieper, West-Vlaanderen, Belgium
Private Joseph Craig   II. E. 5

Wytschaete Military Cemetery, Heuvelland, West-Vlaanderen, Belgium

Corporal **Robert Boyd Rainey**   II. E. 15

Y Farm Military Cemetery, Bois-Grenier, Nord, France

Rifleman **George Jamison**   K. 35

Y Ravine Cemetery, Beaumont-Hamel, Somme, France

Private **Walter Mulholland**   D. 102

Ypres (Menin Gate) Memorial, Ieper, West-Vlaanderen, Belgium

Private **James Best**	Panel 11
Company Sergeant Major **James Campbell**	Panel 40
Rifleman **Thomas Corry**	Panel 40
Rifleman **Robert James Dempster**	Panel 40
Rifleman **Thomas Dines**	Panel 40
Rifleman **Alexander Doggart**	Panel 40
Rifleman **John Foster**	Panel 40
Rifleman **Hans Hamilton**	Panel 40
Rifleman **James Heron**	Panel 40
Lance Corporal **James Holland**	Panel 51 & 53
Lance Corporal **James Irvine**	Panel 22
Rifleman **James Jones**	Panel 40
Private **Daniel Maclean Keith**	Panel 19 & 33
Private **Thomas Alexander Keith**	Panel 24-28-30
Second Lieutenant **George Knox**	Panel 12
Private **John Lynch**	Panel 11
Private **George Turner McAlpine**	Panel 15-16 & 16A
Rifleman **James McClelland**	Panel 40
Rifleman **Joseph McConnell**	Panel 40
Rifleman **Andrew McDonald**	Panel 46-48 & 50
Lance Corporal **Robert John McDowell**	Panel 32
Rifleman **Robert McGimpsey**	Panel 40
Corporal **William Barry Ritchie Millar**	Panel 7-17-23-25-27-29-31
Private **Catherwood Moore**	Panel 19 & 33
Captain **Samuel Valentine Morgan LS&GCM**	Panel 40
Captain **Walter Percy O'Lone DCM MID**	Panel 40
Rifleman **Alexander Pagan**	Panel 40
Rifleman **Reuben Peake**	Panel 40
Corporal **John Russell (Movilla Street)**	Panel 40
Second Lieutenant **Donald SS Smurthwaite**	Panel 37
Rifleman **James Stewart**	Panel 40

Ypres Town Cemetery, Ieper, West-Vlaanderen, Belgium
Captain **The Hon Andrew Edward Somerset Mulholland**　　　E2. 3

Ypres Town Cemetery Extension, Ieper, West-Vlaanderen, Belgium
Captain **Alfred Squire Taylor**　　　III. B. 21

Zuydcoote Military Cemetery, Nord, France
Private **Robert Saunders**　　　II. C. 10

Cemetery and/or CWGC Memorial Not Confirmed To Date
Rifleman **William J Allen**
Rifleman **William Auld**
Rifleman **David Bell**
Quartermaster Sergeant **Andrew Boyd**
Private **Samuel Boyd**
Rifleman **James Brankin**
Rifleman **Hugh Brown**
Private **Archibald Cairns**
Private **A Edward Campbell**
Sergeant **Henry Campbell**
John Campbell
Regimental Sergeant Major **Patrick Campbell**
Rifleman **William Campbell**
Sergeant **George Carson**
Rifleman **James Casey**
Private **James Clarke**
Private **William Clarke**
Thomas Clegg
Robert Close
Sergeant **Hugh Crowe**
Rifleman **Robert Dempster**
Rifleman **Thomas Dorrian**
Rifleman **Thomas Dowdall**
Private **Alfred Fenton**
Rifleman **Thomas Girvin**
A Gracey
Sapper **Thomas Griffiths**
Samuel Hamilton
Stephen Johnson
Rifleman **Robert Kemp**

Not Confirmed To Date continued…

Corporal **Hugh Lawson**

George Ledlie

James Majury

Rifleman **George Mallon**

Engineer Lieutenant **Edward Wilson McBurney**

Rifleman **John McCartan**

Seaman **John McClement**

Rifleman **James McClure**

Robert McConnell

John McCullough

Gunner **John McDonagh**

James W McDowell

Rifleman **John McDowell**

Private **Thomas McGimpsey**

Gunner **Samuel McKendry**

Private **John McKenna**

Rifleman **David McKimm**

Private **George McKnight**

Rifleman **Patrick McMullan**

Rifleman **William McMullan**

Private **Andrew McTaggart**

Sergeant **James Monks**

J Moreland

Private **Walter Morrison**

Rifleman **James Neill**

Private **Robert Palmer**

Sergeant **Charles Pegg**

Rifleman **Robert Poole**

Private **Charles Quigley**

W Regan

William Rice

William Robinson

Rifleman **Robert Russell**

T Scott

Robert Stannage

Rifleman **James Stewart**

Robert D Stewart

Rifleman **William R Strain**

Rifleman **David Stratton**

Rifleman **George Stratton**
John Thompson
Private **William Henry Thompson**
Rifleman **William Vance (East Street)**
Captain **GAC Ward**
Adam White
Private **James Wilson**
T Woodside
Rifleman **Charles Young**

Abbreviations and Glossary of Terms

Abbreviations used in this Book of Honour:

ACC	Army Cyclist Corps
ADS	Advanced Dressing Station
AMC	Armed Merchant Cruiser
ANZAC	Australian and New Zealand Army Corps
ASC	Army Service Corps
attd	attached
AIF	Australian Imperial Force
BC	Bad Character
Bde	Brigade
BEF	British Expeditionary Force
BH	Base Hospital
Bn	Battalion
CB	Companion of the Order of the Bath
CCS	Casualty Clearing Station
CdG (F)	Croix de Guerre (France)
CEF	Canadian Expeditionary Force
CLB	Church Lads' Brigade
Cmdr	Commander
CMG	Companion of the Order of St Michael & St George
Coy	Company
Cpl	Corporal
CQMS	Company Quartermaster Sergeant
CWGC	Commonwealth War Graves Commission
D	Deserter *or* Died
DAH	Disordered action of the Heart
DCM	Distinguished Conduct Medal
Div	Division
DoW	Died of wounds
DSO	Distinguished Service Order
FA	Field Ambulance
GRT	Gross Register Tonnage
HQ	Headquarters
HMML	His Majesty's Motor Launch
HMS	His Majesty's Ship
HMT	His Majesty's Transport
IV	Irish Volunteers (formed in 1913 by Irish Nationalists)

Jnr	Junior
KIA	Killed in Action
L/Cpl	Lance Corporal
LOL	Loyal Orange Lodge
Lt	Lieutenant
Maj	Major
MBE	Member of the Order of the British Empire
MC	Military Cross
MCB	Methodist College Belfast
MGC	Machine Gun Corps
MIA	Missing in Action
MID	Mentioned in Despatches
MM	Military Medal
MT	Mechanical Transport
NCO	Non-Commissioned Officer
NZEF	New Zealand Expeditionary Force
NV	National Volunteers (IV members who fought in the Great War)
OBE	Officer of the Order of the British Empire
OTC	Officers' Training Corps
PCI	Presbyterian Church in Ireland
POW	Prisoner of War
PS	Public Schools
Pte	Private
QMS	Quartermaster Sergeant
QUB	Queen's University Belfast
Q-ship	Armed merchant ship with concealed weaponry
RAF	Royal Air Force
RAMC	Royal Army Medical Corps
RAP	Regimental Aid Post
RAPC	Royal Arch Purple Chapter
RASC	Royal Army Service Corps
RBAI	Royal Belfast Academical Institution
RBL	Royal British Legion
RBP	Royal Black Preceptory
RFA	Royal Field Artillery
RFC	Royal Flying Corps
RGA	Royal Garrison Artillery
Rgt	Regiment
RHA	Royal Horse Artillery
RIC	Royal Irish Constabulary

RMS	Royal Mail Ship
RNAS	Royal Naval Air Service
RNVR	Royal Naval Volunteer Reserve
RSM	Regimental Sergeant Major (the most senior NCO)
SAI	South African Infantry
Sgt	Sergeant
SMLE	Short Magazine Lee Enfield
SMS	Seiner Majestat Schiff (German equivalent of His Majesty's Ship)
Snr	Senior
SS	Steamship
TB	Tuberculosis
transfd	transferred
U-boat	Untersee-boat (German submarine)
UK	United Kingdom (then England, Scotland, Wales and Ireland)
UV	Ulster Volunteers (Unionist militia formed in 1912)
UVF	Ulster Volunteer Force (formally established on 13 January 1913 from Ulster Volunteers)
VAD	Voluntary Aid Detachment
VC	Victoria Cross
VDH	Valvular Disease of the Heart
WAAC	Women's Auxiliary Army Corps
YCV	Young Citizen Volunteers (formed 10 September 1912)
YMCA	Young Men's Christian Association
YWCA	Young Women's Christian Association

Glossary of Military and Other Terms used in this Book of Honour:

Army Structure:

1. **Regiment (Infantry)**: A regiment normally comprised two peace-time regular battalions, one remaining at home and the other serving abroad, along with 2/3 militia battalions. Some did not go overseas and were used as training battalions. When the Great War began each regiment raised a number of new 'service' battalions.

2. **Battalion**: When at full strength a battalion mustered just over 1000 officers and men and was commanded by a Lieutenant Colonel. As the war progressed many battalions operated far below full strength. Some battalions were merged or disbanded altogether.

3. **Company**: Each battalion comprised four companies of around 220 men, each commanded by a Captain or a Major, together with a Headquarters company.

4. **Platoons and Sections**: Each company was divided into four platoons and each platoon was divided into four sections.

5. **Brigade (Infantry)**: A brigade comprised four battalions (reduced to three in 1918) and was commanded by a Brigadier General.

6. **Division (Infantry)**: A division was commanded by a Major General and mustered 19000 men in three brigades. It had 12 infantry battalions, a pioneer battalion, specialist engineers, signallers, medical and supply troops, a squadron of cavalry and four batteries of Royal Field Artillery. Three divisions were formed in Ireland – the 10th (Irish), the 16th (Irish) and the 36th (Ulster) Divisions.

7. **Battery**: A battery was a group of artillery guns and gunners. Several batteries were grouped into an artillery brigade (the equivalent of a regiment). There were three branches in the Royal Artillery – Horse, Field and Garrison.

8. **Regiment (Cavalry)**: Cavalry regiments were smaller (around 550) and did not have battalions.

Battalion and Regimental Names and Mottos

Royal Irish Rifles: Quis separabit *('Who will separate [us]')*
4th Battalion Royal Irish Rifles: Royal North Downs *(HQ in Newtownards)*
13th Battalion Royal Irish Rifles: *1st County Down Volunteers*
16th Battalion Royal Irish Rifles: *2nd County Down Volunteers*
Royal Irish Fusiliers: Faugh-a-Ballaghs *('Clear the way')*

Kitchener's New Armies

When Field Marshal Earl Kitchener of Khartoum took over as Minister of War on 5 August 1914 he issued orders for the expansion of the British Army and he called for men to enlist. The first 100,000 volunteers comprised Kitchener's First New Army, they were known as K1 and they included the 10th (Irish) Division. The second 100,000 volunteers were known as K2 and they included the 16th (Irish) Division. Kitchener's Fifth New Army included the 36th (Ulster) Division.

Service Rank Equivalents across the Services

Army	Navy	Air Force
Field Marshal	Admiral of the Fleet	Marshal of the Air Force
General	Admiral	Air Marshal
Brigadier	Commodore	Air Commodore
Colonel	Captain	Group Captain
Lieutenant Colonel	Commander	Wing Commander
Major	Lieutenant Commander	Squadron Leader
Captain	Lieutenant	Flight Lieutenant
Lieutenant	Sub-Lieutenant	Flying Officer
Second Lieutenant	Ensign	Pilot Officer
Officer Cadet	Midshipman	Officer Cadet
Sergeant Major	Warrant Officer	Warrant Officer
Sergeant	Petty Officer	Sergeant
Corporal	Leading Seaman	Corporal
Private	Seaman	Aircraftman

Adjutant — *Officer in charge of Battalion administration*

Quartermaster — *Sergeant responsible for stores and transport*

Additional Information

This Section provides additional information about some of the men with Ards connections.

Adair, James
Died on Tuesday 7 August 1928 (aged 35)
Newtownards (Movilla) Cemetery, Co. Down

DEATHS.

ADAIR—August 7th 1928, at 42A Church Street, Newtownards, James, late Copl. R.F.A., eldest and only surviving son of the late Robert and Margaret Adair. His remains were interred in Movilla Cemetery on the 9th inst. Deeply regretted by his sorrowing Sisters.
KATHLEEN M'CULLOUGH, ANNIE ADAIR.
12 Robert Street, Newtownards.

James Adair was born on 26 November 1892 and he was the eldest son of Robert and Margaret (Maggie) Adair (nee Mullen) who were married on 11 November 1890 in Ballyblack Presbyterian Church. They lived in the townland of Corporation South, Newtownards before moving to the townland of Ballyharry, Newtownards. Robert Adair worked as an agricultural labourer and he and Maggie had at least five children – Kathleen (1891), James (1892), Edward (1895), Alice (1898) and Ann Jane Bleakly (Annie) (1903). They were baptised in First Newtownards Presbyterian Church. Prior to the outbreak of the Great War, James and Edward Adair both worked as agricultural labourers.

James Adair's death was reported in the 18 August 1928 edition of the *Newtownards Chronicle*. Corporal James Adair served with the Royal Field Artillery and he died on 7 August 1928 aged 35. He was buried in Movilla Cemetery. James's wife Elizabeth (Lizzie) and his sisters Kathleen McCullough and Annie Adair placed separate death notices. Lizzie Adair had two children and they lived at 35 Robert Street, Newtownards.

Algie, James
Died on Monday 15 October 1928 (aged 56)
Newtownards (Movilla) Cemetery, Co. Down

DEATHS.

ALGIE—October 15, 1928, at the County Infirmary, Downpatrick, James Algie. The remains of my beloved husband were interred in Movilla Cemetery on Wednesday afternoon, 17th inst. Deeply regretted by his sorrowing Wife and Family.
4, Balfour Street, Newtownards.

James Algie died on Monday 15 October 1928 at the County Infirmary in Downpatrick and he was buried in Movilla Cemetery, Newtownards. In subsequent years there were 'In Memoriam' notices in the *Newtownards Chronicle* from various family members – his wife Mary living at 4 Balfour Street, Newtownards; his son John and daughter-in-law Eva Algie living at 2 Railway Park Buildings, Newtownards; his sister Polly and brother-in-law Hugh Dunlop living at 17 Ann Street Newtownards and his brother John and sister-in-law Sarah Algie living at 39 Little Francis Street, Newtownards.

Auld, William

William Auld who worked as a dealer died of bronchitis on 15 April 1924 at his home, 74 Mill Street, Newtownards, and he was buried in Movilla New Cemetery. Desk studies and public appeals to date have not confirmed a connection between these data and the soldier who is commemorated on Newtownards and District War Memorial.

Bell, William
Died on Thursday 10 November 1927
Newtownards (Movilla) Cemetery, Co. Down

> **DEATH.**
>
> BELL—November 10, 1927 (in hospital), William Bell, 102, East Street, Newtownards, ex-13th Batt. R.I. Rifles. The remains of my beloved husband will be removed from above address for interment in Movilla Cemetery on to-day (Saturday), at 3 p.m. Friends will please accept this intimation.
> MARGARET BELL.

William Bell of 102 East Street Newtownards and ex-13th Battalion Royal Irish Rifles died in hospital on Thursday 10 November 1927 and his wife Margaret placed a death notice in the *Newtownards Chronicle*. William was buried in Movilla Cemetery Newtownards.

Bennett, David
Sergeant
Durham Light Infantry
Died of cardiac failure on Friday 27 May 1921
Newtownards (Movilla) Cemetery, Co. Down (Grave 2. 25)

> **DEATHS.**
>
> BENNETT.—27th May, 1921, at the residence of his sister, 138 Mill Street, Newtownards, David Bennett, ex-Sergt. Durham Light Infantry. His remains were interred in Movilla Cemetery on Sunday, 29th ult.
> Inserted by his Nephew.
> DAVID BENNETT.
> 58 Church Street, Newtownards.

Sergeant David Bennett served with the Durham Light Infantry and he died on 27 May 1921 at his sister's residence, 138 Mill Street, Newtownards. He was buried in Newtownards (Movilla) Cemetery.

Burns, Joseph
Died on Friday 19 March 1920
Donaghadee Parish Church Graveyard, Donaghadee, Co. Down

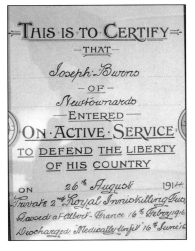

DEATHS.

BURNS—March 19th, 1920, at 54 Movilla Street, Newtownards, Joseph Burns, date private 3/4606, 3rd Battalion Royal Innis. Fusiliers. His remains were interred in Donaghadee Churchyard on Sunday afternoon, 21st inst.
God took him to His home above,
  Out of this world of pain ;
'Tis only but a little while,
  And we shall meet again,
Deeply regretted by his Mother and Brother John,

Joseph Burns enlisted on 26 August 1914. He was gassed at Albert in France on 16 February 1916 and he was discharged as medically unfit on 16 June 1916. Joseph Burns died on 19 March 1920 at 54 Movilla Street, Newtownards and he was buried in Donaghadee Parish Church Graveyard. His mother and brother John placed a death notice in the *Newtownards Chronicle* and it contained the verse:

> 'God took him to His home above,
> Out of this world of pain;
> Tis only but a little while,
> And we shall meet again'

Cairns, William John
Died on Wednesday 12 July 1922 (aged 44)
Newtownards (Movilla) Cemetery, Co. Down

CAIRNS—July 12th, 1922, at the U.V.F. Hospital, Belfast, William John, son of the late John Cairns, Newtownards. The remains of my beloved husband will be removed from above Institution for interment in the family burying-ground, Movilla, to-day (Saturday), at 2 p.m., passing through Newtownards about 3 p.m.
SARAH CAIRNS.

William John Cairns was born on 18 September 1877 and he was a son of John and Annie Cairns (nee McKee). He was baptised in Greenwell Street Presbyterian Church Newtownards. William John Cairns and Sarah Walsh were married on 29 October 1900 in Regent Street Methodist Church Newtownards and they had at least five children – Alexander, John, Ellen Jane, Sarah and George. William John Cairns died on 12 July 1922 in the UVF Hospital in Belfast and he was buried in Newtownards (Movilla) Cemetery.

Carson, George

DEATHS.

CARSON—September 6, 1930, at the Royal Victoria Hospital, Belfast, George, the dearly-beloved husband of Rachel Carson, 10, Bangor Road, Newtownards. His remains were interred in Movilla Cemetery on 8th inst. Deeply regretted by his sorrowing Wife and Family.
RACHEL CARSON.

A George Carson died on 6 September 1930 in the Royal Victoria Hospital Belfast and his wife Rachel placed a death notice in the *Newtownards Chronicle*. 'In Memoriam' notices in subsequent years indicate that the family lived at 35 Bangor Road in Newtownards. Desk studies and public appeals to date have not conclusively confirmed a connection between these data and the soldier who is commemorated on Newtownards and District War Memorial.

Caughey, William James

IRISH FEDERATION OF DISCHARGED AND DEMOBILISED SAILORS AND SOLDIERS. NEWTOWNARDS BRANCH.

CAUGHEY—The Members of the above Branch regret to learn of the death of their esteemed Brother, Wm. Caughey, and desire to place same on record.
JAMES WALLACE, Secretary.
A. C. TATE, Treasurer.

After William James Caughey died, the Officers and Members of the Newtownards Branch of the Irish Federation of Discharged and Demobilised Sailors and Soldiers placed a sympathy notice in the *Newtownards Chronicle*.

Crooks, Joseph
Died on Wednesday 4 May 1932
Killysuggan Graveyard, Newtownards, Co Down

CROOKS—May 4, 1932, at the U.V.F. Hospital, Joseph, beloved husband of Elizabeth Blaney Crooks, 23, Bangor Road, Newtownards.—R.I.P. His remains were interred in Killysuggan Cemetery on Friday afternoon, 6th inst. " On his soul, Sweet Jesus, have mercy."
Deeply regretted by his sorrowing Wife and Family; also his Sister and Brother-in-law.

Joseph Crooks died on 4 May 1932 at the UVF Hospital, Craigavon House in Belfast and he was buried in Killysuggan Graveyard, Newtownards. His wife Eleanor Blaney Crooks lived at 23 Bangor Road, Newtownards.

Dines, Alexander

Dorrian, Hugh John M

Hugh John M Dorrian was baptised on 5 December 1896 in Ballyphilip Roman Catholic Church Portaferry. He was a son of John and Eliza Jane Dorrian who had at least nine children – William (1889), Daniel (1890), Mary (1892), Thomas (1894; like Hugh John, he also fought in the Great War), Hugh John (1896), James (1898), Francis (1901) and Richard (1907). All of the Dorrian children were baptised in Ballyphilip Roman Catholic Church Portaferry.

Fenton, Alfred

FENTON—August 11th, 1924, at his residence 116, Mill Street, Newtownards, Alfred Fenton. The remains of my beloved husband were interred in Movilla Cemetery on Tuesday, 12th inst.

Sadly missed.
ANNIE FENTON.

An Alfred Fenton, husband of Annie Fenton, died on 11 August 1924 at his home in 116 Mill Street, Newtownards and he was buried in Movilla Cemetery. A connection with the soldier who is commemorated on Newtownards and District War Memorial has not as yet been conclusively confirmed.

Fisher Brothers: George and Hugh

George and Hugh Fisher had another sister and her name was Rose. Rose was baptised on 1 October 1897 in St Patrick's Roman Catholic Church Ballygalget.

Fitzsimmons, James

James Fitzsimmons was baptised on 21 April 1875 in Ballyphilip Roman Catholic Church Portaferry and he was a son of George and Mary Fitzsimmons who had at least seven children – Mary (1867), Margaret (1870), Georgina (1872), James (1875), Thomas (1878), William (1879) and Martha (1883). All of the Fitzsimmons children were baptised in Ballyphilip Roman Catholic Church Portaferry.

Fulton, Stewart

This is an additional name.

Stewart Fulton is commemorated in the PCI Roll of Honour for St Enoch's Presbyterian Church in Belfast. There it is recorded that he served with the US National Guards and was killed. His address was 11 Rosewood Street, Belfast. Stewart Fulton was born in County Tyrone and he was a son of John and Susan Fulton who had two other children – Frances and John. In 1911 the Fulton family was living at 108 High Street in Comber. John was working as a hackle-maker in a spinning mill and Stewart (aged 17) was working as a clerk in a whiskey distillery.

Stewart Fulton is not listed by the American Battle Monuments Commission; the Commission only has records of those casualties that are buried in their cemeteries or listed on the Walls of the Missing (some 33,717 out of a total of 116,516 American casualties in the Great War). Desk studies and public appeals to date have yielded no further information as to when Stewart Fulton died.

Graham, James

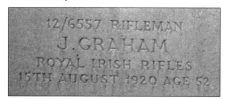

In the CWGC Debt of Honour James Graham's Royal Irish Rifles service number is recorded as 12/6517 and on his CWGC headstone in Newtownards (Movilla) Cemetery it is inscribed as 12/6557.

Kerr, Bernard

Bernard Kerr was a son of Bernard and Mary Kerr (nee Graham)

McAlpine, Francis (Frank)

In 1919 Frank's mother Mary placed an 'Our Heroes – In Memoriam' notice in the *Newtownards Chronicle* and it contained the verse:

'An unknown grave is the bitterest blow,
  None but an aching heart can know;
  A little hillock of blood-stained clay,
  A wooden cross raised two years today'

McCready, John
Died on Thursday 11 April 1929
Newtownards (Movilla) Cemetery, Co. Down

John McCready died at the UVF Hospital, Craigavon House in Belfast on Thursday 11 April 1929 and his wife Mary placed a death notice in the *Newtownards Chronicle*. The funeral was from his home at 47 East Street, Newtownards to Movilla Cemetery Newtownards.

McMullan, Edward
Edward McMullan was born in 1892 and his parents, Richard and Sarah McMullan, had eleven children all of whom were baptised in Portaferry Roman Catholic Church – Sarah in 1884, Elizabeth Anne in 1884 (died), Jane (Jinnie) in 1885, Thomas John in 1887, Richard in 1889, Edward in 1892, Catherine (Kate) in 1894, Nellie in 1897, James in 1900, Hugh in 1903 and Eliza Anne in 1904.

McMullan, John Joseph
John Joseph McMullan was born in 1896 and his parents, James and Rebecca McMullan, had seven children all of whom were baptised in Portaferry Roman Catholic Church – James Joseph on 24 October 1893, Mary Jane on 1 January 1895, John Joseph on 9 December 1896, James on 10 June 1898, Sarah on 6 January 1901, Gerard on 19 April 1903 and William on 3 June 1904.

McNally, Hugh Francis (Hugh)
Hugh Francis McNally was born in 1892 and he was a son of Nicholas and Elizabeth McNally (nee McGrath). Hugh's sister Rose married Patrick Tomelty who was a brother of **Charles Tomelty** who was killed in action on 27 August 1918.

Parfitt, Henry J
Lance Corporal
No. B/164, 7th Battalion, Rifle Brigade
Killed in action on Sunday 20 August 1916
Thiepval Memorial (Pier and Face 16B and 16C)

This is an additional name.

In the 29 August 1925 edition of the *Newtownards Chronicle* there was an 'Our Heroes – In Memoriam' notice for Lance Corporal Henry J Parfitt from his widow Annabella and their children who were living at 26 Church Street in Newtownards and it contained the verse:

'And now he is sleeping his last long sleep,
And his grave I may never see,
But some gentle hand, in a distant land,
May scatter some flowers for me;

And some tender heart may shed a tear
For the wife in anguish sore,
For the life so fair that has ended there,
Away on an alien shore'

Parker, John J

PARKER.—June 5th. 1921 (suddenly), at 46 James Street. Newtownards, John J. Parker late Sergeant-Major, 4th Royal Irish Rifles. The remains of my beloved husband were interred in the family burying ground, Kilmood, on Tuesday afternoon, 7th inst.
                            MAGGIE PARKER.

This is an additional name. In the 11 June 1921 edition of the *Newtownards Chronicle* the sudden death on 5 June 1921 of John J Parker, late Sergeant Major 4th Royal Irish Rifles, was reported. He was buried in the family burying ground, Kilmood.

Parkhill, James

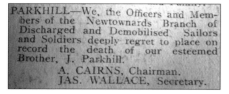

PARKHILL—We, the Officers and Members of the Newtownards Branch of Discharged and Demobilised Sailors and Soldiers deeply regret to place on record the death of our esteemed Brother, J. Parkhill.
    A. CAIRNS, Chairman.
    JAS. WALLACE, Secretary.

After James Parkhill died on 17 February 1919, the Officers and Members of the Newtownards Branch of the Irish Federation of Discharged and Demobilised Sailors and Soldiers placed a sympathy notice in the *Newtownards Chronicle*.

Rilley, James Henry

After James Henry Rilley died on 14 February 1918, his family moved to Ballymoney, Holywood and it was there that his son – affectionately known as 'Wee Sydney' – died on 13 May 1920.

Russell, John
Died on Monday 9 May 1921 (aged 48)
Newtownards (Movilla) Cemetery, Co. Down

John Russell served with the Royal Irish Rifles during the South African War and after his term of duty was complete he was placed on Reserve. At the outbreak of the Great War he rejoined the colours and served throughout the war. Sergeant John Russell was demobilised in 1919 and on 24 January 1921 he joined the 'A' class of the RIC Specials. After training at the Newtownards Camp he was posted to Newry and it was reported in the press that he was 48 years old and a widower with dependent children. John's wife Maggie died just one month before John died and so when John died his children were orphaned.

RUSSELL.—May 9th, 1921 (the result of an accident at Newry), Special Constable John Russell. The remains of our dearly-beloved father were interred in Movilla Cemetery on Thursday afternoon, 12th inst.
Inserted by his sorrowing Family.
36 Frederick Street,
Newtownards.

On the night of 3/4 May 1921 John Russell was on sentry duty in a roof-top listening post in Newry when he accidentally fell off the roof – there was no guard-rail. John suffered serious head injuries and died in hospital. His address in Newtownards was 36 Frederick Street and he was buried in Movilla Cemetery with constabulary honours. A considerable number of ex-servicemen attended his funeral which was conducted by the Rev Thomas McIlwrath from Greenwell Street Presbyterian Church.

Acknowledgements

A great many people have contributed in different ways to the production of this book and their contributions are all gratefully acknowledged. The author extends his apologies to anyone who has been omitted from the following list.

Family details, letters from the front, photographs and memorabilia contributed by relatives of those who died, together with assistance from other people (including members of the North of Ireland Family History Society www.nifhs.org) with the collection and compilation of information:

Valerie Adams, Ellen Adamson, Harry Allen, Amy Anderson, Colin Anderson, Cathie Bailie, John Bailie, Frank Bell, Brian Black, Ann Boston, John Bowley, Helen Boyd, Doreen Brown, Jackie Brown, Richard Bryson, Olive Byers, Bill Cameron, Jim Campbell, David Cargo, John Carlisle, Alison Caruth, Alan Carson, Shirley Cochrane, Brian Cockcroft, Anne Conkey, Sam Conkey, Roy Cooper, David Coffey, Margaret Corry, Norman Corry, Brian Foster Courtney, Ruth Craig, Willie Cromie, Anne Curry, Bill Curry, Bailie Dalzell, Charles Davidson, Margaret Davidson, James Davison, Allen Delamere, Arnold Dick, Bernie Doran, Kerry Douglas, David Drysdale, Barbara Dumbleton, Neil Dumbleton, Helen Dunn, Bridie Ennis, Carol Ferguson, Brian Fitzsimmons, Anne Forbes, Pat Gallon, Jim Galloway, Ian Gamble, Cathy George, Randal Gill, Ian Gilpin, Sandra Gilpin, Meg Graham, Walter Graham, David Gray, Jack Greenald, Brian Gregory, Billy Hamilton, Phyllis Hancox, John Hemphill, Michael Henry, Peter Hirsch, David Hume, Tom Johnston, Shona Kendrick, Graeme Kennedy, Julie Kessler, Elma Kilpatrick, Gerard Lennon, Gerrard Lennon, Liam Lennon, Alvin Little, Rosemary Little, Joseph Long, Frank Mackey, Heather Magowan, Maurice McAuley, Norman McAuley, Vincent McAuley, Trevor McCavery, Brian McClelland, Colin McClelland, Tommy McClimonds, Derek McConnell, Andrew McDonald, Brian McDonald, Fiona McDonald, Tony McHugh, Jim McIlorum, Bill McKenzie, Nick McKnight, David McMullan, Dave McNamara, Hessie McNamara, Kim McNarry, Heather McVeigh, Robert McVeigh, Claire McWhirter, Hannah Millar, David Miskimmin, Margaret Mooney, Annie Moore, Rosie Moorehead, William Morrison, James Morrow, David Murdoch, Samuel Murray, Charlotte Murtagh, Sean Napier, Patrick Neeson, Annes Nel, Anne Niblock, Mark Niblock, Martin O'Hagan, John Parkinson, Raymond Patterson, Derek Patton, Peter Paul Rea, Thomas

Ritchie, William Roulston, Alan Russell, Christine Savage, David Shepherd, Allen Sleith, Ken Smyth, Peter Stevenson, Robert Stevenson, Sheelagh Swain, Catherine Switzer, Ken Switzer, Diana Taggart, Gail Taggart, Ken Tait, Douglas Thompson, Mark Thompson, Brian Tompsett, Jean Tompsett, Ken Tompsett, Mary Tompsett, Christine Tyrrell, Douglas Vance, Carol Walker, Doreen Walker, Claire Wallace, Mark Welsh, Elma Wickens, Lesley-Ann Wilson, Neil Wilson, Gillian Withers, Arron Wright and Jan Zelones.

Information and advice from military experts, including the authors and compilers of other Books of Honour:

Arthur Clarke, Richard Doherty, Ellen Elder, Donal Hall, Paddy Harte, William Henry, John Hewitt, Sam Hudson, James Kane, Stewart McClean, Colin Moffett, Amanda Moreno, Lester Morrow, Terence Nelson, Richard Newell, Ivor Paisley, Mark Ramsey, Derek Smyth, Jimmy Taylor, Robert Thompson, David Truesdale and Gerry White.

Permission to reproduce photographs and/or previously published information from individuals and organisations including the CWGC, the Newtownards Chronicle and County Down Spectator Newspapers, Bangor Grammar School, Campbell College, Methodist College Belfast, Regent House School, Rockport School, Royal Belfast Academical Institution, Sullivan Upper School, North Down Borough Council, Regimental Museums and Military Archives in the United Kingdom, Australia, Canada, South Africa and New Zealand:

Alan Curragh, Peter Donnelly, John Dougan, IG Edwards, Brian Fitzsimons, Paul Flowers, Tony Goddard, Barry Greenaway, Keith Haines, Nigel Henderson, L Jooste, Trevor McCavery, Norman McGimpsey, Lester Morrow, Tom Neill, Brian Todd, George Vance, Alison Weir and Jackie Withers.

Advice and support from Oaklee Housing Association Ltd (including IT advice and support for a battlefield tour):
Ian Elliott, Dominic Griffith and Brian McKenna

Financial support from Ards Borough Council

Development and maintenance of the War Dead of North Down and Ards Website at www.barryniblock.co.uk

Austen Lennon of Austen Lennon Web Design www.AustenLennon.co.uk

Professional and customer-focused publishing service from the team at April Sky Design www.aprilsky.co.uk